HOLY BLOOD,
HOLY GRAIL

HOLY BLOOD, HOLY GRAIL
A Delacorte Press Book published by arrangement with Century

PUBLISHING HISTORY
First published in the United Kingdom in a slightly different form in 1982 by Jonathan Cape
Delacorte Press edition / November 2005

Published by
Bantam Dell
A Division of Random House, Inc.
New York, New York

Book design by Dave Crook

ISBN-10: 0-385-34001-X
ISBN-13: 978-0-385-34001-4

Printed in the United States of America
Published simultaneously in Canada

www.bantamdell.com

10 9 8 7 6 5 4 3 2 1
RRW

HOLY BLOOD, HOLY GRAIL

MICHAEL BAIGENT
RICHARD LEIGH
& HENRY LINCOLN

Delacorte
Press

Henry Lincoln was born in London in 1930. He has been a writer for almost fifty years. He has lectured extensively, and is best known for the presentation of his television documentary films on Rennes-le-Château.

Although he has been exploring historical mysteries and esoteric subjects for over twenty years, *Richard Leigh* is primarily a novelist and short-story writer. Born in New Jersey in 1943, he was educated at Tufts University, the University of Chicago and the State University of New York, where he received his Ph.D. Since then, he has lectured at colleges and universities in the States, in Canada and in Britain.

Born in New Zealand in 1948, *Michael Baigent* has a BA degree in Psychology from Canterbury University, New Zealand and an MA degree in Mysticism and Religious Experience from the University of Kent, England. His dissertation concerned the theurgic use of symbolism in the Renaissance. He has long maintained an active interest in history, religion and esoterica; an interest shared by his wife and children. In 1973, he embarked on a career as a professional photographer which took him to many parts of the world. He came to England in 1976 to research a project on the Knights Templar. Shortly thereafter, he met Richard Leigh and Henry Lincoln, and became involved in the mystery of Rennes-le-Château. Since then he has authored and co-authored twelve books and appeared widely in documentary films and Press interviews.

Also by Michael Baigent, Richard Leigh and Henry Lincoln
THE MESSIANIC LEGACY

and by Michael Baigent and Richard Leigh
THE TEMPLE AND THE LODGE
THE DEAD SEA SCROLLS DECEPTION
SECRET GERMANY: CLAUS VON STAUFFENBERG AND THE MYSTICAL CRUSADE AGAINST HITLER
THE ELIXIR AND THE STONE
THE INQUISITION

and by Michael Baigent
FROM THE OMENS OF BABYLON
ANCIENT TRACES

and by Henry Lincoln
THE HOLY PLACE
KEY TO THE SACRED PATTERN
THE TEMPLARS' SECRET ISLAND

Holy Blood, Holy Grail
Michael Baigent, Richard Leigh and Henry Lincoln

CONTENTS

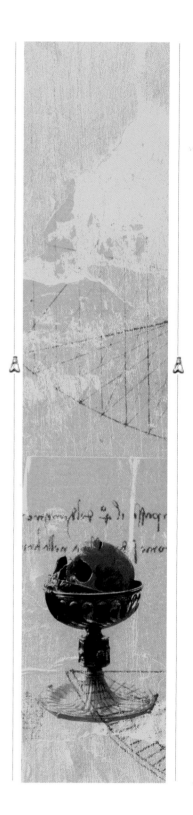

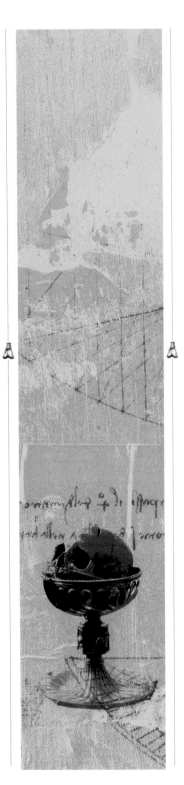

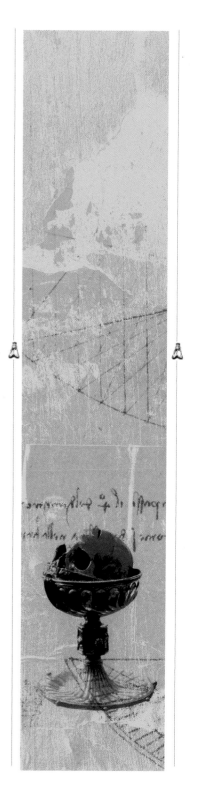

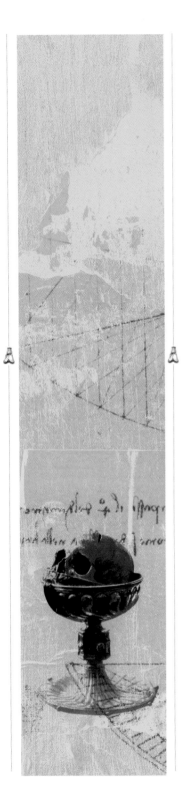

ACKNOWLEDGMENTS

We should like particularly to thank Ann Evans, without whom this book could not have been written. We should also like to thank the following: Jehan l'Ascuiz, Robert Beer, Ean Begg, Dave Bennett, Colin Bloy, Juliet Burke, Henri Buthion, Jean-Luc Chaumeil, Philippe de Chérisey, Jonathan Clowes, Shirley Collins, Chris Cornford, Painton Cowan, Roy Davies, Liz Flower, Janice Glaholm, John Glover, Liz Greene, Margaret Hill, Renee Hinchley, Judy Holland, Paul Johnstone, Patrick Lichfield, Douglas Lockhart, Guy Lovel, Jane McGillivray, Andrew Maxwell-Hyslop, Pam Morris, Lea Olbinson, Pierre Plantard de Saint-Clair, Bob Roberts, David Rolfe, John Saul, Gérard de Sède, Rosalie Siegel, John Sinclair, Jeanne Thomason, Louis Vazart, Colin Waldeck, Anthony Wall, Andy Whitaker, the staff of the British Museum Reading Room and the residents of Rennes-le-Château.

Photographs and paintings were kindly supplied by the following: AGRACI, Paris, p436; Albatross, p80 (Templar's fortress of Castle Pilgrim); Archives Nationales, Paris, p127; Michael Baigent, London, p30, 34, 39, 40, 41, 42, 43, 45, 46, 48, 51; Bibliothèque Nationale, Paris, p190, 271, 272, 273, 325 (Galahad in the Siege Perilous. Manuscript illustration from Li Roumans du bon chevalier Tristan, Ms. Fr. 99, f.563r. France, 15th c.); Michel Bouffard, Carcassonne, p189; www.bridgeman.co.uk , p199 (View of the façade of the Church of Saint-Sulpice. (Photo), French School / Paris, France, Lauros / Giraudo); British Library, London, p74 (85 Folio f.48 Burning of the Templar Grand Master from Chroniques de France ou de St Denis); British Museum, London (reproduced by courtesy of the Trustees of the British Museum), p127, 436; akg-images / Erich Lessing, p36 (Et in Arcadia Ego by Nicolas Poussin), p38 (Les Bergers d'Arcadie by Nicolas Poussin), p101 (The Copper Scroll, Qumran), p450 (The coronation of Napoleon I (1769-1821) by Pope Pius VII in the Cathedral of Notre-Dame de Paris); Jean Dieuzaide/YAN photo, Toulouse, p66 ; Galleria Nazionale d'Arte Antica, Rome, p209; Henry Lincoln, London, p32; National Library of Vienna, p157 (La Fontaine de Fortune by Rene d'Anjou); Scala, p87 (Interior of the rotunda, Temple Church, London).

Permission to quote extracts in copyright was granted by: Le Charivari magazine, Paris for material from issue no. 18, 'Les Archives du Prieuré de Sion'; Victor Gollancz, London and Harper & Row, Publishers, Inc, New York for specified material on pp. 334–36 from pp. 14–17 in The Secret Gospel by Morton Smith copyright © 1973 by Morton Smith; Random House, Inc., New York for material from Parzival by Wolfram von Eschenbach, translated by Helen Mustard and Charles E. Passage, copyright © 1961 by Helen Mustard and Charles Passage.

INTRODUCTION

In 1969, *en route* for a summer holiday in the Cévennes, I made the casual purchase of a paperback. *Le Trésor Maudit* by Gérard de Sède was a mystery story – a lightweight, entertaining blend of historical fact, genuine mystery and conjecture. It might have remained consigned to the post-holiday oblivion of all such reading had I not stumbled upon a curious and glaring omission in its pages.

The 'accursed treasure' of the title had apparently been found in the 1890s by a village priest through the decipherment of certain cryptic documents unearthed in his church. Although the purported texts of two of these documents were reproduced, the 'secret messages' said to be encoded within them were not. The implication was that the deciphered messages had again been lost. And yet, as I found, a cursory study of the documents reproduced in the book reveals at least one concealed message. Surely the author had found it. In working on his book he must have given the documents more than fleeting attention. He was bound, therefore, to have found what I had found. Moreover the message was exactly the kind of titillating snippet of 'proof' that helps to sell a 'pop' paperback. Why had M. de Sède not published it?

During the ensuing months the oddity of the story and the possibility of further discoveries drew me back to it from time to time. The appeal was that of a rather more than usually intriguing crossword puzzle – with the added curiosity of de Sède's silence. As I caught tantalising new glimpses of layers of meaning buried within the text of the documents, I began to wish I could devote more to the mystery of Rennes-le-Château than mere moments snatched from my working life as a writer for television. And so, in the late autumn of 1970, I presented the story as a possible documentary subject to the late Paul Johnstone, executive producer of the BBC's historical and archaeological series 'Chronicle'.

Paul saw the possibilities, and I was dispatched to France to talk to de Sède and explore the prospects for a short film. During Christmas week of 1970 I met de Sède in Paris. At that first meeting, I asked the question which had nagged at me for more than a year, 'Why didn't you publish the message hidden in the parchments?' His reply astounded me. 'What message?'

It seemed to me inconceivable that he was unaware of this elementary message. Why was he fencing with me? Suddenly I found myself reluctant to reveal exactly what I had found. We continued an elliptical verbal fencing match for a few minutes. It thus became apparent that we were both aware of the message. I repeated my question, 'Why didn't you publish it?' This time de Sède's answer was calculated, 'Because we thought it might interest someone like you to find it for yourself.'

That reply, as cryptic as the priest's mysterious documents, was the first clear hint that the mystery of Rennes-le-Château was to prove much more than a simple tale of lost treasure.

With my director, Andrew Maxwell-Hyslop, I began to prepare a 'Chronicle' film in the spring of 1971. It was planned as a simple twenty-minute item for a magazine programme. But as we worked de Sède began to feed us further fragments of information. First came the full text of a major encoded message, which spoke of the painters Poussin and Teniers. This was fascinating. The cipher was unbelievably complex. We were told it had been broken by experts of the French Army Cipher Department, using computers. As I studied the convolutions of the code, I became convinced that this explanation was, to say the least, suspect. I checked with cipher experts of British Intelligence. They agreed with me. 'The cipher does not present a valid problem for a computer.' The code was unbreakable. Someone, somewhere, must have the key.

And then de Sède dropped his second bombshell. A tomb resembling that in Poussin's famous painting, 'Les Bergers d'Arcadie', had been found. He would send details 'as soon as he had them'. Some days later the photographs arrived, and it was clear that our short film on a small local mystery had begun to assume unexpected dimensions. Paul decided to abandon it and committed us to a full-length 'Chronicle' film. Now there would be more time to research and more screen time to explore the story. Transmission was postponed to the spring of the following year.

The Lost Treasure of Jerusalem? was screened in February 1972, and provoked a very strong reaction. I knew that I had found a subject of consuming interest not merely to myself, but to a very large viewing public. Further research would not be self-indulgence. At some time there would have to be a follow-up film. By 1974 I had a mass of new material and Paul assigned Roy Davies to produce my second 'Chronicle' film, *The Priest, the Painter and the Devil.* Again the reaction of the public proved how much the story had caught the popular imagination. But by now it had grown so complex, so far-reaching in its ramifications, that I knew the detailed research was rapidly exceeding the capabilities of any one person. There were too many different leads to follow. The more I pursued one line of investigation, the more conscious I became of the mass of material being neglected. It was at this daunting juncture that Chance, which had first tossed the story so casually into my lap, now made sure that the work would not become bogged down.

In 1975, at a summer school where we were both lecturing on aspects of literature, I had the great good fortune to meet Richard Leigh. Richard is a novelist and short-story writer with post-graduate degrees in Comparative Literature and a deep knowledge of history, philosophy, psychology and esoterica. He had been working for some years as a university lecturer in the United States, Canada and Britain.

Between our summer-school talks we spent many hours discussing subjects of mutual interest. I mentioned the Knights Templar, who had assumed an important role in the background to the mystery of Rennes-le-Château. To my delight, I found that this shadowy order of medieval warrior-monks had already awakened Richard's profound interest, and he had done considerable research into their history. At one stroke months of work which I had seen stretching ahead of me became unnecessary. Richard could answer most of my queries, and was as intrigued as I was by some of the apparent anomalies I had unearthed. More importantly, he too saw the fascination and sensed the significance of the whole research project on which I had embarked. He offered to help me with the aspect involving the Templars. And he brought in Michael Baigent, a psychology graduate who had recently abandoned a successful career in photo-journalism to devote his time to researching the Templars for a film project he had in mind.

Had I set out to search for them, I could not have found two better qualified and more congenial partners with whom to form a team. After years of solitary labour the impetus brought to the project by two fresh brains was exhilarating. The first tangible result of our collaboration was the third 'Chronicle' film on Rennes-le-Château, *The Shadow of the Templars*, which was produced by Roy Davies in 1979.

The work which we did on that film at last brought us face to face with the underlying foundations upon which the entire mystery of Rennes-le-Château had been built. But the film could only hint at what we were beginning to discern. Beneath the surface was something more startling, more significant and more immediately relevant than we could have believed possible when we began our work on the 'intriguing little mystery' of what a French priest might have found in a mountain village.

In 1972 I closed my first film with the words, 'Something extraordinary is waiting to be found . . . and in the not too distant future, it will be.'

This book explains what that 'something' is – and how extraordinary the discovering has been.

H.L.

January 17th, 1981

INTRODUCTION, 1996

For reasons the reader will appreciate after reading it, we wanted *Holy Blood, Holy Grail* to be released on 17 January. That year, unfortunately, 17 January fell on a Sunday. The book accordingly appeared a day later, 18 January, 1982, in Britain. The American edition followed on 26 February, also a day off talismanically. During the month or so subsequent to publication in both countries, we found ourselves embroiled in an increasingly bizarre media circus.

We had written a book which we guessed would probably be controversial. We expected it to be criticised in the usual way – in reviews, for example, by the vested theological and historical interests we had implicitly challenged. We certainly didn't expect more attention than publications tend generally to receive. To our bewilderment, however, we found ourselves attracting as much celebrity – or, to be more accurate, notoriety – as if we'd personally attempted a *coup d'état* at the Vatican. We didn't just elicit reviews. We also attained certifiable shock-horror status as a news story – a full-fledged news story, which actually made the front pages of sundry newspapers.

It was, admittedly, a quiet time. The pre-Christmas turbulence in Poland had given way if not quite to calm, then at least to the kind of robotic docility prevailing elsewhere in the Soviet imperium. No public figures had been shot of late. Argentina had not yet invaded the Falklands. In the absence of anything more catastrophic to galvanise popular attention, we became darlings of the media. Responses and reactions assumed torrential proportions, pouring in the letters columns of newspapers, to our publishers and agent, to ourselves. So diverse was the spectrum of opinion that it seemed to be referring to a number of altogether different books. At one extreme, there was praise on a scale epitomised by a letter extolling our opus as 'the greatest work of the century' – an assessment with which, alas, we couldn't honestly concur. At the opposite extreme, there were statements which, albeit less succinctly, implied it might well be the worst. Seldom in recent publishing history have so many Don Quixotes tilted so vigorously against one small windmill.

Much of the rumpus was precipitated by the BBC's *Omnibus*, on which we were improbably interviewed by a film critic, Barry Norman. He could not, of course, be expected to have much greater knowledge of our subject matter than the average layman. In con-

The major sites of investigation in France

sequence, he was accompanied by two officially recognised experts, the historian Marina Warner and the then Bishop of Birmingham, Hugh Montefiore. Somewhat naively, with a trusting lamb-being-led-to-slaughter acquiescence, we had accepted an invitation to appear on the programme. The producer had earnestly assured us that we'd be participating in a 'discussion' – one that would permit some serious exploration of our book's hypothetical conclusions. His definition of a 'discussion' seemed to us somewhat idiosyncratic. For us, and probably for most people, the word 'ambush' would more accurately convey what ensued.

Barry Norman hurriedly summarised something which bore only a tenuous resemblance to the work we had written. We were then confronted with a pre-arranged scroll of charges long enough to sanction an immediate *auto-da-fé* of both our book and ourselves. Marina Warner comported herself responsibly, concentrating on specific scholarly points and seeming rather abashed by the executioner's rôle assigned to her. She subsequently expressed her embarrassment at having been lured into the 'attempted mugging'. The Bishop of Birmingham, however, displayed no such Christian compunction.

We found ourselves subjected to a veritable blitz. Broad generalities and pedantic trivialities were launched against us like a Luftwaffe of flies. We could have swatted most of them. We did, in fact, swat a great many. But it takes only a moment for a voice, arrogating the resonance of authority, to stigmatise a book – to label it irresponsible, implausible, poorly researched or simply bad. It takes rather longer to refute such charges. One must do so point by point, citing specific examples. One must become embroiled in minutiae and academic quibbles that do not make for good television, for good television revels more in dramatic bloodbaths than in dry exchanges of information. For every half-dozen objections raised by our critics in the studio, we were allowed to reply to only one; and when the programme was transmitted, even our replies had been pruned. Each of us was edited down to one or two perfunctory comments, and that was all. In consequence, the 'discussion' witnessed by BBC viewers was very different from the 'discussion' that actually occurred in the studio. A number of people observed afterwards that it seemed we'd not been given much chance to speak. In reality, we'd been given slightly more chance than was apparent, but most of what we said had ended up on the cutting-room floor.

Such things, of course, constantly happen in the world of television – a world with which we were sufficiently familiar not to be unduly surprised. The pity of it was that some magnificently comic moments were irretrievably lost. At one point, for example, Barry Norman asked the Bishop of Birmingham whether such books as ours were potentially 'dangerous'. 'Absolutely,' replied the bishop, who had only read the last two chapters of it. Our book, he declared, was a shameless exploitation of sex and sensationalism. A stunned silence descended on the studio. Sex? Had we written a book about sex? We gaped at one another in stupefaction, half-wondering whether a deranged printer had bound a few pages of the *Kama Sutra* into our text, or replaced one of our illustrations with a picture of a nude Templar. As far as we could gauge, our book, on a scale of sexiness, ranked somewhere below the Turin Shroud – which is, after all, a full-frontal portrait of a naked man, but has never attracted much purient interest.

Barry Norman twitched his head, as if to shake water out of his ear. Marina Warner looked manifestly embarrassed. Somewhat ironically, we attempted to ascertain precisely which book the bishop had read. Before we could do so, the heavens intervened in the form of a humble technician, who hurried into the studio and requested us to shoot the scene again. Something had gone wrong, he explained – a gremlin had apparently unsprocketed some technical apparatus. Barry Norman accordingly repeated the question. The bishop by now had realised that instead of moistening his fingers with the tip of his tongue, he'd jammed both hands and feet into his mouth simultaneously. Given a second opportunity, he retreated as fast as his tongue could carry him. Was our book potentially 'dangerous'? Not at all, he replied with seraphic serenity. On the contrary, he was confident that Christianity would prove sufficiently robust to withstand the challenge we had posed. As we harboured no particular desire to demolish Christianity, we did not presume to doubt his optimism.

This entire sequence, and a number of others, were entirely excised from what was transmitted. But if the *Omnibus* editing struck us as less than honourable, that could be ascribed to various extenuating circumstances – the format of the programme, the shortage of time, the exigencies of television as a medium. And we had, after all, written a book which we knew would be subject to attack and distortion. What cannot be excused, however, was the producer's apparent attempt to make the Duke of Devonshire look ridiculous, which seemed to have been a *cause célèbre* on his part. In our book – and the wording is very precise – we state that certain members of the Devonshire family seem to have been privy to suggestive fragments of information. This statement was based on material dating from the eighteenth century, as well as on remarks made by a member of the Devonshire family today – by a member of a collateral branch of the family, not directly connected with the duke at all. We had patiently and painstakingly explained this to our producer, who had pressed us insistently on the matter. But he was bent on exhuming some sensational 'English angle', and rather overzealously trundled out to Chatsworth to interview the Duke of Devonshire personally. In order to maximise the drama, he appeared to have confronted the duke with an assertion we never made. According to a forthcoming book, His Grace was told, the Devonshires were directly descended from Jesus. Not surprisingly, the duke was mortified. 'Absolutely obnoxious!' he replied indignantly. Because we had not made it, the assertion to which he was replying had to be cut from the transmission. The television viewer only saw His Grace answering 'Absolutely obnoxious!' to something quite unspecified. Someone might have been asking him about French naval tactics at the Battle of Quiberon Bay in 1759, or the quality of modern English tweed.

During the *Omnibus* interview, the Bishop of Birmingham charged us with no less than '79 errors of fact' in two chapters – the two chapters, that is, which he had read. This indictment, issuing from so august a figure, seemed to be authoritative – an unimpugnable judgment pronounced by the Voice of Truth Itself, and therefore definitively damning. It was accordingly seized by the newspapers, by radio and television, and disseminated across the world. 'You were attacked by a bishop,' someone reported anxiously, ringing us long-distance from the United States. 'Are you in any danger?'

We were not unduly alarmed by the prospect of an episcopal assault team – a cadre of mitred commandos with crosiers converted into blow-pipes and SAS balaclavas above flowing copes and stoles. Yet the charge of 79 errors, when it was first levelled against us, took us momentarily aback. Could we really have got 79 things wrong? We must confess to a fleeting disquiet, an instant of self-doubt. But within the week, the bishop deigned to send us a typed list of the 79 errors he claimed to have found. It was a singular document indeed. The bishop *had*, admittedly, discovered four genuine errors of fact. We had mistakenly said that Palestine, in Jesus' era, was divided into two provinces. As the bishop correctly observed, it was actually divided into one province and two tetrarchies. We had mistakenly ascribed the origin of Jesus' image as a carpenter to Luke's Gospel. As the bishop correctly observed, it actually derives from Mark's. A careless compositor, whose slip we had overlooked in proof-reading, had placed Julius Africanus in the third century rather than in the first; and our manuscript, which alluded to 'the Greek city of Ephesus', had got altered, presumably by a copy editor, to 'the city of Ephesus in Greece'. Ephesus, of course, is in Asia Minor.

On these four points, we could only plead guilty. The bishop was right – we had been in error, and we duly accepted his corrections. But what of the other 75 'errors of fact' for which the media, quoting the bishop, were vociferously taking us to task? Virtually all of them proved not to be errors of fact at all, but errors of faith – or, more specifically, issues of contention and interpretation still being debated by scholars – and we had 'erred' only to the extent that we deviated from established tradition. For example, the bishop listed as 'errors of fact' a number of statements about which, as he said, 'there is much argument', and the explanation we offered 'does not have the support of most scholars' – meaning, of course, the orthodox scholars whom he found most congenial. Then, too, the bishop included in his list of errors our citation of an apocryphal text he did not know and could not find in his library, even though it was readily available in both hardcover and paperback. In other words, it was our 'error' that the bishop's library lacked this particular text. At another point, the bishop had labelled as an error a reference that made no sense to him – because he had not read the earlier chapters of our book, where the meaning was explained. Finally, the bishop castigated as erroneous our assertion that the Gospels 'are historical documents like any other'. 'No,' he declared, 'they are unique documents, telling the good news of Christ under the form of history.' Whatever this might mean, it could hardly incriminate us for a factual error. If we had erred at all, it was simply because we did not share the bishop's view of the Gospels.

These, then, were the issues for which the Bishop of Birmingham condemned us. They render the damning charge of '79 errors of fact' somewhat puerile, not to say misleading. Yet much of the criticism from the theological establishment was of essentially the same order. In our book, we had addressed ourselves to matters of historical possibility, historical probability and, whenever facts were available, historical fact. Our theological critics, most of whom had little historical background, could only assail us from the standpoint of faith. Faith is not the best perspective for appraising history, but many of our critics had no choice. We had, it seemed to them, implicitly challenged vested interests which they felt obliged to defend, however wobbly the foundations of their arguments. 'Your book hasn't met with a favourable response from Church authorities,' radio and television interviewers would say to us earnestly and fatuously. As if things could possibly have been otherwise. As if every bishop in Christendom might have been expected to say 'Fair cop' and summarily surrender his mitre.

We were also chastised for having speculated. We readily admitted it. We had propounded what we explicitly declared to be no more than an hypothesis; and hypotheses must necessarily rest on speculation. The sheer scarcity of reliable information on biblical matters obliges any researcher of the subject to speculate – if, that is, he is not to remain mute. Granted, one must not speculate wildly. One must confine one's speculation to the framework of known historical information. Within this framework, however, one has no choice but to speculate – to *interpret* the meagre and often opaque evidence that exists. All biblical scholarship entails speculation, as does theology. The Gospels are sketchy, ambiguous and often contradictory documents. During the course of the last two thousand years, people have argued, even waged wars over what particular passages might mean. In the coalescence of Christian tradition, one principle has consistently obtained. Confronted by any of the numerous ambiguities in scripture, ecclesiastical authorities would *speculate* about its meaning. Their conclusions, once accepted, were enshrined as dogma and – quite erroneously – came to be regarded over the centuries as established fact. Such conclusions, however, are not fact at all. On the contrary, they are speculation and interpretation congealed into a tradition; and it is this tradition that is constantly mistaken for fact.

A single example should serve to illustrate the process. According to all four Gospels, Pilate alludes to Jesus as 'King of the Jews', and an inscription of that title is affixed to the cross. But this is all the Gospels tell us. They offer no indication of whether the title was warranted or not – no indication of whether Jesus had or made a claim to such a kingship. At some point in the past, it was merely assumed that the title must have been intended mockingly. This assumption was based on speculative interpretation. Yet most Christians today blindly accept as established fact that the title was indeed conferred in derision. But it is not established fact at all. If one reads the Gospels with no preconceptions whatever, there is nothing to suggest the title wasn't used in all seriousness, wasn't perfectly legitimate. In the nativity, after all, we are told the three wise men come in search of the infant 'born King of the Jews', and we don't regard them as being derisive. On the contrary, their homage, and Herod's fear of being deposed by a more legitimate sovereign, would seem to suggest that Jesus did indeed possess some sort of royal pedigree, status or claim – which was recognised as such by his contemporaries, including Pilate. It is only tradition that makes this suggestion sound dubious to Christian commentators today. To assert that Jesus might in reality have been 'King of the Jews' is not, therefore, to be at variance with the evidence. It is merely to be at variance with a long-established tradition, a long-established canon of beliefs based ultimately on someone's speculative interpretation.

'You can't prove your conclusions.' This was another indictment levelled against us by interviewers and theological critics – as if we might have been expected to produce a sworn affidavit signed by Jesus himself, duly witnessed and duly notarised. Of course we couldn't 'prove' our conclusions. As we stressed repeatedly in the book itself, we were simply posing an hypothesis. Had we been able to 'prove' it, it wouldn't have been an hypothesis, but a fact;

and there would have been no controversy at all, only a sensational revelation and *fait accompli.* But what, in the present context, *would* constitute genuine 'proof'? Can such 'proof' be found for any issue of consequence in the New Testament? Obviously not. So far as the New Testament is concerned, there is nothing that can be definitively 'proved'. It cannot even be 'proved' that Jesus ever existed as an historical personage. Certain writers, past and present, have argued, sometimes persuasively, that he didn't.

The question of 'proof' is ultimately beside the point. Given the scarcity of both documentary and archaeological testimony, there is very little, if anything, that can be 'proved' about Jesus. The most the researcher has at his disposal is *evidence,* and evidence is not the same thing as 'proof'. Evidence, in the context of New Testament studies, cannot 'prove' anything. It can only suggest greater or lesser possibilities, greater or lesser plausibilities. One must survey the available evidence, assess it, interpret it and draw responsible conclusions from it – that a particular sequence of events, for instance, is *more likely* to have occurred than various others. If this criterion is employed, the matter becomes one of common sense and what we know of the human condition. It is quite simply more likely that a man would have married, fathered children and attempted to gain a throne than that he would have been born of a virgin, walked on water and risen from the dead.

Contrary to the assertions of both theologians and interviewers, such a statement does not constitute 'an attack on the very core of Christianity and the Christian ethos'. The core of Christianity and the Christian ethos resides in Jesus' teachings. Those teachings are, in many respects, unique. They promulgate values and attitudes that had not previously been expressed on the stage of human history. It is to that extent that they comprise of the 'new message', the 'good news' for humankind, and are valid in themselves. They do not need miraculous biographical details to support them – especially not the kind of miraculous biographical details that characterised rival deities throughout the ancient world. If the teachings *do* require such details, it suggests one of two things – either there is something seriously defective in the teachings or, more likely, there is something defective in the believer's faith. Any thoughtful Christian would concur that Jesus' primary significance resides in the message he sought to communicate. That message would hardly be vitiated if it proved to have issued from a man who was also a husband and a father. Neither would it be any more valid if it issued from a celibate.

The high-level theologians and ecclesiastics who attacked us were almost all Protestant. In fact, the majority were Anglicans, like the Bishop of Birmingham. It is clear, of course, what the Roman Catholic Church would have liked to do to us, and would have been able to do to us in a former age. Being thwarted today of such incendiary ambitions, the Catholic hierarchy had the wisdom to remain sonorously silent and thereby refrain from granting us additional publicity. But an important ex-functionary in the Church confided to us personally that the upper echelons of his institution – though they would never make a public statement on the matter – privately acknowledged the plausibility, if not indeed the veracity, of our conclusions. We were also told by an informed source that our book was being widely, albeit discreetly, circulated throughout the Vatican. And in a radio discussion during our publicity tour of the United States, we explored the implications of our book with Dr. Malachi Martin, one of the leading authorities on Vatican affairs and former member of the Vatican's Pontifical Institute. There was ultimately, Dr. Martin conceded, no theological objection to the suggestion that Jesus might have been married and fathered children.

Such was the spectrum of reactions from the ecclesiastical establishment. But it was only towards the end of our book that we had addressed ourselves to biblical material. A much greater proportion of the text was devoted to aspects of history, particularly French history, between the sixth and the twentieth centuries. If reactions from the ecclesiastical establishment could be fairly well predicted, those from the historical establishment could not, and we awaited them with some curiosity. In fact, however, few established historians deigned to accord us their attention. Hindsight enables us to recognise that this was not especially surprising. Egg, after all, becomes nobody's face, and scholars, like politicians, are especially sensitive to such mishaps. To damn us definitively might have entailed the risk of some future embarrassment – some document perhaps coming to light that might have supported our conclusions. To endorse us would have been even more perilous – a matter of placing one's professional reputation prominently 'on the line' in a matter of potentially explosive controversy. So far as the historians were concerned, therefore, it was altogether more prudent to equivocate, to reserve judgment, to remain conscientiously silent or, on occasion, to adopt a tone of lofty, ironic, Olympian condescension. By such means, our book could be implicitly reduced to the proverbial storm in a teacup and all confrontation with our material dexterously avoided.

There was, nevertheless, the odd barrage here and there, fired with the earnest and urgent desperation of a bastion besieged by uncouth barbarians. If Marina Warner had been graciously temperate in our interview with the BBC's *Omnibus*, her review in *The Sunday Times* was described by one commentator as 'the rudest review of the year', and by another as simply 'hysterical'. Among other slippages of lucidity, Ms. Warner castigated us for relying on questionable sources – sources on which we had not, in fact, relied. In the *Times Literary Supplement*, Jonathan Sumption took us to task on the same grounds. He cited as an unreliable source a reference which, unbeknown to him, we had found in a work by Marina Warner.

The serious historical criticism that appeared was of essentially two kinds. Some was undeniably valid and valuable, correcting us on certain specific matters – statistics, dates, titles, nomenclature and other details which we had indeed got wrong, but which had no bearing on our arguments, hypotheses or conclusions. There were other historians, however, who questioned the validity of our overall approach. We had not proceeded, they maintained, 'by the rules'. Measured by the standards of established academic research, our methods had been highly unorthodox, irregular, even heretical. We had not observed certain enshrined protocols of scholarship, certain dogmatically cautious approaches. We had thereby, apparently, betrayed ourselves as upstarts and amateurs who did not warrant serious consideration – and who had, moreover, committed the transgression of trespassing on the sovereign territory of 'experts'. In consequence, we could only be regarded with solemn, even righteous, disapprobation.

We were all well-trained in the techniques of 'official' academic research and knew effectively enough how to deploy them. If we had recourse to other methods, we had ample reason for doing so. We were not hell-bent on a bestseller, though fundamentalist Christians may have believed us to be – quite literally. At the same time, we did not want to produce a book exclusively for specialists, which would then fester away on the shelves of university libraries. On the contrary, we wanted to produce a work which – while not compromising its integrity – would be accessible to the reading public at large. We had, after all, an exciting story to tell, and wanted to convey not only the story, but also something of its excitement. We took pains to make our research conform to the most fastidious criteria. But we chose to present the results of that research in a form as compellingly readable as possible.

Ultimately, however, our approach was dictated by other, more important factors. Indeed, it was dictated by the essential nature of our subject. Our material spanned an immense and diverse spectrum, in origin, in character and in chronology. It was necessary for us to synthesise in a coherent pattern data extending from the Old Testament to a semi-secret society in Europe today, from the Gospels and Grail romances to accounts of current affairs in modern newspapers. For such an undertaking, the techniques of academic scholarship were sorely inadequate. To make the requisite connections between radically diverse bodies of subject matter, we were obliged to adopt and develop a more comprehensive approach, based on synthesis rather than on conventional analysis.

Such an approach was even more necessary because traditional techniques had already demonstrated their inability to deal with large tracts of our material. Much of what we were exploring lay in spheres deemed academically suspect. If one surveys any period of the past, one will find a number of ostensible anomalies – incidents, movements, phenomena, groups or individuals which call attention to themselves, but cannot apparently be accommodated by the accepted 'mainstream' of history. When confronted by anomalies of this sort, most orthodox historians choose to ignore them – to dismiss them as transient aberrations, as peripheral or incidental. Thus Nostradamus, for example, is deemed an irrelevant oddity, and receives only scant attention in studies of sixteenth-century France. Thus the Knights Templar and many of the questions surrounding them are regarded as a mere footnote to the Crusades. Secret societies, by virtue of their very secrecy, have often kept historians at bay; and the historians, reluctant to confess their ignorance, prefer to diminish the consequence of the subject. Freemasonry, to cite one such instance, is of vital importance to any social, psychological, cultural or political history of eighteenth-century Europe, as well as to the founding of the United States; but most history books do not even mention it. There would almost seem to be an implicit policy in operation – if something cannot be exhaustively and satisfactorily documented, it must be irrelevant, and therefore not worth discussing at all. Yet much of what is most important in history will not be found preserved in documents.

Until quite recently, the seventeenth-century 'Rosicrucians' were dismissed as a mere 'lunatic fringe' sect; and the spectrum of disciplines known collectively as 'esoterica' – astrology, alchemy, the Kabbalah, the Tarot, numerology and sacred geometry – were deemed similarly irrelevant, similarly taboo. Now, however, through the work of the late Dame Frances Yates, of her colleagues and protégés at the Warburg Institute, such subjects can be seen in perspective; and in perspective, they are indeed significant. The mysterious and elusive 'Rosicrucians' can now be discerned as having played a crucial rôle in the events leading to the Thirty Years War and to the foundation of the Royal Society in England. The spectrum of 'esoterica' can now be perceived not as mere quaint marginalia of Western history, but as a vital key to any understanding of the Renaissance. If anything, these 'aberrations' constitute more of a 'mainstream' than what is customarily labelled as such.

Much of our material was as academically suspect as 'esoterica' or the self-styled 'Rosicrucians', and few historians, therefore, had addressed themselves to it. Few reliable books existed; few relevant connections had been made. We

were thus forced to break new ground by confronting and reconsidering historical 'anomalies' with a sufficiently flexible and comprehensive approach. We
were forced to make new connections, to find genuine historical links in hitherto neglected spheres of study, to restore certain taboo subjects to the status they
had actually enjoyed in the context of their own times. We had to explore the
subject matter of 'occult' and mystical writers and place it in its true historical
framework, while not lapsing into their pitfall of credulous gullibility.

Thus was our approach dictated by our material – by the necessity it generated to synthesise, to confront and accommodate historical 'anomalies'
habitually ignored by conventional scholars. It was therefore not surprising that
conventional scholars questioned our approach. But it was also significant, and
not just coincidental, that the most sympathetic responses to our book seemed
to come from literary figures – from novelists like Anthony Burgess, for example, or Anthony Powell and Peter Vansittart. Unlike the professional historian,
the novelist is accustomed to the kind of approach we adopted. He is accustomed to synthesising diverse material, to making connections more elusive
than those explicitly preserved in documents. He recognises that history is not
confined only to recorded facts, but often lies in more intangible domains – in
cultural achievements, in myths, legends and traditions, in the psychic life of
both individuals and entire peoples. For the novelist, knowledge is not sub-
divided into rigidly demarcated compartments, and there are no taboos, no
'disreputable' subjects. History is not for him something frozen, something pet-
rified into precise periods or epochs, each of which can be isolated and
subjected to a controlled laboratory experiment. On the contrary, it is a fluid,
organic and dynamic process, whereby psychology, sociology, politics, art, folklore, religion and many other things as well are interwoven in a single seamless
fabric. It was with a vision akin to that of the novelist that we endeavoured to
produce our book.

At the same time, we were aware that we were engaged in what Umberto
Eco would call a 'semiotic exercise'. In other words, we were confronted by a
multitude of fragments from a number of different jigsaw puzzles, a multitude
of 'indicators', 'signs', 'clues', 'vectors', all of which seemed to reflect an apparently meaningful pattern. Were they ultimately mere random coincidences? Or
did they indeed reflect a pattern? And, if so, was the pattern meaningful? Was
the meaning inherent in the pattern – 'out there', so to speak, in history – or
were we assembling the pattern ourselves and projecting our own meaning into
it? In attempting to answer these questions, we found ourselves embarked on
our own compelling adventure, our own personal 'Grail quest'. But that, after
all, is just another metaphor for what every individual must do to imbue his or

her life with meaning, purpose and direction. Perhaps it was primarily for this reason that *Holy Blood, Holy Grail* spoke as deeply as it did to so many people.

For another two and a half years, until the autumn of 1984, we continued to research additional aspects of the story recounted in *Holy Blood, Holy Grail*. Some of our findings were published in 1986, in *The Messianic Legacy*. By that time, however, we felt we had arrived at a cul-de-sac, at least so far as the broader dimensions of the story – those pertaining to history and to contemporary politics – were concerned. One of our primary sources of information, the semi-secret society known as the Prieuré de Sion, went abruptly silent; and all our attempts to trace it, to investigate its membership and activities, proved, beyond a certain point, futile. In the years that followed, our own works began to diverge, moving in different directions. The geometry associated with Rennes-le-Château, as well as its possible implications, was explored in *The Holy Place* (1991). *The Temple and the Lodge* (1989) and *The Dead Sea Scrolls Deception* (1991) addressed themselves to Freemasonry and to events in first-century Palestine – material tangentially pertinent to the mystery of Rennes-le-Château perhaps, but not directly related to it.

Quite apart from us, however, the mystery of Rennes-le-Château became a booming business of its own. In the summer of 1982, when only the English-language editions of *Holy Blood, Holy Grail* had appeared in print, the little mountain village was inundated by upwards of 10,000 tourists. As the French and other foreign-language editions of our book appeared, that number more than doubled. It has continued increasing until today it exceeds 100,000 visitors each year. Rennes-le-Château is now a veritable pilgrimage centre for a diverse spectrum of pilgrims – curious tourists, zealous entrepreneurs, serious researchers, treasure-hunters, 'esoteric groupies' with dubious interests ranging from ritual magic to UFOs and Atlantis. Some of these have bought land in the vicinity and now live there.

The village is, indeed, enormously changed from the tranquil, lost and isolated hamlet which we first knew in the early 1970s. In 1994 Saunière's property, the Villa Bethania and Tour Magdala, changed hands and major refurbishment is under way. A museum has been installed in his Winter Garden and Rennes-le-Château boasts a well-stocked bookshop. Doubtless, our priest would be delighted, too, to see that his portrait adorns bottles of a Rennes-le-Château wine, the *Cuvee Berenger Souniere*. A village Association, the *Terre de Rhedae*, issues Newsletters and raises funds for the upkeep of church and hamlet. Less welcome, perhaps, are the coach park and the countless rubbish bins which its new status of 'tourist centre' now demands.

To our knowledge, there are currently at least six circles or study groups devoted to discussing and researching the mystery of Rennes-le-Château and related subjects. Certain of them are indubitably serious, scholarly and responsible. Certain others would probably be regarded as certifiably cranky. Two of them are based in the United Kingdom – the Rennes Group and the Saunière Society. Most of them publish journals, bulletins or newsletters containing the latest findings of their members, as well as book reviews and general gossip.

The mystery has gained a wider currency, too, and sometimes an improbable one. It has featured, for example, in full-page colour advertisements for Dubonnet, which appeared in the Sunday supplements of British newspapers. On a more serious note, the story is cited in a recent and authoritative work, *Poussin Paintings – A Catalogue Raisonné* by Christopher Wright (1984). When consulted in 1971, Anthony Blunt had petulantly dismissed our evidence for suggesting the landscape in Poussin's 'Shepherds of Arcadia' was in fact a real landscape near to Rennes-le-Château, and the tomb a real tomb, situated near the village of Arques. It is now acknowledged that the similarities of Poussin's background and the local landscape are 'undeniable'.

The tomb itself, tragically, no longer exists. It was destroyed in 1988 in a misguided attempt to protect it from the rapacious and mindless treasure hunters who have been drawn to the story. The many attempts to break into the tomb at last culminated in a lunatic assault with explosives which led the desperate owner to take a sledgehammer to the structure. All that now remains is a sad and insignificant scattering of rubble. What was destroyed in stone, however, was restored in other mediums. In 1989, for example, the mystery of Rennes-le-Château inspired an opera by Stewart Copeland, which was premiered by the Cleveland Opera. It also, we were told, had begun to figure in the lyrics of several popular songs, and was extolled by such prominent individuals in the music business as Sting and David Bowie. In the realm of classical music, the story found its way into an oratorio by Dominic Muldowney.

Shortly after *Holy Blood, Holy Grail* was published, we were approached by the scriptwriter and director Paul Schrader, who said that he and his colleague, Martin Scorsese, were interested in adapting the material for the screen. An option was accordingly sold to Paramount. Unfortunately, nothing was to come of this project, nor of other attempts to do a screenplay of the story by Franc Roddam and at least two others. We would like to think, however, that our book helped to create a climate which made possible such works as Scorsese's adaptation of Nikos Kazantzakis' novel, *The Last Temptation*.

Even before *Holy Blood, Holy Grail* was published, Liz Greene had drawn upon our research for her novel revolving around Nostradamus, *The Dreamer of the Vine.* She drew on it again for a second novel, *The Puppet Master.* In the years that followed, material from *Holy Blood, Holy Grail* found its way into a multitude of other fictional narratives, from tacky thrillers and potboilers to very serious literature indeed. In reviewing our book when it first appeared, the late Anthony Burgess said he could not help seeing the story as containing ideal components for a novel. So, too, obviously, did Umberto Eco, whom Burgess extolled in another review as having signposted the direction in which the novel of the future must move. Professor Eco clearly discerned the extent to which our research had constituted a species of 'semiotic exercise'. In *Foucault's Pendulum,* he ingeniously adapted aspects of it to a fictitious 'semiotic exercise' of his own.

In the meantime, *Holy Blood, Holy Grail* had been translated into more than twenty languages – and banned by authoritarian regimes as politically divergent as those then presiding in Bulgaria and South Africa. Its dissemination precipitated a positive cascade of books and articles on Rennes-le-Château, as well as on such related subjects as the Cathar heresy and the Knights Templar. Many of these were responsible, scholarly and immensely illuminating. Others attempted to seize the numinous by the hem of its cloak and toppled into certifiable dottiness. In 1985, John Saul and Janice Glaholm produced what comprised at the time a definitive bibliography of publications pertaining to the story. Plans to keep this bibliography up to date had to be abandoned because the task proved impossible. Within two years, the number of existing entries had already been exceeded by new publications, and more were constantly forthcoming. Among those particularly worthy of attention, we would recommend *The Hidden Tradition in Europe* by the Bulgarian scholar and historian Yuri Stoyanov.

Did *Holy Blood, Holy Grail* actually contribute to the Zeitgeist, or merely hitch a ride on it? That, of course, is an impossible question to answer definitively. In the years since the book's publication, however, Christian origins, Christian traditions and Christian institutions have come under ever increasing scrutiny, ever increasing suspicion; and recent scandals within the Church have contributed signally to her own loss of credibility. And yet we could not but marvel at the wilful obliviousness, naiveté and, often, sheer ignorance with which biblical material continued – and continues still – to be treated by the media.

In every other sphere of historical enquiry, new material is acknowledged. It may be disputed. Attempts may be made to disparage or discredit it. Alternatively, it may be digested or assimilated. But at least the media, the reviewing establishment and, thereby, the general public are aware of the existing state of knowledge – aware of what has been discovered, of what was said five or twenty or fifty or a hundred years ago. There is some genuine advance, genuine progression, whereby older discoveries and contentions provide a basis for newer discoveries and contentions. Thus does a corpus of understanding come into being. Revolutionary theories may be accepted or discarded, but cognisance is at least taken of them. A context evolves. Cumulative contributions by successive generations of researchers create an ever more comprehensive framework. It is in this fashion that we acquire our perceptions of history in general, as well as of specific epochs and events. It is in this fashion that we acquire a coherent image of such figures as Alexander or Caesar, King Arthur, Robin Hood or Jeanne d'Arc. Their images are constantly growing, constantly mutating, constantly being augmented by new material as it becomes available.

In biblical history, however, a wilful obliviousness prevails, a perverse sort of induced selective amnesia. Thus, for example, each new pronouncement by the former Bishop of Durham could produce a media sensation, as if such pronouncements had never been heard before. Thus a television showing of Martin Scorsese's film, *The Last Temptation,* could precipitate a public controversy, and even elicit fulminations from a Member of Parliament. Thus a recent leader in the *Daily Telegraph* could offhandedly, in passing, refer to the Bible as a 'factual' work, implying no doubt whatever about its factuality.

In 1963, the late Hugh Schonfield published *The Passover Plot,* in which he argued that Jesus did not die on the cross. This assertion was hardly new, hardly original. It had been promulgated for nearly two millennia by a number of so-called 'heresies'. It had been suggested by novelists, by historians, by biblical scholars for centuries. It was widely accepted throughout the Islamic world. And yet Schonfield's book provoked a controversy, and an indignant uproar, of awesome international proportions. In the wake of its publication, it was on everyone's lips, one was constantly hearing it discussed, and there could have been very few literate individuals in the Western world who had not at least heard of it. By the time debate subsided, more than three million copies of the book were in circulation.

Whether Jesus died on the cross or not was ultimately irrelevant to our conclusions in *Holy Blood, Holy Grail.* In the course of our book, however, we did discuss some of Schonfield's arguments. This provoked an entirely new rumpus. 'Authors claim Jesus did not die on the cross!' the media shrieked – as if Schonfield had not said as much a mere twenty years before, as if *The Passover Plot* had never been published. We were baffled and bemused by such naiveté, or by such shortness of memory.

In 1993, A. N. Wilson produced his own speculative biography of Jesus. In this work, he put forward a perfectly plausible argument to the effect that Jesus was, in all probability, married. A fresh furore erupted, as if *Holy Blood, Holy*

Grail had not made the same suggestion a mere decade previously. In another few years, the suggestion will undoubtedly be made again by another author; and the media will undoubtedly prove as forgetful of Wilson's book as they were of ours. Thus does amnesia prevail in the sphere of biblical commentary. And thus must each successive generation, denied knowledge of the works read by its predecessors, make the same ostensibly startling discoveries over and over again. In this climate of ill-informed commentary and perpetuated ignorance, the wilder excesses of rabid fundamentalism can only thrive.

In the meantime, while the media gawped at books like Wilson's, at pronouncements by the former Bishop of Durham and at *The Last Temptation*, material on Rennes-le-Château continued to flow from presses and photocopiers, particularly in France. Having commitments elsewhere, we could not keep abreast of all of it. We did, however, feel obliged to pay periodic visits to the village on which we had brought down such notoriety, and this enabled us to keep in touch with certain developments. Occasionally, we would hear stories from visitors to the village – such as, for example, the destruction of the tomb at Arques. Occasionally, we would hear fragments of gossip about the latest activities of Pierre Plantard de Saint-Clair and the Prieuré de Sion. And sometimes we ourselves, in the course of our other researches, would stumble upon stray snippets of information which constituted additional pieces of the jigsaw. Again, however, we simply had no time to investigate, much less properly pursue, such new leads as offered themselves. In a very real sense, we felt the story had passed out of our hands – had passed beyond us, into the public domain and the hands of other researchers. This, as we stated at the end of *Holy Blood, Holy Grail*, was just what we hoped would happen. We saw ourselves as merely having scratched the surface of something – of a mystery which extended over at least twenty centuries, and radiated out across the whole of Western civilisation. The depths of that mystery had yet to be properly explored and charted.

And yet, despite our increasing distance from the story, new material continued to come our way. In sheer quantity, that material now comprises a weighty dossier of its own. For this new edition of *Holy Blood, Holy Grail*, we have decided to offer at least some of it to our readers, who will find it in the Postscript to the original text. It amounts, in effect, to a 'do-it-yourself' kit, with the aid of which the reader can embark on his or her own 'semiotic exercise', his or her own personal Grail quest.

CHAPTER ONE

VILLAGE OF MYSTERY

At the start of our search we did not know precisely what we were looking for – or, for that matter, looking at. We had no theories and no hypotheses, we had set out to prove nothing. On the contrary, we were simply trying to find an explanation for a curious little enigma of the late nineteenth century. The conclusions we eventually reached were not postulated in advance. We were led to them, step by step, as if the evidence we accumulated had a mind of its own, was directing us of its own accord.

We believed at first that we were dealing with a strictly local mystery – an intriguing mystery certainly, but a mystery of essentially minor significance, confined to a village in the south of France. We believed at first that the mystery, although it involved many fascinating historical strands, was primarily of academic interest. We believed that our investigation might help to illumine certain aspects of Western history, but we never dreamed that it might entail re-writing them. Still less did we dream that whatever we discovered could be of any real contemporary relevance – and explosive contemporary relevance at that.

Our quest began – for it was indeed a quest – with a more or less straightforward story. At first glance this story was not markedly different from numerous other 'treasure stories' or 'unsolved mysteries' which abound in the history and folklore of almost every rural region. A version of it had been publicised in France, where it attracted considerable interest but was not – to our knowledge at the time – accorded any inordinate consequence. As we subsequently learned, there were a number of errors in this version. For the moment, however, we must recount the tale as it was published during the 1960s, and as we first came to know of it.[1]

RENNES-LE-CHÂTEAU AND BÉRENGER SAUNIÈRE

On June 1st, 1885 the tiny French village of Rennes-le-Château received a new parish priest. The curé's name was Bérenger Saunière.[2] He was a robust, handsome, energetic and, it would seem, highly intelligent man aged thirty-three. In seminary school not long before he had seemed destined for a promising clerical career. Certainly he had seemed destined for something more important than a remote village in the eastern foothills of the Pyrenees. Yet at some point he seems to have incurred the displeasure of his superiors. What precisely he did, if anything, remains unclear, but it soon thwarted all prospects of advancement.

Rennes-le-Château in southwestern France. The château of the Hautpoul family can be seen in the centre of the village. Saunière's library tower hangs over the escarpment to the far left.

Bérenger Saunière, the priest of Rennes-le-Château (standing centre). The mystery of his sudden wealth was the starting point of the investigation.

And it was perhaps to rid themselves of him that his superiors sent him to the parish of Rennes-le-Château.

At the time Rennes-le-Château housed only two hundred people. It was a tiny hamlet perched on a steep mountain-top, approximately twenty-five miles from Carcassonne. To another man, the place might have constituted exile – a life sentence in a remote provincial backwater, far from the civilised amenities of the age, far from any stimulus for an eager and inquiring mind. No doubt it was a blow to Saunière's ambition. Nevertheless there were certain compensations. Saunière was a native of the region, having been born and raised only a few miles distant, in the village of Montazels. Whatever its deficiencies, therefore, Rennes-le-Château must have been very like home, with all the comforts of childhood familiarity.

Between 1885 and 1891 Saunière's income averaged, in francs, the equivalent of six pounds sterling per year – hardly opulence, but pretty much what one would expect for a rural curé in late nineteenth-century France. Together with gratuities provided by his parishioners, it appears to have been sufficient – for survival, if not for any extravagance. During those six years Saunière seems to have led a pleasant enough life, and a placid one. He hunted and fished in the mountains and streams of his boyhood. He read voraciously, perfected his Latin, learned Greek, embarked on the study of Hebrew. He employed, as housekeeper and servant, an eighteen-year-old peasant girl named Marie Denarnaud, who was to be his lifelong companion and confidante. He paid frequent visits to his friend, the Abbé Henri Boudet, curé of the neighbouring village of Rennes-les-Bains. And under Boudet's tutelage he immersed himself in the turbulent history of the region – a history whose residues were constantly present around him.

A few miles to the south-east of Rennes-le-Château, for example, looms another peak, called Bézu, surmounted by the ruins of a medieval fortress, which was once a preceptory of the Knights Templar. On a third peak, a mile or so east of Rennes-le-Château, stand the ruins of the château of Blanchefort, ancestral home of Bertrand de Blanchefort, fourth Grand Master of the Knights Templar, who presided over that famous order in the mid-twelfth century. Rennes-le-Château and its environs had been on the ancient pilgrim route, which ran from Northern Europe to Santiago de Compastela in Spain. And the entire region was steeped in evocative legends, in echoes of a rich, dramatic and often bloodsoaked past.

For some time Saunière had wanted to restore the village church of Rennes-le-Château. Consecrated to the Magdalene in 1059, this dilapidated edifice stood on the foundations of a still older Visigoth structure dating from the sixth century. By the late nineteenth century it was, not surprisingly, in a state of almost hopeless disrepair.

In 1891, encouraged by his friend Boudet, Saunière embarked on a modest restoration, borrowing a small sum from the village funds. In the course of his endeavours he removed the altar-stone, which rested on two archaic Visigoth columns. One of these columns proved to be hollow. Inside the curé found four parchments preserved in sealed wooden tubes. Two of these parchments are said to have comprised genealogies, one dating from 1244, the other from 1644. The two remaining documents had apparently been composed in the 1780s by one of Saunière's predecessors as curé of Rennes-le-Château, the Abbé Antoine Bigou. Bigou had also been personal chaplain to the noble Blanchefort family – who, on the eve of the French Revolution, were still

The Visigothic pillar in which Saunière is said to have found, in 1891, a number of genealogical documents and coded texts.

among the most prominent local landowners.

The two parchments from Bigou's time would appear to be pious Latin texts, excerpts from the New Testament. At least ostensibly. But on one of the parchments the words are run incoherently together, with no space between them, and a number of utterly superfluous letters have been inserted. And on the second parchment lines are indiscriminately truncated – unevenly, sometimes in the middle of a word – while certain letters are conspicuously raised above the others. In reality these parchments comprise a sequence of ingenious ciphers or codes. Some of them are fantastically complex and unpredictable, defying even a computer, and insoluble without the requisite key. The following decipherment has appeared in French works devoted to Rennes-le-Château, and in two of our films on the subject made for the BBC.

BERGERE PAS DE TENTATION QUE POUSSIN TENIERS GARDENT LA CLEF
PAX DCLXXXI PAR LA CROIX ET CE CHEVAL DE DIEU J'ACHEVE CE DAE-
MON DE GARDIEN A MIDI POMMES BLEUES
*(SHEPHERDESS, NO TEMPTATION. THAT POUSSIN, TENIERS, HOLD THE
KEY; PEACE 681. BY THE CROSS AND THIS HORSE OF GOD, I COMPLETE –
OR DESTROY – THIS DAEMON OF THE GUARDIAN AT NOON. BLUE
APPLES.)*

But if some of the ciphers are daunting in their complexity, others are patently, even flagrantly obvious. In the second parchment, for instance, the raised letters, taken in sequence, spell out a coherent message.

A DAGOBERT II ROI ET A SION EST CE TRESOR ET IL EST LA MORT.
*(TO DAGOBERT II, KING, AND TO SION BELONGS THIS TREASURE AND HE
IS THERE DEAD.)*

Although this particular message must have been discernible to Saunière, it is doubtful that he could have deciphered the more intricate codes. Nevertheless, he realised he had stumbled upon something of consequence and, with the consent of the village mayor, brought his discovery to his superior, the bishop of Carcassonne. How much the bishop understood is unclear, but Saunière was immediately dispatched to Paris – at the bishop's expense – with instructions to present himself and the parchments to certain important ecclesiastic authorities. Chief among these were the Abbé Bieil, Director General of the Seminary of Saint Sulpice, and Bieil's nephew, Émile Hoffet. At the time Hoffet was training for the priesthood. Although still in his early twenties, he had already established an impressive reputation for scholarship, especially in linguistics, cryptography and palaeography. Despite his pastoral vocation, he was known to be immersed in esoteric thought, and main-

tained cordial relations with the various occult-oriented groups, sects and secret societies which were proliferating in the French capital. This had brought him into contact with an illustrious cultural circle, which included such literary figures as Stéphane Mallarmé and Maurice Maeterlinck, as well as the composer Claude Debussy. He also knew Emma Calvé, who, at the time of Saunière's appearance, had just returned from triumphant performances in London and Windsor. As a diva, Emma Calvé was the Maria Callas of her age. At the same time she was a high priestess of Parisian esoteric sub-culture, and sustained amorous liaisons with a number of influential occultists.

Having presented himself to Bieil and Hoffet, Saunière spent three weeks in Paris. What transpired during his meetings with the ecclesiastics is unknown. What is known is that the provincial country priest was promptly and warmly welcomed into Hoffet's distinguished circle. It has even been asserted that he became Emma Calvé's lover. Contemporary gossips spoke of an affair between them, and one acquaintance of the singer described her as being 'obsessed' with the curé. In any case there is no question but that they enjoyed a close enduring friendship. In the years that followed she visited him frequently in the vicinity of Rennes-le-Château, where, until recently, one could still find romantic hearts carved into the rocks of the mountainside, bearing their initials.

During his stay in Paris, Saunière also spent some time in the Louvre. This may well be connected with the fact that, before his departure, he purchased reproductions of three paintings. One seems to have been a portrait, by an unidentified artist, of Pope Célestin V, who reigned briefly at the end of the thirteenth century. One was a work by David Teniers – although it is not clear which David Teniers, father or son.[3] The third was perhaps the most famous tableau by Nicolas Poussin, 'Les Bergers d'Arcadie' – 'The Shepherds of Arcadia'.

On his return to Rennes-le-Château, Saunière resumed his restoration of the village church. In the process he exhumed a curiously carved flagstone, dating from the seventh or eighth century, which may have had a crypt beneath it, a burial chamber in which skeletons were said to have been found. Saunière also embarked on projects of a rather more singular kind. In the churchyard, for example, stood the sepulchre of Marie, Marquise d'Hautpoul de Blanchefort. The headstone and flagstone marking her grave had been designed and installed by the Abbé Antoine Bigou – Saunière's predecessor of a century before, who had

'Et in Arcadia Ego' *by the French painter, Nicolas Poussin. This, his first painting on the theme, was completed c 1630.*

'Les Bergers d'Arcadie' *by Nicolas Poussin, c 1640-1642. Christopher Wright, in his* Poussin Paintings - A Catalogue Raisonné, *(1984), says of the remarkable resemblance to the real tomb and landscape near to Rennes-le-Château:* "These similarities are undeniable and are unlikely to have been coincidental."

apparently composed two of the mysterious parchments.

Not knowing that the inscription on the marquise's tomb had already been copied, Saunière obliterated them. Nor was this desecration the only curious behaviour he exhibited. Accompanied by his faithful housekeeper, he began to make long journeys on foot about the countryside, collecting rocks of no apparent value or interest. He also embarked on a voluminous exchange of letters with unknown correspondents throughout France, as well as in Germany, Switzerland, Italy, Austria and Spain. He took to collecting stacks of utterly worthless postage stamps. And he opened certain shadowy transactions with various banks. One of them even dispatched a representative from Paris, who travelled all the way to Rennes-le-Château for the sole purpose of ministering to Saunière's business.

In postage alone Saunière was already spending a substantial sum – more than his previous annual income could possibly sustain. Then, in

Previous page; The 'Tour Magdala', constructed by Saunière at Rennes-le-Château with his new-found wealth and which housed his library.

1896, he began to spend in earnest, on a staggering and unprecedented scale. By the end of his life in 1917 his expenditure would amount to the equivalent of several million pounds at least.

Some of this unexplained wealth was devoted to laudable public works – a modern road was built leading up to the village, for example, and facilities for running water were provided. Other expenditures were more quixotic. A tower was built, the Tour Magdala, overlooking the sheer side of the mountain. An opulent country house was constructed, called the Villa Bethania, which Saunière himself never occupied. And the church was not only redecorated, but redecorated in a most bizarre fashion.

Immediately inside the entrance a hideous statue was erected, a gaudy representation of the demon Asmodeus – custodian of secrets, guardian of hidden treasures and, according to ancient Judaic legend, builder of Solomon's Temple. On the church walls lurid, garishly painted plaques were installed depicting the Stations of the Cross – each was characterised by some odd inconsistency, some inexplicable added detail, some flagrant or subtle deviation from accepted Scriptural account. In Station VIII for example, there is a child swathed in a Scottish plaid. In Station XIV, which portrays Jesus's body being carried into the tomb, there is a background of dark nocturnal sky, dominated by a full moon. It is almost as if Saunière were trying to intimate something. But what? That Jesus's burial occurred after nightfall, several hours later than the Bible tells us it did? Or that the body is being carried out of the tomb, not into it?

Saunière's statue of St Mary Magdalen, patron saint of Rennes-le-Château, in the porch of the village church. She is shown here, in accordance with the legend that 'she came to France bearing the True Cross and the Grail.'

While engaged in this curious adornment, Saunière continued to spend extravagantly. He collected rare china, precious fabrics, antique marbles. He created an orangery and a zoological garden. He assembled a magnificent library. Shortly before his death, he was allegedly planning to build a massive Babel-like tower lined with books, from which he intended to preach. Nor were his parishioners neglected. Saunière regaled them with sumptuous banquets and other forms of largesse, maintaining the life-style of a medieval potentate presiding over an impregnable mountain domain. In his remote and well-nigh inaccessi-

The painted bas-relief of the fourteenth Station of the Cross in Rennes-le-Château Church. By tradition, this Station always depicts Jesus being laid into the Tomb. Saunière's version subtly alters the meaning. The New Testament informs us that Christ was taken down from the Cross before nightfall - the beginning of the Passover. But here Saunière shows us a full moon in a night-dark sky. This is later. Passover has already begun. Could Saunière be suggesting that - concealed in the darkness of night - Jesus was carried out again?

ble eyrie he received a number of notable guests. One, of course, was Emma Calvé. One was the French Secretary of State for Culture. But perhaps the most august and consequential visitor to the unknown country priest was the Archduke Johann von Habsburg, a cousin of Franz-Josef, Emperor of Austria. Bank statements subsequently

*Drawing of the headstone of
the tomb of Marie de Negre
D'Ables, Marquise
d'Hautpoul de Blanchefort.
Saunière is said to have
effaced the inscription.*

revealed that Saunière and the archduke had opened consecutive accounts on the same day, and that the latter had made a substantial sum over to the former.

The ecclesiastical authorities at first turned a blind eye. When Saunière's former superior at Carcassonne died, however, the new bishop attempted to call the priest to account. Saunière responded with startling and brazen defiance. He refused to explain his wealth. He refused to accept the transfer the bishop ordered. Lacking any more substantial charge, the bishop accused him of simony – illicitly selling masses – and a local tribunal suspended him. Saunière appealed to the Vatican, which exonerated and reinstated him.

On January 17th, 1917, Saunière, then in his sixty-fifth year, suffered a sudden stroke. The date of January 17th is perhaps suspicious. The same date appears on the tombstone of the Marquise d'Hautpoul de Blanchefort – the tombstone Saunière had eradicated. And January 17th is also the feast day of Saint Sulpice, who, as we were to discover, figured throughout our story. It was at the Seminary of Saint Sulpice that he confided his parchments to the Abbé Bieil and Émile Hoffet. But what makes Saunière's stroke on January 17th most suspicious is the fact that five days before, on January 12th, his parishioners declared that he had seemed to be in enviable health for a man of his age. Yet on January 12th, according to a receipt in our possession, Marie Denarnaud had ordered a coffin for her master.

As Saunière lay on his deathbed, a priest was called from a neighbouring parish to hear his final confession and administer the last rites. The priest duly arrived and retired into the sickroom. According to eye-witness testimony, he emerged shortly thereafter, visibly shaken. In the words of one account he 'never smiled again'. In the words of another he lapsed into an acute depression that lasted for several months. Whether these accounts are exaggerated or not, the priest, presumably on the basis of Saunière's confession, refused to administer extreme unction.

On January 22nd Saunière died unshriven. The following morning his body was placed upright in an armchair on the terrace of the Tour Magdala, clad in an ornate robe adorned with scarlet tassels. One by one, certain unidentified mourners filed past, many of them plucking tassels of remembrance from the dead man's garment. There has never been any explanation of

The broken remains of the tomb of Marie, Marquise d'Hautpoul de Blanchefort.

this ceremony. Present-day residents of Rennes-le-Château are as mystified by it as everyone else.

The reading of Saunière's will was awaited with great anticipation. To everyone's surprise and chagrin, however, it declared him to be utterly penniless. At some point before his death he had apparently transferred the whole of his wealth to Marie Denarnaud, who had shared his life and secrets for thirty-two years. Or perhaps most of that wealth had been in Marie's name from the very beginning.

Following the death of her master, Marie continued to live a comfortable life in the Villa Bethania until 1946. After the Second World War, however, the newly installed French government issued a new currency. As a means of apprehending tax-evaders, collaborators and wartime profiteers, French citizens, when exchanging old francs for new, were obliged to account for their revenues. Confronted by the prospect of an explanation, Marie chose poverty. She was seen in the garden of the villa, burning vast sheaves of old franc notes.

For the next seven years Marie lived austerely, supporting herself on money obtained from the sale of Villa Bethania. She promised the purchaser, Monsieur Noël Corbu, that she would confide to him, before her death, a 'secret' which would make him not only rich but also 'powerful'. On January 29th, 1953, however, Marie, like her master before her, suffered a sudden and unexpected stroke – which left her prostrate on

The enamel heart which once marked the grave of Saunière's housekeeper and confidant, Marie Denarnaud, who died suddenly in 1953. The original - and its replacement - have since been stolen.

her deathbed, incapable of speech. To Monsieur Corbu's intense frustration, she died shortly thereafter, carrying her secret with her.

THE POSSIBLE TREASURES

This, in its general outlines, was the story published in France during the 1960s. This was the form in which we first became acquainted with it. And it was to the questions raised by the story in this form that we, like other researchers of the subject, addressed ourselves.

The first question is fairly obvious. What was the source of Saunière's money? Whence could such sudden and enormous wealth have come? Was the explanation ultimately banal? Or was there something more exciting involved? The latter possibility imparted a tantalising quality to the mystery, and we could not resist the impulse to play detectives.

We began by considering the explanations suggested by other researchers. According to many of these, Saunière had indeed found a treasure of some kind. This was a plausible enough assumption, for the history of the village and its environs includes many possible sources of hidden gold or jewels.

In prehistoric times, for example, the area around Rennes-le-Château was regarded as a sacred site by the Celtic tribes who lived there; and the village itself, once called Rhédae, derived its name from one of these tribes. In Roman times the area was a large and thriving community, important for its mines and therapeutic hot springs. And the Romans, too, regarded the site as sacred. Later researchers have found traces of several pagan temples.

During the sixth century, the little mountain-top village was supposedly a town with 30,000 inhabitants. At one point it seems to have been the northern capital of the empire ruled by the Visigoths – the Teutonic people who had swept westwards from Central Europe, sacked Rome, toppled the Roman Empire and established their own domain straddling the Pyrenees.

For another five hundred years the town remained the seat of an important county, or comté, the Comté of Razès. Then, at the beginning of the thirteenth century, an army of northern knights descended on the Languedoc to stamp out the Cathar or Albigensian heresy and claim the rich spoils of the region for themselves. During the atrocities of the so-called Albigensian Crusade, Rennes-le-Château was captured and transferred from hand to hand as a fief. A century and a quarter later, in the 1360s, the local population was decimated by plague; and Rennes-le-Château was destroyed shortly thereafter by roving Catalan bandits.[4]

Tales of fantastic treasure are interwoven with many of these historical vicissitudes. The Cathar heretics, for example, were reputed to possess something of fabulous and even sacred value – which according to a number of legends, was the Holy Grail. There was also the vanished treasure of the Knights Templar, whose Grand Master, Bertrand de Blanchefort, commissioned certain mysterious excavations in the vicinity. According to all accounts, these excavations were of a markedly clandestine nature, performed by a specially imported contingent of German miners. If some kind of Templar treasure were indeed concealed around Rennes-le-Château, this might explain the reference to 'Sion' in the parchments discovered by Saunière.

There were other possible treasures as well. Between the fifth and eighth centuries much of modern France was ruled by the Merovingian dynasty, which included King Dagobert II. Rennes-le-Château, in Dagobert's time, was a Visigoth bastion, and Dagobert himself was married to a Visigoth princess. The town might have constituted a sort of royal treasury; and there are documents which speak of great wealth amassed by Dagobert for military conquest and concealed in the environs of Rennes-le-Château. If Saunière discovered some such depository, it would explain the reference in the codes to Dagobert.

The Cathars. The Templars. Dagobert II. And there was yet another possible treasure – the vast booty accumulated by the Visigoths during their tempestuous advance through Europe. This might have included something more than conventional booty, possibly items of immense relevance – both symbolic and literal – to Western religious tradition. It might, in short, have included the legendary treasure of the Temple of Jerusalem – which, even more than the Knights Templar, would warrant the references to 'Sion'.

In A.D. 66 Palestine rose in revolt against the Roman yoke. Four years later, in A.D. 70, Jerusalem was razed by the legions of the emperor, under the command of his son, Titus. The Temple itself was sacked and

Stone head supposedly depicting King Dagobert II ... or his son, Sigebert ... or the 'Head of the Saviour'. It is here seen, mounted in the back wall of the presbytery at Rennes-les-Bains, where it is said to have been placed by Saunière's friend, the Abbé Boudet. It was removed following the disastrous floods of September 1992.

The crumbling château at Rennes-le-Château, formerly the seat of the Hautpoul family.

the contents of the Holy of Holies carried back to Rome. As they are depicted on Titus's triumphal arch, these included the immense gold seven-branched candelabrum so sacred to Judaism, and possibly even the Ark of the Covenant.

Three and a half centuries later, in A.D. 410, Rome in her turn was sacked by the invading Visigoths under Alaric the Great, who pillaged virtually the entire wealth of the Eternal City. As the historian Procopius tells us, Alaric made off with 'the treasures of Solomon, the King of the Hebrews, a sight most worthy to be seen, for they were adorned in the most part with emeralds and in the olden time they had been taken from Jerusalem by the Romans.'[5]

Treasure, then, may well have been the source of Saunière's unexplained wealth. The priest may have discovered any of several treasures, or he may have discovered a single treasure which repeatedly changed hands through the centuries – passing perhaps from the Temple of Jerusalem, to the Romans, to the Visigoths, eventually to the Cathars and/or the Knights Templar. If this were so, it would explain why the treasure in question 'belonged' both to Dagobert II and to Sion.

Thus far our story seemed to be essentially a treasure story. And a treasure story – even one involving the treasure of the Temple of Jerusalem – is ultimately of limited relevance and significance. People are constantly discovering treasures of one kind or another. Such discoveries are often exciting, dramatic and mysterious, and many of them cast important illumination on the past. Few of them, however, exercise any direct influence, political or otherwise, on the present – unless, of course, the treasure in question includes a secret of some sort, and possibly an explosive one.

We did not discount the argument that Saunière discovered treasure. At the same time it seemed clear to us that, whatever else he discovered, he also discovered a secret – an historical secret of immense import to his own time and perhaps to our own as well. Mere money, gold or jewels would not, in themselves, explain a number of facets to his story. They would not account for his introduction to Hoffet's circle, for instance, his association with Debussy and his liaison with Emma Calvé. They would not explain the Church's intense interest in the matter, the impunity with which Saunière defied his bishop or his subsequent exoneration by the Vatican, which seemed to have displayed an urgent concern of its own. They would not explain a priest's refusal to administer the last rites to a dying man, or the visit of a Habsburg archduke to a remote little village in the Pyrenees. The Habsburg archduke in question has since been revealed as Johann Salvator von Habsburg, known by the pseudonym of Jean Orth. He renounced all his rights and titles in 1889 and within two months had been banished from all the territories of the Empire. It was shortly after this that he first appeared in Rennes-le-Château. Said officially to have died in 1890 but in fact died in Argentina in 1910 or 1911. See *Les Maisons Souveraines de L'Autriche* by Dr. Dugast Rouillé, Paris, 1967, page 191. Nor would money, gold or jewels explain the powerful aura of mystification surrounding the whole affair, from the elaborate coded ciphers to Marie Denarnaud burning her inheritance of banknotes. And Marie herself had promised to divulge a 'secret' which conferred not merely wealth but 'power' as well.

On these grounds we grew increasingly convinced that Saunière's story involved more than riches, and that it involved a secret of some kind, one that was almost certainly controversial. In other words it seemed to us that the mystery was not confined to a remote backwater village and nineteenth-century priest. Whatever it was, it appeared to radiate out from Rennes-le-Château and produce ripples – perhaps even a potential tidal wave – in the world beyond. Could Saunière's wealth have come not from anything of intrinsic financial value, but from knowledge of some kind? If so, could this knowledge have been turned to fiscal account? Could it have been used to blackmail somebody, for example? Could Saunière's wealth have been his payment for silence?

We knew that he had received money from Johann von Habsburg. At the same time, however, the priest's 'secret', whatever it was, seemed to be more religious in nature than political. Moreover, his relations with the Austrian archduke, according to all accounts, were notably cordial. On the other hand, there was one institution which, throughout Saunière's later career, seems to have been distinctly afraid of him, and to have treated him with kid gloves – the Vatican. Could Saunière have been blackmailing the Vatican? Granted such blackmail would be

A mysterious pool, once in the centre of a triangular field at Coume-Sourde, near Rennes-le-Château and close to La Valdieu – the Valley of God. It fulfils the requirements for a mikveh *– a bath of ritual purification.*

a presumptuous and dangerous undertaking for one man, however exhaustive his precautions. But what if he were aided and supported in his enterprise by others, whose eminence rendered them inviolable to the church, like the French Secretary of State for Culture, or the Habsburgs? What if the Archduke Johann were only an intermediary, and the money he bestowed on Saunière actually issued from the coffers of Rome?[6]

THE INTRIGUE

In February 1972 *The Lost Treasure of Jerusalem?*, the first of our three films on Saunière and the mystery of Rennes-le-Château, was shown. The film made no controversial assertions, it simply told the 'basic story' as it has been recounted in the preceding pages. Nor was there any speculation about an 'explosive secret' or high-level blackmail. It is also worth mentioning that the film did not cite Émile Hoffet – the young clerical scholar in Paris to whom Saunière confided his parchments – by name.

Not surprisingly perhaps, we received a veritable deluge of mail. Some of it offered intriguing speculative suggestions. Some of it was complimentary. Some of it was dotty. Of all these letters, one, which the writer did not wish us to publicise, seemed to warrant special attention. It came from a retired Anglican priest and seemed a curious and provocative *non sequitur*. Our correspondent wrote with categorical certainty and authority. He made his assertions baldly and definitively, with no elaboration, and with apparent indifference as to whether we believed him or not. The 'treasure', he declared flatly, did not involve gold or precious stones. On the contrary, it consisted of 'incontrovertible proof' that the Crucifixion was a fraud and that Jesus was alive as late as A.D. 45.

This claim sounded flagrantly absurd. What, even to a convinced atheist, could possibly comprise 'incontrovertible proof' that Jesus survived the Crucifixion? We were unable to imagine anything which could not be disbelieved or repudiated – which would not only comprise 'proof', but 'proof' that was truly 'incontrovertible'. At the same time the sheer extravagance of the assertion begged for clarification and elaboration. The writer of the letter had provided a return address. At the earliest opportunity we drove to see him and attempted to interview him.

In person he was rather more reticent than he had been in his letter, and seemed to regret having written to us in the first place. He refused to expand upon his reference to 'incontrovertible proof' and volunteered only one additional fragment of information. This 'proof' he said, or its existence at any rate, had been divulged to him by another Anglican cleric, Canon Alfred Leslie Lilley.

Lilley, who died in 1940, had published widely and was not unknown. During much of his life he had maintained contacts with the Catholic Modernist Movement, based primarily at Saint Sulpice in Paris. In his youth Lilley had worked in Paris, and had been acquainted with Émile Hoffet. The trail had come full circle. Given a connection between Lilley and Hoffet, the claims of the priest, however preposterous, could not be summarily dismissed.

Similar evidence of a monumental secret was forthcoming when we began to research the life of Nicolas Poussin, the great seventeenth-century painter whose name recurred throughout Saunière's story. In 1656 Poussin, who was living in Rome at the time, had received a visit from the Abbé Louis Fouquet, brother of Nicolas Fouquet, Superintendent of Finances to Louis XIV of France. From Rome, the abbé dispatched a letter to his brother, describing his meeting with Poussin. Part of this letter is worth quoting.

> He and I discussed certain things, which I shall with ease be able to explain to you in detail – things which will give you, through Monsieur Poussin, advantages which even kings would have great pains to draw from him, and which, according to him, it is possible that nobody else will ever rediscover in the centuries to come. And what is more, these are things so difficult to discover that nothing now on this earth can prove of better fortune nor be their equal.[7]

Neither historians nor biographers of Poussin or Fouquet have ever been able satisfactorily to explain this letter, which clearly alludes to some mysterious matter of immense import. Not long after receiving it, Nicolas Fouquet was arrested and imprisoned for the duration of his life. According to certain accounts, he was held strictly incommunicado – and some historians regard him as a likely candidate for the Man in the Iron Mask. In the meantime the whole of his correspondence was confiscated by Louis XIV, who inspected all of it personally. In the years

that followed the king went determinedly out of his way to obtain the original of Poussin's painting, 'Les Bergers d'Arcadie'. When he at last succeeded it was sequestered in his private apartments at Versailles.

Whatever its artistic greatness, the painting would seem to be innocent enough. In the foreground three shepherds and a shepherdess are gathered about a large antique tomb, contemplating the inscription in the weathered stone: 'ET IN ARCADIA EGO'. In the background looms a rugged, mountainous landscape of the sort generally associated with Poussin. According to Anthony Blunt, as well as other Poussin experts, this landscape was wholly mythical, a product of the painter's imagination. In the early 1970s, however, an actual tomb was located, identical to the one in the painting – identical in setting, dimensions, proportions, shape, surrounding vegetation, even in the circular outcrop of rock on which one of Poussin's shepherds rests his foot. This actual tomb stands on the outskirts of a village called Arques – approximately six miles from Rennes-le-Château, and three miles from the château of Blanchefort. If one stands before the sepulchre the vista is virtually indistinguishable from that in the painting. And then it becomes apparent that one of the peaks in the background of the painting is Rennes-le-Château.

There is no indication of the age of the tomb. It may, of course, have been erected quite recently – but how did its builders ever locate a setting which matches so precisely that of the painting? In fact it would seem to have been standing in Poussin's time, and 'Les Bergers d'Arcadie' would seem to be a faithful rendering of the actual site. According to local farmers, the tomb has been there for as long as they, their parents and grandparents can remember. And there is said to be specific mention of it in a *mémoire* dating from 1709.[8]

According to records in the village of Arques, the land on which the tomb starts belonged, until his death in the 1950s, to an American, one Louis Lawrence of Boston, Massachusetts. In the 1920s Mr Lawrence opened the sepulchre and found it empty. His wife and mother-in-law were later buried in it.

When preparing the first of our BBC films on Rennes-le-Château, we spent a morning shooting footage of the tomb. We broke off for lunch and returned some three hours later. During our absence, a crude and violent attempt had been made to smash into the sepulchre.

If there was once an inscription on the actual tomb, it had long since been weathered away. As for the inscription on the tomb in Poussin's painting, it would seem to be conventionally elegiac – Death announcing his sombre presence even in Arcadia, the idyllic pastoral paradise of classical myth. And yet the inscription is curious because it lacks a verb. Literally translated, it reads:

AND IN ARCADIA I . . .

Why should the verb be missing? Perhaps for a philosophical reason – to preclude all tense, all indication of past, present or future, and thereby to imply something eternal? Or perhaps for a reason of a more practical nature.

The codes in the parchments found by Saunière had relied heavily on anagrams, on the transposition and rearrangement of letters. Could 'ET IN ARCADIA EGO' also perhaps be an anagram? Could the verb have been omitted so that the inscription would consist only of certain precise letters? One of our television viewers, in writing to us, suggested that this might indeed be so – and then rearranged the letters into a coherent Latin statement. The result was:

I TEGO ARCANA DEI
(BEGONE! I CONCEAL THE SECRETS OF GOD)

We were pleased and intrigued by this ingenious exercise. We did not realise at the time how extraordinarily appropriate the resulting admonition was.

CHAPTER TWO

THE CATHARS AND THE GREAT HERESY

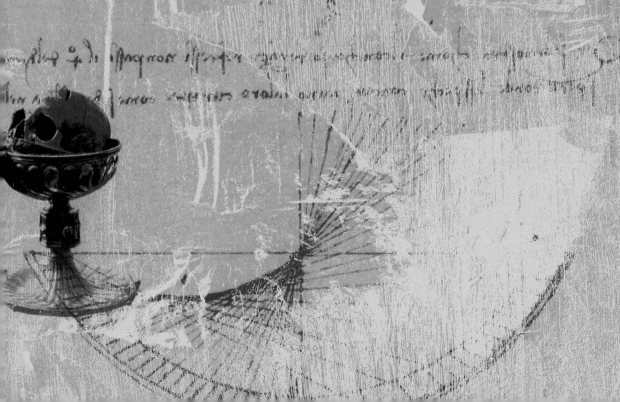

We began our investigation at a point with which we already had a certain familiarity – the Cathar or Albigensian heresy and the crusade it provoked in the thirteenth century. We were already aware that the Cathars figured somehow in the mystery surrounding Saunière and Rennes-le-Château. In the first place the medieval heretics had been numerous in the village and its environs, which suffered brutally during the course of the Albigensian Crusade. Indeed, the whole history of the region is soaked in Cathar blood, and the residues of that blood, along with much bitterness, persist to the present day. Many local farmers in the area now, with no inquisitors to fall upon them, openly proclaim Cathar sympathies. There is even a Cathar church and a so-called 'Cathar pope' who, until his death in 1978, lived in the village of Arques.

We knew that Saunière had immersed himself in the history and folklore of his native soil, so he could not possibly have avoided contact with Cathar thought and traditions. He could not have been unaware that Rennes-le-Château was an important town in the twelfth and thirteenth centuries, and something of a Cathar bastion. Saunière must also have been familiar with the numerous legends attached to the Cathars. He must have known of the rumours connecting them with that fabulous object, the Holy Grail. And if Richard Wagner, in quest of something pertaining to the Grail, did indeed visit Rennes-le-Château, Saunière could not have been ignorant of that fact either.

In 1890, moreover, a man named Jules Doinel became librarian at Carcassonne and established a neo-Cathar church.[1] Doinel himself wrote prolifically on Cathar thought, and by 1896 had become a prominent member of a local cultural organisation, the Society of Arts and Sciences of Carcassonne. In 1898 he was elected its secretary. This society included a number of Saunière's associates, among them his best friend, the Abbé Henri Boudet. And Doinel's own personal circle included Emma Calvé. It is therefore very probable that Doinel and Saunière were acquainted.

There is a further, and more provocative, reason for linking the Cathars with the mystery of Rennes-le-Château. In one of the parchments found by Saunière, the text is sprinkled with a handful of small letters – eight, to be precise – quite deliberately different from all the others. Three of the letters are towards the top of the page, five towards the bottom. These eight letters have only to be read in sequence for them to spell out two words – 'REX MUNDI'. This is unmistakably a Cathar term, which is immediately recognisable to anyone familiar with Cathar thought.

Given these factors, it seemed reasonable enough to commence our investigation with the Cathars. We therefore began to research into them, their beliefs and traditions, their history and milieu in detail. Our inquiry opened new dimensions of mystery, and generated a number of tantalising questions.

THE ALBIGENSIAN CRUSADE

In 1209 an army of some 30,000 knights and foot-soldiers from Northern Europe descended like a whirlwind on the Languedoc – the mountainous north-eastern foothills of the Pyrenees in what is now southern France. In the ensuing war the whole territory was ravaged, crops were destroyed, towns and cities were razed, a whole population was put to the sword. This extermination occurred on so vast, so terrible a scale that it may well constitute the first case of 'genocide' in modern European history. In the town of Béziers alone, for example, at least 15,000 men, women and children were slaughtered wholesale – many of them in the sanctuary of the church itself. When an officer inquired of the pope's representative how he might distinguish heretics from true believers, the reply was, 'Kill them all. God will recognise His own.' This quotation, though widely reported, may be apocryphal. Nevertheless, it typifies the fanatical zeal and bloodlust with which the atrocities were perpetrated. The same papal representative, writing to Innocent III in Rome, announced proudly that 'neither age nor sex nor status was spared'.

After Béziers, the invading army swept through the whole of the Languedoc. Perpignan fell, Narbonne fell, Carcassonne fell, Toulouse fell. And, wherever the victors passed, they left a trail of blood, death and carnage in their wake.

This war, which lasted for nearly forty years, is now known as the Albigensian Crusade. It was a crusade in the true sense of the word. It had been called by the pope himself. Its participants wore a cross on their tunics, like crusaders in Palestine. And the rewards were the same as they were for crusaders in the Holy Land – remission of all sins, an expiation of penances, an assured place in Heaven and all the booty one could plunder. In this Crusade, moreover, one did not even have to cross the sea. And in accordance with feudal law, one was obliged to fight for no more than forty days – assuming, of course, that one had no interest in plunder.

By the time the Crusade was over, the Languedoc had been utterly transformed, plunged back into the barbarity that characterised the rest of Europe. Why? For what had all this havoc, brutality and devastation occurred?

At the beginning of the thirteenth century the area now known as the Languedoc was not officially a part of France. It was an independent principality, whose language, culture and political institutions had less in common with the north than they had with Spain – with the kingdoms of León, Aragon and Castile. The principality was ruled by a handful of noble families, chief of whom were the counts of Toulouse and the powerful house of Trencavel. And within the confines of this principality, there flourished a culture which, at the time, was the most advanced and sophisticated in Christendom, with the possible exception of Byzantium.

The Languedoc had much in common with Byzantium. Learning, for example, was highly esteemed, as it was not in Northern Europe. Philosophy and other intellectual activities flourished; poetry and courtly love were extolled; Greek, Arabic and Hebrew were enthusiastically studied; and at Lunel and Narbonne, schools devoted to the Kabbalah – the ancient esoteric tradition of Judaism – were thriving. Even the nobility was literate and literary, at a time when most Northern nobles could not even sign their names.

Like Byzantium, too, the Languedoc practised a civilised, easy-going religious tolerance – in contrast to the fanatical zeal that characterised other parts of Europe. Skeins of Islamic and Judaic thought, for instance, were imported through maritime commercial centres like Marseilles, or made their way across the Pyrenees from Spain. At the same time, the Roman Church enjoyed no very high esteem; Roman clerics in the Languedoc, by virtue of their notorious corruption, succeeded primarily in alienating the populace. There were churches, for example, in which no mass had been said for more than thirty years. Many priests ignored their parishioners and ran businesses or large estates. One archbishop of Narbonne never even visited his diocese.

Whatever the corruption of the church, the Languedoc had reached an apex of culture that would not be seen in Europe again until the Renaissance. But, as in Byzantium, there were elements of complacency, decadence and tragic weakness which rendered the region unprepared for the onslaught subsequently unleashed upon it. For some time both the Northern European nobility and the Roman Church had been aware of its vulnerability, and were eager to exploit it. The Northern nobility had for many years coveted the wealth and luxury of the Languedoc. And the Church was interested for its own reasons. In the first place its authority in the region was slack. And while culture flourished in the Languedoc, something else flourished as well – the major heresy of medieval Christendom.

In the words of Church authorities the Languedoc was 'infected' by the Albigensian heresy, 'the foul leprosy of the South'. And although the adherents of this heresy were essentially non-violent, they constituted a severe threat to Roman authority, the most severe threat, indeed, that Rome would experience until three centuries later when teachings of Martin Luther began the Reformation. By 1200 there was a very real prospect of this heresy displacing Roman Catholicism as the dominant form of Christianity in the Languedoc. And what was more ominous still in the Church's eyes, it was already radiating out to other parts of Europe, especially to urban centres in Germany, Flanders and Champagne.

The heretics were known by a variety of names. In 1165 they had been condemned by an ecclesiastical council at the Languedoc town of Albi. For this reason, or perhaps because Albi continued to be one of their centres, they were often called Albigensians. On other occasions they were called Cathars or Cathares or Cathari. In Italy they were called Patarines. Not infrequently they were also branded or stigmatised with the names of much earlier heresies – Arian, Marcionite and Manichaean.

'Albigensian' and 'Cathar' were essentially generic names. In other words they did not refer to a single coherent church, like that of Rome, with a fixed, codified and definitive body of doctrine and theology. The heretics in question comprised a multitude of diverse sects – many under the direction of an independent leader, whose followers would assume his name. And while these sects may have held to certain common principles, they diverged radically from one another in detail. Moreover, much of our information about the heretics derives from ecclesiastical sources like the Inquisition. To form a picture of them from such sources is like trying to form a picture of, say, the French Resistance from the reports of the SS and Gestapo. It is therefore virtually impossible to present a coherent and definitive summary of what actually constituted 'Cathar thought'.

In general the Cathars subscribed to a doctrine of reincarnation and to a recognition of the feminine principle in religion. Indeed, the preachers and teachers of Cathar congregations, known as *parfaits* ('perfected ones'), were of both sexes. At the same time, the Cathars rejected the orthodox Catholic Church and denied the validity of all clerical hierarchies, or official and ordained intercessors between man and God. At the core of this position lay an important Cathar tenet – the repudiation of 'faith', at least as the Church insisted on it. In the place of 'faith' accepted at second hand, the Cathars insisted on direct and personal knowledge, a religious or mystical experience apprehended at first hand. This experience had been called 'gnosis', from the Greek word for 'knowledge', and for the Cathars it took precedence over all creeds and dogma. Given such an emphasis on direct personal contact with God, priests, bishops and other clerical authorities became superfluous.

The Cathars were also dualists. All Christian thought, of course, can ultimately be seen as dualistic, insisting on a conflict between two opposing principles – good and evil, spirit and flesh, higher and lower. But the Cathars carried this dichotomy much further than orthodox Catholicism was prepared to. For the Cathars, men were the swords that spirits fought with, and no one saw the hands. For them, a perpetual war was being waged throughout the whole of creation between two irreconcilable principles – light and darkness, spirit and matter, good and evil. Catholicism posits one supreme God, whose adversary, the Devil, is ultimately inferior to Him. The Cathars, however, proclaimed the existence not of one god, but of two, with more or less comparable status. One of these gods – the 'good' one – was entirely disincarnate, a being or principle of pure spirit, unsullied by the taint of matter. He was the god of love. But love was deemed wholly incompatible with power; and material creation was a manifestation of power. Therefore, for the Cathars, material creation – the world itself – was intrinsically evil. All matter was intrinsically evil. The universe, in short, was the handiwork of a 'usurper god', the god of evil – or, as the Cathars called him, 'Rex Mundi', 'King of the World'.

Catholicism rests on what might be called an 'ethical dualism'. Evil, though issuing ultimately perhaps from the Devil, manifests itself primarily through man and his actions. In contrast, the Cathars maintained a form of 'cosmological dualism', a dualism that pervaded the whole of reality. For the Cathars, this was a basic premise, but their response to it varied from sect to sect. According to some Cathars, the purpose of man's life on earth was to transcend matter, to renounce perpetually anything connected with the principle of power and thereby to attain union with the principle of love. According to other Cathars, man's purpose was to reclaim and redeem matter, to spiritualise and transform it. It is important to note the absence of any fixed dogma, doctrine or theology. As in most deviations from established orthodoxy there are only certain loosely defined attitudes, and the moral obligations attendant on these attitudes were subject to individual interpretation.

In the eyes of the Roman Church the Cathars were committing serious heresies in regarding material creation, on behalf of which Jesus had supposedly died, as intrinsically evil, and implying that God, whose 'word' had created the world 'in the beginning', was a usurper. Their most serious heresy, however, was their attitude towards Jesus himself. Since matter was intrinsically evil, the Cathars denied that Jesus could partake of matter, become incarnate in the flesh, and still be the Son of God. By some Cathars he was therefore deemed to be wholly incorporeal, a 'phantasm', an entity of pure spirit, which, of course, could not possibly be crucified. The majority of Cathars seem to have regarded him as a prophet no different from any other – a mortal being who, on behalf of the principle of love, died on the cross. There was, in short, nothing mystical, nothing supernatural, nothing divine about the Crucifixion – if, indeed, it was relevant at all, which many Cathars appear to have doubted.

In any case, all Cathars vehemently repudiated the significance of both the Crucifixion and the cross – perhaps because they felt these doctrines were irrelevant, or because Rome extolled them so fervently, or because the brutal circumstances of a prophet's death did not seem worthy of worship. And the cross – at least in association with Calvary and the Crucifixion – was regarded as an emblem of Rex Mundi, lord of the material world, the very antithesis of the true redemptive principle. Jesus, if mortal at all, had been a prophet of AMOR, the principle of love. And AMOR, when inverted or perverted or twisted into power, became ROMA – Rome, whose opulent, luxurious Church seemed to the Cathars a palpable embodiment and manifestation on earth of Rex Mundi's sovereignty. In consequence the Cathars not only refused to worship the cross, they also denied such sacraments as baptism and communion.

Despite these subtle, complex, abstract and, to a modern mind perhaps, irrelevant theological positions, most Cathars were not unduly fanatical about their creed. It is intellectually fashionable nowadays to regard the Cathars as a congregation of sages, enlightened mystics or initiates in arcane wisdom, all of whom were privy to some great cosmic secret. In actual fact, however, most Cathars were more or less 'ordinary' men and women, who found in their creed a refuge from the stringency of orthodox Catholicism – a respite from the endless tithes, penances, obsequies, strictures and other impositions of the Roman Church.

However abstruse their theology, the Cathars were eminently realistic people in practice. They condemned procreation, for example, since the propagation of the flesh was a service not to the principle of love, but to Rex Mundi; but they were not so naive as to advocate the abolition of sexuality. True, there was a specific Cathar 'sacrament', or the equivalent thereof, called the *Consolamentum*, which compelled one to chastity. Except for the *parfaits*, however, who were usually ex-family men and women anyway, the *Consolamentum* was not administered until one was on one's death-bed; and it is not inordinately difficult to be chaste when one is dying. So far as the congregation at large was concerned, sexuality was tolerated, if not explicitly sanctioned. How does one condemn procreation while condoning sexuality? There is evidence to suggest that the Cathars practised both birth control and abortion.[2] When Rome subsequently charged the heretics with 'unnatural sexual practices', this was taken to refer to sodomy. However, the Cathars, in so far as records survive, were extremely strict in their prohibition of homosexuality. 'Unnatural sexual practices' may well have referred to various methods of birth control and abortion. We know Rome's position on those issues today. It is not difficult to imagine the energy and vindictive zeal with which that position would have been enforced during the Middle Ages.

Generally, the Cathars seem to have adhered to a life of extreme devotion and simplicity. Deploring churches, they usually conducted their rituals and services in the open air or in any readily available building – a barn, a house, a municipal hall. They also practised what we, today, would call meditation. They were strict vegetarians, although the eating of fish was allowed. And when travelling about the countryside, *parfaits* would always do so in pairs, thus lending credence to the rumours of sodomy sponsored by their enemies.

THE SIEGE OF MONTSÉGUR

This, then, was the creed which swept the Languedoc and adjacent provinces on a scale that threatened to displace Catholicism itself. For a number of comprehensible reasons, many nobles found the creed attractive. Some warmed to its general tolerance. Some were anticlerical anyway. Some were disillusioned with the Church's corruption. Some had lost patience with the tithe system, whereby the income from their estates vanished into the distant coffers of Rome. Thus many nobles, in their old age, became *parfaits*. Indeed, it is estimated that 30 per cent of all *parfaits* were drawn from Languedoc nobility.

In 1145, half a century before the Albigensian Crusade, Saint Bernard himself had journeyed to the Languedoc, intending to preach against the heretics. When he arrived, he was less appalled by the heretics than by the corruption of his own Church. So far as the heretics were concerned, Bernard was clearly impressed by them. 'No sermons are more Christian than theirs,' he declared, 'and their morals are pure.'[3]

By 1200, needless to say, Rome had grown distinctly alarmed by the situation. Nor was she unaware of the envy with which the barons of Northern Europe regarded the rich lands and cities to the south. This envy could readily be exploited, and the Northern lords would constitute the Church's storm-troops. All that was needed was some provocation, some excuse to ignite popular opinion.

Such an excuse was soon forthcoming. On January 14th, 1208, one of the Papal Legates to the Languedoc, Pierre de Castelnau, was murdered. The crime seems to have been committed by anticlerical rebels with no Cathar affiliations whatever. Furnished with the excuse she needed, however, Rome did not hesitate to blame the Cathars. At once Pope Innocent III ordered a Crusade. Although there had been intermittent persecution of heretics all through the previous century, the Church now mobilised her forces in earnest. The heresy was to be extirpated once and for all.

A massive army was mustered under the command of the abbot of Cîteaux. Military operations were entrusted largely to Simon de Montfort – father of the man who was subsequently to play so crucial a role in English history. And under Simon's leadership the pope's crusaders set out to reduce the highest European culture of the Middle Ages to destitution and rubble. In this holy undertaking they were aided by a new and useful ally, a Spanish fanatic named Dominic

Guzmán. Spurred by a rabid hatred of heresy, Guzmán, in 1216, created the monastic order subsequently named after him, the Dominicans. And in 1233 the Dominicans spawned a more infamous institution – the Holy Inquisition. The Cathars were not to be its sole victims. Before the Albigensian Crusade, many Languedoc nobles – especially the influential houses of Trencavel and Toulouse – had been extremely friendly to the region's large indigenous Jewish population. Now all such protection and support was withdrawn by order.

In 1218 Simon de Montfort was killed besieging Toulouse. Nevertheless, the depredation of the Languedoc continued, with only brief respites, for another quarter of a century. By 1243, however, all organised resistance – in so far as there had ever been any – had effectively ceased. By 1243 all major Cathar towns and bastions had fallen to the Northern invaders, except for a handful of remote and isolated strong points. Chief among these was the majestic mountain citadel of Montségur, poised like a celestial ark above the surrounding valleys.

For ten months Montségur was besieged by the invaders, withstanding repeated assaults and maintaining tenacious resistance. At length, in March 1244, the fortress capitulated, and Catharism, at least ostensibly, ceased to exist in the south of France. But ideas can never be stamped out definitively. In his best-selling book, *Montaillou*, for example, Emmanuel Le Roy Ladurie, drawing extensively on documents of the period, chronicles the activities of surviving Cathars nearly half a century after the fall of Montségur. Small enclaves of heretics continued to survive in the mountains, living in caves, adhering to their creed and waging a bitter guerrilla war against their persecutors. In many areas of the Languedoc – including the environs of Rennes-le-Château – the Cathar faith is generally acknowledged to have persisted. And many writers have traced subsequent European heresies to offshoots of Cathar thought – the Waldensians, for instance, the Hussites, the Adamites or Brethren of the Free Spirit, the Anabaptists and the strange Camisards, numbers of whom found refuge in London during the early eighteenth century.

THE CATHAR TREASURE

During the Albigensian Crusade and afterwards, a mystique grew up around the Cathars which still persists today. In part this can be put down to the element of romance that surrounds any lost and tragic cause – that of Bonnie Prince Charlie, for example – with a magical lustre, with a haunting nostalgia, with the 'stuff of legend'. But at the same time, we discovered, there were some very real mysteries associated with the Cathars. While the legends might be exalted and romanticised, a number of enigmas remained.

One of these pertains to the origins of the Cathars; and although this at first seemed an academic point to us, it proved subsequently to be of considerable importance. Most recent historians have argued that the Cathars derived from the Bogomils, a sect active in Bulgaria during the tenth and eleventh centuries, whose missionaries migrated westwards. There is no question that the heretics of the Languedoc included a number of Bogomils. Indeed a known Bogomil preacher was prominent in the political and religious affairs of the time. And yet our research disclosed substantial evidence that the Cathars did not derive from the Bogomils. On the contrary, they seemed to represent the flowering of something already rooted in French soil for centuries. They seemed to have issued, almost directly, from heresies established and entrenched in France at the very advent of the Christian era.[4]

There are other, considerably more intriguing, mysteries associated with the Cathars. Jean de Joinville, for example, an old man writing of his acquaintance with Louis IX during the thirteenth century, writes, 'The king (Louis IX) once told me how several men from among the Albigenses had gone to the Comte de Montfort . . . and asked him to come and look at the body of Our Lord, which had become flesh and blood in the hands of their priest.'[5] Montfort, according to the anecdote, seems somewhat taken aback by the invitation. Rather huffily, he declared that his entourage may go if they wish, but he will continue to believe in accordance with the tenets of 'Holy Church'. There is no further elaboration or explanation of this incident. Joinville himself merely recounts it in passing. But what are we to make of that enigmatic invitation? What were the Cathars doing? What kind of ritual was involved? Leaving aside the Mass, which the Cathars repudiated anyway, what could possibly make 'the body of Our Lord . . . become flesh and blood'? Whatever it might be, there is certainly something disturbingly literal in the statement.

Another mystery surrounds the legendary Cathar 'treasure'. It is known that the Cathars were extremely wealthy. Technically, their creed forbade them to bear arms; and though many ignored this prohibition, the fact remains that large numbers of mercenaries were employed at considerable expense. At the same time, the sources of Cathar wealth – the allegiance they commanded from powerful landowners, for instance – were obvious and explicable. Yet rumours arose, even during the course of the Albigensian Crusade, of a fantastic mystical Cathar treasure, far beyond material wealth. Whatever it was, this treasure was reputedly kept at Montségur. When Montségur fell, however, nothing of consequence was found. And yet there are certain extremely singular incidents connected with the siege and the capitulation of the fortress.

During the siege, the attackers numbered upwards of ten thousand. With this vast force the besiegers attempted to surround the entire mountain, precluding all entry and exit and hoping to starve out the defenders. Despite their numerical strength, however, they lacked sufficient manpower to make their ring completely secure. Many troops were local, moreover, and sympathetic to the Cathars. And many troops were simply unreliable. In consequence, it was not difficult to pass undetected through the attackers' lines. There were many gaps through which men slipped to and fro, and supplies found their way up to the fortress.

The Cathars took advantage of these gaps. In January, nearly three months before the fall of the fortress, two *parfaits* escaped. According to reliable accounts, they carried with them the bulk of the Cathars' material wealth – a load of gold, silver and coin which they carried first to a fortified cave in the mountains and from there to a castle stronghold. After that the treasure vanished and has never been heard of again.

On March 1st Montségur finally capitulated. By then its defenders numbered less than four hundred – between 150 and 180 of them were *parfaits*, the rest being knights, squires, men-at-arms and their families. They were granted surprisingly lenient terms. The fighting men were to receive full pardon for all previous 'crimes'. They would be allowed to depart with their arms, baggage and any gifts, including money, they might receive from their employers. The *parfaits* were also accorded unexpected generosity. Provided they abjured their heretical beliefs and confessed their 'sins' to the Inquisition, they would be freed and subjected only to light penances.

The defenders requested a two-week truce, with a complete halt to hostilities, to consider the terms. In a further display of uncharacteristic generosity, the attackers agreed. In return the defenders voluntarily offered hostages. It was agreed that if anyone attempted to escape from the fortress the hostages would be executed.

Were the *parfaits* so committed to their beliefs that they willingly chose martyrdom instead of conversion? Or was there something they could not – or dared not – confess to the Inquisition? Whatever the answer, not one of the *parfaits*, as far as is known, accepted the besiegers' terms. On the contrary, all of them chose martyrdom. Moreover, at least twenty of the other occupants of the fortress, six women and some fifteen fighting men, voluntarily received the *Consolamentum* and became *parfaits* as well, thus committing themselves to certain death.

On March 15th the truce expired. At dawn the following day more than two hundred *parfaits* were dragged roughly down the mountainside. Not one recanted. There was no time to erect individual stakes, so they were locked into a large wood-filled stockade at the foot of the mountain and burned *en masse*. Confined to the castle, the remainder of the garrison was compelled to look on. They were warned that if any of them sought to escape it would mean death for all of them, as well as for the hostages.

Despite this risk, however, the garrison had connived in hiding four *parfaits* among them. And on the night of March 16th these four men, accompanied by a guide, made a daring escape – again with the knowledge and collusion of the garrison. They descended the sheer western face of the mountain, suspended by ropes and letting themselves down drops of more than a hundred metres at a time.[6]

What were these men doing? What was the purpose of their hazardous escape, which entailed such risk to both the garrison and the hostages? On the next day they could have walked freely out of the fortress, at liberty to resume their lives. Yet for some unknown reason, they embarked on a perilous nocturnal escape which might easily have entailed death for themselves and their colleagues.

According to tradition, these four men carried with them the legendary Cathar treasure. But the Cathar treasure had been smuggled out of Montségur three months before. And how much 'treasure', in any case – how much gold, silver or coin – could three or four men carry on their backs, dangling from ropes on a sheer mountainside? If the four escapees were indeed carrying something, it would seem clear that they were carrying something other than material wealth.

What might they have been carrying? Accoutrements of the Cathar faith perhaps – books, manuscripts, secret teachings, relics, religious objects of some kind; perhaps something which, for one reason or another, could not be permitted to fall into hostile hands. That might

Opposite; The Cathar castle of Montségur in the Languedoc. It became the refuge for the leaders of the Cathar movement in 1232 who built a small village close to its walls. It fell to the northern French crusaders in 1244; over 200 Cathars, men and women, were burned alive in a field at the foot of the hill.

explain why an escape was undertaken – an escape that entailed such risk for everyone involved. But if something of so precious a nature had, at all costs, to be kept out of hostile hands, why was it not smuggled out before? Why was it not smuggled out with the bulk of the material treasure three months previously? Why was it retained in the fortress until this last and most dangerous moment?

The precise date of the truce permitted us to deduce a possible answer to these questions. It had been requested by the defenders, who voluntarily offered hostages to obtain it. For some reason, the defenders seem to have deemed it necessary – even though all it did was delay the inevitable for a mere two weeks.

Perhaps, we concluded, such a delay was necessary to purchase time. Not time in general, but that specific time, that specific date. It coincided with the spring equinox – and the equinox may well have enjoyed some ritual status for the Cathars. It also coincided with Easter. But the Cathars, who questioned the relevance of the Crucifixion, ascribed no particular importance to Easter. And yet it is known that a festival of some sort was held on March 14th, the day before the truce expired.[7] There seems little doubt that the truce was requested in order that this festival might be held. And there seems little doubt that the festival could not be held on a date selected at random. It apparently had to be on March 14th. Whatever the festival was, it clearly made some impression on the hired mercenaries – some of whom, defying inevitable death, converted to the Cathar creed. Could this fact hold at least a partial key to what was smuggled out of Montségur two nights later? Could whatever was smuggled out then have been necessary, in some way, for the festival on the 14th? Could it somehow have been instrumental in persuading at least twenty of the defenders to become *parfaits* at the last moment? And could it in some fashion have ensured the subsequent collusion of the garrison, even at the risk of their lives? If the answer is yes to all these questions, that would explain why whatever was removed on the 16th was not removed earlier – in January, for example, when the monetary treasure was carried to safety. It would have been needed for the festival. And it would then have had to be kept out of hostile hands.

THE MYSTERY OF THE CATHARS

As we pondered these conclusions, we were constantly reminded of the legends linking the Cathars and the Holy Grail.[8] We were not prepared to regard the Grail as anything more than myth. We were certainly not prepared to assert that it ever existed in actuality. Even if it did, we could not imagine that a cup or bowl, whether it held Jesus's blood or not, would be so very precious to the Cathars – for whom Jesus, to a significant degree, was incidental. Nevertheless, the legends continued to haunt and perplex us.

Elusive though it is, there does seem to be some link between the Cathars and the whole cult of the Grail as it evolved during the twelfth and thirteenth centuries. A number of writers have argued that the Grail romances – those of Chrétien de Troyes and Wolfram von Eschenbach, for example – are an interpolation of Cathar thought, hidden in elaborate symbolism, into the heart of orthodox Christianity. There may be some exaggeration in that assertion, but there is also some truth. During the Albigensian Crusade ecclesiastics fulminated against the Grail romances, declaring them to be pernicious, if not heretical. And in some of these romances there are isolated passages which are not only highly unorthodox, but quite unmistakably dualist – in other words, Cathar.

What is more, Wolfram von Eschenbach, in one of his Grail romances, declares that the Grail castle was situated in the Pyrenees – an assertion which Richard Wagner, at any rate, would seem to have taken literally. According to Wolfram, the name of the Grail castle was Munsalvaesche – a Germanicised version apparently of Montsalvat, a Cathar term. And in one of Wolfram's poems the lord of the Grail castle is named Perilla. Interestingly enough, the lord of Montségur was Raimon de Pereille – whose name, in its Latin form, appears on documents of the period as Perilla.[9]

If such striking coincidences persisted in haunting us, they must also, we concluded, have haunted Saunière – who was, after all, steeped in the legends and folklore of the region. And like any other native of the region, Saunière must have been constantly aware of the proximity of Montségur, whose poignant and tragic fate still dominates local consciousness. But for Saunière the very nearness of the fortress may well have entailed certain practical implications.

Something had been smuggled out of Montségur just after the truce expired. According to tradition, the four men who escaped from the doomed citadel carried with them the Cathar treasure. But the monetary treasure had been smuggled out three months earlier. Could the Cathar 'treasure', like the 'treasure' Saunière discovered, have consisted primarily of a secret? Could that secret have been related, in some unimaginable way, to something that became known as the Holy Grail? It seemed inconceivable to us that the Grail romances could possibly be taken literally.

In any case, whatever was smuggled out of Montségur had to have been taken somewhere. According to tradition, it was taken to the fortified caves of Ornolac in the Ariège, where a band of Cathars was exterminated shortly after. But nothing save skeletons has ever been found at Ornolac. On the other hand, Rennes-le-Château is only half a day's ride on horseback from Montségur. Whatever was smuggled out of Montségur might well have been brought to Rennes-le-Château, or, more likely, to one of the caves which honeycomb the surrounding mountains. And if the 'secret' of Montségur was what Saunière subsequently discovered, that would obviously explain a great deal.

In the case of the Cathars, as with Saunière, the word 'treasure' seems to hide something else – knowledge or information of some kind. Given the tenacious adherence of the Cathars to their creed and their militant antipathy to Rome, we wondered if such knowledge or information (assuming it existed) related in some way to Christianity – to the doctrines and theology of Christianity, perhaps to its history and origins. Was it possible, in short, that the Cathars (or at least certain Cathars) knew something – something that contributed to the frenzied fervour with which Rome sought their extermination? The priest who had written to us had referred to 'incontrovertible proof'. Could such 'proof' have been known to the Cathars?

At the time, we could only speculate idly. And information on the Cathars was in general so meagre that it precluded even a working hypothesis. On the other hand our research into the Cathars had repeatedly impinged on another subject, even more enigmatic and mysterious, and surrounded by evocative legends. This subject was the Knights Templar.

It was therefore to the Templars that we next directed our investigation. And it was with the Templars that our inquiries began to yield concrete documentation, and the mystery began to assume far greater proportions than we had ever imagined.

CHAPTER THREE

THE WARRIOR MONKS

To research the Knights Templar proved a daunting undertaking. The voluminous quantity of written material devoted to the subject was intimidating; and we could not at first be sure how much of this material was reliable. If the Cathars had engendered a welter of spurious and romantic legend, the mystification surrounding the Templars was even greater.

On one level they were familiar enough to us – the fanatically fierce warrior-monks, knight-mystics clad in white mantle with splayed red cross, who played so crucial a role in the Crusades. Here, in some sense, were the archetypal crusaders – the storm-troopers of the Holy Land, who fought and died heroically for Christ in their thousands. Yet many writers, even today, regarded them as a much more mysterious institution, an essentially secret order, intent on obscure intrigues, clandestine machinations, shadowy conspiracies and designs. And there remained one perplexing and inexplicable fact. At the end of their two-century-long career, these white-garbed champions of Christ were accused of denying and repudiating Christ, of trampling and spitting on the cross.

In Scott's *Ivanhoe* the Templars are depicted as haughty and arrogant bullies, greedy and hypocritical despots shamelessly abusing their power, cunning manipulators orchestrating the affairs of men and kingdoms. By other nineteenth-century writers they are depicted as vile satanists, devil-worshippers, practitioners of all manner of obscene, abominable and/or heretical rites. More recent historians have been inclined to view them as hapless victims, sacrificial pawns in the high-level political manoeuvrings of Church and state. And there are yet other writers, especially in the tradition of Freemasonry, who regard the Templars as mystical adepts and initiates, custodians of an arcane wisdom that transcends Christianity itself.

Whatever the particular bias or orientation of such writers, no one disputes the heroic zeal of the Templars or their contribution to history. Nor is there any question that their order is one of the most glamorous and enigmatic institutions in the annals of Western culture. No account of the Crusades – or, for that matter, of Europe during the twelfth and thirteenth centuries – will neglect to mention the Templars. At their zenith they were the most powerful and influential organisation in the whole of Christendom, with the single possible exception of the papacy.

And yet certain haunting questions remain. Who and what were the Knights Templar? Were they merely what they appeared to be, or were they something else? Were they simple soldiers on to whom an aura of legend and mystification was subsequently grafted? If so, why? Alternatively was there a genuine mystery connected with them? Could there have been some foundation for the later embellishments of myth?

We first considered the accepted accounts of the Templars – the accounts offered by respected and responsible historians. On virtually every point these accounts raised more questions than they answered. They not only collapsed under scrutiny, but suggested some sort of 'cover-up'. We could not escape the suspicion that something had been deliberately concealed and a 'cover story' manufactured, which later historians had merely repeated.

A seal of the Knights Templar, England, 1303, showing the cross pattée, the crescent moon of the Mother Goddess and stars.

KNIGHTS TEMPLAR – THE ORTHODOX ACCOUNT

So far as is generally known, the first historical information on the Templars is provided by a Frankish historian, Guillaume de Tyre, who wrote between 1175 and 1185. This was at the peak of the Crusades, when Western armies had already conquered the Holy Land and established the Kingdom of Jerusalem – or, as it was called by the Templars themselves, 'Outremer', the 'Land Beyond the Sea'. But by the time Guillaume de Tyre began to write, Palestine had been in Western hands for seventy years, and the Templars had already been in existence for more than fifty. Guillaume was therefore writing of events which predated his own lifetime – events which he had not personally witnessed or experienced, but had learnt of at second or even third hand. At second or third hand and, moreover, on the basis of uncertain authority. For there were no Western chroniclers in Outremer between 1127 and 1144. Thus there are no written records for those crucial years.

We do not, in short, know much of Guillaume's sources, and this may well call some of his statements into question. He may have been drawing on popular word of mouth, on a none too reliable oral tradition. Alternatively, he may have consulted the Templars themselves and recounted what they told him. If this is so, it means he is reporting only what the Templars wanted him to report.

Granted, Guillaume does provide us with certain basic information;

and it is this information on which all subsequent accounts of the Templars, all explanations of their foundation, all narratives of their activities have been based. But because of Guillaume's vagueness and sketchiness, because of the time at which he was writing, because of the dearth of documented sources, he constitutes a precarious basis on which to build a definitive picture. Guillaume's chronicles are certainly useful. But it is a mistake – and one to which many historians have succumbed – to regard them as unimpugnable and wholly accurate. Even Guillaume's dates, as Sir Steven Runciman stresses, 'are confused and at times demonstrably wrong'.[1]

According to Guillaume de Tyre, the Order of the Poor Knights of Christ and the Temple of Solomon was founded in 1118. Its founder is said to be one Hugues de Payen, a nobleman from Champagne and vassal of the count of Champagne.[2] One day Hugues, unsolicited, presented himself with eight comrades at the palace of Baudouin I – king of Jerusalem, whose elder brother, Godfroi de Bouillon, had captured the Holy City nineteen years before. Baudouin seems to have received them most cordially, as did the Patriarch of Jerusalem – the religious leader of the new kingdom and special emissary of the pope.

The declared objective of the Templars, Guillaume de Tyre continues, was, 'as far as their strength permitted, they should keep the roads and highways safe . . . with especial regard for the protection of pilgrims'.[3] So worthy was this objective apparently that the king placed an entire wing of the royal palace at the knights' disposal. And, despite their declared oath of poverty, the knights moved into this lavish accommodation. According to tradition, their quarters were built on the foundations of the ancient Temple of Solomon, and from this the fledgling Order derived its name.

For nine years, Guillaume de Tyre tells us, the nine knights admitted no new candidates to their Order. They were still supposed to be living in poverty – such poverty that official seals show two knights riding a single horse, implying not only brotherhood, but also a penury that precluded separate mounts. This style of seal is often regarded as the most famous and distinctive of Templar devices, descending from the first days of the Order. However, it actually dates from a full century later, when the Templars were hardly poor – if, indeed, they ever were.

According to Guillaume de Tyre, writing a half century later, the Templars were established in 1118 and moved into the king's palace – presumably sallying out from here to protect pilgrims on the Holy

Land's highways and byways. And yet there was, at this time, an official royal historian, employed by the king. His name was Fulk de Chartres, and he was writing not fifty years after the Order's purported foundation but during the very years in question. Curiously enough, Fulk de Chartres makes no mention whatever of Hugues de Payen, Hugues's companions or anything even remotely connected with the Knights Templar. Indeed there is a thunderous silence about Templar activities during the early days of their existence. Certainly there is no record anywhere – not even later – of them doing anything to protect pilgrims. And one cannot but wonder how so few men could hope to fulfil so mammoth a self-imposed task. Nine men to protect the pilgrims on all the thoroughfares of the Holy Land? Only nine? And all pilgrims? If this was their objective, one would surely expect them to welcome new recruits. Yet, according to Guillaume de Tyre, they admitted no new candidates to the Order for nine years.

None the less, within a decade the Templars' fame seems to have spread back to Europe. Ecclesiastical authorities spoke highly of them and extolled their Christian undertaking. By 1128, or shortly thereafter, a tract lauding their virtues and qualities was issued by no less a person than Saint Bernard, abbot of Clairvaux and the age's chief spokesman for Christendom. Bernard's tract, 'In Praise of the New Knighthood', declares the Templars to be the epitome and apotheosis of Christian values.

After nine years, in 1127, most of the nine knights returned to Europe and a triumphal welcome, orchestrated in large part by Saint Bernard. In January 1128 a Church council was convened at Troyes – court of the count of Champagne, Hugues de Payen's liege lord – at which Bernard was again the guiding spirit. At this council the Templars were officially recognised and incorporated as a religious-military order. Hugues de Payen was given the title of Grand Master. He and his subordinates were to be warrior-monks, soldier-mystics, combining the austere discipline of the cloister with a martial zeal tantamount to fanaticism – a 'militia of Christ', as they were called at the time. And it was again Saint Bernard who helped to draw up, with an enthusiastic preface, the rule of conduct to which the knights would adhere – a rule based on that of the Cistercian monastic order, in which Bernard himself was a dominant influence.

The Templars were sworn to poverty, chastity and obedience. They were obliged to cut their hair but forbidden to cut their beards, thus distinguishing themselves in an age when most men were clean-shaven. Diet, dress and other aspects of daily life were stringently regulated in accordance with both monastic and military routines. All members of the Order were obliged to wear white habits or surcoats and cloaks, and these soon evolved into the distinctive white mantle for which the Templars became famous. 'It is granted to none to wear white habits, or to have white mantles, excepting the . . . Knights of Christ.'[4] So stated the Order's rule, which elaborated on the symbolic significance of this apparel, 'To all the professed knights, both in winter and in summer, we give, if they can be procured, white garments, that those who have cast behind them a dark life may know that they are to commend themselves to their creator by a pure and white life.'[5]

In addition to these details, the rule established a loose administrative hierarchy and apparatus. And behaviour on the battlefield was strictly controlled. If captured, for instance, Templars were not allowed to ask for mercy or to ransom themselves. They were compelled to fight to the death. Nor were they permitted to retreat, unless the odds against them exceeded three to one.

In 1139[6] a Papal Bull was issued by Pope Innocent II – a former Cistercian monk at Clairvaux and protégé of Saint Bernard. According to this Bull, the Templars would owe allegiance to no secular or ecclesiastical power other than the pope himself. In other words, they were rendered totally independent of all kings, princes and prelates, and all interference from both political and religious authorities. They had become, in effect, a law unto themselves, an autonomous international empire.

During the two decades following the Council of Troyes, the Order expanded with extraordinary rapidity and on an extraordinary scale. When Hugues de Payen visited England in late 1128, he was received with 'great worship' by King Henry I. Throughout Europe, younger sons of noble families flocked to enrol in the Order's ranks, and vast donations – in money, goods and land – were made from every quarter of Christendom. Hugues de Payen donated his own properties, and all new recruits were obliged to do likewise. On admission to the Order, a man was compelled to sign over all his possessions.

Given such policies, it is not surprising that Templar holdings proliferated. Within a mere twelve months of the Council of Troyes, the Order held substantial estates in France, England, Scotland, Flanders, Spain and Portugal. Within another decade, it also held territory in Italy,

Austria, Germany, Hungary, the Holy Land and points east. Although individual knights were bound to their vow of poverty, this did not prevent the Order from amassing wealth, and on an unprecedented scale. All gifts were welcomed. At the same time, the Order was forbidden to dispose of anything – not even to ransom its leaders. The Temple received in abundance but, as a matter of strict policy, it never gave. When Hugues de Payen returned to Palestine in 1130, therefore, with an entourage – quite considerable for the time – of some three hundred knights, he left behind, in the custody of other recruits, vast tracts of European territory.

In 1146 the Templars adopted the famous splayed red cross – the cross pattée. With this device emblazoned on their mantles, the knights accompanied King Louis VII of France on the Second Crusade. Here they established their reputation for martial zeal coupled with an almost insane foolhardiness, and a fierce arrogance as well. On the whole, however, they were magnificently disciplined – the most disciplined fighting force in the world at the time. The French king himself wrote that it was the Templars alone who prevented the Second Crusade – ill-conceived and mismanaged as it was – from degenerating into a total débâcle.

During the next hundred years the Templars became a power with international influence. They were constantly engaged in high-level diplomacy between nobles and monarchs throughout the Western world and the Holy Land. In England, for example, the Master of the Temple was regularly called to the king's Parliament, and was regarded as head of all religious orders, taking precedence over all priors and abbots in the land. Maintaining close links with both Henry II and Thomas à Becket, the Templars were instrumental in trying to reconcile the sovereign and his estranged archbishop. Successive English kings, including King John, often resided in the Temple's London preceptory, and the Master of the Order stood by the monarch's side at the signing of the Magna Carta.[7]

Nor was the Order's political involvement confined to Christendom alone. Close links were forged with the Muslim world as well – the world so often opposed on the battlefield – and the Templars commanded a respect from Saracen leaders exceeding that accorded any other Europeans. Secret connections were also maintained with the Hashishim or Assassins, the famous sect of militant and often fanatical adepts who were Islam's equivalent of the Templars. The Hashishim paid tribute to the Templars and were rumoured to be in their employ.

On almost every political level the Templars acted as official arbiters in disputes, and even kings submitted to their authority. In 1252 Henry III of England dared to challenge them, threatening to confiscate certain of their domains. 'You Templars . . . have so many liberties and charters that your enormous possessions make you rave with pride and haughtiness. What was imprudently given must therefore be prudently revoked; and what was inconsiderately bestowed must be considerately recalled.' The Master of the Order replied, 'What sayest thou, O King? Far be it that thy mouth should utter so disagreeable and silly a word. So long as thou dost exercise justice, thou wilt reign. But if thou infringe it, thou wilt cease to be King.'[8] It is difficult to convey to the modern mind the enormity and audacity of this statement. Implicitly the Master is taking for his Order and himself a power that not even the papacy dared explicitly claim – the power to make or depose monarchs.

At the same time, the Templars' interests extended beyond war, diplomacy and political intrigue. In effect they created and established the institution of modern banking. By lending vast sums to destitute monarchs they became the bankers for every throne in Europe – and for certain Muslim potentates as well. With their network of preceptories throughout Europe and the Middle East, they also organised, at modest interest rates, the safe and efficient transfer of money for merchant traders, a class which became increasingly dependent upon them. Money deposited in one city, for example, could be claimed and withdrawn in another, by means of promissory notes inscribed in intricate codes. The Templars thus became the primary money-changers of the age, and the Paris preceptory became the centre of European finance.[9] It is even probable that the cheque, as we know and use it today, was invented by the Order.

And the Templars traded not only in money, but in thought as well. Through their sustained and sympathetic contact with Islamic and Judaic culture, they came to act as a clearing-house for new ideas, new dimensions of knowledge, new sciences. They enjoyed a veritable monopoly on the best and most advanced technology of their age – the best that could be produced by armourers, leather-workers, stonemasons, military architects and engineers. They contributed to the development of surveying, map-making, road-building and navigation. They possessed their own sea-ports, shipyards and fleet – a fleet both commercial and military, which was among the first to use the magnetic compass. And as soldiers, the Templars' need to treat wounds and illness made them adept in the use of drugs. The Order maintained its own hospitals with its own physicians and surgeons – whose use of mould extract suggests an understanding of the properties of antibiotics. Modern principles of hygiene and cleanliness were understood. And with an understanding also in advance of their time they regarded epilepsy not as demonic possession but as a controllable disease.[10]

Inspired by its own accomplishments, the Temple in Europe grew increasingly wealthy, powerful and complacent. Not surprisingly perhaps, it also grew increasingly arrogant, brutal and corrupt. 'To drink like a Templar' became a cliché of the time. And certain sources assert that the Order made a point of recruiting excommunicated knights.

But while the Templars attained both prosperity and notoriety in Europe, the situation in the Holy Land had seriously deteriorated. In 1185 King Baudouin IV of Jerusalem died. In the dynastic squabble that followed, Gérard de Ridefort, Grand Master of the Temple, betrayed an oath made to the dead monarch, and thereby brought the European community in Palestine to the brink of civil war. Nor was this Ridefort's only questionable action. His cavalier attitude towards the Saracens precipitated the rupture of a long-standing truce, and provoked a new cycle of hostilities. Then, in July 1187, Ridefort led his knights, along with the rest of the Christian army, into a rash, misconceived and, as it transpired, disastrous battle at Hattin. The Christian forces were virtually annihilated; and two months later Jerusalem itself – captured nearly a century before – was again in Saracen hands.

Castle Pilgrim, a Templar fortress near Athlit, Israel, built in 1218 and evacuated in 1291 after the fall of Acre. It had its own seaport and was a major part of the Templar logistic network supporting their campaigns in the Holy Land. Tombs of Templar maritime leaders have been found in the large graveyard.

During the following century the situation became increasingly hopeless. By 1291 nearly the whole of Outremer had fallen, and the Holy Land was almost entirely under Muslim control. Only Acre remained, and in May 1291 this last fortress was lost as well. In defending the doomed city, the Templars showed themselves at their most heroic. The Grand Master himself, though severely wounded, continued fighting until his death. As there was only limited space in the Order's galleys, the women and children were evacuated, while all knights, even the wounded, chose to remain behind. When the last bastion in Acre

Templar gravestone of a Templar master mason showing the square and mason's hammer.

fell, it did so with apocalyptic intensity, the walls collapsing and burying attackers and defenders alike.

The Templars established their new headquarters in Cyprus; but with the loss of the Holy Land, they had effectively been deprived of their *raison d'être*. As there were no longer any accessible infidel lands to conquer, the Order began to turn its attention towards Europe, hoping to find there a justification for its continued existence.

A century before, the Templars had presided over the foundation of another chivalric, religious-military order, the Teutonic Knights. The latter were active in small numbers in the Middle East, but by the mid-thirteenth century had turned their attention to the north-eastern frontiers of Christendom. Here they had carved out an independent principality for themselves – the *Ordenstaat* or *Ordensland*, which encompassed almost the whole of the eastern Baltic. In this principality – which extended from Prussia to the Gulf of Finland and what is now Russian soil – the Teutonic Knights enjoyed an unchallenged sovereignty, far from the reach of both secular and ecclesiastical control.

From the very inception of the *Ordenstaat*, the Templars had envied the independence and immunity of their kindred order. After the fall of the Holy Land, they thought increasingly of a state of their own in which they might exercise the same untrammelled authority and autonomy as the Teutonic Knights. Unlike the Teutonic Knights, however, the Templars were not interested in the harsh wilderness of Eastern Europe. By now they were too accustomed to luxury and opulence. Accordingly, they dreamed of founding their state on more accessible, more congenial soil – that of the Languedoc.[11]

From its earliest years, the Temple had maintained a certain warm rapport with the Cathars, especially in the Languedoc. Many wealthy landowners – Cathars themselves or sympathetic to the Cathars – had donated vast tracts of land to the Order. According to a recent writer, at least one of the co-founders of the Temple was a Cathar. This seems somewhat improbable, but it is beyond dispute that Bertrand de Blanchefort, fourth Grand Master of the Order, came from a Cathar family. Forty years after Bertrand's death, his descendants were fighting side by side with other Cathar lords against the Northern invaders of Simon de Montfort.[12]

During the Albigensian Crusade, the Templars ostensibly remained neutral, confining themselves to the role of witnesses. At the same time, however, the Grand Master at the time would seem to have made the

Order's position clear when he declared there was in fact only one true Crusade – the Crusade against the Saracens. Moreover, a careful examination of contemporary accounts reveals that the Templars provided a haven for many Cathar refugees.[13] On occasion they do seem to have taken up arms on these refugees' behalf. And an inspection of the Order's rolls towards the beginning of the Albigensian Crusade reveals a major influx of Cathars into the Temple's ranks – where not even Simon de Montfort's crusaders would dare to challenge them. Indeed, the Templar rolls of the period show that a significant proportion of the Order's high-ranking dignitaries were from Cathar families.[14] In the Languedoc Temple officials were more frequently Cathar than Catholic. What is more, the Cathar nobles who enrolled in the Temple do not appear to have moved about the world as much as their Catholic brethren. On the contrary, they appear to have remained for the most part in the Languedoc, thus creating for the Order a long-standing and stable base in the region.

By virtue of their contact with Islamic and Judaic cultures, the Templars had already absorbed a great many ideas alien to orthodox Roman Christianity. Templar Masters, for example, often employed Arab secretaries, and many Templars, having learnt Arabic in captivity, were fluent in the language. A close rapport was also maintained with Jewish communities, financial interests and scholarship. The Templars had thus been exposed to many things Rome would not ordinarily countenance. Through the influx of Cathar recruits, they were now exposed to Gnostic dualism as well – if, indeed, they had ever really been strangers to it.

By 1306 Philippe IV of France – Philippe le Bel – was acutely anxious to rid his territory of the Templars. They were arrogant and unruly. They were efficient and highly trained, a professional military force much stronger and better organised than any he himself could muster. They were firmly established throughout France, and by this time even their allegiance to the pope was only nominal. Philippe had no control over the Order. He owed it money. He had been humiliated when, fleeing a rebellious Paris mob, he was obliged to seek abject refuge in the Temple's preceptory. He coveted the Templars' immense wealth, which his sojourn in their premises made flagrantly apparent to him. And, having applied to join the Order as a postulant, he had suffered the indignity of being haughtily rejected. These factors – together, of course, with the alarming prospect of an independent Templar state at his back door – were sufficient to spur the king to action. And heresy was a convenient excuse.

Philippe first had to enlist the co-operation of the pope, to whom, in theory at any rate, the Templars owed allegiance and obedience. Between 1303 and 1305, the French king and his ministers engineered the kidnapping and death of one pope (Boniface VIII) and quite possibly the murder by poison of another (Benedict XI). Then, in 1305, Philippe managed to secure the election of his own candidate, the archbishop of Bordeaux, to the vacant papal throne. The new pontiff took the name Clement V. Indebted as he was to Philippe's influence, he could hardly refuse the king's demands. And these demands included the eventual suppression of the Knights Templar.

Philippe planned his moves carefully. A list of charges was compiled, partly from the king's spies who had infiltrated the Order, partly from the voluntary confession of an alleged renegade Templar. Armed with these accusations, Philippe could at last move; and when he delivered his blow, it was sudden, swift, efficient and lethal. In a security operation worthy of the SS or Gestapo, the king issued sealed and secret orders to his seneschals throughout the country. These orders were to be opened everywhere simultaneously and implemented at once. At dawn on Friday, October 13th, 1307, all Templars in France were to be seized and placed under arrest by the king's men, their preceptories placed under royal sequestration, their goods confiscated. But although Philippe's objective of surprise might seem to have been achieved, his primary interest – the Order's immense wealth – eluded him. It was never found, and what became of the fabulous 'treasure of the Templars' has remained a mystery.

In fact it is doubtful whether Philippe's surprise attack on the Order was as unexpected as he, or subsequent historians, believed. There is considerable evidence to suggest the Templars received some kind of advance warning. Shortly before the arrests, for example, the Grand Master, Jacques de Molay, called in many of the Order's books and extant rules, and had them burnt. A knight who withdrew from the Order at this time was told by the treasurer that he was extremely 'wise', as catastrophe was imminent. An official note was circulated to all French preceptories, stressing that no information regarding the Order's customs and rituals was to be released.

In any case, whether the Templars were warned in advance or whether they deduced what was in the wind, certain precautions were definitely taken.[15] In the first place the knights who were captured seem to have submitted passively, as if under instructions to do so. At no point is there any record of the Order in France actively resisting the king's seneschals. In the second place there is persuasive evidence of some sort of organised flight by a particular group of knights – virtually all of whom were in some way connected with the Order's Treasurer. It is not perhaps surprising, therefore, that the treasure of the Temple, together with almost all its documents and records, should have disappeared. Persistent but unsubstantiated rumours speak of the treasure being smuggled by night from the Paris preceptory, shortly before the arrests. According to these rumours, it was transported by wagons to the coast – presumably to the Order's naval base at La Rochelle – and loaded into eighteen galleys, which were never heard of again. Whether this is true or not, it would seem that the Templars' fleet escaped the king's clutches because there is no report of any of the Order's ships being taken. On the contrary, those ships appear to have vanished totally, along with whatever they might have been carrying.[16]

Manuscript depiction of the burning alive over a slow fire on a small island in the Seine, Paris, of the last Templar Grand Master, Jacques de Molay, and the Commander of Normandy, Geoffroi de Charney, on 18 March, 1314. This island now provides support for Pont Neuf, Paris.

In France the arrested Templars were tried and many subjected to torture. Strange confessions were extracted and even stranger accusations made. Grim rumours began to circulate about the country. The Templars supposedly worshipped a devil called Baphomet. At their secret ceremonies they supposedly prostrated themselves before a bearded male head, which spoke to them and invested them with occult powers. Unauthorised witnesses of these ceremonies were never seen again. And there were other charges as well, which were even more vague: of infanticide; of teaching women how to abort; of obscene kisses at the induction of postulants; of homosexuality. But of all the charges levelled against these soldiers of Christ, who had fought and laid down their lives for Christ, one stands out as most bizarre and seemingly improbable. They were accused of ritually denying Christ, of repudiating, trampling and spitting on the cross.

In France, at least, the fate of the arrested

Templars was effectively sealed. Philippe harried them savagely and mercilessly. Many were burned, many more imprisoned and tortured. At the same time the king continued to bully the pope, demanding ever more stringent measures against the Order. After resisting for a time, the pope gave way in 1312, and the Knights Templar were officially dissolved – without a conclusive verdict of guilt or innocence ever being pronounced. But in Philippe's domains, the trials, inquiries and investigations continued

Above; Enigmatic Templar graffiti still remaining in the prison tower at the castle of Chinon, on the Vienne river, France. The leaders of the Knights Templar were imprisoned here in 1308 and interrogated by Vatican officials for the Pope who had grave suspicions over the truth of the accusations brought against the Order by the French king.

Below; The prison tower at the castle of Chinon.

for another two years. At last, in March 1314, Jacques de Molay, the Grand Master, and Geoffroi de Charnay, Preceptor of Normandy, were roasted to death over a slow fire. With their execution, the Templars ostensibly vanish from the stage of history. Nevertheless, the Order did not cease to exist. Given the number of knights who escaped, who remained at large or who were acquitted, it would be surprising if it had.

Philippe had tried to influence his fellow monarchs, hoping thereby to ensure that no Templar, anywhere in Christendom, should be spared. Indeed, the king's zeal in this respect is almost suspicious. One can perhaps understand him wanting to rid his own domains of the Order's presence. It is rather less clear why he should have been so intent on exterminating Templars elsewhere. Certainly he himself was no model of virtue; and it is difficult to imagine a monarch who arranged for the deaths of two popes being genuinely distressed by infringements of faith. Did Philippe simply fear vengeance if the Order remained intact outside France? Or was there something else involved?

In any case, his attempt to eliminate Templars outside France was not altogether successful. Philippe's own son-in-law, for example, Edward II of England, at first rallied to the Order's defence. Eventually, pressured by both the pope and the French king, he complied with their demands, but only partially and tepidly. Although most Templars in England seem to have escaped completely, a

Previous page; The church of the Knights Templar in the Temple, London. The round nave was consecrated in 1185 by the Patriarch of Jerusalem.

Above; Fenestella in the Initiatory Chapel at Garway.

Below;The Templar church at Garway, Herefordshire. The original church was circular but this was dismantled and rebuilt in the late thirteenth century.

number were arrested. Of these, however, most received only light sentences – sometimes no more than a few years penance in abbeys and monasteries, where they lived in generally comfortable conditions. Their lands were eventually consigned to the Knights Hospitaller of Saint John, but they themselves were spared the vicious persecution visited upon their brethren in France.

Elsewhere the elimination of the Templars met with even greater difficulty. Scotland, for instance, was at war with England at the time, and the consequent chaos left little opportunity for implementing legal niceties. Thus the Papal Bulls dissolving the Order were never proclaimed in Scotland – and in Scotland, therefore, the Order was never technically dissolved. Many English and, it would appear, French Templars found a Scottish refuge, and a sizeable contingent is said to have fought at Robert Bruce's side at the Battle of Bannockburn in 1314. According to legend – and there is evidence to support it – the Order maintained itself as a coherent body in Scotland for another four centuries. In the fighting of 1688–91, James II of England was deposed by William of Orange. In Scotland supporters of the beleaguered Stuart monarch rose in revolt and, at the Battle of Killiecrankie in 1689, John Claverhouse, Viscount of Dundee, was killed on the field. When his body was recovered, he was reportedly found to be wearing the Grand Cross of the Order of the Temple – not a recent device supposedly, but

one dating from before 1307.[17]

In Lorraine, which was part of Germany at the time, not part of France, the Templars were supported by the duke of the principality. A few were tried and exonerated. Most, it seems, obeyed their Preceptor, who reputedly advised them to shave their beards, don secular garb and assimilate themselves into the local populace.

In Germany proper the Templars openly defied their judges, threatening to take up arms. Intimidated, their judges pronounced them innocent; and when the Order was officially dissolved, many German Templars found a haven in the Hospitallers of Saint John and in the Teutonic Order. In Spain, too, the Templars resisted their persecutors and found a refuge in other orders.

In Portugal the Order was cleared by an inquiry and simply modified its name, becoming Knights of Christ. Under this title they functioned well into the sixteenth century, devoting themselves to maritime activity. Vasco da Gama was a Knight of Christ, and Prince Henry the Navigator was a Grand Master of the Order. Ships of the Knights of Christ sailed under the familiar red pattée cross. And it was under the same cross that Christopher Columbus's three caravels crossed the Atlantic to the New World. Columbus himself was married to the daughter of a former Knight of Christ, and had access to his father-in-law's charts and diaries.

Thus, in a number of diverse ways, the Templars survived the attack of October 13th, 1307. And in 1522 the Templars' Prussian progeny, the Teutonic Knights, secularised themselves, repudiated their allegiance to Rome and threw their support behind an upstart rebel and heretic named Martin Luther. Two centuries after their dissolution, the Templars, however vicariously, were exacting revenge on the Church which had betrayed them.

KNIGHTS TEMPLAR – THE MYSTERIES

In greatly abridged form, this is the history of the Knights Templar as writers have accepted and presented it, and as we encountered it in our research. But we quickly discovered that there was another dimension to the Order's history, considerably more elusive, more provocative and more speculative. Even during their existence, a mystique had come to surround the knights. Some said they were sorcerers and magicians, secret adepts and alchemists. Many of their contemporaries shunned them, believing them to be in league with unclean powers. As early as 1208, at the beginning of the Albigensian Crusade, Pope Innocent III had admonished the Templars for un-Christian behaviour, and referred explicitly to necromancy. On the other hand, there were individuals who praised them with extravagant enthusiasm. In the late twelfth century Wolfram von Eschenbach, greatest of medieval *Minnesänger* or *romanciers*, paid a special visit to Outremer, to witness the Order in action. And when, between 1195 and 1220, Wolfram composed his epic romance *Parzival*, he conferred on the Templars a most exalted status. In Wolfram's poem the knights who guard the Holy Grail, the Grail castle and the Grail family, are Templars.[18]

After the Temple's demise, the mystique surrounding it persisted. The final recorded act in the Order's history had been the burning of the last Grand Master, Jacques de Molay, in March 1314. As the smoke from the slow fire choked the life from his body, Jacques de Molay is said to have issued an imprecation from the flames. According to tradition, he called his persecutors – Pope Clement and King Philippe – to join him and account for themselves before the court of God within the year. Within a month Pope Clement was dead, supposedly from a sudden onslaught of dysentery. By the end of the year Philippe was dead as well, from causes that remain obscure to this day. There is, of course, no need to look for supernatural explanations. The Templars possessed great expertise in the use of poisons. And there were certainly enough people about – refugee knights travelling incognito, sympathisers of the Order or relatives of persecuted brethren – to exact the appropriate vengeance. Nevertheless, the apparent fulfilment of the Grand Master's curse lent credence to belief in the Order's occult powers. Nor did the curse end there. According to legend, it was to cast a pall over the French royal line far into the future. And thus echoes of the Templars' supposed mystic power reverberated down the centuries.

By the eighteenth century various secret and semi-secret confraternities were lauding the Templars as both precursors and mystical initiates. Many Freemasons of the period appropriated the Templars as their own antecedents. Certain Masonic 'rites' or 'observances' claimed direct lineal descent from the Order, as well as authorised custody of its arcane secrets. Some of these claims were patently preposterous. Others – resting, for example, on the Order's possible survival in Scotland – may well have a core of validity, even if the attendant trappings are spurious.

By 1789 the legends surrounding the Templars had attained posi-

Masonic tomb of the 17th century. Skull and crossbones indicate that the buried man was a Master Mason. Many such tombs predate the founding of the English Grand Lodge in 1717.

tively mythic proportions, and their historical reality was obscured by an aura of obfuscation and romance. They were regarded us occult adepts, illumined alchemists, magi and sages, master masons and high initiates – veritable supermen endowed with an awesome arsenal of arcane power and knowledge. They were also regarded as heroes and martyrs, harbingers of the anticlerical spirit of the age; and many French Freemasons, in conspiring against Louis XVI, felt they were helping to implement Jacques de Molay's dying curse on the French line. When the king's head fell beneath the guillotine, an unknown man is reported to have leaped on to the scaffold. He dipped his hand in the monarch's blood, flung it out over the surrounding throng and cried, 'Jacques de Molay, thou art avenged!'

Since the French Revolution the aura surrounding the Templars has not diminished. At least three contemporary organisations today call themselves Templars, claiming to possess a pedigree from 1314 and charters whose authenticity has never been established. Certain Masonic lodges have adopted the grade of 'Templar', as well as rituals and appellations supposedly descended from the original Order. Towards the end of the nineteenth century, a sinister 'Order of the New Templars' was established in Germany and Austria, employing the swastika as one of its emblems. Figures like H. P. Blavatsky, founder of Theosophy, and Rudolf Steiner, founder of Anthroposophy, spoke of an esoteric 'wisdom tradition' running back through the Rosicrucians to the Cathars and Templars – who were purportedly repositories of more ancient secrets still. In the United States teenage boys are admitted into the De Molay Society, without either they or their mentors having much notion whence the name derives. In Britain, as well as elsewhere in the West, recondite rotary clubs dignify themselves with the name 'Templar' and include eminent public figures. From the heavenly kingdom he sought to conquer with his sword, Hugues de Payen must now look down with a certain wry perplexity on the latter-day knights, balding, paunched and bespectacled, that he engendered. And yet he must also be impressed by the durability and vitality of his legacy.

In France this legacy is particularly powerful. Indeed, the Templars are a veritable industry in France, as much as Glastonbury, ley-lines or the Loch Ness Monster are in Britain. In Paris bookshops are filled with histories and accounts of the Order – some valid, some plunging enthusiastically into lunacy. During the last quarter-century or so a number of extravagant claims have been advanced on behalf of the Templars, some of which may not be wholly without foundation. Certain writers have credited them, at least in large part, with the building of the Gothic cathedrals – or at least with providing an impetus of some sort to that burst of architectural energy and genius. Other writers have argued that the Order established commercial contact with the Americas as early as 1269, and derived much of its wealth from imported Mexican silver. It has frequently been asserted that the Templars were privy to some sort of secret concerning the origins of Christianity. It has been said that they were Gnostic, that they were heretical, that they were defectors to Islam. It has been declared that they sought a creative unity between bloods, races and religions – a systematic policy of fusion between Islamic, Christian and Judaic thought. And again and again it is maintained, as Wolfram von Eschenbach maintained nearly eight centuries ago, that the Templars were guardians of the Holy Grail, whatever the Holy Grail might be.

The claims are often ridiculous. At the same time there are unquestionably mysteries associated with the Templars and, we became convinced, secrets of some kind as well. It was clear that some of these secrets pertained to what is now called 'esoterica'. Symbolic carvings in Templar preceptories, for instance, suggest that some officials in the Order's hierarchy were conversant with such disciplines as astrology, alchemy, sacred geometry and numerology, as well, of course, as astronomy – which, in the twelfth and thirteenth centuries, was inseparable from astrology, and every bit as 'esoteric'.

But it was neither the extravagant claims nor the esoteric residues that intrigued us. On the contrary, we found ourselves fascinated by something much more mundane, much more prosaic – the welter of contradictions, improbabilities, inconsistencies and apparent 'smokescreens' in the accepted history. Esoteric secrets the Templars may well have had. But something else about them was being concealed as well – something rooted in the religious and political currents of their epoch. It was on this level that we undertook most of our investigation.

We began with the end of the story, the fall of the Order and the charges levelled against it. Many books have been written exploring and evaluating the possible truth of these charges; and from the evidence we, like most researchers, concluded there seems to have been some basis for them. Subjected to interrogation by the Inquisition, for example, a number of knights referred to something called 'Baphomet' – too many, and in too many different places, for Baphomet to be the invention of a single individual or even a single preceptory. At the same time, there is no indication of who or what Baphomet might have been, what he or it represented, why he or it should have had any special significance. It would appear that Baphomet was regarded with reverence, a reverence perhaps tantamount to idolatry. In some instances the name is associated with the gargoyle-like, demonic sculptures found in various preceptories. On other occasions Baphomet seems to be associated with an apparition of a bearded head. Despite the claims of certain older historians, it seems clear that Baphomet was not a corruption of the name Muhammad. On the other hand, it might have been a corruption of the Arabic *abufihamet*, pronounced in Moorish Spanish as *bufihimat*. This means 'Father of Understanding' or 'Father of Wisdom', and 'father' in Arabic is also taken to imply 'source'.[19] If this is indeed the origin of Baphomet, it would therefore refer presumably to some supernatural or divine principle. But what might have differentiated Baphomet from any other supernatural or divine principle remains unclear. If Baphomet was simply God or Allah, why did the Templars bother to re-christen Him? And if Baphomet was not God or Allah, who or what was he?

In any case, we found indisputable evidence for the charge of secret ceremonies involving a head of some kind. Indeed the existence of such a head proved to be one of the dominant themes running through the Inquisition records. As with Baphomet, however, the significance of the head remains obscure. It may perhaps pertain to alchemy. In the alchemical process there was a phase called the 'Caput Mortuum' or 'Dead Head' – the 'Nigredo' or 'Blackening' which was said to occur before the precipitation of the Philosopher's Stone. According to other accounts, however, the head was that of Hugues de Payen, the Order's founder and first Grand Master; and it is suggestive that Hugues's shield consisted of three black heads on a gold field.

The head may also be connected with the famous Turin Shroud, which seems to have been in the possession of the Templars between 1204 and 1307, and which, if folded, would have appeared as nothing more than a head. Indeed, at the Templar preceptory of Templecombe in Somerset a reproduction of a head was found which bears a striking resemblance to that on the Turin Shroud. At the same time recent speculation had linked the head, at least tentatively, with the severed head of John the Baptist; and certain writers have suggested that the Templars were 'infected' with the Johannite or Mandaean heresy – which denounced Jesus as a 'false prophet' and acknowledged John as the true Messiah. In the course of their activities in the Middle East the Templars undoubtedly established contact with Johannite sects, and the possibility of Johannite tendencies in the Order is not altogether unlikely. But one cannot say that such tendencies obtained for the Order as a whole, nor that they were a matter of official policy.

During the interrogations following the arrests in 1307, a head also figured in two other connections. According to the Inquisition records, among the confiscated goods of the Paris preceptory a reliquary in the shape of a woman's head was found. It was hinged on top, and contained what appeared to have been relics of a peculiar kind. It is described as follows:

> a great head of gilded silver, most beautiful, and constituting the image of a woman. Inside were two head-bones, wrapped in a cloth of white linen, with another red cloth around it. A label was attached, on which was written the legend caput lviiim. The bones inside were those of a rather small woman.[20]

A curious relic – especially for a rigidly monastic, military institution like the Templars. Yet a knight under interrogation, when confronted with this feminine head, declared it had no relation to the bearded male head used in the Order's rituals. CAPUT LVIIIm – 'Head 58m' – remains a baffling enigma. But it is worth noting that the 'm' may not be an 'm' at all, but ♍, the astrological symbol for Virgo.[21]

The head figures again in another mysterious story traditionally linked with the Templars. It is worth quoting in one of its several variants:

> A great lady of Maraclea was loved by a Templar, a Lord of Sidon; but she died in her youth, and on the night of her burial, this wicked lover crept to the grave, dug up her body and violated it. Then a voice from the void bade him return in nine months time for he would find a son. He obeyed the injunction and at the appointed time he opened the grave again and found a head on the leg bones of the skeleton (skull and crossbones). The same voice bade him 'guard it well, for it would be the giver of all good things', and so he carried it away with him. It became his protecting genius, and he was able to defeat his enemies by merely showing them the magic head. In due course, it passed into the possession of the Order.[22]

This grisly narrative can be traced at least as far back as one Walter Map, writing in the late twelfth century. But neither he nor another writer, who recounts the same tale nearly a century later, specifies that the necrophiliac rapist was a Templar.[23] Nevertheless, by 1307 the story had become closely associated with the Order. It is mentioned repeatedly in the Inquisition's records, and at least two knights under interrogation confessed their familiarity with it. In subsequent accounts, like the one quoted above, the rapist himself is identified as a Templar, and he remains so in the versions preserved by Freemasonry – which adopted the skull and crossbones, and often employed it as a device on tombstones.

In part the tale might almost seem to be a grotesque travesty of the Virgin Birth. In part it would seem to be a garbled symbolic account of some initiation rite, some ritual involving a figurative death and resurrection. One chronicler cites the name of the woman in the story – Yse, which would seem quite clearly to derive from Isis. And certainly the tale evokes echoes of the mysteries associated with Isis, as well as those of Tammuz or Adonis, whose head was flung into the sea, and of Orpheus, whose head was flung into the river of the Milky Way. The magical properties of the head also evoke the head of Bran the Blessed in Celtic mythology and in the *Mabinogion*. And it is Bran's mystical cauldron that numerous writers have sought to identify as the pagan precursor of the Holy Grail.

Whatever significance might be ascribed to the 'cult of the head', the Inquisition clearly believed it to be important. In a list of charges drawn up on August 12th, 1308, there is the following:

> Item, that in each province they had idols, namely heads . . .
> Item, that they adored these idols . . .
> Item, that they said that the head could save them.
> Item, that [it could] make riches . . .
> Item, that it made the trees flower.
> Item, that it made the land germinate.
> Item, that they surrounded or touched each head of the aforesaid idols with small cords, which they wore around themselves next to the shirt or the flesh.[24]

The cord mentioned in the last item is reminiscent of the Cathars, who were also alleged to have worn a sacred cord of some kind. But most striking in the list is the head's purported capacity to engender riches, make trees flower and bring fertility to the land. These properties coincide remarkably with those ascribed in the romances to the Holy Grail.

Of all the charges levelled against the Templars, the most serious were those of blasphemy and heresy – of denying, trampling and spitting on the cross. It is not clear precisely what this alleged ritual was intended to signify – what, in other words, the Templars were actually repudiating. Were they repudiating Christ? Or were they simply repudiating the Crucifixion? And whatever they repudiated, what exactly did they extol in its stead? No one has satisfactorily answered these questions, but it seems clear that a repudiation of some sort did occur, and was an integral principle of the Order. One knight, for example, testified that on his induction into the Order he was told, 'You believe wrongly, because he [Christ] is indeed a false prophet. Believe only in God in heaven, and not in him.'[25] Another Templar declared that he was told, 'Do not believe that the man Jesus whom the Jews crucified in Outremer is God and that he can save you.'[26] A third knight similarly claimed he was instructed not to believe in Christ, a false prophet, but only in a 'higher God'. He was then shown a crucifix and told, 'Set not much faith in this, for it is too young.'[27]

Such accounts are frequent and consistent enough to lend credence to the charge. They are also relatively bland; and if the Inquisition desired to concoct evidence, it could have devised something far more dramatic, more incriminating, more damning. There thus seems little doubt that the Templars' attitude towards Jesus did not concur with that of Catholic orthodoxy, but it is uncertain precisely what the Order's attitude was. In any case, there is evidence that the ritual ascribed to the Templars – trampling and spitting on the cross – was in the air at least half a century before 1307. Its context is confusing, but it is mentioned in connection with the Sixth Crusade, which occurred in 1249.[28]

KNIGHTS TEMPLAR – THE HIDDEN SIDE

If the end of the Knights Templar was fraught with baffling enigmas, the foundation and early history of the Order seemed to us to be even more so. We were already plagued by a number of inconsistencies and improbabilities. Nine knights, nine 'poor' knights, appeared as if from nowhere and – among all the other crusaders swarming about the Holy Land – promptly had the king's quarters turned over to them! Nine 'poor' knights – without admitting any new recruits to their ranks – presumed, all by themselves, to defend the highways of Palestine. And there was no record at all of them actually doing anything, not even from Fulk de Chartres, the king's official chronicler, who must surely have known about them! How, we wondered, could their activities, their move into the royal premises, for instance, have escaped Fulk's notice? It would seem incredible, yet the chronicler says nothing. No one says anything, in fact, until Guillaume de Tyre, a good half century later. What could we conclude from this? That the knights were not engaged in the laudable public service ascribed to them? That they were perhaps involved instead in some more clandestine activity, of which not even the official chronicler was aware? Or that the chronicler himself was muzzled? The latter would seem to be the most likely explanation. For the knights were soon joined by two most illustrious noblemen, noblemen whose presence could not have gone unnoticed.

According to Guillaume de Tyre, the Order of the Temple was established in 1118, originally numbered nine knights and admitted no new recruits for nine years. It is clearly on record, however, that the count of Anjou – father of Geoffrey Plantagenet – joined the Order in 1120, only two years after its supposed foundation. And in 1124 the count of Champagne, one of the wealthiest lords in Europe, did likewise. If Guillaume de Tyre is correct, there should have been no new members until 1127; but by 1126 the Templars had in fact admitted four new members to their ranks.[29] Is Guillaume wrong, then, in saying that no new members were admitted for nine years? Or is he perhaps correct in that assertion, but wrong in the date he attributes to the Order's foundation? If the count of Anjou became a Templar in 1120, and if the Order admitted no new members for nine years after its foundation, its foundation would date not from 1118, but at the latest, from 1111 or 1112.

Indeed there is very persuasive evidence for this conclusion. In 1114 the count of Champagne was preparing for a journey to the Holy Land. Shortly before his departure, he received a letter from the bishop of Chartres. At one point, the bishop wrote, 'We have heard that . . . before leaving for Jerusalem you made a vow to join "la milice du Christ", that you wish to enrol in this evangelical soldiery.'[30] 'La milice du Christ' was the name by which the Templars were originally known, and the name by which Saint Bernard alludes to them. In the context of the bishop's letter the appellation cannot possibly refer to any other institution. It cannot mean, for example, that the count of Champagne simply decided to become a crusader, because the bishop goes on to speak of a vow of chastity which his decision has entailed. Such a vow would hardly have been required of an ordinary crusader. From the bishop of Chartres's letter, then, it is clear that the Templars already existed, or had at least been planned, as early as 1114, four years before the date generally accepted; and that as early as 1114, the count of Champagne was already intending to join their ranks – which he eventually did a decade later. One historian who noted this letter drew the rather curious conclusion that the bishop cannot have meant what he said.[31] He could not have meant to refer to the Templars, the historian in question argues, because the Templars were not founded until four years later in 1118. Or perhaps the bishop did not know the year of Our Lord in which he was writing? But the bishop died in 1115. How, in 1114, could he 'mistakenly' refer to something which did not yet exist? There is only one possible, and very obvious, answer to the question – that it is not the bishop who is wrong, but Guillaume de Tyre, as well as all subsequent historians who insist on regarding Guillaume as the unimpeachable voice of authority.

In itself an earlier foundation date for the Order of the Temple need not necessarily be suspicious. But there are other circumstances and singular coincidences which decidedly are. At least three of the nine founding knights, including Hugues de Payen, seem to have come from adjacent regions, to have had family ties, to have known each other previously and to have been vassals of the same lord. This lord was the count of Champagne, to whom the bishop of Chartres addressed his letter in 1114 and who became a Templar in 1124, pledging obedience to his own vassal! In 1115 the count of Champagne donated the land on which Saint Bernard, patron of the Templars, built the famous Abbey of Clairvaux; and one of the nine founding knights, André de Montbard, was Saint Bernard's uncle.

In Troyes, moreover, the court of the count of Champagne, an influential school of Cabalistic and esoteric studies had flourished since 1070.[32] At the Council of Troyes in 1128 the Templars were officially incorporated. For the next two centuries Troyes remained a strategic centre for the Order; and even today there is a wooded expanse adjacent

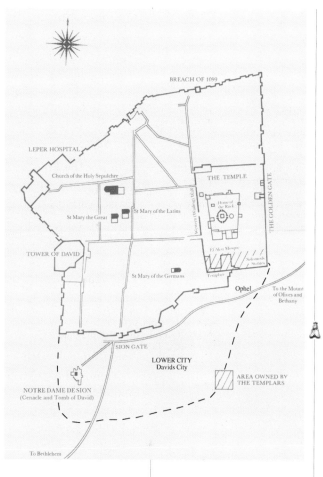

Jerusalem - the temple and the area of Mount Sion in the Mid-Twelfth century.

to the city called the *Forêt du Temple*. And it was from Troyes, court of the count of Champagne, that one of the earliest Grail romances issued – quite possibly the earliest, composed by Chrétien de Troyes.

Amid this welter of data, we could begin to see a tenuous web of connections – a pattern that seemed more than mere coincidence. If such a pattern did exist, it would certainly support our suspicion that the Templars were involved in some clandestine activity. Nevertheless, we could only speculate as to what that activity might have been. One basis for our speculation was the specific site of the knights' domicile – the wing of the royal palace, the Temple Mount, so inexplicably conferred upon them. In A.D. 70 the Temple which then stood there was sacked by Roman legions under Titus. Its treasure was plundered and brought to Rome, then plundered again and perhaps brought to the Pyrenees. But what if there were something else in the Temple as well – something even more important than the treasure pillaged by the Romans? It is certainly possible that the Temple's priests, confronted by an advancing phalanx of centurions, would have left to the looters the booty they expected to find. And if there were something else, it might well be concealed somewhere near by. Beneath the Temple, for instance.

Among the Dead Sea Scrolls found at Qumrán, there is one now known as the 'Copper Scroll'. This scroll, deciphered at Manchester University in 1955–6, makes explicit references to great quantities of bullion, sacred vessels, additional unspecified material and 'treasure' of an indeterminate kind. It cites twenty-four different hoards buried beneath the Temple itself.[33]

In the mid-twelfth century a pilgrim to the Holy Land, one Johann von Würzburg, wrote of a visit to the so-called 'Stables of Solomon'. These stables, situated directly beneath the Temple itself, are still visible. They were large enough, Johann reported, to hold two thousand horses; and it was in these stables that the Templars quartered their mounts. According to at least one other historian, the Templars were using these stables for their horses as early as 1124, when they still supposedly numbered only nine. It would thus seem likely that the fledgling Order, almost immediately after its inception, undertook excavations beneath the Temple.

Such excavations might well imply that the knights were actively looking for something. It might even imply that they were deliberately sent to the Holy Land, with the express commission of finding something. If this supposition is valid, it would explain a number of anom-

The Copper Scroll, one of the Dead Sea Scrolls found in Cave Three, 1952, near the ruins of Qumran on the Dead Sea, Israel.

alies – their installation in the royal palace, for example, and the silence of the chronicler. But if they were sent to Palestine, who sent them?

In 1104 the count of Champagne had met in conclave with certain high-ranking nobles, at least one of whom had just returned from Jerusalem.[34] Among those present at this conclave were representatives of certain families – Brienne, Joinville and Chaumont – who, we later discovered, figured significantly in our story. Also present was the liege lord of André de Montbard, André being one of the co-founders of the Temple and Saint Bernard's uncle.

Shortly after the conclave, the count of Champagne departed for the Holy Land himself and remained there for four years, returning in 1108.[35] In 1114 he made a second journey to Palestine, intending to join the 'milice du Christ', then changing his mind and returning to Europe a year later. On his return, he immediately donated a tract of land to the Cistercian Order, whose pre-eminent spokesman was Saint Bernard. On this tract of land Saint Bernard built the Abbey of Clairvaux, where he established his own residence and then consolidated the Cistercian Order.

Prior to 1112 the Cistercians were dangerously close to bankruptcy. Then, under Saint Bernard's guidance, they underwent a dazzling change of fortune. Within the next few years half a dozen abbeys were established. By 1153 there were more than three hundred, of which Saint Bernard himself personally founded sixty-nine. This extraordinary growth directly parallels that of the Order of the Temple, which was expanding in the same way during the same years. And, as we have said, one of the co-founders of the Order of the Temple was Saint Bernard's uncle, André de Montbard.

It is worth reviewing this complicated sequence of events. In 1104 the count of Champagne departed for the Holy Land after meeting with certain nobles, one of whom was connected with André de Montbard. In 1112 André de Montbard's nephew, Saint Bernard, joined the Cistercian Order. In 1114 the count of Champagne departed on a second journey to the Holy Land, intending to join the Order of the Temple – which was co-founded by his own vassal together with André de Montbard, and which, as the bishop of Chartres's letter attests, was already in existence or in process of being established. In 1115 the count of Champagne returned to Europe, having been gone for less than a year, and donated land for the Abbey of Clairvaux – whose abbot was André de Montbard's nephew. In the years that followed both the Cistercians and the Templars – both Saint Bernard's order and André de Montbard's – became immensely wealthy and enjoyed phases of phenomenal growth.

As we pondered this sequence of events, we became increasingly convinced that there was some pattern underlying and governing such an intricate web. It certainly did not appear to be random, nor wholly coincidental. On the contrary we seemed to be dealing with the vestiges of some complex and ambitious overall design, the full details of which had been lost to history. In order to reconstruct these details, we developed a tentative hypothesis – a 'scenario', so to speak, which might accommodate the known facts.

We supposed that something was discovered in the Holy Land, either by accident or design – something of immense import, which aroused the interest of some of Europe's most influential noblemen. We further supposed that this discovery involved, directly or indirectly, a great deal of potential wealth – as well, perhaps, as something else, something that had to be kept secret, something which could only be divulged to a small number of high-ranking lords. Finally, we supposed that this discovery was reported and discussed at the conclave of 1104.

Immediately thereafter the count of Champagne departed for the Holy Land himself, perhaps to verify personally what he had heard, perhaps to implement some course of action – the foundation, for example, of what subsequently became the Order of the Temple. In 1114, if not before, the Templars were established with the count of Champagne playing some crucial role, perhaps acting as guiding spirit and sponsor. By 1115 money was already flowing back to Europe and into the coffers of the Cistercians, who, under Saint Bernard and from their new position of strength, endorsed and imparted credibility to the fledgling Order of the Temple.

Under Bernard the Cistercians attained a spiritual ascendancy in Europe. Under Hugues de Payen and André de Montbard, the Templars attained a military and administrative ascendancy in the Holy Land which quickly spread back to Europe. Behind the growth of both orders loomed the shadowy presence of uncle and nephew, as well as the wealth, influence and patronage of the count of Champagne. These three individuals constitute a vital link. They are like markers breaking the surface of history, indicating the dim configurations of some elaborate, concealed design.

If such a design actually existed, it cannot, of course, be ascribed to these three men alone. On the contrary, it must have entailed a great deal of co-operation from certain other people and a great deal of meticulous organisation. Organisation is perhaps the key word; for if our hypothesis was correct, it would presuppose a degree of organisation amounting to an order in itself – a third and secret order behind the known and documented Orders of the Cistercians and the Temple. Evidence for the existence of such a third order was not long in arriving.

In the meantime, we devoted our attention to the hypothetical 'discovery' in the Holy Land – the speculative basis on which we had established our 'scenario'. What might have been found there? To what might the Templars, along with Saint Bernard and the count of Champagne, have been privy? At the end of their history the Templars kept inviolate the secret of their treasure's whereabouts and nature. Not even documents survived. If the treasure in question were simply financial – bullion, for example – it would not have been necessary to destroy or conceal all records, all rules, all archives. The implication is that the Templars had something else in their custody, something so precious that not even torture would wring an intimation of it from their lips.

Wealth alone could not have prompted such absolute and unanimous secrecy. Whatever it was had to do with other matters, like the Order's attitude towards Jesus.

On October 13th, 1307, all Templars throughout France were arrested by Philippe le Bel's seneschals. But that statement is not quite true. The Templars of at least one preceptory slipped unscathed through the king's net – the preceptory of Bézu, adjacent to Rennes-le-Château. How and why did they escape? To answer that question, we were compelled to investigate the Order's activities in the vicinity of Bézu. Those activities proved to have been fairly extensive. Indeed, there were some half dozen preceptories and other holdings in the area, which covered some twenty square miles.

In 1153 a nobleman of the region – a nobleman with Cathar sympathies – became fourth Grand Master of the Order of the Temple. His name was Bertrand de Blanchefort, and his ancestral home was situated on a mountain peak a few miles away from both Bézu and Rennes-le-Château. Bertrand de Blanchefort, who presided over the Order from 1153 until 1170, was probably the most significant of all Templar Grand Masters. Before his régime the Order's hierarchy and administrative structure were, at best, nebulous. It was Bertrand who transformed the Knights Templar into the superbly efficient, well-organised and magnificently disciplined hierarchical institution they then became. It was Bertrand who launched their involvement in high-level diplomacy and international politics. It was Bertrand who created for them a major sphere of interest in Europe, and particularly in France. And according to the evidence that survives, Bertrand's mentor – some historians even list him as the Grand Master immediately preceding Bertrand – was André de Montbard.

Within a few years of the Templars' incorporation, Bertrand had not only joined their ranks, but also conferred on them lands in the environs of Rennes-le-Château and Bézu. And in 1156, under Bertrand's régime as Grand Master, the Order is said to have imported to the area a contingent of German-speaking miners. These workers were supposedly subjected to a rigid, virtually military discipline. They were forbidden to fraternise in any way with the local population and were kept strictly segregated from the surrounding community. A special judicial body, 'la Judicature des Allemands', was even created to deal with legal technicalities pertaining to them. And their alleged task was to work the gold mines on the slopes of the mountain at Blanchefort – gold mines

which had been utterly exhausted by the Romans nearly a thousand years before.[36]

During the seventeenth century engineers were commissioned to investigate the mineralogical prospects of the area and draw up detailed reports. In the course of his report one of them, César d'Arcons, discussed the ruins he had found, remains of the German workers' activity. On the basis of his research, he declared that the German workers did not seem to have been engaged in mining.[37] In what, then, were they engaged? César d'Arcons was unsure – smelting perhaps, melting something down, constructing something out of metal, perhaps even excavating a subterranean crypt of some sort and creating a species of depository.

Whatever the answer to this enigma, there had been a Templar presence in the vicinity of Rennes-le-Château since at least the mid-twelfth century. By 1285 there was a major preceptory a few miles from Bézu, at Campagne-sur-Aude. Yet near the end of the thirteenth century, Pierre de Voisins, lord of Bézu and Rennes-le-Château, invited a separate detachment of Templars to the area, a special detachment from the Aragonese province of Roussillon.[38] This fresh detachment established itself on the summit of the mountain of Bézu, erecting a lookout post and a chapel. Ostensibly, the Roussillon Templars had been invited to Bézu to maintain the security of the region and protect the pilgrim route which ran through the valley to Santiago de Compastela in Spain. But it is unclear why these extra knights should have been required. In the first place they cannot have been very numerous – not enough to make a significant difference. In the second place there were already Templars in the neighbourhood. Finally, Pierre de Voisins had troops of his own, who, together with the Templars already there, could guarantee the safety of the environs. Why, then, did the Roussillon Templars come to Bézu? According to local tradition, they came to spy. And to exploit or bury or guard a treasure of some sort.

Whatever their mysterious mission, they obviously enjoyed some kind of special immunity. Alone of all Templars in France, they were left unmolested by Philippe le Bel's seneschals on October 13th, 1307. On that fateful day the commander of the Templar contingent at Bézu was a Seigneur de Goth.[39] And before taking the name of Pope Clement V, the archbishop of Bordeaux – King Philippe's vacillating pawn – was Bertrand de Goth. Moreover, the new pontiff's mother was Ida de Blanchefort, of the same family as Bertrand de Blanchefort. Was the pope then privy to some secret entrusted to the custody of his family – a secret which remained in the Blanchefort family until the eighteenth century, when the Abbé Antoine Bigou, curé of Rennes-le-Château and confessor to Marie de Blanchefort, composed the parchments found by Saunière? If this were the case, the pope might well have extended some sort of immunity to his relative commanding the Templars at Bézu.

The history of the Templars near Rennes-le-Château was clearly as fraught with perplexing enigmas as the history of the Order in general. Indeed, there were a number of factors – the role of Bertrand de Blanchefort, for example – which seemed to constitute a discernible link between the general and the more localised enigmas.

In the meantime, however, we were confronted with a daunting array of coincidences – coincidences too numerous to be truly coincidental. Were we in fact dealing with a calculated pattern? If so, the obvious question was who devised it, for patterns of such intricacy do not devise themselves. All the evidence available to us pointed to meticulous planning and careful organisation – so much so that increasingly we suspected there must be a specific group of individuals, perhaps comprising an order of some sort, working assiduously behind the scenes. We did not have to seek confirmation for the existence of such an order. The confirmation thrust itself upon us.

CHAPTER FOUR

SECRET DOCUMENTS

Confirmation of a third order – an order behind both the Templars and the Cistercians – thrust itself upon us. At first, however, we could not take it seriously. It seemed to issue from too unreliable, too vague and nebulous a source. Until we could authenticate the veracity of this source, we could not believe its claims.

In 1956 a series of books, articles, pamphlets and other documents relating to Bérenger Saunière and the enigma of Rennes-le-Château began to appear in France. This material has steadily proliferated, and is now voluminous. Indeed, it has come to constitute the basis for a veritable 'industry'. And its sheer quantity, as well as the effort and resources involved in producing and disseminating it, implicitly attest to something of immense but as yet unexplained import.

Not surprisingly, the affair has served to whet the appetites of numerous independent researchers like ourselves, whose works have added to the corpus of material available. The original material, however, seems to have issued from a single specific source. Someone clearly has a vested interest in 'promoting' Rennes-le-Château, in drawing public attention to the story, in generating publicity and further investigation. Whatever else it might be, this vested interest does not appear to be financial. On the contrary, it would appear to be more in the order of propaganda – propaganda which establishes credibility for something. And whoever the individuals responsible for this propaganda may be, they have endeavoured to focus spotlights on certain issues while keeping themselves scrupulously in the shadows.

Since 1956 a quantity of relevant material has been deliberately and systematically 'leaked', in a piecemeal fashion, fragment by fragment. Most of these fragments purport to issue, implicitly or explicitly, from some 'privileged' or 'inside' source. Most contain additional information, which supplements what was known before and thus contributes to the overall jigsaw. Neither the import nor the meaning of the overall jigsaw has yet been made clear, however. Instead, every new snippet of information has done more to intensify than to dispel the mystery. The result has been an ever-proliferating network of seductive allusions, provocative hints, suggestive cross-references and connections. In confronting the welter of data now available, the reader may well feel he is being toyed with, or being ingeniously and skilfully led from conclusion to conclusion by successive carrots dangled before his nose. And underlying it all is the constant, pervasive intimation of a secret – a secret of monumental and explosive proportions.

The material disseminated since 1956 has taken a number of forms. Some of it has appeared in popular, even best-selling books, more or less sensational, more or less cryptically teasing. Thus, for example, Gérard de Sède has produced a sequence of works on such apparently divergent topics as the Cathars, the Templars, the Merovingian dynasty, the Rose-Croix, Saunière and Rennes-le-Château. In these works, M. de Sède is often arch, coy, deliberately mystifying and coquettishly evasive. His tone implies constantly that he knows more than he is saying – perhaps a device for concealing that he does not know as much as he pretends. But his books contain enough verifiable details to forge a link between their respective themes. Whatever else one may think of M. de Sède, he effectively establishes that the diverse subjects to which he addresses himself somehow overlap and are interconnected.

On the other hand, we could not but suspect that M. de Sède's work drew heavily on information provided by an informant – and indeed, M. de Sède more or less acknowledges as much himself. Quite by accident, we learned who this informant was. In 1971, when we embarked on our first BBC film on Rennes-le-Château, we wrote to M. de Sède's Paris publisher for certain visual material. The photographs we requested were accordingly posted to us. Each of them, on the back, was stamped 'Plantard'. At that time the name meant little enough to us. But the appendix to one of M. de Sède's books consisted of an interview with one Pierre Plantard. And we subsequently obtained evidence that Pierre Plantard had been involved with certain of M. de Sède's works. Eventually Pierre Plantard began to emerge as one of the dominant figures in our investigation.

The information disseminated since 1956 has not always been contained in as popular and accessible a form as M. de Sède's. Some of it has appeared in weighty, daunting, even pedantic tomes, diametrically opposed to M. de Sède's journalistic approach. One such work was produced by René Descadeillas, former Director of the Municipal Library of Carcassonne. M. Descadeillas's book is strenuously anti-sensational. Devoted to the history of Rennes-le-Château and its environs, it contains a plethora of social and economic minutiae – for example, the births, deaths, marriages, finances, taxes and public works between the years 1730 and 1820.[1] On the whole, it could not possibly differ more from the mass-market books of M. de Sède – which M. Descadeillas elsewhere subjects to scathing criticism.[2]

In addition to published books, including some which have been published privately, there have been a number of articles in newspapers and magazines. There have been interviews with various individuals claiming to be conversant with one or another facet of the mystery. But the most interesting and important information has not, for the most part, appeared in book form. Most of it has surfaced elsewhere – in documents and pamphlets not intended for general circulation. Many of these documents and pamphlets have been deposited, in limited, privately printed editions, at the Bibliothèque Nationale in Paris. They seem to have been produced very cheaply. Some, in fact, are mere typewritten pages, photo-offset and reproduced on an office duplicator.

Even more than the marketed works, this body of ephemera seems to have issued from the same source. By means of cryptic asides and footnotes pertaining to Saunière, Rennes-le-Château, Poussin, the Merovingian dynasty and other themes, each piece of it complements, enlarges on and confirms the others. In most cases the ephemera are of uncertain authorship, appearing under a variety of

Authors with Pierre Plantard de Saint-Clair, Paris, 1982. (Left to right: Henry Lincoln, Michael Baigent, Richard Leigh, Pierre Plantard.)

transparent, even 'cute' pseudonyms – Madeleine Blancassal, for example, Nicolas Beaucéan, Jean Delaude and Antoine l'Ermite. 'Madeleine', of course, refers to Marie-Madeleine, the Magdalene, to whom the church at Rennes-le-Château is dedicated and to whom Saunière consecrated his tower, the Tour Magdala. 'Blancassal' is formed from the names of two small rivers that converge near the village of Rennes-les-Bains – the Blanque and the Sals. 'Beaucéan' is a variation of 'Beauséant', the official battle-cry and battle-standard of the Knights Templar. 'Jean Delaude' is 'Jean de l'Aude' or 'John of the Aude', the department in which Rennes-le-Château is situated. And 'Antoine l'Ermite' is Saint Anthony the Hermit, whose statue adorns the church at Rennes-le-Château and whose feast day is January 17th – the date on Marie de Blanchefort's tombstone and the date on which Saunière suffered his fatal stroke.

The work ascribed to Madeleine Blancassal is entitled *Les*

Descendants mérovingiens et l'énigme du Razès wisigoth ('The Merovingian Descendants and the Enigma of the Visigoth Razès') – Razès being the old name for Saunière's region. According to its title page, this work was originally published in German and translated into French by Walter Celse-Nazaire – another pseudonym compounded from Saints Celse and Nazaire, to whom the church at Rennes-les-Bains is dedicated. And according to the title page, the publisher of the work was the Grande Loge Alpina, the supreme Masonic lodge of Switzerland – the Swiss equivalent of Grand Lodge in Britain or Grand Orient in France. There is no indication as to why a modern Masonic lodge should display such interest in the mystery surrounding an obscure nineteenth-century French priest and the history of his parish a millennium and a half ago. One of our colleagues and an independent researcher both questioned Alpina officials. They disclaimed all knowledge not only of the work's publication, but also of its existence. Yet an independent researcher claims personally to have seen the work on the shelves of Alpina's library.[3] And subsequently we discovered that the Alpina imprint appeared on two other pamphlets as well.

Of all the privately published documents deposited in the Bibliothèque Nationale, the most important is a compilation of papers entitled collectively *Dossiers secrets* ('Secret Dossiers'). Catalogued under number 4° lm^1 249, this compilation is now on microfiche. Until recently, however, it comprised a thin, nondescript volume, a species of folder with stiff covers which contained a loose assemblage of ostensibly unrelated items – news clippings, letters pasted to backing-sheets, pamphlets, numerous genealogical trees and the odd printed page apparently extracted from the body of some other work. Periodically some of the individual pages would be removed. At different times other pages would be freshly inserted. On certain pages additions and corrections would sometimes be made in a minuscule longhand. At a later date, these pages would be replaced by new ones, printed and incorporating all previous emendations.

The bulk of the *Dossiers*, which consists of genealogical trees, is ascribed to one Henri Lobineau, whose name appears on the title page. Two additional items in the folder declare that Henri Lobineau is yet another pseudonym – derived perhaps from a street, the Rue Lobineau, which runs outside Saint Sulpice in Paris – and that the genealogies are actually the work of a man named Leo Schidlof, an Austrian historian and antiquarian who purportedly lived in Switzerland and died in

1966. On the basis of this information we undertook to learn what we could about Leo Schidlof.

In 1978 we managed to locate Leo Schidlof's daughter, who was living in England. Her father, she said, was indeed Austrian. He was not a genealogist, historian or antiquarian, however, but an expert and dealer in miniatures, who had written two works on the subject. In 1948 he had settled in London, where he lived until his death in Vienna in 1966 – the year and place specified in the *Dossiers secrets*.

Miss Schidlof vehemently maintained that her father had never had any interest in genealogies, the Merovingian dynasty, or mysterious goings-on in the south of France. And yet, she continued, certain people obviously believed he had. During the 1960s, for example, he had received numerous letters and telephone calls from unidentified individuals in both Europe and the United States, who wished to meet with him and discuss matters of which he had no knowledge whatever. On his death in 1966 there was another barrage of messages, most of them inquiring about his papers.

Whatever the affair in which Miss Schidlof's father had become unwittingly embroiled, it seemed to have struck a sensitive chord with the American government. In 1946 – a decade before the *Dossiers secrets* are said to have been compiled – Leo Schidlof applied for a visa to enter the United States. The application was refused, on grounds of suspected espionage or some other form of clandestine activity. Eventually the matter seems to have been sorted out, the visa issued and Leo Schidlof was admitted to the States. It may all have been a typical bureaucratic mix-up. But Miss Schidlof seemed to suspect that it was somehow connected with the arcane preoccupations so perplexingly ascribed to her father.

Miss Schidlof's story gave us pause. The refusal of an American visa might well have been more than coincidental, for there were, among the papers in the *Dossiers secrets*, references that linked the name Leo Schidlof with some sort of international espionage. In the meantime, however, a new pamphlet had appeared in Paris – which, during the months that followed, was confirmed by other sources. According to this pamphlet the elusive Henri Lobineau was not Leo Schidlof after all, but a French aristocrat of distinguished lineage, Comte Henri de Lénoncourt.

The question of Lobineau's real identity was not the only enigma associated with the *Dossiers secrets*. There was also an item which referred to 'Leo Schidlof's leather briefcase'. This briefcase supposedly contained a number of secret papers relating to Rennes-le-Château between 1600 and 1800. Shortly after Schidlof's death, the briefcase was said to have passed into the hands of a courier, a certain Fakhar ul Islam – who, in February 1967, was to rendezvous in East Germany with an 'agent delegated by Geneva' and entrust it to him. Before the transaction could be effected, however, Fakhar ul Islam was reportedly expelled from East Germany and returned to Paris 'to await further orders'. On February 20th, 1967, his body was found on the railway tracks at Melun, having been hurled from the Paris–Geneva express. The briefcase had supposedly vanished.

We set out to check this lurid story as far as we could. A series of articles in French newspapers of February 21st did confirm most of it.[4] A decapitated body had indeed been found on the tracks at Melun. It was identified as that of a young Pakistani named Fakhar ul Islam. For reasons that remained obscure, the dead man had been expelled from East Germany and was travelling from Paris to Geneva – engaged, it appeared, in some form of espionage. According to the newspaper reports, the authorities suspected foul play, and the affair was being investigated by the DST (Directorate of Territorial Surveillance, or Counter-Espionage).

On the other hand, the newspapers made no mention of Leo Schidlof, a leather briefcase or anything else that might connect the occurrence with the mystery of Rennes-le-Château. As a result, we found ourselves confronted with a number of questions. On the one hand, it was possible that Fakhar ul Islam's death was linked with Rennes-le-Château – that, the item in the *Dossiers secrets* in fact drew upon 'inside information' inaccessible to the newspapers. On the other hand the item in the *Dossiers secrets* might have been deliberate and spurious mystification. One need only find any unexplained or suspicious death and ascribe it, after the fact, to one's own hobby-horse. But if this were indeed the case, what was the purpose of the exercise? Why should someone deliberately try to create an atmosphere of sinister intrigue around Rennes-le-Château? What might be gained by the creation of such an atmosphere? And who might gain from it?

These questions perplexed us all the more because Fakhar ul Islam's death was not, apparently, an isolated occurrence. Less than a month later another privately printed work was deposited in the Bibliothèque Nationale. It was called *Le Serpent rouge* ('The Red Serpent') and dated, symbolically and significantly enough, January 17th. Its title page ascribed it to three authors – Pierre Feugère, Louis Saint-Maxent and Gaston de Koker.

Le Serpent rouge is a singular work. It contains one Merovingian genealogy and two maps of France in Merovingian times, along with a cursory commentary. It also contains a ground plan of Saint Sulpice in Paris, which delineates the chapels of the church's various saints. But the bulk of the text consists of thirteen short prose poems of impressive literary quality – many of them reminiscent of the work of Rimbaud. Each of these prose poems is no more than a paragraph long, and each corresponds to a sign of the Zodiac – a zodiac of thirteen signs, with the thirteenth, Ophiuchus or the Serpent Holder, inserted between Scorpio and Sagittarius.

Narrated in the first person, the thirteen prose poems are a type of symbolic or allegorical pilgrimage, commencing with Aquarius and ending with Capricorn – which, as the text explicitly states, presides over January 17th. In the otherwise cryptic text there are familiar references – to the Blanchefort family, to the decorations in the church at Rennes-le-Château, to some of Saunière's inscriptions there, to Poussin and the painting of 'Les Bergers d'Arcadie', to the motto on the tomb, 'Et in Arcadia Ego'. At one point, there is mention of a red snake, 'cited in the parchments', uncoiling across the centuries – an explicit allusion, it would seem, to a bloodline or a lineage. And for the astrological sign of Leo, there is an enigmatic paragraph worth quoting in its entirety:

From she whom I desire to liberate, there wafts towards me the fragrance of the perfume which impregnates the Sepulchre. Formerly, some named her: ISIS, queen of all sources benevolent. COME UNTO ME ALL YE WHO SUFFER AND ARE AFFLICTED, AND I SHALL GIVE YE REST. To others, she is MAGDALENE, of the celebrated vase filled with healing balm. The initiated know her true name: NOTRE DAME DES CROSS.[5]

The implications of this paragraph are extremely interesting. Isis, of course, is the Egyptian Mother Goddess, patroness of mysteries – the 'White Queen' in her benevolent aspects, the 'Black Queen' in her malevolent ones. Numerous writers, on mythology, anthropology, psychology, theology, have traced the cult of the Mother Goddess from pagan times to the Christian epoch. And according to these writers she is said to have survived under Christianity in the guise of the Virgin Mary – the 'Queen of Heaven', as Saint Bernard called her, a designation applied in the Old Testament to the Mother Goddess Astarte, the Phoenician equivalent of Isis. But according to the text in *Le Serpent rouge*, the Mother Goddess of Christianity would not appear to be the Virgin. On the contrary, she would appear to be the Magdalene – to whom the church at Rennes-le-Château is dedicated and to whom Saunière consecrated his tower. Moreover, the text would seem to imply that 'Notre Dame' does not apply to the Virgin either. That resonant title – conferred on all the great cathedrals of France – would also seem to refer to the Magdalene. But why should the Magdalene be revered as 'Our Lady' – and, still more, as a Mother Goddess? Maternity is the last thing generally associated with the Magdalene. In popular Christian tradition she is a prostitute who finds redemption by apprenticing herself to Jesus. And she figures most noticeably in the Fourth Gospel, where she is the first person to behold Jesus after the Resurrection. In consequence she is extolled as a saint, especially in France – where, according to medieval legends, she is said to have brought the Holy Grail. And indeed the 'vase filled with healing balm' might well be intended to suggest the Grail. But to enshrine the Magdalene in the place usually reserved for the Virgin would seem, at very least, to be heretical.

Whatever their point, the authors of *Le Serpent rouge* – or, rather, the alleged authors – met with a fate as gruesome as that of Fakhar ul Islam. On March 6th, 1967, Louis Saint-Maxent and Gaston de Koker were found hanged. And the following day, March 7th, Pierre Feugère was found hanged as well.

One might immediately assume, of course, that these deaths were in some way connected with the composition and public release of *Le Serpent rouge*. As in the case of Fakhar ul Islam, however, we could not discount an alternative explanation. If one wished to engender an aura of sinister mystery, it would be easy enough to do. One need only comb the newspapers until one found a suspicious death – or, in this instance, three suspicious deaths. After the fact, one might then append the names of the deceased to a pamphlet of one's own concoction and deposit that pamphlet in the Bibliothèque Nationale – with an earlier date (January 17th) on the title page. It would be virtually impossible to expose such a hoax, which would certainly produce the desired intimation of foul play. But why perpetrate such a hoax at all? Why should someone want to invoke an aura of violence, murder and intrigue? Such a ploy would hardly deter investigators. On the contrary, it would only further attract them.

If, on the other hand, we were not dealing with a hoax, there were still a number of baffling questions. Were we to believe, for example, that the three hanged men were suicides or victims of murder? Suicide, in the circumstances, would seem to make little sense. And murder would not seem to make much more. One could understand three people being dispatched lest they divulge certain explosive information. But in this case the information had already been divulged, already deposited in the Bibliothèque Nationale. Could the murders – if that was what they were – have been a form of punishment, of retribution? Or perhaps a means of precluding any subsequent indiscretions? Neither of these explanations is satisfactory. If one is angered by the disclosure of certain information, or if one wishes to forestall additional disclosures, one does not attract attention to the matter by committing a trio of lurid and sensational murders unless one is reasonably confident that there will be no very assiduous inquiry.

Our own adventures in the course of our investigation were mercifully less dramatic, but equally mystifying. In our research, for example, we had encountered repeated references to a work by one Antoine l'Ermite entitled *Un Trésor mérovingien à Rennes-le-Château* ('A Merovingian Treasure at Rennes-le-Château'). We endeavoured to locate this work and quickly found it listed in the Bibliothèque Nationale catalogue; but it proved inordinately difficult to obtain. Every day, for a week, we went to the library and filled out the requisite fiche requesting the work. On each occasion the fiche was returned marked 'communiqué' – indicating that the work was being used by someone else. In itself this was not necessarily unusual. After a fortnight, however, it began to become so – and exasperating as well, for we could not remain in Paris much longer. We sought the assistance of a librarian. He told us the book would be 'communiqué' for three months – an extremely unusual situation – and that we could not order it in advance of its return.

In England not long afterwards a friend of ours announced that she was going to Paris for a holiday. We accordingly asked her to try to obtain the elusive work of Antoine l'Ermite and at least make a note of what it contained. At the Bibliothèque Nationale, she requested the book. Her fiche was not even returned. The next day she tried again, and with the same result.

When we were next in Paris, some four months later, we made another attempt. Our fiche was again returned marked 'communiqué'. At this point, we began to feel the game had been somewhat overplayed and began to play one of our own. We made our way down the catalogue room, adjacent to the 'stacks' – which are, of course, inaccessible to the public. Finding an elderly and kindly looking library assistant, we assumed the role of bumbling English tourists with Neanderthal command of French. Asking his help, we explained that we were seeking a particular work but were unable to obtain it, no doubt because of our imperfect understanding of the library's procedures.

The genial old gentleman agreed to help. We gave him the work's catalogue number and he disappeared into the 'stacks'. When he emerged, he apologised, saying there was nothing he could do – the book had been stolen. What was more, he added, a compatriot of ours was apparently responsible for the theft – an Englishwoman. After some badgering, he consented to give us her name. It was that of our friend!

On returning to England again, we sought the assistance of the library service in London, and they agreed to look into the bizarre affair. On our behalf, the National Central Library wrote to the Bibliothèque Nationale requesting an explanation for what appeared to be deliberate obstruction of legitimate research. No explanation was forthcoming. Shortly thereafter, however, a Xerox copy of Antoine l'Ermite's work was at last dispatched to us – along with emphatic instructions that it be returned immediately. This in itself was extremely singular, for libraries do not generally request return of Xerox copies. Such copies are usually deemed mere waste paper and disposed of accordingly.

The work, when it was finally in our hands, proved distinctly disappointing – hardly worth the complicated business of obtaining it. Like Madeleine Blancassal's work, it bore the imprint of the Swiss Grande Loge Alpina. But it said nothing in any way new. Very briefly, it recapitulated the history of the Comté of Razès, of Rennes-le-Château and Bérenger Saunière. In short, it rehashed all the details with which we had long been familiar. There seemed to be no imaginable reason why anyone should have been using it, and keeping it 'communiqué', for a solid week. Nor did there seem any imaginable reason for withholding it from us. But most puzzling of all, the work itself was not original. With the exception of a few words altered here and there, it was a verbatim text, reset and reprinted, of a chapter in a popular paperback – a facile best-seller, available at news-stands for a few francs, on lost treasures throughout the world. Either Antoine l'Ermite had shamelessly plagiarised the published book, or the published book had plagiarised Antoine l'Ermite.

The chateau of Gisors, Normandy, showing the octagonal keep. Gisors was said to be the headquarters of the Prieuré de Sion after 1188.

Such occurrences are typical of the mystification that has attended the material which, since 1956, has been appearing fragment by fragment in France. Other researchers have encountered similar enigmas. Ostensibly plausible names have proved to be pseudonyms. Addresses, including addresses of publishing houses and organisations, have proved not to exist. References have been cited to books which no one, to our knowledge, has ever seen. Documents have disappeared, been altered, or inexplicably miscatalogued in the Bibliothèque Nationale. At times one is tempted to suspect a practical joke. If so, however, it is a practical joke on an enormous scale, involving an impressive array of resources – financial and otherwise. And whoever might be perpetrating such a joke would seem to be taking it very seriously indeed.

In the meantime new material has continued to appear, with the familiar themes recurring like *leitmotifs* – Saunière, Rennes-le-Château, Poussin, 'Les Bergers d'Arcadie', the Knights Templar, Dagobert II and the Merovingian dynasty. Allusions to viticulture – the grafting of vines – figure prominently, presumably in some allegorical sense. At the same time, more and more information has been added. The identification of Henri Lobineau as the count of Lénoncourt is one example. Another is an increasing but unexplained insistence on the significance of the Magdalene. And two other locations have been stressed repeatedly, assuming a status now apparently commensurate with Rennes-le-Château. One of these is Gisors, a fortress in Normandy which was of vital strategic and political importance at the peak of the Crusades. The other is Stenay, once called Satanicum, on the fringe of the Ardennes – the old capital of the Merovingian dynasty, near which Dagobert II was assassinated in 679.

The corpus of material now available cannot be adequately reviewed or discussed in these pages. It is too dense, too confusing, too disconnected, most of all too copious. But from this ever-proliferating welter of information, certain key points emerge which constitute a foundation for further research. They are presented as indisputable historical fact, and can be summarised as follows:

1) There was a secret order behind the Knights Templar, which created the Templars as its military and administrative arm. This order, which has functioned under a variety of names, is most frequently known as the Prieuré de Sion ('Priory of Sion').

2) The Prieuré de Sion has been directed by a sequence of Grand Masters whose names are among the most illustrious in Western history and culture.

3) Although the Knights Templar were destroyed and dissolved between 1307 and 1314, the Prieuré de Sion remained unscathed. Although itself periodically torn by internecine and factional strife, it has continued to function through the centuries. Acting in the shadows, behind the scenes, it has orchestrated certain of the critical events in Western history.

4) The Prieuré de Sion exists today and is still operative. It is influential and plays a role in high-level international affairs, as well as in the domestic affairs of certain European countries. To some significant extent it is responsible for the body of information disseminated since 1956.

5) The avowed and declared objective of the Prieuré de Sion is the restoration of the Merovingian dynasty and bloodline – to the throne not only of France, but to the thrones of other European nations as well.

6) The restoration of the Merovingian dynasty is sanctioned and justifiable, both legally and morally. Although deposed in the eighth century, the Merovingian bloodline did not become extinct. On the contrary it perpetuated itself in a direct line from Dagobert II and his son, Sigisbert IV. By dint of dynastic alliances and intermarriages, this line came to include Godfroi de Bouillon, who captured Jerusalem in 1099, and various other noble and royal families, past and present – Blanchefort, Gisors, Saint-Clair (Sinclair in England), Montesquiou, Montpézat, Poher, Luisignan, Plantard and Habsburg-Lorraine. At present, the Merovingian bloodline enjoys a legitimate claim to its rightful heritage.

Here, in the so-called Prieuré de Sion, was a possible explanation for the reference to 'Sion' in the parchments found by Bérenger Saunière. Here, too, was an explanation for the curious signature, 'P.S.', which appeared on one of those parchments, and on the tombstone of Marie de Blanchefort.

Nevertheless, we were extremely sceptical, like most people, about 'conspiracy theories of history'; and most of the above assertions struck us as irrelevant, improbable and/or absurd. But the fact remained that certain people were promulgating them, and doing so quite seriously; quite seriously and, there was reason to believe, from positions of considerable power. And whatever the truth of the assertions, they were clearly connected in some way with the mystery surrounding Saunière and Rennes-le-Château.

We, therefore, embarked on a systematic examination of what we had begun to call, ironically, the 'Prieuré documents', and of the assertions they contained. We endeavoured to subject these assertions to careful critical scrutiny and determine whether they could be in any way substantiated. We did so with a cynical, almost derisory scepticism, fully convinced the outlandish claims would wither under even cursory investigation. Although we could not know it at the time, we were to be greatly surprised.

CHAPTER FIVE

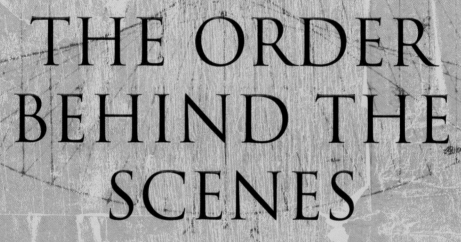

THE ORDER BEHIND THE SCENES

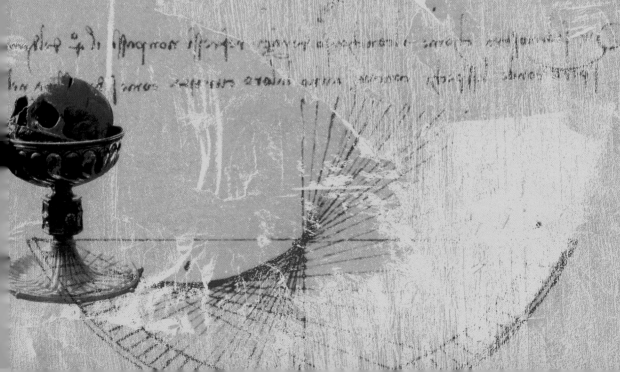

We had already suspected the existence of a group of individuals, if not a coherent 'order', behind the Knights Templar. The claim that the Temple was created by the Prieuré de Sion thus seemed slightly more plausible than the other assertions in the 'Prieuré documents'. It was with this claim, therefore, that we started our examination.

As early as 1962 the Prieuré de Sion had been mentioned, briefly, cryptically and in passing, in a work by Gérard de Sède. The first detailed reference to it that we found, however, was a single page in the *Dossiers secrets*. At the top of this page there is a quotation from René Grousset, one of the foremost twentieth-century authorities on the Crusades, whose monumental opus on the subject, published during the 1930s, is regarded as a seminal work by such modern historians as Sir Steven Runciman. The quotation refers to Baudouin I, younger brother of Godfroi de Bouillon, Duke of Lorraine and conqueror of the Holy Land. On Godfroi's death, Baudouin accepted the crown offered him and thereby became the first official king of Jerusalem. According to René Grousset, there existed, through Baudouin I, a 'royal tradition'. And because it was 'founded on the rock of Sion',[1] this tradition was 'equal' to the reigning dynasties in Europe – the Capetian dynasty of France, the Anglo-Norman (Plantagenet) dynasty of England, the Hohenstauffen and Habsburg dynasties which presided over Germany and the old Holy Roman Empire. But Baudouin and his descendants were elected kings, not kings by blood. Why, then, should Grousset speak of a 'royal tradition' which 'existed through' him? Grousset himself does not explain. Nor does he explain why this tradition, because it was 'founded on the rock of Sion', should be 'equal' to the foremost dynasties of Europe.

On the page in the *Dossiers secrets* Grousset's quotation is followed by an allusion to the mysterious Prieuré de Sion – or Ordre de Sion, as it was apparently called at the time. According to the text, the Ordre de Sion was founded by Godfroi de Bouillon in 1090, nine years before the conquest of Jerusalem – although there are other 'Prieuré documents' which give the founding date as 1099. According to the text, Baudouin, Godfroi's younger brother, 'owed his throne' to the Order. And according to the text, the Order's official seat, or 'headquarters', was a specific abbey – the Abbey of Notre Dame du Mont de Sion in Jerusalem. Or perhaps just outside Jerusalem – on Mount Sion, the famous 'high hill' just south of the city.

On consulting all standard twentieth-century works on the Crusades, we found no mention whatever of any Ordre de Sion. We therefore undertook to establish whether or not such an Order ever existed – and whether it could have had the power to confer thrones. To do that, we were obliged to rummage through sheaves of antiquated documents and charters. We did not just seek explicit references to the Order. We also sought some trace of its possible influence and activities. And we endeavoured to confirm whether or not there was an abbey called Notre Dame du Mont de Sion.

To the south of Jerusalem looms the 'high hill' of Mount Sion. In 1099, when Jerusalem fell to Godfroi de Bouillon's crusaders, there stood on this hill the ruins of an old Byzantine basilica, dating supposedly from the fourth century and called 'the Mother of all Churches' – a most suggestive title. According to numerous extant charters, chronicles and contemporary accounts, an abbey was built on the site of these ruins. It was built at the express command of Godfroi de Bouillon. It must have been an imposing edifice, a self-contained community. According to one chronicler, writing in 1172, it was extremely well fortified, with its own walls, towers and battlements. And this structure was called the Abbey of Notre Dame du Mont de Sion.

Someone, obviously, had to occupy the premises. Could they have been an autonomous 'order', taking their name from the site itself? Could the occupants of the abbey indeed have been the Ordre de Sion? It was not unreasonable to assume so. The knights and monks who occupied the Church of the Holy Sepulchre, also installed by Godfroi, were formed into an official and duly constituted 'order' – the Order of the Holy Sepulchre. The same principle might well have obtained for the occupants of the abbey on Mount Sion, and it would seem to have done so. According to the leading nineteenth-century expert on the subject, the abbey 'was inhabited by a chapter of Augustinian canons, charged with serving the sanctuaries under the direction of an abbot. The community assumed the double name of "Sainte-Marie du Mont Syon et du Saint-Esprit".[2] And another historian, writing in 1698, is more explicit still: 'There were in Jerusalem during the Crusades . . . knights attached to the Abbey of Notre Dame de Sion who took the name of "Chevaliers de l'Ordre de Notre Dame de Sion".[3]

If this were not sufficient confirmation, we also discovered documents of the period – original documents – bearing the seal and signature of one or another prior of 'Notre Dame de Sion'. There is a charter,

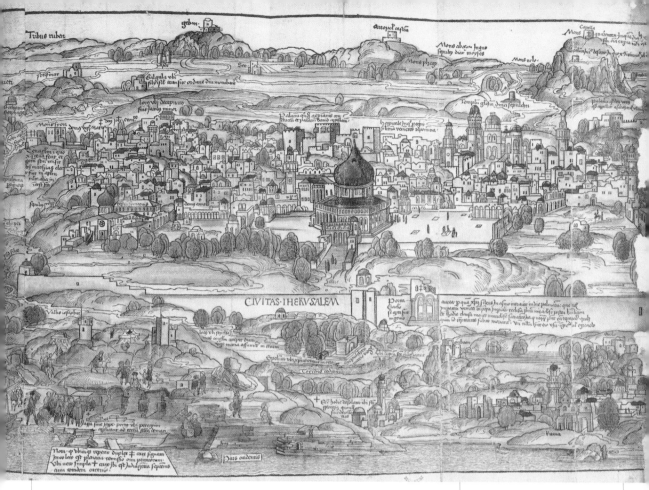

for example, signed by a Prior Arnaldus and dated July 19th, 1116.[4] On another charter, dated May 2nd, 1125, Arnaldus's name appears in conjunction with that of Hugues de Payen, first Grand Master of the Temple.[5]

So far the 'Prieuré documents' had proved valid, and we could assert that an Ordre de Sion did exist by the turn of the twelfth century. Whether or not the Order had actually been formed earlier, however, remained an open question. There is no consistency about which comes first, an order or the premises in which it is housed. The Cistercians, for instance, took their name from a specific place, Cîteaux. On the other hand, the Franciscans and Benedictines – to cite but two examples – took their names from individuals, and pre-dated any fixed abode. The most we could say, therefore, was that an abbey existed by 1100 and housed an order of the same name – which may have been formed earlier.

127

A nineteenth-century engraving of Isis with the pentagram in the correct form depicting the occultations of Venus during its eight-year cycle.

The 'Prieuré documents' imply that it was, and there is some evidence to suggest, albeit vaguely and obliquely, that this may indeed have been the case. It is known that in 1070, twenty-nine years before the First Crusade, a specific band of monks, from Calabria in southern Italy, arrived in the vicinity of the Ardennes Forest, part of Godfroi de Bouillon's domains.[6] According to Gérard de Sède, this band of monks was led by an individual called 'Ursus' – a name which the 'Prieuré documents' consistently associate with the Merovingian bloodline. On their arrival in the Ardennes, the Calabrian monks obtained the patronage of Mathilde de Toscane, Duchess of Lorraine – who was Godfroi de Bouillon's aunt and, in effect, foster-mother. From Mathilde the monks received a tract of land at Orval, not far from Stenay, where Dagobert II had been assassinated some five hundred years earlier. Here an abbey was established to house them. Nevertheless they did not remain at Orval very long. By 1108 they had mysteriously disappeared, and no record of their whereabouts survives. Tradition says they returned to Calabria. Orval, by 1131, had become one of the fiefs owned by Saint Bernard.

Before their departure from Orval, however, the Calabrian monks may have left a crucial mark on Western history. According to Gérard de Sède, at least, they included the man subsequently known as Peter the Hermit. If this is so, it would be extremely significant, for Peter the Hermit is often believed to have been Godfroi de Bouillon's personal tutor.[7] Nor is that his only claim to fame. In 1095, along with Pope Urban II, Peter made himself known throughout Christendom by charismatically preaching the need for a crusade – a holy war which would reclaim Christ's sepulchre and the Holy Land from the hands of the Muslim infidel. Today Peter the Hermit is regarded as one of the chief instigators of the Crusades.

Previous page; Statue of the Virgin Mary in the modern monastic quarters of the Abbey of Orval. When first constructed the pentagram on her head pointed downwards - a symbol of the occultations of Venus - but subsequently someone was sufficiently outraged to go to the effort of twisting the pentagram around to point upwards.

When Islam was established in the seventh century, it was at first accommodating to the Christian communities in its midst – communities sometimes orthodox, sometimes heterodox, sometimes 'heretical'. During the eighth and ninth centuries, however, these communities were subjected to increasing persecution, and substantial numbers of Christians fled – taking with them their sacred texts and establishing new monasteries in Sicily and Calabria, then under the rule of the Byzantine Empire. In 1070, persecution of those few remaining in the Holy Land intensified when Arab Muslims were overrun by Turks from the northeast; and this precipitated a new exodus to Sicily and Calabria. A year later, in 1071, the last possessions of the Byzantine Empire in Italy fell to the Normans and the House of Anjou. Sicily and Calabria were now Norman territory.

Against this background, the origins of the monastic order at Orval become clearer, more comprehensible and more plausible. It is certainly conceivable that an order of monks with long-suppressed information about Jesus could have found their way to Calabria from Egypt, from Syria or Lebanon, from Asia Minor, perhaps from the Holy Land itself. And it is equally conceivable that an Italian noblewoman, Mathilde de Toscane, could have granted them land in her husband's fiefdom of the Ardennes. In the process, she and her family could well have become privy to whatever secrets her beneficiaries harboured. Her beneficiaries may, indeed, have become beneficiaries in exchange for their information. If the monks at Orval had been driven from the Holy Land, their preaching of a crusade to reclaim their lost domain would be explicable enough. And if Mathilde knew of Godfroi de Bouillon's claim to Davidic descent, she would have had all the more reason to become the monks' protectress. This would explain the central legend of Orval – the ring lost in a pool, then found in the belly of a fish – which so closely echoes the story associated with King Solomon.

On the basis of hints intimated in the 'Prieuré documents', we began to wonder whether there might have been some sort of shadowy continuity between the monks of Orval, Peter the Hermit and the Ordre de Sion. It would certainly seem that the monks at Orval were not just a random band of itinerant religious devotees. On the contrary their movements – their collective arrival in the Ardennes from Calabria and their mysterious disappearance *en masse* – attest to some kind of cohesion, some kind of organisation and perhaps a permanent base somewhere. And if Peter were a member of this band of monks, his preaching of a crusade might have been a manifestation not of rampant fanaticism, but of calculated policy. If he was Godfroi's personal tutor, moreover, he might well have played some role in convincing his pupil to embark for the Holy Land. And when the monks vanished from Orval, they might not have returned to Calabria after all. They might have established themselves in Jerusalem, perhaps in the Abbey of Notre Dame de Sion.

This, of course, was only a speculative hypothesis, with no documentary confirmation. Again, however, we soon found fragments of circumstantial evidence to support it. When Godfroi de Bouillon embarked for the Holy Land, he is known to have been accompanied by an entourage of anonymous figures who acted as advisors and administrators – the equivalent, in effect, of a modern general staff. But Godfroi's was not the only Christian army to embark for Palestine. There were no less than three others, each commanded by an illustrious and influential Western potentate. If the crusade proved successful, if Jerusalem did fall and a Frankish kingdom were established, any one of these four potentates would have been eligible to occupy its throne. And yet Godfroi seems to have known beforehand that he would be selected. Alone among the European commanders, he renounced his fiefs, sold all his goods and made it apparent that the Holy Land, for the duration of his life, would be his domain.

In 1099, immediately after the capture of Jerusalem, a group of anonymous figures convened in secret conclave. The identity of this group has eluded all historical inquiry – although Guillaume de Tyre, writing three-quarters of a century later, reports that the most important of them was 'a certain bishop from Calabria'.[8] In any case the purpose of the meeting was clear – to elect a king of Jerusalem. And despite a persuasive claim by Raymond, Count of Toulouse, the mysterious and obviously influential electors promptly offered the throne to Godfroi de Bouillon. With uncharacteristic modesty, Godfroi declined the title, accepting instead that of 'Defender of the Holy Sepulchre'. In other words, he was a king in everything but name. And when he died, in 1100, his brother, Baudouin, did not hesitate to accept the name as well.

Could the mysterious conclave which elected Godfroi ruler have been the elusive monks from Orval – including perhaps Peter the

Hermit, who was in the Holy Land at the time and enjoyed considerable authority? And could this same conclave have occupied the abbey on Mount Sion? In short, could those three ostensibly distinct groups of individuals – the monks from Orval, the conclave who elected Godfroi and the occupants of Notre Dame de Sion – have been one and the same? The possibility cannot be proved, but neither can it be dismissed out of hand. And if it is true, it would certainly attest to the Ordre de Sion's power – a power which included the right to confer thrones.

THE MYSTERY SURROUNDING THE FOUNDATION OF THE KNIGHTS TEMPLAR

The text in the *Dossiers secrets* goes on to refer to the Order of the Temple. The founders of the Temple are specifically listed as, 'Hugues de Payen, Bisol de St. Omer and Hugues, Comte de Champagne, along with certain members of the Ordre de Sion, André de Montbard, Archambaud de Saint-Aignan, Nivard de Montdidier, Gondemar and Rossal'.[9]

We were already familiar with Hugues de Payen and André de Montbard, Saint Bernard's uncle. We were also familiar with Hugues, Count of Champagne – who donated the land for Saint Bernard's abbey at Clairvaux, became a Templar himself in 1124 (pledging fealty to his own vassal) and received from the bishop of Chartres the letter quoted in Chapter 3. But although the count of Champagne's connection with the Templars was well known, we had never before seen him cited as one of their founders. In the *Dossiers secrets* he is. And André de Montbard, Saint Bernard's shadowy uncle, is listed as belonging to the Ordre de Sion, in other words to another Order, which predates the Order of the Temple and plays an instrumental role in the Temple's creation.

Nor is that all. The text in the *Dossiers secrets* states that in March 1117, Baudouin I, 'who owed his throne to Sion', was 'obliged' to negotiate the constitution of the Order of the Temple – at the site of Saint Léonard of Acre. Our own research revealed that Saint Léonard of Acre was in fact one of the fiefs of the Ordre de Sion. But we were uncertain why Baudouin should have been 'obliged' to negotiate the Temple's constitution. In French the verb certainly connotes a degree of coercion or pressure. And the implication in the *Dossiers secrets* was that this pressure was brought to bear by the Ordre de Sion – to whom Baudouin

'owed his throne'. If this were the case, the Ordre de Sion would have been a most influential and powerful organisation – an organisation which could not only confer thrones, but also, apparently, compel a king to do its bidding.

If the Ordre de Sion was in fact responsible for Godfroi de Bouillon's election, then Baudouin, Godfroi's younger brother, would have 'owed his throne' to its influence. As we had already discovered, moreover, there was indisputable evidence that the Order of the Temple existed, at least in embryonic form, a good four years before the generally accepted foundation date of 1118. In 1117 Baudouin was a sick man, whose death was patently imminent. It is therefore possible that the Knights Templar were active, albeit in an *ex officio* capacity, long before 1118 – as, say, a military or administrative arm of the Ordre de Sion, housed in its fortified abbey. And it is possible that King Baudouin, on his deathbed, was compelled – by illness, by the Ordre de Sion or by both – to grant the Templars some official status, to give them a constitution and make them public.

In researching the Templars we had already begun to discern a web of intricate, elusive and provocative connections, the shadowy vestiges perhaps of some ambitious design. On the basis of these connections, we had formulated a tentative hypothesis. Whether our hypothesis was accurate or not, we could not know; but the vestiges of a design had now become even more apparent. We assembled the fragments of the pattern as follows:

1) In the late eleventh century a mysterious group of monks from Calabria appears in the Ardennes, where they are welcomed, patronised and given land at Orval by Godfroi de Bouillon's aunt and foster-mother.
2) A member of this group may have been Godfroi's personal tutor and may have co-instigated the First Crusade.
3) Some time before 1108 the monks at Orval decamp and disappear. Although there is no record of their destination, it may well have been Jerusalem. Certainly Peter the Hermit embarked for Jerusalem; and if he was one of the monks at Orval, it is probable that his brethren later joined him.
4) In 1099 Jerusalem falls and Godfroi is offered a throne by an anonymous conclave – a leader of whom, like the monks of Orval, is of Calabrian origin.

5) An abbey is built at Godfroi's behest on Mount Sion, which houses an order of the same name as itself – an order which may comprise the individuals who offered him the throne.

6) By 1114 the Knights Templar are already active, perhaps as the Ordre de Sion's armed entourage; but their constitution is not negotiated until 1117, and they themselves are not made public until the following year.

7) In 1115 Saint Bernard – member of the Cistercian Order, then on the brink of economic collapse – emerges as the pre-eminent spokesman of Christendom. And the formerly destitute Cistercians rapidly become one of the most prominent, influential and wealthy institutions in Europe.

8) In 1131 Saint Bernard receives the abbey of Orval, vacated some years before by the monks from Calabria. Orval then becomes a Cistercian house.

9) At the same time certain obscure figures seem to move constantly in and out of these events, stitching the tapestry together in a manner that is not altogether clear. The count of Champagne, for example, donates the land for Saint Bernard's abbey at Clairvaux, establishes a court at Troyes, whence the Grail romances subsequently issue and, in 1114, contemplates joining the Knights Templar – whose first recorded Grand Master, Hugues de Payen, is already his vassal.

10) André de Montbard – Saint Bernard's uncle and an alleged member of the Ordre de Sion – joins Hugues de Payen in founding the Knights Templar. Shortly thereafter André's two brothers join Saint Bernard at Clairvaux.

11) Saint Bernard becomes an enthusiastic public relations exponent for the Templars, contributes to their official incorporation and the drawing-up of their rule – which is essentially that of the Cistercians, Bernard's own order.

12) Between approximately 1115 and 1140, both Cistercians and Templars begin to prosper, acquiring vast sums of money and tracts of land.

Again we could not but wonder whether this multitude of intricate connections was indeed wholly coincidental. Were we looking at a number of essentially disconnected people, events and phenomena – which just 'happened', at intervals, to overlap and cross each other's paths? Or were we dealing with something that was not random or coincidental at all? Were we dealing with a plan of some sort, conceived and engineered by some human agency? And could that agency have been the Ordre de Sion?

Could the Ordre de Sion have actually stood behind both Saint Bernard and the Knights Templar? And could both have been acting in accordance with some carefully evolved policy?

LOUIS VII AND THE PRIEURÉ DE SION

The 'Prieuré documents' gave no indication of the Ordre de Sion's activities between 1118 – the public foundation of the Templars – and 1152. For the whole of that time, it would seem, the Ordre de Sion remained based in the Holy Land, in the abbey outside Jerusalem. Then, on his return from the Second Crusade, Louis VII of France is said to have brought with him ninety-five members of the Order. There is no indication of the capacity in which they might have attended the king, nor why he should have extended his bounty to them. But if the Ordre de Sion was indeed the power behind the Temple, that would constitute an explanation – since Louis VII was heavily indebted to the Temple, both for money and military support. In any case the Ordre de Sion, created half a century previously by Godfroi de Bouillon, in 1152 established – or re-established – a foothold in France. According to the text, sixty-two members of the Order were installed at the 'large priory' of Saint-Samson at Orleans, which King Louis had donated to them. Seven were reportedly incorporated into the fighting ranks of the Knights Templar. And twenty-six – two groups of thirteen each – are said to have entered the 'small Priory of the Mount of Sion', situated at Saint Jean le Blanc on the outskirts of Orleans.[10]

In trying to authenticate these statements, we suddenly found ourselves on readily provable ground. The charters by which Louis VII installed the Ordre de Sion at Orleans are still extant. Copies have been reproduced in a number of sources, and the originals can be seen in the municipal archives of Orleans. In the same archives there is also a Bull dated 1178, from Pope Alexander III, which officially confirms the Ordre de Sion's possessions. These possessions attest to the Order's wealth, power and influence. They include houses and large tracts of land in Picardy, in France (including Saint-Samson at Orleans), in Lombardy, Sicily, Spain and Calabria, as well, of course, as a number of sites in the Holy Land, including Saint Léonard at Acre. Until the

Second World War, in fact, there were in the archives of Orleans[11] no less than twenty charters specifically citing the Ordre de Sion. During the bombing of the city in 1940 all but three of these disappeared.

THE 'CUTTING OF THE ELM' AT GISORS

If the 'Prieuré documents' can be believed, 1188 was a year of crucial importance for both Sion and the Knights Templar. A year before, in 1187, Jerusalem had been lost to the Saracens – chiefly through the impetuosity and ineptitude of Gérard de Ridefort, Grand Master of the Temple. The text in the *Dossiers secrets* is considerably more severe. It speaks not of Gérard's impetuosity or ineptitude, but of his 'treason' – a very harsh word indeed. What constituted this 'treason' is not explained. But as a result of it the 'initiates' of Sion are said to have returned *en masse* to France – presumably to Orleans. Logically this assertion is plausible enough. When Jerusalem fell to the Saracens, the abbey on Mount Sion would obviously have fallen as well. Deprived of their base in the Holy Land, it would not be surprising if the abbey's occupants had sought refuge in France – where a new base already existed.

The events of 1187 – Gérard de Ridefort's 'treason' and the loss of Jerusalem – seem to have precipitated a disastrous rift between the Ordre de Sion and the Order of the Temple. It is not clear precisely why this should have occurred; but according to the *Dossiers secrets* the following year witnessed a decisive turning-point in the affairs of both orders. In 1188 a formal separation supposedly occurred between the two institutions. The Ordre de Sion, which had created the Knights Templar, now washed its hands of its celebrated protégés. The 'parent', in other words, officially disowned the 'child'. This rupture is said to have been commemorated by a ritual or ceremony of some sort. In the *Dossiers secrets* and other 'Prieuré documents', it is referred to as 'the cutting of the elm', and allegedly took place at Gisors.

Accounts are garbled and obscure, but history and tradition both confirm that something extremely odd occurred at Gisors in 1188 which did involve the cutting of an elm. On the land adjacent to the fortress there was a meadow called the Champ Sacré – the Sacred Field. According to medieval chroniclers, the site had been deemed sacred since pre-Christian times, and during the twelfth century had provided the setting for numerous meetings between the kings of England and

France. In the middle of the Sacred Field stood an ancient elm. And in 1188, during a meeting between Henry II of England and Philippe II of France, for some unknown reason this elm became an object of serious, even bloody, contention.

According to one account, the elm afforded the only shade on the Sacred Field. It was said to be more than eight hundred years old, and so large that nine men, linking hands, could barely encompass its trunk. Under the shade of this tree Henry II and his entourage supposedly took shelter, leaving the French monarch, who arrived later, to the merciless sunlight. By the third day of negotiations French tempers had become frayed by the heat, insults were exchanged by the men-at-arms and an arrow flew from the ranks of Henry's Welsh mercenaries. This provoked a full-scale onslaught by the French, who greatly outnumbered the English. The latter sought refuge within the walls of Gisors itself, while the French are said to have cut down the tree in frustration. Philippe II then stormed back to Paris in a huff, declaring he had not come to Gisors to play the role of woodcutter.

The story has a characteristic medieval simplicity and quaintness, contenting itself with superficial narrative while hinting between the lines at something of greater import – explanations and motivations which are left unexplored. In itself it would almost seem to be absurd – as absurd and possibly apocryphal as, say, the tales associated with the founding of the Order of the Garter. And yet there is confirmation of the story, if not its specific details, in other accounts.

According to another chronicle, Philippe seems to have given notice to Henry that he intended to cut down the tree. Henry supposedly responded by reinforcing the trunk of the elm with bands of iron. On the following day the French armed themselves and formed a phalanx of five squadrons, each commanded by a distinguished lord of the realm, who advanced on the elm, accompanied by slingmen, as well as carpenters equipped with axes and hammers. A struggle is said to have ensued, in which Richard Coeur de Lion, Henry's eldest son and his heir, participated, attempting to protect the tree and spilling considerable blood in the process. Nevertheless, the French held the field at the end of the day, and the tree was cut down.

This second account implies something more than a petty squabble or minor skirmish. It implies a full-scale engagement, involving substantial numbers and possibly substantial casualties. Yet no biography of Richard makes much of the affair, still less explores it.

Again, however, the 'Prieuré documents' were confirmed by both recorded history and tradition – to the extent, at least, that a curious dispute did occur at Gisors in 1188, which involved the cutting of an elm. There is no external confirmation that this event was related in any way to either the Knights Templar or the Ordre de Sion. On the other hand, the existing accounts of the affair are too vague, too scant, too incomprehensible, too contradictory to be accepted as definitive. It is extremely probable that Templars were present at the incident – Richard I was frequently accompanied by knights of the Order, and, moreover, Gisors, thirty years before, had been entrusted to the Temple.

Given the existing evidence, it is certainly possible, if not likely, that the cutting of the elm involved something more – or something other – than the accounts which have been preserved for posterity imply. Indeed, given the sheer oddness of surviving accounts, it would not be surprising if there were something else involved – something overlooked, or perhaps never made public, by history, something, in short, of which the surviving accounts are a species of allegory, simultaneously intimating and concealing an affair of much greater import.

ORMUS

From 1188 onwards, the 'Prieuré documents' maintain, the Knights Templar were autonomous – no longer under the authority of the Ordre de Sion, or acting as its military and administrative arm. From 1188 onwards the Templars were officially free to pursue their own objectives and ends, to follow their own course through the remaining century or so of their existence to their grim doom in 1307. And in the meantime, as of 1188, the Ordre de Sion is said to have undergone a major administrative restructuring of its own.

Until 1188 the Ordre de Sion and the Order of the Temple are said to have shared the same Grand Master. Hugues de Payen and Bertrand de Blanchefort, for example, would thus have presided over both institutions simultaneously. Commencing in 1188, however, after the 'cutting of the elm', the Ordre de Sion reportedly selected its own Grand Master, who had no connection with the Temple. The first such Grand Master, according to the 'Prieuré documents', was Jean de Gisors.

In 1188 the Ordre de Sion is also said to have modified its name, adopting the one which has allegedly obtained to the present – the Prieuré de Sion. And, as a kind of subtitle, it is said to have adopted the curious name 'Ormus'. This subtitle was supposedly used until 1306 – a year before the arrest of the French Templars. The device for 'Ormus' was ♍ and involves a kind of acrostic or anagram which combines a number of key words and symbols. 'Ours' means bear in French – 'Ursus' in Latin, an echo, as subsequently became apparent, of Dagobert II and the Merovingian dynasty. 'Orme' is French for 'elm'. 'Or', of course, is 'gold'. And the 'M' which forms the frame enclosing the other letters is not only an 'M', but also the astrological sign for Virgo – connoting, in the language of medieval iconography, Notre Dame.

Our researches revealed no reference anywhere to a medieval order or institution bearing the name 'Ormus'. In this case we could find no external substantiation for the text in the *Dossiers secrets*, nor even any circumstantial evidence to argue its veracity. On the other hand, 'Ormus' does occur in two other – radically different – contexts. It figures in Zoroastrian thought and in Gnostic texts, where it is synonymous with the principle of light. And it surfaces again among the pedigrees claimed by late eighteenth-century Freemasonry. According to Masonic teachings, Ormus was the name of an Egyptian sage and mystic, a Gnostic 'adept' of Alexandria. He lived, supposedly, during the early years of the Christian epoch. In A.D. 46 he and six of his followers were supposedly converted to a form of Christianity by one of Jesus's disciples, Saint Mark in most accounts. From this conversion a new sect or order is said to have been born, which fused the tenets of early Christianity with the teachings of other, even older mystery schools. To our knowledge this story cannot be authenticated. At the same time, however, it is certainly plausible. During the first century A.D. Alexandria was a veritable hotbed of mystical activity, a crucible in which Judaic, Mithraic, Zoroastrian, Pythagorean, Hermetic and Neo-Platonic doctrines suffused the air and combined with innumerable others. Teachers of every conceivable kind abounded; and it would hardly be surprising if one of them adopted a name implying the principle of light.

According to Masonic tradition, in A.D. 46 Ormus is said to have conferred on his newly constituted 'order of initiates' a specific identifying symbol – a red or a rose cross. Granted, the red cross was subsequently to find an echo in the blazon of the Knights Templar, but the import of the text in the *Dossiers secrets*, and in other 'Prieuré documents', is unequivocally clear. One is intended to see in Ormus the origins of the so-called Rose-Croix, or Rosicrucians. And in 1188 the Prieuré de Sion is said to have adopted a second subtitle, in addition to 'Ormus'. It is said to have called itself l'Ordre de la Rose-Croix Veritas.

At this point we seemed to be in very questionable territory, and the text in the 'Prieuré documents' began to appear highly suspect. We were familiar with the claims of the modern 'Rosicrucians' in California and other contemporary organisations, who claim for themselves, after the fact, a pedigree harking back to the mists of antiquity which includes most of the world's great men. An 'Order of the Rose-Croix' dating from 1188 appeared equally spurious.

Pentagram

As Frances Yates had demonstrated convincingly, there is no known evidence of any 'Rosicrucians' (at least by that name) before the early seventeenth century – or perhaps the last years of the sixteenth.[12] The myth surrounding the legendary order dates from approximately 1605, and first gained impetus a decade later with the publication of three inflammatory tracts. These tracts, which appeared in 1614, 1615 and 1616 respectively, proclaimed the existence of a secret brotherhood or confraternity of mystical 'initiates', allegedly founded by one Christian Rosenkreuz – who, it was maintained, was born in 1378 and died, at the hoary age of 106, in 1484. Christian Rosenkreuz and his secret confraternity are now generally acknowledged to have been fictitious – a hoax of sorts, devised for some purpose no one has yet satisfactorily explained, although it was not without political repercussions at the time. Moreover, the author of one of the three tracts, the famous *Chemical Wedding of Christian Rosenkreuz,* which appeared in 1616, is now known. He was Johann Valentin Andrea, a German writer and theologian living in Württemberg, who confessed that he composed *The Chemical Wedding* as a 'ludibrium' – a 'joke', or perhaps a 'comedy' in Dante's and Balzac's sense of the word. There is reason to believe that Andrea, or one of his associates, composed the other 'Rosicrucian' tracts as well; and it is to this source that 'Rosicrucianism', as it evolved and as one thinks of it today, can be traced.

If the 'Prieuré documents' were accurate, however, we would have to reconsider, and think in terms of something other than a seventeenth-century hoax. We would have to think in terms of a secret order or society that actually existed, a genuine clandestine brotherhood or confraternity. It need not have been wholly or even primarily mystical. It might well have been largely political. But it would have existed a full 425 years before its name ever became public, and a good two centuries before its legendary founder is alleged to have lived.

Again we found no substantiating evidence. Certainly the rose has been a mystical symbol from time immemorial, and enjoyed a particular vogue during the Middle Ages – in the popular *Romance of the Rose* by Jean de Meung, for instance, and in Dante's *Paradiso*. And the red cross was also a traditional symbolic motif. Not only was it the blazon of the Knights Templar. It subsequently became the Cross of Saint George and, as such, was adopted by the Order of the Garter – created some thirty years after the fall of the Temple. But though roses and red crosses abounded as symbolic motifs, there was no evidence of an institution or an order, still less of a secret society.

On the other hand, Frances Yates maintains that there were secret societies functioning long before the seventeenth-century 'Rosicrucians' – and that these earlier societies were, in fact, 'Rosicrucian' in political and philosophical orientation, if not necessarily in name.[13] Thus, in conversation with one of our researchers, she described Leonardo as a 'Rosicrucian' – using the term as a metaphor to define his values and attitudes.

In 1629, when 'Rosicrucian' interest in Europe was at its zenith, a man named Robert Denyau, curé of Gisors, composed an exhaustive history of Gisors and the Gisors family, the *Histoire polytique de Gisors et du pays de Vulcsain*. This manuscript is now in the Bibliothèque de Rouen[14]. In this manuscript, according to a note by Gerard de Sède, is the information that the Rose-Croix was founded by Jean de Gisors in 1188. In other words there was apparently a verbatim seventeenth-century confirmation of the claims made by the 'Prieuré documents'. Granted, Denyau's manuscript was composed some four and a half centuries after the alleged fact. But, if true, it constitutes an extremely important fragment of evidence. And the fact that it issues from Gisors renders it all the more important.

We looked at this manuscript. It was immediately clear that there were major difficulties in verifying this information. Of some 575 handwritten pages, the majority are barely legible and many pages are missing while others have been cut or have had sections removed; only the *Calendarium Martyrology* is clearly legible. It was, or course, a conveniently difficult text to proffer as a source of important information.

We were left, therefore, with no confirmation, only a possibility. But in every respect so far the 'Prieuré documents' had proved astonishingly accurate. Thus it would have been rash to dismiss them out of hand. We were not prepared to accept them on blind, unquestioning faith. But we did feel obliged to reserve judgment.

THE PRIEURÉ AT ORLEANS

In addition to their more grandiose claims, the 'Prieuré documents' offered information of a very different kind, minutiae so apparently trivial and inconsequential that their significance eluded us. At the same time the sheer unimportance of this information argued in favour of its veracity. Quite simply there seemed to be no point in inventing or concocting such minor details. And what was more, the authenticity of many of these details could be confirmed.

Thus, for example, Girard, abbot of the 'little priory' at Orleans between 1239 and 1244, is said to have ceded a tract of land at Acre to the Teutonic Knights. Why this should warrant mention is unclear, but it can be definitively established. The actual charter exists, dating from 1239 and bearing Girard's signature.

Information of a similar, albeit more suggestive, kind is offered on an abbot named Adam, who presided over the 'little priory' at Orleans in 1281. In that year, according to the 'Prieuré documents', Adam ceded a tract of land near Orval to the monks then occupying the abbey there – Cistercians, who had moved in under the aegis of Saint Bernard a century and a half before. We could not find written evidence of this particular transaction, but it would seem plausible enough – there are charters attesting to numerous other transactions of the same nature. What makes this one interesting, of course, is the recurrence of Orval, which had figured earlier in our inquiry. Moreover, the tract of land in question would seem to have been of special import, for the 'Prieuré documents' tell us that Adam incurred the wrath of the brethren of Sion for his donation – so much so that he was apparently compelled to renounce his position. The act of abdication, according to the *Dossiers secrets,* was formally witnessed by Thomas de Sainville, Grand Master of the Order of Saint Lazarus. Immediately afterwards Adam is said to have gone to Acre, then to have fled the city when it fell to the Saracens and to have died in Sicily in 1291.

Again we could not find the actual charter of abdication. But Thomas de Sainville was Grand Master of the Order of Saint Lazarus in 1281, and the headquarters of Saint Lazarus were near Orleans – where Adam's abdication would have taken place. And there is no question that Adam went to Acre. Two proclamations and two letters were in fact signed by him there, the first dated August 1281,[15] the second March 1289.[16]

THE 'HEAD' OF THE TEMPLARS

According to the 'Prieuré documents', the Prieuré de Sion was not, strictly speaking, a perpetuation or continuation of the Order of the Temple: on the contrary, the text stresses emphatically that the separation between the two orders dates from the 'cutting of the elm' in 1188. Apparently, however, some kind of rapport continued to exist, and, 'in 1307, Guillaume de Gisors received the golden head, Caput LVIII ♍, from the Order of the Temple.'[17]

Our investigation of the Templars had already acquainted us with this mysterious head. To link it with Sion, however, and with the seemingly important Gisors family, again struck us as dubious – as if the 'Prieuré documents' were straining to make powerful and evocative connections. And yet it was precisely on this point that we found some of our most solid and intriguing confirmation. According to the official records of the Inquisition:

> The guardian and administrator of the goods of the Temple at Paris, after the arrests, was a man of the King named Guillaume Pidoye. Before the Inquisitors on May 11th, 1308, he declared that at the time of the arrest of the Knights Templar, he, together with his colleague Guillaume de Gisors and one Raynier Bourdon, had been ordered to present to the Inquisition all the figures of metal or wood they had found. Among the goods of the Temple they had found a large head of silver gilt . . . the image of a woman, which Guillaume, on May 11th, presented before the Inquisition. The head carried a label, 'CAPUT LVIIIm'.[18]

If the head continued to baffle us, the context in which Guillaume de Gisors appeared was equally perplexing. He is specifically cited as being a colleague of Guillaume Pidoye, one of King Philippe's men. In other words he, like Philippe, would seem to have been hostile to the Templars and participated in the attack upon them. According to the 'Prieuré documents', however, Guillaume was Grand Master of the Prieuré de Sion at the time. Did this mean that Sion endorsed Philippe's action against the Temple, perhaps even collaborated in it? There are certain 'Prieuré documents' which hint that this may have been the case – that Sion, in some unspecified way, authorised and presided over the dissolution of its unruly protégés. On the other hand, the 'Prieuré documents' also imply that Sion exercised a kind of paternal protectiveness towards at least certain Templars during the Order's last days. If this is true, Guillaume de Gisors might well have been a 'double-agent'. He might well have been responsible for the 'leak' of Philippe's plans, the means whereby the Templars received advance warning of the king's machinations against them. If, after the formal separation in 1188, Sion did in fact continue to exercise some clandestine control over Temple affairs, Guillaume de Gisors might have been partially responsible for the careful destruction of the Order's documents – and the unexplained disappearance of its treasure.

THE GRAND MASTERS OF THE TEMPLARS

In addition to the fragmentary information discussed above, the text in the *Dossiers secrets* includes three lists of names. The first of these is straightforward enough – the least interesting, and the least open to controversy or doubt, being merely a list of abbots who presided over Sion's lands in Palestine between 1152 and 1281. Our research confirmed its veracity; it appears elsewhere, independent of the *Dossiers secrets,* and in accessible, unimpugnable sources.[19] The lists in these sources agree with that in the *Dossiers secrets,* except that two names are missing in the sources. In this case, then, the 'Prieuré documents' not only agree with verifiable history, but are more comprehensive in that they fill certain lacunae.

The second list in the *Dossiers secrets* is a list of the Grand Masters of the Knights Templar from 1118 until 1190 – in other words, from the Temple's public foundation until its separation from Sion and the 'cutting of the elm' at Gisors. At first there seemed nothing unusual or extraordinary about this list. When we compared it to other lists, however – those cited by acknowledged historians writing on the Templars, for instance – certain obvious discrepancies quickly emerged.

According to virtually all other known lists, there were ten Grand Masters between 1118 and 1190. According to the *Dossiers secrets,* there were only eight. According to most other lists, André de Montbard – Saint Bernard's uncle – was not only a co-founder of the Order, but also its Grand Master between 1153 and 1156. According to the *Dossiers secrets*, however, André was never Grand Master, but would seem to have continued functioning as he does all through his career – behind the scenes. According to most other lists, Bertrand de Blanchefort appears as sixth Grand Master of the Temple, assuming his office after André de Montbard, in 1156. According to the *Dossiers secrets*, Bertrand is not sixth, but fourth in succession, becoming Grand Master in 1153. There were other such discrepancies and contradictions, and we were uncertain what to make of them or how seriously to take them. Because it disagreed with those compiled by established historians, were we to regard the list in the *Dossiers secrets* as wrong?

It must be emphasised that no official or definitive list of the Temple's Grand Masters exists. Nothing of the sort has been preserved or handed down to posterity. The Temple's own records were destroyed or disappeared, and the earliest known compilation of the Order's Grand Masters dates from 1342 – thirty years after the Order itself was suppressed, and 225 years after its foundation. As a result historians compiling lists of Grand Masters have based their findings on contemporary chroniclers – on a man writing in 1170, for example, who makes a passing allusion to one or another individual as 'Master' or 'Grand Master' of the Temple. And additional evidence can be obtained by examining documents and charters of the period, in which one or another Templar official would append one or another title to his signature. It is thus hardly surprising that the sequence and dating of Grand Masters should engender considerable uncertainty and confusion. Nor is it surprising that sequence and dating should vary, sometimes dramatically, from writer to writer, account to account.

Nevertheless, there were certain crucial details – like those summarised above – in which the 'Prieuré documents' deviated significantly from all other sources. We could not, therefore, ignore such deviations. We had to determine, as far as we could, whether the list in the *Dossiers secrets* was based on sloppiness, ignorance or both; or, alternatively, whether this list was indeed the definitive one, based on 'inside' information, inaccessible to historians. If Sion did create the Knights Templar, and if Sion (or at least its records) did survive to the present day, we could reasonably expect it to be privy to details unobtainable elsewhere.

Most of the discrepancies between the list in the *Dossiers secrets* and those in other sources can be explained fairly easily. At this point, it is not worth exploring each such discrepancy and accounting for it. But a single example should serve to illustrate how and why such discrepancies might occur. In addition to the Grand Master, the Temple had a multitude of local masters – a master for England, for Normandy, for Aquitaine, for all the territories comprising its domains. There was also an overall European master, and, it would appear, a maritime master as well. In documents and charters these local or regional masters would invariably sign themselves 'Magister Templi' – 'Master of the Temple'. And on most occasions the Grand Master – through modesty, carelessness, indifference or slapdash insouciance – would also sign himself as nothing more than 'Magister Templi'. In other words André de Montbard, regional Master of Jerusalem, would, on a charter, have the same designation after his name as the Grand Master, Bertrand de Blanchefort.

It is thus not difficult to see how an historian, working with one or two charters alone and not cross-checking his references, might readily misconstrue André's true status in the Order. By virtue of precisely this kind of error, many lists of Templar Grand Masters include a man named Everard des Barres. But the Grand Master, by the Temple's own constitutions, had to be elected by a general chapter in Jerusalem and had to reside there. Our research revealed that Everard des Barres was a regional master, elected and resident in France, who did not set foot in the Holy Land until much later. On this basis he could be excised from the list of Grand Masters – as indeed he was in the *Dossiers secrets*. It was specifically on such academic fine points that the 'Prieuré documents' displayed a meticulous accuracy and precision we could not imagine being contrived after the fact.

We spent more than a year considering and comparing various lists of Templar Grand Masters. We consulted all writers on the Order, in English, French and German, and then checked their sources as well. We examined the chronicles of the time – like those of Guillaume de Tyre – and other contemporary accounts. We consulted all the charters we could find and obtained comprehensive information on all those known to be still extant. We compared signatories and titles on numerous proclamations, edicts, deeds and other Templar documents. As a result of this exhaustive inquiry, it became apparent that the list in the *Dossiers secrets* was more accurate than any other – not only on the identity of the Grand Masters, but on the dates of their respective régimes as well. If a definitive list of the Temple's Grand Masters did exist, it was in the *Dossiers secrets*.[20]

The accuracy of this list was not only important in itself. The implications attending it were much broader. Granted, such a list might perhaps have been compiled by an extremely careful researcher, but the task would have been monumental. It seemed much more likely to us that a list of such accuracy attested to some repository of privileged or 'inside' information – information hitherto inaccessible to historians.

Whether our conclusion was warranted or not, we were confronted by one indisputable fact – someone had obtained access, somehow, to a list which was more accurate than any other. And since that list – despite its divergence from others more accepted – proved so frequently to be correct, it lent considerable credibility to the 'Prieuré documents' as a whole. If the *Dossiers secrets* were demonstrably reliable in this critical respect, there was somewhat less reason to doubt them in others.

Such reassurance was both timely and necessary. Without it, we might well have dismissed the third list in the *Dossiers secrets* – the Grand Masters of the Prieuré de Sion – out of hand. For this third list, even at a cursory glance, seemed absurd.

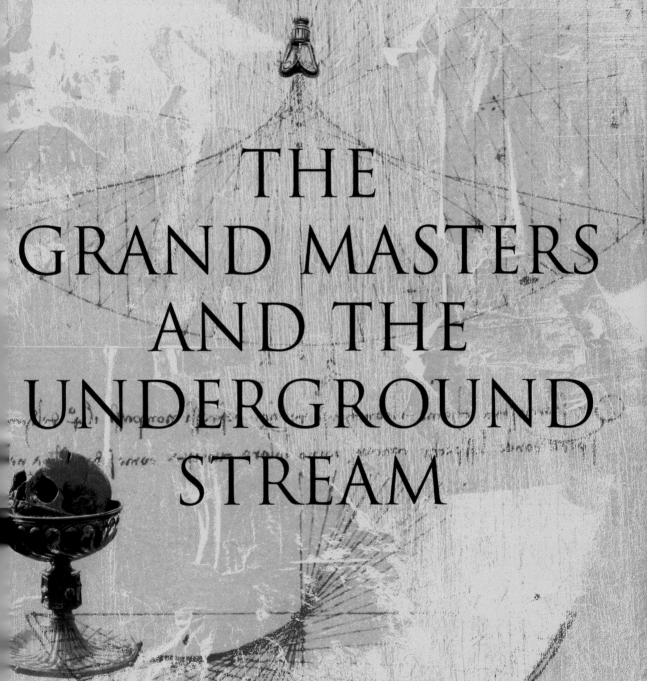

CHAPTER SIX

THE GRAND MASTERS AND THE UNDERGROUND STREAM

In the *Dossiers secrets*,[1] the following individuals are listed as successive Grand Masters of the Prieuré de Sion – or, to use the official term, 'Nautonnier', an old French word which means 'navigator' or 'helmsman':

Jean de Gisors	1188–1220
Marie de Saint-Clair	1220–66
Guillaume de Gisors	1266–1307
Edouard de Bar	1307–36
Jeanne de Bar	1336–51
Jean de Saint-Clair	1351–66
Blanche d'Evreux	1366–98
Nicolas Flamel	1398–1418
René d'Anjou	1418–80
Iolande de Bar	1480–83
Sandro Filipepi	1483–1510
Léonard de Vinci	1510–19
Connétable de Bourbon	1519–27
Ferdinand de Gonzague	1527–75
Louis de Nevers	1575–95
Robert Fludd	1595–1637
J. Valentin Andrea	1637–54
Robert Boyle	1654–91
Isaac Newton	1691–1727
Charles Radclyffe	1727–46
Charles de Lorraine	1746–80
Maximilian de Lorraine	1780–1801
Charles Nodier	1801–44
Victor Hugo	1844–85
Claude Debussy	1885–1918
Jean Cocteau	1918–

When we first saw this list, it immediately provoked our scepticism. On the one hand it includes a number of names which one would automatically expect to find on such a list – names of famous individuals associated with the 'occult' and 'esoteric'. On the other hand it includes a number of illustrious and improbable names – individuals whom, in certain cases, we could not imagine presiding over a secret society. At the same time, many of these latter names are precisely the kind that twentieth-century organisations have often attempted to appropriate for themselves, thus establishing a species of spurious 'pedigree'. There are, for example, lists published by AMORC, the modern 'Rosicrucians' based in California, which include virtually every important figure in Western history and culture whose values, even if only tangentially, happened to coincide with the Order's own. An often haphazard overlap or convergence of attitudes is deliberately misconstrued as something tantamount to 'initiated membership'. And thus one is told that Dante, Shakespeare, Goethe and innumerable others were 'Rosicrucians' – implying that they were card-carrying members who paid their dues regularly.

Our initial attitude towards the above list was equally cynical. Again, there are the predictable names – names associated with the 'occult' and 'esoteric'. Nicolas Flamel, for instance, is perhaps the most famous and well-documented of medieval alchemists. Robert Fludd, seventeenth-century philosopher, was an exponent of Hermetic thought and other arcane subjects. Johann Valentin Andrea, German contemporary of Fludd, composed, among other things, some of the works which spawned the myth of the fabulous Christian Rosenkreuz. And there are also names like Leonardo da Vinci and Sandro Filipepi, who is better known as Botticelli. There are names of distinguished scientists, like Robert Boyle and Sir Isaac Newton. During the last two centuries the Prieuré de Sion's Grand Masters are alleged to have included such important literary and cultural figures as Victor Hugo, Claude Debussy and Jean Cocteau.

By including such names, the list in the *Dossiers secrets* could not but appear suspect. It was almost inconceivable that some of the individuals cited had presided over a secret society – and still more, a secret society devoted to 'occult' and 'esoteric' interests. Boyle and Newton, for example, are hardly names that people in the twentieth century associate with the 'occult' and 'esoteric'. And though Hugo, Debussy and Cocteau were immersed in such matters, they would seem to be too well known, too well researched and documented, to have exercised a 'Grand Mastership' over a secret order. Not, at any rate, without some word of it somehow leaking out.

On the other hand the distinguished names are not the only names on the list. Most of the other names belong to high-ranking European nobles, many of whom are extremely obscure – unfamiliar not only to the general reader, but even to the professional historian. There is

Guillaume de Gisors, for instance, who in 1306 is said to have organised the Prieuré de Sion into an 'hermetic freemasonry'. And there is Guillaume's grandfather, Jean de Gisors, who is said to have been Sion's first independent Grand Master, assuming his position after the 'cutting of the elm' and the separation from the Temple in 1188. There is no question that Jean de Gisors existed historically. He was born in 1133 and died in 1220. He is mentioned in charters and was at least nominal lord of the famous fortress in Normandy – where meetings traditionally convened between English and French kings took place, as did the cutting of the elm in 1188. Jean seems to have been an extremely powerful and wealthy landowner and, until 1193, a vassal of the king of England. He is also known to have possessed property in England – in Sussex, and the manor of Titchfield in Hampshire.[2] According to the *Dossiers secrets*, he met Thomas à Becket at Gisors in 1169 – though there is no indication of the purpose of this meeting. We were able to confirm that Becket was indeed at Gisors in 1169,[3] and it is therefore probable that he had some contact with the lord of the fortress; but we could find no record of any actual encounter between the two men.

In short, Jean de Gisors, apart from a few bland details, proved virtually untraceable. He seemed to have left no mark whatever on history, save his existence and his title. We could find no indication of what he did – what might have constituted his claim to fame, or have warranted his assumption of Sion's Grand Mastership. If the list of Sion's purported Grand Masters was authentic, what, we wondered, did Jean do to earn his place on it? And if the list were a latter-day fabrication, why should someone so obscure be included at all?

There seemed to us only one possible explanation – which did not really explain very much in fact. Like the other aristocratic names on the list of Sion's Grand Masters, Jean de Gisors appeared in the complicated genealogies which figured elsewhere in the 'Prieuré documents'. Together with those other elusive nobles, he apparently belonged to the same dense forest of family trees – ultimately descended, supposedly, from the Merovingian dynasty. It thus seemed evident to us that the Prieuré de Sion – to a significant extent, at least – was a domestic affair. In some way the Order appeared to be intimately associated with a bloodline and a lineage. And it was their connection with this bloodline or lineage that perhaps accounted for the various titled names on the list of Grand Masters.

From the list quoted above, it would seem that Sion's Grand

Mastership has recurrently shifted between two essentially distinct groups of individuals. On the one hand there are the figures of monumental stature who – through esoterica, the arts or sciences – have produced some impact on Western tradition, history and culture. On the other hand, there are members of a specific and interlinked network of families – noble, and sometimes royal. In some degree this curious juxtaposition imparted plausibility to the list. If one merely wished to 'concoct a pedigree', there would be no point in including so many unknown or long-forgotten aristocrats. There would be no point, for instance, in including a man like Charles de Lorraine – Austrian field-marshal in the eighteenth century, brother-in-law to the Empress Maria Theresa, who proved himself signally inept on the battlefield and was trounced in one engagement after another by Frederick the Great of Prussia.

In this respect, at least, the Prieuré de Sion would seem to be both modest and realistic. It does not claim to have functioned under the auspices of unqualified geniuses, superhuman 'masters', illumined 'initiates', saints, sages or immortals. On the contrary, it acknowledges its Grand Masters to have been fallible human beings, a representative cross-section of humanity – a few geniuses, a few notables, a few 'average specimens', a few nonentities, even a few fools.

Why, we could not but wonder, would a forged or fabricated list include such a spectrum? If one wishes to contrive a list of Grand Masters, why not make all the names on it illustrious? If one wishes to 'concoct a pedigree' which includes Leonardo, Newton and Victor Hugo, why not also include Dante, Michelangelo, Goethe and Tolstoi – instead of obscure people like Edouard de Bar and Maximilian de Lorraine? Why, moreover, were there so many 'lesser lights' on the list? Why a relatively minor writer like Charles Nodier, rather than contemporaries like Byron or Pushkin? Why an apparent 'eccentric' like Cocteau rather than men of such international prestige as André Gide or Albert Camus? And why the omission of individuals like Poussin, whose connection with the mystery had already been established? Such questions nagged at us, and argued that the list warranted consideration before we dismissed it as an arrant fraud.

We therefore embarked on a lengthy and detailed study of the alleged Grand Masters – their biographies, activities and accomplishments. In conducting this study we tried, as far as we could, to subject each name on the list to certain critical questions:

1) Was there any personal contact, direct or indirect, between each alleged Grand Master, his immediate predecessor and immediate successor?

2) Was there any affiliation, by blood or otherwise, between each alleged Grand Master and the families who figured in the genealogies of the 'Prieuré documents' – with any of the families of purported Merovingian descent, and especially the ducal house of Lorraine?

3) Was each alleged Grand Master in any way connected with Rennes-le-Château, Gisors, Stenay, Saint Sulpice or any of the other sites that had recurred in the course of our previous investigation?

4) If Sion defined itself as an 'Hermetic freemasonry', did each alleged Grand Master display a predisposition towards Hermetic thought or an involvement with secret societies?

Although information on the alleged Grand Masters before 1400 was difficult, sometimes impossible to obtain, our investigation of the later figures yield some astonishing results and consistency. Many of them were associated, in one way or another, with one or more of the sites that seemed to be relevant – Rennes-le-Château, Gisors, Stenay or Saint Sulpice. Most of the names on the list were either allied by blood to the house of Lorraine or associated with it in some other fashion; even Robert Fludd, for example, served as tutor to the sons of the duke of Lorraine. From Nicolas Flamel on, every name on the list, without exception, was steeped in Hermetic thought, and often also associated with secret societies – even men whom one would not readily associate with such things, like Boyle and Newton. And with only one exception, each alleged Grand Master had some contact – sometimes direct, sometimes through close mutual friends – with those who preceded and succeeded him. As far as we could determine, there was only one apparent 'break in the chain'. And even this – which seems to have occurred around the French Revolution, between Maximilian of Lorraine and Charles Nodier – is not by any means conclusive.

In the context of this chapter it is not feasible to discuss each alleged Grand Master in detail. Some of the more obscure figures assume significance only against the background of a given age, and to explain this significance fully would entail lengthy digressions into forgotten byways of history. In the case of the more famous names, it would be impossible to do them justice in a few pages. In consequence the relevant biographical material on the alleged Grand Masters and the connections between them have been consigned to an appendix (see pp. 441–65). The present chapter will dwell on broader social and cultural developments, in which a succession of alleged Grand Masters played a collective part. It was in such social and cultural developments that our research seemed to yield a discernible trace of the Prieuré de Sion's hand.

RENÉ D'ANJOU

Although little known today, René d'Anjou – 'Good King René' as he was known – was one of the most important figures in European culture during the years immediately preceding the Renaissance. Born in 1408, during his life he came to hold an awesome array of titles. Among the most important were count of Bar, count of Provence, count of Piedmont, count of Guise, duke of Calabria, duke of Anjou, duke of Lorraine, king of Hungary, king of Naples and Sicily, king of Aragon, Valencia, Majorca and Sardinia – and, perhaps most resonant of all, king of Jerusalem. This last was, of course, purely titular. Nevertheless it invoked a continuity extending back to Godfroi de Bouillon, and was acknowledged by other European potentates. One of Rene's daughters, Marguerite d'Anjou, in 1445 married Henry VI of England and played a prominent role in the Wars of the Roses.

In its earlier phases René d'Anjou's career seems to have been in some obscure way associated with that of Jeanne d'Arc. As far as is known, Jeanne was born in the town of Domrémy, in the duchy of Bar, making her René's subject. She first impressed herself on history in 1429, when she appeared at the fortress of Vaucouleurs, a few miles up the Meuse from Domrémy. Presenting herself to the commandant of the fortress, she announced her 'divine mission' – to save France from the English invaders and ensure that the dauphin, subsequently Charles VII, was crowned king. In order to perform this mission, she would have had to join the dauphin at his court at Chinon, on the Loire, far to the south-west. But she did not request a passage to Chinon of the commandant at Vaucouleurs; she requested a special audience with the duke of Lorraine – René's father-in-law and great uncle.

In deference to her request, Jeanne was granted an audience with the duke at his capital in Nancy. When she arrived there, René d'Anjou is known to have been present. And when the duke of Lorraine asked her what she wished, she replied explicitly, in words that have constantly

'La Fontaine de Fortune' painted in 1457 by René d'Anjou, alleged Grand Master of the Prieuré de Sion, 1418 - 1480. The inscription says that the sorcerer Virgil brought the spring forth. René's contemporaries would have associated Virgil with Arcadia. This is the first sur-facing of Arcadia's under-ground stream, Alpheus, as a symbol in modern western culture.

perplexed historians, 'Your son [in-law], a horse and some good men to take me into France'.[4]

Both at the time and later, speculation was rife about the nature of René's connection with Jeanne. According to some sources, probably inaccurate, the two were lovers. But the fact remains that they knew each other, and that René was present when Jeanne first embarked on her mission. Moreover, contemporary chroniclers maintain that when Jeanne departed for the Dauphin's court at Chinon, René accompanied her. And not only that. The same chroniclers assert that René was actu-ally present at her side during the siege of Orleans.[5] In the centuries that followed a systematic attempt seems to have been made to expunge all trace of René's possible role in Jeanne's life. Yet René's later biographers cannot account for his whereabouts or activities between 1429 and 1431 – the apex of Jeanne's career. It is usually and tacitly assumed that he was vegetating at the ducal court in Nancy, but there is no evidence to support this assumption.

Circumstances argue that René did accompany Jeanne to Chinon. For if there was any one dominant personality at Chinon at the time, that personality was Iolande d'Anjou. It was Iolande who provided the febrile, weak-willed dauphin with incessant transfusions of morale. It was Iolande who inexplicably appointed herself Jeanne's official patroness and sponsor. It was Iolande who overcame the court's resistance to the visionary girl and obtained authorisation for her to accompany the army to Orleans. It was Iolande who convinced the dauphin that Jeanne might indeed be the saviour she claimed to be. It was Iolande who contrived the dauphin's marriage – to her own daughter. And Iolande was René d'Anjou's mother.

As we studied these details, we became increasingly convinced, like many modern historians, that something was being enacted behind the scenes – some intricate, high-level intrigue, or audacious design. The more we examined it, the more Jeanne d'Arc's meteoric career began to suggest a 'put-up job' – as if someone, exploiting popular legends of a 'virgin from Lorraine' and playing ingeniously on mass psychology, had engineered and orchestrated the Maid of Orleans's so-called mission. This did not, of course, presuppose the existence of a secret society. But it rendered the existence of such a society decidedly more plausible. And if such a society did exist, the man presiding over it might well have been René d'Anjou.

RENÉ AND THE THEME OF ARCADIA

If René was associated with Jeanne d'Arc, his later career, for the most part, was distinctly less bellicose. Unlike many of his contemporaries, René was less a warrior than a courtier. In this respect he was misplaced in his own age; he was, in short, a man ahead of his time, anticipating the cultured Italian princes of the Renaissance. An extremely literate person, he wrote prolifically and illuminated his own books. He composed poetry and mystical allegories, as well as compendiums of tournament rules. He sought to promote the advancement of knowledge and at one time employed Christopher Columbus. He was steeped in esoteric tradition, and his court included a Jewish astrologer, Cabalist and physician known as Jean de Saint-Rémy. According to a number of accounts, Jean de Saint-Rémy was the grandfather of Nostradamus, the famous sixteenth-century prophet who was also to figure in our story.

René's interests included chivalry and the Arthurian and Grail romances. Indeed he seems to have had a particular preoccupation with the Grail. He is said to have taken great pride in a magnificent cup of red porphyry, which, he asserted, had been used at the wedding at Cana. He had obtained it, he claimed, at Marseilles – where the Magdalene, according to tradition, landed with the Grail. Other chroniclers speak of a cup in René's possession – perhaps the same one – which bore a mysterious inscription incised into the rim:

> Qui bien beurra
> Dieu voira.
> Qui beurra tout d'une baleine
> Voira Dieu et la Madeleine.[6]

> *(He who drinks well*
> *Will see God.*
> *He who quaffs at a single draught*
> *Will see God and the Magdalene.)*

It would not be inaccurate to regard René d'Anjou as a major impetus behind the phenomenon now called the Renaissance. By virtue of his numerous Italian possessions he spent some years in Italy; and through his intimate friendship with the ruling Sforza family of Milan he established contact with the Medicis of Florence. There is good reason to believe that it was largely René's influence which prompted Cosimo de' Medici to embark on a series of ambitious projects – projects destined to transform Western civilisation.

In 1439, while René was resident in Italy, Cosimo de' Medici began sending his agents all over the world in quest of ancient manuscripts. Then, in 1444, Cosimo founded Europe's first public library, the Library of San Marco, and thus began to challenge the Church's long monopoly of learning. At Cosimo's express commission, the corpus of Platonic, Neo-Platonic, Pythagorean, Gnostic and Hermetic thought found its way into translation for the first time and became readily accessible. Cosimo also instructed the University of Florence to begin teaching Greek, for the first time in Europe for some seven hundred years. And he undertook to create an academy of Pythagorean and Platonic studies. Cosimo's academy quickly generated a multitude of similar institutions throughout the Italian peninsula, which became bastions of Western esoteric tradition. And from them the high culture of the

Opposite; 'La Primavera'
('Spring') painted around
1480 by Sandro Botticelli,
alleged Grand Master of the
Prieuré de Sion, 1483 - 1510.
Botticelli was a student of the
Hermetic and Platonic
philosopher, Marsilio Ficino
who lived in Florence during
the fifteenth-century under
the patronage of the Medici
family. The painting depicts
the eternal circulation of
Divine energy from the heav-
ens (on the right), through
the earth and its life, and back
to the heavens again via the
wand of Hermes (on the left).
The whole process mediated
by the Goddess.

Renaissance began to blossom.

René d'Anjou not only contributed in some measure to the formation of the academies, but also seems to have conferred upon them one of their favourite symbolic themes – that of Arcadia. Certainly it is in René's own career that the motif of Arcadia appears to have made its début in post-Christian Western culture. In 1449, for example, at his court of Tarascon, René staged a series of *pas d'armes* – curious hybrid amalgams of tournament and masque, in which knights tilted against each other and, at the same time, performed a species of drama or play. One of René's most famous *pas d'armes* was called 'The *Pas d'Armes* of the Shepherdess'. Played by his mistress at the time, the 'Shepherdess' was an explicitly Arcadian figure, embodying both romantic and philosophical attributes. She presided over a tourney in which knights assumed allegorical identities representing conflicting values and ideas. The event was a singular fusion of the pastoral Arcadian romance with the pageantry of the Round Table and the mysteries of the Holy Grail.

Arcadia figures elsewhere in René's work as well. It is frequently denoted by a fountain or a tombstone, both of which are associated with an underground stream. This stream is usually equated with the river Alpheus – the central river in the actual geographical Arcadia in Greece, which flows underground and is said to surface again at the Fountain of Arethusa in Sicily. From the most remote antiquity to Coleridge's 'Kubla Khan', the river Alpheus has been deemed sacred. Its very name derives from the same root as the Greek word 'Alpha', meaning 'first' or 'source'.

For René, the motif of an underground stream seems to have been extremely rich in symbolic and allegorical resonances. Among other things, it would appear to connote the 'underground' esoteric tradition of Pythagorean, Gnostic, Cabalistic and Hermetic thought. But it might also connote something more than a general corpus of teachings, perhaps some very specific factual information – a 'secret' of some sort, transmitted in clandestine fashion from generation to generation. And it might connote an unacknowledged and thus 'subterranean' bloodline.

In the Italian academies the image of the 'underground stream' appears to have been invested with all these levels of meaning. And it recurs consistently – so much so, indeed, that the academies themselves have often been labelled 'Arcadian'. Thus, in 1502, a major work was published, a long poem entitled *Arcadia*, by Jacopo Sannazaro – and René d'Anjou's Italian entourage of some years before included one

Jacques Sannazar, probably the poet's father. In 1553 Sannazaro's poem was translated into French. It was dedicated, interestingly enough, to the cardinal of Lénoncourt – ancestor of the twentieth-century count of Lénoncourt who compiled the genealogies in the 'Prieuré documents'.

During the sixteenth century Arcadia and the 'underground stream' became a prominent cultural fashion. In England they inspired Sir Philip Sidney's most important work, *Arcadia*.[7] In Italy they inspired such illustrious figures as Torquato Tasso – whose masterpiece, *Jerusalem Delivered*, deals with the capture of the Holy City by Godfroi de Bouillon. By the seventeenth century the motif of Arcadia had culminated in Nicolas Poussin and 'Les Bergers d'Arcadie'.

The more we explored the matter, the more apparent it became that something – a tradition of some sort, a hierarchy of values or attitudes,

perhaps a specific body of information – was constantly being intimated by the 'underground stream'. This image seems to have assumed obsessive proportions in the minds of certain eminent political families of the period – all of whom, directly or indirectly, figure in the genealogies of the 'Prieuré documents'. And the families in question seem to have transmitted the image to their protégés in the arts. From René d'Anjou, something seems to have passed to the Medicis, the Sforzas, the Estes and the Gonzagas – the last of whom, according to the 'Prieuré documents', provided Sion with two Grand Masters, Ferrante de Gonzaga and Louis de Gonzaga, Duke of Nevers. From them it appears to have found its way into the work of the epoch's most illustrious poets and painters, including Botticelli and Leonardo da Vinci.

THE ROSICRUCIAN MANIFESTOS

A somewhat similar dissemination of ideas occurred in the seventeenth century, first in Germany, then spreading to England. In 1614 the first of the so-called 'Rosicrucian manifestos' appeared, followed by a second tract a year later. These manifestos created a furore at the time, provoking fulminations from the Church and the Jesuits, and eliciting fervently enthusiastic support from liberal factions in Protestant Europe. Among the most eloquent and influential exponents of 'Rosicrucian' thought was Robert Fludd, who is listed as the Prieuré de Sion's sixteenth Grand Master, presiding between 1595 and 1637.

Among other things, the 'Rosicrucian manifestos'[8] promulgated the story of the legendary Christian Rosenkreuz. They purported to issue from a secret, 'invisible' confraternity of 'initiates' in Germany and France. They promised a transformation of the world and of human knowledge in accordance with esoteric, Hermetic principles – the 'underground stream' which had flowed from René d'Anjou through the Renaissance. A new epoch of spiritual freedom was heralded, an epoch in which man would liberate himself from his former shackles, would unlock hitherto dormant 'secrets of nature', and would govern his own destiny in accord with harmonious, all-pervading universal and cosmic laws. At the same time, the manifestos were highly inflammatory politically, fiercely attacking the Catholic Church and the old Holy Roman Empire. These manifestos are now generally believed to have been written by a German theologian and esotericist, Johann Valentin Andrea, listed as Grand Master of the Prieuré de Sion after

Robert Fludd. If they were not written by Andrea, they were certainly written by one or more of his associates.

In 1616 a third 'Rosicrucian' tract appeared, *The Chemical Wedding of Christian Rosenkreuz*. Like the two previous works, *The Chemical Wedding* was originally of anonymous authorship; but Andrea himself later confessed to having composed it as a 'joke' or comedy.

The Chemical Wedding is a complex Hermetic allegory, which subsequently influenced such works as Goethe's *Faust*. As Frances Yates has demonstrated, it contains unmistakable echoes of the English esotericist, John Dee, who also influenced Robert Fludd. Andrea's work also evokes resonances of the Grail romances and of the Knights Templar – Christian Rosenkreuz, for instance, is said to wear a white tunic with a red cross on the shoulder. In the course of the narrative a play is performed – an allegory within an allegory. This play involves a princess, of unspecified 'royal' lineage, whose rightful domains have been usurped by the Moors and who is washed ashore in a wooden chest. The rest of the play deals with her vicissitudes and her marriage to a prince who will help her regain her heritage.

Our research revealed assorted second- and third-hand links between Andrea and the families whose genealogies figure in the 'Prieuré documents'. We discovered no first-hand or direct links, however, except perhaps for Frederick, Elector Palatine of the Rhine. Frederick was the nephew of an important French Protestant leader, Henri de la Tour d'Auvergne, Viscount of Turenne and Duke of Bouillon – Godfroi de Bouillon's old title. Henri was also associated with the Longueville family, which figured prominently in both the 'Prieuré documents' and our own inquiry. And in 1591 he had taken great trouble to acquire the town of Stenay.

In 1613 Frederick of the Palatinate had married Elizabeth Stuart, daughter of James I of England, granddaughter of Mary Queen of Scots and great-granddaughter of Marie de Guise – and Guise was the cadet branch of the house of Lorraine. Marie de Guise, a century before, had been married to the duke of Longueville and then, on his death, to James V of Scotland. This created a dynastic alliance between the houses of Stuart and Lorraine. In consequence the Stuarts began to figure, if

Robert Fludd. Alleged Grand Master of the Prieuré de Sion, 1595-1637.

only peripherally, in the genealogies of the 'Prieuré documents'; and Andrea, as well as the three alleged Grand Masters who followed him, displayed varying degrees of interest in the Scottish royal house. During this period the house of Lorraine was, to a significant degree, in eclipse. If Sion was a coherent and active order at the time, it might therefore have transferred its allegiance – at least partially and temporarily – to the decidedly more influential Stuarts.

In any case Frederick of the Palatinate, after his marriage to Elizabeth Stuart, established an esoterically oriented court at his capital of Heidelberg. As Frances Yates writes:

> A culture was forming in the Palatinate which came straight out of the Renaissance but with more recent trends added, a culture which may be defined by the adjective 'Rosicrucian'. The prince around whom these deep currents were swirling was Friedrich, Elector Palatine, and their exponents were hoping for a politico-religious expression of their aims . . . The Frederickian movement . . . was an attempt to give those currents politico-religious expression, to realise the ideal of Hermetic reform centred on a real prince . . . It . . . created a culture, a 'Rosicrucian' state with its court centred on Heidelberg.[9]

In short the anonymous 'Rosicrucians' and their sympathisers seem to have invested Frederick with a sense of mission, both spiritual and political. And Frederick seems to have readily accepted the role imposed upon him, together with the hopes and expectations it entailed. Thus, in 1618, he accepted the crown of Bohemia, offered him by that country's rebellious nobles. In doing so he incurred the wrath of the papacy and the Holy Roman Empire and precipitated the chaos of the Thirty Years War. Within two years he and Elizabeth had been driven into exile in Holland, and Heidelberg was overrun by Catholic troops. And for the ensuing quarter of a century Germany became the major battleground for the most bitter, bloody and costly conflict in European history before the twentieth century – a conflict in which the Church almost managed to re-impose the hegemony she had enjoyed during the Middle Ages.

Amidst the turmoil raging around him, Andrea created a network of more or less secret societies known as the Christian Unions. According to Andrea's blueprint, each society was headed by an anonymous prince, assisted by twelve others divided into groups of three – each of whom was to be a specialist in a given sphere of study.[10] The original purpose of the Christian Unions was to preserve threatened knowledge – especially the most recent scientific advances, many of which the Church deemed heretical. At the same time, however, the Christian Unions also functioned as a refuge for persons fleeing the Inquisition – which accompanied the invading Catholic armies, and was intent on rooting out all vestiges of 'Rosicrucian' thought. Thus numerous scholars, scientists, philosophers and esotericists found a haven in Andrea's institutions. Through them many were smuggled to safety in England – where Freemasonry was just beginning to coalesce. In some significant sense Andrea's Christian Unions may have contributed to the organisation of the Masonic lodge system.

Among the displaced Europeans finding their way to England were a number of Andrea's personal associates: Samuel Hartlib, for example; Johann Komensky, better known as Comenius, with whom Andrea maintained a continuing correspondence; Theodore Haak, who was also a personal friend of Elizabeth Stuart and maintained a correspondence with her; and Doctor John Wilkins, formerly personal chaplain to the son of Frederick of the Palatinate and subsequently bishop of Chester.

Once in England, these men became closely associated with Masonic circles. They were intimate with Robert Moray, for instance, whose induction into a Masonic lodge in 1641 is one of the earliest on record; with Elias Ashmole, antiquarian and expert on chivalric orders, who was inducted in 1646; with the young but precocious Robert Boyle – who, though not himself a Freemason, was a member of another, more elusive secret society.[11] There is no concrete evidence that this secret society was the Prieuré de Sion, but Boyle, according to the 'Prieuré documents', succeeded Andrea as Sion's Grand Master.

During Cromwell's Protectorate, these dynamic minds, both English and European, formed what Boyle – in a deliberate echo of the 'Rosicrucian' manifestos – called an 'invisible college'. And with the restoration of the monarchy in 1660, the 'invisible college' became the Royal Society[12] with the Stuart ruler, Charles II, as its patron and sponsor. One could reasonably argue that the Royal Society itself, at least in its inception, was a quasi-masonic institution – derived, through Andrea's Christian Unions, from the 'invisible Rosicrucian brotherhood'. But this was not to be the culmination of the 'underground stream'. On the contrary, it was to flow from Boyle to Sir Isaac Newton, listed as Sion's next Grand Master, and thence into the complex tributaries of eighteenth-century Freemasonry.

THE STUART DYNASTY

According to the 'Prieuré documents', Newton was succeeded as Sion's Grand Master by Charles Radclyffe. The name was hardly as resonant to us as Newton's or Boyle's or even Andrea's. Indeed, we were not at first certain who Charles Radclyffe was. As we began to research into him, however, he emerged as a figure of considerable, if subterranean, consequence in eighteenth-century cultural history.

Since the sixteenth century the Radclyffes had been an influential Northumbrian family. In 1688, shortly before he was deposed, James II had created them earls of Derwentwater. Charles Radclyffe himself was born in 1693. His mother was an illegitimate daughter of Charles II by his mistress, Moll Davies. Radclyffe was thus, on his mother's side, of royal blood – a grandson of the next-to-last Stuart monarch. He was a cousin of Bonnie Prince Charlie and of George Lee, Earl of Lichfield – another illegitimate grandson of Charles II. Not surprisingly, therefore, Radclyffe devoted much of his life to the Stuart cause.

In 1715 this cause rested with the 'Old Pretender', James III, then in exile and residing at Bar-le-Duc, under the special protection of the duke of Lorraine. Radclyffe and his elder brother, James, both participated in the Scottish rebellion of that year. Both were captured and imprisoned, and James was executed. Charles, in the meantime, apparently aided by the earl of Lichfield, made a dashing and unprecedented escape from Newgate prison, and found refuge in the Jacobite ranks in France. In the years that followed he became personal secretary to the 'Young Pretender', Bonnie Prince Charlie.

In 1745 the latter landed in Scotland and embarked on his quixotic attempt to reinstate the Stuarts on the British throne. In the same year Radclyffe, *en route* to join him, was captured in a French ship off the Dogger Bank. A year later, in 1746, the 'Young Pretender' was disastrously defeated at the Battle of Culloden Moor. A few months thereafter, Charles Radclyffe died beneath the headsman's axe at the Tower of London.

During their stay in France the Stuarts had been deeply involved in the dissemination of Freemasonry. Indeed they are generally regarded as the source of the particular form of Freemasonry known as 'Scottish Rite'. 'Scottish Rite' Freemasonry introduced higher degrees than those offered by other Masonic systems at the time. It promised initiation into greater and more profound mysteries – mysteries supposedly preserved and handed down in Scotland. It established more direct connections between Freemasonry and the various activities – alchemy, Cabalism and Hermetic thought, for instance – which were regarded as 'Rosicrucian'. And it elaborated not only on the antiquity but also on the illustrious pedigree of the 'craft'.

It is probable that 'Scottish Rite' Freemasonry was originally promulgated, if not indeed devised, by Charles Radclyffe. In any case Radclyffe, in 1725, is said to have founded the first Masonic lodge on the continent, in Paris. During the same year, or perhaps in the year following, he seems to have been acknowledged Grand Master of all French lodges, and it is still cited as such a decade later, in 1736. The dissemination of eighteenth-century Freemasonry owes more, ultimately, to Radclyffe than to any other man.

This has not always been readily apparent because Radclyffe, especially after 1738, kept a relatively 'low profile'. To a very significant degree, he seems to have worked through intermediaries and 'mouthpieces'. The most important of these, and the most famous, was the enigmatic individual known as the Chevalier Andrew Ramsay.[13]

Ramsay was born in Scotland sometime during the 1680s. As a young man he was a member of a quasi-Masonic, quasi-'Rosicrucian' society called the Philadelphians. Among the other members of this society were at least two close friends of Isaac Newton. Ramsay himself regarded Newton with unmitigated reverence, deeming him a kind of high mystical 'initiate' – a man who had rediscovered and reconstructed the eternal truths concealed in the ancient mysteries.

Ramsay had other links with Newton. He was associated with Jean Desaguliers, one of Newton's closest friends. In 1707 he studied mathematics under one Nicolas Fatio de Duillier, the most intimate of all Newton's companions. Like Newton, he displayed a sympathetic interest in the Camisards – a sect of Cathar-like heretics then suffering persecution in southern France, and a kind of *cause célèbre* for Fatio de Duillier.

By 1710 Ramsay was in Cambrai and on intimate terms with the mystical philosopher Fénelon, formerly curé of Saint Sulpice – which, even at that time, was a bastion of rather questionable orthodoxy. It is not known precisely when Ramsay made Charles Radclyffe's acquaintance, but by the 1720s he was closely affiliated with the Jacobite cause. For a time he even served as Bonnie Prince Charlie's tutor.

Despite his Jacobite connections, Ramsay returned to England in 1729 where – notwithstanding an apparent lack of appropriate qualifications – he was promptly admitted to the Royal Society. He also became a member of a rather more obscure institution called the Gentleman's Club of Spalding. This 'club' included men like Desaguliers, Alexander Pope and, until his death in 1727, Isaac Newton.

By 1730 Ramsay was back in France and increasingly active on behalf of Freemasonry. He is on record as having attended lodge meetings with a number of notable figures, including Desaguliers. And he received special patronage from the Tour d'Auvergne family, the viscounts of Turenne and dukes of Bouillon – who, three-quarters of a century before, had been related to Frederick of the Palatinate. In Ramsay's time the duke of Bouillon was a cousin of Bonnie Prince Charlie and among the most prominent figures in Freemasonry. He conferred an estate and a town-house on Ramsay, whom he also appointed tutor to his son.

In 1737 Ramsay delivered his famous 'Oration' – a lengthy disquisition on the history of Freemasonry, which subsequently became a seminal document for the 'craft'.[14] On the basis of this 'Oration' Ramsay became the pre-eminent Masonic spokesman of his age. Our research convinced us, however, that the real voice behind Ramsay was that of Charles Radclyffe – who presided over the lodge at which Ramsay delivered his discourse and who appeared again, in 1743, as chief signatory at Ramsay's funeral. But if Radclyffe was the power behind Ramsay, it would seem to have been Ramsay who constituted the link between Radclyffe and Newton.

Despite Radclyffe's premature death in 1746, the seeds he had sown in Europe continued to bear fruit. Early in the 1750s a new ambassador of Freemasonry appeared – a German named Karl Gottlieb von Hund. Hund claimed to have been initiated in 1742 – a year before Ramsay's death, four years before Radclyffe's. At his initiation, he claimed, he had been introduced to a new system of Freemasonry, confided to him by 'unknown superiors'.[15] These 'unknown superiors', Hund maintained, were closely associated with the Jacobite cause. Indeed, he even believed at first that the man who presided over his initiation was Bonnie Prince Charlie. And although this proved not to be the case,

Hund remained convinced that the unidentified personage in question was intimately connected with the 'Young Pretender'. It seems reasonable to suppose that the man who actually presided was Charles Radclyffe.

The system of Freemasonry to which Hund was introduced – a further extension of the 'Scottish Rite' – was subsequently called 'Strict Observance'. Its name derived from the oath it demanded, an oath of unswerving, unquestioning obedience to the mysterious 'unknown superiors'. And the basic tenet of the 'Strict Observance' was that it had descended directly from the Knights Templar, some of whom had purportedly survived the purge of 1307–14 and perpetuated their Order in Scotland.

We were already familiar with this claim. On the basis of our own research we could allow it some truth. A contingent of Templars had allegedly fought on Robert Bruce's side at the Battle of Bannockburn. Because the Papal Bull dissolving the Templars was never promulgated in Scotland, the Order was never officially suppressed there. And we ourselves had located what seemed to be a Templar graveyard in Argyllshire. The earliest of the stones in this graveyard dated from the thirteenth century, the later ones from the eighteenth. The earlier stones bore certain unique carvings and incised symbols identical to those found at known Templar preceptories in England and France. The later stones combined these symbols with specifically Masonic motifs, attesting thereby to some sort of fusion. It was thus not impossible, we concluded, that the Order had indeed perpetuated itself in the trackless wilderness of medieval Argyll – maintaining a clandestine existence, gradually secularising itself and becoming associated with both Masonic guilds and the prevailing clan system.

The pedigree Hund claimed for the 'Strict Observance' did not, therefore, seem to us altogether improbable. To his own embarrassment and subsequent disgrace, however, he was unable to elaborate further on his new system of Freemasonry. As a result his contemporaries dismissed him as a charlatan, and accused him of having fabricated the story of his initiation, his meeting with 'unknown superiors', his mandate to disseminate the 'Strict Observance'. To these charges Hund could only reply that his 'unknown superiors' had inexplicably abandoned him. They had promised to contact him again and give him further instructions, he protested, but they had never done so. To the end of his life he affirmed his integrity, maintaining he had been deserted by his original sponsors – who, he insisted, had actually existed.

The more we considered Hund's assertions, the more plausible they sounded and he appeared to have been a hapless victim – not so much of deliberate betrayal as of circumstances beyond everyone's control. For according to his own account, Hund had been initiated in 1742, when the Jacobites were still a powerful political force in continental affairs. By 1746, however, Radclyffe was dead. So were many of his colleagues, while others were in prison or exile – as far away, in some cases, as North America. If Hund's 'unknown superiors' failed to re-establish contact with their protégé, the omission does not seem to have been voluntary. The fact that Hund was abandoned immediately after the collapse of the Jacobite cause would seem, if anything, to confirm his story.

There is another fragment of evidence which lends credence not only to Hund's claims but to the 'Prieuré documents' as well. This evidence is a list of Grand Masters of the Knights Templar, which Hund insisted he had obtained from his 'unknown superiors'.[16] On the basis of our own research, we had concluded that the list of Templar Grand Masters in the *Dossiers secrets* was accurate – so accurate, in fact, that it appeared to derive from 'inside information'. Save for the spelling of a single surname, the list Hund produced agreed with the one in the *Dossiers secret*. In short, Hund had somehow obtained a list of Templar Grand Masters more accurate than any other known at the time. Moreover, he obtained it when many documents on which we relied – charters, deeds, proclamations – were still sequestered in the Vatican and unobtainable. This would seem to confirm that Hund's story of 'unknown superiors' was not a fabrication. It would also seem to indicate that those 'unknown superiors' were extraordinarily knowledgeable about the Order of the Temple – more knowledgeable than they could possibly have been without access to 'privileged sources'.

In any case, despite the charges levelled against him Hund was not left completely friendless. After the collapse of the Jacobite cause he found a sympathetic patron, and a close companion, in no less a person than the Holy Roman Emperor. The Holy Roman Emperor at this time was François, Duke of Lorraine – who, by his marriage to Maria Theresa of Austria in 1735, had linked the houses of Habsburg and Lorraine and inaugurated the Habsburg-Lorraine dynasty. And according to the 'Prieuré documents', it was Francois's brother, Charles de Lorraine, who succeeded Radclyffe as Sion's Grand Master.

François was the first European prince to become a Mason and to publicise his Masonic affiliations. He was initiated in 1731 at the Hague – a bastion of esoteric activity since 'Rosicrucian' circles had installed themselves there during the Thirty Years War. And the man who presided over François's initiation was Jean Desaguliers, intimate associate of Newton, Ramsay and Radclyffe. Shortly after his initiation moreover, François embarked for a lengthy stay in England. Here he became a member of that innocuous-sounding institution, the Gentleman's Club of Spalding.

In the years that followed, François de Lorraine was probably more responsible than any other European potentate for the spread of Freemasonry. His court at Vienna became, in a sense, Europe's Masonic capital, and a centre for a broad spectrum of other esoteric interests as well. François himself was a practising alchemist, with an alchemical laboratory in the imperial palace, the Hofburg. On the death of the last Medici he became grand duke of Tuscany, and deftly thwarted the Inquisition's harassment of Freemasons in Florence. Through François, Charles Radclyffe, who had founded the first Masonic lodge on the continent, left a durable legacy.

CHARLES NODIER AND HIS CIRCLE

Compared to the important cultural and political figures who preceded him, compared even to a man like Charles Radclyffe, Charles Nodier seemed a most unlikely choice for Grand Master. We knew him primarily as a kind of literary curiosity – a relatively minor belle-lettrist, a somewhat garrulous essayist, a second-rate novelist and short-story writer in the bizarre tradition of E. T. A. Hoffmann and, later, Edgar Allan Poe. In his own time, however, Nodier was regarded as a major cultural figure, and his influence was enormous. Moreover, he proved to be connected with our inquiry in a number of surprising ways.

By 1824 Nodier was already a literary celebrity. In that year he was appointed the chief librarian at the Arsenal Library, the major French depository for medieval and specifically occult manuscripts. Among its various treasures the Arsenal was said to have contained the alchemical works of Nicolas Flamel – the medieval alchemist listed as one of Sion's earlier Grand Masters. The Arsenal also contained the library of Cardinal Richelieu – an exhaustive collection of works on magical, Cabalistic and Hermetic thought. And there were other treasures, too.

On the outbreak of the French Revolution monasteries throughout the country had been plundered, and all books and manuscripts sent to Paris for storage. Then in 1810 Napoleon, as part of his ambition to create a definitive world library, confiscated and brought to Paris almost the entire archive of the Vatican. There were more than three thousand cases of material, some of which – all the documents pertaining to the Templars, for example – had been specifically requested. Although some of these papers were subsequently returned to Rome, a great many remained in France. And it was material of this sort – occult books and manuscripts, works plundered from monasteries and the archive of the Vatican – that passed through the hands of Nodier and his associates. Methodically they sifted it, catalogued it, explored it.

Among Nodier's colleagues in this task were Eliphas Lévi and Jean Baptiste Pitois, who adopted the nom de plume of Paul Christian. The works of these two men, over the years that followed, engendered a major renaissance of interest in esoterica. It is to these two men, and to Charles Nodier, their mentor, that the French 'occult revival' of the nineteenth century, as it has been called, can ultimately be traced. Indeed, Pitois's *History and Practice of Magic* became a bible for nineteenth-century students of the arcane. Recently re-issued in English translation – complete with its original dedication to Nodier – it is now a coveted work among modern students of the occult.

During his tenure at the Arsenal Nodier continued to write and publish prolifically. Among the most important of his later works is a massive, lavishly illustrated, multi-volume opus of antiquarian interest, devoted to sites of particular consequence in ancient France. In this monumental compendium Nodier devoted considerable space to the Merovingian epoch – a fact all the more striking in that no one at the time displayed the least interest in the Merovingians. There are also lengthy sections on the Templars, and there is a special article on Gisors – including a detailed account of the mysterious 'cutting of the elm' in 1188, which, according to the 'Prieuré documents', marked the separation between the Knights Templar and the Prieuré de Sion.[17]

At the same time Nodier was more than a librarian and a writer. He was also a gregarious, egocentric and flamboyant individual who constantly sought the centre of attention and did not hesitate to exaggerate his own importance. In his quarters at the Arsenal Library he inaugurated a salon which established him as one of the most influential and prestigious 'aesthetic potentates' of the epoch. By the time of his death in 1844, he had served as mentor for a whole generation — many of whom quite eclipsed him in their subsequent achievements. For example, Nodier's chief disciple and closest friend was the young Victor Hugo – Sion's next Grand Master according to the 'Prieuré documents'. There was François-René de Chateaubriand – who made a special pilgrimage to Poussin's tomb in Rome and had a stone erected there bearing a reproduction of 'Les Bergers d'Arcadie'. There were Balzac, Delacroix, Dumas *père*, Lamartine, Musset, Théophile Gautier, Gérard de Nerval and Alfred de Vigny. Like the poets and painters of the Renaissance, these men often drew heavily on esoteric, and especially Hermetic, tradition. They also incorporated in their works a number of motifs, themes, references and allusions to the mystery which, for us, commenced with Saunière and Rennes-le-Château. In 1832, for instance, a book was published entitled *A Journey to Rennes-les-Bains*, which speaks at length of a legendary treasure associated with Blanchefort and Rennes-le-Château. The author of this obscure book, Auguste de Labouïsse-Rochefort, also produced another work, *The Lovers – To Eléonore*. On the title page there appears, without any explanation, the motto 'Et in Arcadia Ego'.

Nodier's literary and esoteric activities were quite clearly pertinent to our investigation. But there was another aspect of his career which was, if anything, more pertinent still. For Nodier, from his childhood, was deeply involved in secret societies. As early as 1790, for instance, at the age of ten he is known to have been involved in a group called the Philadelphes.[18] Around 1793 he created another group – or perhaps an inner circle of the first – which included one of the subsequent plotters against Napoleon. A charter dated 1797 attests to the foundation of yet another group – also called the Philadelphes – in that year.[19] In the library of Besançon there is a cryptic essay composed and recited to this group by one of Nodier's closest friends. It is entitled *Le berger arcadien ou première accents d'une flute champêtre* ('The Arcadian Shepherd Sounds the First Accents of a Rustic Flute').[20]

In Paris in 1802 Nodier wrote of his affiliation with a secret society which he described as 'Biblical and Pythagorean'.[21] Then, in 1815, he published anonymously one of his most curious and influential works, the *History of Secret Societies in the Army*. In this book Nodier is deliberately ambiguous. He does not clarify definitively whether he is writing pure fiction or pure fact. If anything, he implies, the book is a species of thinly disguised allegory of actual historical occurrences. In any case it develops a comprehensive philosophy of secret societies. And it credits such societies with a number of historical accomplishments, including the downfall of Napoleon. There are a great many secret societies in operation, Nodier declares. But there is one, he adds, that takes precedence over all others, that in fact presides over all the others. According to Nodier, this 'supreme' secret society is called the Philadelphes. At the same time, however, he speaks of 'the oath which binds me to the Philadelphes and which forbids me to make them known under their social name'.[22] Nevertheless, there is a hint of Sion in an address which Nodier quotes. It was supposedly made to an assembly of Philadelphes by one of the plotters against Napoleon. The man in question is speaking of his newly born son:

> He is too young to engage himself to you by the oath of
> Annibal; but remember I have named him Eliacin, and that I
> delegate to him the guard of the temple and the altar, if I should
> die ere I have seen fall from his throne the last of the oppressors
> of Jerusalem.[23]

Nodier's book burst on the scene when fear of secret societies had assumed virtually pathological proportions. Such societies were often blamed for instigating the French Revolution; and the atmosphere of post-Napoleonic Europe was similar, in many respects, to that of the 'McCarthy Era' in the United States during the 1950s. People saw, or imagined they saw, conspiracies everywhere. Witch-hunts abounded. Every public disturbance, every minor disruption, every untoward occurrence was attributed to 'subversive activity' – to the work of highly organised clandestine organisations working insidiously behind the scenes, eroding the fabric of established institutions, perpetrating all manner of devious sabotage. This mentality engendered measures of extreme repression. And the repression, directed often at a fictitious threat, in turn engendered real opponents, real groups of subversive conspirators – who would form themselves in accordance with the fictitious blueprints. Even as figments of the imagination, secret societies fostered a pervasive paranoia in the upper echelons of government; and this paranoia frequently accomplished more than any secret society itself could possibly have done. There is no question that the myth of the secret society, if not the secret society itself, played a major role in nineteenth-century European history. And one of the chief architects of that myth, and possibly of a reality behind it, was Charles Nodier.[24]

DEBUSSY AND THE ROSE-CROIX

The trends to which Nodier gave expression – a fascination with secret societies and a renewed interest in the esoteric – continued to gain influence and adherents throughout the nineteenth century. Both trends reached a peak in the Paris of the *fin de siècle* – the milieu of Claude Debussy, Sion's alleged Grand Master when Bérenger Saunière, in 1891, discovered the mysterious parchments at Rennes-le-Château.

Debussy seems to have made Victor Hugo's acquaintance through the symbolist poet Paul Verlaine. Subsequently he set a number of Hugo's works to music. He also became an integral member of the symbolist circles which, by the last decade of the century, had come to dominate Parisian cultural life. These circles were sometimes illustrious, sometimes odd, sometimes both. They included the young cleric Émile Hoffet and Emma Calvé – through whom Debussy came to meet Saunière. There was also the enigmatic magus of French symbolist poetry, Stéphane Mallarmé – one of whose masterpieces, *L'Après-Midi d'un Faune*, Debussy set to music. There was the symbolist playwright, Maurice Maeterlinck, whose Merovingian drama, *Pelléas et Mélisande*, Debussy turned into a world-famous opera. There was the flamboyant Comte Philippe Auguste Villiers de l'Isle-Adam, whose 'Rosicrucian' play, *Axel*, became a bible for the entire Symbolist Movement. Although his death in 1918 prevented its completion, Debussy began to compose a libretto for Villiers's occult drama, intending to turn it, too, into an opera. Among his other associates were the luminaries who attended Mallarmé's famous Tuesday night soirées – Oscar Wilde, W. B. Yeats, Stefan George, Paul Valéry, the young André Gide and Marcel Proust.

In themselves Debussy's and Mallarmé's circles were steeped in esoterica. At the same time, they overlapped circles that were more esoteric still. Thus Debussy consorted with virtually all the most prominent names in the so-called French 'occult revival'. One of these was the Marquis Stanislas de Guaïta, an intimate of Emma Calvé and founder of the so-called Cabalistic Order of the Rose-Croix. A second was Jules Bois, a notorious satanist, another intimate of Emma Calvé and a friend of MacGregor Mathers. Prompted by Jules Bois, Mathers established the most famous British occult society of the period, the Order of the Golden Dawn.

Another occultist of Debussy's acquaintance was Doctor Gérard Encausse – better known as Papus,[25] under which name he published what is still considered one of the definitive works on the Tarot. Papus was not only a member of numerous esoteric orders and societies, but also a confidant of the czar and czarina, Nicholas and Alexandra of Russia. And among Papus's closest associates was a name which had already figured in our inquiry – that of Jules Doinel. In 1890 Doinel had become librarian at Carcassonne and established a neo-Cathar church in the Languedoc – in which he and Papus functioned as bishops. Doinel in fact proclaimed himself Gnostic bishop of Mirepoix, which included the parish of Montségur, and of Alet, which included the parish of Rennes-le-Château.

Doinel's church was supposedly consecrated by an eastern bishop in Paris – at the home, interestingly enough, of Lady Caithness, wife of the earl of Caithness, Lord James Sinclair. In retrospect this church seems to have been merely another innocuous sect or cult, like so many of the *fin de siècle*. At the time, however, it caused considerable alarm in official quarters. A special report was prepared for the Holy Office of the Vatican on the 'resurgence of Cathar tendencies'. And the pope issued an explicit condemnation of Doinel's institution, which he militantly denounced as a new manifestation of 'the ancient Albigensian heresy'.

Notwithstanding the Vatican's condemnation, Doinel, by the mid-1890s, was active in Saunière's home territory – and at precisely the time that the curé of Rennes-le-Château began to flaunt his wealth. The two men may well have been introduced by Debussy. Or by Emma Calvé. Or by the Abbé Henri Boudet – curé of Rennes-les-Bains, best friend of Saunière and colleague of Doinel in the Society of Arts and Sciences of Carcassonne.

One of the closest of Debussy's occult contacts was Joséphin Péladan – another friend of Papus and, predictably enough, another intimate of Emma Calvé. In 1889 Péladan embarked on a visit to the Holy Land. When he returned he claimed to have discovered Jesus's tomb – not at the traditional site of the Holy Sepulchre but under the Mosque of Omar, formerly part of the Templars' enclave. In the words of an enthusiastic admirer, Péladan's alleged discovery was 'so astonishing that at any other era it would have shaken the Catholic world to its foundations'.[26] Neither Péladan nor his associates, however, volunteered any indication of how Jesus's tomb could have been so definitively identified and verified as such, nor why its discovery should necessarily shake the Catholic world – unless, of course, it contained something significant, controversial, perhaps even explosive. In any case, Péladan did not elaborate on his purported discovery. But though a self-professed Catholic, he nevertheless insisted on Jesus's mortality.

In 1890 Péladan founded a new order – the Order of the Catholic Rose-Croix, the Temple and the Grail. And this order, unlike the other Rose-Croix institutions of the period, somehow escaped papal condemnation. In the meantime, Péladan turned his attention increasingly to the arts. The artist, he declared, should be 'a knight in armour, eagerly engaged in the symbolic quest for the Holy Grail'. And in adherence to this principle, Péladan embarked on a fully fledged aesthetic crusade. It took the form of a highly publicised series of annual exhibitions, known as the Salon de la Rose + Croix – whose avowed purpose was 'to ruin realism, reform Latin taste and create a school of idealist art'. To that end certain themes and subjects were autocratically and summarily rejected as unworthy – 'no matter how well executed, even if perfectly'. The list of rejected themes and subjects included 'prosaic' history painting, patriotic and military painting, representations of contemporary life, portraits, rustic scenes and 'all landscapes except those composed in the manner of Poussin'.[27]

Nor did Péladan confine himself to painting. On the contrary, he attempted to promulgate his aesthetic in music and the theatre as well. He formed his own theatre company, which performed specially composed works on such subjects as Orpheus, the Argonauts and the Quest for the Golden Fleece, the 'Mystery of the Rose-Croix' and the 'Mystery of the Grail'. One of the regular promoters and patrons of these productions was Claude Debussy.

Among Péladan's and Debussy's other associates was Maurice Barrès – who, as a young man, had been involved in a 'Rose-Croix' circle with Victor Hugo. In 1912 Barrès published his most famous novel, *La Colline inspirée* ('The Inspired Mount'). Certain modern commentators have suggested that his work is in fact a thinly disguised allegory of Bérenger Saunière and Rennes-le-Château. Certainly there are parallels which would seem too striking to be wholly coincidental. But Barrès does not situate his narrative in Rennes-le-Château, or any other place in the Languedoc. On the contrary, the 'inspired mount' of the title is a mountain surmounted by a village in Lorraine. And the village is the old pilgrimage centre of Sion.

JEAN COCTEAU

More than Charles Radclyffe, more than Charles Nodier, Jean Cocteau seemed to us a most unlikely candidate for the Grand Mastership of an influential secret society. In Radclyffe's and Nodier's cases, however, our investigation had yielded certain connections of considerable interest. In Cocteau's we discovered very few.

Certainly he was raised in a milieu close to the 'corridors of power' – his family were politically prominent and his uncle was an important diplomat. But Cocteau, at least ostensibly, abandoned this world, leaving home at the age of fifteen and plunging into the seedy sub-culture of Marseilles. By 1908 he had established himself in bohemian artistic circles. In his early twenties he became associated with Proust, Gide and Maurice Barrès. He was also a close friend of Victor Hugo's great-grandson, Jean, with whom he embarked on assorted excursions into spiritualism and the occult. He quickly became versed in esoterica; and Hermetic thinking shaped not only much of his work, but also his entire aesthetic. By 1912, if not earlier, he had begun to consort with Debussy, to whom he alludes frequently, if non-committally, in his journals. In 1926 he designed the set for a production of the opera *Pelléas et Mélisande* because, according to one commentator, he was 'unable to resist linking his name for all time to that of Claude Debussy'.

Cocteau's private life – which included bouts of drug addiction and a sequence of homosexual affairs – was notoriously erratic. This has fostered an image of him as a volatile and recklessly irresponsible individual. In fact, however, he was always acutely conscious of his public persona; and whatever his personal escapades, he would not let them impede his access to people of influence and power. As he himself admitted, he had always craved public recognition, honour, esteem, even admission to the Académie Française. And he made a point of conforming sufficiently to assure him of the status he sought. Thus he was never far removed from prominent figures like Jacques Maritain and André Malraux. Although never ostensibly interested in politics, he denounced the Vichy government during the war and seems to have been quietly in league with the Resistance. In 1949 he was made a Chevalier of the Legion of Honour. In 1958 he was invited by de Gaulle's brother to make a public address on the general subject of France. It is not the kind of role one generally attributes to Cocteau, but he appears to have played it frequently enough and to have relished doing so.

For a good part of his life, Cocteau was associated – sometimes intimately, sometimes peripherally – with royalist Catholic circles. Here he frequently hobnobbed with members of the old aristocracy – including some of Proust's friends and patrons. At the same time, however, Cocteau's Catholicism was highly suspect, highly unorthodox, and seems to have been more an aesthetic than a religious commitment. In the latter part of his life, he devoted much of his energy to redecorating churches – curious echo, perhaps, of Bérenger Saunière. Yet even then his piety was questionable: 'They take me for a religious painter because I've decorated a chapel. Always the same mania for labelling people.'[28]

Like Saunière, Cocteau, in his redecorations, incorporated certain curious and suggestive details. Some are visible in the church of Notre Dame de France, around the corner from Leicester Square in London. The church itself dates from 1865 – and may, at its consecration, have had certain Masonic connections. In 1940, at the peak of the blitz, it was seriously damaged. Nevertheless, it remained the favourite centre of worship for many important members of the Free French Forces; and after the war it was restored and redecorated by artists from all over France. Among them was Cocteau, who, in 1960, three years before his death, executed a mural depicting the Crucifixion. It is an extremely singular Crucifixion. There is a black sun, and a sinister, green-tinged and unidentified figure in the lower right-hand corner. There is a Roman soldier holding a shield with a bird emblazoned on it – a highly stylised bird suggesting an Egyptian rendering of Horus. Among the mourning women and dice-throwing centurions, there are two incongruously modern figures – one of whom is Cocteau himself, presented as a self-portrait, with his back significantly turned on the cross. Most striking of all is the fact that the mural depicts only the lower portion of the cross. Whoever hangs upon it is visible only as far up as the knees – so that one cannot see the face, or determine the identity of who is being crucified. And fixed to the cross, immediately below the anonymous victim's feet, is a gigantic rose. The design, in short, is a flagrant Rose-Croix device. And if nothing else, it is a very singular motif for a Catholic church.

THE TWO JOHN XXIIIS

The *Dossiers secrets*, in which the list of Sion's alleged Grand Masters appeared, were dated 1956. Cocteau did not die until 1963. There was thus no indication of who might have succeeded him, or of who might preside over the Prieuré de Sion at present. But Cocteau himself posed one additional point of immense interest.

Until the 'cutting of the elm' in 1188, the 'Prieuré documents' asserted, Sion and the Order of the Temple shared the same Grand Master. After 1188 Sion is said to have chosen a Grand Master of its own, the first of them being Jean de Gisors. According to the 'Prieuré documents', every Grand Master, on assuming his position, has adopted the name of Jean (John) – or, since there were four women, Jeanne (Joan). Sion's Grand Masters are therefore alleged to have comprised a continuous succession of Jeans and Jeannes, from 1188 to the present. This succession was clearly intended to imply an esoteric and Hermetic papacy based on John, in contrast (and perhaps opposition) to the exoteric one based on Peter.

One major question, of course, was which John. John the Baptist? John the Evangelist – the 'Beloved Disciple' in the Fourth Gospel? Or John the Divine, author of the Book of Revelation? It seemed it must be one of these three because Jean de Gisors in 1188 had purportedly taken the title of Jean II. Who, then, was Jean I?

Whatever the answer to that question, Jean Cocteau appeared on the list of Sion's alleged Grand Masters as Jean XXIII. In 1959, while Cocteau still presumably held the Grand Mastership, Pope Pius XII died and the assembled cardinals elected, as their new pontiff, Cardinal Angelo Roncalli of Venice. Any newly elected pope chooses his own name; and Cardinal Roncalli caused considerable consternation when he chose the name of John XXIII. Such consternation was not unjustified. In the first place the name 'John' had been implicitly anathematised since it was last used in the early fifteenth century – by an antipope. Moreover, there had already been a John XXIII. The antipope who abdicated in 1415 – and who, interestingly enough, had previously been bishop of Alet – was in fact John XXIII. It was thus unusual, to say the least, for Cardinal Roncalli to assume the same name.

In 1976 an enigmatic little book was published in Italy and soon after translated into French. It was called *The Prophecies of Pope John XXIII* and contained a compilation of obscure prophetic prose poems reputedly composed by the pontiff who had died thirteen years before – in 1963, the same year as Cocteau. For the most part these 'prophecies' are extremely opaque and defy any coherent interpretation. Whether they are indeed the work of John XXIII is also open to question. But the introduction to the work maintains that they are Pope John's work. And it maintains something further as well – that John XXIII was secretly a member of the 'Rose-Croix', with whom he had become affiliated while acting as Papal Nuncio to Turkey in 1935.

Needless to say, this assertion sounds incredible. Certainly it cannot be proved, and we found no external evidence to support it. But why, we wondered, should such an assertion even have been made in the first place?

Could it be true after all? Could there be at least a grain of truth in it? In 1188 the Prieuré de Sion is said to have adopted the subtitle of 'Rose-Croix Veritas'. If Pope John was affiliated with a 'Rose-Croix' organisation, and if that organisation was the Prieuré de Sion, the implications would be extremely intriguing. Among other things they would suggest that Cardinal Roncalli, on becoming pope, chose the name of his own secret Grand Master – so that, for some symbolic reason, there would be a John XXIII presiding over Sion and the papacy simultaneously.

In any case the simultaneous rule of a John (or Jean) XXIII over both Sion and Rome would seem to be an extraordinary coincidence. Nor could the 'Prieuré documents' have devised a list to create such a coincidence – a list which culminated with Jean XXIII at the same time that a man with that title occupied the throne of Saint Peter. For the list of Sion's alleged Grand Masters had been composed and deposited in the Bibliothèque Nationale no later than 1956 – three years before John XXIII became pope.

There was another striking coincidence. In the twelfth century an Irish monk named Malachi compiled a series of Nostradamus-like prophecies. In these prophecies – which, incidentally, are said to be highly esteemed by many important Roman Catholics, including the present pope, John-Paul II – Malachi enumerates the pontiffs who will occupy the throne of Saint Peter in the centuries to come. For each pontiff he offers a species of descriptive motto. And for John XXIII the motto, translated into French, is 'Pasteur et Nautonnier' – 'Shepherd and Navigator'.[29] The official title of Sion's alleged Grand Master is also 'Nautonnier'.

Whatever the truth underlying these strange coincidences, there is no question that more than any other man Pope John XXIII was responsible for re-orienting the Roman Catholic Church – and bringing it, as commentators have frequently said, into the twentieth century. Much of this was accomplished by the reforms of the Second Vatican Council, which John inaugurated. At the same time, however, John was responsible for other changes as well. He revised the Church's position on Freemasonry, for example – breaking with at least two centuries of entrenched tradition and allowing that a Catholic might be a Freemason. And in June 1960 he issued a profoundly important apostolic letter.[30] This missive addressed itself specifically to the subject of 'The Precious Blood of Jesus'. It ascribed a hitherto unprecedented significance to that blood. It emphasised Jesus's suffering as a human being, and maintained that the redemption of mankind had been effected by the shedding of his blood. In the context of Pope John's letter, Jesus's human Passion, and the shedding of his blood, assume a greater consequence than the Resurrection or even than the mechanics of the Crucifixion.

The implications of this letter are ultimately enormous. As one commentator has observed, they alter the whole basis of Christian belief. If man's redemption was achieved by the shedding of Jesus's blood, his death and resurrection became incidental – if not, indeed, superfluous. Jesus need not have died on the cross for the faith to retain its validity.

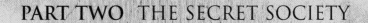

PART TWO THE SECRET SOCIETY

CHAPTER SEVEN

CONSPIRACY THROUGH THE CENTURIES

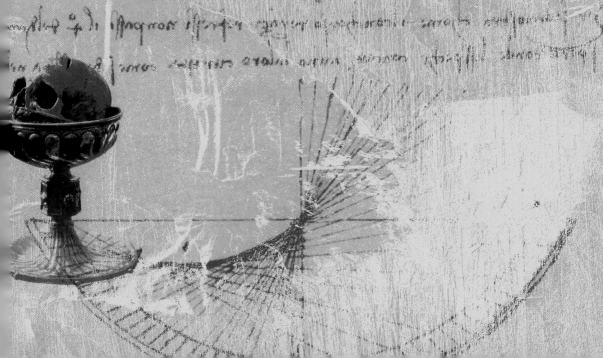

How were we to synthesise the evidence we had accumulated? Much of it was impressive and seemed to bear witness to something – some pattern, some coherent design. The list of Sion's alleged Grand Masters, however improbable it had originally appeared, now displayed some intriguing consistencies. Most of the figures on the list, for example, were connected, either by blood or personal association, with the families whose genealogies figured in the 'Prieuré documents' – and particularly with the house of Lorraine. Most of the figures on the list were involved with orders of one kind or another, or with secret societies. Virtually all the figures on the list, even when nominally Catholic, held unorthodox religious beliefs. Virtually all of them were immersed in esoteric thought and tradition. And in almost every case there had been some species of close contact between an alleged Grand Master, his predecessor and his successor.

Nevertheless, these consistencies, impressive though they might be, did not necessarily prove anything. They did not prove, for instance, that the Prieuré de Sion, whose existence during the Middle Ages we had confirmed, had actually continued to survive through the subsequent centuries. Still less did they prove that the individuals cited as Grand Masters actually held that position. It still seemed incredible to us that some of them really did. So far as certain individuals were concerned, the age at which they allegedly became Grand Master argued against them. Granted, it was possible that Edouard de Bar might have been selected Grand Master at the age of five, or René d'Anjou at the age of eight, on the basis of some hereditary principle. But no such principle seemed to obtain for Robert Fludd or Charles Nodier, who both supposedly became Grand Master at the age of twenty-one, or for Debussy, who supposedly did so aged twenty-three. Such individuals would not have had time to 'work their way up through the ranks', as one might, for example, in Freemasonry. Nor had they even become solidly established in their own spheres. This anomaly made no apparent sense. Unless one assumed that Sion's Grand Mastership was often purely symbolic, a ritual position occupied by a figurehead – a figurehead who, perhaps, was not even aware of the status accorded him.

However, it proved futile to speculate – at least on the basis of the information we possessed. We therefore turned back to history again, seeking evidence of the Prieuré de Sion elsewhere, in quarters other than the list of alleged Grand Masters. We turned particularly to the fortunes of the house of Lorraine, and some of the other families cited in the 'Prieuré documents'. We sought to verify other statements made in those documents. And we sought additional evidence for the work of a secret society, acting more or less covertly behind the scenes.

If it was indeed genuinely secret, we did not, of course, expect to find the Prieuré de Sion explicitly mentioned by that name. If it had continued to function through the centuries, it would have done so under a variety of shifting guises and masks, 'fronts' and façades – just as it purportedly functioned for a time under the name Ormus, which it discarded. Nor would it have displayed a single obvious and specific policy, political position or prevailing attitude. Indeed, any such cohesive and unified stance, even if it could be gleaned, would have seemed highly suspect. If we were dealing with an organisation which had survived for some nine centuries, we would have to credit it with considerable flexibility and adaptability. Its very survival would have hinged on these qualities; and without them it would have degenerated into an empty form, as devoid of any real power as, say, the Yeomen of the Guard. In short, the Prieuré de Sion could not have remained rigid and immutable for the whole of its history. On the contrary, it would have been compelled to change periodically, modify itself and its activities, adjust itself and its objectives to the shifting kaleidoscope of world affairs – just as cavalry units during the last century have been compelled to exchange their horses for tanks and armoured cars. In its capacity to conform to a given age and exploit and master its technology and resources, Sion would have constituted a parallel to what seemed its exoteric rival, the Roman Catholic Church; or perhaps, to cite a deceptively sinister example, to the organisation known as the Mafia. We did not, of course, see the Prieuré de Sion as unadulterated villains. But the Mafia at least provided testimony of how, by adapting itself from age to age, a secret society could exist, and of the kind of power it could exercise.

THE PRIEURÉ DE SION IN FRANCE

According to the 'Prieuré documents', Sion between 1306 and 1480 possessed nine commanderies. In 1481 – when René d'Anjou died – this number was supposedly expanded to twenty-seven. The most important are listed as having been situated at Bourges, Gisors, Jarnac, Mont-Saint-Michel, Montréval, Paris, Le Puy, Solesmes and Stenay. And, the *Dossiers secrets* add cryptically, there was 'an arch called Beth-Ania –

The 'Villa Bethania' built by Bérenger Saunière, the priest of Rennes-le-Château with his mysteriously gained funds. He can be seen, seated on the edge of the pool, bottom right, with Marie, his housekeeper standing behind him (centre).

house of Anne – situated at Rennes-le-Château'.[1] It is not clear precisely what this passage means, except that Rennes-le-Château would appear to enjoy some kind of highly special significance. And surely it cannot be coincidental that Saunière, on building his villa, then christened it Villa Bethania.

According to the *Dossiers secrets*, the commandery at Gisors dated from 1306 and was situated in the rue de Vienne. From here it supposedly communicated, via an underground passageway, with the local cemetery and with the subterranean chapel of Sainte-Catherine located beneath the fortress. In the sixteenth century this chapel, or perhaps a crypt adjacent to it, is said to have become a depository for the archives of the Prieuré de Sion, housed in thirty coffers.

Early in 1944, when Gisors was occupied by German personnel, a special military mission was sent from Berlin, with instructions to plan a series of excavations beneath the fortress. The Allied invasion of Normandy thwarted any such undertaking; but not long after, a French workman named Roger Lhomoy embarked on excavations of his own. In 1946 Lhomoy announced to the Mayor of Gisors that he had found an underground chapel containing nineteen sarcophagi of stone and thirty coffers of metal. His petition to excavate further, and make public

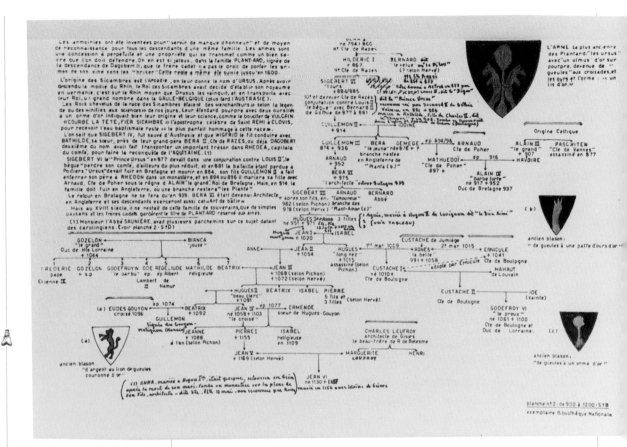

One page of the genealogies in the Dossiers Secrets *found in the Bibliothèque Nationale, Paris, under the pseudonym of Henri Lobineau.*

his discovery, was delayed – almost deliberately, it might seem – by a welter of official red tape. At last, in 1962, Lhomoy commenced his requested excavations at Gisors. They were conducted under the auspices of André Malraux, French Minister of Culture at the time, and were not officially open to the public. Certainly no coffers or sarcophagi were found. Whether the underground chapel was found has been debated – in the press, as well as in various books and articles. Lhomoy insisted he did find his way again to the chapel, but its contents had been removed. Whatever the truth of the matter, there is mention of the subterranean chapel of Sainte-Catherine in two old manuscripts, one dated 1696 and the other 1375.[2]

On this basis, Lhomoy's story at least becomes plausible. So does the assertion that the subterranean chapel was a depository for Sion's archives. For we, in our own research, found conclusive proof that the Prieuré de Sion continued to exist for at least three centuries after the Crusades and the dissolution of the Knights Templar. Between the early fourteenth and early seventeenth centuries, for example, documents pertinent to Orleans, and to Sion's base there at Saint-Samson, make sporadic references to the Order. Thus it is on record that in the early sixteenth century members of the Prieuré de Sion at Orleans – by flouting their 'rule' and 'refusing to live in common' – incurred the displeasure of the pope and the king of France. Towards the end of the fifteenth century the Order was also accused of a number of offences – failing to observe their rule, living 'individually' rather than 'in common', being licentious, residing outside the walls of Saint-Samson, boycotting divine services and neglecting to rebuild the walls of the house, which had been seriously damaged in 1562. By 1619 the authorities seemed to have lost patience. In that year, according to the records, the Prieuré de Sion was evicted from Saint-Samson and the house was made over to the Jesuits.[3]

A medieval charter on parchment listing the possessions in Palestine, Sicily, Spain, Italy and France of the Order de Sion. Drawn up by Pope Alexander III in 1173 this is an official copy from the thirteenth century.

From 1619 onwards we could find no reference to the Prieuré de Sion – not, at any rate, under that name. But if nothing else, we could at least prove its existence until the seventeenth century. And yet the proof itself, such as it was, raised a number of crucial questions. In the first place the references we found cast no light whatever on Sion's real activities, objectives, interests or possible influence. In the second place these references, it seemed, bore witness only to something of trifling consequence – a curiously elusive fraternity of monks or religious devotees whose behaviour, though unorthodox and perhaps clandestine, was of relatively minor import. We could not reconcile the apparently remiss occupants of Saint-Samson with the celebrated and legendary Rose-Croix, or a band of wayward monks with an institution whose Grand Masters supposedly comprised some of the most illustrious names in Western history and culture. According to the 'Prieuré documents', Sion was an organisation of considerable power and influence, responsible for creating the Templars and manipulating

Medieval charter on parchment by which King Louis VII of France confirms that he has taken a number of members of the Order de Sion to France and established them in a Prieuré at Saint-Samson, Orleans. This charter confirms the foundation of the historical Prieuré de Sion.

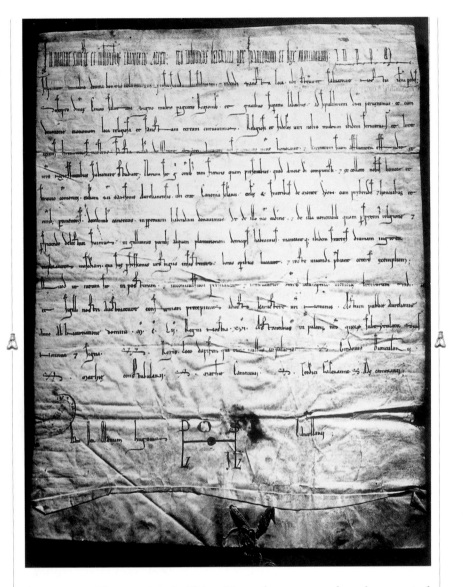

the course of international affairs. The references we found suggested nothing of such magnitude.

One possible explanation, of course, was that Saint-Samson at Orleans was but an isolated seat, and probably a minor one, of Sion's activities. And indeed, the list of Sion's important commanderies in the *Dossiers secrets* does not even include Orleans. If Sion was in fact a force to be reckoned with, Orleans can only have been one small fragment of a much broader pattern. And if this were the case, we would have to look for traces of the Order elsewhere.

THE DUKES OF GUISE AND LORRAINE

During the sixteenth century the house of Lorraine and its cadet branch, the house of Guise, made a concerted and determined attempt to topple the Valois dynasty of France – to exterminate the Valois line and claim the French throne. This attempt, on several occasions, came within a hair's breadth of dazzling success. In the course of some thirty years all Valois rulers, heirs and princes were wiped out, and the line driven to extinction.

The Duchy of Lorraine in the Mid-Sixteenth century.

The attempt to seize the French throne extended across three generations of the Guise and Lorraine families. It came closest to success in the 1550s and 1560s under the auspices of Charles, Cardinal of Lorraine and his brother, François, Duke of Guise. Charles and François were related to the Gonzaga family of Mantua and to Charles de Montpensier, Constable of Bourbon – listed in the *Dossiers secrets* as Grand Master of Sion until 1527. Moreover, François, Duke of Guise, was married to Anne d'Esté, Duchess of Gisors. And in his machinations for the throne he seems to have received covert aid and support from Ferrante de Gonzaga, allegedly Grand Master of Sion from 1527 until 1575.

Both François and his brother, the cardinal of Lorraine, have been stigmatised by later historians as rabidly bigoted and fanatic Catholics, intolerant, brutal and bloodthirsty. But there is substantial evidence to suggest that this reputation is to some extent unwarranted, at least so far as adherence to Catholicism is concerned. François and his brother appear, quite patently, to have been brazen, if cunning, opportunists, courting both Catholics and Protestants in the name of their ulterior design.[4] In 1562, for example, at the Council of Trent, the cardinal of Lorraine launched an attempt to decentralise the papacy – to confer autonomy on local bishops and restore the ecclesiastical hierarchy to what it had been in Merovingian times.

By 1563 François de Guise was already virtually king when he fell to an assassin's bullet. His brother, the cardinal of Lorraine, died twelve years later, in 1575. But the vendetta against the French royal line did not cease. In 1584 the new duke of Guise and new cardinal of Lorraine embarked on a fresh assault against the throne. Their chief ally in this enterprise was Louis de Gonzaga, Duke of Nevers – who, according to the 'Prieuré documents', had become Grand Master of Sion nine years before. The banner of the conspirators was the Cross of Lorraine – the former emblem of René d'Anjou.[5]

The feud continued. By the end of the century the Valois were at last extinct. But the house of Guise had bled itself to death in the process, and could put forward no eligible candidate for a throne that finally lay within its grasp.

It is simply not known whether there was an organised secret society, or secret order, supporting the houses of Guise and Lorraine. Certainly they were aided by an international network of emissaries, ambassadors, assassins, *agents provocateurs*, spies and agents who might well have comprised such a clandestine institution. According to Gérard de Sède, one of these agents was Nostradamus; and there are other 'Prieuré documents' which echo M. de Sède's contention. In any case, there is abundant evidence to suggest that Nostradamus was indeed a secret agent working for François de Guise and Charles, Cardinal of Lorraine.[6]

If Nostradamus was an agent for the houses of Guise and Lorraine, he would have been responsible not only for providing them with important information concerning the activities and plans of their adversaries, but he would also, in his capacity as astrologer to the French court, have been privy to all manner of intimate secrets, as well as quirks and weaknesses of personality. By playing on vulnerabilities with which he had become acquainted, he could have psychologically manipulated the Valois into the hands of their enemies. And by virtue of his familiarity with their horoscopes, he might well have advised their enemies on, say, an apparently propitious moment for assassination. Many of Nostradamus's prophecies, in short, may not have been prophecies at all. They may have been cryptic messages, ciphers, schedules, timetables, instructions, blueprints for action.

Whether this was actually the case or not, there is no question that some of Nostradamus's prophecies were not prophecies but referred, quite explicitly, to the past – to the Knights Templar, the Merovingian dynasty, the history of the house of Lorraine. A striking number of them refer to the Razès – the old comté of Rennes-le-Château.[7] And the numerous quatrains which refer to the advent of 'le Grand Monarch' –

CONSPIRACY THROUGH THE CENTURIES

the Great Monarch – indicate that this sovereign will derive ultimately from the Languedoc.

Our research revealed an additional fragment which linked Nostradamus even more directly to our investigation. According to Gérard de Sède,[8] as well as to popular legend, Nostradamus, before embarking on his career as prophet, spent considerable time in Lorraine. This would appear to have been some sort of novitiate, or period of probation, after which he was supposedly 'initiated' into some portentous secret. More specifically he is said to have been shown an ancient and arcane book, on which he based all his own subsequent work. And this book was reportedly divulged to him at a very signifi-cant place – the mysterious Abbey of Orval, donated by Godfroi de Bouillon's foster-mother, where our research suggested that the Prieuré de Sion may have had its inception. In any case, Orval continued, for another two centuries, to be associated with the name of Nostradamus. As late as the French Revolution and the Napoleonic era books of prophecies, purportedly authored by Nostradamus, were issuing from Orval.

THE BID FOR THE THRONE OF FRANCE

By the mid-1620s the throne of France was occupied by Louis XIII. But the power behind the throne, and the real architect of French policy, was the king's prime minister, Cardinal Richelieu. Richelieu is generally acknowledged to have been the arch-Machiavel, the supreme machina-tor, of his age. He may have been something more as well.

While Richelieu established an unprecedented stability in France, the rest of Europe – and especially Germany – flamed in the throes of the Thirty Years War. In its origins the Thirty Years War was not essen-tially religious. Nevertheless, it quickly became polarised in religious terms. On one side were the staunchly Catholic forces of Spain and Austria. On the other were the Protestant armies of Sweden and the small German principalities – including the Palatinate of the Rhine, whose rulers, Elector Frederick and his wife Elizabeth Stuart, were in exile at the Hague. Frederick and his allies in the field were endorsed and supported by 'Rosicrucian' thinkers and writers both on the conti-nent and in England.

In 1633 Cardinal Richelieu embarked on an audacious and seeming-ly incredible policy. He brought France into the Thirty Years War – but

not on the side one would expect. For Richelieu, a number of considerations took precedence over his religious obligations as cardinal. He
sought to establish French supremacy in Europe. He sought to neu-
tralise the perpetual and traditional threat posed to French security by
Austria and Spain. And he sought to shatter the Spanish hegemony
which had obtained for more than a century – especially in the old
Merovingian heartland of the Low Countries and parts of modern
Lorraine. As a result of these factors, Europe was taken aback by the
unprecedented action of a Catholic cardinal, presiding over a Catholic
country, dispatching Catholic troops to fight on the Protestant side –
against other Catholics. No historian has ever suggested that Richelieu
was a 'Rosicrucian'. But he could not possibly have done anything more
in keeping with 'Rosicrucian' attitudes, or more likely to win him
'Rosicrucian' favour.

In the meantime the house of Lorraine had again begun to aspire,
albeit obliquely, to the French throne. This time the claimant was Gaston
d'Orléans, younger brother of Louis XIII. Gaston was not himself of the
house of Lorraine. In 1632, however, he had married the duke of
Lorraine's sister. His heir would thus carry Lorraine blood on the mater-
nal side; and if Gaston ascended the throne Lorraine would preside
over France within another generation. This prospect was sufficient to
mobilise support. Among those asserting Gaston's right of succession
we found an individual we had encountered before – Charles, Duke of
Guise. Charles had been tutored by the young Robert Fludd. And he
had married Henriette-Catherine de Joyeuse, owner of Couiza and
Arques – where the tomb identical to the one in Poussin's painting is
located.

Attempts to depose Louis in favour of Gaston failed, but time it
seemed was on Gaston's side; or at least on the side of Gaston's heirs,
for Louis XIII and his wife, Anne of Austria, remained childless.
Rumours were already in circulation that the king was homosexual or
sexually incapacitated; and indeed, according to certain reports following his subsequent autopsy, he was pronounced incapable of begetting
children. But then, in 1638, after twenty-three years of sterile marriage,
Anne of Austria suddenly produced a child. Few people at the time
believed in the boy's legitimacy, and there is still considerable doubt
about it. According to both contemporary and later writers, the child's
true father was Cardinal Richelieu, or perhaps a 'stud' employed by
Richelieu, quite possibly his protégé and successor, Cardinal Mazarin. It

has even been claimed that after Louis XIII's death, Mazarin and Anne of Austria were secretly married.

In any case the birth of an heir to Louis XIII was a serious blow to the hopes of Gaston d'Orléans and the house of Lorraine. And when Louis and Richelieu both died in 1642, the first in a series of concerted attempts was launched to oust Mazarin and keep the young Louis XIV from the throne. These attempts, which began as popular uprisings, culminated in a civil war that flared intermittently for ten years. To historians that war is known as the Fronde. In addition to Gaston d'Orléans, its chief instigators included a number of names, families and titles already familiar to us. There was Frédéric-Maurice de la Tour d'Auvergne, Duke of Bouillon. There was the viscount of Turenne. There was the duke of Longueville – grandson of Louis de Gonzaga, Duke of Nevers and alleged Grand Master of Sion half a century before. The headquarters and capital of the *frondeurs* was, significantly enough, the ancient Ardennes town of Stenay.

THE COMPAGNIE DU SAINT-SACREMENT

According to the 'Prieuré documents', the Prieuré de Sion, during the mid-seventeenth century, 'dedicated itself to deposing Mazarin'. Quite clearly it would seem to have been unsuccessful. The Fronde failed, Louis XIV did mount the throne of France and Mazarin, though briefly removed, was quickly reinstated, presiding as prime minister until his death in 1660. But if Sion did in fact devote itself to opposing Mazarin, we at last had some vector on it, some means of locating and identifying it. Given the families involved in the Fronde – families whose genealogies also figured in the 'Prieuré documents' – it seemed reasonable to associate Sion with the instigators of that turmoil.

The 'Prieuré documents' had asserted that Sion actively opposed Mazarin. They also asserted that certain families and titles – Lorraine, for example, Gonzaga, Nevers, Guise, Longueville and Bouillon – had not only been intimately connected with the Order, but also provided it with some of its Grand Masters. And history confirmed that it was these names and titles which had loomed in the forefront of resistance to the cardinal. It thus seemed that we had located the Prieuré de Sion, and that we had identified at least some of its members. If we were right, Sion – during the period in question, at any rate – was simply another name for a movement and a conspiracy which historians had long recognised and acknowledged.

But if the *frondeurs* constituted an enclave of opposition to Mazarin, they were not the only such enclave. There were others as well, overlapping enclaves which functioned not only during the Fronde but long afterwards. The 'Prieuré documents' themselves refer repeatedly and insistently to the Compagnie du Saint-Sacrement. They imply, quite clearly, that the Compagnie was in fact Sion, or a façade for Sion, operating under another name. And certainly the Compagnie – in its structure, organisation, activities and modes of operation – conformed to the picture we had begun to form of Sion.

The Compagnie du Saint-Sacrement was a highly organised and efficient secret society. There is no question of it being fictitious. On the contrary, its existence has been acknowledged by its contemporaries, as well as by subsequent historians. It has been exhaustively documented, and numerous books and articles have been devoted to it. Its name is familiar enough in France, and it continues to enjoy a certain fashionable mystique. Some of its own papers have even come to light.

The Compagnie is said to have been founded, between 1627 and 1629, by a nobleman associated with Gaston d'Orléans. The individuals who guided and shaped its policies remained scrupulously anonymous, however, and are still so today. The only names definitively associated with it are those of intermediate or lower-ranking members of its hierarchy – the 'front men', so to speak, who acted on instructions from above. One of these was the brother of the duchess of Longueville. Another was Charles Fouquet, brother of Louis XIV's Superintendent of Finances. And there was the uncle of the philosopher Fénelon who, half a century later, exerted a profound influence on Freemasonry through the Chevalier Ramsay. Among those most prominently associated with the Compagnie were the mysterious figures now known as Saint Vincent de Paul, and Nicolas Pavillon, bishop of Alet, the town a few miles from Rennes-le-Château, and Jean-Jacques Olier, founder of the Seminary of Saint Sulpice. Indeed Saint Sulpice is now generally acknowledged to have been the Compagnie's 'centre of operations'.[9]

In its organisation and activities the Compagnie echoed the Order of the Temple and prefigured later Freemasonry. Working from Saint Sulpice, it established an intricate network of provincial branches or chapters. Provincial members remained ignorant of their directors' identities. They were often manipulated on behalf of objectives they themselves did not share. They were even forbidden to contact each

other except via Paris, thus ensuring a highly centralised control. And even in Paris the architects of the society remained unknown to those who obediently served them. In short the Compagnie comprised a hydra-headed organisation with an invisible heart. To this day it is not known who constituted the heart. Nor what constituted the heart. But it is known that the heart beat in accordance with some veiled and weighty secret. Contemporary accounts refer explicitly to 'the Secret which is the core of the Compagnie'. According to one of the society's statutes, discovered long afterwards, 'The primary channel which shapes the spirit of the Compagnie, and which is essential to it, is the Secret.'[10]

So far as uninitiated novice members were concerned, the Compagnie was ostensibly devoted to charitable work, especially in regions devastated by the Wars of Religion and subsequently by the Fronde – in Picardy, for instance, Champagne and Lorraine. It is now generally accepted, however, that this

Base of the astronomical gnomon, Saint Sulpice Church. Note the brass strip, which has run across the church floor to bisect the monument. Part of both text and design have been chiselled out, as if in an attempt at concealment.

'charitable work' was merely a convenient and ingenious façade, which had little to do with the Compagnie's real *raison d'être*. The real *raison d'être* was twofold – to engage in what was called 'pious espionage', gathering 'intelligence information', and to infiltrate the most important offices in the land, including circles in direct proximity to the throne.

In both of these objectives the Compagnie seems to have enjoyed a signal success. As a member of the royal 'Council of Conscience', for example, Vincent de Paul became confessor to Louis XIII. He was also an intimate adviser to Louis XIV – until his opposition to Mazarin forced him to resign this position. And the queen mother, Anne of Austria, was, in many respects, a hapless pawn of the Compagnie, who – for a time at any rate – managed to turn her against Mazarin. But the Compagnie did not confine itself exclusively to the throne. By the mid-seventeenth century, it could wield power through the aristocracy, the *parlement*, the judiciary and the police – so much so, that on a number of

The brass strip which crosses the floor of Saint Sulpice. On a specific date, originally January 17th, the sun shines through a small, clear glass panel to strike the brass strip. As the sun rises, the ray moves along the strip, eventually reaching the top of the gnomon.

occasions these bodies openly dared to defy the king.

In our researches we found no historian, writing either at the time or more recently, who adequately explained the Compagnie du Saint-Sacrement. Most authorities depict it as a militant arch-Catholic organisation, a bastion of rigidly entrenched and fanatic orthodoxy. The same authorities claim that it devoted itself to weeding out heretics. But, why, in a devoutly Catholic country, should such an organisation have had to function with such strict secrecy? And who constituted a 'heretic' at that time? Protestants? Jansenists? In fact, there were numerous Protestants and Jansenists within the ranks of the Compagnie.

In 1988, the Canadian writer Michael Bradley published a book entitled *Holy Grail across the Atlantic*[i] in which he traced aspects of our story to North America. According to Bradley, the 'real power behind the founding of Montreal' was the Compagnie du Saint-Sacrement. In 1641, the Compagnie despatched 50 settlers under conditions of rigorous secrecy. These settlers established the centre of Montreal and proceeded to maintain it. In 1650, they incorporated the future city as the 'Societé de Montréal', or the Company of Montreal. For the next five decades or so, Montreal was sustained by constant injections of money from the Compagnie – some 200,000 livres in the first 30 years. Among those named as joint owners of the island of Montreal was Jean-Jacques Olier.[i] Olier, it will be remembered, is repeatedly cited by the Prieuré documents as representing their interests and forming a secret conclave at Saint Sulpice – a conclave which included Vincent de Paul, as well as Nicolas Pavillon, then Bishop of Alet, the town a few miles away from Rennes-le-Château. Among those with a particular interest in Montreal was Louis XIV's minister of finances, Nicolas Fouquet – who, along with his brother, Louis, plays a crucial role in our story. Fouquet at one point fancied claiming for himself the title 'King of America'.[ii]

i: Bradley, M., *Holy Grail across the Atlantic*, Willowdale, 1988, pp.270–280.

ii: Marcel, G., *Le Surintendent Fouquet. Vice-Roi d'Amerique*, Paris, 1885.

If the Compagnie was piously Catholic, it should, in theory, have endorsed Cardinal Mazarin – who, after all, embodied Catholic interests at the time. Yet the Compagnie militantly opposed Mazarin – so much so that the cardinal, losing his temper, vowed he would employ all his resources to destroy it. What is more, the Compagnie provoked vigorous hostility in other conventional quarters as well. The Jesuits, for instance, assiduously campaigned against it. Other Catholic authorities accused the Compagnie of 'heresy' – the very thing the Compagnie itself purported to oppose. In 1651 the bishop of Toulouse charged the Compagnie with 'impious practices' and hinted at something highly irregular in its induction ceremonies[11] – a curious echo of the charges levelled against the Templars. He even threatened members of the society with excommunication. Most of them brazenly defied this threat – an extremely singular response from supposedly 'pious' Catholics.

The Compagnie had been formed when the 'Rosicrucian' furore was still at its zenith. The 'invisible confraternity' was believed to be everywhere, omnipresent – and this engendered not only panic and paranoia, but also the inevitable witch-hunts. And yet no trace was ever found of a card-carrying 'Rosicrucian' – nowhere, least of all in Catholic France. So far as France was concerned, the 'Rosicrucians' remained figments of an alarmist popular imagination. Or did they? If there were indeed 'Rosicrucian' interests determined to establish a foothold in France, what better façade could there be than an organisation dedicated to hunting out 'Rosicrucians'? In short the 'Rosicrucians' may have furthered their objectives, and gained a following in France, by posing as their own arch-enemy.

The Compagnie successfully defied both Mazarin and Louis XIV. In 1660, less than a year before Mazarin's death, the king officially pronounced against the Compagnie and ordered its dissolution. For the next five years the Compagnie cavalierly ignored the royal edict. At last, in 1665, it concluded that it could not continue to operate in its 'present form'. Accordingly all documents pertinent to the society were recalled and concealed in some secret Paris depository. This depository has never been located, although it is generally believed to have been Saint Sulpice.[12] If it was, the Compagnie's archives would thus have been available, more than two centuries later, to men like Abbé Émile Hoffet.

But though the Compagnie ceased to exist in what was then its 'present form', none the less it continued to operate at least until the beginning of the next century, still constituting a thorn in Louis XIV's side.

According to unconfirmed traditions, it survived well into the twentieth century.

Whether this last assertion is true or not, there is no question that the Compagnie survived its supposed demise in 1665. In 1667 Molière, a loyal adherent of Louis XIV, attacked the Compagnie through certain veiled but pointed allusions in *Le Tartuffe*. Despite its apparent extinction, the Compagnie retaliated by getting the play suppressed – and keeping it so for two years, despite Molière's royal patronage. And the Compagnie seems to have employed its own literary spokesmen as well. It is rumoured, for example, to have included La Rochefoucauld – who was certainly active in the Fronde. According to Gérard de Sède, La Fontaine was also a member of the Compagnie, and his charming, ostensibly innocuous fables were in fact allegorical attacks on the throne. This is not inconceivable. Louis XIV disliked La Fontaine intensely, and actively opposed his admission to the Académie Française. And La Fontaine's sponsors and patrons included the duke of Guise, the duke of Bouillon, the viscount of Turenne and the widow of Gaston d'Orléans.

In the Compagnie du Saint-Sacrement we thus found an actual secret society, much of whose history was on record. It was ostensibly Catholic, but was nevertheless linked with distinctly un-Catholic activities. It was intimately associated with certain important aristocratic families – families who had been active in the Fronde and whose genealogies figured in the 'Prieuré documents'. It was closely connected with Saint Sulpice. It worked primarily by infiltration and came to exercise enormous influence. And it was actively opposed to Cardinal Mazarin. In all these respects, it conformed almost perfectly to the image of the Prieuré de Sion as presented in the 'Prieuré documents'. If Sion was indeed active during the seventeenth century, we could reasonably assume it to have been synonymous with the Compagnie. Or perhaps with the power behind the Compagnie.

CHÂTEAU BARBERIE

According to the 'Prieuré documents', Sion's opposition to Mazarin provoked bitter retribution from the cardinal. Among the chief victims of this retribution are said to have been the Plantard family – lineal descendants of Dagobert II and the Merovingian dynasty. In 1548, the 'Prieuré documents' state, Jean des Plantard had married Marie de

Saint-Clair – thus forging another link between his family and that of the Saint-Clair/Gisors. By that time, too, the Plantard family was supposedly established at a certain Château Barberie near Nevers, in the Nivernais region of France. This château supposedly constituted the Plantards' official residence for the next century. Then, on July 11th, 1659, according to the 'Prieuré documents', Mazarin ordered the razing and total destruction of the château. In the ensuing conflagration, the Plantard family is said to have lost all its possessions.[13]

No established or conventional history book, no biography of Mazarin, confirmed these assertions. Our researches yielded no mention whatever of a Plantard family in the Nivernais, or, at first, of any Château Barberie. And yet Mazarin, for some unspecified reason, did covet the Nivernais and the duchy of Nevers. Eventually he managed to purchase them – and the contract is signed July 11th, 1659,[14] the very day on which Château Barberie is said to have been destroyed.

This prompted us to investigate the matter further. Eventually we exhumed a few disparate fragments of evidence. They were not enough to explain things, but they did attest to the veracity of the 'Prieuré documents'. In a compilation, dated 1506, of estates and holdings in the Nivernais a Barberie was indeed mentioned. A charter of 1575 mentioned a hamlet in the Nivernais called Les Plantards.[15]

Most convincing of all, it transpired that the existence of Château Barberie had in fact been definitively established. During 1874–5 members of the Society of Letters, Sciences and Arts of Nevers undertook an exploratory excavation on the site of certain ruins. It was a difficult enterprise, for the ruins were almost unrecognisable as such, the stones had been vitrified by fire and the site itself was thickly overgrown with trees. Eventually, however, remnants of a town wall and of a château were uncovered. This site is now acknowledged to have been Barberie. Before its destruction it apparently consisted of a small fortified town and château.[16] And it is within a short distance of the old hamlet of Les Plantards.

We could now say that Château Barberie indisputably existed and was destroyed by fire. And, given the hamlet of Les Plantards, there was no reason to doubt it had been owned by a family of that name. The curious fact was that there was no record of when the château had been destroyed, nor by whom. If Mazarin was responsible, he would seem to have taken extraordinary pains to eradicate all traces of his action. Indeed there seemed to have been a methodical and systematic attempt to wipe Château Barberie from the map and from history. Why embark on such a process of obliteration, unless there was something to hide?

NICOLAS FOUQUET

Mazarin had other enemies besides the *frondeurs* and the Compagnie du Saint-Sacrement. Among the most powerful of them was Nicolas Fouquet, who in 1653, had become Superintendent of Finances to Louis XIV. A gifted, precocious and ambitious man, Fouquet, within the next few years, had become the wealthiest and most powerful individual in the kingdom. He was sometimes called 'the true king of France'. And he was not without political aspirations. It was rumoured that he intended to make Brittany an independent duchy and himself its presiding duke.

Fouquet's mother was a prominent member of the Compagnie du Saint-Sacrement. So was his brother Charles, Archbishop of Narbonne in the Languedoc. His younger brother, Louis, was also an ecclesiastic. In 1656 Nicolas Fouquet dispatched Louis to Rome, for reasons which – though not necessarily mysterious – have never been explained. From Rome, Louis wrote the enigmatic letter quoted in Chapter 1 – the letter that speaks of a meeting with Poussin and a secret 'which even kings would have great pains to draw from him'. And indeed, if Louis was indiscreet in correspondence, Poussin gave nothing whatever away. His personal seal bore the motto 'Tenet Confidentiam'.

In 1661 Louis XIV ordered the arrest of Nicolas Fouquet. The charges were extremely general and nebulous. There were vague accusations of misappropriation of funds, and others, even more vague, of sedition. On the basis of these accusations, all Fouquet's goods and properties were placed under royal sequestration. But the king forbade his officers to touch the Superintendent's papers or correspondence. He insisted on sifting through these documents himself – personally and in private.

The ensuing trial dragged on for four years and became the sensation of France at the time, violently splitting and polarising public opinion. Louis Fouquet – who had met with Poussin and written the letter from Rome – was dead by then. But the Superintendent's mother and surviving brother mobilised the Compagnie de Saint-Sacrement, whose membership also included one of the presiding judges. The Compagnie threw the whole of its support behind the Superintendent, working actively through the courts and the popular mind. Louis XIV – who was not usually bloodthirsty – demanded nothing less than the death sentence. Refusing to be intimidated by him, the court passed a sentence of perpetual banishment. Still demanding death, the enraged king removed the recalcitrant judges and replaced them with others more obedient; but the Compagnie still seems to have defied him. Eventually, in 1665, Fouquet was sentenced to perpetual imprisonment. On the king's orders he was kept in rigorous isolation. He was forbidden all writing implements, all means whereby he might communicate with anyone. And any soldiers who conversed with him were allegedly consigned to prison ships or, in some cases, hanged.[17]

In 1665, the year of Fouquet's imprisonment, Poussin died in Rome. During the years that followed, Louis XIV persistently endeavoured through his agents to obtain a single painting – 'Les Bergers d'Arcadie'. In 1685 he finally managed to do so. But the painting was not placed on display – not even in the royal residence. On the contrary, it was sequestered in the king's private apartments, where no one could view it without the monarch's personal authority.

There is a footnote to Fouquet's story, for his own disgrace, whatever its causes and magnitude, was not visited on his children. By the middle of the following century Fouquet's grandson, the marquis of Belle-Isle, had become, in effect, the single most important man in France. In 1718 the marquis of Belle-Isle ceded Belle-Isle itself – a fortified island off the Breton coast – to the crown. In return he obtained certain interesting territories. One was Longueville, whose former dukes and duchesses had figured recurrently in our investigation. And another was Gisors. In 1718 the marquis of Belle-Isle became count of Gisors. In 1742 he became duke of Gisors. And in 1748 Gisors was raised to the exalted status of premier duchy.

NICOLAS POUSSIN

Poussin himself was born in 1594 in a small town called Les Andelys – a few miles, we discovered, from Gisors. As a young man he left France and established residence in Rome, where he spent the duration of his life, returning only once to his native country. He returned to France in the early 1640s at the request of Cardinal Richelieu, who had invited him to undertake a specific commission.

Although he was not actively involved in politics, and few historians have touched on his political interests, Poussin was in fact closely associated with the Fronde. He did not leave his refuge in Rome. But his correspondence of the period reveals him to have been deeply committed to the anti-Mazarin movement, and on surprisingly familiar terms with a number of influential *frondeurs* – so much so, indeed, that, in speaking of them, he repeatedly uses the word 'we', thus clearly implicating himself.[18]

We had already traced the motifs of the underground stream Alpheus, of Arcadia and Arcadian shepherds, to René d'Anjou. We now undertook to find an antecedent for the specific phrase in Poussin's painting – 'Et in Arcadia Ego'. It appeared in an earlier painting by Poussin, in which the tomb is surmounted by a skull and does not constitute an edifice of its own, but is embedded in the side of a cliff. In the foreground of this painting a bearded water-deity reposes in an attitude of brooding moroseness – the river god Alpheus, lord of the underground stream. The work dates from 1630 or 1635, five or ten years earlier than the more familiar version of 'Les Bergers d'Arcadie'.

The phrase 'Et in Arcadia Ego' made its public début between 1618 and 1623 in a painting by Giovanni Francesco Guercino – a painting which constitutes the real basis for Poussin's work. In Guercino's painting two shepherds, entering a clearing in a forest, have just happened upon a stone sepulchre. It bears the now famous inscription, and there is a large skull resting on top of it. Whatever the symbolic significance of this work, Guercino himself raised a number of questions. Not only was he well versed in esoteric tradition. He also seems to have been

Carved symbols on an external beam in the medieval 'House of the Jews' at Alet-les-Bains. A curiosity is the addition of the Chinese yin-yang symbol.

conversant with the lore of secret societies, and some of his other paintings deal with themes of a specifically Masonic character – a good twenty years before lodges started proliferating in England and Scotland. One painting, 'The Raising of the Master', pertains explicitly to the Masonic legend of Hiram Abiff, architect and builder of Solomon's temple. It was executed nearly a century before the Hiram legend is generally believed to have found its way into Masonry.[19]

In the 'Prieuré documents', 'Et in Arcadia Ego' is said to have been the official device of the Plantard family since at least the twelfth centu-

'Et in Arcadia Ego' by Guercino, c.1618. This is the first recorded appearance of this phrase.

209

Window in the shape of the Star of David in the church at Alet-les-Bains, near Rennes-le-Château.

ry, when Jean de Plantard married Idoine de Gisors. According to one source quoted in the 'Prieuré documents', it is cited as such as early as 1210 by one Robert, Abbot of Mont-Saint-Michel.[20] We were unable to obtain access to the archives of Mont-Saint-Michel, and so could not verify this assertion. Our research convinced us, however, that the date of 1210 was demonstrably wrong. In point of fact, there was no abbot of Mont-Saint-Michel named Robert in 1210. On the other hand, one Robert de Torigny was indeed abbot of Mont-Saint-Michel between 1154 and 1186. And Robert de Torigny is known to have been a prolific and assiduous historian – whose hobbies included collecting mottoes, devices, blazons and coats-of-arms of noble families throughout Christendom.[21]

Whatever the origin of the phrase, 'Et in Arcadia Ego' seems, for both Guercino and Poussin, to have been more than a line of elegiac poetry. Quite clearly it seems to have enjoyed some important secret significance, which was recognisable or identifiable to certain other people – the equivalent, in short, of a Masonic sign or password. And it is precisely in such terms that one statement in the 'Prieuré documents' defines the character of symbolic or allegorical art:

> Allegorical works have this advantage, that a single word suffices to illumine connections which the multitude cannot grasp. Such works are available to everyone, but their significance addresses itself to an élite. Above and beyond the masses, sender and receiver understand each other. The inexplicable success of certain works derives from this quality of allegory, which constitutes not a mere fashion, but a form of esoteric communication.[22]

In its context, this statement was made with reference to Poussin. As Frances Yates has demonstrated, however, it might equally well be applied to the works of Leonardo, Botticelli and other Renaissance artists. It might also be applied to later figures – to Nodier, Hugo, Debussy, Cocteau and their respective circles.

ROSSLYN CHAPEL AND SHUGBOROUGH HALL

Opposite; The 'Apprentice Pillar' inside Rosslyn Chapel

In our previous research we had found a number of important links between Sion's alleged Grand Masters of the seventeenth and eigh-

Rosslyn Chapel, 3 miles south of Edinburgh, Scotland. Construction began in 1446 and it was intended to be part of a large collegiate church which was never built although some foundations remain.

teenth centuries and European Freemasonry. In the course of our study of Freemasonry we discovered certain other links as well. These additional links did not relate to the alleged Grand Masters as such, but they did relate to other aspects of our investigation.

Thus, for example, we encountered repeated references to the Sinclair family – Scottish branch of the Norman Saint-Clair/Gisors family. Their domain at Rosslyn was only a few miles from the former Scottish headquarters of the Knights Templar, and the chapel at Rosslyn – built between 1446 and 1486 – has long been associated with both Freemasonry and the Rose-Croix. In a charter believed to date from 1601, moreover, the Sinclairs are recognised as 'hereditary Grand Masters of Scottish Masonry'[23]. According to Masonic sources, however, the hereditary Grand Mastership was conferred on the Sinclairs by James II, who ruled between 1437 and 1460 – the age of René d'Anjou.

Another and rather more mysterious piece of our jigsaw puzzle also surfaced in Britain – this time in Staffordshire, which had been a hotbed for Masonic activity in the early and mid-seventeenth century. When Charles Radclyffe, alleged Grand Master of Sion, escaped from

Newgate Prison in 1714, he was aided by his cousin, the earl of Lichfield. Later in the century the earl of Lichfield's line became extinct and his title lapsed. It was bought in the early nineteenth century by descendants of the Anson family, who are the present earls of Lichfield.

The seat of the present earls of Lichfield is Shugborough Hall in Staffordshire. Formerly a bishop's residence, Shugborough was purchased by the Anson family in 1697. During the following century it was the residence of the brother of George Anson, the famous admiral who circumnavigated the globe. When George Anson died in 1762, an elegiac poem was read aloud in Parliament. One stanza of this poem reads:

> Upon that storied marble cast thine eye.
> The scene commands a moralising sigh.
> E'en in Arcadia's bless'd Elysian plains,
> Amidst the laughing nymphs and sportive swains,
> See festal joy subside, with melting grace,
> And pity visit the half-smiling face;
> Where now the dance, the lute, the nuptial feast,
> The passion throbbing in the lover's breast,
> Life's emblem here, in youth and vernal bloom,
> But reason's finger pointing at the tomb![24]

This would seem to be an explicit allusion to Poussin's painting and the inscription 'Et in Arcadia Ego' – right down to the 'finger pointing at the tomb'. And in the grounds of Shugborough there is an imposing marble bas-relief, executed at the command of the Anson family between 1761 and 1767. This bas-relief comprises a reproduction – reversed, mirror-fashion – of Poussin's 'Les Bergers d'Arcadie'. And immediately below it, there is an enigmatic inscription, which no one has ever satisfactorily deciphered:

O.U.O.S.V.A.V.V.

D   M

THE POPE'S SECRET LETTER

In 1738 Pope Clement XII issued a Papal Bull condemning and excommunicating all Freemasons, whom he pronounced 'enemies of the Roman Church'. It has never been altogether clear why they should have been regarded as such – especially as many of them, like the

Jacobites at the time, were ostensibly Catholic. Perhaps the pope was aware of the connection we had discovered between early Freemasonry and the anti-Roman 'Rosicrucians' of the seventeenth century. In any case some light may be shed on the matter by a letter released and published for the first time in 1962. This letter had been written by Pope Clement XII and addressed to an unknown correspondent. In its text the pope declares that Masonic thought rests on a heresy we had encountered repeatedly before – the denial of Jesus's divinity. And he further asserts that the guiding spirits, the 'masterminds', behind Freemasonry are the same as those who provoked the Lutheran Reformation.[25] The pope may well have been paranoid; but it is important to note that he is not speaking of nebulous currents of thought or vague traditions. On the contrary, he is speaking of a highly organised group of individuals – a sect, an order, a secret society – who, through the ages, have dedicated themselves to subverting the edifice of Catholic Christianity.

THE ROCK OF SION

In the late eighteenth century, when different Masonic systems were proliferating wildly, the so-called Oriental Rite of Memphis[26] made its appearance. In this rite the name Ormus occurred, to our knowledge, for the first time – the name allegedly adopted by the Prieuré Sion between 1188 and 1307. According to the Oriental Rite of Memphis, Ormus was an Egyptian sage who, around A.D. 46, amalgamated pagan and Christian mysteries and, in so doing, founded the Rose-Croix.

In other eighteenth century Masonic rites there are repeated references to the 'Rock of Sion' – the same Rock of Sion which, as the 'Prieuré documents' quote, rendered the 'royal tradition' established by Godfroi and Baudouin de Bouillon 'equal' to that of any other reigning dynasty in Europe. We had previously assumed that the Rock of Sion was simply Mount Sion – the 'high hill' south of Jerusalem on which Godfroi built an abbey to house the order which became the Prieuré de Sion. But Masonic sources ascribe an additional significance to the Rock of Sion. Given their preoccupation with the Temple of Jerusalem, it is not surprising that they refer one to specific passages in the Bible. And in these passages the Rock of Sion is something more than a high hill. It is a particular stone overlooked or unjustifiably neglected during the building of the Temple, which must subsequently be retrieved and incorporated as the structure's keystone. According to Psalm 118, for example:

The stone which the builders refused is become the head stone of the corner.

In Matthew 21:42 Jesus alludes specifically to this psalm:

Did ye never read in the scriptures, The stone which the builders rejected, the same is become the head of the corner.

In Romans 9:33 there is another reference, rather more ambiguous:

Behold, I lay in Sion a stumblingstone and rock of offence: and whosoever believeth on him shall not be ashamed.

In Acts 4:11 the Rock of Sion might well be interpreted as a metaphor for Jesus himself:

by the name of Jesus Christ of Nazareth . . . doth this man stand here before you whole. This is the stone which was set at nought of you builders, which is become the head of the corner.

In Ephesians 2:20 the equation of Jesus with the Rock of Sion becomes more apparent:

built upon the foundation of the apostles and prophets, Jesus Christ himself being the chief corner stone.

And in 1 Peter 2:3–8 this equation is made even more explicit:

the Lord is gracious. To whom coming, as unto a living stone, disallowed indeed of men, but chosen of God, and precious. Ye also, as lively stones, are built up a spiritual house, an holy priesthood, to offer up spiritual sacrifices, acceptable to God by Jesus Christ. Wherefore it is also contained in the scripture, Behold, I lay in Sion a chief corner stone, elect, precious: and he that believeth on him shall not be confounded. Unto you therefore which believe he is precious: but unto them which be disobedient, the stone which the builders disallowed, the same is made the head of the corner, And a stone of stumbling, and a rock of offence, even to them which stumble at the word, being disobedient; whereunto also they were appointed.

In the very next verse, the text goes on to stress themes whose significance did not become apparent to us until later. It speaks of an elect line of kings who are both spiritual and secular leaders, a line of priest-kings:

> But you are a chosen generation, a royal priesthood, an holy nation, a peculiar people . . .

What were we to make of these baffling passages? What were we to make of the Rock of Sion – the keystone of the Temple, which seemed to figure so saliently among the 'inner secrets' of Freemasonry? What were we to make of the explicit identification of this keystone with Jesus himself? And what were we to make of that 'royal tradition' which – because founded on the Rock of Sion or on Jesus himself – was 'equal' to the reigning dynasties of Europe during the Crusades?[27]

THE CATHOLIC MODERNIST MOVEMENT

In 1833 Jean Baptiste Pitois, Charles Nodier's former disciple at the Arsenal Library, was an official in the Ministry of Public Education.[28] And in that year the Ministry undertook an ambitious project – to publish all hitherto suppressed documents pertinent to the history of France. Two committees were formed to preside over the enterprise. These committees included, among others, Victor Hugo, Jules Michelet and an authority on the Crusades, Baron Emmanuel Rey.

Among the works subsequently published under the auspices of the Ministry of Public Education was Michelet's monumental *Le Procès des Templiers* – an exhaustive compilation of Inquisition records dealing with the trials of the Knights Templar. Under the same auspices Baron Rey published a number of works dealing with the Crusades and the Frankish kingdom of Jerusalem. In these works there appeared in print for the first time original charters pertaining to the Prieuré de Sion. At certain points the texts Rey quotes are almost verbatim with passages in the 'Prieuré documents'.

In 1875 Baron Rey co-founded the Société de l'Orient Latin ('Society of the Latin – or Frankish – Middle East'). Based in Geneva, this society devoted itself to ambitious archaeological projects. It also published its own magazine, the *Revue de l'Orient Latin*, which is now one of the primary sources for modern historians like Sir Steven Runciman. The *Revue de l'Orient Latin* reproduced a number of additional charters of the Prieuré de Sion.

Rey's research was typical of a new form of historical scholarship appearing in Europe at the time, most prominently in Germany, which constituted an extremely serious threat to the Church. The dissemination of Darwinian thought and agnosticism had already produced a 'crisis of faith' in the late nineteenth century, and the new scholarship magnified the crisis. In the past, historical research had been, for the most part, an unreliable affair, resting on highly tenuous foundations – on legend and tradition, on personal memoirs, on exaggerations promulgated for the sake of one or another cause. Only in the nineteenth century did German scholars begin introducing the rigorous, meticulous techniques that are now accepted as commonplace, the stock-in-trade of any responsible historian. Such preoccupation with critical examination, with investigation of first-hand sources, with cross-references and exact chronology, established the conventional stereotype of the Teutonic pedant. But if German writers of the period tended to lose themselves in minutiae, they also provided a solid basis for inquiry. And for a number of major archaeological discoveries as well. The most famous example, of course, is Heinrich Schliemann's excavation of the site of Troy.

It was only a matter of time before the techniques of German scholarship were applied, with similar diligence, to the Bible. And the Church, which rested on unquestioning acceptance of dogma, was well aware that the Bible itself could not withstand such critical scrutiny. In his best-selling and highly controversial *Life of Jesus,* Ernest Rénan had already applied German methodology to the New Testament, and the results, for Rome, were extremely embarrassing.

The Catholic Modernist Movement arose initially as a response to this new challenge. Its original objective was to produce a generation of ecclesiastical experts trained in the German tradition, who could defend the literal truth of Scripture with all the heavy ordnance of critical scholarship. As it transpired, however, the plan backfired. The more the Church sought to equip its younger clerics with the tools for combat in the modern polemical world, the more those same clerics began to desert the cause for which they had been recruited. Critical examination of the Bible revealed a multitude of inconsistencies, discrepancies and implications that were positively inimical to Roman dogma. And by the end of the century the Modernists were no longer the élite shock-troops the Church had hoped they would be, but defectors and incipient heretics. Indeed, they posed the most serious threat the Church had experienced since Martin Luther, and brought the entire edifice of Catholicism to the brink of a schism unparalleled for centuries.

The hotbed for Modernist activity – as it had been for the Compagnie du Saint-Sacrement – was Saint Sulpice in Paris. Indeed, one of the most resonant voices in the Modernist movement was the man who was director of the Seminary of Saint Sulpice from 1852 to 1884.[29] From Saint Sulpice Modernist attitudes spread rapidly to the rest of France, and to Italy and Spain. According to these attitudes, Biblical texts were not unimpugnably authoritative, but had to be understood in the specific context of their time. And the Modernists also rebelled against the increasing centralisation of ecclesiastical power – especially the recently instituted doctrine of papal infallibility,[30] which ran flagrantly counter to the new trend. Before long Modernist attitudes were being disseminated not only by intellectual clerics, but by distinguished and influential writers as well. Figures like Roger Martin du Gard in France, and Miguel de Unamuno in Spain, were among the primary spokesmen for Modernism.

The Church responded with predictable vigour and wrath. The Modernists were accused of being Freemasons. Many of them were suspended or even excommunicated, and their books were placed on the Index. In 1903 Pope Leo XIII established the Pontifical Biblical Commission to monitor the work of scriptural scholars. In 1907 Pope Pius X issued a formal condemnation of Modernism. And on September 1st, 1910, the Church demanded of its clerics an oath against Modernist tendencies.

Nevertheless Modernism continued to flourish until the First World War diverted public attention to other concerns. Until 1914 it remained a *cause célèbre*. One Modernist author, the Abbé Turmel, proved a particularly mischievous individual. While ostensibly behaving impeccably at his teaching post in Brittany, he published a series of Modernist works under no less than fourteen different pseudonyms. Each of them was placed on the Index, but not until 1929 was Turmel identified as their author. Needless to say, he was then summarily excommunicated.

In the meantime Modernism spread to Britain, where it was warmly welcomed and endorsed by the Anglican Church. Among its Anglican adherents was William Temple, later archbishop of Canterbury, who declared that Modernism 'is what most educated people already believe'.[31] One of Temple's associates was Canon A. L. Lilley. And Lilley knew the priest from whom we had received that portentous letter – which spoke of 'incontrovertible proof' that Jesus did not die on the cross.

Lilley, as we knew, had worked for some time in Paris, where he made the acquaintance of the Abbé Émile Hoffet – the man to whom Saunière brought the parchments found at Rennes-le-Château. With his expertise in history, language and linguistics, Hoffet was the typical young Modernist scholar of his age. He had not been trained at Saint Sulpice, however. On the contrary, he had been trained in Lorraine. At the Seminary School of Sion: *La Colline inspirée*.[32]

THE PROTOCOLS OF SION

One of the most persuasive testimonials we found to the existence and activities of the Prieuré de Sion dated from the late nineteenth century. The testimonial in question is well enough known – but it is not recognised as a testimonial. On the contrary it has always been associated with more sinister things. It has played a notorious role in recent history and still tends to arouse such violent emotions, bitter antagonisms and gruesome memories that most writers are happy to dismiss it out of hand. To the extent that this testimonial has contributed significantly to human prejudice and suffering, such a reaction is perfectly understandable. But if the testimonial has been criminally misused, our researches convinced us that it has also been seriously misunderstood.

The role of Rasputin at the court of Nicholas and Alexandra of Russia is more or less generally known. It is not generally known, however, that there were influential, even powerful esoteric enclaves at the Russian court long before Rasputin. During the 1890s and 1900s one such enclave formed itself around an individual known as Monsieur Philippe, and around his mentor, who made periodic visits to the imperial court at Petersburg. And Monsieur Philippe's mentor was none other than the man called Papus[33] – the French esotericist associated with Jules Doinel (founder of the neo-Cathar church in the Languedoc), Péladan (who claimed to have discovered Jesus's tomb), Emma Calvé and Claude Debussy. In a word, the 'French occult revival' of the late nineteenth century had not only spread to Petersburg. Its representatives also enjoyed the privileged status of personal confidants to the czar and czarina.

However, the esoteric enclave of Papus and Monsieur Philippe was actively opposed by certain other powerful interests – the Grand Duchess Elizabeth, for example, who was intent on installing her own favourites in proximity to the imperial throne. One of the grand duchess's favourites was a rather contemptible individual known to posterity under the pseudonym of Sergei Nilus. Sometime around 1903 Nilus presented a highly controversial document to the czar – a document that supposedly bore witness to a dangerous conspiracy. But if Nilus expected the czar's gratitude for his disclosure, he must have been grievously disappointed. The czar declared the document to be an outrageous fabrication, and ordered all copies of it to be destroyed. And Nilus was banished from the court in disgrace.

Of course the document – or, at any rate, a copy of it – survived. In 1903 it was serialised in a newspaper but failed to attract any interest. In 1905 it was published again – this time as an appendix to a book by a distinguished mystical philosopher, Vladimir Soloviov. At this point it began to attract attention. In the years that followed it became one of the single most infamous documents of the twentieth century.

The document in question was a tract, or, more strictly speaking, a purported social and political programme. It has appeared under a variety of slightly differing titles, the most common of which is *The Protocols of the Elders of Sion*.[34] The *Protocols* allegedly issued from specifically Jewish sources. And for a great many anti-Semites at the time they were convincing proof of an 'international Jewish conspiracy'. In 1919, for example, they were distributed to troops of the White Russian Army – and these troops, during the next two years, massacred some 60,000 Jews who were held responsible for the 1917 Revolution. By 1919 the *Protocols* were also being circulated by Alfred Rosenberg, later the chief racial theoretician and propagandist for the National Socialist Party in Germany. In *Mein Kampf* Hitler used the *Protocols* to fuel his own fanatical prejudices, and is said to have believed unquestioningly in their authenticity. In England the *Protocols* were immediately accorded credence by the *Morning Post*. Even *The* Times, in 1921, took them seriously and only later admitted its error. Experts today concur – and rightly so, we concluded – that the *Protocols*, at least in their present form, are a vicious and insidious forgery. Nevertheless, they are still being circulated – in Latin America, in Spain, even in Britain – as anti-Semitic propaganda.[35]

The *Protocols* propound in outline a blueprint for nothing less than total world domination. On first reading they would seem to be the Machiavellian programme – a kind of inter-office memo, so to speak – for a group of individuals determined to impose a new world order, with themselves as supreme despots. The text advocates a many-tentacled hydra-headed conspiracy dedicated to disorder and anarchy, to toppling certain existing régimes, infiltrating Freemasonry and other such organisations, and eventually seizing absolute control of the Western world's social, political and economic institutions. And the anonymous authors of the *Protocols* declare explicitly that they 'stage-managed' whole peoples 'according to a political plan which no one has so much as guessed at in the course of many centuries'.[36]

To a modern reader the *Protocols* might seem to have been devised by some fictitious organisation like SPECTRE – James Bond's adversary in Ian Fleming's novels. When they were first publicised, however, the *Protocols* were alleged to have been composed at an International Judaic Congress which convened in Basle in 1897. This allegation has long since been disproved. The earliest copies of the *Protocols*, for example, are known to have been written in French – and the 1897 Congress in Basle did not include a single French delegate. Moreover, a copy of the *Protocols* is known to have been in circulation as early as 1884 – a full thirteen years before the Basle Congress met. The 1884 copy of the *Protocols* surfaced in the hands of a member of a Masonic lodge – the same lodge of which Papus was a member and subsequently Grand Master.[37] Moreover, it was in this same lodge that the tradition of Ormus had first appeared – the legendary Egyptian sage who amalgamated pagan and Christian mysteries and founded the Rose-Croix.

Modern scholars have established in fact that the *Protocols*, in their published form, are based at least in part on a satirical work written and printed in Geneva in 1864. The work was composed as an attack on Napoleon III by a man named Maurice Joly, who was subsequently imprisoned. Joly is said to have been a member of a Rose-Croix order. Whether this is true or not, he was a friend of Victor Hugo; and Hugo, who shared Joly's antipathy to Napoleon III, was a member of a Rose-Croix order.

It can thus be proved conclusively that the *Protocols* did not issue from the Judaic Congress at Basle in 1897. That being so, the obvious question is whence they did issue. Modern scholars have dismissed them as a total forgery, a wholly spurious document concocted by anti-

Semitic interests intent on discrediting Judaism. And yet the *Protocols* themselves argue strongly against such a conclusion. They contain, for example, a number of enigmatic references – references that are clearly not Judaic. But these references are so clearly not Judaic that they cannot plausibly have been fabricated by a forger either. No anti-Semitic forger with even a modicum of intelligence would possibly have concocted such references in order to discredit Judaism. For no one would have believed these references to be of Judaic origin.

Thus, for instance, the text of the *Protocols* ends with a single statement, 'Signed by the representatives of Sion of the 33rd Degree.'[38]

Why would an anti-Semitic forger have made up such a statement? Why would he not have attempted to incriminate all Jews, rather than just a few – the few who constitute 'the representatives of Sion of the 33rd Degree'? Why would he not declare that the document was signed by, say, the representatives of the International Judaic Congress? In fact, the 'representatives of Sion of the 33rd Degree' would hardly seem to refer to Judaism at all, or to any 'international Jewish conspiracy'. If anything, it would seem to refer to something specifically Masonic. And the 33rd Degree in Freemasonry is that of the so-called 'Ancient and Accepted Scottish Rite' which emerges mysteriously out of French Freemasonry in the mid eighteenth century.

The *Protocols* contain other even more flagrant anomalies. The text speaks repeatedly, for example, of the advent of a 'Masonic Kingdom', and of a 'King of the blood of Sion', who will preside over this 'Masonic Kingdom'. It asserts that the future king will be of 'the dynastic roots of King David'. It affirms that 'the King of the Jews will be the real Pope' and 'the patriarch of an international church'. And it concludes in a most cryptic fashion, 'Certain members of the seed of David will prepare the Kings and their heirs . . . Only the King and the three who stood sponsor for him will know what is coming.'[39]

As an expression of Judaic thought, real or fabricated, such statements are blatantly absurd. Since Biblical times no king has figured in Judaic tradition, and the very principle of kingship has become utterly irrelevant. The concept of a king would have been as meaningless to Jews of 1897 as it would be to Jews today; and no forger can have been ignorant of this fact. Indeed the references quoted would appear to be more Christian than Judaic. For the last two millennia the only 'King of the Jews' has been Jesus himself – and Jesus, according to the Gospels, was of the 'dynastic roots of David'. If one is fabricating a document and ascribing it to a Jewish conspiracy, why include such patently Christian echoes? Why speak of so specifically and uniquely Christian a concept as a pope? Why speak of an 'international church' rather than an international synagogue or an international temple? And why include the enigmatic allusion to 'the King and the three who stood sponsor' – which is less suggestive of Judaism and Christianity than it is of the secret societies of Johann Valentin Andrea and Charles Nodier? If the *Protocols* issued wholly from a propagandist's anti-Semitic imagination, it is difficult to imagine a propagandist so inept, or so ignorant and uninformed.

On the basis of prolonged and systematic research, we reached certain conclusions about the *Protocols of the Elders of Sion*. They are as follows.

1) There was an original text on which the published version of the Protocols was based. This original text was not a forgery. On the contrary it was authentic. But it had nothing whatever to do with Judaism or an 'international Jewish conspiracy'. It issued rather from some Masonic organisation or Masonically oriented secret society which incorporated the word 'Sion'.

2) The original text on which the published version of the Protocols was based need not have been provocative or inflammatory in its language. But it may well have included a programme for gaining power, for infiltrating Freemasonry, for controlling social, political and economic institutions. Such a programme would have been perfectly in keeping with the secret societies of the Renaissance, as well as with the Compagnie du Saint-Sacrement and the institutions of Andrea and Nodier.

3) The original text on which the published version of the Protocols was based fell into the hands of Sergei Nilus. Nilus did not at first intend it to discredit Judaism. On the contrary, he brought it to the czar with the intention of discrediting the esoteric enclave at the imperial court – the enclave of Papus, Monsieur Philippe and others who were members of the secret society in question. Before doing so, he almost certainly doctored the language, rendering it far more venomous and inflammatory than it initially was. When the czar spurned him, Nilus then released the Protocols in their doctored form for publication. They had failed in their primary objective of compromising Papus and Monsieur Philippe. But they might still serve a secondary purpose – that of fostering anti-Semitism. Although Nilus's chief tar-

gets had been Papus and Monsieur Philippe, he was hostile to Judaism as well.

4) The published version of the Protocols is not, therefore, a totally fabricated text. It is rather a radically altered text. But despite the alterations certain vestiges of the original version can be discerned – as in a palimpsest, or as in passages of the Bible. These vestiges – which referred to a king, a pope, an international church, and to Sion – probably meant little or nothing to Nilus. He certainly would not have invented them himself. But if they were already there, he would have had no reason, given his ignorance, to excise them. And while such vestiges might have been irrelevant to Judaism, they might have been extremely relevant to a secret society. As we learned subsequently, they were – and still are – of paramount importance to the Prieuré de Sion.

THE HIÉRON DU VAL D'OR

While we pursued our independent research, new 'Prieuré documents' had continued to appear. Some of them – privately printed works, like the *Dossiers secrets*, and intended for limited circulation – were made available to us through the offices of friends in France or through the Bibliothèque Nationale. Others appeared in book form, newly published and released on the market for the first time.

In some of these works there was additional information on the late nineteenth century, and specifically on Bérenger Saunière. According to one such 'up-dated' account, Saunière did not discover the fateful parchments in his church by accident. On the contrary he is said to have been directed to them by emissaries of the Prieuré de Sion – who visited him at Rennes-le-Château and enlisted him as their factotum. In late 1916 Saunière is reported to have defied the emissaries of Sion and quarrelled with them.[40] If this is true, the curé's death in January 1917 acquires a more sinister quality than is generally ascribed to it. Ten days before his death he had been in satisfactory health. Nevertheless ten days before his death a coffin was ordered on his behalf. The receipt for the coffin, dated January 12th, 1917, is made out to Saunière's confidante and housekeeper, Marie Denarnaud.

A more recent and, if anything, more apparently authoritative 'Prieuré' publication elaborates further on Saunière's story – and would seem to confirm, at least in part, the account summarised above.

According to this publication, Saunière himself was little more than a pawn and his role in the mystery of Rennes-le-Château has been much exaggerated. The real force behind the events at the mountain village is said to have been Saunière's friend, the Abbé Henri Boudet, curé of the adjacent village of Rennes-le-Bains.[41]

Boudet is said to have provided Saunière with all his money – a total of thirteen million francs between 1887 and 1915. And Boudet is said to have guided Saunière on his various projects – the public works, the construction of the Villa Bethania and the Tour Magdala. He is also said to have supervised the restoration of the church at Rennes-le-Château, and to have designed Saunière's perplexing Stations of the Cross – as a kind of illustrated version, or visual equivalent, of a cryptic book of his own.

According to this recent 'Prieuré' publication, Saunière remained essentially ignorant of the real secret for which he acted as custodian – until Boudet, in the throes of approaching death, confided it to him in March 1915. According to the same publication, Marie Denarnaud, Saunière's housekeeper, was in fact Boudet's agent. It was through her that Boudet supposedly transmitted instructions to Saunière. And it was to her that all money was made payable. Or, rather, most money. For Boudet, between 1885 and 1901, is said to have paid 7,655,250 francs to the bishop of Carcassonne – the man who, at his own expense, dispatched Saunière to Paris with the parchments. The bishop, too, would seem then to have been essentially in Boudet's employ. It is certainly an incongruous situation – an important regional bishop being the paid servitor of a humble, backwater parish priest. And the parish priest himself? For whom was Boudet working? What interests did he represent? What can have given him the power to enlist the services, and the silence, of his ecclesiastical superior? And who can have furnished him with such vast financial resources to be dispensed so prodigally? These questions are not answered explicitly. But the answer is constantly implicit – the Prieuré de Sion.

Further light on the matter was shed by another recent work – which, like its predecessors, seemed to draw on 'privileged sources' of information. The work in question is *Le Trésor du triangle d'or* ('The Treasure of the Golden Triangle') by Jean-Luc Chaumeil, published in 1979. According to M. Chaumeil, a number of clerics involved in the enigma of Rennes-le-Château – Saunière, Boudet, quite probably others like Hoffet, Hoffet's uncle at Saint Sulpice and the bishop of

Two pages from a large archive of Saunière's monthly accounts in the late nineteenth century.

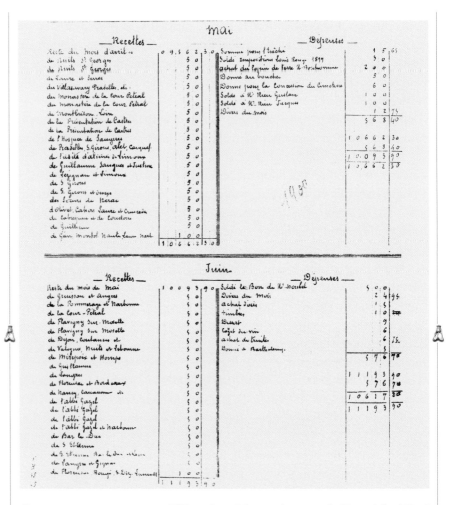

Carcassonne – were affiliated with a form of 'Scottish Rite' Freemasonry. This Freemasonry, M. Chaumeil declares, differed from most other forms in that it was 'Christian, Hermetic and aristocratic'. In short, it did not, like many rites of Freemasonry, consist primarily of free-thinkers and atheists. On the contrary, it seems to have been deeply religious and magically oriented – emphasising a sacred social and political hierarchy, a divine order, an underlying cosmic plan. And the upper grades or degrees of this Freemasonry, according to M. Chaumeil, were the lower grades or degrees of the Prieuré de Sion.[42]

In our own researches we had already encountered a Freemasonry of the sort M. Chaumeil describes. Indeed M. Chaumeil's description could readily be applied to the original 'Scottish Rite' introduced by Charles Radclyffe and his associates. Both Radclyffe's Masonry and the

titres	I'	auteurs	vol.	Prix	Je trouve	

Masonry M. Chaumeil describes would have been acceptable, despite papal condemnation, to devout Catholics – whether eighteenth-century Jacobites or nineteenth-century French priests. In both cases Rome certainly disapproved – and quite vehemently. Nevertheless the individuals involved seem not only to have persisted in regarding themselves as Christians and Catholics. They also seem, on the basis of available evidence, to have received a major and exhilarating transfusion of faith – a transfusion that enabled them to see themselves as, if anything, more truly Christian than the papacy.

Although M. Chaumeil is both vague and evasive, he strongly implies that in the years prior to 1914 the Freemasonry of which Boudet and Saunière were members became amalgamated with another esoteric institution – an institution that might well explain some of the curious references to a monarch in the *Protocols of the Elders of Sion*, especially if, as M. Chaumeil further intimates, the real power behind this other institution was also the Prieuré de Sion.

The institution in question was called the Hiéron du Val d'Or – which would seem to be a verbal transposition of that recurring site, Orval.[43] The Hiéron du Val d'Or was a species of secret political society founded, it would appear, around 1873. It seems to have shared much with other esoteric organisations of the period. There was, for example, a characteristic emphasis on sacred geometry and various sacred sites. There was an insistence on a mystical or Gnostic truth underlying mythological motifs. There was a preoccupation with the origins of men, races, languages and symbols, such as occurs in Theosophy. And like many other sects and societies of the time, the Hiéron du Val d'Or was simultaneously Christian and 'trans-Christian'. It stressed the importance of the Sacred Heart, for instance, yet linked the Sacred Heart with other, pre-Christian symbols. It sought to reconcile – as the legendary Ormus was said to have reconciled – Christian and pagan mysteries. And it ascribed special significance to Druidic thought – which, like many modern experts, it regarded as partially Pythagorean. All of these themes are adumbrated in the published work of Saunière's friend, the Abbé Henri Boudet.

For the purposes of our inquiry, the Hiéron du Val d'Or proved relevant by virtue of its formulation of what M. Chaumeil calls an 'esoteric geo-politics' and an 'ethnarchical world order'. Translated into more mundane terms this entailed, in effect, the establishment of a new Holy Roman Empire in nineteenth-century Europe – a revitalised and reconstituted Holy Roman Empire, a secular state that unified all peoples and rested ultimately on spiritual, rather than social, political or economic foundations. Unlike its predecessor, this new Holy Roman Empire would have been genuinely 'holy', genuinely 'Roman' and genuinely 'imperial' – although the specific meaning of these terms would have differed crucially from the meaning accepted by tradition and convention. Such a state would have realised the centuries-old dream of a 'heavenly kingdom' on earth, a terrestrial replica or mirror-image of the order, harmony and hierarchy of the cosmos. It would have actualised the ancient Hermetic premise, 'As above, so below'. And it was not altogether Utopian or naive. On the contrary, it was at least remotely feasible in the context of late nineteenth-century Europe.

According to M. Chaumeil, the objectives of the Hiéron du Val d'Or were:

> a theocracy wherein nations would be no more than provinces, their leaders but proconsuls in the service of a world occult government consisting of an élite. For Europe, this régime of the Great King implied a double hegemony of the Papacy and the Empire, of the Vatican and of the Habsburgs, who would have been the Vatican's right arm.[44]

By the nineteenth century, of course, the Habsburgs were synonymous with the house of Lorraine. The concept of a 'Great King' would thus have constituted a fulfilment of Nostradamus's prophecies. And it would also have actualised, at least in some sense, the monarchist blueprint outlined in the *Protocols of the Elders of Sion*. At the same time the realisation of so grandiose a design would clearly have entailed a number of changes in existing institutions. The Vatican, for example, would presumably have been a very different Vatican from the one then situated in Rome. And the Habsburgs would have been more than imperial heads of state. They would have become, in effect, a dynasty of priest-kings, like the pharaohs of ancient Egypt. Or like the Messiah anticipated by the Jews at the dawn of the Christian era.

M. Chaumeil does not clarify the extent, if any, to which the Habsburgs themselves were actively involved in these ambitious clandestine designs. There is a quantity of evidence, however – including the visit of a Habsburg archduke to Rennes-le-Château – which seemingly attests to at least some implication. But whatever plans were afoot, they would have been thwarted by the First World War, which, among other things, toppled the Habsburgs from power.

As M. Chaumeil explained them, the objectives of the Hiéron du Val d'Or – or of the Prieuré de Sion – made a certain logical sense in the context of what we had discovered. They shed new light on the *Protocols of the Elders of Sion*. They concurred with the stated objectives of various secret societies, including those of Charles Radclyffe and Charles Nodier. Most important of all, they conformed to the political aspirations which, through the centuries, we had traced in the house of Lorraine.

But if the Hiéron du Val d'Or's objectives made logical sense, they did not make practical political sense. On what basis, we wondered, would the Habsburgs have asserted their right to function as a dynasty of priest-kings? Unless it commanded overwhelming popular support, such a right could not possibly have been asserted against the republican government of France – not to mention the imperial dynasties then presiding over Russia, Germany and Britain. And how could the necessary popular support have been obtained?

In the context of nineteenth-century political realities such a scheme, while logically consistent, seemed to us effectively absurd. Perhaps, we concluded, we had misconstrued the Hiéron du Val d'Or. Or perhaps the members of the Hiéron du Val d'Or were quite simply potty.

Until we obtained further information, we had no choice but to shelve the matter. In the meantime, we turned our attention to the present – to determine whether the Prieuré de Sion existed today. As we quickly discovered, it did. Its members were not at all potty, and they were pursuing, in the post-war twentieth century, a programme essentially similar to that pursued in the nineteenth by the Hiéron du Val d'Or.

CHAPTER EIGHT

THE SECRET SOCIETY TODAY

T he French Journal *Officiel* is a weekly government publication in which all groups, societies and organisations in the country must declare themselves. In the *Journal Officiel* for the week of July 20th, 1956 (Issue Number 167), there is the following entry:

25 JUIN 1956. DÉCLARATION À LA SOUS-PRÉFECTURE DE
SAINT-JULIEN-EN-GENEVOIS. PRIEURÉ DE SION. BUT: ÉTUDES ET
ENTR'AIDE DES MEMBRES. SIÈGE SOCIAL: SOUS-CASSAN, ANNEMASSE
(HAUTE SAVOIE).

*(JUNE 25TH, 1956. DECLARATION TO THE SUB-PREFECTURE OF SAINT-
JULIEN-EN-GENEVOIS. PRIEURÉ DE SION. OBJECTIVES: STUDIES AND
MUTUAL AID TO MEMBERS. HEAD OFFICE: SOUS-CASSAN, ANNEMASSE,
HAUTE SAVOIE.)*

The Prieuré de Sion was officially registered with the police. Here, at any rate, appeared to be definitive proof of its existence in our own age – even though we found it somewhat odd that a supposedly secret society should thus broadcast itself. But perhaps it was not so odd after all. There was no listing for the Prieuré de Sion in any French telephone directory. The address proved too vague to allow us to identify a specific office, house, building or even street. And the Sub-Prefecture, when we rang them, were of little help. There had been numerous inquiries, they said, with weary, long-suffering resignation. But they could provide no further information. As far as they knew, the address was untraceable. If nothing else, this gave us pause. Among other things, it made us wonder how certain individuals had contrived to register a fictitious or non-existent address with the police – and then, apparently, escape all subsequent consequences and prosecution of the matter. Were the police really as insouciant and indifferent as they sounded? Or had Sion somehow enlisted their cooperation and discretion?

The Sub-Prefecture, at our request, provided us with a copy of what purported to be the Prieuré de Sion's statutes. This document, which consisted of twenty-one articles, was neither controversial nor particularly illuminating. It did not, for example, clarify the Order's objectives. It gave no indication of Sion's possible influence, membership or resources. On the whole, it was rather bland – while at the same time compounding our perplexity. At one point, for instance, the statutes declared that admission to the Order was not to be restricted on the basis of language, social origin, class or political ideology. At another point, they stipulated that all Catholics over the age of twenty-one were eligible for candidature. Indeed the statutes in general appeared to have issued from a piously, even fervently Catholic institution. And yet Sion's alleged Grand Masters and past history, in so far as we had been able to trace them, hardly attested to any orthodox Catholicism. For that matter, even the modern 'Prieuré documents', many of them published at the same time as the statutes, were less Catholic in orientation than Hermetic, even heretically Gnostic. The contradiction seemed to make no sense – unless Sion, like the Knights Templar and the Compagnie du Saint-Sacrement, demanded Catholicism as an exoteric prerequisite, which might then be transcended within the Order. At any rate Sion, like the Temple and the Compagnie du Saint-Sacrement, apparently demanded an obedience which, in its absolute nature, subsumed all other commitments, secular or spiritual. According to Article VII of the statutes, 'The candidate must renounce his personality in order to devote himself to the service of a high moral apostolate'.

The statutes further declare that Sion functions under the subtitle of Chevalerie d'Institutions et Règles Catholiques, d'Union Indépendante et Traditionaliste ('Chivalry of Catholic Rules and Institutions of the Independent and Traditionalist Union'). This abbreviates to CIRCUIT,[1] the name of a magazine which, according to the statutes, is published internally by the Order and circulated within its ranks.

Perhaps the most interesting information in the statutes is that since 1956 the Prieuré de Sion would seem to have expanded its membership almost fivefold. According to a page reproduced in the *Dossiers secrets*, printed sometime before 1956, Sion had a total of 1,093 members ranked in seven grades. The structure was traditionally pyramidal. At the top was the Grand Master, or 'Nautonnier'. There were three in the grade below him ('Prince Noachite de Notre Dame'), nine in the grade below that ('Croisé de Saint-Jean'). Each grade from here downwards was three times as large as the grade before it – 27, 81, 243, 729. The three highest grades – the Grand Master and his twelve immediate subordinates – were said to constitute the thirteen 'Rose-Croix'. The number would also, of course, correspond to anything from a satanic coven to Jesus and his twelve disciples.

According to the post-1956 statutes, Sion had a total membership of 9,841, ranked not in seven grades but in nine. The structure seems to have remained essentially the same, although it was clarified, and two new grades had been introduced at the bottom of the hierarchy – thus further insulating the leadership behind a larger network of novices. The Grand Master still retained the title of 'Nautonnier'. The three 'Princes Noachites de Notre Dame' were simply called 'Seneschals'. The nine 'Croisés de Saint-Jean' were called 'Constables'. The organisation of the Order, in the portentously enigmatic jargon of the statutes, was as follows:

The general assembly is composed of all members of the association. It consists of 729 provinces, 27 commanderies and an Arch designated 'Kyria'.

Each of the commanderies, as well as the Arch, must consist of forty members, each province of thirteen members.

The members are divided into two effective groups:
a) The Légion, charged with the apostolate.
b) The Phalange, guardian of the Tradition.

The members compose a hierarchy of nine grades.

The hierarchy of nine grades consists of:
  a) in the 729 provinces
   1) Novices   6561 members
   2) Croisés: 2187 members
  b) in the 27 commanderies
   3) Preux: 729 members
   4) Ecuyers: 243 members
   5) Chevaliers: 81 members
   6) Commandeurs: 27 members
  c) in the Arch 'Kyria':
   7) Connétables: 9 members
   8) Sénéchaux: 3 members
   9) Nautonnier: 1 member[2]

Apparently for official bureaucratic and legal purposes, four individuals were listed as comprising 'The Council'. Three of the names were unfamiliar to us and, quite possibly, pseudonyms – André Bonhomme, born December 7th, 1934, President; Jean Deleaval, born March 7th, 1931, Vice-Président; Armand Defago, born December 11th, 1928, Treasurer. One name, however, we had encountered before – Pierre Plantard, born March 18th, 1920, Secretary-General. According to the research of another writer, M. Plantard's official title was Secretary-General of the Department of Documentation – which implies, of course, that there are other departments as well.

ALAIN POHER

By the early 1970s the Prieuré de Sion had become a modest *cause célèbre* among certain people in France. There were a number of magazine articles and some newspaper coverage. On February 13th, 1973, the *Midi Libre* published a lengthy feature on Sion, Saunière and the mystery of Rennes-le-Château. This feature specifically linked Sion with a possible survival of the Merovingian bloodline into the twentieth century. It also suggested that the Merovingian descendants included a 'true pretender to the throne of France', whom it identified as M. Alain Poher.[3]

While not especially well known in Britain or the United States Alain Poher was (and still is) a household name in France. During the Second World War he won the Resistance Medal and the Croix de Guerre. Following the resignation of de Gaulle, he was Provisional President of France from April 28th to June 19th, 1969. He occupied the same position on the death of Georges Pompidou, from April 2nd to May 27th, 1974. In 1973, when the feature in the *Midi Libre* appeared, M. Poher was President of the French Senate.

As far as we know, M. Poher never commented, one way or the other, on his alleged connections with the Prieuré de Sion and/or the Merovingian bloodline. In the genealogies of the 'Prieuré documents', however, there is mention of Arnaud, Count of Poher, who, sometime between 894 and 896, intermarried with the Plantard family – the direct descendants supposedly of Dagobert II. Arnaud de Poher's grandson, Alain, became duke of Brittany in 937. Whether or not M. Poher acknowledges Sion, it would thus seem clear that Sion acknowledges him – as being, at the very least, of Merovingian descent.

THE LOST KING

In the meantime, while we pursued our research and the French media accorded periodic flurries of attention to the whole affair, new 'Prieuré documents' continued to appear. As before, some appeared in book form, others as privately printed pamphlets or articles deposited in the Bibliothèque Nationale. If anything, they only compounded the mystification. Someone was obviously producing this material, but their real objective remained unclear. At times we nearly dismissed the whole affair as an elaborate joke, a hoax of extravagant proportions. If this were true, however, it was a hoax that certain people seemed to have been sustaining for centuries – and if one invests so much time, energy and resources in a hoax, can it really be called a hoax at all? In fact the interlocking skeins and the overall fabric of the 'Prieuré documents' were less a joke than a work of art – a display of ingenuity, suspense, brilliance, intricacy, historical knowledge and architectonic complexity worthy of, say, James Joyce. And while *Finnegans Wake* may be regarded as a joke of sorts, there is no question that its creator took it very seriously indeed.

It is important to note that the 'Prieuré documents' did not constitute a conventional 'bandwagon' – a lucrative fashion which burgeoned into a profitable industry, spawning sequels, 'prequels' and assorted other derivatives. They could not be compared, for example, to von Däniken's *Chariots of the Gods*, the sundry accounts of the Bermuda Triangle or the works of Carlos Castaneda. Whatever the motivation behind the 'Prieuré documents', it was clearly not financial gain. Indeed, money seemed to be only an incidental factor, if a factor at all. Although they would have proved extremely lucrative in book form, the most important 'Prieuré documents' were not published as such. Despite their commercial potential, they were confined to private printings, limited editions and discreet deposition at the Bibliothèque Nationale – where, for that matter, they were not even always available. And the information that did appear in conventional book form was not haphazard or arbitrary – and for the most part it was not the work of independent researchers. Most of it seemed to issue from a single source. Most of it was based on the testimony of very specific informants, who measured out precise quantities of new information as if with an eyedropper – and according to some prearranged plan. Each new fragment of information added at least one modification, one further piece to the overall jigsaw. Many of these fragments were released under different names. A superficial impression was thus conveyed of an array of separate writers, each of whom confirmed and imparted credibility to the others.

There appeared to us only one plausible motivation for such a procedure – to attract public attention to certain matters, to establish credibility, to engender interest, to create a psychological climate or atmosphere that kept people waiting with bated breath for new revelations. In short, the 'Prieuré documents' seemed specifically calculated to 'pave the way' for some astonishing disclosure. Whatever this disclosure might eventually prove to be, it apparently dictated a prolonged process of 'softening up' – of preparing people. And whatever this disclosure might eventually prove to be, it somehow involved the Merovingian dynasty, the perpetuation of that dynasty's bloodline to the present day and a clandestine kingship. Thus, in a magazine article purportedly written by a member of the Prieuré de Sion, we found the following statement, 'Without the Merovingians, the Prieuré de Sion would not exist, and without the Prieuré de Sion, the Merovingian dynasty would be extinct.' The relationship between the Order and the bloodline is partly clarified, partly further confused, by the following elaboration:

> The King *is*, shepherd and pastor at the same time. Sometimes he dispatches some brilliant ambassador to his vassal in power, his factotum, one who has the felicity of being subject to death. Thus René d'Anjou, Connétable de Bourbon, Nicolas Fouquet . . . and numerous others for whom astonishing success is followed by inexplicable disgrace – for these emissaries are both terrible and vulnerable. Custodians of a secret, one can only exalt them or destroy them. Thus people like Gilles de Rais, Leonardo da Vinci, Joseph Balsamo, the dukes of Nevers and Gonzaga, whose wake is attended by a perfume of magic in which sulphur is mingled with incense – the perfume of the Magdalene.
>
> If King Charles VII, on the entrance of Jeanne d'Arc into the great hall of his castle at Chinon, hid himself among the throng of his courtiers, it was not for the sake of a frivolous joke – where was the humour in it? – but because he already knew of whom she was the ambassadress. And that, before her, he was scarcely more than one courtier among the others. The secret she delivered to him in private was contained in these words: 'Gentle lord, I come on behalf of the King.'[4]

The implications of this passage are provocative and intriguing. One is that the King – the 'Lost King', presumably of the Merovingian blood-line – continues in effect to rule, simply by virtue of who he is. Another, and perhaps even more startling, implication is that temporal sovereigns are aware of his existence, acknowledge him, respect him and fear him. A third implication is that the Grand Master of the Prieuré de Sion, or some other member of the Order, acts as ambassador between the 'Lost King' and his temporal deputies or surrogates. And such ambassadors, it would seem, are deemed expendable.

CURIOUS PAMPHLETS IN THE BIBLIOTHÈQUE NATIONALE, PARIS

In 1966 a curious exchange of letters occurred concerning the death of Leo Schidlof – the man who, under the pseudonym of Henri Lobineau, was at that time alleged to have composed the genealogies in some of the 'Prieuré documents'. The first letter, which appeared in the *Catholic Weekly of Geneva*, is dated October 22nd, 1966. It is signed by one Lionel Burrus, who claims to speak on behalf of an organisation called Swiss Christian Youth. M. Burrus announces that Leo Schidlof, alias Henri Lobineau, died in Vienna the week before, on October 17th. He then defends the deceased against a slanderous attack which, he claims, appeared in a recent Roman Catholic bulletin. M. Burrus registers his indignation at this attack. In his eulogy on Schidlof he declares that the latter, under the name of Lobineau, compiled, in 1956, 'a remarkable study . . . on the genealogy of the Merovingian kings and the affair of Rennes-le-Château'.

Rome, M. Burrus asserts, did not dare asperse Schidlof when he was alive, even though it had a comprehensive dossier on the man and his activities. But even now, despite his death, Merovingian interests continue to be furthered. To support this contention, M. Burrus seems to wax more than a little preposterous. He cites what, in 1966, was the emblem of Antar, one of France's leading petrol companies. This emblem is said to embody a Merovingian device and depict, albeit in cartoon fashion, a Merovingian king. And this emblem, according to M. Burrus, proves that information and propaganda on behalf of the Merovingians is being effectively disseminated; and even the French clergy, he adds with imperfect relevance, do not always jump at the behest of the Vatican. As for Leo Schidlof, M. Burrus concludes (with echoes of Freemasonry and Cathar thought), 'For all those who knew

Henri Lobineau, who was a great voyager and a great seeker, a loyal and good man, he remains in our hearts as the symbol of a "maître parfait", whom one respects and venerates.'[5]

This letter from Lionel Burrus would seem distinctly cranky. Certainly it is extremely curious. More curious still, however, is the alleged attack on Schidlof in a Roman Catholic bulletin, from which M. Burrus quotes liberally. The bulletin, according to M. Burrus, accuses Schidlof of being 'pro-Soviet, a notorious Freemason actively preparing the way for a popular monarchy in France'.[6] It is a singular and seemingly contradictory accusation – for one does not usually combine Soviet sympathies with an attempt to establish a monarchy. And yet the bulletin, as M. Burrus claims to quote it, makes charges that are even more extravagant:

> The Merovingian descendants have always been behind all heresies, from Arianism, through the Cathars and the Templars, to Freemasonry. At the beginning of the Protestant Reformation, Cardinal Mazarin, in July 1659, had their château of Barberie, dating from the twelfth century, destroyed. For the house and family in question, all through the centuries, had spawned nothing but secret agitators against the Church.[7]

M. Burrus does not specifically identify the Roman Catholic bulletin in which this quotation supposedly appeared, so we could not verify its authenticity. If it is authentic, however, it would be of considerable significance. It would constitute independent testimony, from Roman Catholic sources, of the razing of Château Barberie in Nevers. It would also seem to suggest at least a partial *raison d'être* for the Prieuré de Sion. We had already come to see Sion, and the families associated with it, as manoeuvring for power on their own behalf – and in the process repeatedly clashing with the Church. According to the above quotation, however, opposition to the Church would not seem to have been a matter of chance, circumstances or even politics. On the contrary it would seem to have been a matter of on-going policy. This confronted us with another contradiction. For the statutes of the Prieuré de Sion had issued, at least ostensibly, from a staunchly Catholic institution.

Not long after the publication of this letter, Lionel Burrus was killed in a car accident which claimed six other victims as well. Shortly before his death, however, his letter elicited a response even more curious and provocative than that which he himself had written. This response was published as a privately printed pamphlet under the name of S. Roux,[8]

In certain respects S. Roux's text would appear to echo the original attack on Schidlof which prompted M. Burrus's letter. It also chastises M. Burrus for being young, over-zealous, irresponsible and prone to talk too much. But while seeming to condemn M. Burrus's position, not only does S. Roux's pamphlet confirm his facts, but it actually elaborates on them. Leo Schidlof, S. Roux affirms, was a dignitary of the Swiss Grande Loge Alpina – the Masonic lodge whose imprint appeared on certain of the 'Prieuré documents'. According to S. Roux, Schidlof 'did not conceal his sentiments of friendship for the Eastern Bloc'.[9] As for M. Burrus's statements about the Church, S. Roux continues:

> one cannot say that the Church is ignorant of the line of the
> Razès, but it must be remembered that all its descendants, since
> Dagobert, have been secret agitators against both the royal line
> of France and against the Church – and that they have been the
> source of all heresies. The return of a Merovingian descendant
> to power would entail for France the proclamation of a popular
> monarchy allied to the USSR, and the triumph of Freemasonry –
> in short, the disappearance of religious freedom.[10]

If all of this sounds rather extraordinary, the concluding statements of S. Roux's pamphlet are even more so:

> As for the question of Merovingian propaganda in France, every-
> one knows that the publicity of Antar Petrol, with a Merovingian
> king holding a Lily and a Circle, is a popular appeal in favour of
> returning the Merovingians to power. And one cannot but won-
> der what Lobineau was preparing at the time of his decease in
> Vienna, on the eve of profound changes in Germany. Is it not also
> true that Lobineau prepared in Austria a future reciprocal accord
> with France? Was not this the basis of the Franco-Russian
> accord?[11]

Not surprisingly we were utterly bewildered, wondering what the devil S. Roux was talking about; if anything, he appeared to have outdone M. Burrus in nonsense. Like the bulletin M. Burrus had attacked, S. Roux links together political objectives as apparently diverse and discordant as Soviet hegemony and popular monarchy. He goes further than M. Burrus by declaring that 'everyone knows' the emblem of a petrol company to be a subtle form of propaganda – for an unknown and apparently ludicrous cause. He hints at sweeping changes in France, Germany and Austria as if these changes were already 'on the cards', if not indeed *faits accomplis.* And he speaks of a mysterious 'Franco-Russian' accord as if this accord were a matter of public knowledge.

On first reading S. Roux's pamphlet appeared to make no sense whatever. A closer scrutiny convinced us that it was, in fact, another ingenious 'Prieuré document' – deliberately calculated to mystify, to confuse, to tease, to sow hints of something portentous and monumental. In any case it offered, in its wildly eccentric way, an intimation of the magnitude of the issues involved. If S. Roux was correct the subject of our inquiry was not confined to the activities of some elusive but innocuous latter-day chivalric order. If S. Roux was correct the subject of our inquiry pertained in some way to the upper echelons of high-level international politics.

THE CATHOLIC TRADITIONALISTS

In 1977 a new and particularly significant 'Prieuré document' appeared – a six-page pamphlet entitled *Le Cercle d'Ulysse* written by one Jean Delaude. In the course of his text the writer addresses himself explicitly to the Prieuré de Sion. And although he rehashes much older material, he also furnishes certain new details about the Order:

> In March 1177 Baudouin was compelled, at Saint Léonard d'Acre, to negotiate and prepare the constitution of the Order of the Temple, under the directives of the Prieuré de Sion. In 1118 the Order of the Temple was then established by Hugues de Payen. From 1118 to 1188 the Prieuré de Sion and the Order of the Temple shared the same Grand Masters. Since the separation of the two institutions in 1188, the Prieuré de Sion had counted twenty-seven Grand Masters to the present day. The most recent were:
>
> Charles Nodier   from 1801 to 1644
> Victor Hugo   from 1844 to 1885

Claude Debussy   from 1885 to 1918
Jean Cocteau   from 1918 to 1963

and from 1963 until the advent of the new order, the Abbé Ducaud-Bourget.

For what is the Pieuré de Sion preparing? I do not know, but it represents a power capable of confronting the Vatican in the days to come. Monsignor Lefebvre is a most active and redoubtable member, capable of saying: 'You make me Pope and I will make you King.'[12]

There are two important new fragments of information in this extract. One is the alleged affiliation with the Prieuré de Sion of Archbishop Marcel Lefebvre. Monsignor Lefebvre, of course, represents the extreme conservative wing of the Roman Catholic Church. He was vociferously outspoken against Pope Paul VI, whom he flagrantly and flamboyantly defied. In 1976 and 1977, in fact, he was explicitly threatened with excommunication; and his brazen indifference to this threat nearly precipitated a full-scale ecclesiastical schism. But how could we reconcile a militant 'hard-line' Catholic like Monsignor Lefebvre with a movement and an Order that was Hermetic, if not downright heretical, in orientation? There seemed to be no explanation for this contradiction: unless Monsignor Lefebvre was a modern-day representative of the nineteenth-century Freemasonry associated with the Hiéron du Val d'Or – the 'Christian, aristocratic and Hermetic Freemasonry' which presumed to regard itself as more Catholic than the pope.

The second major point in the extract quoted above is, of course, the identification of the Prieuré de Sion's Grand Master at that time as Abbé Ducaud-Bourget. François Ducaud-Bourget was born in 1897 and trained for the priesthood at – predictably enough – the Seminary of Saint Sulpice. He is thus likely to have known many of the Modernists there at the time – and, quite possibly, Emile Hoffet. Subsequently he was Conventual Chaplain of the Sovereign Order of Malta. For his activities during the Second World War he received the Resistance Medal and the Croix de Guerre. Today he is recognised as a distinguished man of letters – a member of the Académie Française, a biographer of important French Catholic writers like Paul Claudel and François Mauriac, and a highly esteemed poet in his own right.

Like Monsignor Lefebvre the Abbé Ducaud-Bourget assumed a

stance of militant opposition to Pope Paul VI. Like Monsignor Lefebvre he is an adherent of the Tridentine Mass. Like Monsignor Lefebvre he has proclaimed himself a 'traditionalist', adamantly opposed to ecclesiastical reform or any attempt to 'modernise' Roman Catholicism. On May 22nd, 1976 he was forbidden to administer confession or absolution – and, like Monsignor Lefebvre, he boldly defied the interdict imposed on him by his superiors. On February 27th, 1977 he led a thousand Catholic traditionalists in their occupation of the Church of Saint-Nicolas-du-Chardonnet in Paris.

If Marcel Lefebvre and François Ducaud-Bourget appear to be 'right-wing' theologically, they would seem to be equally so politically. Before the Second World War, Monsignor Lefebvre was associated with Action Française – the extreme right of French politics at the time, which shared certain attitudes in common with National Socialism in Germany. More recently the 'rebel archbishop' attracted considerable notoriety by warmly endorsing the military régime in Argentina. When questioned on this position, he replied that he had made a mistake. He had not meant Argentina, he said, but Chile! François Ducaud-Bourget would not appear to be quite so extreme; and his medals, at any rate, attest to patriotic anti-German activity during the war. Nevertheless he has expressed a high regard for Mussolini, and the hope that France would 'recover its sense of values under the guidance of a new Napoleon'.[13]

Our first suspicion was that Marcel Lefebvre and François Ducaud-Bourget were not, in fact, affiliated with the Prieuré de Sion at all, but that someone had deliberately attempted to embarrass them by aligning them with the very forces they would, in theory, most vigorously oppose. And yet according to the statutes we had obtained from the French police, the subtitle of the Prieuré de Sion was Chevalerie d'Institutions et Règles Catholiques; d'Union Indépendante et Traditionaliste. An institution with such a name might very well accommodate individuals like Marcel Lefebvre and François Ducaud-Bourget.

There seemed to us a second possible explanation – a far-fetched explanation admittedly, but one that would at least account for the contradiction confronting us. Perhaps Marcel Lefebvre and François Ducaud-Bourget were not what they appeared to be. Perhaps they were something else. Perhaps, in actuality, they were *agents provocateurs* – whose objective was systematically to create turmoil, sow dissent, foment an incipient schism that threatened Pope Paul's pontificate.

Such tactics would be in keeping with the secret societies described by Charles Nodier, as well as with the *Protocols of the Elders of Sion.* And a number of recent commentators – journalists as well as ecclesiastical authorities – have declared Archbishop Lefebvre to be working for, or manipulated by, someone else.[14]

Far-fetched though our hypothesis might be, there was a coherent logic underlying it. If Pope Paul were regarded as 'the enemy', and one wished to force him into a more liberal position, how would one go about it? Not by agitating from a liberal point of view. That would only have entrenched the pope more firmly in his conservatism. But what if one publicly adopted a position even more rabidly conservative than Paul's? Would this not, despite his wishes to the contrary, force him into an increasingly liberal position? And that, certainly, is what Archbishop Lefebvre and his colleagues accomplished – the unprecedented feat of casting the pope as a liberal.

Whether our conclusions were valid or not, it seemed clear that Archbishop Lefebvre, like so many other individuals in our investigation, was privy to some momentous and explosive secret. In 1976, for example, his excommunication seemed imminent. The press, indeed, was expecting it any day, for Pope Paul, confronted by brazen and repeated defiance, seemed to have no alternative. And yet, at the very last minute, the pope backed down. It is still unclear precisely why he did so: but the following excerpt from the *Guardian,* dated August 30th, 1976, suggests a clue:

> The Archbishop's team of priests in England . . . believe that their leader still has a powerful ecclesiastical weapon to use in his dispute with the Vatican. No one will give any hint of its nature, but Father Peter Morgan, the group's leader . . . describes it as being something 'earth-shaking'.[15]

What kind of 'earth-shaking' matter or 'secret weapon' could thus intimidate the Vatican? What kind of Damoclean sword, invisible to the world at large, could have been held over the pontiff's head? Whatever it was, it certainly seems to have proved effective. It seems, in fact, to have rendered the archbishop wholly immune to punitive action from Rome. As Jean Delaude wrote, Marcel Lefebvre did indeed seem to 'represent a power capable of confronting the Vatican' – head-on, if necessary.

But to whom did he – or will he – allegedly say: 'You make me Pope and I will make you King'?

THE CONVENT OF 1981 AND COCTEAU'S STATUTES

More recently, some of the issues surrounding François Ducaud-Bourget seem to have been clarified. This clarification has resulted from a sudden glare of publicity which the Prieuré de Sion, during late 1980 and early 1981, has received in France. This publicity has made it something of a household name.

In August 1980 the popular magazine *Bonne Soirée* – a kind of amalgam between a British Sunday supplement and the American *TV Guide* – published a two-part feature on the mystery of Rennes-le-Château and the Prieuré de Sion. In this feature both Marcel Lefebvre and François Ducaud-Bourget are explicitly linked with Sion. Both are said to have paid a special visit fairly recently to one of Sion's sacred sites, the village of Sainte-Colombe in Nevers, where the Plantard domain of Château Barberie was situated before its destruction by Cardinal Mazarin in 1659.

By this time we ourselves had established both telephone and postal contact with the Abbé Ducaud-Bourget. He proved courteous enough. But his answers to most of our questions were vague, if not evasive; and, not surprisingly, he disavowed all affiliation with the Prieuré de Sion. This disavowal was reiterated in a letter which, shortly thereafter, he addressed to *Bonne Soirée*.

On January 22nd, 1981, a short article appeared in the French press,[16] of which it is worth quoting the greater part:

A veritable secret society of 121 dignitaries, the Prieuré de Sion, founded by Godfroi de Bouillon in Jerusalem in 1099, has numbered among its Grand Masters Leonardo da Vinci, Victor Hugo and Jean Cocteau. This Order convened its Convent at Blois on 17 January, 1981 (the previous Convent dating from 5 June 1956, in Paris).

As a result of this recent Convent at Blois, Pierre Plantard de Saint-Clair was elected Grand Master of the Order by 83 out of 92 votes on the third ballot.

This choice of Grand Master marks a decisive step in the evolution of the Order's conception and spirit in relation to the world; for the 121 dignitaries of the Prieuré de Sion are all *eminences grises* of high finance and of international political or philosophical societies; and Pierre Plantard is the direct descendant, through Dagobert II, of the Merovingian kings. His descent has been proved legally by the parchments of Queen Blanche of Castile, discovered by the Abbé Saunière in his church at Rennes-le-Château (Aude) in 1891.

These documents were sold by the priest's niece in 1965 to Captain Roland Stanmore and Sir Thomas Frazer, and were deposited in a safe-deposit box of Lloyds Bank Europe Limited of London.[17]

Shortly before this item appeared in the press, we had written to Philippe de Chérisey, with whom we had already established contact and whose name figured as frequently as Pierre Plantard's as a spokesman for the Prieuré de Sion. In reply to one of the questions we asked him, M. de Chérisey declared that François Ducaud-Bourget had not been elected Grand Master by a proper quorum. Moreover, he added, the Abbé Ducaud-Bourget had publicly repudiated his affiliation with the Order. This latter assertion seemed unclear. It made more sense, however, in the context of something M. de Chérisey enclosed in his letter.

Some time before, we had obtained, from the Sub-Prefecture of Saint-Julien, the statutes of the Prieuré de Sion. A copy of these same statutes had been published in 1973 by a French magazine.[18] However, we had been told in Paris by Jean-Luc Chaumeil that these statutes were fraudulent. In his letter to us M. de Chérisey enclosed a copy of what were said to be the Prieuré de Sion's true statutes – translated from the Latin. These statutes bore the signature af Jean Cocteau; and unless it had been executed by an extremely skilful forger, the signature was authentic. We certainly could not distinguish it from other specimens of Cocteau's signature. And on this basis, we are inclined to accept the statutes to which the signature is appended as genuine.[19] They are set out below:

ARTICLE ONE – There is formed, between the undersigned to this present constitution and those who shall subsequently join and fulfil the following conditions, an initiatory order of chivalry, whose usages and customs rest upon the foundation made by

Godfroi VI, called the Pious, Duc de Bouillon, at Jerusalem in 1099 and recognised in 1100.

ARTICLE TWO – The Order is called 'Sionis Prioratus' or 'Prieuré de Sion'.

ARTICLE THREE – The Prieuré de Sion has as its objectives the perpetuation of the traditionalist order of chivalry, its initiatory teaching and the creation between members of mutual assistance, as much moral as material, in all circumstances.

ARTICLE FOUR – The duration of the Prieuré de Sion is unlimited.

ARTICLE FIVE – The Prieuré de Sion adopts, as its representative office, the domicile of the Secretary-General named by the Convent. The Prieuré de Sion is not a secret society. All its decrees, as well as its records and appointments, are available to the public in Latin text.

ARTICLE SIX – The Prieuré de Sion comprises 121 members. Within these limits, it is open to all adult persons who recognise its aims and accept the obligations specified in this present constitution. Members are admitted without regard to sex, race or philosophical, religious or political ideas.

ARTICLE SEVEN – Nevertheless, in the event that a member should designate in writing one of his descendants to succeed him, the Convent shall accede to this request and may, if necessary in the case of minority, undertake the education of the above designated.

ARTICLE EIGHT – A future member must provide, for his induction to the first grade, a white robe with cord, at his own expense. From the time of his admission to the first grade, the member holds the right to vote. On admission, the new member must swear to serve the Order in all circumstances, as well as to work for PEACE and the respect of human life.

ARTICLE NINE – On his admission, the member must pay a token fee, the amount being discretionary. Each year, he must forward to the Secretariat General a voluntary contribution to the Order of a sum to be decided by himself.

ARTICLE TEN – On admission, the member must provide a birth certificate and a specimen of his signature.

ARTICLE ELEVEN – A member of the Prieuré de Sion against whom a sentence has been pronounced by a tribunal for a common-law offence may be suspended from his duties and titles, as well as his membership.

ARTICLE TWELVE – The general assembly of members is designated the Convent. No deliberation of Convent shall be deemed valid if the number of members present is less than eighty-one. The vote is secret and is cast by means of white and black balls. To be adopted, all motions must receive eighty-one white balls. All motions not receiving sixty-one white balls in a vote may not be re-submitted.

ARTICLE THIRTEEN – The Convent of the Prieuré de Sion alone decides, on a majority of 81 votes out of 121 members, all changes to the constitution and the internal regulation of ceremonial.

ARTICLE FOURTEEN – All admissions shall be decided by the 'Council of the thirteen Rose-Croix'. Titles and duties shall be conferred by the Grand Master of the Prieuré de Sion. Members are admitted to their office for life. Their titles revert by right to one of their children chosen by themselves without consideration of sex. The child thus designated may make an act of renunciation of his rights, but he cannot make this act in favour of a brother, sister, relative or any other person. He may not be readmitted to the Prieuré de Sion.

ARTICLE FIFTEEN – Within twenty-seven full days, two members shall be required to contact a future member to obtain his assent or his renunciation. In default of a deed of acceptance after a period of reflection of eighty-one full days, renunciation shall be legally recognised and the place considered vacant.

ARTICLE SIXTEEN – By virtue of hereditary right confirmed by the preceding articles, the duties and titles of Grand Master of the Prieuré de Sion shall be transmitted to his successor according to the same prerogatives. In the case of a vacancy in the office of Grand Master, and the absence of a direct successor, the Convent must proceed to an election within eighty-one days.

ARTICLE SEVENTEEN – All decrees must be voted by Convent and receive validation by the Seal of the Grand Master. The Secretary-General is named by Convent for three years, renewable by tacit consent. The Secretary-General must be of the grade of Commander to undertake his duties. The functions and duties are unpaid.

ARTICLE EIGHTEEN – The hierarchy of the Prieuré de Sion is composed of five grades:

1st	Nautonnier	number:	1	Arche of the
2nd	Croisé	number:	3	13 Rose-Croix
3rd	Commandeur	number:	9	
4th	Chevalier	number:	27	The nine
5th	Ecuyer	number:	81	commanderies
total	number:		121	of the Temple

ARTICLE NINETEEN – There are 243 Free Brothers, called Preux or, since the year 1681, *Enfants* de *Saint Vincent,* who participate neither in the vote nor in Convents, but to whom the Prieuré de Sion accords certain rights and privileges in conformity with the decree of January 17th, 1681.

ARTICLE TWENTY – The funds of the Prieuré de Sion are composed of gifts and fees of members. A reserve, called the 'patrimony of the Order', is settled upon the Council of the thirteen Rose-Croix. This treasure may only be used in case of absolute necessity and grave danger to the Prieuré and its members.

ARTICLE TWENTY-ONE – The Convent is convoked by the Secretary-

General when the Council of the Rose-Croix deems it useful.

ARTICLE TWENTY-TWO – Disavowal of membership in the Prieuré de Sion, manifested publicly and in writing, without cause or personal danger, shall incur exclusion of the member, which shall be pronounced by the Convent.

Text of the constitution in XXII articles, conforming to the original and to the modifications of the Convent of June 5th, 1956.

Signature of the Grand Master

JEAN COCTEAU

In certain details, these statutes are at odds both with the statutes we received from the French police and with the information relating to Sion in the 'Prieuré documents'. The latter shows a total membership of 1,093, the former of 9,841. According to the articles quoted above, Sion's total membership, including the 243 'Children of Saint Vincent', is only 364. The 'Prieuré documents', moreover, establish a hierarchy of seven grades. In the statutes we received from the French police, this hierarchy has been expanded to nine. According to the articles quoted above, there are only five grades in the hierarchy. And the specific appellations of these grades differ from those in the two previous sources as well.

These contradictions might well be evidence of some sort of schism, or incipient schism, within the Prieuré de Sion, dating from around 1956 – when the 'Prieuré documents' first began to appear in the Bibliothèque Nationale. And indeed, Philippe de Chérisey alludes to just such a schism in a recent article.[20] It occurred between 1956 and 1958, he says, and threatened to assume the proportions of the rift between Sion and the Order of the Temple in 1188 – the rift marked by the 'cutting of the elm'. According to M. de Chérisey, the schism was averted by the diplomatic skill of M. Plantard, who brought the potential defectors back into the fold. In any case, and whatever the internal politics of the Prieuré de Sion, the Order, as of the January 1981 Convent, would seem to constitute a unified and coherent whole.

If François Ducaud-Bourget was the Prieuré de Sion's Grand Master, it would appear clear that he is not so at present. M. de Chérisey declared that he had not been elected by the requisite quorum. This may mean that he was elected by the incipient schismatics. It is uncertain whether he is subject to or in violation of Article Twenty-Two of the statutes. We may assume that his affiliation with Sion – whatever it may have been in the past – no longer exists.

The statutes quoted might seem to clarify the status of François Ducaud-Bourget. They make clear, anyway, the principle of selection governing the Prieuré de Sion's Grand Masters. It is now comprehensible why there should have been Grand Masters aged five or eight. It is also comprehensible why the Grand Mastership should move, as it does, in and out of a particular bloodline and network of interlinked genealogies. In principle, the title would seem to be hereditary, transmitted down the centuries through an intertwined cluster of families all claiming Merovingian descent. When there was no eligible claimant, however, or when the designated claimant declined the status offered him, the Grand Mastership, presumably in accordance with the procedures outlined in the statutes, was conferred on a chosen outsider. It would be on this basis that individuals like Leonardo, Newton, Nodier and Cocteau found their way on to the list.

M. PLANTARD DE SAINT-CLAIR

Among the names that figured most prominently and recurrently in the various 'Prieuré documents' was that of the Plantard family. And among the numerous individuals associated with the mystery of Saunière and Rennes-le-Château, the most authoritative seemed to be Pierre Plantard de Saint-Clair.[21] According to the genealogies in the 'Prieuré documents', M. Plantard is a lineal descendant of King Dagobert II and the Merovingian dynasty. According to the same genealogies, he is also a lineal descendant of the owners of Château Barberie, the property destroyed by Cardinal Mazarin in 1659.

Throughout the course of the inquiry we had repeatedly encountered M. Plantard's name. Indeed, so far as release of information during the last twenty-five years or so was concerned, all trails seemed to lead ultimately to him. In 1960, for example, he was interviewed by Gérard de Sède and spoke of an 'international secret' concealed at Gisors.[22] During the subsequent decade he seems to have been a major source of information for M. de Sède's books on both Gisors and Rennes-le-Château.[23] According to recent disclosures, M. Plantard's grandfather was a personal acquaintance of Bérenger Saunière. And M. Plantard himself proved to own a number of tracts of land in the vicinity of Rennes-le-Château and Rennes-les-Bains, including the mountain of Blanchefort. When we interviewed the town antiquarian at Stenay, in the Ardennes, we were told that the site of the Old Church of Saint Dagobert was also owned by M. Plantard. And according to the statutes we obtained from the French police, M. Plantard was listed as Secretary-General of the Prieuré de Sion.

In 1973 a French magazine published what seems to have been the transcript of a telephone interview with M. Plantard. Not surprisingly he did not give very much away. As might be expected, his statements were allusive, cryptic and provocative – raising, in fact, more questions than they answered. Thus, for example, when speaking of the Merovingian bloodline and its royal claims, he declared, 'You must explore the origins of certain great French families, and you will then comprehend how a personage named Henri de Montpézat could one day become king.'[24] And when asked the objectives of the Prieuré de Sion, M. Plantard replied in a manner whose evasiveness was predictable, 'I cannot tell you that. The society to which I am attached is extremely ancient. I merely succeed others, a point in a sequence. We are guardians of certain things. And without publicity.'[25]

The same French magazine also published a character sketch of M. Plantard, written by his first wife, Anne Lea Hisler, who died in 1971. If the magazine is to be believed, this sketch first appeared in *Circuit*, the Prieuré de Sion's own internal publication – for which M. Plantard is said to have written regularly under the pseudonym of 'Chyren':

> Let us not forget that this psychologist was the friend of personages as diverse as Comte Israël Monti, one of the brothers of the Holy Vehm, Gabriel Trarieux d'Egmont, one of the thirteen members of the Rose-Croix, Paul Lecour, the philosopher on Atlantis, the Abbé Hoffet of the Service of Documentation of the Vatican, Th. Moreaux, the director of the Conservatory at Bourges, etc. Let us remember that during the Occupation, he was arrested, suffered torture by the Gestapo and was interned as a political prisoner for long months. In his capacity of doctor of arcane sciences, he learned to appreciate the value of secret information, which no doubt led to his receiving the title of honorary member in several hermetic societies. All this has gone to form a singular personage, a mystic of peace, an apostle of liberty, an ascetic whose ideal is to serve the well-being of humanity. Is it astonishing therefore that he should become one of the *émi-*

nences grises from whom the great of this world seek counsel?
Invited in 1947 by the Federal Government of Switzerland, he
resided for several years there, near Lake Léman, where numerous *chargés de missions* and delegates from the entire world are
gathered.[26]

Madame Hisler undoubtedly intended this to be a glowing portrait.
What emerges, however, is the sense of an individual more singular
than anything else. In some places Madame Hisler's language becomes
both vague and hyperbolic. Moreover, the diverse people listed as M.
Plantard's distinguished acquaintances are, to say the least, a fairly odd
lot.

On the other hand, M. Plantard's contretemps with the Gestapo
would seem to point to some, laudable activity during the Occupation.
And our own researches eventually yielded documentary evidence. As
early as 1941 Pierre Plantard had begun editing the resistance journal
Vaincre, published in a suburb of Paris. He was imprisoned by the
Gestapo for more than a year, from October 1943 until the end of 1944.[27]

M. Plantard's friends and associates proved to include individuals
rather better known than those listed by Madame Hisler. They included
André Malraux and Charles de Gaulle. Indeed M. Plantard's connections apparently extended well into the corridors of power. In 1958, for
example, Algeria rose in revolt and General de Gaulle sought to be
returned to the Presidency of France. He seems to have turned specifically to M. Plantard for aid. M. Plantard, together with André Malraux
and others, seems to have responded by mobilising the so-called
'Committees of Public Safety' – which played a critical role in returning
de Gaulle to the Élysee Palace. In a letter dated July 29th, 1958, de
Gaulle personally thanked M. Plantard for his services. In a second letter, dated five days later, the General requested of M. Plantard that the
committees, having attained their objective, be disbanded. By an official
communiqué in the press and on the radio, M. Plantard dissolved the
committees.[28]

Needless to say, we became increasingly anxious, as our research pro-
gressed, to make M. Plantard's acquaintance. There did not at first seem
much likelihood of our doing so, however. M. Plantard appeared to be
untraceable, and there seemed no way whereby we, as private individuals, could possibly locate him. Then, during the early spring of 1979,

we embarked on another film about Rennes-le-Château for the BBC, who placed their resources at our disposal. It was under the auspices of the BBC that we at last managed to establish contact with M. Plantard and the Prieuré de Sion.

Initial inquiries were undertaken by an Englishwoman, a journalist living in Paris, who had worked on various projects for the BBC and had acquired an imposing network of connections throughout France, through which she attempted to find the Prieuré de Sion. At first, pursuing her quest through Masonic lodges and the Parisian esoteric 'subculture', she encountered a predictable smoke-screen of mystification and contradiction. One jounalist warned her, for example, that anyone probing Sion too closely sooner or later got killed. Another journalist told her that Sion had indeed existed during the Middle Ages, but no longer did today. An official of Grande Loge Alpina, on the other hand, reported that Sion did exist today but was a modern organisation – it had never, he said, existed in the past.

Threading her way through this welter of confusion, our researcher at last established contact with Jean-Luc Chaumeil – who had interviewed M. Plantard for a magazine and written extensively on Saunière, Rennes-le-Château and the Prieuré de Sion. He was not himself a member of Sion, M. Chaumeil said, but he could contact M. Plantard and possibly arrange a meeting with us. In the meantime, he provided our researcher with additional fragments of information.

According to M. Chaumeil the Prieuré de Sion was not, strictly speaking, a 'secret society'. It merely wished to be discreet about its existence, its activities and its membership. The entry in the *Journal Officiel*, M. Chaumeil declared, was spurious, placed there by certain 'defecting members' of the Order. According to M. Chaumeil, the statutes registered with the police were also spurious, issuing from the same 'defecting members'.

M. Chaumeil confirmed our suspicions that Sion entertained ambitious political plans for the near future. Within a few years, he asserted, there would be a dramatic change in the French Government – a change that would pave the way for a popular monarchy with a Merovingian ruler on the throne. And Sion, he asserted further, would be behind this change – as it had been behind numerous other important changes for centuries. According to M. Chaumeil, Sion was anti-materialistic and intent on presiding over a restoration of 'true values' – values, it would appear, of a spiritual, perhaps esoteric character. These values, M.

Chaumeil explained, were ultimately pre-Christian – despite Sion's ostensibly Christian orientation, despite the Catholic emphasis in the statutes. M. Chaumeil also reiterated that Sion's Grand Master at that time was François Ducaud-Bourget. When asked how the latter's Catholic traditionalism could be reconciled with pre-Christian values, M. Chaumeil replied cryptically that we would have to ask the Abbé Ducaud-Bourget himself.

M. Chaumeil emphasised the antiquity of the Prieuré de Sion, as well as the breadth of its membership. It included, he said, members from all spheres of life. Its objectives, he added, were not exclusively confined to restoring the Merovingian bloodline. And at this point, M. Chaumeil made a very curious statement to our researcher. Not all members of the Prieuré de Sion, he said, were Jewish. The implication of this apparent *non sequitur* is obvious – that some members of the Order, if not indeed many, are Jewish. And again we were confronted with a baffling contradiction. Even if the statutes were spurious, how could we

French Journalist, Jean-Luc Chaumeil and co-author of Holy Blood, Holy Grail, *Michael Baigent, Paris, 1985.*

reconcile an Order with Jewish membership and a Grand Master who embraced extreme Catholic traditionalism – and whose close friends included Marcel Lefebvre, a man known for statements verging on anti-Semitism?

M. Chaumeil made other perplexing statements as well. He spoke, for instance, of the 'Prince de Lorraine', who was descended from the Merovingian bloodline and whose 'sacred mission was therefore obvious'. This assertion is all the more baffling in that there is no known Prince of Lorraine today, not even a titular one. Was M. Chaumeil implying that such a Prince did actually exist, living perhaps incognito? Or did he mean 'prince' in the broader sense of 'scion'? In that case, the present prince (as opposed to Prince) of Lorraine is Dr. Otto von Habsburg, who is titular duke of Lorraine.

On the whole, M. Chaumeil's answers were less answers than they were bases for further questions – and our researcher, in the short time of preparation allowed her, did not know precisely which questions to ask. She made considerable headway, however, by stressing the BBC's interest in the matter; for the BBC, on the continent, enjoys considerably more prestige than it does in Britain and is still a name to be conjured with. In consequence the prospect of BBC involvement was not to be taken lightly. 'Propaganda' is too strong a word, but a BBC film which emphasised and authenticated certain facts would certainly have been attractive – a powerful means of gaining credence and creating a psychological climate or atmosphere, especially in the English-speaking world. If the Merovingians and the Prieuré de Sion became accepted as 'historical givens' or generally acknowledged facts – like, say, the Battle of Hastings or the murder of Thomas à Becket – this would patently have been to Sion's advantage. It was undoubtedly such considerations that prompted M. Chaumeil to telephone M. Plantard.

Eventually, in March 1979, with our BBC producer, Roy Davies, and his researcher functioning as liaison, a meeting was arranged between M. Plantard and ourselves. When it occurred, it had something of the character of a meeting between Mafia godfathers. It was held on 'neutral ground' in a Paris cinema rented by the BBC for the occasion, and all parties were accompanied by an entourage.

M. Plantard proved to be a dignified, courteous man of discreetly aristocratic bearing, unostentatious in appearance, with a gracious, volatile but soft-spoken manner. He displayed enormous erudition and impressive nimbleness of mind – a gift for dry, witty, mischievous but not in any way barbed repartee. There was frequently a gently amused, indulgent twinkle in his eyes, an almost avuncular quality. For all his modest, unassertive manner, he exercised an imposing authority over his companions. And there was a marked quality of asceticism and austerity about him. He did not flaunt any wealth. His apparel was conservative, tasteful, insouciantly informal, but neither ostentatiously elegant nor manifestly expensive. As far as we could gather, he did not even drive a car.

At our first, and two subsequent meetings with him, M. Plantard made it clear to us that he would say nothing whatever about the Prieuré de Sion's activities or objectives at the present time. On the other hand he offered to answer any questions we might have about the Order's past history. And although he refused to discuss the future in any public statements – on film, for example – he did vouchsafe us a few hints in conversation. He declared, for example, that the Prieuré de Sion did in fact hold the lost treasure of the Temple of Jerusalem – the booty plundered by Titus's Roman legions in AD. 70. These items he stated, would be 'returned to Israel when the time is right'. But whatever the historical, archaeological or even political significance of this treasure, M. Plantard dismissed it as incidental. The true treasure, he insisted, was 'spiritual'. And he implied that this 'spiritual treasure' consisted, at least in part, of a secret. In some unspecified way the secret in question would facilitate a major social change. M. Plantard echoed M. Chaumeil in stating that, in the near future, there would be a dramatic upheaval in France – not a revolution, but a radical change in French institutions which would pave the way for the reinstatement of a monarchy. This assertion was not made with any prophetic histrionics. On the contrary, M. Plantard simply assured us of it, very quietly, very matter-of-factly – and very definitively.

In M. Plantard's discourse there were certain curious inconsistencies. At times, for instance, he seemed to be speaking on behalf of the Prieuré de Sion – he would say 'we' and thereby indicate the Order. At other times, he would seem to dissociate himself from the Order – would speak of himself, alone, as a Merovingian claimant, a rightful king, and Sion as his allies or supporters. We seemed to be hearing two quite distinct voices – which were not always compatible. One was the voice of Sion's Secretary-General. The other was the voice of an incognito king who 'rules but does not govern' – and who regarded Sion as one might a sort of privy council. This dichotomy between the two voices was never satisfactorily resolved, and M. Plantard could not be prevailed upon to clarify it.

After three meetings with M. Plantard and his associates, we were not significantly wiser than we had been before. Apart from the Committees of Public Safety and the letters from Charles de Gaulle, we received no indication of Sion's political influence or power, or that the men we had met were in any position to transform the government and institutions of France. And we received no indication of why the Merovingian bloodline should be taken any more seriously than the various attempts to restore any other royal dynasty. There are several Stuart claimants to the British throne, for example – and their claims, at least so far as modern historians are concerned, rest on a more solid basis than that of the Merovingians. For that matter, there are numerous other claimants to vacant crowns and thrones throughout Europe; and there are surviving members of the Bourbon, Habsburg, Hohenzollern and Romanov dynasties. Why should they be accorded any less credibility than the Merovingians? In terms of 'absolute legitimacy', and from a purely technical point of view, the Merovingian claim might indeed take precedence. But the matter would still appear to be academic in the modern world – as academic, say, as a contemporary Irishman proving descent from the High Kings of Tara.

Again we considered dismissing the Prieuré de Sion as a minor 'lunatic fringe' sect, if not an outright hoax. And yet all our own research had indicated that the Order, in the past, had had real power and been involved in matters of high-level international import. Even today there was clearly more to it than met the eye. There was nothing mercenary about it, for example, or exploitative in any way. Had M. Plantard so desired, he could have turned the Prieuré de Sion into an extremely lucrative affair – like many other fashionable 'new age' cults, sects and institutions. Yet most of the seminal 'Prieuré documents' remained confined to private printings. And Sion itself did not solicit recruits – not even in the way that a Masonic lodge might. Its membership, as far as we could determine, remained rigorously fixed at a precise number, and new members were admitted only as vacancies occurred. Such 'exclusiveness' attested, among other things, to an extraordinary self-confidence, a certainty that it simply did not need to enrol swarms of novices – for financial gain or any other reason. In other words, it already 'had something going for it' – something that seems to have enlisted the allegiance of men like Malraux and de Gaulle. But could we seriously believe that men like Malraux and de Gaulle were intent on restoring the Merovingian bloodline?

The modern-day Prieuré de Sion first became public in 1956, when it was listed in the French *Journal Officiel*. We subsequently discovered that 1955 and 1956 were apparently significant years in the story we were investigating. In *The Messianic Legacy*, we attempted to trace the circumstances in which the genealogical documents allegedly found by Saunière were secretly spirited to England. We obtained officially notarised papers dating from 1956, asserting that the documents in question had been entrusted by Saunière's niece to three City of London businessmen, who had then deposited them in a London bank. Parts of these documents were attested as valid by the authorities we consulted but we proved that in one of them, at least, material concerning the genealogical documents had been fraudulently added at a later date. But to what purpose; and how had the forger obtained the original documents to tamper with? The most recent document was stamped and dated 25 August 1956, by the French Consulate in London. The French Consulate confirmed to us personally that the stamp, date and signature were authentic. We were left with the question of whether the year 1956 was in some way important or relevant. Could all the subterfuge and intrigue involved in smuggling the documents to England have occurred at any time, and had 1956 been purely random, purely haphazard? Or was there a specific context, a specific constellation of events in 1956 that made the matter particularly consequential at that precise time? What, we pondered, had happened in 1956 that might have some bearing on the affair we were researching? The only things of any apparent pertinence were France's general instability just then, and her intensifying troubles in Algeria.

On 6 September 1987 the *Sunday Times* provided a possible and provocative answer to our question. A banner headline on that day announced that 'France tried to join the Commonwealth'. There followed an account derived from government papers only recently released, which had been investigated by an historian, Dr. John Zametica.

In 1940, in the period immediately preceding and following the fall of France, there had apparently been some tentative high-level discussion about amalgamating France and Britain, with the British Crown exercising sovereignty over both countries. At the time, the idea had been discarded. In 1956, however, it was resurrected. On 11 September 1956, the French prime Minister, Guy Mollet, suggested to Sir Anthony Eden that France and Britain form a political union. France, Mollet reportedly said, would be prepared to accept the sovereignty of Elizabeth II and the British Crown.

Eden established a Cabinet committee to study the matter. This committee first met on 24 September 1956 – and, on advice from the Treasury and the Foreign Office, quickly rejected the French suggestion. The French Prime Minister then proposed an alternative – that France at least be allowed to join the Commonwealth, still recognising the Queen as official Head of State. Eden was said to be sympathetic to this proposal, but those opposed to it on the committee he had established thwarted it in time-honoured fashion – by setting up a sub-committee to study it further. The sub-committee was instituted on 2 October 1956. Thirty-four days later, before any conclusions could be formulated, British and French forces invaded Suez. In the international furore that ensued, all suggestions of Anglo-French amalgamation vanished, never to be heard of again.

The mere fact that such proposals were being discussed, however, imparts a new significance to Saunière's genealogies being brought to England in 1956. If there were indeed high-level discussions about amalgamating Britain and France, or about France joining the Commonwealth, the genealogies would have been important documents indeed – to be used or withheld as various vested interests found expedient. In anything pertaining to the question of French sovereignty, documents concerning the Merovingian bloodline – its origins, its survival and its status as the oldest and 'most legitimate' in Europe – could hardly have been ignored. It is not too far-fetched to suggest that the very existence of such documents, if known, would have been sufficient to deter Britain from any form of union with France.

THE POLITICS OF THE PRIEURÉ DE SION

In 1973 a book was published entitled *Les Dessous d'une ambition politique* ('The Undercurrents of a Political Ambition'). This book, written by a Swiss journalist named Mathieu Paoli, recounts the author's exhaustive attempts to investigate the Prieuré de Sion. Like us, M. Paoli eventually established contact with a representative of the Order – whom he does not identify by name. But M. Paoli did not have the prestige of the BBC behind him, and the representative he met – if we can gauge by his account – would seem to have been of lesser status than M. Plantard. Nor was this representative as communicative as M. Plantard was with us. At the same time, M. Paoli, being based on the continent and enjoying a greater mobility than we do, was able to pursue certain leads and undertake 'on the spot' research in a way that we could not. As a result his book was extremely valuable and contains much new information – so much, in fact, that it appeared to warrant a sequel, and we wondered why M. Paoli had not written one. When we inquired about him, we were told that in 1977 or 1978 he had been shot as a spy

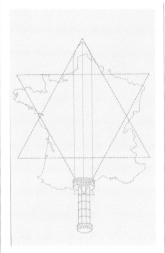

The cover design of the novel,
Circuit.

by the Israeli government for attempting to sell certain secrets to the Arabs.[29]

M. Paoli's approach, as he describes it in his book, was in many respects similar to our own. He too contacted the daughter of Leo Schidlof in London; and he too was told by Miss Schidlof that her father, to her knowledge, had no connection whatever with secret societies, Freemasonry or Merovingian genealogies. Like our BBC researcher, M. Paoli also contacted Grande Loge Alpina and met with the Loge's Chancellor, and each received an ambiguous reply. According to M. Paoli, the Chancellor denied all knowledge of anyone named 'Lobineau' or 'Schidlof'. As for the various works bearing the Alpina imprint, the Chancellor asserted quite categorically that they did not exist. And yet a personal friend of M. Paoli's who was also a member of Alpina, claimed to have seen the works in the Loge's library. M. Paoli's conclusion is as follows:

> There is one of two possibilities. Given the specific character of the works of Henri Lobineau, Grande Loge Alpina – which forbids all political activity both within Switzerland and without – does not want known its involvement in the affair. Or another movement has availed itself of the name of the Grande Loge in order to camouflage its own activities.[30]

In the Versailles Annexe of the Bibliothèque Nationale, M. Paoli discovered four issues of *Circuit*,[31] the magazine mentioned in the Prieuré de Sion's statutes. The first one was dated July 1st, 1959, and its director was listed as Pierre Plantard. But the magazine itself did not purport to be connected with the Prieuré de Sion. On the contrary it declared itself the official organ of something called the Federation of French Forces. There was even a seal, which M. Paoli reproduces in his book, and the following data:

Publication périodique culturelle de la Fédération des Forces
Françaises
116 Rue Pierre Jouhet, 116
Aulnay-sous-Bois – (Seine-et-Oise)
Tél: 929–72–49

M. Paoli checked the above address. No magazine had ever been published there. The telephone number, too, proved to be false. And all M.

Paoli's attempts to track the Federation of French Forces proved futile. To this day no information on any such organisation has been forthcoming. But it would hardly seem coincidental that the French headquarters of the Committees of Public Safety were also Aulnay-sous-Bois.[32] The Federation of French Forces would thus appear to have been in some way connected with the committees. There would seem to be considerable basis for this assumption. M. Paoli reports that Volume 2 of *Circuit* alludes to a letter from de Gaulle to Pierre Plantard, thanking the latter for his service. The service in question would seem to have been the work of the Committees of Public Safety.

According to M. Paoli, most of the articles in *Circuit* dealt with esoteric matters. They were signed by Pierre Plantard – under both his own name and the pseudonym 'Chyren' – Anne Lea Hisler and others with whom we were already familiar. At the same time, however, there were other articles of a very different kind. Some of them, for example, spoke of a secret science of vines and viticulture – the grafting of vines – which, apparently, had some crucial bearing on politics. This seemed to make no sense unless we assumed that vines and viticulture were to be understood allegorically – a metaphor perhaps for genealogies, for family trees and dynastic alliances.

When the articles in *Circuit* were not arcane or obscure, they were, according to M. Paoli, fervently nationalistic. In one of them, for instance, signed Adrian Sevrette, the author asserts that no solution for existing problems will be forthcoming

> except through new methods and new men, for politics are
> dead. The curious fact remains that men do not wish to recog-
> nise this. There exists only one question: economic organisation.
> But do there still exist men who are capable of thinking *France*,
> as during the Occupation, when patriots and resistance fighters
> did not bother themselves about the political tendencies of their
> comrades in the fight?[33]

And from Volume 4 of *Circuit*, M. Paoli quotes the following passage:

> We desire that the 1500 copies of *Circuit* be a contact which kin-
> dles a light, we desire that the voice of patriots be able to tran-
> scend obstacles as in 1940, when they left invaded France to
> come and knock on the office door of the *leader* of Free France.

Today, it is the same, before all we are French, we are that force which fights in one way or another to construct a France cleansed and new. This must be done in the same patriotic spirit, with the same will and solidarity of action. Thus we cite here what we declare to be an old philosophy.[34]

There then follows a detailed plan of government to restore to France a lost lustre. It insists, for example, on the dismantling of departments and the restoration of provinces:

The department is but an arbitrary system, created at the time of the Revolution, dictated and determined by the era in accordance with the demands of locomotion (the horse). Today, it no longer represents anything. In contrast, the province is a living portion of France; it is a whole vestige of our past, the same basis as that which formed the existence of our nation; it has its own folklore, its customs, its monuments, often its local dialects, which we wish to reclaim and promulgate. The province must have its own specific apparatus for defence and administration, adapted to its specific needs, with the national unit.[35]

M. Paoli then quotes eight pages that follow. The material they contain is organised under the following subheadings:

Council of the Provinces
Council of State
Parliamentary Council
Taxes
Work and Production
Medical
National Education
Age of Majority
Housing and Schools

The plan of government proposed under these subheadings is not inordinately controversial, and could probably be instituted with a minimum of upheaval. Nor can the plan be labelled politically. It cannot be called 'left-wing' or 'right-wing', liberal or conservative, radical or reactionary. On the whole, it seems fairly innocuous; and one is at a loss to see how it would necessarily restore any particular lost lustre to France. As M. Paoli says, 'The propositions . . . are not revolutionary. However, they rest on a realistic analysis of the actual structures of the French state, and are impregnated with a solid good sense.'[36] But then the plan of government outlined in *Circuit* makes no explicit mention of the real basis on which, if implemented, it would presumably ultimately rest – the restoration of a popular monarchy ruled by the Merovingian bloodline. In *Circuit* there would be no need to state this, for it would constitute an underlying 'given', a premise on which everything published in the magazine pivoted. For the magazine's intended readers the restoration of the Merovingian bloodline was clearly too obvious and accepted an objective to need belabouring.

At this point in his book M. Paoli poses a crucial question – a question that had haunted us as well:

> We have, on the one hand, a concealed descent from the Merovingians and, on the other, a secret movement, the Prieuré de Sion, whose goal is to facilitate the restoration of a popular monarchy of the Merovingian line . . . But it is necessary to know if this movement contents itself with esoterico-political speculations (whose unavowed end is to make much money by exploiting the world's gullibility and naiveté) or whether this movement is genuinely active.[37]

M. Paoli then considers this question, reviewing the evidence at his disposal. His conclusion is as follows:

> Unquestionably, the Prieuré de Sion seems to possess powerful connections. In actuality, any creation of an association is submitted to a preliminary inquiry by the Minister of the Interior. This obtains as well for a magazine, a publishing house. And yet these people are able to publish, under pseudonyms, at false addresses, through non-existent publishing houses, works which cannot be found in circulation either in Switzerland or in France. There are two possibilities. Either government authorities are not doing their jobs. Or else . . .[38]

M. Paoli does not spell out the alternative. At the same time it is apparent that he personally regards the unstated alternative as the more probable of the two. M. Paoli's conclusion, in short, is that government officials, and a great many other powerful people as well, are either members of Sion or obedient to it. If this is so, Sion must be a very influential organisation indeed.

Having conducted extensive research of his own, M. Paoli is satisfied with the Merovingian claim to legitimacy. To that extent, he admits, he can make sense of Sion's objectives. Beyond this point, however, he confesses himself to be profoundly puzzled. What is the point, he wonders, of restoring the Merovingian bloodline today, 1300 years after it was deposed? Would a modern-day Merovingian régime be different from any other modern-day régime? If so, how and why? What is so special about the Merovingians? Even if their claim is legitimate, it would seem to be irrelevant. Why should so many powerful and intelligent people, both today and in the past, accord it not only their attention, but their allegiance as well?

We, of course, were posing precisely the same questions. Like M. Paoli, we were prepared to acknowledge the Merovingian claim to legitimacy. But what possible significance could such a claim enjoy today? Could the technical legitimacy of a monarchy really be so persuasive and convincing an argument? Why, in the late twentieth century, should any monarchy, legitimate or not, command the kind of allegiance the Merovingians seemed to command?

If we were dealing only with a group of idiosyncratic cranks, we could dismiss the matter out of hand. But we were not. On the contrary, we seemed to be dealing with an extremely influential organisation which included in its ranks some of the most important, most distinguished, most acclaimed and most responsible men of our age. And these men, in many cases, seemed to regard the restoration of the Merovingian dynasty as a sufficiently valid goal to transcend their personal political, social and religious differences.

It seemed to make no sense – that the restoration of a 1300-year-old bloodline should constitute so vital a *cause célèbre* for so many public and highly esteemed people. Unless, of course, we were overlooking something. Unless legitimacy was not the only Merovingian claim. Unless there was something else of immense consequence that differentiated the Merovingians from other dynasties. Unless, in short, there was something very special indeed about the Merovingian blood royal.

CHAPTER NINE

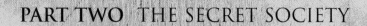

THE LONG-HAIRED MONARCHS

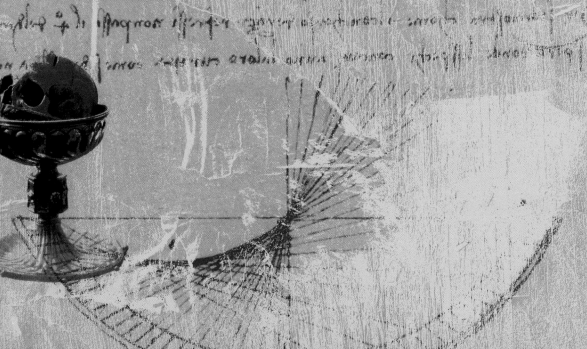

B y this time, of course, we had already researched the Merovingian dynasty. As far as we could we had groped our way through a mist of fantasy and obscurity even more opaque than that surrounding the Cathars and the Knights Templar. We had spent some months endeavouring to disentangle complex strands of intertwined history and fable. Despite our efforts, however, the Merovingians remained for the most part shrouded in mystery.

The Merovingian dynasty issued from the Sicambrians, a tribe of the Germanic people collectively known as the Franks. Between the fifth and seventh centuries the Merovingians ruled large parts of what are now France and Germany. The period of their ascendancy coincides with the period of King Arthur – a period which constitutes the setting for the romances of the Holy Grail. It is probably the most impenetrable period of what are now called the Dark Ages. But the Dark Ages, we discovered, had not been truly dark. On the contrary it quickly became apparent to us that someone had deliberately obscured them. To the extent that the Roman Church exercised a veritable monopoly on learning, and especially on writing, the records that survived represent certain vested interests. Almost everything else has been lost – or censored. But here and there something from time to time slipped through the curtain drawn across the past, seeped out to us despite the official silence. From these shadowy vestiges, a reality could be reconstructed – a reality of a most interesting kind, and one very discordant with the tenets of orthodoxy.

LEGEND AND THE MEROVINGIANS

We encountered a number of enigmas surrounding the origins of the Merovingian dynasty. One usually thinks of a dynasty, for example, as a ruling family or house which not merely succeeds another ruling family or house, but does so by virtue of having displaced, deposed or supplanted its predecessors. In other words one thinks of dynasties as commencing with a *coup d'état* of one sort or another, often entailing the extinction of the previous ruling line. The Wars of the Roses in England, for instance, marked the change of a dynasty. A century or so later the Stuarts mounted the English throne only when the Tudors were extinct. And the Stuarts themselves were deposed forcibly by the houses of Orange and Hanover.

In the case of the Merovingians, however, there was no such violent or abrupt transition, no usurpation, no displacement, no extinction of an earlier régime. On the contrary the house that came to be called Merovingian seems already to have ruled over the Franks. The Merovingians were already rightful and duly acknowledged kings. But there appears to have been something special about one of them – so much so that he conferred his name on the entire dynasty.

The ruler from whom the Merovingians derived their name is most elusive, his historical reality eclipsed by legend. Mérovée (Merovech or Meroveus) was a semi-supernatural figure worthy of classical myth. Even his name bears witness to his miraculous origin and character. It echoes the French word for 'mother', as well as both the French and Latin words for 'sea'.

According to both the leading Frankish chronicler and to subsequent tradition, Mérovée was born of two fathers. When already pregnant by her husband, King Clodio, Mérovée's mother supposedly went swimming in the ocean. In the water she is said to have been seduced and/or raped by an unidentified marine creature from beyond the sea – 'bestea Neptuni Quinotauri similis', a 'beast of Neptune similar to a Quinotaur', whatever a Quinotaur may have been. This creature apparently impregnated the lady a second time. And when Mérovée was born, there allegedly flowed in his veins a commingling of two different bloods – the blood of a Frankish ruler and of a mysterious aquatic creature.

Such fantastic legends are quite common, of course, not only in the ancient world, but in later European tradition as well. Usually they are not entirely imaginary, but symbolic or allegorical, masking some concrete historical fact behind their fabulous façade. In the case of Mérovée the fabulous façade might well indicate an intermarriage of some sort – a pedigree transmitted through the mother, as in Judaism, for instance, or a mingling of dynastic lines whereby the Franks became allied by blood with someone else; quite possibly with a source from 'beyond the sea' – a source which, for one or another reason, was transformed by subsequent fable into a sea-creature.

In any case by virtue of his dual blood Mérovée was said to have been endowed with an impressive array of superhuman powers. And whatever the historical actuality behind the legend, the Merovingian dynasty continued to be mantled in an aura of magic, sorcery and the supernatural. According to tradition, Merovingian monarchs were occult adepts, initiates in arcane sciences, practitioners of esoteric arts –

worthy rivals of Merlin, their fabulous near-contemporary. They were often called 'the sorcerer kings' or 'thaumaturge kings'. By virtue of some miraculous property in their blood they could allegedly heal by laying on of hands; and according to one account the tassels at the fringes of their robes were deemed to possess miraculous curative powers. They were said to be capable of clairvoyant or telepathic communication with beasts and with the natural world around them, and to wear a powerful magical necklace. They were said to possess an arcane spell which protected them and granted them phenomenal longevity – which history, incidentally, does not seem to confirm. And they all supposedly bore a distinctive birthmark, which distinguished them from all other men, which rendered them immediately identifiable and which attested to their semi-divine or sacred blood. This birthmark reputedly took the form of a red cross, either over the heart – a curious anticipation of the Templar blazon – or between the shoulder blades.

The Merovingians were also frequently called 'the long-haired kings'. Like Samson in the Old Testament, they were loath to cut their hair. Like Samson's, their hair supposedly contained their *vertu* – the essence and secret of their power. Whatever the basis for this belief in the power of the Merovingians' hair, it seems to have been taken quite seriously, and as late as A.D. 754. When Childeric III was deposed in that year and imprisoned, his hair was ritually shorn at the pope's express command.

However extravagant the legends surrounding the Merovingians, they would seem to rest on some concrete basis, some status enjoyed by the Merovingian monarchs during their own lifetime. In fact the Merovingians were not regarded as kings in the modern sense of that word. They were regarded as priest-kings – embodiments of the divine, in other words, not unlike, say, the ancient Egyptian pharaohs. They did not rule simply by God's grace. On the contrary they were apparently deemed the living embodiment and incarnation of God's grace – a status usually reserved exclusively for Jesus. And they seem to have engaged in ritual practices which partook, if anything, more of priesthood than of kingship. Skulls found of Merovingian monarchs, for example, bear what appears to be a ritual incision or hole in the crown. Similar incisions can be found in the skulls of high priests of early Tibetan Buddhism – to allow the soul to escape on death, and to open direct contact with the divine. There is

Crystal ball found in the grave of Merovingian king Childeric I, the father of Clovis who was the first of the line to convert to Christianity. Many similar to this have been found in other Merovingian tombs. Their use is unknown.

Two gold bees - all that now remain of the three hundred found in king Childeric's grave.

reason to suppose that the clerical tonsure is a residue of the Merovingian practice.

In 1653 an important Merovingian tomb was found in the Ardennes – the tomb of King Childeric I, son of Mérovée and father of Clovis, most famous and influential of all Merovingian rulers. The tomb contained arms, treasure and regalia, such as one would expect to find in a royal tomb. It also contained items less characteristic of kingship than of magic, sorcery and divination – a severed horse's head, for instance, a bull's head made of gold and a crystal ball.[1]

One of the most sacred of Merovingian symbols was the bee; and King Childeric's tomb contained no less than three hundred miniature bees made of solid gold. Along with the tomb's other contents, these bees were entrusted to Leopold Wilhelm von Habsburg, military governor of the Austrian Netherlands at the time and brother of the Emperor Ferdinand III.[2] Eventually most of Childeric's treasure was returned to France. And when he was crowned emperor in 1804 Napoleon made a special point of having the golden bees affixed to his coronation robes.

This incident was not the only manifestation of Napoleon's interest in the Merovingians. He commissioned a compilation of genealogies by one Abbé Pichón, to determine whether or not the Merovingian bloodline had survived the fall of the dynasty. It was on these genealogies, commissioned by Napoleon, that the genealogies in the 'Prieuré documents' were in large part based.[3]

The Marquis de Chérisey began to drop recurring allusions to the painter Jacques Louis David (1748–1825). We had noted David's paintings – the care, for instance, with which he emphasised the golden Merovingian bees on Napoleon's coronation robe. But David's name had not previously occurred in relation to the mystery of Rennes-le-Château and had not previously figured in what we called 'the Prieuré documents'.

As is well known, David was the 'neo-classical' court painter to Napoleon, famous for his depictions of Napoleon's coronation (reproduced for years in cognac advertisements) and of Marat's assassination, as well as for his portrayal of Marie Antoinette on her way to execution. His first significant commission as a painter had come in 1782 from the wife of the then Minister of War, the Marshal de Noailles. She was Catherine de Cossé-Brissac. The Noailles family had often been cited in 'the Prieuré documents', as having a valid claim to Merovingian descent. They had figured repeatedly in our story, up to the twentieth century, when Cocteau's patron was the Comtesse de Noailles. The Cossé-Brissac family had been associated with the Noailles as early as the sixteenth century, and had subsequently become one of the families most closely associated with French Freemasonry. It was in the archives of the Cossé-Brissac family that the 1656 'Fouquet letter' came to light.

Around 1795, David began to gather a circle of pupils at his studio in Paris. Among this circle was a certain Maurice Quay. Quay was the founder of an unnamed secret society. He was also a close friend of the young Charles Nodier, alleged to have been Grand Master of the Prieuré between 1801 and 1844. The secret society founded by Quay, and attended by Nodier, would meet regularly in a room directly above David's studio.[i] David can hardly have been unaware of its existence and its activities, especially given the involvement of one of his pupils. It is likely, indeed, that his circle of disciples provided other recruits. And in one instance, at least, that circle leads directly back to the mystery of Rennes-le-Château.

The list of David's pupils includes, among others, the name of a future military commander, the Marquis d'Hautpoul.[ii] The marquis, Armand d'Hautpoul, was a member of the Hautpoul-Blanchefort family who, until the French Revolution, had owned Rennes-le-Château. Armand was in fact the nephew of Marie de Negri d'Ables, or Marie de Blanchefort, whose enigmatic enciphered tombstone provides one of the starting points for any investigation of the mystery.

Armand d'Hautpoul never exhibited any of his paintings, and nothing is known about his period of apprenticeship to David. From 1803 on, when he was commissioned a lieutenant in a regiment of horse artillery, he pursued a military career. He fought at Ulm, Austerlitz and in Spain. He was wounded at Wagram. He was 'at the side of the Emperor', as a staff officer of ordnance, on Napoleon's invasion of Russia; and on the subsequent retreat, he fought at Lützen and Dresden, where he was wounded again, this time severely. In 1814, he resigned from Napoleon's army and transferred his allegiance to the restored Bourbon monarchy, eventually

Gold sword hilt and scabbard parts set with garnets, found in the grave of king Childeric.

becoming a general and commander of the Staff College. Towards the end of his life, he resigned this post in protest against serving the government of Louis-Philippe.

Armand d'Hautpoul's uncle, Joseph-Marie, Marquis d'Hautpoul, had been the husband of Marie de Negri d'Ables, or Marie de Blanchefort, or, as she was also known, Marie d'Hautpoul-Rennes. This marriage had reunited two sides of the ancient Hautpoul family which had been separated since 1418.[iii] But Joseph-Marie d'Hautpoul had died at a relatively early age, in 1753. Marie died in 1781. The future general, Armand d'Hautpoul, would thus have been her heir – and eventual custodian of the family's secrets. The links associating him directly with David, and, through David, with Nodier, assume, in consequence, a dramatic new significance.

i: Delécluze, M.E.J., *Louis David, son école et son temps*, Paris, 1855, p.73.

ii: "D'Hautpoult (Marquis General d')" listed in Delécluze, *op. cit*, p.415; "D'Hautpoul (le marquis)" listed in David, J.L.L., *Le Peintre Louis David*, Paris, 1880, p.627.

iii: General Amand d'Hautpoul's father was Jean-Henri d'Hautpoul, brother of Joseph-Marie d'Hautpoul who on 24 September 1752 married Marie de Hautpoul-Rennes who is titled Marie de Negri d'Ablès (after her mother) in the *Dossiers Secrets*. By this marriage, the two branches of the family and all their lands, separated since 1418, were brought back together. See: *Dictionnaire de la Noblesse*, Paris, 1865, X, p.443. See also *Dossiers Secrets*, planche No.22.

THE BEAR FROM ARCADIA

The legends surrounding the Merovingians proved worthy of the age of Arthur and the Grail romances. At the same time they constituted a daunting rampart between us and the historical reality we wanted to explore. When we at last gained access to it – or what little of it survived – this historical reality was somewhat different from the legends. But it was not any the less mysterious, extraordinary or evocative.

We could find little verifiable information about the true origins of the Merovingians. They themselves claimed descent from Noah, whom they regarded, even more than Moses, as the source of all Biblical wisdom – an interesting position, which surfaced again a thousand years later in European Freemasonry. The Merovingians also claimed direct descent from ancient Troy – which, whether true or not, would serve to explain the occurrence in France of Trojan names like Troyes and Paris. More contemporary writers – including the authors of the 'Prieuré documents' – have endeavoured to trace the Merovingians to ancient Greece, and specifically to the region known as Arcadia. According to these documents, the ancestors of the Merovingians were connected with Arcadia's royal house. At some unspecified date towards the advent of the Christian era they supposedly migrated up the Danube, then up the Rhine, and established themselves in what is now western Germany.

Whether the Merovingians derived ultimately from Troy or from Arcadia would now seem to be academic, and there is not necessarily a conflict between the two claims. According to Homer a substantial contingent of Arcadians was present at the siege of Troy. According to early Greek histories, Troy was in fact founded by settlers from Arcadia. It is also worth noting in passing that the bear, in ancient Arcadia, was a sacred animal – a totem on which mystery cults were based and to which ritual sacrifice was made.[4] Indeed, the very name 'Arcadia' derives from 'Arkades', which means 'People of the Bear'. The ancient Arcadians claimed descent from Arkas, the patron deity of the land, whose name also means 'bear'. According to Greek myth, Arkas was the son of Kallisto, a nymph connected with Artemis, the Huntress. To the modern mind Kallisto is most familiar as the constellation Ursa Major – the Great Bear.

For the Sicambrian Franks, from whom the Merovingians issued, the bear enjoyed a similar exalted status. Like the ancient Arcadians they worshipped the bear in the form of Artemis – or, more specifically, the form of her Gallic equivalent, Arduina, patron goddess of the Ardennes. The mystery cult of Arduina persisted well into the Middle Ages, one centre of it being the town of Lunéville, not far from two other sites recurring repeatedly in our investigation – Stenay and Orval. As late as 1304 statutes were still being promulgated by the Church forbidding worship of the heathen goddess.[5]

Given the magical, mythic and totemic status of the bear in the Merovingian heartland of the Ardennes, it is not surprising that the name 'Ursus' – Latin for 'bear' – should be associated in the 'Prieuré documents' with the Merovingian royal line. Rather more surprising is the fact that the Welsh word for bear is 'arth' – from whence the name 'Arthur' derives. Although we did not pursue the matter at this point, the coincidence intrigued us – that Arthur should not only be contemporary with the Merovingians, but also, like them, associated with the bear.

THE SICAMBRIANS ENTER GAUL

In the early fifth century the invasion of the Huns provoked large-scale migrations of almost all European tribes. It was at this time that the Merovingians – or, more accurately, the Sicambrian ancestors of the Merovingians – crossed the Rhine and moved *en masse* into Gaul, establishing themselves in what is now Belgium and northern France, in the vicinity of the Ardennes. A century later this region came to be called the kingdom of Austrasie. And the core of the kingdom of Austrasie was what is now known as Lorraine.

The Sicambrian influx into Gaul did not consist of a horde of wild unkempt barbarians tumultuously overrunning the land. On the contrary it was a placid and civilised affair. For centuries the Sicambrians had maintained close contact with the Romans; and though they were pagans, they were not savages. Indeed, they were well versed in Roman customs and administration, and followed Roman fashions. Some Sicambrians had become high-ranking officers in the imperial army. Some had even become Roman consuls. Thus, the Sicambrian influx was less an onslaught or an invasion than a kind of peaceful absorption. And when, towards the end of the fifth century, the Roman empire collapsed, the Sicambrians filled the vacuum. They did not do so violently or by force. They retained the old customs and altered very little. With no upheaval whatever, they assumed control of the already existing but vacant administrative apparatus. The régime of the early Merovingians thus conformed fairly closely to the model of the old Roman empire.

MÉROVÉE AND HIS DESCENDANTS

Our research exhumed mention of at least two historical figures named Mérovée, and it is not altogether clear which of them legend credits with descent from a sea-creature. One Mérovée was a Sicambrian chieftain, alive in 417, who fought under the Romans and died in 438. It has been suggested by at least one modern expert on the period that this Mérovée actually visited Rome and caused something of a sensation. There is certainly a record of a visit by an imposing Frankish leader, conspicuous for his flowing yellow hair.

In 448 the son of this first Mérovée, bearing the same name as his father, was proclaimed king of the Franks at Tournai and reigned until his death ten years later. He may have been the first official king of the Franks as a united people. By virtue of this perhaps, or of whatever was symbolised by his fabulous dual birth, the dynasty which succeeded him has since been called Merovingian.

Under Mérovée's successors the kingdom of the Franks flourished. It was not the crude barbaric culture often imagined. On the contrary, it warrants comparison in many respects with the 'high civilisation' of Byzantium. Even secular literacy was encouraged. Under the Merovingians secular literacy was more widespread than it would be two dynasties and five hundred years later. This literacy extended up to the rulers themselves – a most surprising fact, given the rude, untutored and unlettered character of later medieval monarchs. King Chilperic, for example, who reigned during the sixth century, not only built lavish Roman-style amphitheatres at Paris and Soissons, but was also a dedicated and accomplished poet, who took considerable pride in his craft. And there are verbatim accounts of his discussions with ecclesiastical authorities which reflect an extraordinary subtlety, sophistication and learning – hardly qualities one would associate with a king of the time. In many of these discussions Chilperic proves himself more than equal to his clerical interlocutors.[6]

Under Merovingian rule the Franks were often brutal, but they were not really a warlike people by nature or disposition. They were not like the Vikings, for instance, or the Vandals, Visigoths or Huns. Their main activities were farming and commerce. Much attention was devoted to maritime trade, especially in the Mediterranean. And the artefacts of the Merovingian epoch reflect a quality of workmanship which is truly amazing – as the Sutton Hoo treasure ship attests.

The wealth accumulated by the Merovingian kings was enormous, even by later standards. Much of this wealth was in gold coins of superb quality, produced by royal mints at certain important sites including what is now Sion in Switzerland. Specimens of such coins were found in the Sutton Hoo treasure ship, and can now be seen in the British Museum. Many of the coins bear a distinctive equal-armed cross, identical to the one subsequently adopted during the Crusades for the Frankish kingdom of Jerusalem.

BLOOD ROYAL

Although Merovingian culture was both temperate and surprisingly modern, the monarchs who presided over it were another matter. They were not typical even of rulers of their own age, for the atmosphere of mystery and legend, magic and the supernatural, surrounded them even during their lifetimes. If the customs and economy of the Merovingian world did not differ markedly from others of the period, the aura about the throne and the royal bloodline was quite unique.

Sons of the Merovingian blood were not 'created' kings. On the contrary they were automatically regarded as such on the advent of their twelfth birthday. There was no public ceremony of anointment, no coronation of any sort. Power was simply assumed, as by sacred right. But while the king was supreme authority in the realm, he was never obliged – or even expected – to sully his hands with the mundane business of governing. He was essentially a ritualised figure, a priest-king, and his role was not necessarily to *do* anything, simply to *be*. The king ruled, in short, but did not govern. In this respect, his status was somewhat similar to that of the present British royal family. Government and administration were left to a non-royal official, the equivalent of a chancellor, who held the title 'Mayor of the Palace'. On the whole the structure of the Merovingian régime had many things in common with modern constitutional monarchies.

Even after their conversion to Christianity the Merovingian rulers, like the Patriarchs of the Old Testament, were polygamous. On occasion they enjoyed harems of oriental proportions. Even when the aristocracy, under pressure from the Church, became rigorously monogamous, the monarchy remained exempt. And the Church, curiously enough, seems to have accepted this prerogative without any inordinate protest. According to one modern commentator:

> Why was it [polygamy] tacitly approved by the Franks themselves? We may here be in the presence of ancient usage of polygamy in a royal family – a family of such rank that its blood could not be ennobled by any match, however advantageous, nor degraded by the blood of slaves . . . It was a matter of indifference whether a queen were taken from a royal dynasty or from among courtesans . . . The fortune of the dynasty rested in its blood and was shared by all who were of that blood.[7]

And again, 'It is just possible that, in the Merovingians, we may have a dynasty of Germanic Heerkönige derived from an ancient kingly family of the migration period.'[8]

But how many families can there possibly have been in the whole of world history which enjoyed such extraordinary and exalted status? Why should the Merovingians do so? Why should their blood come to be invested with such immense power? These questions continued to perplex us.

CLOVIS AND HIS PACT WITH THE CHURCH

The most famous of all Merovingian rulers was Mérovée's grandson, Clovis I, who reigned between 481 and 511. Clovis's name is familiar to any French schoolchild, for it was under Clovis that the Franks were converted to Roman Christianity. And it was through Clovis that Rome began to establish her undisputed supremacy in Western Europe – a supremacy that would remain unchallenged for a thousand years.

By 496 the Roman Church was in a precarious situation. During the course of the fifth century, its very existence had been severely threatened. Between 384 and 399 the bishop of Rome had already begun to call himself the pope, but his official status was no greater than that of any other bishop, and quite different from that of the pope today. He was not, in any sense, the spiritual leader or supreme head of Christendom. He merely represented a single body of vested interests, one of many divergent forms of Christianity – and one which was desperately fighting for survival against a multitude of conflicting schisms and theological points of view. Officially the Roman Church had no greater authority than, say, the Celtic church – with which it was constantly at odds. It had no greater authority than heresies such as Arianism, which denied Jesus's divinity and insisted on his humanity. Indeed during much of the fifth century every bishopric in Western Europe was either Arian or vacant.

If the Roman Church was to survive, still more assert its authority, it would need the support of a champion – a powerful secular figure who might represent it. If Christianity was to evolve in accordance with Roman doctrine, that doctrine would have to be disseminated, implemented and imposed by secular force – a force sufficiently powerful to withstand and eventually extirpate the challenge of rival Christian creeds. Not surprisingly the Roman Church, in its most acute moment

279

of need, turned to Clovis.

By 486 Clovis had significantly increased the extent of Merovingian domains, striking out from the Ardennes to annex a number of adjacent kingdoms and principalities, vanquishing a number of rival tribes. As a result, many important cities – Troyes, for instance, Rheims and Amiens – were incorporated into his realm. Within a decade it was apparent that Clovis was well on his way to becoming the most powerful potentate in Western Europe.

The conversion and baptism of Clovis proved to be of crucial importance to our investigation. An account of it was compiled, in all its particulars and details, around the time it happened. Two and a half centuries later this account, called *The Life of Saint Rémy,* was destroyed, except for a few scattered manuscript pages. And the evidence suggests that it was destroyed deliberately. Nevertheless the fragments that survive bear witness to the importance of what was involved.

According to tradition, Clovis's conversion was a sudden and unexpected affair, effected by the king's wife, Clothilde – a fervent devotee of Rome, who seems to have badgered her husband until he accepted her faith and who was subsequently canonised for her efforts. In these efforts she was said to have been guided and assisted by her confessor, Saint Rémy. But behind these traditions, there lies a very practical and mundane historical reality. When Clovis was converted to Roman Christianity and became first Catholic king of the Franks, he had more to gain than his wife's approbation, and a kingdom more tangibly substantial than the kingdom of Heaven.

It is known that in 496 a number of secret meetings occurred between Clovis and Saint Rémy. Immediately thereafter an accord was ratified between Clovis and the Roman Church. For Rome this accord constituted a major political triumph. It would ensure the Church's survival, and establish that Church as supreme spiritual authority in the West. It would consolidate Rome's status as an equal to the Greek Orthodox faith based in Constantinople. It would offer a prospect of Roman hegemony and an effective means of eradicating the hydra heads of heresy. And Clovis would be the means of implementing these things – the sword of the Church of Rome, the instrument whereby Rome imposed her spiritual dominion, the secular arm and palpable manifestation of Roman power.

In return Clovis was granted the title of 'Novus Constantinus' – 'New Constantine'. In other words, he was to preside over a unified

empire – a 'Holy Roman Empire' intended to succeed the one suppos-
edly created under Constantine and destroyed by the Visigoths and
Vandals not long before. According to one modern expert of the period,
Clovis, prior to his baptism, was, 'fortified . . . with visions of an empire
in succession to that of Rome, which should be the inheritance of the
Merovingian race'.[9]

According to another modern writer, 'Clovis must now become a
kind of western emperor, a patriarch to the western Germans, reigning
over, though not governing, all peoples and kings.'[10]

The pact between Clovis and the Roman Church, in short, was one
of momentous consequence to Christendom – not only the Christendom
of the time, but also the Christendom of the next millennium. Clovis's
baptism was deemed to mark the birth of a new Roman empire – a
Christian empire, based on the Roman Church and administered, on the
secular level, by the Merovingian bloodline. In other words, an indis-
soluble bond was established between church and state, each pledging
allegiance to the other, each binding itself to the other in perpetuity. In
ratification of this bond, in 496, Clovis allowed himself to be formally
baptised by Saint Rémy at Rheims. At the climax of the ceremony, Saint
Rémy pronounced his famous words:

MITIS DEPONE COLLA, SICAMBER, ADORA QUOD INCENDISTI, INCENDI
QUOD ADORASTI.

(BOW THY HEAD HUMBLY, SICAMBRIAN, REVERE WHAT THOU HAST
BURNED AND WHAT THOU HAST REVERED.)

It is important to note that Clovis's baptism was not a coronation – as
historians sometimes suggest. The Church did not make Clovis a king.
He was already that, and all the Church could do was recognise him as
such. By virtue of so doing, the Church officially bound itself not to
Clovis alone, but to his successors as well – not to a single individual,
but to a bloodline. In this respect the pact resembled the covenant which
God, in the Old Testament, makes with King David – a pact which can
be modified, as in Solomon's case, but not revoked, broken or betrayed.
And the Merovingians did not lose sight of the parallel.

During the remaining years of his life Clovis fully realised Rome's
ambitious expectations of him. With irresistible efficiency, faith was
imposed by the sword; and with the sanction and spiritual mandate of

the Church, the Frankish kingdom expanded to both east and south, encompassing most of modern France and much of modern Germany. Among Clovis's numerous adversaries the most important were the Visigoths, who adhered to Arian Christianity. It was against the empire of the Visigoths – which straddled the Pyrenees and extended as far north as Toulouse – that Clovis directed his most assiduous and concerted campaigns. In 507 he decisively defeated the Visigoths at the Battle of Vouillé. Shortly thereafter Aquitaine and Toulouse fell into Frankish hands. The Visigoth empire north of the Pyrenees effectively collapsed before the Frankish onslaught. From Toulouse, the Visigoths fell back to Carcassonne. Driven from Carcassonne, they established their capital, and last remaining bastion, in the Razès, at Rhédae – now the village of Rennes-le-Château.

DAGOBERT II

In 511 Clovis died, and the empire he had created was divided, according to Merovingian custom, between his four sons. For more than a century thereafter the Merovingian dynasty presided over a number of disparate and often warring kingdoms, while lines of succession became increasingly tangled and claims to thrones increasingly confused. The authority once centralised in Clovis became progressively more diffuse, progressively more inchoate, and secular order deteriorated. Intrigues, machinations, kidnappings and political assassination became ever more commonplace. And the court chancellors, or 'Mayors of the Palace', accumulated more and more power – a factor which would eventually contribute to the fall of the dynasty.

Bereft increasingly of authority the later Merovingian rulers have often been called 'les rois fainéants' – 'the enfeebled kings'. Posterity has contemptuously stigmatised them as weak, ineffectual monarchs, effeminate and pliably helpless in the hands of cunning and wily counsellors. Our research revealed that this stereotype was not strictly accurate. It is true that the constant wars, vendettas and internecine strife thrust a number of Merovingian princes on to the throne at an extremely youthful age – and they were thus easily manipulated by their advisers. But those who did attain manhood proved as strong and decisive as any of their predecessors. This certainly seems to have been the case with Dagobert II.

Dagobert II was born in 651, heir to the kingdom of Austrasie. On his father's death in 656 extravagant attempts were made to preclude his inheritance of the throne. Indeed Dagobert's early life reads like a medieval legend, or a fairy tale. But it is well documented history.[11]

On his father's death Dagobert was kidnapped by the presiding Mayor of the Palace, an individual named Grimoald. Attempts to find the five-year-old child proved fruitless, and it was not difficult to convince the court that he was dead. On this basis Grimoald then engineered his own son's acquisition of the throne, claiming this had been the wish of the former monarch, Dagobert's deceased father. The ruse worked effectively. Even Dagobert's mother, believing her son dead, deferred to the ambitious Mayor of the Palace.

However, Grimoald had apparently balked at actually murdering the young prince. In secret Dagobert had been confided to the charge of the bishop of Poitiers. The bishop, it seems, was equally reluctant to murder the child. Dagobert was therefore consigned to permanent exile in Ireland. He grew into manhood at the Irish monastery of Slane,[12] not far from Dublin; and here, at the school attached to the monastery, he received an education unobtainable in France at the time. At some point during this period he is supposed to have attended the court of the High King of Tara. And he is said to have made the acquaintance of three Northumbrian princes, also being educated at Slane. In 666, probably still in Ireland, Dagobert married Mathilde, a Celtic princess. Not long after he moved from Ireland to England, establishing residence at York, in the kingdom of Northumbria. Here he formed a close friendship with Saint Wilfrid, bishop of York, who became his mentor.

During the period in question a schism still existed between the Roman and Celtic Churches, with the latter refusing to acknowledge the

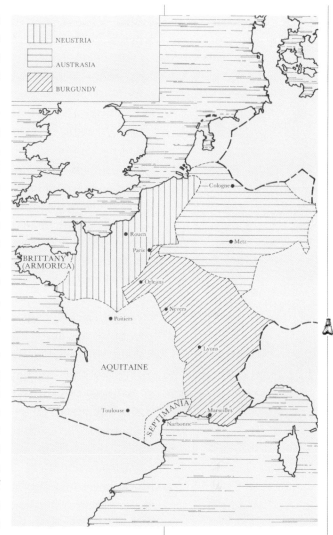

The Merovingian Kingdoms

former's authority. In the interests of unity Wilfrid was intent on bring-ing the Celtic Church into the Roman fold. This he had already accom-plished at the famous Council of Whitby in 664. But his subsequent friendship and patronage of Dagobert II may not have been devoid of ulterior motive. By Dagobert's time Merovingian allegiance to Rome – as dictated by the Church's pact with Clovis a century and a half before – was somewhat less fervent than it might have been. As a loyal adher-ent of Rome, Wilfrid was eager to consolidate Roman supremacy – not only in Britain, but on the continent as well. Were Dagobert to return to France and reclaim the kingdom of Austrasie, it would have been expe-dient to ensure his fealty. Wilfrid may well have seen the exiled king as a possible future sword-arm of the Church.

In 670 Mathilde, Dagobert's Celtic wife, died giving birth to her third daughter. Wilfrid hastened to arrange a new match for the recently bereft monarch, and in 671 Dagobert married for the second time. If his first alliance was of potential dynastic import, his second was even more so. Dagobert's new wife was Giselle de Razès, daughter of the count of Razès and niece of the king of the Visigoths.[13] In other words the Merovingian bloodline was now allied to the royal bloodline of the Visigoths. Herein lay the seeds of embryonic empire which would have united much of modern France extending from the Pyrenees to the Ardennes. Such an empire, moreover, would have brought the Visigoths – still with strong Arian tendency – firmly under Roman con-trol.

When Dagobert married Giselle, he had already returned to the con-tinent. According to existing documentation, the marriage was celebrat-ed at Giselle's official residence of Rhédae, or Rennes-le-Château. Indeed, the marriage was reputedly celebrated in the church of Saint Madeleine – the structure on the site of which Bérenger Saunière's church was subsequently erected.

Dagobert's first marriage had produced three daughters but no male heir. By Giselle, Dagobert had two more daughters and at last, in 676, one son – the infant Sigisbert IV. And by the time Sigisbert was born, Dagobert was once more a king.

For some three years he seems to have bided his time at Rennes-le-Château, watching the vicissitudes of his domains to the north. Finally, in 674, the opportunity had presented itself. With the support of his mother and her advisers, the long-exiled monarch announced himself, reclaimed his realm and was officially proclaimed king of Austrasie.

Wilfrid of York was instrumental in his reinstatement. According to Gérard de Sède, so too was a much more elusive, much more mysterious figure, about whom there is little historical information – Saint Amatus, bishop of Sion in Switzerland.[14]

Once restored to the throne, Dagobert was no *roi fainéant*. On the contrary, he proved to be a worthy successor to Clovis. At once he set about asserting and consolidating his authority, taming the anarchy that prevailed throughout Austrasie and re-establishing order. He ruled firmly, breaking the control of various rebellious nobles who had mobilised sufficient military and economic power to challenge the throne. And at Rennes-le-Château he is said to have amassed a substantial treasury. These resources were to be used to finance the reconquest of Aquitaine,[15] which had seceded from Merovingian hands some forty years previously and declared itself an independent principality.

At the same time Dagobert must have been a severe disappointment to Wilfrid of York. If Wilfrid had expected him to be a sword-arm of the Church, Dagobert proved nothing of the sort. On the contrary he seems to have curbed attempted expansion on the part of the Church within his realm, and thereby incurred ecclesiastical displeasure. A letter from an irate Frankish prelate to Wilfrid exists, condemning Dagobert for levying taxes, for 'scorning the churches of God together with their bishops'.[16]

Nor was this the only respect in which Dagobert seems to have run foul of Rome. By virtue of his marriage to a Visigoth princess he had acquired considerable territory in what is now the Languedoc. He may also have acquired something else. The Visigoths were only nominally loyal to the Roman Church. In fact their allegiance to Rome was extremely tenuous, and a tendency towards Arianism still obtained in the royal family. There is evidence to suggest that Dagobert absorbed something of this tendency.

By 679, after three years on the throne, Dagobert had made a number of powerful enemies, both secular and ecclesiastic. By curbing their rebellious autonomy, he had incurred the hostility of certain vindictive nobles. By thwarting its attempted expansion, he had roused the antipathy of the Church. By establishing an effective and centralised régime, he had provoked the envy and alarm of other Frankish potentates – the rulers of adjacent kingdoms. Some of these rulers had allies and agents within Dagobert's realm. One such was the king's own Mayor of the Palace, Pepin the Fat. And Pepin, clandestinely aligning himself with

Dagobert's political foes, did not shrink from either treachery or assassination.

Like most Merovingian rulers, Dagobert had at least two capital cities. The most important of these was Stenay,[17] on the fringe of the Ardennes. Near the royal palace at Stenay stretched a heavily wooded expanse, long deemed sacred, called the Forest of Woëvres. It was in this forest, on December 23rd, 679, that Dagobert is said to have gone hunting. Given the date, the hunt may well have been a ritual occasion of some sort. In any case, what followed evokes a multitude of archetypal echoes, including the murder of Siegfried in the *Nibelungenlied*.

Towards midday, succumbing to fatigue, the king lay down to rest beside a stream, at the foot of a tree. While he slept, one of his servants – supposedly his godson – stole furtively up to him and, acting under Pepin's orders, pierced him with a lance through the eye. The murderers then returned to Stenay, intent on exterminating the rest of the family in residence there. How successful they were in this latter undertaking is not clear. But there is no question that the reign of Dagobert and his family came to an abrupt and violent end. Nor did the Church waste much time grieving. On the contrary, it promptly endorsed the actions of the king's assassins. There is even a letter from a Frankish prelate to Wilfrid of York, which attempts to rationalise and justify the regicide.[18]

Dagobert's body and posthumous status both underwent a curious number of vicissitudes. Immediately after his death, he was buried at Stenay, in the Royal Chapel of Saint Rémy. In 872 – nearly two centuries later – he was exhumed and moved to another church. This new church became the Church of Saint Dagobert, for in the same year the dead king was canonised – not by the pope (who did not claim this right exclusively until 1159), but by a Metropolitan Conclave. The reason for Dagobert's canonisation remains unclear. According to one source, it was because his relics were believed to have preserved the vicinity of Stenay against Viking raids – though this explanation begs the question, for it is not clear why the relics should have possessed such powers in the first place. Ecclesiastical authorities seem embarrassingly ignorant concerning the matter. They admit that Dagobert, for some reason, became the object of a fully fledged cult and had his own feast day – December 23rd, the anniversary of his death.[19] But they seem utterly at a loss as to why he should have been so exalted. It is possible, of course, that the Church felt guilty about its role in the king's death. Dagobert's canonisation may therefore have been an attempt to make amends. If so, however, there is no indication of why such a gesture should have been deemed necessary, nor why it should have had to wait for two centuries.

Stenay, the Church of Saint Dagobert and perhaps the relics it contained were all accorded great significance by a number of illustrious figures in the centuries that followed. In 1069, for example, the duke of Lorraine – Godfroi de Bouillon's grandfather – accorded special protection to the church and placed it under the auspices of the near-by Abbey of Gorze. Some years later the church was appropriated by a local nobleman. In 1093 Godfroi de Bouillon mobilised an army and subjected Stenay to a full-scale siege – for the sole purpose, it would appear, of regaining the church and returning it to the Abbey of Gorze.

During the French Revolution, the church was destroyed and the relics of Saint Dagobert, like so many others throughout France, were dispersed. Today a ritually incised skull said to be Dagobert's is in the custody of a convent at Mons. All other relics of the king have disappeared. But in the mid-nineteenth century a most curious document came to light. It was a poem, a twenty-one verse litany, entitled 'De sancta Dagoberto martyre prose' – implying that Dagobert was martyred to, or for, something. This poem is believed to date from at least the Middle Ages, possibly much earlier. Significantly enough, it was found at the Abbey of Orval.[20]

THE USURPATION BY THE CAROLINGIANS

Strictly speaking Dagobert was not the last ruler of the Merovingian dynasty. In fact Merovingian monarchs retained at least nominal status for another three-quarters of a century. But these last Merovingians did warrant the appellation of *rois fainéants*. Many of them were extremely young. In consequence they were often weak, helpless pawns in the hands of the Mayors of the Palace, incapable of asserting their authority or of making decisions of their own. They were really little more than victims; and more than a few became sacrifices.

Moreover, the later Merovingians were of cadet branches, not scions of the main line descended from Clovis and Mérovée. The main line of Merovingian descent had been deposed with Dagobert II. To all intents and purposes, therefore, Dagobert's assassination may be regarded as signalling the end of the Merovingian dynasty. When Childeric III died in 754, it was a mere formality so far as dynastic power was concerned.

As rulers of the Franks the Merovingian bloodline had been effectively extinct long before.

As power seeped from the hands of the Merovingians, it passed into the hands of the Mayors of the Palace – a process that had already commenced before Dagobert's reign. It was a Mayor of the Palace, Pepin the Fat, who engineered Dagobert's death. And Pepin the Fat was followed by his son, the famous Charles Martel.

In the eyes of posterity Charles Martel is one of the most heroic figures in French history. There is certainly some basis for the acclaim given him. Under Charles the Moorish invasion of France was checked at the Battle of Poitiers in 732; and Charles, by virtue of this victory, was, in some sense, both 'defender of the Faith' and 'saviour of Christendom'. What is curious is that Charles Martel, strong man though he was, never seized the throne – which certainly lay within his grasp. In fact he seems to have regarded the throne with a certain superstitious awe – and, in all probability, as a specifically Merovingian prerogative. Certainly Charles's successors, who did seize the throne, went out of their way to establish their legitimacy by marrying Merovingian princesses.

Charles Martel died in 741. Ten years later his son, Pepin III, Mayor of the Palace to King Childeric III, enlisted the support of the Church in laying formal claim to the throne. 'Who should be king?' Pepin's ambassadors asked the pope. 'The man who actually holds power, or he, though called king, who had no power at all?' The pope pronounced in Pepin's favour. By apostolic authority he ordered that Pepin be created king of the Franks – a brazen betrayal of the pact ratified with Clovis two and a half centuries before. Thus endorsed by Rome, Pepin deposed Childeric III, confined the king to a monastery and – to humiliate him, to deprive him of his 'magical powers' or both – had him shorn of his sacred hair. Four years later Childeric died, and Pepin's claim to the throne was undisputed.[21]

A year before a crucial document had conveniently made its appearance, which subsequently altered the course of Western history. This document was called the 'Donation of Constantine'. Today there is no question that it was a forgery, concocted – and not very skilfully – within the papal Chancery. At the time, however, it was deemed genuine, and its influence was enormous.

The 'Donation of Constantine' purported to date from Constantine's alleged conversion to Christianity in A.D. 312. According to the

A silver reliquary containing the trepanned skull of Merovingian king Dagobert II who was assassinated near Stenay, France, 23rd December 679. This reliquary is kept in a convent at Mons, Belgium.

'Donation', Constantine had officially given to the bishop of Rome his imperial symbols and regalia, which thus became the Church's property. The 'Donation' further alleged that Constantine, for the first time, had declared the bishop of Rome to be 'Vicar of Christ' and offered him the status of emperor. In his capacity as 'Vicar of Christ' the bishop had supposedly returned the imperial regalia to Constantine, who wore them subsequently with ecclesiastical sanction and permission – more or less in the manner of a loan.

The implications of this document are clear enough. According to the 'Donation of Constantine', the bishop of Rome exercised supreme secular as well as supreme spiritual authority over Christendom. He was, in effect, a papal emperor, who could dispose as he wished of the imperial crown, who could delegate his power or any aspect thereof as he saw fit. In other words he possessed, through Christ, the unchallengeable right to create or depose kings. It is from the 'Donation of Constantine' that the subsequent power of the Vatican in secular affairs ultimately derives.

Claiming authority from the 'Donation of Constantine', the Church deployed its influence on behalf of Pepin III. It devised a ceremony whereby the blood of usurpers, or anyone else for that matter, could be made sacred. This ceremony came to be known as coronation and anointment – as those terms were understood during the Middle Ages and on into the Renaissance. At Pepin's coronation, bishops for the first time were authorised to attend, with rank equal to that of secular nobles. And the coronation itself no longer entailed the recognition of a king, or a pact with a king. It now consisted of nothing less than the creation of a king.

The ritual of anointment was similarly transformed. In the past, when practised at all, it was a ceremonial accoutrement – an act of recognition and ratification. Now, however, it assumed a new significance. Now it took precedence over blood, and could 'magically', as it were, sanctify blood. Anointment became something more than a symbolic gesture. It became the literal act whereby divine grace was conferred upon a ruler. And the pope, by performing this act, became supreme mediator between God and kings. Through the ritual of anointment, the Church arrogated to itself the right to make kings. Blood was now subordinate to oil. And all monarchs were rendered ultimately subordinate, and subservient, to the pope.

In 754 Pepin III was officially anointed at Ponthion, thus inaugurating the Carolingian dynasty. The name derives from Charles Martel, although it is generally associated with the most famous of Carolingian rulers, Charles the Great, Carolus Magnus or, as he is best known, Charlemagne. And in 800 Charlemagne was proclaimed Holy Roman Emperor – a title which, by virtue of the pact with Clovis three centuries before, should have been reserved exclusively for the Merovingian bloodline. Rome now became the seat of an empire that embraced the whole of Western Europe, whose rulers ruled only with the sanction of the pope.

In 496 the Church had pledged itself in perpetuity to the Merovingian bloodline. In sanctioning the assassination of Dagobert, in devising the ceremonies of coronation and anointment, in endorsing Pepin's claim to the throne, it had clandestinely betrayed its pact. In crowning Charlemagne it had made its betrayal not only public, but a *fait accompli*. In the words of one modern authority:

> We cannot therefore be sure that the anointing with chrism of
> the Carolingians was intended to compensate for the loss of
> magical properties of the blood symbolised by long hair. If it
> compensated for anything, it was probably for loss of faith
> incurred in breaking an oath of fidelity in a particularly shock-
> ing way.[22]

And again, 'Rome showed the way by providing in unction a king-mak-ing rite . . . that somehow cleared the consciences of "all the Franks".'[23]

Not all consciences, however. The usurpers themselves seem to have felt, if not a sense of guilt, at least an acute need to establish their legit-imacy. To this end Pepin III, immediately before his anointment, had ostentatiously married a Merovingian princess. And Charlemagne did likewise.

Charlemagne, moreover, seems to have been painfully aware of the betrayal involved in his coronation. According to contemporary accounts, the coronation was a carefully stage-managed affair, engi-neered by the pope behind the Frankish monarch's back; and Charlemagne appears to have been both surprised and profoundly embarrassed. A crown of some sort had already been clandestinely pre-pared. Charlemagne had been lured to Rome and there persuaded to attend a special mass. When he took his place in the church, the pope, without warning, placed a crown upon his head, while the populace acclaimed him as 'Charles, Augustus, crowned by God, the great and peace-loving emperor of the Romans'. In the words of a chronicler writing at the time, Charlemagne 'made it clear that he would not have entered the Cathedral that day at all, although it was the greatest of all festivals of the Church, if he had known in advance what the Pope was planning to do.'[24]

But whatever Charlemagne's responsibility in the affair, the pact with Clovis and the Merovingian bloodline had been shamelessly betrayed. And all our inquiries indicated that this betrayal, even though it occurred more than 1100 years ago, continued to rankle for the Prieuré de Sion. Mathieu Paoli, the independent researcher quoted in the preceding chapter, reached a similar conclusion:

> For them [the Prieuré de Sion], the only authentic nobility is the nobility of Visigothic/Merovingian origin. The Carolingians, then all others, are but usurpers. In effect, they were but functionaries of the king, charged with administering lands – who, after transmitting by heredity their right to govern these lands, then purely and simply seized power for themselves. In consecrating Charlemagne in the year 800, the Church perjured itself, for it had concluded, at the baptism of Clovis, an alliance with the Merovingians which had made France the eldest daughter of the Church.[25]

THE EXCLUSION OF DAGOBERT II FROM HISTORY

With the murder of Dagobert II in 679 the Merovingian dynasty effectively ended. With the death of Childeric III in 755 the Merovingians seemed to vanish from the stage of world history completely. According to the 'Prieuré documents', however, the Merovingian bloodline in fact survived. According to the 'Prieuré documents', it was perpetuated to the present day, from the infant Sigisbert IV – Dagobert's son by his second wife, Giselle de Razès.

There is no question that Sigisbert existed and that he was Dagobert's heir. According to all sources other than the 'Prieuré documents', however, it is unclear what happened to him. Certain chroniclers have tacitly assumed that he was murdered along with his father and other members of the royal family. One highly dubious account asserts that he died in a hunting accident a year or two before his father's death. If that is true Sigisbert must have been a precocious hunter, for he cannot possibly have been much more than three years old at the time.

There is no record whatever of Sigisbert's death. Nor is there any record – apart from the evidence in the 'Prieuré documents' – of his survival. The whole issue seems to have been lost in 'the mists of time', and no one seems to have been much concerned about it – except, of course, for the Prieuré de Sion. In any case Sion appeared to be privy to certain information which was not available elsewhere; or was deemed of too little consequence to warrant much investigation; or was deliberately suppressed.

It is hardly surprising that no account of Sigisbert's fate has been filtered down to us. There was no publicly accessible account even of Dagobert until the seventeenth century. At some point during the Middle Ages a systematic attempt was apparently made to erase Dagobert from history, to deny that he ever existed. Today Dagobert II can be found in any encyclopaedia. Until 1646, however, there was no acknowledgment whatever that he had ever lived.[26] Any list or genealogy of French rulers compiled before 1646 simply omits him, jumping (despite the flagrant inconsistency) from Dagobert I to Dagobert III – one of the last Merovingian monarchs, who died in 715. And not until 1655 was Dagobert II reinstated in accepted lists of French kings. Given this process of eradication, we were not unduly astonished at the dearth of information relating to Sigisbert. And we could not but suspect that whatever information did exist had been deliberately suppressed.

But why, we wondered, should Dagobert II have been excised from history? What was being concealed by such an excision? Why should one wish to deny the very existence of a man? One possibility, of course, is to negate thereby the existence of his heirs. If Dagobert never lived, Sigisbert cannot have lived either. But why should it have been important, as late as the seventeenth century, to deny that Sigisbert had ever lived? Unless he had indeed survived, and his descendants were still regarded as a threat.

It seemed to us that we were clearly dealing with some sort of 'cover-up'. Quite patently there were vested interests which had something of import to lose if knowledge of Sigisbert's survival were made public. In the ninth century and perhaps as late as the Crusades, these interests would seem to have been the Roman Church and the French royal line. But why should the issue have continued to matter as late as the age of

Louis XIV? It would surely have been an academic point by then, for three French dynasties had come and gone, while Protestantism had broken Roman hegemony. Unless there was indeed something very special about the Merovingian blood. Not 'magical properties', but something else – something that retained its explosive potency even after superstitions about magical blood had fallen by the wayside.

PRINCE GUILLEM DE GELLONE, COMTE DE RAZÈS

According to the 'Prieuré documents', Sigisbert IV, on the death of his father, was rescued by his sister and smuggled southwards to the domain of his mother – the Visigoth princess, Giselle de Razès. He is said to have arrived in the Languedoc in 681 and, at some point shortly thereafter, to have adopted – or inherited – his uncle's titles, duke of Razès and count of Rhédae. He is also said to have adopted the surname, or nickname, of 'Plant-Ard' (subsequently Plantard) from the appellation *'réjeton ardent'* – 'ardently flowering shoot' of the Merovingian vine. Under this name, and under the titles acquired from his uncle, he is said to have perpetuated his lineage. And by 886 one branch of that lineage is said to have culminated in a certain Bernard Plantavelu – apparently derived from Plant-ard or Plantard – whose son became the first duke of Aquitaine.

As far as we could ascertain, no independent historian either confirmed or disputed these assertions. The whole matter was simply ignored. But the circumstantial evidence argued persuasively that Sigisbert did indeed survive to perpetuate his lineage. The assiduous eradication of Dagobert from history lends credence to this conclusion. By denying his existence, any line of descent from him would have been invalidated. This constitutes a motive for an otherwise inexplicable action. Among the other fragments of evidence is a charter, dated 718, which pertains to the foundation of a monastery – a few miles from Rennes-le-Château – by 'Sigebert, Comte de Rhédae and his wife, Magdala'.[27] Apart from this charter nothing is heard of the Rhédae or Razès titles for another century. When one of them reappears, however, it does so in an extremely interesting context.

By 742 there was an independent and fully autonomous state in the south of France – a princedom according to some accounts, a fully fledged kingdom according to others. Documentation is sketchy and history is vague about it – most historians, in fact, are unaware of its

existence – but there is no question of its reality. It was officially recognised by Charlemagne and his successors, and by the caliph of Baghdad
and the Islamic world. It was grudgingly recognised by the Church,
some of whose lands it confiscated. And it survived until the late ninth
century.

Sometime between 759 and 768 the ruler of this state – which included the Razès and Rennes-le-Château – was officially pronounced a king.
Despite Rome's disapprobation, he was recognised as such by the
Carolingians, to whom he pledged himself as vassal. In existing
accounts he figures most frequently under the name of Theodoric, or
Thierry. And most modern scholars regard him as being of Merovingian
descent.[28] There is no definitive evidence from where such descent
might have derived. It might well have derived from Sigisbert. In any
case, there is no question that by 790 Theodoric's son, Guillem de
Gellone, held the title of count of Razès – the title Sigisbert is said to
have possessed and passed on to his descendants.

Guillem de Gellone was one of the most famous men of his time, so
much so, indeed, that his historical reality – like that of Charlemagne
and Godfroi de Bouillon – has been obscured by legend. Before the
epoch of the Crusades, there were at least six major epic poems composed about him, *chansons de geste* similar to the famous *Chanson de
Roland*. In *The Divine Comedy* Dante accorded him a uniquely exalted
status. But even before Dante, Guillem had again become an object of
literary attention. In the early thirteenth century he figured as the protagonist of *Willehalm*, an unfinished epic romance composed by
Wolfram von Eschenbach – whose most famous work, *Parzival*, is probably the most important of all romances dealing with the mysteries of
the Holy Grail. It seemed to us somewhat curious at first that Wolfram
– all of whose other work deals with the Grail, the 'Grail family' and the
lineage of the 'Grail family' – should suddenly devote himself to so radically different a theme as Guillem de Gellone. On the other hand,
Wolfram stated in another poem that the 'Grail castle', abode of the
'Grail family', was situated in the Pyrenees – in what, at the beginning
of the ninth century, was Guillem de Gellone's domain.

Guillem maintained a close rapport with Charlemagne. His sister, in
fact, was married to one of Charlemagne's sons, thus establishing a
dynastic link with the imperial blood. And Guillem himself was one of
Charlemagne's most important commanders in the incessant warfare
against the Moors. In 803, shortly after Charlemagne's coronation as

Holy Roman Emperor, Guillem captured Barcelona, doubling his own territory and extending his influence across the Pyrenees. So grateful was Charlemagne for his services that his principality was confirmed by the emperor as a permanent institution. The charter ratifying this has been lost or destroyed, but there is abundant testimony to its existence.

Independent and unimpugnable authorities have provided detailed genealogies of Guillem de Gellone's line – his family and descendants.[29] These sources, however, provide no indication of Guillem's antecedents, except for his father, Theodoric. In short, the real origins of the family were shrouded in mystery. And contemporary scholars and historians are generally somewhat puzzled about the enigmatic appearance, as if by spontaneous combustion, of so influential a noble house. But one thing, at any rate, is certain. By 886 the line of Guillem de Gellone culminated in a certain Bernard Plantavelu, who established the duchy of Aquitaine. In other words Guillem's line culminated in precisely the same individual as the line ascribed by the 'Prieuré documents' to Sigisbert IV and his descendants.

On Friday 13 October 1307, Templars throughout France were arrested in what was supposed to be a surprise swoop on their preceptories. Orders for similar arrests elsewhere swiftly followed – in Aragón, for example, in December. Some of the Aragonese Templars fled, discarding their habits, cutting their beards and vanishing into the civilian populace. Most, however, retired to their fortified castles in the kingdom, and in adjacent Catalonia, where they prepared to defend themselves.

In January 1308, forces loyal to the king laid siege to the Templar fortress of Miravet. The defending knights held out until the following November, when they finally surrendered on favourable terms. On entering the preceptory, the besiegers found, among other objects, an iron lance which had apparently been accorded some kind of special, if not indeed sacred, status, and revered, it would seem, as a relic. The lance had allegedly been passed down through the family of the Counts of Barcelona.[i]

Why should this lance have been significant? One can only speculate. But the first Count of Barcelona was the figure who appears in our text as Guillem de Gellone, Prince of Orange, Count of Toulouse and of Razès (Rennes-le-Château) – one of the Peers of Charlemagne and ruler of the Judaic principality in the south of

France. Guillam was also cited by Wolfram von Eschenbach as a member of the 'Grail family', and figures as the protagonist in Wolfram's *Willehalm*. Could the lance have been connected in some way with the lance in the Grail story, which Wolfram recounted in *Parzival*? Wolfram claimed to have heard the Grail story, it will be remembered, from one Guiot de Provins – who supposedly learned it in turn from an individual known as Flegetanis, in Spain.

i: Alart, M., "Suppression de l'Ordre du Temple en Roussillon", *Bulletin de la Société agricole, scientifique et littéraire de Pyrénées Orientales*, 15, 1867, p.42.

We were tempted, of course, to jump to conclusions, and use the genealogies in the 'Prieuré documents' to bridge the gap left by accepted history. We were tempted to assume that the elusive progenitors of Guillem de Gellone were Dagobert II, and Sigisbert IV and the main line of the deposed Merovingian dynasty – the line cited in the 'Prieuré documents' under the name Plant-Ard or Plantard.

Unfortunately we could not do so. Given the confused state of existing records, we could not definitively establish the precise connection between the Plantard line and the line of Guillem de Gellone. They might indeed have been one and the same. On the other hand, they might have intermarried at some point. What remained certain, however, was that both lines, by 886, had culminated in Bernard Plantavelu and the dukes of Aquitaine.

Although they did not always match precisely in dating and translation of names, the genealogies connected with Guillem de Gellone did constitute a certain independent confirmation for the genealogies in the 'Prieuré documents'. We could thus tentatively accept, in the absence of any contradictory evidence, that the Merovingian bloodline did continue, more or less as the 'Prieuré documents' maintained. We could tentatively accept that Sigisbert did survive his father's murder, did adopt the family name of Plantard and, as count of Razès, did perpetuate his father's lineage.

PRINCE URSUS

By 886, of course, the 'flowering shoot of the Merovingian vine' had blossomed into a large and complicated family tree. Bernard Plantavelu and the dukes of Aquitaine constitute one branch. There were other branches as well. Thus the 'Prieuré documents' declare that Sigisbert IV's grandson, Sigisbert VI, was known by the name of 'Prince Ursus'. Between 877 and 879 'Prince Ursus' is said to have been officially proclaimed 'King Ursus'. Aided by two nobles – Bernard d'Auvergne and the marquis of Gothie – he is said to have undertaken an insurrection against Louis II of France in an attempt to regain his rightful heritage.

Independent historians confirm that such an insurrection did indeed occur between 877 and 879. These same historians refer to Bernard d'Auvergne and the marquis of Gothie. The leader, or instigator, of the insurrection is not specifically named as Sigisbert VI. But there are references to an individual known as 'Prince Ursus'. Moreover, 'Prince Ursus' is known to have been involved in a curious and elaborate ceremony in Nîmes, at which five hundred assembled ecclesiastics chanted the Te Deum.[30] From all accounts of it, this ceremony would seem to have been a coronation. It may well have been the coronation to which the 'Prieuré documents' alluded – the proclamation of 'Prince Ursus' as king.

Once again, the 'Prieuré documents' received independent support. Once again, they seemed to draw on information unobtainable elsewhere – information which supplemented and sometimes even helped explain caesuras in accepted history. In this case, they had apparently told us who the elusive 'Prince Ursus' actually was – the lineal descendant, through Sigisbert IV, of the murdered Dagobert II. And the insurrection, of which historians had hitherto made no sense, could now be seen as a perfectly comprehensible attempt by the deposed Merovingian dynasty to regain its heritage – the heritage conferred upon it by Rome through the pact with Clovis, and then subsequently betrayed.

According to both the 'Prieuré documents' and independent sources, the insur-

The Merovingian Dynasty - The Counts of Razès. From Henri Lobineau's work based on the Abbé Pichon and De Hervé.

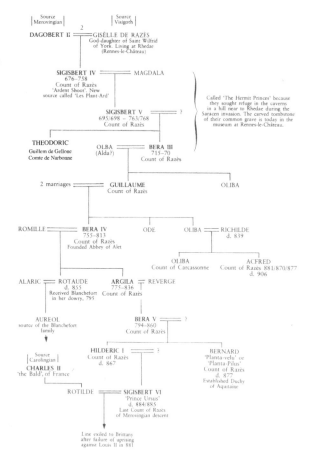

rection failed, 'Prince Ursus' and his supporters being defeated at a battle near Poitiers in 881. With this setback, the Plantard family is said to have lost its possessions in the south of France – although it still clung to the now purely titular status of duke of Rhédae and count of Razès. 'Prince Ursus' is said to have died in Brittany, while his line became allied by marriage with the Breton ducal house. By the late ninth century, then, the Merovingian blood had flowed into the duchies of both Brittany and Aquitaine.

In the years that followed, the family – including Alain, later duke of Brittany – is said to have sought refuge in England, establishing an English branch called 'Planta'. Independent authorities again confirm that Alain, his family and entourage, fled from the Vikings to England. According to the 'Prieuré documents', one of the English branch of the family, listed as Bera VI, was nicknamed 'the Architect'. He and his descendants, having found a haven in England under King Athelstan, are said to have practised 'the art of building' – a seemingly enigmatic reference. Interestingly enough, Masonic sources date the origin of Freemasonry in England from the reign of King Athelstan.[31] Could the Merovingian bloodline, we wondered, in addition to its claim to the French throne, be in some way connected with something at the core of Freemasonry?

THE GRAIL FAMILY

The Middle Ages abound with a mythology as rich and resonant as those of ancient Greece and Rome. Some of this mythology pertains, although wildly exaggerated in form, to actual historical personages – to Arthur, to Roland and Charlemagne, to Rodrigo Díaz of Vivar, popularly known as El Cid. Other myths – like those relating to the Grail, for example – would seem at first to rest on a more tenuous foundation.

Among the most popular and evocative of medieval myths is that of Lohengrin, the 'Swan Knight'. On the one hand it is closely linked with the fabulous Grail romances; on the other it cites specific historical personages. In its mingling of fact and fantasy it may well be unique. And through such works as Wagner's opera it continues to exert its archetypal appeal even today.

According to medieval accounts, Lohengrin – sometimes called Helias, implying solar associations – was a scion of the elusive and mysterious 'Grail family'. In Wolfram von Eschenbach's poem, he is in fact the son of Parzival, the supreme 'Knight of the Grail'. One day, in the sacred temple or castle of the Grail at Munsalvaesche, Lohengrin is said to have heard the chapel bell tolling without the intervention of human hands – a signal that his aid was urgently required somewhere in the world. It was required, predictably enough, by a damsel in distress – the duchess of Brabant[32] according to some sources, the duchess of Bouillon according to others. The lady desperately needed a champion, and Lohengrin hastened to her rescue in a boat drawn by heraldic swans. In single combat he defeated the duchess's persecutor, then married the lady. At their nuptials, however, he issued a stringent warning. Never was his bride to query him about his origins or ancestry, his background or the place whence he came. And for some years the lady obeyed her husband's edict. At last, however, goaded to fatal curiosity by the scurrilous insinuations of rivals, she presumed to ask the forbidden question. Thereupon, Lohengrin was compelled to depart, vanishing in his swan-drawn boat into the sunset. And behind him, with his wife, he left a child of uncertain lineage. According to the various accounts, this child was either the father or the grandfather of Godfroi de Bouillon.

It is difficult for the modern mind to appreciate the magnitude of Godfroi's status in popular consciousness – not only in his own time but even as late as the seventeenth century. Today, when one thinks of the Crusades, one thinks of Richard Coeur de Lion, King John, perhaps Louis IX (Saint Louis) or Frederick Barbarossa. But until relatively recently, none of these individuals enjoyed Godfroi's prestige or acclaim. Godfroi, leader of the First Crusade, was the supreme popular hero, the hero *par excellence*. It was Godfroi who inaugurated the Crusades. It was Godfroi who captured Jerusalem from the Saracens. It was Godfroi who rescued Christ's sepulchre from infidel hands. It was Godfroi, above all others, who, in people's imaginations, reconciled the ideals of high chivalric enterprise and fervent Christian piety. Not surprisingly, therefore, Godfroi became the object of a cult which persisted long after his death.

Given this exalted status, it is understandable that Godfroi should be credited with all manner of illustrious mythical pedigrees. It is even understandable that Wolfram von Eschenbach, and other medieval *romanciers*, should link him directly with the Grail – should depict him as a lineal descendant of the mysterious 'Grail family'. And such fabulous pedigrees are rendered even more comprehensible by the fact that Godfroi's true lineage is obscure. History remains uncomfortably uncertain about his ancestry.[33]

The 'Prieuré documents' furnished us with the most plausible – perhaps, indeed, the first plausible – genealogy of Godfroi de Bouillon that has yet come to light. As far as this genealogy could be checked – and much of it could be – it proved accurate. We found no evidence to contradict it, much to support it; and it convincingly bridged a number of perplexing historical gaps.

According to the genealogy in the 'Prieuré documents', Godfroi de Bouillon – by virtue of his great-grandmother, who married Hugues de Plantard in 1009 – was a lineal descendant of the Plantard family. In other words Godfroi was of Merovingian blood, directly descended from Dagobert II, Sigisbert IV and the line of Merovingian 'lost kings' – 'les rois perdus'. For four centuries the Merovingian blood royal appears to have flowed through gnarled and numerous family trees. At last, through a process analogous to the grafting of vines in viticulture, it would seem to have borne fruit in Godfroi de Bouillon, Duke of Lorraine. And here, in the house of Lorraine, it established a new patrimony.

This revelation cast a significant new light on the Crusades. We could now perceive the Crusades from a new perspective, and discern in them something more than the symbolic gesture of reclaiming Christ's supulchre from the Saracens.

In his own eyes, as well as those of his supporters, Godfroi would have been more than duke of Lorraine. He would, in fact, have been a rightful king – a legitimate claimant of the dynasty deposed with Dagobert II in 679. But if Godfroi was a rightful king, he was also a king without a kingdom; and the Capetian dynasty in France, supported by the Roman Church, was by then too well entrenched to be dethroned.

What can one do if one is a king without a kingdom? Perhaps find a kingdom. Or create a kingdom. The most precious kingdom in the entire world – Palestine, the Holy Land, the soil trodden by Jesus himself. Would not the ruler of such a kingdom be comparable to any in Europe? And would he not, in presiding over that most sacred of earthly sites, obtain sweet revenge on the Church which betrayed his ancestors four centuries before?

THE ELUSIVE MYSTERY

Gradually certain pieces of the puzzle were beginning to fall into place.

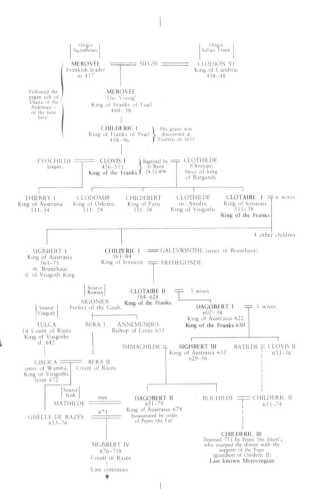

The Merovingian Dynasty -
The lost Kings.
From the work of Henri
Lobineau's (Henri de
Lénoncort).

If Godfroi was of Merovingian blood, a number of seemingly disconnected fragments ceased to be disconnected and assumed a coherent continuity. We could thus explain the emphasis accorded such apparently disparate elements as the Merovingian dynasty and the Crusades, Dagobert II and Godfroi, Rennes-le-Château, the Knights Templar, the house of Lorraine, the Prieuré de Sion. We could even trace the Merovingian bloodlines up to the present day – to Alain Poher, to Henri de Montpézat (consort of the queen of Denmark), to Pierre Plantard de Saint-Clair, to Otto von Habsburg, titular duke of Lorraine and king of Jerusalem.

And yet the really crucial question continued to elude us. We still could not see why the Merovingian bloodline should be so inexplicably important today. We still could not see why its claim should be in any way relevant to contemporary affairs, or why it should command the allegiance of so many distinguished men through the centuries. We still could not see why a modern Merovingian monarchy, however technically legitimate it might be, warranted such urgent endorsement. Quite clearly we were overlooking something.

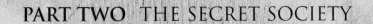

PART TWO THE SECRET SOCIETY

CHAPTER TEN

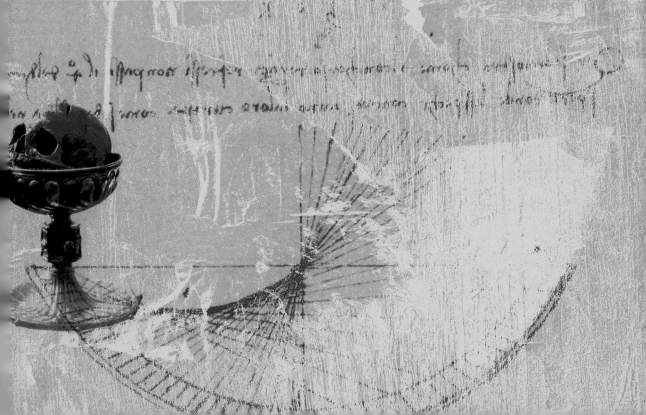

THE
EXILED TRIBE

Could there be something special about the Merovingian bloodline – something more than an academic, technical legitimacy? Could there really be something which, in some way, might genuinely matter to people today? Could there be something that might affect, perhaps even alter, existing social, political or religious institutions? These questions continued to nag at us. As yet, however, there appeared to be no answer to them.

Once again we sifted through the compilation of 'Prieuré documents', and especially the all-important *Dossiers secrets*. We re-read passages which had meant nothing to us before. Now they made sense, but they did not serve to explain the mystery, nor to answer what had now become the critical questions. On the other hand there were other passages whose relevance was still unclear to us. These passages by no means resolved the enigma; but, if nothing else, they set us thinking along certain lines – lines which eventually proved to be of paramount significance.

As we had already discovered, the Merovingians themselves, according to their own chroniclers, claimed descent from ancient Troy. But according to certain of the 'Prieuré documents' the Merovingian pedigree was older than the siege of Troy. According to certain of the 'Prieuré documents', the Merovingian pedigree could in fact be traced back to the Old Testament.

Among the genealogies in the *Dossiers secrets*, for example, there were numerous footnotes and annotations. Many of these referred specifically to one of the twelve tribes of ancient Israel, the Tribe of Benjamin. One such reference cites, and emphasises, three Biblical passages – Deuteronomy 33, Joshua 18 and Judges 20 and 21.

Deuteronomy 33 contains the blessing pronounced by Moses on the patriarchs of each of the twelve tribes. Of Benjamin, Moses says, 'The beloved of the Lord shall dwell in safety by him; and the Lord shall cover him all the day long, and he shall dwell between his shoulders.' (33:12) In other words Benjamin and his descendants were singled out for a very special and exalted blessing. That much, at any rate, was clear. We were, of course, puzzled by the promise of the Lord dwelling 'between Benjamin's shoulders'. Should we associate it with the legendary Merovingian birthmark – the red cross between the shoulders? The connection seemed somewhat far-fetched. On the other hand, there were other clearer similarities between Benjamin in the Old Testament and the subject of our investigation. According to Robert Graves, for example, the day sacred to Benjamin was December 23rd[1] – Dagobert's feast day. Among the three clans which comprised the Tribe of Benjamin, there was the clan of Ahiram – which might in some obscure way pertain to Hiram, builder of the Temple of Solomon and central figure in Masonic tradition. Hiram's most devoted disciple, moreover, was named Benoni; and Benoni, interestingly enough, was the name originally conferred upon the infant Benjamin by his mother, Rachel, before she died.

The second Biblical reference in the *Dossiers secrets*, to Joshua 18, is rather more clear. It deals with the arrival of Moses's people in the Promised Land and the apportionment to each of the twelve tribes of particular tracts of territory. According to this apportionment, the territory of the Tribe of Benjamin included what subsequently became the sacred city of Jerusalem. Jerusalem, in other words, even before it became the capital of David and Solomon, was the allocated birthright of the Tribe of Benjamin. According to Joshua 18:28, the birthright of the Benjamites encompassed 'Zelah, Eleph and Jebusi, which is Jerusalem, Gibeath and Kirjath; fourteen cities with their villages. This is the inheritance of the children of Benjamin according to their families.'

The third Biblical passage cited by the *Dossiers secrets* involves a fairly complex sequence of events. A Levite, travelling through Benjamite territory, is assaulted, and his concubine ravished, by worshippers of Belial – a variant of the Sumerian Mother Goddess, known as Ishtar by the Babylonians and Astarte by the Phoenicians. Calling representatives of the twelve tribes to witness, the Levite demands vengeance for the atrocity; and at a council, the Benjamites are instructed to deliver the malefactors to justice. One might expect the Benjamites to comply readily. For some reason, however, they do not, and undertake, by force of arms, to protect the 'sons of Belial'. The result is a bitter and bloody war between the Benjamites and the remaining eleven tribes. In the course of hostilities a curse is pronounced by the latter on any man who gives his daughter to a Benjamite. When the war is over, however, and the Benjamites virtually exterminated, the victorious Israelites repent of their malediction – which, however, cannot be retracted:

Now the men of Israel had sworn in Mizpeh, saying, There shall not any of us give his daughter unto Benjamin to wife. And the people came to the house of God, and abode there till even before God, and lifted up their voices, and wept sore; And said,

O Lord God of Israel, why is this come to pass in Israel, that
there should be today one tribe lacking in Isreal? (Judges 21:1–3)

A few verses later, the lament is repeated:

And the children of Israel repented them for Benjamin their
brother, and said, There is one tribe cut off from Israel this day.
How shall we do for wives for them that remain, seeing we
have sworn by the Lord that we will not give them of our
daughters to wives? (Judges 21:6–7)

And yet again:

And the people repented them for Benjamin, because that the
Lord had made a breach in the tribes of Israel. Then the elders
of the congregation said, How shall we do for wives for them
that remain, seeing the women are destroyed out of Benjamin?
And they said, There must be an inheritance for them that be
escaped out of Benjamin, that a tribe be not destroyed out of
Israel. Howbeit we may not give them wives of our daughters:
for the children of Israel have sworn, saying, Cursed be he that
giveth a wife to Benjamin. (Judges 21:15–18)

Confronted by the possible extinction of an entire tribe, the elders
quickly devise a solution. At Shiloh, in Bethel, there is to be a festival
shortly; and the women of Shiloh – whose menfolk had remained neutral in the war – are to be considered fair game. The surviving
Benjamites are instructed to go to Shiloh and wait in ambush in the
vineyards. When the women of the town congregate to dance in the
forthcoming festival, the Benjamites are to pounce upon them and take
them to wife.

It is not at all clear why the *Dossiers secrets* insist on calling attention
to this passage. But whatever the reason, the Benjamites, so far as
Biblical history is concerned, are clearly important. Despite the devastation of the war, they quickly recover in prestige, if not in numbers.
Indeed, they recover so well that in 1 Samuel they furnish Israel with
her first king, Saul.

Whatever recovery the Benjamites may have made, however, the
Dossiers secrets imply that the war over the followers of Belial was a cru-

cial turning point. It would seem that in the wake of this conflict many, if not most, Benjamites went into exile. Thus, there is a portentous note in the *Dossiers secrets*, in capital letters:

ONE DAY THE DESCENDANTS OF BENJAMIN LEFT THEIR COUNTRY; CERTAIN REMAINED; TWO THOUSAND YEARS LATER GODFROI VI [DE BOUILLON] BECAME KING OF JERUSALEM AND FOUNDED THE ORDRE DE SION.[2]

At first there appeared to be no connection between these apparent *non sequiturs*. When we assembled the diverse and fragmentary references in the *Dossiers secrets*, however, a coherent story began to emerge. According to this account most Benjamites did go into exile. Their exile supposedly took them to Greece, to the central Peloponnese – to Arcadia, in short, where they supposedly became aligned with the Arcadian royal line. Towards the advent of the Christian era, they are then said to have migrated up the Danube and the Rhine, inter-marrying with certain Teutonic tribes and eventually engendering the Sicambrian Franks – the immediate forebears of the Merovingians.

According to the 'Prieuré documents', then, the Merovingians were descended, via Arcadia, from the Tribe of Benjamin. In other words the Merovingians, as well as their subsequent descendants – the bloodlines of Plantard and Lorraine, for example – were ultimately of Semitic or Israelite origin. And if Jerusalem was indeed the hereditary birthright of the Benjamites, Godfroi de Bouillon, in marching on the Holy City, would in fact have been reclaiming his ancient and rightful heritage. Again it is significant that Godfroi, alone among the august Western princes who embarked on the First Crusade, disposed of all his property before his departure – implying thereby that he did not intend to return to Europe.

Needless to say, we had no way of ascertaining whether the Merovingians were of Benjamite origin or not. The information in the 'Prieuré documents', such as it was, related to too remote, too obscure a past, for which no confirmation, no records of any sort could be obtained. But the assertions were neither particularly unique nor particularly new. On the contrary they had been around, in the form of vague rumours and nebulous traditions, for a long time. To cite but one instance, Proust draws upon them in his opus; and more recently, the novelist Jean d'Ormesson suggests a Judaic origin for certain noble

French families. And in 1965 Roger Peyrefitte, who seems to like scandalising his country-men, did so with resounding éclat in a novel affirming all French and most European nobil-ity to be ultimately Judaic.

In fact the argument, although unprovable, is not altogether implausible, nor are the exile and migration ascribed to the Tribe of Benjamin in the 'Prieuré documents'. The Tribe of Benjamin took up arms on behalf of the followers of Belial – a form of the Mother Goddess often associated with images of a bull or calf. There is reason to believe that the Benjamites themselves revered the same deity. Indeed, it is possible that the worship of the Golden Calf in Exodus – the subject, signifi-cantly enough, of one of Poussin's most famous paintings – may have been a specifi-cally Benjamite ritual.

Following their war against the other eleven tribes of Israel, Benjamites fleeing into exile would, of necessity, have had to flee westwards, towards the Phoenician coast. The Phoenicians possessed ships capable of trans-porting large numbers of refugees. And they would have been obvious allies for fugitive Benjamites – for they, too, worshipped the Mother Goddess in the form of Astarte, Queen of Heaven.

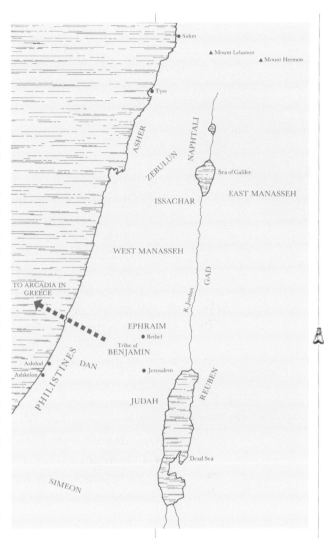

Judaea, showing the only avenue of escape for the Tribe of Benjamin.

If there was actually an exodus of Benjamites from Palestine, one might hope to find some vestigial record of it. In Greek myth one does. There is the legend of King Belus's son, one Danaus, who arrives in Greece, with his daughters, by ship. His daughters are said to have introduced the cult of the Mother Goddess, which became the estab-lished cult of the Arcadians. According to Robert Graves, the Danaus myth records the arrival in the Peloponnesus of 'colonists from Palestine'.[3] Graves states that King Belus is in fact Baal, or Bel – or per-haps Belial from the Old Testament. It is also worthy of note that one of the clans of the Tribe of Benjamin was the clan of Bela.

In Arcadia the cult of the Mother Goddess not only prospered but survived longer than in any other part of Greece. It became associated with worship of Demeter, then of Diana or Artemis. Known regionally as Arduina, Artemis became tutelary deity of the Ardennes; and it was from the Ardennes that the Sicambrian Franks first issued into what is now France. The totem of Artemis was the she-bear – Kallisto, whose son was Arkas, the bear-child and patron of Arcadia. And Kallisto, transported to the heavens by Artemis, became the constellation Ursa Major, the Great Bear. There might thus be something more than coincidence in the appellation 'Ursus', applied repeatedly to the Merovingian bloodline.

In any case there is other evidence, apart from mythology, suggesting a Judaic migration to Arcadia. In classical times the region known as Arcadia was ruled by the powerful, militaristic state of Sparta. The Spartans absorbed much of the older Arcadian culture; and indeed, the legendary Arcadian Lycaeus may in fact be identified with Lycurgus, who codified Spartan Law. On reaching manhood, the Spartans, like the Merovingians, ascribed a special, magical significance to their hair – which, like the Merovingians, they wore long. According to one authority, 'the length of hair denoted their physical vigour and became a sacred symbol.'[4] What is more, both books of Maccabees in the Apocrypha stress the link between Spartans and Jews. Maccabees 2 speaks of certain Jews 'having embarked to go to the Lacedaemonians, in hope of finding protection there because of their kinship.'[5] And Maccabees 1 states explicitly, 'It has been found in writing concerning the Spartans and the Jews that they are brethren and are of the family of Abraham.'[6]

We could thus acknowledge at least the possibility of a Judaic migration to Arcadia – so that the 'Prieuré documents', if they could not be proved correct, could not be dismissed either. As for Semitic influence on Frankish culture, there was solid archaeological evidence. Phoenician or Semitic trade routes traversed the whole of southern France, from Bordeaux to Marseilles and Narbonne. They also extended up the Rhone. As early as 700–800 B.C., there were Phoenician settlements not only along the French coast but inland as well, at such sites as Carcassonne and Toulouse. Among the artefacts found at these sites were many of Semitic origin. This is hardly surprising. In the ninth century B.C. the Phoenician kings of Tyre had intermarried with the kings of Israel and Judah, thus establishing a dynastic alliance that would have engendered a close contact between their respective peoples.

The sack of Jerusalem in A.D. 70, and the destruction of the Temple, prompted a massive exodus of Jews from the Holy Land. Thus the city of Pompeii, buried by the eruption of Vesuvius in A.D. 79, included a Jewish community. Certain cities in southern France – Arles, for example, Lunel and Narbonne – provided a haven for Jewish refugees around the same time. And yet the influx of Judaic peoples into Europe, and especially France, predated the fall of Jerusalem in the first century. In fact it had been in progress from before the Christian era. Between 106 and 48 B.C. a Jewish colony was established in Rome. Not long after another such colony was founded far up the Rhine, at Cologne. Certain Roman legions included contingents of Jewish slaves, who accompanied their masters all over Europe. Many of these slaves eventually won, purchased or, in some other fashion, obtained their freedom and formed communities.

In consequence there are many specifically Semitic place names scattered about France. Some of them are situated squarely in the Old Merovingian heartland. A few kilometres from Stenay, for example, on the fringe of the Forest of Woëvres where Dagobert was assassinated, there is a village called Baalon. Between Stenay and Orval, there is a town called Avioth. And the mountain of Sion in Lorraine – 'la colline inspirée' – was originally Mount Semita.[7]

Again then, while we could not prove the claims in the 'Prieuré documents', we could not discount them either. Certainly there was enough evidence to render them at least plausible. We were compelled to acknowledge that the 'Prieuré documents' might be correct – that the Merovingians, and the various noble families descended from them, might have stemmed from Semitic sources.

But could this, we wondered, really be all there was to the story? Could this really be the portentous secret which had engendered so much fuss and intrigue, so much machination and mystery, so much controversy and conflict through the centuries? Merely another lost tribe legend? And even if it were not legend but true, could it really explain the motivation of the Prieuré de Sion and the claim of the Merovingian dynasty? Could it really explain the adherence of men like Leonardo and Newton or the activities of the houses of Guise and Lorraine, the covert endeavours of the Compagnie du Saint-Sacrement, the elusive secrets of 'Scottish Rite' Freemasonry? Obviously not. Why should descent from the Tribe of Benjamin constitute so explosive a secret? And, perhaps most crucially, why should descent from the Tribe of Benjamin matter today? How could it possibly clarify the Prieuré de Sion's present-day activities and objectives?

If our inquiry involved vested interests that were specifically Semitic or Judaic, moreover, why did it involve so many components of a specifically, even fervently, Christian character? The pact between Clovis and the Roman Church, for example; the avowed Christianity of Godfroi de Bouillon and the conquest of Jerusalem; the heretical, perhaps, but none the less Christian thought of the Cathars and Knights Templar; pious institutions like the Compagnie du Saint-Sacrement; Freemasonry that was 'Hermetic, aristocratic and Christian', and the implication of so many Christian ecclesiastics, from high-ranking princes of the Church to local village curés like Boudet and Saunière?

It might be that the Merovingians were ultimately of Judaic origin, but if this were so it seemed to us essentially incidental. Whatever the real secret underlying our investigation, it appeared to be inextricably associated not with Old Testament Judaism, but with Christianity. In short, the Tribe of Benjamin – for the moment, at least – seemed to be a red herring. However important it might be, there was something of even greater importance involved. We were still overlooking something.

PART THREE THE BLOODLINE

CHAPTER ELEVEN

THE
HOLY GRAIL

What might we have been overlooking? Or, alternatively, what might we have been seeking in the wrong place? Was there perhaps some fragment that had been before our eyes all along – which, for one reason or another, we had failed to notice? As far as we could determine, we had overlooked no item, no data of accepted historical scholarship. But might there be something else – something that lay 'beyond the pale' of documented history, the concrete facts to which we had endeavoured to confine ourselves?

Certainly there was one motif, admittedly fabulous, which had threaded itself through our investigation, recurring repeatedly, with insistent and intriguing consistency. This was the mysterious object known as the Holy Grail. By their contemporaries, for example, the Cathars were believed to have been in possession of the Grail. The Templars, too, were often regarded as the Grail's custodians; and the Grail romances had originally issued from the court of the count of Champagne, who was intimately associated with the foundation of the Knights Templar. When the Templars were suppressed, moreover, the bizarre heads they supposedly worshipped enjoyed, according to the official Inquisition reports, many of the attributes traditionally ascribed to the Grail – providing sustenance, for example, and imbuing the land with fertility.

In the course of our investigation we had run across the Grail in numerous other contexts as well. Some had been relatively recent, such as the occult circles of Joséphin Péladan and Claude Debussy at the end of the nineteenth century. Others were considerably older. Godfroi de Bouillon, for instance, was descended according to medieval legend and folklore from Lohengrin, the Knight of the Swan; and Lohengrin, in the romances, was the son of Perceval or Parzival, protagonist of all the early Grail stories. Guillem de Gellone, moreover, ruler of the medieval principality in southern France during the reign of Charlemagne, was the hero of a poem by Wolfram von Eschenbach, most important of the Grail chroniclers. Indeed, the Guillem in Wolfram's poem was said to have been associated in some way with the mysterious 'Grail family'.

Were these intrusions of the Grail into our inquiry, and others like them, merely random and coincidental? Or was there a continuity underlying and connecting them – a continuity which, in some unimaginable way, did link our inquiry to the Grail, whatever the Grail might really be? At this point, we were confronted by a staggering question. Could the Grail be something more than pure fantasy? Could it actually have existed in some sense? Could there really have been such a thing as the Holy Grail? Or something concrete, at any rate, for which the Holy Grail was employed as a symbol?

The question was certainly exciting and provocative – to say the least. At the same time it threatened to take us too far afield, into spheres of spurious speculation. It did, however, serve to direct our attention to the Grail romances themselves. And in themselves the Grail romances posed a number of perplexing and distinctly relevant conundrums.

It is generally assumed that the Holy Grail relates in some way to Jesus. According to some traditions, it was the cup from which Jesus and his disciples drank at the Last Supper. According to other traditions, it was the cup in which Joseph of Arimathea caught Jesus's blood as he hung on the cross. According to other traditions still, the Grail was both of these. But if the Grail was so intimately associated with Jesus, or if it did indeed exist, why was there no reference to it whatever for more than a thousand years? Where was it during all that time? Why did it not figure in earlier literature, folklore or tradition? Why should something of such intense relevance and immediacy to Christendom remain buried for as long as it apparently did?

More provocatively still, why should the Grail finally surface precisely when it did – at the very peak of the Crusades? Was it coincidence that this enigmatic object, ostensibly non-existent for ten centuries, should assume the status it did at the very time it did – when the Frankish kingdom of Jerusalem was in its full glory, when the Templars were at the apex of their power, when the Cathar heresy was gaining a momentum which actually threatened to displace the creed of Rome? Was this convergence of circumstances truly coincidental? Or was there some link between them?

Inundated and somewhat daunted by questions of this kind, we turned our attention to the Grail romances. Only by examining these 'fantasies' closely could we hope to determine whether their recurrence in our inquiry was indeed coincidental, or the manifestation of a pattern – a pattern which might, in some way, prove significant.

THE LEGEND OF THE HOLY GRAIL

Most twentieth-century scholarship concurs in the belief that the Grail romances rest ultimately on a pagan foundation – a ritual connected with the cycle of the seasons, the death and rebirth of the year. In its most primordial origins it would appear to involve a vegetation cult, closely related in form to, if not directly derived from those of Tammuz, Attis, Adonis and Osiris in the Middle East. Thus, in both Irish and Welsh mythology, there are repeated references to death, rebirth and renewal, as well as to a similar regenerative process in the land – sterility and fertility. The theme is central to the anonymous fourteenth-century English poem, *Sir Gawain and the Green Knight*. And in the *Mabinogion*, a compilation of Welsh legends roughly contemporary with the Grail romances though obviously drawing on much earlier material, there is a mysterious 'cauldron of rebirth' – in which dead warriors, thrown at nightfall, are resurrected the following morning. This cauldron is often associated with a giant hero named Bran. Bran also possessed a platter and 'whatever food one wished thereon was instantly obtained' – a property also sometimes ascribed to the Grail. At the end of his life, moreover, Bran was supposedly decapitated and his head placed, as a sort of talisman, in London. Here it was said to perform a number of magical functions – not only ensuring fertility of the land but also, by some occult power, repelling invaders.

Many of these motifs were subsequently incorporated into the Grail romances. There is no question that Bran, with his cauldron and platter, contributed something to later conceptions of the Grail. And Bran's head shares attributes not only with the Grail, but also with the heads allegedly worshipped by the Knights Templar.

The pagan foundation for the Grail romances has been exhaustively explored by scholars, from Sir James Frazer in *The Golden Bough* up to the present. But during the mid to late twelfth century the originally pagan foundation for the Grail romances underwent a curious and extremely important transformation. In some obscure way that has eluded the investigation of researchers, the Grail became very uniquely and specifically associated with Christianity – and with a rather unorthodox form of Christianity at that. On the basis of some elusive amalgamation, the Grail became inextricably linked with Jesus. And there seems to have been something more involved than a facile grafting of pagan and Christian traditions.

As a relic linked mystically with Jesus, the Grail engendered a voluminous quantity of romances, or lengthy narrative poems, which, even today, tease the imagination. Despite clerical disapprobation, these romances flourished for nearly a century, becoming a fully fledged cult of their own – a cult whose lifespan, interestingly enough, closely paralleled that of the Order of the Temple after its separation from the Prieuré de Sion in 1188. With the fall of the Holy Land in 1291, and the dissolution of the Templars between 1307 and 1314, the Grail romances also vanished from the stage of history, for another two centuries or so, at any rate. Then, in 1470, the theme was taken up again by Sir Thomas Malory in his famous *Le Morte d'Arthur*; and it has remained more or less prominent in Western culture ever since. Nor has its context always been wholly literary. There seems to be abundant documentary evidence that certain members of the National Socialist hierarchy in Germany actually believed in the Grail's physical existence, and excavations for it were actually undertaken during the war in the south of France.[1]

By Malory's time the mysterious object known as the Grail had assumed the more or less distinct identity ascribed to it today. It was alleged to be the cup of the Last Supper, in which Joseph of Arimathea later caught Jesus's blood. According to certain accounts, the Grail was brought by Joseph of Arimathea to England – more specifically, to Glastonbury. According to other accounts, it was brought by the Magdalene to France. As early as the fourth century legends describe the Magdalene fleeing the Holy Land and being set ashore near Marseilles – where, for that matter, her purported relics are still venerated. According to medieval legends, she carried with her to Marseilles the Holy Grail. By the fifteenth century this tradition had clearly assumed immense importance for such individuals as King René d'Anjou, who collected 'Grail cups'.

But the early legends say that the Magdalene brought the Grail into France, not a cup. In other words, the simple association of Grail and cup was a relatively late development. Malory perpetuated this facile association, and it has been a truism ever since. But Malory, in fact, took considerable liberties with his original sources. In these original sources, the Grail is something much more than a cup. And the mystical aspects of the Grail are far more important than the chivalric, which Malory extols.

In the opinion of most scholars the first genuine Grail romance dates from the late twelfth century, from around 1188 – that crucial year which witnessed the fall of Jerusalem and the alleged rupture between the Order of the Temple and the Prieuré de Sion. The romance in question is entitled *Le Roman de Perceval* or *Le Conte del Graal*. It was composed by

one Chrétien de Troyes, who seems to have been attached, in some indeterminate capacity, to the court of the count of Champagne.

Little is known of Chrétien's biography. His association with the
court of Champagne is apparent from numerous works composed
before his Grail romance – works dedicated to Marie, Countess of
Champagne. Through this corpus of courtly romances – including one
dealing with Lancelot, which makes no mention of anything resembling
a Grail – Chrétien by the 1180s had established an imposing reputation
for himself. And, given his earlier work, one might have expected him
to continue in a similar vein. Towards the end of his life, however,
Chrétien turned his attention to a new, hitherto unarticulated theme;
and the Holy Grail, as it has come down to us today, made its official
début in Western culture and consciousness.

Chrétien's Grail romance was dedicated not to Marie de
Champagne, but to Philippe d'Alsace, Count of Flanders.[2] At the beginning of his poem Chrétien declares that his work has been composed
specifically at Philippe's request, and that it was from Philippe that he
heard the story in the first place. The work itself furnishes a general pattern, and constitutes a prototype, for subsequent Grail narratives. Its
protagonist is named Perceval, who is described as the 'Son of the
Widow Lady'. This appellation is, in itself, both significant and intriguing. It had long been employed by certain of the dualist and Gnostic
heresies – sometimes for their own prophets, sometimes for Jesus himself. Subsequently it became a cherished designation in Freemasonry.

Leaving his widowed mother, Perceval sallies forth to win his
knighthood. During his travels, he comes upon an enigmatic fisherman
– the famous 'Fisher King' – in whose castle he is offered refuge for the
night. That evening the Grail appears. Neither at this point nor at any
other in the poem is it linked in any way whatever with Jesus. In fact the
reader learns very little about it. He is not even told what it is. But whatever it is, it is carried by a damsel, is golden and studded with gems.
Perceval does not know that he is expected to ask a question of this mysterious object – he is expected to ask 'whom one serves with it'. The
question is obviously ambiguous. If the Grail is a vessel or a dish of
some kind, the question may mean 'who is intended to eat from it'.
Alternatively the question might be rephrased: 'Whom does one serve
(in a chivalric sense) by virtue of serving the Grail?' Whatever the meaning of the question, Perceval neglects to ask it; and the next morning
when he wakes, the castle is empty. His omission, he learns subse-

quently, causes a disastrous blight on the land. Later still he learns that he himself is of the 'Grail family', and that the mysterious 'Fisher King', who was 'sustained' by the Grail, was in fact his own uncle. At this point Perceval makes a curious confession. Since his unhappy experience with the Grail, he declares, he has ceased to love or believe in God.

Chrétien's poem is rendered all the more perplexing by the fact that it is unfinished. Chrétien himself died around 1188, quite possibly before he could complete the work; and even if he did complete it no copy has survived. If such a copy ever existed, it may well have been destroyed in a fire at Troyes in 1188. The point need not be laboured, but certain scholars have found this fire, coinciding as it did with the poet's death, vaguely suspicious.

In any case Chrétien's version of the Grail story is less important in itself than in its role as precursor. During the next half century the motif he had introduced at the court of Troyes was to spread through Western Europe like a brush-fire. At the same time, however, modern experts on the subject agree that the later Grail romances do not seem to have derived wholly from Chrétien, but seem to have drawn on at least one other source as well – a source which, in all probability, pre-dated Chrétien. And during its proliferation the Grail story became much more closely linked with King Arthur – who was only a peripheral figure in Chrétien's version. And it also became linked with Jesus.

Of the numerous Grail romances which followed Chrétien's version, there were three that proved of special interest and relevance to us. One of these, the *Roman de l'Estoire dou Saint Graal,* was composed by Robert de Boron, sometime between 1190 and 1199. Justifiably or not, Robert is often credited with making the Grail a specifically Christian symbol. Robert himself states that he is drawing on an earlier source – and one quite different from Chrétien. In speaking of his poem, and particularly of the Grail's Christian character, he alludes to a 'great book', the secrets of which have been revealed to him.[3]

It is thus uncertain whether Robert himself Christianised the Grail, or whether someone else did so before him. Most authorities today incline towards the second of these possibilities. However, there is no question that Robert de Boron's account is the first to furnish a history of the Grail. The Grail, he explains, was the cup of the Last Supper. It then passed into the hands of Joseph of Arimathea, who, when Jesus was removed from the cross, filled it with the Saviour's blood – and it is this sacred blood which confers on the Grail a magical quality. After the Crucifixion, Robert continues, Joseph's family became the keepers of the Grail. And for Robert the Grail romances involve the adventures and vicissitudes of this particular family. Thus Galahad is said to be Joseph of Arimathea's son. And the Grail itself passes to Joseph's brother-in-law, Brons, who carries it to England and becomes the Fisher King. As in Chrétien's poem, Perceval is the 'Son of the Widow Lady', but he is also the grandson of the Fisher King.

> It seems that there may have been some Grail 'source document' to which Philippe d'Alsace, Count of Flanders had access, and which formed the basis of both Chrétien's and Robert de Boron's romances. Professor Loomis says that one is forced to assume a common source for the *Quest* and Robert de Boron's romance. He feels that Robert de Boron was telling the truth when he referred to a book about the secrets of the Grail which provided the bulk of his information. See Loomis, *The Grail*, pp. 233 ff.

Robert's version of the Grail story thus deviates in a number of important respects from Chrétien's. In both versions Perceval is a 'Son of the Widow Lady', but in Robert's version he is the grandson, not the nephew, of the Fisher King – and thus even more directly related to the Grail family. And while Chrétien's narrative is vague in its chronology, set sometime during the Arthurian age, Robert's is quite precise. For Robert, the Grail story is set in England, and is not contemporary with Arthur but with Joseph of Arimathea.

There is another Grail romance which has much in common with Robert's. Indeed it would seem to draw upon the same sources, but its utilisation of these sources is very different and decidedly more interesting. The romance in question is known as the *Perlesvaus*. It was composed around the same time as Robert's poem, between 1190 and 1212, by an author who, contrary to the conventions of the time, chose to remain anonymous. It is odd that he should have done so, given the exalted status accorded poets, unless he was involved in some calling – a monastic or military order, for example – which would have rendered composition of such romances unseemly or inappropriate. And, in fact, the weight of textual evidence concerning the *Perlesvaus* suggests this to be the case. According to at least one modern expert, the *Perlesvaus* may actually have been written by a Templar.[4] And there is certainly evidence to support such a conjecture. It is known, for instance, that the

Teutonic Knights encouraged and sponsored anonymous poets in their ranks, and such a precedent could well have been established by the Templars. What is more, the author of the *Perlesvaus* reveals, in the course of the poem, an almost extraordinarily detailed knowledge of the realities of fighting – of armour and equipment, strategy and tactics, and weaponry and its effects on human flesh. The graphic description of wounds, for example, would seem to attest to a first-hand experience of the battlefield – a realistic, unromanticised experience uncharacteristic of any other Grail romance.

If the *Perlesvaus* was not actually composed by a Templar, it nevertheless provides a solid basis for linking the Templars with the Grail. Although the Order is not mentioned by name, its appearance in the poem would seem to be unmistakable. Thus Perceval, in his wanderings, happens upon a castle. This castle does not house the Grail, but it does house a conclave of 'initiates' who are obviously familiar with the Grail. Perceval is received here by two 'masters' – who clap their hands and are joined by thirty-three other men. 'They were clad in white garments, and not one of them but had a red cross in the midst of his breast, and they seemed to be all of an age.'[5] One of these mysterious 'masters' states that he has personally seen the Grail – an experience vouchsafed only to an elect few. And he also states that he is familiar with Perceval's lineage.

Like Chrétien's and Robert's poems, the *Perlesvaus* lays an enormous stress on lineage. At numerous points Perceval's is described as 'most holy'. Elsewhere it is stated explicitly that Perceval 'was of the lineage of Joseph of Arimathea', and that 'this Joseph was his [Perceval's] mother's uncle, that had been a soldier of Pilate seven years'.[6]

Nevertheless the *Perlesvaus* is not set in Joseph's lifetime. On the contrary it takes place, like Chrétien's version, during the age of Arthur. Chronology is further scrambled by the fact that the Holy Land is already in the hands of the 'infidel' – which it wasn't until nearly two centuries after Arthur. And by the fact that the Holy Land is apparently to be identified with Camelot.

To a greater degree than either Chrétien's or Robert's poems, the *Perlesvaus* is magical in nature. In addition to his knowledge of the battlefield, the anonymous author displays a knowledge, quite surprising for the time, of conjuration and invocation. There are also numerous alchemical references – to two men, for instance, 'made of copper by art of nigromancy'.[7] And some of the magical and alchemical references resonate with echoes of the mystery surrounding the Templars. Thus, one of the 'masters' of the white-clad Templar-like company says to Perceval, 'There are the heads sealed in silver, and the heads sealed in lead, and the bodies whereunto these heads belonged; I tell you that you must make come thither the head both of the King and of the Queen.'[8]

If the *Perlesvaus* abounds in magical allusions, it also abounds in other allusions that are both heretical and/or pagan. Again Perceval is designated by the dualist appellation, 'Son of the Widow Lady'. There are references to a sanctioned ritual of king-sacrifice, most incongruous in a purportedly Christian poem. There are references to the roasting and devouring of children – a crime of which the Templars were popularly accused. And at one point there is a singular rite, which again evokes memories of the Templar trials. At a red cross erected in a forest, a beautiful white beast of indeterminate nature is torn apart by hounds. While Perceval watches, a knight and a damsel appear with golden vessels, collect the fragments of mutilated flesh and, having kissed the cross, disappear into the trees. Perceval himself then kneels before the cross and kisses it:

> and there came to him a smell so sweet of the cross and of the place, such as no sweetness can be compared therewith. He looketh and seeth coming from the forest two priests all afoot; and the first shouteth to him: 'Sir Knight, withdraw yourself away from the cross, for no right have you to come nigh it': Perceval draweth him back, and the priest kneeleth before the cross and adoreth it and boweth down and kisseth it more than a score times, and manifesteth the most joy in the world. And the other priest cometh after, and bringeth a great rod, and setteth the first priest aside by force, and beateth the cross with the rod in every part, and weepeth right passing sore.
>
> Perceval beholdeth him with right great wonderment and saith unto him, 'Sir, herein seem you to be no priest! wherefore do you so great shame?' 'Sir,' saith the priest, 'It nought concerneth you of whatsoever we may do, nor nought shall you know thereof for us!' Had he not been a priest, Perceval would have been right wroth with him, but he had no will to do him any hurt.[9]

Such abuse of the cross evokes distinct echoes of the accusations levelled against the Templars. But not of the Templars alone. It might also reflect a skein of dualist or Gnostic thought – the thought of the Cathars, for instance, who also repudiated the cross.

In the *Perlesvaus* this skein of dualist or Gnostic thought extends, in some sense, to the Grail itself. For Chrétien the Grail was something unspecified, made of gold and encrusted with gems. For Robert de Boron it was identified as the cup used at the Last Supper and subsequently to collect Jesus's blood. In the *Perlesvaus*, however, the Grail assumes a most curious and significant dimension. At one point, Sir Gawain is warned by a priest, 'for behoveth not discover the secrets of the Saviour, and them also to whom they are committed behoveth keep them covertly'.[10] The Grail, then, involves a secret in some way related to Jesus; and the nature of this secret is entrusted to a select company.

When Gawain eventually does see the Grail, it 'seemeth him that in the midst of the Graal he seeth the figure of a child . . . he looketh up and it seemeth him to be the Graal all in flesh, and he seeth above, as he thinketh, a King crowned, nailed upon a rood.'[11] And some time later, the Grail

> appeared at the sacring of the mass, in five several manners that none ought not to tell, for the secret things of the sacrament ought none tell openly, but he unto whom God hath given it. King Arthur beheld all the changes, the last whereof was the change into a chalice.[12]

In short the Grail, in the *Perlesvaus*, consists of a changing sequence of images or visions. The first of these is a crowned king, crucified. The second is a child. The third is a man wearing a crown of thorns, bleeding from his forehead, his feet, his palms and his side.[13] The fourth manifestation is not specified. The fifth is a chalice. On each occasion the manifestation is attended by a fragrance and a great light.

From this account the Grail, in the *Perlesvaus*, would seem to be several things simultaneously – or something that can be interpreted on several different levels. On the mundane level, it might well be an object of some kind – like a cup, bowl or chalice. It would also, in some metaphorical sense, appear to be a lineage – or perhaps certain individuals who comprise this lineage. And quite obviously the Grail would also seem to be an experience of some sort – quite likely a Gnostic illumination such as that extolled by the Cathars and other dualist sects of the period.

Galahad and the Holy Grail: a 15th century depiction of the Grail as a mystical experience. At the time, recommending mystical experience would have been close to heresy, as it involved questioning the need for the Church.

325

THE STORY OF WOLFRAM VON ESCHENBACH

Of all the Grail romances the most famous, and the most artistically significant, is *Parzival*, composed sometime between 1195 and 1216. Its author was Wolfram von Eschenbach, a knight of Bavarian origin. At first we thought that this might distance him from his subject, rendering his account less reliable than various others. Before long, however, we concluded that if anyone could speak authoritatively of the Grail, it was Wolfram.

At the beginning of *Parzival*, Wolfram boldly asserts that Chrétien's version of the Grail story is wrong, while his own is accurate because based on privileged information. This information, he later explains, he obtained from one Kyot de Provence – who received it in turn supposedly from one Flegetanis. It is worth quoting Wolfram's words in full:

> Anyone who asked me before about the Grail and took me to task for not telling him was very much in the wrong. Kyot asked me not to reveal this, for Adventure commanded him to give it no thought until she herself, Adventure, should invite the telling, and then one must speak of it, of course.
>
> Kyot, the well-known master, found in Toledo, discarded, set down in heathen writing, the first source of this adventure. He first had to learn the abc's, but without the art of black magic . . .
>
> A heathen, Flegetanis, had achieved high renown for his learning. This scholar of nature was descended from Solomon and born of a family which had long been Israelite until baptism became our shield against the fire of Hell. He wrote the adventure of the Grail. On his father's side, Flegetanis was a heathen, who worshipped a calf . . .
>
> The heathen Flegetanis could tell us how all the stars set and rise again . . . To the circling course of the stars man's affairs and destiny are linked. Flegetanis the heathen saw with his own eyes in the constellations things he was shy to talk about, hidden mysteries. He said there was a thing called the Grail, whose name he had read clearly in the constellations. A host of angels left it on the earth.
>
> Since then, baptised men have had the task of guarding it, and with such chaste discipline that those who are called to the service of the Grail are always noble men. Thus wrote Flegetanis

326

of these things.

Kyot, the wise master, set about to trace this tale in Latin books, to see where there ever had been a people, dedicated to purity and worthy of caring for the Grail. He read the chronicles of the lands, in Britain and elsewhere, in France and in Ireland, and in Anjou he found the tale. There he read the true story of Mazadan, and the exact record of all his family was written there.[14]

Of the numerous items that beg for comment in this passage, it is important to note at least four. One is that the Grail story apparently involves the family of an individual named Mazadan. A second is that the house of Anjou is in some way of paramount consequence. A third is that the original version of the story seems to have filtered into Western Europe over the Pyrenees, from Muslim Spain – a perfectly plausible assertion, given the status Toledo enjoyed as a centre for esoteric studies, both Judaic and Muslim. But the most striking element in the passage quoted is that the Grail story, as Wolfram explains its derivation, would seem ultimately to be of Judaic origin. If the Grail is so awesome a Christian mystery, why should its secret be transmitted by Judaic initiates? For that matter, why should Judaic writers have had access to specifically Christian material of which Christendom itself was unaware?

Scholars have wasted considerble time and energy debating whether Kyot and Flegetanis are real or fictitious. In fact the identity of Kyot, as we had learned from our study of the Templars, can be fairly solidly established. Kyot de Provence would seem, almost certainly, to have been Guiot de Provins – a troubadour, monk and spokesman for the Templars who did live in Provence and who wrote love songs, attacks on the Church, paeans in praise of the Temple and satirical verses. Guiot is known to have visited Mayence, in Germany, in 1184. The occasion was the chivalric festival of Pentecost, at which the Holy Roman Emperor, Frederick Barbarossa, conferred knighthood on his sons. As a matter of course the ceremony was attended by poets and troubadours from all over Christendom. As a knight of the Holy Roman Empire, Wolfram would almost certainly have been present; and it is certainly reasonable to suppose that he and Guiot met. Learned men were not so very common at the time. Inevitably they would have clustered together, sought each other out, made each other's acquaintance; and Guiot may well have found in Wolfram a kindred spirit – to whom he perhaps confided certain information, even if only in symbolic form. And if Guiot permits Kyot to be accepted as genuine, it is at least plausible to assume that Flegetanis was genuine as well. If he was not, Wolfram and/or Guiot must have had some special purpose in creating him. And in giving him the distinctive background and pedigree he is said to have had.

In addition to the Grail story, Wolfram may have obtained from Guiot a consuming interest in the Templars. In any case it is known that Wolfram possessed such an interest. Like Guiot he even made a pilgrimage to the Holy Land, where he could observe the Templars in action, at first hand. And in *Parzival* he emphasises that the guardians of the Grail and the Grail family are Templars. This might, of course, be the sloppy chronology and cavalier anachronism of poetic licence – such as can be discerned in some of the other Grail romances. But Wolfram is much more careful about such things than other writers of his time. Moreover there are the patent allusions to the Temple in the *Perlesvaus*. Would both Wolfram and the author of the *Perlesvaus* be guilty of the same glaring anachronism? Possibly. But it is also possible that something is being implied by these ostentatious connections of the Templars with the Grail. For if the Templars are indeed guardians of the Grail, there is one flagrant implication – that the Grail existed not only in Arthurian times, but also during the Crusades, when the romances about it were composed. By introducing the Templars, both Wolfram and the author of the *Perlesvaus* may be suggesting that the Grail was not just something of the past, but also something which, for them, possessed contemporary relevance.

The background to Wolfram's poem is thus as important, in some obscure way, as the text of the poem itself. Indeed the role of the Templars, like the identity of both Kyot and Flegetanis, would seem to be crucial; and these factors may well hold a key to the whole mystery surrounding the Grail. Unfortunately, the text of *Parzival* does little to resolve these questions, while posing a good many others.

In the first place Wolfram not only maintains that his version of the Grail story, in contrast to Chrétien's, is the correct one. He also maintains that Chrétien's account is merely fantastic fable, whereas his is in fact a species of 'initiation document'. In other words, as Wolfram states quite unequivocally, there is more to the Grail mystery than meets the eye. And he makes it clear, with numerous references throughout his poem, that the Grail is not merely an object of gratuitous mystification and fantasy, but a means of concealing something of immense consequence. Again and again, he hints to his audience to read between the lines, dropping here and there suggestive hints. At the same time, he constantly reiterates the urgency of secrecy, 'For no man can ever win the Grail unless he is known in Heaven and he be called by name to the Grail.'[15] And 'the Grail is unknown save to those who have been called by name . . . to the Grail's company.'[16]

Wolfram is both precise and elusive in identifying the Grail. When it first appears, on Parzival's sojourn in the Fisher King's castle, there is no real indication of what it is. It would seem, however, to have something in common with Chrétien's vague description of it:

> She [the Queen of the Grail family] was clothed in a dress of Arabian silk. Upon a deep green achmardi she bore the Perfection of Paradise, both root and branch. That was a thing called the Grail, which surpasses all earthly perfection. Repanse de Schoye was the name of her whom the Grail permitted to be its bearer. Such was the nature of the Grail that she who watched over it had to preserve her purity and renounce all falsity.[17]

Among other things, the Grail, at this point, would seem to be a kind of magical cornucopia or horn of plenty:

> A hundred squires, so ordered, reverently took bread in white napkins from before the Grail, stepped back in a group and, separating, passed the bread to all the tables. I was told, and I tell you too, but on your oath, not mine – hence if I deceive you, we are liars all of us – that whatsoever one reached out his hand for, he found it ready, in front of the Grail, food warm or food cold, dishes new or old, meat tame or game. 'There never was anything like that,' many will say. But they will be wrong in their angry protest, for the Grail was the fruit of blessedness, such abundance of the sweetness of the world that its delights were very like what we are told of the kingdom of heaven.[18]

All of this is rather mundane in its way, even pedestrian, and the Grail would appear to be an innocuous enough affair. But later, when Parzival's hermit-uncle expounds on the Grail, it becomes decidedly more powerful. After a lengthy disquisition, which includes strands of flagrantly Gnostic thought, the hermit describes the Grail thus:

> Well I know that many brave knights dwell with the Grail at Munsalvaesche. Always when they ride out, as they often do, it is to seek adventure. They do so for their sins, these templars, whether their reward be defeat or victory. A valiant host lives there, and I will tell you how they are sustained. They live from a stone of purest kind. If you do not know it, it shall here be named to you. It is called *lapsit exillis*. By the power of that stone the phoenix burns to ashes, but the ashes give him life again. Thus does the phoenix molt and change its plumage, which afterwards is bright and shining and as lovely as before. There never was a human so ill but that, if he one day sees that stone, he cannot die within the week that follows. And in looks he will not fade. His appearance will stay the same, be it maid or man, as on the day he saw the stone, the same as when the best years of his life began, and though he should see the stone for two hundred years, it will never change, save that his hair might perhaps turn grey. Such power does the stone give a man that flesh and bones are at once made young again. The stone is also called the Grail.[19]

According to Wolfram, then, the Grail is a stone of some kind. But such a definition of the Grail is far more provocative than satisfying. Scholars have a number of interpretations of the phrase 'lapsit exillis', all of which are more or less plausible. 'Lapsit exillis' might be a corruption of 'lapis ex caelis' – 'stone from the heavens'. It might also be a corruption of 'lapsit ex caelis' – 'it fell from the heavens', or of 'lapis lapsus ex caelus' – 'a stone fallen from heaven', or, finally, of 'lapis elixir' – the fabulous Philosopher's Stone of alchemy.[20] Certainly the passage quoted, like the whole of Wolfram's poem for that matter, is laden with alchemical symbolism. The phoenix, for example is established alchemical shorthand for resurrection or rebirth – and also, in medieval iconography, is an emblem of the dying and resurrected Jesus.

If the phoenix is indeed somehow representative of Jesus, Wolfram is implicitly associating him with a stone. Such an association is, of course, hardly unique. There is Peter (Pierre or 'stone' in French) – the 'stone' or 'rock' on which Jesus establishes his church. And as we had discovered, Jesus, in the New Testament, explicitly equates himself with 'the keystone neglected by the builders' – the keystone of the Temple, the Rock of Sion. Because it was 'founded' on this rock, there was supposedly a royal tradition descended from Godfroi de Bouillon which was equal to the reigning dynasties of Europe.

In the passage immediately following the one quoted, Wolfram links the Grail specifically with the Crucifixion – and, through the symbol of the dove, with the Magdalene:

> This very day, there comes to it [the Grail] a message wherein lies its greatest power. Today is Good Friday, and they await there a dove, winging down from Heaven. It brings a small white wafer, and leaves it on the stone. Then, shining white, the dove soars up to Heaven again. Always on Good Friday it brings to the stone what I have just told you, and from that the stone derives whatever good fragrances of drink and food there are on earth, like to the perfection of Paradise. I mean all things the earth may bear. And further the stone provides whatever game lives beneath the heavens, whether it flies or runs or swims. Thus, to the knightly brotherhood, does the power of the Grail give sustenance.[21]

In addition to its other extraordinary attributes the Grail, in Wolfram's poem, would almost seem to possess a certain sentience. It has the capacity to call individuals into its service – to call them, that is, in an active sense:

> Hear now how those called to the Grail are made known. On the stone, around the edge, appear letters inscribed, giving the name and lineage of each one, maid or boy, who is to take this blessed journey. No one needs to rub out the inscription, for once he had read the name, it fades away before his eyes. All those now grown to maturity came there as children. Blessed is the mother who bore a child destined to do service there. Poor and rich alike rejoice if their child is summoned to join the company. They are brought there from many lands. From sinful shame they are more protected than others, and receive good reward in heaven. When life dies for them here they are given perfection there.[22]

If the Grail's guardians are Templars, its actual custodians would appear to be members of a specific family. This family seems to possess numerous collateral branches, some of which – their identity often unknown even to themselves – are scattered about the world. But other members of the family inhabit the Grail castle of Munsalvaesche – fairly obviously linked with the legendary Cathar castle of Montsalvat, which at least one writer has identified as Montségur.[23] Within Munsalvaesche dwell a number of enigmatic figures. There is the Grail's actual keeper and bearer, Repanse de Schoye ('Réponse de Choix' or 'Chosen Response'). And there is, of course, Anfortas, the Fisher King and lord of the Grail castle, who is wounded in the genitals and unable to procreate or, alternatively, to die. As in Chrétien's Grail romance, Anfortas, for Wolfram, is Parzival's uncle. And when, at the end of the poem, the curse is lifted and Anfortas can at last die, Parzival becomes heir to the Grail castle.

The Grail, or the Grail family, calls certain individuals into its service from the outside world – individuals who must be initiated into some sort of mystery. At the same time it sends its trained servitors out into the world to perform actions on its behalf – and sometimes to occupy a throne. For the Grail, apparently, possesses the power to create kings:

> Maidens are appointed to care for the Grail . . . That was God's decree, and these maidens performed their service before it. The Grail selects only noble company. Knights, devout and good, are chosen to guard it. The coming of the high stars brings this people great sorrow, young and old alike. God's anger at them has lasted all too long. When shall they ever say yes to joy? . . . I will tell you something more, whose truth you may well believe. A twofold chance is often theirs; they both give and receive profit. They receive young children there, of noble lineage and beautiful. And if anywhere a land loses its lord, if the people there acknowledge the Hand of God, and seek a new lord, they are granted one from the company of the Grail. They must treat him with courtesy, for the blessing of God protects him.[24]

From the above passage, it would seem that at some point in the past the Grail family somehow incurred God's wrath. The allusion to 'God's anger at them' echoes numerous medieval statements about the Jews. It also echoes the title of a mysterious book associated with Nicolas Flamel – *The Sacred Book of Abraham the Jew, Prince, Priest, Levite, Astrologer and Philosopher to that Tribe of Jews who by the Wrath of God were Dispersed amongst the Gauls.* And Flegetanis, who Wolfram says wrote the original account of the Grail, is said to be descended from Solomon. Could the Grail family possibly be of Judaic origin?

Whatever the curse formerly visited upon the Grail family, it has unquestionably come, by Parzival's time, to enjoy divine favour – and a great deal of power as well. And yet it is rigorously enjoined, at least in certain respects to secrecy about its identity.

> The men [of the Grail family] God sends forth secretly; the maid-ens leave openly . . . Thus the maids are sent out openly from the Grail, and the men in secret, that they may have children who will in turn one day enter the service of the Grail, and serving, enhance its company. God can teach them how to do this.[25]

Women of the Grail family, then, when they intermarry with the outside world, may disclose their pedigree and identity. The men, however, must keep this information scrupulously concealed – so much so, in fact, that they may not even allow questions about their origins. The point, apparently, is a crucial one, for Wolfram returns to it most emphatically at the very end of the poem.

> Upon the Grail it was now found written that any templar whom God's hand appointed master over foreign people should forbid the asking of his name or race, and that he should help them to their rights. If the question is asked of him they shall have his help no longer.[26]

From this, of course, derives the dilemma of Lohengrin, Parzival's son, who, when queried on his origin, must abandon his wife and children and retire into the seclusion from whence he came. But why should such stringent secrecy be required? What 'skeleton in the closet', so to speak, might conceivably dictate it? If the Grail family were, in fact, of Judaic origin, that – for the age in which Wolfram was writing – might constitute a possible explanation. And such an explanation gains at least some credence from the Lohengrin story. For there are many variants of the Lohengrin story, and Lohengrin is not always identified by the same name. In some versions, he is called Helios – implying the sun. In other versions, he is called Elie or Eli[27] – an unmistakably Judaic name.

In Robert de Boron's romance and in the *Perlesvaus*, Perceval is of Judaic lineage – the 'holy lineage' of Joseph of Arimathea. In Wolfram's poem this status, so far as Parzival is concerned, would seem to be incidental. True, Parzival is the nephew of the wounded Fisher King and thus related by blood to the Grail family. And though he does not marry into the Grail family – he is, in fact, already married – he still inherits the Grail castle and becomes its new lord. But for Wolfram the protagonist's pedigree would seem to be less important than the means whereby he proves himself worthy of it. He must, in short, conform to certain criteria dictated by the blood he carries in his veins. And this emphasis would clearly seem to indicate the importance Wolfram ascribes to that blood.

There is no question that Wolfram does ascribe immense significance to a particular bloodline. If there is a single dominant theme pervading not only *Parzival*, but his other works as well, it is not so much the Grail as the Grail family. Indeed the Grail family seems to dominate Wolfram's mind to an almost obsessive degree, and he devotes far more attention to them and their genealogy than to the mysterious object of which they are custodians.

The genealogy of the Grail family can be reconstructed from a close reading of *Parzival*. Parzival himself is a nephew of Anfortas, the maimed Fisher King and lord of the Grail castle. Anfortas, in turn, is the son of one Frimutel, and Frimutel the son of Titurel. At this point the lineage becomes more entangled. Eventually, however, it leads back to a certain Laziliez – which may be a derivation of Lazarus, the brother, in the New Testament, of Mary and Martha. And Laziliez's parents, the original progenitors of the Grail family, are named Mazadan and Terdelaschoye. The latter is obviously a Germanic version of a French phrase, 'Terre de la Choix' – 'Chosen Land'. Mazadan is rather more obscure. It might conceivably derive from the Zoroastrian Ahura Mazda, the dualist principle of Light. At the same time, it also, if only phonetically perhaps, suggests Masada – a major bastion during the Judaic revolt against Roman occupation in A.D. 68.

The names Wolfram ascribes to members of the Grail family are thus often provocative and suggestive. At the same time, however, they told us nothing that was historically useful. If we hoped to find an actual historical prototype for the Grail family, we would have to look elsewhere.

The clues were meagre enough. We knew, for example, that the Grail family supposedly culminated in Godfroi de Bouillon; but that did not cast much light on Godfroi's mythical antecedents – except, of course, that (like his real antecedents) they kept their identity scrupulously secret. But according to Wolfram, Kyot found an account of the Grail story in the annals of the house of Anjou, and Parzival himself is said to be of Angevin blood. At the least this was extremely interesting, for the house of Anjou was closely associated with both the Templars and the Holy Land. Indeed Fulques, Count of Anjou, himself became, so to speak, an 'honorary' or 'part-time' Templar. In 1131, moreover, he married Godfroi de Bouillon's niece, the legendary Melusine, and became king of Jerusalem. According to the 'Prieuré documents', the lords of Anjou – the Plantagenet family – were thus allied to the Merovingian bloodline. And the name of Plantagenet may even have been intended to echo 'Plant-Ard' or Plantard.

Such connections were patchy and tenuous. But additional clues were provided for us by the geographical setting of Wolfram's poem. For the most part this setting is France. In contrast to later Grail chroniclers Wolfram even maintains that Arthur's court, Camelot, is situated in France – quite specifically at Nantes. Nantes, now in Brittany, was the westernmost boundary of the old Merovingian realm at the apex of its power.[28]

In a manuscript of Chrétien's version of the Grail story, Perceval declares he was born in 'Scaudone' or 'Sinadon', or some such place that appears in a number of orthographic variants – and the region is described as mountainous. According to Wolfram, Parzival comes from 'Waleis'. Most scholars have taken Waleis to be Wales and Sinadon, in its various spellings, as Snowdon or Snowdonia. If this is so, however, certain insurmountable problems arise, and, as one modern commentator remarks, 'maps fail us'. For characters move constantly between Waleis and Arthur's court at Nantes, as well as other French locations, without crossing any water! They move overland, in short, and through regions whose inhabitants speak French. Was Wolfram's geography simply sloppy? Can it possibly have been that careless? Or might Waleis not be Wales after all? Two scholars have suggested that it might be Valois, the region of France to the north-east of Paris – but there are no mountains in Valois, nor does the rest of the landscape conform in any way to Wolfram's description. At the same time, however, there is another possible location for Waleis – a location that is mountainous, that does conform precisely to Wolfram's other topographical descriptions and whose inhabitants do speak French. This location is the Valais in Switzerland, on the shores of Lake Léman to the east of Geneva. It would seem, in short, that Parzival's homeland is neither Wales nor Valois, but Valais. And his actual birthplace of Sinadon would not be Snowdon or Snowdonia, but Sidonensis, the capital of the Valais. And the modern name of Sidonensis, capital of the Valais, is Sion.

According to Wolfram, then, Arthur's court is in Brittany. Parzival would seem to have been born in Switzerland. And the Grail family itself? The Grail castle? Wolfram provides an answer in his most ambitious work, left unfinished at his death and entitled *Der Junge Titurel*. In this evocative fragment Wolfram addressed himself to the life of Titurel, father of Anfortas, and the original builder of the Grail castle. *Der Junge Titurel* is very specific not only about genealogical detail, but also about the dimensions, the components, the materials, the configuration of the Grail castle – its circular chapel, for example, like those of the Templars. And the castle itself is situated in the Pyrenees.

In addition to *Der Junge Titurel*, Wolfram left another work unfinished at his death – the poem known as *Willehalm,* whose protagonist is Guillem de Gellone, Merovingian ruler of the ninth-century principality straddling the Pyrenees. Guillem is said to be associated with the Grail family.[29] He would thus seem to be the only figure in Wolfram's works whose historical identity can actually be determined. Yet even in his treatment of the unidentifiable figures, Wolfram's meticulous precision is astonishing. The more one studies him, the more likely it seems that he is referring to an actual group of people – not a mythic or fictionalised family, but one that did exist historically, and may well have included Guillem de Gellone. This conclusion becomes all the more plausible when Wolfram admits he is hiding something – that *Parzival* and his other works are not merely romances, but also initiation documents, depositories of secrets.

THE GRAIL AND CABALISM

As the *Perlesvaus* suggests, the Grail, at least in part, would seem to be an experience of some kind. In his excursus on the Grail's curative properties and its power to ensure longevity, Wolfram would also seem to be implying something experiential as well as symbolic – a state of mind or a state of being. There seems little question that on one level the Grail is an initiatory experience which in modern terminology would be described as a 'transformation' or 'altered state of consciousness'. Alternatively it might be described as a 'Gnostic experience', a 'mystical experience', 'illumination' or 'union with God'. It is possible to be even more precise and place the experiential aspect of the Grail in a very specific context. That context is the Cabala and Cabalistic thought. Certainly such thought was much 'in the air' at the time the Grail romances were composed. There was a famous Cabalistic school at Toledo, for instance, where Kyot is said to have learned of the Grail. There were other schools at Gerona, Montpellier and elsewhere in the south of France. And it would hardly seem coincidental that there was also such a school at Troyes. It dated from 1070 – Godfroi de Bouillon's time – and was conducted by one Rashi, perhaps the most famous of medieval Cabalists.

It is impossible here, of course, to do justice to the Cabala or Cabalistic thought. Nevertheless certain points must be made in order to establish the connection between Cabalism and the Grail romances. Very briefly then, Cabalism might be described as 'esoteric Judaism' – a practical psychological methodology of uniquely Judaic origin designed to induce a dramatic transformation of consciousness. In this respect it may be viewed as a Judaic equivalent of similar methodologies or disciplines in Hindu, Buddhist and Taoist tradition – certain forms of yoga, for example, or of Zen.

Like its Eastern equivalents, Cabalistic training entails a series of rituals – a structured sequence of successive initiatory experiences leading the practitioner to ever more radical modifications of consciousness and cognition. And though the meaning and significance of such modifications is subject to interpretation, their reality, as psychological phenomena, is beyond dispute. Of the 'stages' of Cabalistic initiation, one of the most important is the stage known as *Tiferet*. In the *Tiferet* experience the individual is said to pass beyond the world of form into the formless – or, in contemporary terms, to 'transcend his ego'. Symbolically speaking this consists of a kind of sacrificial 'death' – the 'death' of the ego, of one's sense of individuality and the isolation such individuality entails; and, of course, a rebirth, or resurrection, into another dimension, of all-encompassing unity and harmony. In Christian adaptations of Cabalism *Tiferet* was therefore associated with Jesus.

For medieval Cabalists the initiation into *Tiferet* was associated with certain specific symbols. These included a hermit or guide or wise old man, a majestic king, a child, a sacrificed god.[30] In time other symbols were added as well – a truncated pyramid, for example, a cube and a rose cross. The relation of these symbols to the Grail romances is sufficiently apparent. In every Grail narrative there is a wise old hermit – Perceval's or Parzival's uncle frequently – who acts as a spiritual guide. In Wolfram's poem the Grail as 'stone' may possibly correspond to the cube. And in the *Perlesvaus* the various manifestations of the Grail correspond almost precisely to the symbols of *Tiferet*. Indeed, the *Perlesvaus* in itself establishes a crucial link between the *Tiferet* experience and the Grail.[31]

THE PLAY ON WORDS

We could thus identify the experiential aspect of the Grail and connect it quite precisely with Cabalism. This imparted another seemingly incongruous Judaic element to the Grail's supposedly Christian character. But whatever the Grail's experiential aspects, there were other aspects as well – aspects which we could not ignore and which were of paramount importance to our story. These aspects were historical and genealogical.

Again and again, the Grail romances had confronted us with a pattern of a distinctly mundane and unmystical nature. Again and again, there was a callow knight who, by dint of certain tests that proved him 'worthy', was initiated into some monumental secret. Again and again, this secret was closely guarded by an order of some sort, apparently chivalric in composition. Again and again, the secret was in some way associated with a specific family. Again and again, the protagonist – by intermarriage with this family, by his own lineage or by both – became lord of the Grail and everything connected with it. On this level, at least, we seemed to be dealing with something of a concrete historical character. One can become lord of a castle or a group of people. One can become heir to certain lands or even a certain heritage. But one cannot become lord or heir to an experience.

Was it relevant, we wondered, that the Grail romances, when subjected to close scrutiny, rested so crucially on matters of lineage and genealogy, pedigree, heritage and inheritance? Was it relevant that the lineage and genealogy in question should overlap at certain key points those which had figured so saliently in our inquiry – the house of Anjou, for instance, Guillem de Gellone and Godfroi de Bouillon?

Could the mystery attached to Rennes-le-Château and the Prieuré de Sion relate, in some as yet obscure way, to that mysterious object called the Holy Grail? Had we, in fact, been following in Parzival's footsteps and conducting our own modern Grail quest?

The evidence suggested that this was a very real possibility. And indeed there was one more crucial piece of evidence which tilted the balance decisively in favour of such a conclusion. In many of the earlier manuscripts, the Grail is called the 'Sangraal'; and even in the later version by Malory, it is called the 'Sangreal'. It is likely that some such form – 'Sangraal' or 'Sangreal' – was in fact the original one. It is also likely that that one word was subsequently broken in the wrong place. In other words 'Sangraal' or 'Sangreal' may not have been intended to divide into 'San Graal' or 'San Greal' – but into 'Sang Raal' or 'Sang Réal'. Or, to employ the modern spelling, Sang Royal. Royal blood.

In itself, such wordplay might be provocative but hardly conclusive. Taken in conjunction with the emphasis on genealogy and lineage, however, there is not much room for doubt. And, for that matter, the traditional associations – the cup which caught Jesus's blood, for instance – would seem to reinforce this supposition. Quite clearly, the Grail would appear to pertain in some way to blood and a bloodline.

This raises, of course, certain obvious questions. Whose blood? And whose bloodline?

THE LOST KINGS AND THE GRAIL

The Grail romances were not the only poems of their kind to find a receptive audience in the late twelfth and early thirteenth centuries. There were many others – *Tristan and Isolde*, for instance, and *Eric and Enide* – composed in some cases by Chrétien himself, in some cases by contemporaries and countrymen of Wolfram, such as Hartmann von Aue and Gottfried von Strassburg. These romances make no mention whatever of the Grail. But they are clearly set in the same mythico-historical period as the Grail romances, because they depend more or less heavily on Arthur. As far as he can be dated, Arthur seems to have lived in the late fifth and/or early sixth centuries. In other words, Arthur lived at the peak of Merovingian ascendancy in Gaul, and was, in fact, closely contemporary with Clovis. If the term 'Ursus' – 'bear' – was applied to the Merovingian royal line, the name 'Arthur', which also means 'bear' may have been an attempt to confer a comparable dignity on a British chieftain.

For the writers at the time of the Crusades, the Merovingian era seems to have been of some crucial importance – so much so, in fact, that it provided the backdrop for romances which had nothing to do with either Arthur or the Grail. One such is the national epic of Germany, the *Nibelungenlied* or *Song of the Nibelungen*, on which, in the nineteenth century, Wagner drew so heavily for his monumental oper-atic sequence, *The Ring*. This musical opus, and the poem from which it derives, are generally dismissed as pure fantasy. Yet the Nibelungs were a real people, a Germanic tribe who lived in late Merovingian times. Moreover, many of the names in the *Nibelungenlied* – Siegmund, for instance, Siegfried, Sieglinde, Brünhilde and Kriemhild – are patently Merovingian names. Many episodes in the poem closely parallel, and may even refer to, specific events of Merovingian times.

Although it has nothing to do with either Arthur or the Grail, the *Nibelungenlied* is further evidence that the Merovingian epoch exercised a powerful hold on the imaginations of twelfth- and thirteenth-century poets – as if they knew something crucial about that epoch which later writers and historians did not. In any case, modern scholars concur that the Grail romances, like the *Nibelungenlied*, refer to the Merovingian age. In part, of course, this conclusion would appear self-evident, given the prominence of Arthur. But it also rests on specific indications provided by the Grail romances themselves. *The Queste del Saint Graal*, for exam-ple, composed between 1215 and 1230, declares explicitly that the events of the Grail story occurred precisely 454 years after the resurrec-tion of Jesus.[32] Assuming Jesus died in A.D. 33, the Grail saga would thus have enacted itself in A.D. 487 – during the first flush of Merovingian power, and a mere nine years before the baptism of Clovis.

There was nothing revolutionary or controversial, therefore, in con-necting the Grail romances with the Merovingian age. None the less we felt that something had been overlooked. Essentially it was a question of emphasis – which, because of Arthur, has been placed primarily on Britain. As a result of this distinctly British emphasis, we had not auto-matically associated the Grail with the Merovingian dynasty. And yet Wolfram insists that Arthur's court is at Nantes and that his poem is set in France. The same assertion is made by other Grail romances – the *Queste del Saint Graal*, for instance. And there are medieval traditions which maintain the Grail was not brought to Britain by Joseph of Arimathea, but to France by the Magdalene.

We now began to wonder whether the pre-eminence assigned to Britain by commentators on the Grail romances had not perhaps been misplaced,[33] and whether the romances in fact referred primarily to events on the continent – more particularly to events in France. And we began to suspect that the Grail itself, the 'blood royal', actually referred to the blood royal of the Merovingian dynasty – a blood which was deemed to be sacred and invested with magical or miraculous properties.

Perhaps the Grail romances constituted, at least in part, a symbolic or allegorical account of certain events of the Merovingian epoch. And perhaps we had already encountered some of those events in the course of our investigation. A marriage with some special family, for example, which, shrouded by time, engendered the legends attending the dual paternity of Mérovée. Or perhaps, in the Grail family, a representation of the clandestine perpetuation of the Merovingian bloodline – *les rois perdus* or 'lost kings' – in the mountains and caves of the Razés. Or perhaps that bloodline's exile in England during the late ninth and early tenth centuries. And the secret but august dynastic alliances whereby the Merovingian vine, like that of the Grail family, eventually bore fruit in Godfroi de Bouillon and the house of Lorraine. Perhaps Arthur himself – the 'bear' – was only incidentally related to the Celtic or Gallo-Roman chieftain. Perhaps the Arthur in the Grail romances was really 'Ursus' – another name for 'bear'. Perhaps the legendary Arthur in the chronicles of Geoffrey of Monmouth had been appropriated by writers on the Grail and deliberately transformed into the vehicle for a quite different, and secret, tradition. If so, this would explain why the Templars – established by the Prieuré de Sion as guardians of the Merovingian bloodline – were declared to be guardians of the Grail and the Grail family. If the Grail family and the Merovingian bloodline were one and the same, the Templars would indeed have been the guardians of the Grail – at the time, more or less, that the Grail romances were composed. Their presence in the Grail romances would not, therefore, have been anachronistic.

The hypothesis was intriguing, but it raised one extremely crucial question. The romances may have been set in Merovingian times, but they linked the Grail quite explicitly to the origins of Christianity – to Jesus, to Joseph of Arimathea, to the Magdalene. Some of them, in fact, go even further. In Robert de Boron's poem, Galahad is said to be Joseph of Arimathea's son – although the identity of the knight's mother is unclear. And the *Queste del Saint Graal* calls Galahad, like Jesus, a scion of the house of David, and identifies Galahad with Jesus himself. Indeed, the very name Galahad, according to modern scholars, derives from the name Gilead, which was deemed a mystical designation for Jesus.[34]

If the Grail could be identified with the Merovingian bloodline, what was its connection with Jesus? Why should something so intimately associated with Jesus also be associated with the Merovingian epoch? How were we to reconcile the chronological discrepancy – the relation between something so pertinent to Jesus and events that occurred at least four centuries later? How could the Grail refer, on the one hand, to the Merovingian age and, on the other, to something brought by Joseph of Arimathea to England or the Magdalene to France?

Even on a symbolic level such questions asserted themselves. The Grail, for example, pertained in some way to blood. Even without the breaking of 'Sangraal' into 'Sang raal', the Grail was said to have been a receptacle for Jesus's blood. How could this be related to the Merovingians? And why should it be related to them at precisely the time it was – during the Crusades, when Merovingian heads wore the crown of the kingdom of Jerusalem, protected by the Order of the Temple and the Prieuré de Sion?

The Grail romances stress the importance of Jesus's blood. They also stress a lineage of some kind. And, given such factors as the Grail family's culmination in Godfroi de Bouillon, they would seem to pertain to Merovingian blood.

Could there possibly be some connection between these two apparently discordant elements? Could the blood of Jesus in some way be related to the blood royal of the Merovingians? Could the lineage connected with the Grail, brought into Western Europe shortly after the Crucifixion, be intertwined with the lineage of the Merovingians?

THE NEED TO SYNTHESISE

At this point we paused to review the evidence at our disposal. It was leading us in a startling yet unmistakable direction. But why, we wondered, had this evidence never been subpoenaed by scholars before? It had certainly been readily available, and for centuries. Why had no one, to our knowledge, ever synthesised it and drawn what would seem to be fairly obvious, if only speculative, conclusions? Granted, such conclusions a few centuries ago would have been rigorously taboo – and, if published, severely punished. But there had been no such danger for at least the last two hundred years. Why, then, had the fragments of the puzzle not hitherto been assembled into a coherent whole?

The answers to these questions, we realised, lay in our own age and the modes or habits of thought which characterise it. Since the so-called 'Enlightenment' of the eighteenth century, the orientation of Western culture and consciousness had been towards analysis, rather than synthesis. As a result, our age is one of ever-increasing specialisation. In accordance with this tendency, modern scholarship lays inordinate emphasis on specialisation – which, as the modern university attests, implies and entails the segregation of knowledge into distinct 'disciplines'. In consequence, the diverse spheres covered by our inquiry have traditionally been segmented into quite separate compartments. In each compartment the relevant material has been duly explored and evaluated by specialists, or 'experts' in the field. But few, if any, of these 'experts' have endeavoured to establish a connection between their particular field and others that may overlap it. Indeed such 'experts' tend generally to regard fields other than their own with considerable suspicion – spurious at worst, at best irrelevant. And eclectic or 'interdisciplinary' research is often actively discouraged as being, among other things, too speculative.

There have been numerous treatises on the Grail romances, their origins and development, their cultural impact, their literary quality. And there have been numerous studies, valid and otherwise, of the Templars and the Crusades. But few experts on the Grail romances have been historians, while fewer still have displayed much interest in the complex, often sordid and not very romantic history behind the Templars and the Crusades. Similarly historians of the Templars and the Crusades have, like all historians, adhered closely to 'factual' records and documents. The Grail romances have been dismissed as mere fiction, as nothing more than a 'cultural phenomenon', a species of 'by-product' generated by the 'imagination of the age'. To suggest to such an historian that the Grail romances might contain a kernel of historical truth would be tantamount to heresy – even though Schliemann, more than a century ago, discovered the site of Troy by dint of careful reading of Homer.

True, various occult writers, proceeding primarily on the basis of wishful thinking, have given literal credence to the legends, claiming that, in some mystical way, the Templars were custodians of the Grail –

whatever the Grail might be. But there has been no serious historical study that endeavours to establish any real connection. The Templars are regarded as fact, the Grail as fiction, and no association between the two is acknowledged possible. And if the Grail romances have thus been neglected by scholars and historians of the period in which they were written, it is hardly surprising that they have been neglected by experts on earlier epochs. Quite simply, it would not occur to a specialist in the Merovingian age to suspect that the Grail romances might, in any way, shed light on the subject of his study, if, indeed, he has any knowledge whatever of the Grail romances. But is it not a serious omission that no Merovingian scholar we have encountered even makes mention of the Arthurian legends – which, chronologically speaking, refer to the very epoch in which he claims expertise?

If historians are unprepared to make such connections, Biblical scholars are even less prepared to do so. During the last few decades a welter of books has appeared – according to which Jesus was a pacifist, an Essene, a mystic, a Buddhist, a sorcerer, a revolutionary, a homosexual, even a mushroom. But despite this plethora of material on Jesus and the historical context of the New Testament, not one author, to our knowledge, has touched on the question of the Grail. Why should he? Why should an expert on Biblical history have any interest in, or knowledge of, a spate of fantastic romantic poems composed in Western Europe more than a thousand years later? It would seem inconceivable that the Grail romances could in any way elucidate the mysteries surrounding the New Testament.

But reality, history and knowledge cannot be segmented and compartmentalised according to the arbitrary filing system of the human intellect. And while documentary evidence may be hard to come by, it is self-evident that traditions may survive for a thousand years, then surface in a written form that does illuminate previous events. Certain Irish sagas, for instance, can reveal a great deal about the shift from matriarchal to patriarchal society in Ancient Ireland. Without Homer's work, composed long after the fact, no one would even have heard of the siege of Troy. And *War and Peace* – although written more than half a century later – can tell us more than most history books, more even than most official documents, about Russia during the Napoleonic era.

Any responsible researcher must, like a detective, pursue whatever clues come to hand, however seemingly improbable. One should not dismiss material *a priori*, out of hand, because it threatens to lead into unlikely or unfamiliar territory. The events of the Watergate scandal, for instance, were reconstructed initially from a multitude of ostensibly disparate fragments, each meaningless in itself, and with no apparent connection between them. Indeed, some of the often childish 'dirty tricks' must have seemed, to investigators at the time, as divorced from the broader issues as the Grail romances might seem from the New Testament. And the Watergate scandal was confined to a single country and a time-span of a few short years. The subject of our investigation encompasses the whole of Western culture, and a time-span of two millennia.

What is necessary is an interdisciplinary approach to one's chosen material – a mobile and flexible approach that permits one to move freely between disparate disciplines, across space and time. One must be able to link data and make connections between people, events and phenomena widely divorced from each other. One must be able to move, as necessity dictates, from the third to the twelfth to the seventh to the eighteenth centuries, drawing on a varied spectrum of sources – early ecclesiastical texts, the Grail romances, Merovingian records and chronicles, the writings of Freemasonry. In short, one must synthesise – for only by such synthesis can one discern the underlying continuity, the unified and coherent fabric, which lies at the core of any historical problem. Such an approach is neither particularly revolutionary, in principle, nor particularly controversial. It is rather like taking a tenet of contemporary Church dogma – the Immaculate Conception, for instance, or the obligatory celibacy of priests – and using it to illumine early Christianity. In much the same way the Grail romances may be used to shed some significant light on the New Testament – on the career and identity of Jesus.

Finally it is not sufficient to confine oneself exclusively to facts. One must also discern the repercussions and ramifications of facts, as those repercussions and ramifications radiate through the centuries – often in the form of myth and legend. True, the facts themselves may be distorted in the process, like an echo reverberating among cliffs. But if the voice itself cannot be located, the echo, however distorted, may yet point the way to it. Facts, in short, are like pebbles dropped into the pool of history. They disappear quickly, often without a trace. But they generate ripples which, if one's perspective is broad enough, enable one to pinpoint where the pebble originally fell. Guided by the ripples, one may then dive or dredge or adopt whatever approach one wishes. The point is that the ripples permit one to locate what might otherwise be irrecoverable.

It was now becoming apparent to us that everything we had studied during our investigation was but a ripple – which, monitored correctly, might direct us to a single stone cast into the pool of history two thousand years ago.

OUR HYPOTHESIS

The Magdalene had figured prominently throughout our inquiry. According to certain medieval legends, the Magdalene brought the Holy Grail – or 'Blood Royal' – into France. The Grail is closely associated with Jesus. And the Grail, on one level at least, relates in some way to blood – or, more specifically, to a bloodline and lineage. The Grail romances are for the most part, however, set in Merovingian times. But they were not composed until after Godfroi de Bouillon – fictional scion of the Grail family and actual scion of the Merovingians – was installed, in everything but name, as king of Jerusalem.

If we had been dealing with anyone other than Jesus – if we had been dealing with a personage such as Alexander, for example, or Julius Caesar – these fragmentary shreds of evidence alone would have led, almost ineluctably, to one glaring self-evident conclusion. We drew that conclusion, however controversial and explosive it might be. We began to test it at least as a tentative hypothesis.

Perhaps the Magdalene – that elusive woman in the Gospels – was in fact Jesus's wife. Perhaps their union produced offspring. After the Crucifixion, perhaps the Magdalene, with at least one child, was smuggled to Gaul – where established Jewish communities already existed and where, in consequence, she might have found a refuge. Perhaps there was, in short, an hereditary bloodline descended directly from Jesus. Perhaps this bloodline, this supreme *sang réal*, then perpetuated itself, intact and incognito, for some four hundred years – which is not, after all, a very long time for an important lineage. Perhaps there were dynastic intermarriages not only with other Jewish families, but with Romans and Visigoths as well. And perhaps in the fifth century Jesus's lineage became allied with the royal line of the Franks, thereby engendering the Merovingian dynasty.

If this sketchy hypothesis was in any sense true, it would serve to explain a great many elements in our investigation. It would explain the extraordinary status accorded the Magdalene, and the cult significance she attained during the Crusades. It would explain the sacred status accorded the Merovingians. It would explain the legendary birth of Mérovée – child of two fathers, one of them a symbolic marine creature from beyond the sea, a marine creature which, like Jesus, might be equated with the mystical fish. It would explain the pact between the Roman Church and Clovis's bloodline – for would not a pact with Jesus's lineal descendants be the obvious pact for a church founded in his name? It would explain the apparently incommensurate stress laid on the assassination of Dagobert II – for the Church, by being party to that murder, would have been guilty not only of regicide, but, according to its own tenets, of a form of deicide as well. It would explain the attempt to eradicate Dagobert from history. It would explain the Carolingians' obsession to legitimise themselves, as Holy Roman Emperors, by claiming a Merovingian pedigree.

A bloodline descended from Jesus through Dagobert would also explain the Grail family in the romances – the secrecy which surrounds it, its exalted status, the impotent Fisher King unable to rule, the process whereby Parzival or Perceval became heir to the Grail castle. Finally, it would explain the mystical pedigree of Godfroi de Bouillon – son or grandson of Lohengrin, grandson or great-grandson of Parzival, scion of the Grail family. And if Godfroi were descended from Jesus, his triumphant capture of Jerusalem in 1099 would have entailed far more than simply rescuing the Holy Sepulchre from the infidel. Godfroi would have been reclaiming his own rightful heritage.

We had already guessed that the references to viticulture throughout our investigation symbolised dynastic alliances. On the basis of our hypothesis, viticulture now seemed to symbolise the process whereby Jesus – who identifies himself repeatedly with the vine – perpetuated his lineage. As if in confirmation, we discovered a carved door depicting Jesus as a cluster of grapes. This door was in Sion, Switzerland.

Our hypothetical scenario was both logically consistent and intriguing. As yet, however, it was also preposterous. Attractive though it might be, it was, as yet, much too sketchy and rested on far too flimsy a foundation. Although it explained many things, it could not yet in itself be supported. There were still too many holes in it, too many inconsistencies and anomalies, too many loose ends. Before we could seriously entertain or consider it, we would have to determine whether there was any real evidence to sustain it. In an attempt to find such evidence we began to explore the Gospels, the historical context of the New Testament and the writings of the early Church fathers.

CHAPTER TWELVE

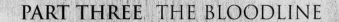

THE PRIEST-KING WHO NEVER RULED

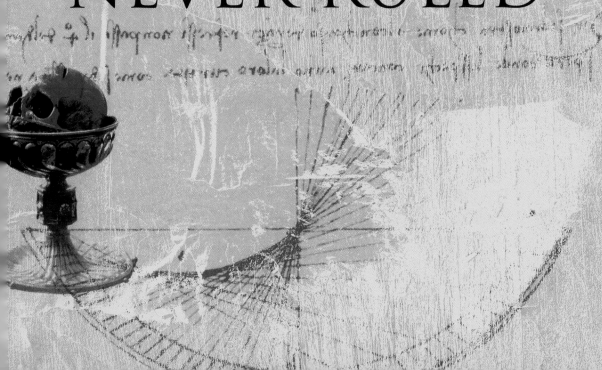

Most people today speak of 'Christianity' as if it were a single specific thing – a coherent, homogeneous and unified entity. Needless to say 'Christianity' is nothing of the sort. As everyone knows, there are numerous forms of 'Christianity': Roman Catholicism, for example, or the Church of England initiated by Henry VIII. There are the various other denominations of Protestantism – from the original Lutheranism and Calvinism of the sixteenth century to such relatively recent developments as Unitarianism. There are multitudinous 'fringe' or 'evangelical' congregations, such as the Seventh Day Adventists and Jehovah's Witnesses. And there are assorted contemporary sects and cults, like the Children of God and the Unification Church of the Reverend Moon. If one surveys this bewildering spectrum of beliefs – from the rigidly dogmatic and conservative to the radical and ecstatic – it is difficult to determine what exactly constitutes 'Christianity'.

If there is a single factor that does permit one to speak of 'Christianity', a single factor that does link the otherwise diverse and divergent 'Christian' creeds, it is the New Testament, and more particularly the unique status ascribed by the New Testament to Jesus, his Crucifixion and Resurrection. Even if one does not subscribe to the literal or historical truth of those events, acceptance of their symbolic significance generally suffices for one to be considered a Christian.

If there is any unity, then, in the diffuse phenomenon called Christianity, it resides in the New Testament – and, more specifically, in the accounts of Jesus known as the Four Gospels. These accounts are popularly regarded as the most authoritative on record: and for many Christians they are assumed to be both coherent and unimpugnable. From childhood one is led to believe that the 'story' of Jesus, as it is preserved in the Four Gospels, is, if not God-inspired, at least definitive. The four evangelists, supposed authors of the Gospels, are deemed to be unimpeachable witnesses who reinforce and confirm each other's testimony. Of the people who today call themselves Christians, relatively few are aware of the fact that the Four Gospels not only contradict each other, but, at times, violently disagree.

So far as popular tradition is concerned, the origin and birth of Jesus are well enough known. But in reality the Gospels, on which that tradition is based, are considerably more vague on the matter. Only two of the Gospels – Matthew and Luke – say anything at all about Jesus's origins and birth; and they are flagrantly at odds with each other.

According to Matthew, for example, Jesus was an aristocrat, if not a rightful and legitimate king – descended from David via Solomon. According to Luke, on the other hand, Jesus's family, though descended from the house of David, was of somewhat less exalted stock; and it is on the basis of Mark's account that the legend of the 'poor carpenter' came into being. The two genealogies, in short, are so strikingly discordant that they might well be referring to two quite different individuals.

The discrepancies between the Gospels are not confined to the question of Jesus's ancestry and genealogy. According to Luke, Jesus, on his birth, was visited by shepherds. According to Matthew, he was visited by wise men. According to Luke, Jesus's family lived in Nazareth. From here they are said to have journeyed – for a census which history suggests never in fact occurred – to Bethlehem, where Jesus was born in the poverty of a manger. But according to Matthew, Jesus's family had been fairly well-to-do residents of Bethlehem all along, and Jesus himself was born in a house. In Matthew's version Herod's persecution of the innocents prompts the family to flee into Egypt, and only on their return do they make their home in Nazareth.

The information in each of these accounts is quite specific and – assuming the census did occur – perfectly plausible. And yet the information itself simply does not agree. This contradiction cannot be rationalised. There is no possible means whereby the two conflicting narratives can both be correct, and there is no means whereby they can be reconciled. Whether one cares to admit it or not, the fact must be recognised that one or both of the Gospels is wrong. In the face of so glaring and inevitable a conclusion, the Gospels cannot be regarded as unimpugnable. How can they be unimpugnable when they impugn each other?

The more one studies the Gospels, the more the contradictions between them become apparent. Indeed they do not even agree on the day of the Crucifixion. According to John's Gospel, the Crucifixion occurred on the day before the Passover. According to the Gospels of Mark, Luke and Matthew, it occurred on the day after. Nor are the Gospels in accord on the personality and character of Jesus. Each depicts a figure who is patently at odds with the figure depicted in the others – a meek lamblike saviour in Luke, for example, a powerful and majestic sovereign in Matthew who comes 'not to bring peace but a sword'. And there is further disagreement about Jesus's last words on the cross. In Matthew and Mark these words are, 'My God, my God, why hast thou forsaken me?' In Luke they are, 'Father, into thy hands I commend my spirit.' And in John, they are simply, 'It is finished.'

Given these discrepancies, the Gospels can only be accepted as a highly questionable authority, and certainly not as definitive. They do not represent the perfect word of any God; or, if they do, God's words have been very liberally censored, edited, revised, glossed and rewritten by human hands. The Bible, it must be remembered – and this applies to both the Old and New Testaments – is only a selection of works, and, in many respects, a somewhat arbitrary one. In fact, it could well include far more books and writings than it actually does. Nor is there any question of the missing books having been 'lost'. On the contrary they were deliberately excluded. In A.D. 367 Bishop Athanasius of Alexandria compiled a list of works to be included in the New Testament. This list was ratified by the Church Council of Hippo in 393 and again by the Council of Catharge four years later. At these councils a selection was agreed upon. Certain works were assembled to form the New Testament as we know it today, and others were cavalierly ignored. How can such a process of selection possibly be regarded as definitive? How could a conclave of clerics infallibly decide that certain books 'belonged' in the Bible while others did not? Especially when some of the excluded books have a perfectly valid claim to historical veracity?

As it exists today, moreover, the Bible is not only a product of a more or less arbitrary selective process. It has also been subjected to some fairly drastic editing, censorship and revision. In 1958, for example, Professor Morton Smith of Columbia University discovered, in a monastery near Jerusalem, a letter which contained a missing fragment of the Gospel of Mark. The missing fragment had not been lost. On the contrary, it had apparently been deliberately suppressed – at the instigation, if not the express behest, of Bishop Clement of Alexandria, one of the most venerated of the early Church fathers.

Clement, it seems, had received a letter from one Theodore, who complained of a Gnostic sect, the Carpocratians. The Carpocratians appear to have been interpreting certain passages of the Gospel of Mark in accordance with their own principles – principles that did not concur with the position of Clement and Theodore. In consequence, Theodore apparently attacked them and reported his action to Clement. In the letter found by Professor Smith, Clement replies to his disciple as follows:

You did well in silencing the unspeakable teachings of the Carpocratians. For these are the 'wandering stars' referred to in the prophecy, who wander from the narrow road of the commandments into a boundless abyss of the carnal and bodily sins. For, priding themselves in knowledge, as they say, 'of the deep [things] of Satan', they do not know that they are casting themselves away into 'the nether world of the darkness' of falsity, and, boasting that they are free, they have become slaves of servile desires. Such [men] are to be opposed in all ways and altogether. For, even if they should say something true, one who loves the truth should not, even so, agree with them. For not all true [things] are the truth, nor should that truth which [merely] seems true according to human opinions be preferred to the true truth, that according to the faith.[1]

It is an extraordinary statement for a Church father. In effect Clement is saying nothing less than, 'If your opponent happens to tell the truth, you must deny it and lie in order to refute him.' But that is not all. In the following passage, Clement's letter goes on to discuss Mark's Gospel and its 'misuse', in his eyes, by the Carpocratians:

[As for] Mark, then, during Peter's stay in Rome he wrote [an account of] the Lord's doings; not, however, declaring all [of them], nor yet hinting at the secret [ones], but selecting those he thought most useful for increasing the faith of those who were being instructed. But when Peter died as a martyr, Mark came over to Alexandria, bringing both his own notes and those of Peter, from which he transferred to his former book the things suitable to whatever makes for progress towards knowledge [gnosis]. [Thus] he composed a more spiritual Gospel for the use of those who were being perfected. Nevertheless, he yet did not divulge the things not to be uttered, nor did he write down the hierophantic teachings of the Lord, but to the stories already written he added yet others and, moreover, brought in certain sayings of which he knew the interpretation would, as a mystagogue, lead the hearers into the innermost sanctuary of that truth hidden by seven [veils]. Thus, in sum, he prearranged matters, neither grudgingly nor incautiously, in my opinion, and, dying, he left his composition to the church in Alexandria, where it even yet is most carefully guarded, being read only to those who are being initiated into the great mysteries.

But since the foul demons are always devising destruction for the race of men, Carpocrates, instructed by them and using deceitful arts, so enslaved a certain presbyter of the church in Alexandria that he got from him a copy of the secret Gospel, which he both interpreted according to his blasphemous and carnal doctrine and, moreover, polluted, mixing with the spotless and holy words utterly shameless lies.[2]

Clement thus freely acknowledges that there is an authentic secret Gospel of Mark. He then instructs Theodore to deny it:

To them [the Carpocratians], therefore, as I said above, one must never give way, nor, when they put forward their falsifications, should one concede that the secret Gospel is by Mark, but should even deny it on oath. For 'not all true [things] are to be said to all men'.[3]

What was this 'secret Gospel' that Clement ordered his disciple to repudiate and that the Carpocratians were 'misinterpreting'? Clement answers the question by including a word-for-word transcription of the text in his letter:

To you, therefore, I shall not hesitate to answer the [questions] you have asked, refuting the falsifications by the very words of the Gospel. For example after 'And they were in the road going up to Jerusalem,' and what follows, until 'After three days he shall arise', [the secret Gospel] brings the following [material] word for word:

'And they came into Bethany, and a certain woman, whose brother had died, was there. And, coming, she prostrated herself before Jesus and says to him, "Son of David, have mercy on me". But the disciples rebuked her. And Jesus, being angered, went off with her into the garden where the tomb was, and straightway a great cry was heard from the tomb. And going near, Jesus rolled away the stone from the door of the tomb. And straightway, going in where the youth was, he stretched forth his hand and raised him, seizing his hand. But the youth,

looking upon him, loved him and began to beseech him that he
might be with him. And going out of the tomb they came into
the house of the youth, for he was rich. And after six days, Jesus
told him what to do and in the evening the youth comes to him,
wearing a linen cloth over [his] naked [body]. And he remained
with him that night, for Jesus taught him the mystery of the
kingdom of God. And thence arising, he returned to the other
side of the Jordan.'[4]

This episode appears in no existing version of the Gospel of Mark. In its
general outlines, however, it is familiar enough. It is, of course, the raising of Lazarus, described in the Fourth Gospel, ascribed to John. In the
version quoted, however, there are some significant variations. In the
first place there is a 'great cry' from the tomb before Jesus rolls the rock
aside or instructs the occupant to come forth. This strongly suggests
that the occupant was not dead and thereby, at a single stroke, contra-
venes any element of the miraculous. In the second place there would
clearly seem to be something more involved than accepted accounts of
the Lazarus episode lead one to believe. Certainly the passage quoted
attests to some special relation between the man in the tomb and the
man who 'resurrects' him. A modern reader might perhaps be tempted
to see a hint of homosexuality. It is possible that the Carpocratians – a
sect who aspired to transcendence of the sense by means of satiation of
the senses – discerned precisely such a hint. But, as Professor Smith
argues, it is in fact much more likely that the whole episode refers to a
typical mystery school initiation – a ritualised and symbolic death and
rebirth of the sort so prevalent in the Middle East at the time.

In any case the point is that the episode, and the passage quoted
above, do not appear in any modern or accepted version of Mark.
Indeed, the only references to Lazarus or a Lazarus figure in the New
Testament are in the Gospel ascribed to John. It is thus clear that
Clement's advice was accepted – not only by Theodore, but by subsequent authorities as well. Quite simply the entire Lazarus incident was
completely excised from the Gospel of Mark.

If Mark's Gospel was so drastically expurgated, it was also burdened
with spurious additions. In its original version it ends with the
Crucifixion, the burial and the empty tomb. There is no Resurrection
scene, no reunion with the disciples. Granted, there are certain modern
Bibles which do contain a more conventional ending to the Gospel of

Mark – an ending which does include the Resurrection. But virtually all modern Biblical scholars concur that this expanded ending is a later addition, dating from the late second century and appended to the original document.[5]

The Gospel of Mark thus provides two instances of a sacred document – supposedly inspired by God – which has been tampered with, edited, censored, revised by human hands. Nor are these two cases speculative. On the contrary, they are now accepted by scholars as demonstrable and proven. Can one then suppose that Mark's Gospel was unique in being subjected to alteration? Clearly if Mark's Gospel was so readily doctored, it is reasonable to assume that the other Gospels were similarly treated.

For the purposes of our investigation, then, we could not accept the Gospels as definitive and unimpugnable authority, but, at the same time we could not discard them. They were certainly not wholly fabricated, and they furnished some of the few clues available to what really happened in the Holy Land two thousand years ago. We therefore undertook to look more closely, to winnow through them, to disengage fact from fable, to separate the truth they contained from the spurious matrix in which that truth was often embedded. And in order to do this effectively, we were first obliged to familiarise ourselves with the historical reality and circumstances of the Holy Land at the advent of the Christian era. For the Gospels are not autonomous entities, conjured out of the void and floating, eternal and universal, over the centuries. They are historical documents, like any other – like the Dead Sea Scrolls, the epics of Homer and Virgil, the Grail romances. They are products of a very specific place, a very specific time, a very specific people and very specific historical factors.

PALESTINE AT THE TIME OF JESUS

Palestine in the first century was a very troubled corner of the globe. For some time the Holy Land had been fraught with dynastic squabbles, internecine strife and, on occasion, full-scale war. During the second century B.C. a more or less unified Judaic kingdom was transiently established – as chronicled by the two Apocryphal Books of Maccabees. By 63 B.C., however, the land was in upheaval again, and ripe for conquest.

More than half a century before Jesus's birth, Palestine fell to the

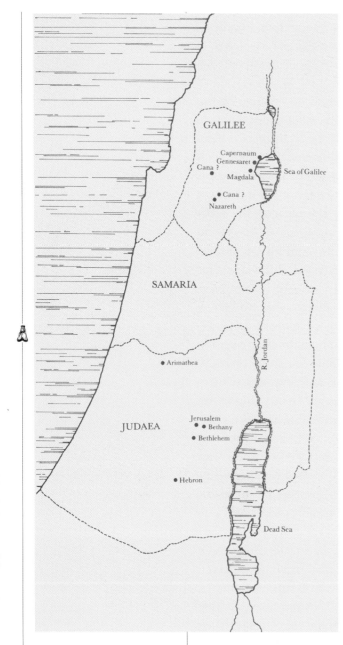

Palestine at the time of Jesus.

armies of Pompey, and Roman rule was imposed. But Rome at the time was over-extended, and too preoccupied with her own affairs, to install the administrative apparatus necessary for direct rule. She therefore created a line of puppet kings to rule under her aegis. This line was that of the Herodians – who were not Jewish, but Arab. The first of the line was Antipater, who assumed the throne of Palestine in 63 B.C. On his death in 37 B.C., he was succeeded by his son, Herod the Great, who ruled until 4 B.C. One must visualise, then, a situation analogous to that of France under the Vichy government between 1940 and 1944. One must visualise a conquered land and a conquered people, ruled by a puppet régime which was kept in power by military force. The people of the country were allowed to retain their own religion and customs. But the final authority was Rome. This authority was implemented according to Roman law and enforced by Roman soldiery – as it was in Britain not long after.

In A.D. 6 the situation became more critical. In this year the country was split administratively into one province (Judaea and Samaria) and two tetrarchies (Peraea and Galilee). Herod Antipas became ruler of the latter. But Judaea – the spiritual and secular capital – was rendered subject to direct Roman rule, administered by a Roman Prefect based at Caesarea. The Roman régime was brutal and autocratic. When it assumed direct control of Judaea more than three thousand rebels were summarily crucified. The Temple was plundered and defiled. Heavy taxation was imposed. Torture was frequently employed, and many of the populace committed suicide. This state of affairs was not improved by Pontius Pilate, who presided as prefect of Judaea from A.D. 26 to 36. In contrast to the Biblical portraits of him, existing records indicate that Pilate was a cruel and corrupt man, who not only perpetuated, but intensified, the abuses of his predecessor.[6] It is thus all the more surprising – at least on first glance – that there should be no criticism of Rome in the Gospels, no mention even of the burden of the Roman yoke. Indeed the Gospel accounts suggest that the inhabitants of Judaea were placid and contented with their lot.

In point of fact very few were contented, and many were far from placid. The Jews in the Holy Land at the time could be loosely divided into several sects and sub-sects. There were, for example, the Sadducees – a small but wealthy land-owning class who, to the anger of their compatriots, collaborated, Quisling-fashion, with the Romans. There were the Pharisees – a progressive group who introduced much reform into Judaism and who, despite the portrait of them in the Gospels, placed themselves in staunch, albeit largely passive, opposition to Rome. There were the Essenes – an austere, mystically oriented sect, whose teachings were much more prevalent and influential than is generally acknowledged or supposed. Among the smaller sects and sub-sects there were many whose precise character has long been lost to history, and which, therefore, are difficult to define. It is worth citing the Nazorites, however, of whom Samson, centuries before, had been a member, and who were still in existence during Jesus's time. And it is worth citing the Nazoreans or Nazarenes – a term which seems to have been applied to Jesus and his followers. Indeed the original Greek version of the New Testament refers to Jesus as 'Jesus of Nazarene' – which is mistranslated in English as 'Jesus of Nazareth'. 'Nazarene', in short, is a specifically sectarian word and has no connection with Nazareth.

There were numerous other groups and sects as well, one of which proved of particular relevance to our inquiry. In A.D. 6, when Rome assumed direct control of Judaea, a Pharisee rabbi known as Judas of Galilee had created a highly militant revolutionary group composed, it would appear, of both Pharisees and Essenes. This following became known as Zealots. The Zealots were not, strictly speaking, a sect. They were a movement, whose membership was drawn from a number of sects. By the time of Jesus's mission, the Zealots had assumed an increasingly prominent role in the Holy Land's affairs. Their activities formed perhaps the most important political backdrop against which Jesus's drama enacted itself. Long after the Crucifixion, Zealot activity continued unabated. By A.D. 44 this activity had so intensified that some sort of armed struggle already seemed inevitable. In A.D. 66 the struggle erupted, the whole of Judaea rising in organised revolt against Rome. It was a desperate, tenacious but ultimately futile conflict – reminiscent in certain respects of, say, Hungary in 1956. At Caesarea alone 20,000 Jews were massacred by the Romans. Within four years Roman legions had occupied Jerusalem, razed the city, and sacked and plundered the Temple. Nevertheless the mountain fortress of Masada held out for yet another three years, commanded by a lineal descendant of Judas of Galilee.

The aftermath of the revolt in Judaea witnessed a massive exodus of Jews from the Holy Land. Nevertheless enough remained to foment another rebellion some sixty years later in A.D. 132. At last, in 135, the Emperor Hadrian decreed that all Jews be expelled by law from Judaea, and Jerusalem became essentially a Roman city. It was renamed Aelia Capitolina.

Jesus's lifetime spanned roughly the first thirty-five years of a turmoil extending over 140 years. The turmoil did not cease with his death, but continued for another century. And it engendered the psychological and cultural adjuncts inevitably attending any such sustained defiance of an oppressor. One of these adjuncts was the hope and longing for a Messiah who would deliver his people from the tyrant's yoke. It was only by virtue of historical and semantic accident that this term came to be applied specifically and exclusively to Jesus.

For Jesus's contemporaries, no Messiah would ever have been regarded as divine. Indeed the very idea of a divine Messiah would have been preposterous if not unthinkable. The Greek word for Messiah is 'Christ' or 'Christos'. The term – whether in Hebrew or Greek – meant simply 'the anointed one' and generally referred to a king. Thus David, when he was anointed king in the Old Testament, became, quite explicitly, a 'Messiah' or a 'Christ'. And every subsequent Jewish king of the house of David was known by the same appellation. Even during the Roman occupation of Judaea, the Roman-appointed high priest was known as the 'Priest Messiah' or 'Priest Christ'.[7]

For the Zealots, however, and for other opponents of Rome, this puppet priest was, of necessity, a 'false Messiah'. For them the 'true Messiah' implied something very different – the legitimate *roi perdu* or 'lost king', the unknown descendant of the house of David who would deliver his people from Roman tyranny. During Jesus's lifetime anticipation of the coming of such a Messiah attained a pitch verging on mass hysteria. And this anticipation continued after Jesus's death. Indeed the revolt of A.D. 66 was prompted in large part by Zealot agitation and propaganda on behalf of a Messiah whose advent was said to be imminent.

The term 'Messiah', then, implied nothing in any way divine. Strictly defined, it meant nothing more than an anointed king; and in the popular mind it came to mean an anointed king who would also be a liberator. In other words, it was a term with specifically political connotations – something quite different from the later Christian idea of a 'Son of God'. It was this mundane political term that was applied to Jesus. He was called 'Jesus the Messiah' or – translated into Greek – 'Jesus the Christ'. Only later was this designation contracted to 'Jesus Christ' and a purely functional title distorted into a proper name.

THE HISTORY OF THE GOSPELS

The Gospels issued from a recognisable and concrete historical reality. It was a reality of oppression, of civic and social discontent, of political unrest, of incessant persecution and intermittent rebellion. It was also a reality suffused with perpetual and tantalising promises, hopes and dreams – that a rightful king would appear, a spiritual and secular leader who would deliver his people into freedom. So far as political freedom was concerned, such aspirations were brutally extinguished by the devastating war between A.D. 66 and 74. Transposed into a wholly religious form, however, the aspirations were not only perpetuated by the Gospels, but given a powerful new impetus.

Modern scholars are unanimous in concurring that the Gospels do not date from Jesus's lifetime. For the most part they date from the period between the two major revolts in Judaea – 66 to 74 and 132 to 135 – although they are almost certainly based on earlier accounts. These earlier accounts may have included written documents since lost – for there was a wholesale destruction of records in the wake of the first rebellion. But there would certainly have been oral traditions as well. Some of these were undoubtedly grossly exaggerated and/or distorted, received and transmitted at second, third or fourth hand. Others, however, may have derived from individuals who were alive in Jesus's lifetime and may even have known him personally. A young man at the time of the Crucifixion might well have been alive when the Gospels were composed.

The earliest of the Gospels is generally considered to be Mark's, composed sometime during the revolt of 66–74 or shortly thereafter – except for its treatment of the Resurrection, which is a later and spurious addition. Although not himself one of Jesus's original disciples, Mark seems to have come from Jerusalem. He seems to have been a companion of Saint Paul, and his Gospel bears an unmistakable stamp of Pauline thought. But if Mark was a native of Jerusalem, his Gospel – as Clement of Alexandria states – was composed in Rome, and addressed to a Greco-Roman audience. This, in itself, explains a great deal. At the time that Mark's Gospel was composed, Judaea was, or had recently been, in open revolt, and thousands of Jews were being crucified for rebellion against the Roman régime. If Mark wished his Gospel to survive and impress itself on a Roman audience, he could not possibly present Jesus as anti-Roman. Indeed, he could not feasibly present Jesus as politically oriented at all. In order to ensure the survival of his message, he would have been obliged to exonerate the Romans of all guilt for Jesus's death – to whitewash the existing and entrenched régime and blame the death of the Messiah on certain Jews. This device was adopted not only by the authors of the other Gospels, but by the early Christian Church as well. Without such a device neither Gospels nor Church would have survived.

The Gospel of Luke is dated by scholars at around A.D. 80. Luke himself appears to have been a Greek doctor, who composed his work for a high-ranking Roman official at Caesarea, the Roman capital of Palestine. For Luke, too, therefore, it would have been necessary to placate and appease the Romans and transfer the blame elsewhere. By the time the Gospel of Matthew was composed – approximately A.D. 85 – such a transference seems to have been accepted as an established fact and gone unquestioned. More than half of Matthew's Gospel, in fact, is derived directly from Mark's, although it was composed originally in Greek and reflects specifically Greek characteristics. The author seems to have been a Jew, quite possibly a refugee from Palestine. He is not to be confused with the disciple named Matthew, who would have lived much earlier and would probably have known only Aramaic.

The Gospels of Mark, Luke and Matthew are known collectively as the 'Synoptic Gospels', implying that they see 'eye to eye' or 'with one eye' – which, of course, they do not. Nevertheless there is enough overlap between them to suggest that they derived from a single common source – either an oral tradition or some other document subsequently lost. This distinguishes them from the Gospel of John, which betrays significantly different origins.

Nothing whatever is known about the author of the Fourth Gospel. Indeed there is no reason to assume his name was John. Except for John the Baptist, the name John is mentioned at no point in the Gospel itself, and its attribution to a man called John is generally accepted as later tradition. The Fourth Gospel is the latest of those in the New Testament – composed around A.D. 100 in the vicinity of the Greek city of Ephesus. It displays a number of quite distinctive features. There is no nativity scene, for example, no description whatever of Jesus's birth, and the opening is almost Gnostic in character. The text is of a decidedly more mystical nature than the other Gospels, and the content differs as well. The other Gospels, for instance, concentrate primarily on Jesus's activities in the northern province of Galilee and reflect what appears to be only a second- or third-hand knowledge of events to the south, in Judaea and Jerusalem – including the Crucifixion. The Fourth Gospel, in contrast, says relatively little about Galilee. It dwells exhaustively on the events in Judaea and Jerusalem which concluded Jesus's career, and its account of the Crucifixion may well rest ultimately on some first-hand eye-witness testimony. It also contains a number of episodes and incidents which do not figure in the other Gospels at all – the wedding at Cana, the roles of Nicodemus and Joseph of Arimathea, and the raising of Lazarus (although the last was once included in Mark's Gospel). On the basis of such factors modern scholars have suggested that the Gospel of John, despite its late composition, may well be the most reliable and historically accurate of the four. More than the other Gospels, it seems to draw upon traditions current among contemporaries of Jesus, as well as other material unavailable to Mark, Luke and Matthew. One modern researcher points out that it reflects an apparently first-hand topographical knowledge of Jerusalem prior to the revolt of A.D. 66. The same author concludes, 'Behind the Fourth Gospel lies an ancient tradition independent of the other Gospels.'[8] This is not an isolated opinion. In fact, it is the most prevalent in modern Biblical scholarship. According to another writer, 'The Gospel of John, though not adhering to the Markian chronological framework and being much later in date, appears to know a tradition concerning Jesus that must be primitive and authentic.'[9]

On the basis of our own research we, too, concluded that the Fourth Gospel was the most reliable of the books in the New Testament – even though it, like the others, had been subjected to doctoring, editing, expurgation and revision. In our inquiry we had occasion to draw upon all four Gospels, and much collateral material as well. But it was in the Fourth Gospel that we found the most persuasive evidence for our, as yet, tentative hypothesis.

THE MARITAL STATUS OF JESUS

It was not our intention to discredit the Gospels. We sought only to winnow through them – to locate certain fragments of possible or probable truth and extract them from the matrix of embroidery surrounding them. We were seeking fragments, moreover, of a very precise character – fragments that might attest to a marriage between Jesus and the woman known as the Magdalene. Such attestations, needless to say, would not be explicit. In order to find them, we realised, we would be obliged to read between the lines, fill in certain gaps, account for certain caesuras and ellipses. We would have to deal with omissions, with innuendoes, with references that were, at best, oblique. And we would not only have to look for evidence of a marriage. We would also have to look for evidence of circumstances that might have been conducive to a marriage. Our inquiry would thus have to encompass a number of distinct but closely related questions. We began with the most obvious of them.

1) Is there any evidence in the Gospels, direct or indirect, to suggest that Jesus was indeed married?

There is, of course, no explicit statement to the effect that he was. On the other hand, there is no explicit statement to the effect that he was not – and this is both more curious and more significant than it might first appear. As Dr. Geza Vermes of Oxford University points out, 'There is complete silence in the Gospels concerning the marital status of Jesus . . . Such a state of affairs is sufficiently unusual in ancient Jewry to prompt further enquiry.'[10]

The Gospels state that many of the disciples – Peter, for example – were married. And at no point does Jesus himself advocate celibacy. On the contrary, in the Gospel of Matthew he declares, 'Have ye not read, that he which made them at the beginning made them male and female . . . For this cause shall a man leave father and mother, and shall cleave to his wife: and they twain shall be one flesh?' (19:4–5) Such a statement can hardly be reconciled with an injunction to celibacy. And if Jesus did not preach celibacy, there is no reason either to suppose that he practised it. According to Judaic custom at the time it was not only usual, but almost mandatory, that a man be married. Except among certain Essenes in certain communities, celibacy was vigorously condemned. During the late first century, one Jewish writer even compared deliberate celibacy with murder, and he does not seem to have been alone in this attitude. And it was as obligatory for a Jewish father to find a wife for his son as it was to ensure that his son be circumcised.

If Jesus were not married, this fact would have been glaringly conspicuous. It would have drawn attention to itself, and been used to characterise and identify him. It would have set him apart, in some significant sense, from his contemporaries. If this were the case, surely one at least of the Gospel accounts would make some mention of so marked a deviation from custom? If Jesus were indeed as celibate as later tradition claims, it is extraordinary that there is no reference to any such celibacy. The absence of any such reference strongly suggests that Jesus, as far as the question of celibacy was concerned, conformed to the conventions of his time and culture – suggests, in short, that he was married. This alone would satisfactorily explain the silence of the Gospels on the matter. The argument is summarised by a respected contemporary theological scholar:

> Granted the cultural background as witnessed . . . it is highly improbable that Jesus was not married well before the beginning of his public ministry. If he had insisted upon celibacy, it would have created a stir, a reaction which would have left some trace. So, the lack of mention of Jesus's marriage in the Gospels is a strong argument not against but for the hypothesis of marriage, because any practice or advocacy of voluntary celibacy would in the Jewish context of the time have been so unusual as to have attracted much attention and comment.[11]

The hypothesis of marriage becomes all the more tenable by virtue of the title of 'Rabbi', which is frequently applied to Jesus in the Gospels. It is possible, of course, that this term is employed in its very broadest sense, meaning simply a self-appointed teacher. But Jesus's literacy – his display of knowledge to the elders in the Temple, for example – strongly suggests that he was more than a self-appointed teacher. It suggests that he underwent some species of formal rabbinical training and was officially recognised as a rabbi. This would conform to tradition, which depicts Jesus as a rabbi in the strict sense of the word. But if Jesus was a rabbi in the strict sense of the word, a marriage would not only have been likely, but virtually certain. The Jewish Mishnaic Law is quite explicit on the subject: 'An unmarried man may not be a teacher.'[12]

In the Fourth Gospel there is an episode related to a marriage which may, in fact, have been Jesus's own. This episode is, of course, the wedding at Cana – a familiar enough story. But for all its familiarity, there are certain salient questions attending it which warrant consideration.

From the account in the Fourth Gospel, the wedding at Cana would seem to be a modest local ceremony – a typical village wedding, whose bride and groom remain anonymous. To this wedding Jesus is specifically 'called' – which is slightly curious perhaps, for he has not yet really embarked on his ministry. More curious still, however, is the fact that his mother 'just happens', as it were, to be present. And her presence would seem to be taken for granted. It is certainly not in any way explained.

What is more, it is Mary who not merely suggests to her son, but in effect orders him, to replenish the wine. She behaves quite as if she were the hostess: 'And when they wanted wine, the mother of Jesus saith unto him, They have no wine. Jesus saith unto her, Woman, what have I to do with thee? mine hour is not yet come.' (John 2:3–4) But Mary, thoroughly unperturbed, ignores her son's protest: 'His mother saith unto the servants, Whatsoever he saith unto you, do it.' (5) And the servants promptly comply – quite as if they were accustomed to receiving orders from both Mary and Jesus.

Despite Jesus's ostensible attempt to disown her, Mary prevails; and Jesus thereupon performs his first major miracle, the transmutation of water into wine. So far as the Gospels are concerned, he has not hitherto displayed his powers; and there is no reason for Mary to assume he even possesses them. But even if there were, why should such unique and holy gifts be employed for so banal a purpose? Why should Mary make such a request of her son? More important still, why should two 'guests' at a wedding take on themselves the responsibility of catering – a responsibility that, by custom, should be reserved for the host? Unless, of course, the wedding at Cana is Jesus's own wedding. In that case, it would indeed be his responsibility to replenish the wine.

There is further evidence that the wedding at Cana is in fact Jesus's own. Immediately after the miracle has been performed, the 'governor of the feast' – a kind of major-domo or master of ceremonies – tastes the newly produced wine, 'the governor of the feast *called the bridegroom*, And saith unto him, Every man at the beginning doth set forth good wine; and when men have well drunk, then that which is worse: but *thou* hast kept the good wine until now.' (John 2:9–10; our italics.) These words would clearly seem to be addressed to Jesus. According to the Gospel, however, they are addressed to the 'bridegroom'. An obvious conclusion is that Jesus and the 'bridegroom' are one and the same.

THE WIFE OF JESUS

2) If Jesus was married, is there any indication in the Gospels of the identity of his wife?

On first consideration there would appear to be two possible candidates – two women, apart from his mother, who are mentioned repeatedly in the Gospels as being of his entourage. The first of these is the Magdalene – or, more precisely, Mary from the village of the Migdal, or Magdala, in Galilee. In all four Gospels this woman's role is singularly ambiguous and seems to have been deliberately obscured. In the accounts of Mark and Matthew she is not mentioned by name until quite late. When she does appear it is in Judaea, at the time of the Crucifixion, and she is numbered among Jesus's followers. In the Gospel of Luke, however, she appears relatively early in Jesus's ministry, while he is still preaching from Galilee. It would thus seem that she accompanies him from Galilee to Judaea – or, if not, that she at least moves between the two provinces as readily as he does. This in itself strongly suggests that she was married to someone. In the Palestine of Jesus's time it would have been unthinkable for an unmarried woman to travel unaccompanied – and, even more so, to travel unaccompanied with a religious teacher and his entourage. A number of traditions seem to have taken cognisance of this potentially embarrassing fact. Thus it is sometimes claimed that the Magdalene was married to one of Jesus's disciples. If that were the case, however, her special relationship with Jesus and her proximity to him would have rendered both of them subject to suspicions, if not charges, of adultery.

Popular tradition notwithstanding, the Magdalene is not, at any point in any of the Gospels, said to be a prostitute. When she is first mentioned in the Gospel of Luke, she is described as a woman 'out of whom went seven devils'. It is generally assumed that this phrase refers to a species of exorcism on Jesus's part, implying that the Magdalene was 'possessed'. But the phrase may equally refer to some sort of conversion and/or ritual initiation. The cult of Ishtar or Astarte – the Mother Goddess and 'Queen of Heaven' – involved, for example, a seven-stage initiation. Prior to her affiliation with Jesus, the Magdalene may well have been associated with such a cult.

One chapter before he speaks of the Magdalene, Luke alludes to a woman who anointed Jesus. In the Gospel of Mark there is a similar anointment by an unnamed woman. Neither Luke nor Mark explicitly identify this woman with the Magdalene. But Luke reports that she was a 'fallen woman' a 'sinner'. Subsequent commentators have assumed that the Magdalene, since she apparently had seven devils cast out of her, must have been a sinner. On this basis the woman who anoints Jesus and the Magdalene came to be regarded as the same person. In fact they may well have been. If the Magdalene were associated with a pagan cult, that would certainly have rendered her a 'sinner' in the eyes not only of Luke, but of later writers as well.

If the Magdalene was a 'sinner', she was also, quite clearly, something more than the 'common prostitute' of popular tradition. Quite clearly she was a woman of means. Luke reports, for example, that her friends included the wife of a high dignitary at Herod's court – and that both women, together with various others, supported Jesus and his disciples with their financial resources. The woman who anointed Jesus was also a woman of means. In Mark's Gospel great stress is laid upon the costliness of the spikenard ointment with which the ritual was performed.

The whole episode of Jesus's anointing would seem to be an affair of considerable consequence. Why else would it be emphasised by the Gospels to the extent it is? Given its prominence, it appears to be something more than an impulsive spontaneous gesture. It appears to be a carefully premeditated rite. One must remember that anointing was the traditional prerogative of kings – and of the 'rightful Messiah', which means 'the anointed one'. From this, it follows that Jesus becomes an authentic Messiah by virtue of his anointing. And the woman who consecrates him in that august role can hardly be unimportant.

In any case it is clear that the Magdalene, by the end of Jesus's ministry, has become a figure of immense significance. In the three Synoptic Gospels her name consistently heads the lists of women who followed Jesus, just as Simon Peter heads the lists of male disciples. And, of course, she was the first witness to the empty tomb following the

Crucifixion. Among all his devotees, it was to the Magdalene that Jesus first chose to reveal his Resurrection.

Throughout the Gospels Jesus treats the Magdalene in a unique and preferential manner. Such treatment may well have induced jealousy in other disciples. It would seem fairly obvious that later tradition endeavoured to blacken the Magdalene's background, if not her name. The portrayal of her as a harlot may well have been the overcompensation of a vindictive following, intent on impugning the reputation of a woman whose association with Jesus was closer than their own and thus inspired an all too human envy. If other 'Christians', either during Jesus's lifetime or afterwards, grudged the Magdalene her unique bond with their spiritual leader, there might well have been an attempt to diminish her in the eyes of posterity. There is no question that she was so diminished. Even today one thinks of her as a harlot, and during the Middle Ages houses for reformed prostitutes were called Magdalenes. But the Gospels themselves bear witness that the woman who imparted her name to these institutions did not deserve to be so stigmatised.

Whatever the status of the Magdalene in the Gospels, she is not the only possible candidate for Jesus's wife. There is one other, who figures most prominently in the Fourth Gospel and who may be identified as Mary of Bethany, sister of Martha and Lazarus. She and her family are clearly on very familiar terms with Jesus. They are also wealthy, maintaining a house in a fashionable suburb of Jerusalem large enough to accommodate Jesus and his entire entourage. What is more, the Lazarus episode reveals that this house contains a private tomb – a somewhat flamboyant luxury in Jesus's time, not only a sign of wealth but also a status symbol attesting to aristocratic connections. In Biblical Jerusalem, as in any modern city, land was at a premium; and only a very few could afford the self-indulgence of a private burial site.

When, in the Fourth Gospel, Lazarus falls ill, Jesus has left Bethany for a few days and is staying with his disciples on the Jordan. Hearing of what has happened, he nevertheless delays for two days – a rather curious reaction – and then returns to Bethany, where Lazarus lies in the tomb. As he approaches, Martha rushes forth to meet him and cries, 'Lord, if thou hadst been here, my brother had not died.' (John 11:21) It is a perplexing assertion, for why should Jesus's physical presence necessarily have prevented the man's death? But the incident is significant because Martha, when she greets Jesus, is alone. One would expect Mary, her sister, to be with her. Mary, however, is sitting in the house –

and does not emerge until Jesus explicitly commands her to do so. The point becomes clearer in the 'secret' Gospel of Mark, discovered by Professor Morton Smith and cited earlier in this chapter. In the suppressed account by Mark, it would appear that Mary does emerge from the house before Jesus instructs her to do so. And she is promptly and angrily rebuked by the disciples, whom Jesus is obliged to silence.

It would be plausible enough for Mary to be sitting in the house when Jesus arrives in Bethany. In accordance with Jewish custom, she would be 'sitting Shiveh' – sitting in mourning. But why does she not join Martha and rush to meet Jesus on his return? There is one obvious explanation. By the tenets of Judaic law at the time, a woman 'sitting Shiveh' would have been strictly forbidden to emerge from the house except at the express bidding of her husband. In this incident the behaviour of Jesus and Mary of Bethany conforms precisely to the traditional comportment of a Jewish man and wife.

There is additional evidence for a possible marriage between Jesus and Mary of Bethany. It occurs, more or less as a *non sequitur*, in the Gospel of Luke:

> Now it came to pass, as they went, that he entered into a certain village: and a certain woman named Martha received him into her house.
> And she had a sister called Mary, which also sat at Jesus' feet, and heard his word.
> But Martha was cumbered about much serving, and came to him, and said, Lord dost thou not care that my sister hath left me to serve alone? bid her therefore that she help me.
> And Jesus answered and said unto her, Martha, Martha, thou art careful and troubled about many things:
> But one thing is needful: and Mary hath chosen that good part, which shall not be taken away from her. (Luke 10:38–42)

From Martha's appeal, it would seem apparent that Jesus exercises some sort of authority over Mary. More important still, however, is Jesus's reply. In any other context one would not hesitate to interpret this reply as an allusion to a marriage. In any case it clearly suggests that Mary of Bethany was as avid a disciple as the Magdalene.

There is substantial reason for regarding the Magdalene and the woman who anoints Jesus as one and the same person. Could this person, we wondered, also be one and the same with Mary of Bethany, sister of Lazarus and Martha? Could these women who, in the Gospels, appear in three different contexts in fact be a single person? The medieval Church certainly regarded them as such, and so did popular tradition. Many Biblical scholars today concur. There is abundant evidence to support such a conclusion.

The Gospels of Matthew, Mark and John, for example, all cite the Magdalene as being present at the Crucifixion. None of them cites Mary of Bethany. But if Mary of Bethany was as devoted a disciple as she appears to be, her absence would seem to be, at the least, remiss. Is it credible that she – not to mention her brother, Lazarus – would fail to witness the climactic moment of Jesus's life? Such an omission would be both inexplicable and reprehensible – unless, of course, she was present and cited by the Gospels as such under the name of the Magdalene. If the Magdalene and Mary of Bethany are one and the same, there is no question of the latter having been absent from the Crucifixion.

The Magdalene can be identified with Mary of Bethany. The Magdalene can also be identified with the woman who anoints Jesus. The Fourth Gospel identifies the woman who anoints Jesus with Mary of Bethany. Indeed, the author of the Fourth Gospel is quite explicit on the matter:

> Now a certain man was sick, named Lazarus, of Bethany, the town of Mary and her sister Martha.
> (It was that Mary which anointed the Lord with ointment, and wiped his feet with her hair, whose brother Lazarus was sick.) (John 11:1–2)

And again, one chapter later:

> Then Jesus six days before the Passover came to Bethany, where Lazarus was which had been dead, whom he raised from the dead.
> There they made him a supper; and Martha served: but Lazarus was one of them that sat at the table with him.
> Then took Mary a pound of ointment of spikenard, very costly, and anointed the feet of Jesus, and wiped his feet with her hair: and the house was filled with the odour of the ointment. (John 12:1–3)

It is thus clear that Mary of Bethany and the woman who anoints Jesus are the same woman. If not equally clear, it is certainly probable that this woman is also the Magdalene. If Jesus was indeed married, there would thus seem to be only one candidate for his wife – one woman who recurs repeatedly in the Gospels under different names and in different roles.

THE BELOVED DISCIPLE

3) If the Magdalene and Mary of Bethany are the same woman, and if this woman was Jesus's wife, Lazarus would have been Jesus's brother-in-law. Is there any evidence in the Gospels to suggest that Lazarus did indeed enjoy such a status?

Lazarus does not figure by name in the Gospels of Luke, Matthew and Mark – although his 'resurrection from the dead' was originally contained in Mark's account and then excised. As a result Lazarus is known to posterity only through the Fourth Gospel – the Gospel of John. But here it is clear that he does enjoy some species of preferential treatment – which is not confined to being 'raised from the dead'. In this and a number of other respects, he would appear, if anything, to be closer to Jesus than the disciples themselves. And yet, curiously enough, the Gospels do not even number him among the disciples.

Unlike the disciples, Lazarus is actually menaced. According to the Fourth Gospel, the chief priests, on resolving to dispatch Jesus, decided to kill Lazarus as well (John 12:10). Lazarus would seem to have been active in some way on Jesus's behalf – which is more than can be said of some of the disciples. In theory this should have qualified him to be a disciple himself – and yet he is still not cited as such. Nor is he said to have been present at the Crucifixion – an apparently shameless display of ingratitude in a man who, quite literally, owed Jesus his life. Granted, he might have gone into hiding, given the threat directed against him. But it is extremely curious that there is no further reference to him in the Gospels. He seems to have vanished completely, and is never mentioned again. Or is he? We attempted to examine the matter more closely.

After staying in Bethany for three months, Jesus retires with his disciples to the banks of the Jordan, not much more than a day's distance away. Here a messenger hastens to him with the news that Lazarus is ill. But the messenger does not refer to Lazarus by name. On the contrary, he portrays the sick man as someone of very special importance, 'Lord, behold, he whom thou lovest is sick.' (John 11:3) Jesus's reaction to this news is distinctly odd. Instead of returning post-haste to the succour of the man he supposedly loves, he blithely dismisses the matter: 'When Jesus heard that, he said, This sickness is not unto death, but for the glory of God, that the Son of God might be glorified thereby.' (11:4) And if his words are perplexing, his actions are even more so: 'When he heard therefore that he was sick, he abode two days still in the same place where he was.' (11:6) In short Jesus continues to dally at the Jordan for another two days despite the alarming news he has received. At last he resolves to return to Bethany. And then he flagrantly contradicts his previous statement by telling the disciples that Lazarus is dead. He is still unperturbed however. Indeed, he states plainly that Lazarus's 'death' had served some purpose and is to be turned to account: 'Our friend Lazarus sleepeth; but I go, that I may awake him out of sleep.' (11:11) And four verses later he virtually admits that the whole affair has been carefully stage-managed and arranged in advance: 'And I am glad for your sakes that I was not there, to the intent ye may believe; nevertheless, let us go unto him.' (11:15) If such behaviour is bewildering, the reaction of the disciples is no less so: 'Then said Thomas, which is called Didymus, unto his fellow disciples, Let us also go, that we may die with him.' (11:16) What does this mean? If Lazarus is literally dead, surely the disciples have no intention of joining him by a collective suicide! And how is one to account for Jesus's own carelessness – the blasé indifference with which he hears of Lazarus's illness and his delay in returning to Bethany?

The explanations of the matter would seem to lie, as Professor Morton Smith suggests, in a more or less standard 'mystery school' initiation. As Professor Smith demonstrates, such initiations and their accompanying rituals were common enough in the Palestine of Jesus's era. They often entailed a symbolic death and rebirth, which were called by those names; sequestration in a tomb, which became a womb for the acolyte's rebirth; a rite, which is now called baptism – a symbolic immersion in water; and a cup of wine, which was identified with the blood of the prophet or magician presiding over the ceremony. By drinking from such a cup, the disciple consummated a symbolic union with his teacher, the former becoming mystically 'one' with the latter. Significantly enough, it is precisely in these terms that Saint Paul explains the purpose of baptism. And Jesus himself uses the same terms at the Last Supper.

As Professor Smith points out, Jesus's career is very similar to those of other magicians, healers, wonder-workers and miracle-workers of the period.[13] Throughout the Four Gospels, for example, he consistently meets secretly with the people he is about to heal, or speaks quietly with them alone. Afterwards he often asks them not to divulge what transpired. And so far as the general public is concerned, he speaks habitually in allegories and parables.

It would seem, then, that Lazarus, during Jesus's sojourn at the Jordan, has embarked on a typical initiation rite, leading as such rites traditionally did to a symbolic resurrection and rebirth. In this light the disciples' desire to 'die with him' becomes perfectly comprehensible – as does Jesus's otherwise inexplicable complacency about the whole affair. Granted, Mary and Martha would appear to be genuinely distraught – as would a number of other people. But they may simply have misunderstood or misconstrued the point of the exercise. Or perhaps something seemed to have gone wrong with the initiation – a not uncommon occurrence. Or perhaps the whole affair was a skilfully contrived piece of stagecraft, whose true nature and purpose were known only to a very few.

If the Lazarus incident does reflect a ritual initiation, he is clearly receiving very preferential treatment. Among other things, he is apparently being initiated before any of the disciples – who, indeed, seem decidedly envious of his privilege. But why should this hitherto unknown man of Bethany thus be singled out? Why should he undergo an experience in which the disciples are so eager to join him? Why should later, mystically oriented 'heretics' like the Carpocratians have made so much of the matter? And why should the entire episode have been expurgated from the Gospel of Mark? Perhaps because Lazarus was 'he whom Jesus loved' – more than the other disciples. Perhaps because Lazarus had some special connection with Jesus – like that of brother-in-law. Perhaps both. It is possible that Jesus came to know and love Lazarus precisely because Lazarus was his brother-in-law. In any case the love is repeatedly stressed. When Jesus returns to Bethany and weeps, or feigns to weep, for Lazarus's death, the bystanders echo the words of the messenger: 'Behold how he loved him!' (John 11:36)

The author of the Gospel of John – the Gospel in which the Lazarus story figures – does not at any point identify himself as 'John'. In fact he does not name himself at all. He does, however, refer to himself by a most distinctive appellation. He constantly calls himself 'the beloved disciple', 'the one whom Jesus loved', and clearly implies that he enjoys a unique and preferred status over his comrades. At the Last Supper, for example, he flagrantly displays his personal proximity to Jesus, and it is to him alone that Jesus confides the means whereby betrayal will occur:

> Now there was leaning on Jesus' bosom one of his disciples, whom Jesus loved.
> Simon Peter therefore beckoned to him, that he should ask who it should be of whom he spake.
> He then lying on Jesus' breast saith unto him, Lord, who is it?
> Jesus answered, He it is, to whom I shall give a sop, when I have dipped it. And when he had dipped the sop, he gave it to Judas Iscariot, the son of Simon. (John 13:23–6)

Who is this 'beloved disciple', on whose testimony the Fourth Gospel is based? All the evidence suggests that he is in fact Lazarus – 'he whom Jesus loved'. It would seem, then, that Lazarus and the 'beloved disciple' are one and the same person, and that Lazarus is the real identity of 'John'. This conclusion would seem to be almost inevitable. Nor were we alone in reaching it. According to Professor William Brownlee, a leading Biblical scholar and one of the foremost experts on the Dead Sea Scrolls: 'From internal evidence in the Fourth Gospel . . . the conclusion is that the beloved disciple is Lazarus of Bethany.'[14]

If Lazarus and the 'beloved disciple' are one and the same, it would explain a number of anomalies. It would explain Lazarus's mysterious disappearance from the Scriptural account, and his apparent absence during the Crucifixion. For if Lazarus and the 'beloved disciple' were one and the same, Lazarus would have been present at the Crucifixion. And it would have been to Lazarus that Jesus entrusted the care of his mother. The words with which he did so might well be the words of a man referring to his brother-in-law:

> When Jesus therefore saw his mother, and the disciple standing by, whom he loved, he saith unto his mother, Woman, behold thy son!
> Then saith he to the disciple, Behold thy mother! And from that hour that disciple took her unto his own home. (John 19:26–7)

The last word of this quotation is particularly revelatory. For the other disciples have left their homes in Galilee and, to all intents and purposes, are homeless. Lazarus, however, does have a home – that crucial house in Bethany, where Jesus himself was accustomed to stay.

After the priests are said to have decided on his death, Lazarus is not again mentioned by name. He would appear to vanish completely. But if he is indeed the 'beloved disciple', he does not vanish at all, and his movements and activities can be traced to the very end of the Fourth Gospel. And here, too, there is a curious episode that warrants examination. At the end of the Fourth Gospel Jesus forecasts Peter's death and instructs Peter to 'follow' him:

> Then Peter, turning about, seeth the disciple whom Jesus loved following; which also leaned on his breast at supper, and said, Lord, which is he that betrayeth thee?
>
> Peter seeing him saith to Jesus, Lord, and what shall this man do?
>
> Jesus saith unto him, If I will that he tarry till I come, what is that to thee? follow thou me.
>
> Then went this saying abroad among the brethren, that that disciple should not die: yet Jesus said not unto him, He shall not die, but, if I will that he tarry till I come, what is that to thee?
>
> This is the disciple which testifieth of these things, and wrote these things: and we know that his testimony is true. (John 21:20–24)

Despite its ambiguous phraseology, the import of this passage would seem to be clear. The 'beloved disciple' has been explicitly instructed to wait for Jesus's return. And the text itself is quite emphatic in stressing that this return is not to be understood symbolically in the sense of a 'second coming'. On the contrary, it implies something much more mundane. It implies that Jesus, after dispatching his other followers out into the world, must soon return with some special commission for the 'beloved disciple'. It is almost as if they have specific, concrete arrangements to conclude and plans to make.

If the 'beloved disciple' is Lazarus, such collusion, unknown to the other disciples, would seem to have a certain precedent. In the week before the Crucifixion, Jesus undertakes to make his triumphal entry into Jerusalem; and in order to do so in accordance with Old Testament prophecies of a Messiah, he must be riding astride an ass. (Zechariah 9:9–10) Accordingly an ass must be procured. In Luke's Gospel Jesus dispatches two disciples to Bethany, where, he tells them, they will find an ass awaiting them. They are instructed to tell the beast's owner that the 'Master has need of it'. When everything transpires precisely as Jesus has forecast, it is regarded as a sort of miracle. But is there really anything very extraordinary about it? Does it not merely attest to carefully laid plans? And would not the man from Bethany who provides an ass at the appointed time seem to be Lazarus?

This, certainly, is the conclusion of Doctor Hugh Schonfield.[15] He argues convincingly that the arrangements for Jesus's triumphal entry into Jerusalem were entrusted to Lazarus, and that the other disciples had no knowledge of them. If this was indeed the case, it attests to an inner circle of Jesus's followers, a core of collaborators, co-conspirators or family members who, alone, are admitted into their master's confidence. Doctor Schonfield believes that Lazarus is part of just such a circle. And his belief concurs with Professor Smith's insistence on the preferential treatment Lazarus receives by virtue of his initiation, or symbolic death, at Bethany. It is possible that Bethany was a cult centre, a place reserved for the unique rituals over which Jesus presided. If so, this might explain the otherwise enigmatic occurrence of Bethany elsewhere in our investigation. The Prieuré de Sion had called its 'arch' at Rennes-le-Château 'Béthanie'. And Saunière, apparently at the Prieuré de Sion's request, had christened his villa Villa Bethania.

In any case, the collusion which seems to elicit an ass from the 'man from Bethany' may well be displaying itself again at the mysterious end of the Fourth Gospel – when Jesus orders the 'beloved disciple' to tarry until he returns. It would seem that he and the 'beloved disciple' have plans to make. And it is not unreasonable to assume that these plans included the care of Jesus's family. At the Crucifixion he had already entrusted his mother to the 'beloved disciple's' custody. If he had a wife and children, they, presumably, would have been entrusted to the 'beloved disciple' as well. This, of course, would be all the more plausible if the 'beloved disciple' were indeed his brother-in-law.

According to much later tradition, Jesus's mother eventually died in exile at Ephesus – from whence the Fourth Gospel is said to have subsequently issued. There is no indication, however, that the 'beloved disciple' attended Jesus's mother for the duration of her life. According to Doctor Schonfield, the Fourth Gospel was probably not composed at

Ephesus, only reworked, revised and edited by a Greek elder there – who made it conform to his own ideas.[16]

If the 'beloved disciple' did not go to Ephesus, what became of him? If he and Lazarus were one and the same that question can be answered, for tradition is quite explicit about what became of Lazarus. According to tradition, as well as certain early Church writers, Lazarus, the Magdalene, Martha, Joseph of Arimathea and a few others, were transported by ship to Marseilles.[17] Here Joseph was supposedly consecrated by Saint Philip and sent on to England, where he established a church at Glastonbury. Lazarus and the Magdalene, however, are said to have remained in Gaul. Tradition maintains that the Magdalene died at either Aix-en-Provence or Saint Baume, and Lazarus at Marseilles after founding the first bishopric there. One of their companions, Saint Maximin, is said to have founded the first bishopric of Narbonne.

If Lazarus and the 'beloved disciple' were one and the same, there would thus be an explanation for their joint disappearance. Lazarus, the true 'beloved disciple', would seem to have been set ashore at Marseilles, together with his sister – who, as tradition subsequently maintains, was carrying with her the Holy Grail, the 'blood royal'. And the arrangements for this escape and exile would seem to have been made by Jesus himself, together with the 'beloved disciple', at the end of the Fourth Gospel.

THE DYNASTY OF JESUS

4) If Jesus was indeed married to the Magdalene, might such a marriage have served some specific purpose? In other words, might it have been something more than a conventional marriage? Might it have been a dynastic alliance of some kind, with political implications and repercussions? Might a bloodline resulting from such a marriage, in short, have fully warranted the appellation 'blood royal'?

The Gospel of Matthew states explicitly that Jesus was of royal blood – a genuine king, the lineal descendant of Solomon and David. If this is true, he would have enjoyed a legitimate claim to the throne of a united Palestine – and perhaps even *the* legitimate claim. And the inscription affixed to the cross would have been much more than mere sadistic derision, for Jesus would indeed have been 'King of the Jews'. His position, in many respects, would have been analogous to that of, say, Bonnie Prince Charlie in 1745. And thus he would have engendered the opposition he did precisely by virtue of his role – the role of a priest-king who might possibly unify his country and the Jewish people, thereby posing a serious threat to both Herod and Rome.

Certain modern Biblical scholars have argued that Herod's famous 'Massacre of the Innocents' never in fact took place. Even if it did, it was probably not of the garish and appalling proportions ascribed to it by the Gospels and subsequent tradition. And yet the very perpetuation of the story would seem to attest to something – some genuine alarm on Herod's part, some very real anxiety about being deposed. Granted, Herod was an extremely insecure ruler, hated by his enslaved subjects and sustained in power only by Roman cohorts. But however precarious his position might have been, it cannot, realistically speaking, have been seriously threatened by rumours of a mystical or spiritual saviour – of the kind with which the Holy Land at the time already abounded anyway. If Herod was indeed worried, it can only have been by a very real, concrete, political threat – the threat posed by a man who possessed a more legitimate claim to the throne than his own, and who could muster substantial popular support. The 'Massacre of the Innocents' may never have occurred, but the traditions relating to it reflect some concern on Herod's part – about a rival claim and, quite possibly, some action intended to forestall or preclude it. Such a claim can only have been political in nature. And it must have warranted being taken seriously.

To suggest that Jesus enjoyed such a claim is, of course, to challenge the popular image of the 'poor carpenter from Nazareth'. But there are persuasive reasons for doing so. In the first place it is not altogether certain that Jesus was from Nazareth. 'Jesus of Nazareth' is in fact a corruption, or mistranslation, of 'Jesus the Nazorite' or 'Jesus the Nazorean' or perhaps 'Jesus of Gennesareth'. In the second place there is considerable doubt as to whether the town of Nazareth actually existed in Jesus's time. It does not occur in any Roman maps, documents or records. It is not mentioned in the Talmud. It is not mentioned, still less associated with Jesus, in any of the writings of Saint Paul – which were, after all, composed before the Gospels. And Flavius Josephus – the foremost chronicler of the period, who commanded troops in Galilee and listed the province's towns – makes no mention of Nazareth either. It would seem, in short, that Nazareth did not appear as a town until sometime after the revolt of A.D. 68–74, and that Jesus's name became associated with it by virtue of the semantic confusion – accidental or deliberate – which characterises so much of the New Testament.

Whether Jesus was 'of Nazareth' or not there is no indication that he was ever a 'poor carpenter'.[18] Certainly none of the Gospels portrays him as such. Indeed their evidence suggests quite the contrary. He seems to be well-educated, for example. He seems to have undergone training for the rabbinate, and to have consorted as frequently with wealthy and influential people as with the poor – Joseph of Arimathea, for instance, and Nicodemus. And the wedding at Cana would seem to bear further witness to Jesus's status and social position.

This wedding does not appear to have been a modest, humble festival conducted by the 'common people'. On the contrary it bears all the marks of an extravagant aristocratic union, a 'high society' affair, attended by at least several hundred guests. There are abundant servants, for example – who hasten to do both Mary's and Jesus's bidding. There is a 'master of the feast' or 'master of ceremonies' – who, in the context, would have been a kind of chief butler or perhaps even an aristocrat himself. Most clearly there is a positively enormous quantity of wine. When Jesus 'transmutes' the water into wine, he produces, according to the 'Good News Bible', no less than six hundred litres, which is more than eight hundred bottles! And this is in addition to what has already been consumed.

All things considered, the wedding at Cana would seem to have been a sumptuous ceremony of the gentry or aristocracy. Even if the wedding were not Jesus's own, his presence at it, and his mother's, would suggest that they were members of the same caste. This alone would explain the servants' obedience to them.

If Jesus was an aristocrat, and if he was married to the Magdalene, it is probable that she was of comparable social station. And indeed, she would appear to be so. As we have seen she numbered among her friends the wife of an important official at Herod's court. But she may have been more important still.

As we had discovered by tracing references in the 'Prieuré documents', Jerusalem – the Holy City and capital of Judaea – had originally been the property of the Tribe of Benjamin. Subsequently the Benjamites were decimated in their war with the other tribes of Israel, and many of them went into exile – although, as the 'Prieuré documents' maintain, 'certain of them remained'. One descendant of this remnant was Saint Paul, who states explicitly that he is a Benjamite. (Romans 11:1)

Despite their conflict with the other tribes of Israel, the Tribe of Benjamin appears to have enjoyed some special status. Among other things, it provided Israel with her first king – Saul, anointed by the prophet Samuel – and with her first royal house. But Saul was eventually deposed by David, of the Tribe of Judah. And David not only deprived the Benjamites of their claim to the throne. By establishing his capital at Jerusalem he deprived them of their rightful inheritance as well.

According to all New Testament accounts, Jesus was of the line of David and thus also a member of the Tribe of Judah. In Benjamite eyes this might have rendered him, at least in some sense, a usurper. Any such objection might have been surmounted, however, if he were married to a Benjamite woman. Such a marriage would have constituted an important dynastic alliance, and one filled with political consequence. It would not only have provided Israel with a powerful priest-king. It would also have performed the symbolic function of returning Jerusalem to its original and rightful owners. Thus it would have served to encourage popular unity and support, and consolidated whatever claim to the throne Jesus might have possessed.

In the New Testament there is no indication of the Magdalene's tribal affiliation. In subsequent legends, however, she is said to have been of royal lineage. And there are other traditions which state specifically that she was of the Tribe of Benjamin.

At this point, the outlines of a coherent historical scenario began to be discernible. And, as far as we could see, it made sound political sense. Jesus would have been a priest-king of the line of David, who possessed a legitimate claim to the throne. He would have consolidated his position by a symbolically important dynastic marriage. He would then have been poised to unify his country, mobilise the populace behind him, drive out the oppressors, depose their abject puppet and restore the glory of the monarchy as it was under Solomon. Such a man would indeed have been 'King of the Jews'.

THE CRUCIFIXION

5) As Gandhi's accomplishments bear witness, a spiritual leader, given sufficient popular support, can pose a threat to an existing régime. But a married man, with a rightful claim to the throne and children through whom to establish a dynasty, is a threat of a decidedly more serious

nature. Is there any evidence in the Gospels that Jesus was in fact regarded by the Romans as such a threat?

During his interview with Pilate, Jesus is repeatedly called 'King of the Jews'. In accordance with Pilate's instructions, an inscription of this title is also affixed to the cross. As Professor S. G. F. Brandon of Manchester University argues, the inscription affixed to the cross must be regarded as genuine – as much so as anything in the New Testament. In the first place it figures, with virtually no variation, in all four Gospels. In the second place it is too compromising, too embarrassing an episode for subsequent editors to have invented it.

In the Gospel of Mark, Pilate, after interrogating Jesus, asks the assembled dignitaries, 'What will ye then that I shall do unto him whom ye call the King of the Jews?' (Mark 15:12) This would seem to indicate that at least some Jews do actually refer to Jesus as their king. At the same time, however, in all four Gospels Pilate also accords Jesus that title. There is no reason to suppose that he does so ironically or derisively. In the Fourth Gospel he insists on it quite adamantly and seriously, despite a chorus of protests. In the three Synoptic Gospels, moreover, Jesus himself acknowledged his claim to the title: 'And Pilate asked him, Art thou the King of the Jews? And he answering said unto him, Thou sayest it.' (Mark 15:2) In the English translation this reply may sound ambivalent – perhaps deliberately so. In the original Greek, however, its import is quite unequivocal. It can only be interpreted as 'Thou hast spoken correctly'. And thus the phrase is interpreted whenever it appears elsewhere in the Bible.

The Gospels were composed during and after the revolt of A.D. 68–74, when Judaism had effectively ceased to exist as an organised social, political and military force. What is more, the Gospels were composed for a Greco-Roman audience – for whom they had, of necessity, to be made acceptable. Rome had just fought a bitter and costly war against the Jews. In consequence it was perfectly natural to cast the Jews in the role of villains. In the wake of the Judaean revolt, moreover, Jesus could not possibly be portrayed as a political figure – a figure in any way linked to the agitation which culminated in the war. Finally the role of the Romans in Jesus's trial and execution had to be whitewashed and presented as sympathetically as possible. Thus Pilate is depicted in the Gospels as a decent, responsible and tolerant man, who consents only reluctantly to the Crucifixion.[19] But despite these liberties taken with history, Rome's true position in the affair can be discerned.

According to the Gospels, Jesus is initially condemned by the Sanhedrin – the Council of Jewish Elders – who then bring him to Pilate and beseech the Procurator to pronounce against him. Historically this makes no sense at all. In the three Synoptic Gospels Jesus is arrested and condemned by the Sanhedrin on the night of the Passover. But by Judaic law the Sanhedrin was forbidden to meet over the Passover.[20] In the Gospels Jesus's arrest and trial occur at night, before the Sanhedrin. By Judaic law the Sanhedrin was forbidden to meet at night, in private houses, or anywhere outside the precincts of the Temple. In the Gospels the Sanhedrin is apparently unauthorised to pass a death sentence – and this would ostensibly be the reason for bringing Jesus to Pilate. However, the Sanhedrin was authorised to pass death sentences – by stoning, if not by Crucifixion. If the Sanhedrin had wished to dispose of Jesus, therefore, it could have sentenced him to death by stoning on its own authority. There would have been no need to bother Pilate at all.

There are numerous other attempts by the authors of the Gospels to transfer guilt and responsibility from Rome. One such is Pilate's apparent offer of a dispensation – his readiness to free a prisoner of the crowd's choosing. According to the Gospels of Mark and Matthew, this was a 'custom of the Passover festival'. In fact it was no such thing.[21] Modern authorities agree that no such policy ever existed on the part of the Romans, and that the offer to liberate either Jesus or Barabbas is sheer fiction. Pilate's reluctance to condemn Jesus, and his grudging submission to the bullying pressure of the mob, would seem to be equally fictitious. In reality it would have been unthinkable for a Roman Procurator – and especially a Procurator as ruthless as Pilate – to bow to the pressure of a mob. Again, the purpose of such fictionalisation is clear enough – to exonerate the Romans, to transfer blame to the Jews and thereby to make Jesus acceptable to a Roman audience.

It is possible, of course, that not all Jews were entirely innocent. Even if the Roman administration feared a priest-king with a claim to the throne, it could not embark overtly on acts of provocation – acts that might precipitate a full-scale rebellion. Certainly it would have been more expedient for Rome if the priest-king were ostensibly betrayed by his own people. It is thus conceivable that the Romans employed certain Sadducees as, say, *agents provocateurs*. But even if this were the case, the inescapable fact remains that Jesus was the victim of a Roman administration, a Roman court, a Roman sentence, Roman soldiery and a Roman execution – an execution which, in form, was reserved exclusively for enemies of Rome. It was not for crimes against Judaism that Jesus was crucified, but for crimes against the empire.[22]

WHO WAS BARABBAS?

6) Is there any evidence in the Gospels that Jesus actually did have children?

There is nothing explicit. But rabbis were expected, as a matter of course, to have children; and if Jesus was a rabbi, it would have been most unusual for him to remain childless. Indeed, it would have been unusual for him to remain childless whether he was a rabbi or not. Granted, these arguments, in themselves, do not constitute any positive evidence. But there is evidence of a more concrete, more specific kind. It consists of the elusive individual who figures in the Gospels as Barabbas, or, to be more precise, as Jesus Barabbas – for it is by this name that he is identified in the Gospel of Matthew. If nothing else, the coincidence is striking.

Modern scholars are uncertain about the derivation and meaning of 'Barabbas'. 'Jesus Barabbas' may be a corruption of 'Jesus Berabbi'. 'Berabbi' was a title reserved for the highest and most esteemed rabbis and was placed after the rabbi's given name.[23] 'Jesus Berabbi' might therefore refer to Jesus himself. Alternatively, 'Jesus Barabbas' might originally have been 'Jesus bar Rabbi' – 'Jesus, son of the Rabbi'. There is no record anywhere of Jesus's own father having been a rabbi. But if Jesus had a son named after himself, that son would indeed have been 'Jesus bar Rabbi'. There is one other possibility as well. 'Jesus Barabbas' may derive from 'Jesus bar Abba'; and since 'Abba' is 'father' in Hebrew, 'Barabbas' would then mean 'son of the father' – a fairly pointless designation unless the 'father' is in some way special. If the 'father' were actually the 'Heavenly Father', then 'Barabbas' might again refer to Jesus himself. On the other hand, if Jesus himself is the 'father', 'Barabbas' would again refer to his son.

Whatever the meaning and derivation of the name, the figure of Barabbas is extremely curious. And the more one considers the incident concerning him, the more apparent it becomes that something irregular is going on and someone is attempting to conceal something. In the first place Barabbas's name, like the Magdalene's, seems to have been subjected to a deliberate and systematic blackening. Just as popular tradition depicts the Magdalene as a harlot, so it depicts Barabbas as a 'thief'.

But if Barabbas was any of the things his name suggests, he is hardly likely to have been a common thief. Why then blacken his name? Unless he was something else in reality – something which the editors of the New Testament did not want posterity to know.

Strictly speaking the Gospels themselves do not describe Barabbas as a thief. According to Mark and Luke he is a political prisoner, a rebel charged with murder and insurrection. In the Gospel of Matthew, however, Barabbas is described as a 'notable prisoner'. And in the Fourth Gospel Barabbas is said to be (in the Greek) a *lestai*. (John 18:40) This can be translated as either 'robber' or 'bandit'. In its historical context, however, it meant something quite different. *Lestes* was in fact the term habitually applied by the Romans to the Zealots[24] – the militant nationalist revolutionaries who for some time had been fomenting social upheaval. Since Mark and Luke agree that Barabbas is guilty of insurrection, and since Matthew does not contradict this assertion, it is safe to conclude that Barabbas was a Zealot.

But this is not the only information available on Barabbas. According to Luke, he had been involved in a recent 'disturbance', 'sedition' or 'riot' in the city. History makes no mention of any such turmoil in Jerusalem at the time. The Gospels, however, do. According to the Gospels, there had been a civic disturbance in Jerusalem, only a few days before – when Jesus and his followers overturned the tables of the money-lenders at the Temple. Was this the disturbance in which Barabbas was involved, and for which he was imprisoned? It certainly seems likely. And in that case there is one obvious conclusion – that Barabbas was one of Jesus's entourage.

According to modern scholars, the 'custom' of releasing a prisoner on the Passover did not exist. But even if it did, the choice of Barabbas over Jesus would make no sense. If Barabbas were indeed a common criminal, guilty of murder, why would the people choose to have his life spared? And if he were indeed a Zealot or a revolutionary, it is hardly likely that Pilate would have released so potentially dangerous a character, rather than a harmless visionary – who was quite prepared, ostensibly, to 'render unto Caesar'. Of all the discrepancies, inconsistencies and improbabilities in the Gospels, the choice of Barabbas is among the most striking and most inexplicable. Something would clearly seem to lie behind so clumsy and confusing a fabrication.

One modern writer has proposed an intriguing and plausible explanation. He suggests that Barabbas was the son of Jesus and Jesus a legitimate king.[25] If this were the case, the choice of Barabbas would suddenly make sense. One must imagine an oppressed populace confronted with the imminent extermination of their spiritual and political ruler – the Messiah, whose advent had formerly promised so much. In such circumstances, would not the dynasty be more important than the individual? Would not the preservation of the bloodline be paramount, taking precedence over everything else? Would not a people, faced with the dreadful choice, prefer to see their king sacrificed in order that his offspring and his line might survive? If the line survived, there would at least be hope for the future. It is certainly not impossible that Barabbas was Jesus's son. Jesus is generally believed to have been born around 6 B.C. The Crucifixion occurred no later than A.D. 36, which would make Jesus, at most, forty-two years of age. But even if he was only thirty-three when he died, he might still have fathered a son. In accordance with the customs of the time, he might have married as early as sixteen or seventeen. Yet even if he did not marry until aged twenty, he might still have had a son aged thirteen – who, by Judaic custom, would have been considered a man. And, of course, there may well have been other children too. Such children could have been conceived at any point up to within a day or so of the Crucifixion.

THE CRUCIFIXION IN DETAIL

7) Jesus could well have sired a number of children prior to the Crucifixion. If he survived the Crucifixion, however, the likelihood of offspring would be still further increased. Is there any evidence that Jesus did indeed survive the Crucifixion – or that the Crucifixion was in some way a fraud?

Given the portrait of him in the Gospels, it is inexplicable that Jesus was crucified at all. According to the Gospels, his enemies were the established Jewish interests in Jerusalem. But such enemies, if they in fact existed, could have stoned him to death of their own accord and on their own authority, without involving Rome in the matter. According to the Gospels, Jesus had no particular quarrel with Rome and did not violate Roman law. And yet he was punished by the Romans, in accordance with Roman law and Roman procedures. And he was punished by crucifixion – a penalty exclusively reserved for those guilty of crimes against the empire. If Jesus was indeed crucified, he cannot have been as apolitical as the Gospels depict him. On the contrary, he must, of necessity, have done something to provoke Roman – as opposed to Jewish – wrath.

Whatever the trespasses for which Jesus was crucified, his apparent death on the cross is fraught with inconsistencies. There is, quite simply, no reason why his Crucifixion, as the Gospels depict it, should have been fatal. The contention that it was warrants closer scrutiny.

The Roman practice of crucifixion adhered to very precise procedures.[26] After sentence a victim would be flogged – and consequently weakened by loss of blood. His outstretched arms would then be fastened – usually by thongs but sometimes by nails – to a heavy wooden beam placed horizontally across his neck and shoulders. Bearing this beam, he would then be led to the place of execution. Here, with the victim hanging from it, the beam would be raised and attached to a vertical post or stake.

Hanging thus from his hands, it would be impossible for the victim to breathe – unless his feet were also fixed to the cross, thus enabling him to press down on them and relieve the pressure on his chest. But, despite the agony, a man suspended with his feet fixed – and especially a fit and healthy man – would usually survive for at least a day or two. Indeed, the victim would often take as much as a week to die – from exhaustion, from thirst, or, if nails were used, from blood poisoning. The attenuated agony could be terminated more quickly by breaking the victim's legs or knees – which, in the Gospels, Jesus's executioners are about to do before they are forestalled. Breaking of the legs or knees was not an additional sadistic torment. On the contrary, it was an act of mercy – a *coup de grâce* which caused a very rapid death. With nothing to support him, the pressure on the victim's chest would become intolerable, and he would quickly asphyxiate.

There is consensus among modern scholars that only the Fourth Gospel rests on an eyewitness account of the Crucifixion. According to the Fourth Gospel, Jesus's feet were affixed to the cross – thus relieving the pressure on his chest muscles – and his legs were not broken. He should therefore, in theory at least, have survived for a good two or three days. And yet he is on the cross for no more than a few hours before being pronounced dead. In the Gospel of Mark, even Pilate is astonished by the rapidity with which death occurs (Mark 15:44).

What can have constituted the cause of death? Not the spear in his side, for the Fourth Gospel maintains that Jesus was already dead when this wound was inflicted on him. (John 19:33) There is only one expla-

Station VIII of Saunière's Stations of the Cross, Rennes-le-Château. Note that the pattern of the child's clothing appears closely to resemble a Scottish tartan.

nation – a combination of exhaustion, fatigue, general debilitation and the trauma of the scourging. But not even these factors should have proved fatal so soon. It is possible, of course, that they did – despite the laws of physiology, a man will sometimes die from a single relatively innocuous blow. But there would still seem to be something suspicious about the affair. According to the Fourth Gospel, Jesus's executioners are on the verge of breaking his legs, thus accelerating his death. Why bother, if he was already moribund? There would, in short, be no point in breaking Jesus's legs unless death were not in fact imminent.

In the Gospels Jesus's death occurs at a moment that is almost too convenient, too felicitously opportune. It occurs just in time to prevent his executioners breaking his legs. And by doing so, it permits him to fulfil an Old Testament prophecy. Modern authorities agree that Jesus, quite unabashedly, modelled and perhaps contrived his life in accordance with such prophecies, which heralded the coming of a Messiah. It was for this reason that an ass had to be procured from Bethany on which he could make his triumphal entry into Jerusalem. And the details of the Crucifixion seem likewise engineered to enact the prophecies of the Old Testament.[27]

In short Jesus's apparent and opportune 'demise' – which, in the nick of time, saves him from certain death and enables him to fulfil a prophecy – is, to say the least, suspect. It is too perfect, too precise to be coincidence. It must either be a later interpolation after the fact, or part of a carefully contrived plan. There is much additional evidence to suggest the latter.

In the Fourth Gospel Jesus, hanging on the cross, declares that he thirsts. In reply to this complaint he is proffered a sponge allegedly soaked in vinegar – an incident that also occurs in the other Gospels. This sponge is generally interpreted as another act of sadistic derision. But was it really? Vinegar – or soured wine – is a temporary stimulant, with effects not unlike smelling salts. It was often used at the time to resuscitate flagging slaves on galleys. For a wounded and exhausted man, a sniff or taste of vinegar would induce a restorative effect, a momentary surge of energy. And yet in Jesus's case, the effect is just the contrary. No sooner does he inhale or taste the sponge then he pronounces his final words and 'gives up the ghost'. Such a reaction to vinegar is physiologically inexplicable. On the other hand such a reaction would be perfectly compatible with a sponge soaked not in vinegar, but in some type of soporific drug – a compound of opium and/or belladonna, for instance, commonly employed in the Middle East at the time. But why proffer a soporific drug? Unless the act of doing so, along with all the other components of the Crucifixion, were elements of a complex and ingenious stratagem – a stratagem designed to produce a semblance of death when the victim, in fact, was still alive. Such a stratagem would not only have saved Jesus's life, but also have realised the Old Testament prophecies of a Messiah.

There are other anomalous aspects of the Crucifixion which point to precisely such a stratagem. According to the Gospels Jesus is crucified at a place called Golgotha, 'the place of the skull'. Later tradition attempts to identify Golgotha as a barren, more or less skull-shaped hill to the north-west of Jerusalem. And yet the Gospels themselves make it clear that the site of the Crucifixion is very different from a barren skull-shaped hill. The Fourth Gospel is most explicit on the matter: 'Now in the place where he was crucified there was a garden; and in the garden a new sepulchre, wherein was never man yet laid.' (John 19:41) Jesus, then, was crucified not on a barren skull-shaped hill, nor, for that matter, in any 'public place of execution'. He was crucified in or immediately adjacent to a garden containing a private tomb. According to Matthew (27:60) this tomb and garden were the personal property of Joseph of Arimathea – who, according to all four Gospels, was both a man of wealth and a secret disciple of Jesus.

Popular tradition depicts the Crucifixion as a large-scale public affair, accessible to the multitude and attended by a cast of thousands. And yet the Gospels themselves suggest very different circumstances. According to Matthew, Mark and Luke, the Crucifixion is witnessed by most people, including the women, from 'afar off' (Luke 23:49). It would thus seem clear that Jesus's death was not a public event, but a private one – a private crucifixion performed on private property. A number of modern scholars argue that the actual site was probably the Garden of Gethsemane. If Gethsemane were indeed the private land of one of Jesus's secret disciples, this would explain why Jesus, prior to the Crucifixion, could make such free use of the place.[28]

Needless to say a private crucifixion on private property leaves considerable room for a hoax – a mock crucifixion, a skilfully stage-managed ritual. There would have been only a few eye-witnesses immediately present. To the general populace the drama would only have been visible, as the Synoptic Gospels confirm, from some distance. And from such a distance, it would not have been apparent who in fact was being crucified. Or if he was actually dead.

Such a charade would, of course, have necessitated some connivance and collusion on the part of Pontius Pilate – or of someone influential in the Roman administration. And indeed such connivance and collusion is highly probable. Granted, Pilate was a cruel and tyrannical man. But he was also corrupt and susceptible to bribes. The historical Pilate, as opposed to the one depicted in the Gospels, would not have been above sparing Jesus's life – in exchange for a sizeable sum of money and perhaps a guarantee of no further political agitation.

Whatever his motivation, there is, in any case, no question that Pilate is somehow intimately involved in the affair. He acknowledges Jesus's claim as 'King of the Jews'. He also expresses, or feigns to express, surprise that Jesus's death occurs as quickly as it apparently does. And, perhaps most important of all, he grants Jesus's body to Joseph of Arimathea.

According to Roman law at the time, a crucified man was denied all burial.[29] Indeed guards were customarily posted to prevent relatives or friends removing the bodies of the dead. The victim would simply be left on the cross, at the mercy of the elements and carrion birds. Yet Pilate, in a flagrant breach of procedure, readily grants Jesus's body to Joseph of Arimathea. This clearly attests to some complicity on Pilate's part. And it may attest to other things as well.

In English translations of Mark's Gospel Joseph asks Pilate for Jesus's body. Pilate expresses surprise that Jesus is dead, checks with a centurion, then, satisfied, consents to Joseph's request. This would appear straightforward enough at first glance; but in the original Greek version of Mark's Gospel, the matter becomes rather more complicated. In the Greek version when Joseph asks for Jesus's body, he uses the word *soma* – a word applied only to a living body. Pilate, assenting to the request, employs the word *ptoma* – which means 'corpse'.[30] According to the Greek, then, Joseph explicitly asks for a living body and Pilate grants him what he thinks, or pretends to think, is a dead one.

Given the prohibition against burying crucified men, it is also extraordinary that Joseph receives any body at all. On what grounds does he receive it? What claim does he have to Jesus's body? If he was a secret disciple, he could hardly plead any claim without disclosing his secret discipleship – unless Pilate was already aware of it, or unless there was some other factor involved which militated in Joseph's favour.

There is little information about Joseph of Arimathea. The Gospels report only that he was a secret disciple of Jesus, possessed great wealth and belonged to the Sanhedrin – the Council of Elders which ruled the Judaic community of Jerusalem under Roman auspices. It would thus seem apparent that Joseph was an influential man. And this conclusion receives confirmation from his dealings with Pilate, and from the fact that he possesses a tract of land with a private tomb.

Medieval tradition portrays Joseph of Arimathea as a custodian of the Holy Grail; and Perceval is said to be of his lineage. According to other later traditions, he is in some way related by blood to Jesus and Jesus's family. If this was indeed the case, it would, at very least, have furnished him with some plausible claim to Jesus's body – for while Pilate would hardly grant the corpse of an executed criminal to a random stranger, he might well do so, with the incentive of a bribe, to the dead man's kin. If Joseph – a wealthy and influential member of the Sanhedrin – was indeed Jesus's kin, he bears further testimony to Jesus's aristocratic pedigree. And if he was Jesus's kin, his association with the Holy Grail – the 'blood royal' – would be all the more explicable.

THE SCENARIO

We had already sketched a tentative hypothesis which proposed a bloodline descended from Jesus. We now began to enlarge on that hypothesis and – albeit still provisionally – fill in a number of crucial details. As we did so, the overall picture began to gain both coherence and plausibility.

It seemed increasingly clear that Jesus was a priest-king – an aristocrat and legitimate claimant to the throne – embarking on an attempt to regain his rightful heritage. He himself would have been a native of Galilee, a traditional hotbed of opposition to the Roman régime. At the same time, he would have had numerous noble, rich and influential supporters throughout Palestine, including the capital city of Jerusalem; and one of these supporters, a powerful member of the Sanhedrin, may also have been his kin. In the Jerusalem suburb of Bethany, moreover, was the home of either his wife or his wife's family; and here, on the eve of his triumphal entry into the capital, the aspiring priest-king resided. Here he established the centre for his mystery cult. Here he augmented his following by performing ritual initiations, including that of his brother-in-law.

Such an aspiring priest-king would have generated powerful opposition in certain quarters – inevitably among the Roman administration and perhaps among entrenched Judaic interests represented by the

Sadducees. One or both of these interests apparently contrived to thwart his bid for the throne. But in their attempt to exterminate him they were not as successful as they had hoped to be. For the priest-king would seem to have had friends in high places; and these friends, working in collusion with a corrupt, easily bribed Roman Procurator, appear to have engineered a mock crucifixion – on private grounds, inaccessible to all but a select few. With the general populace kept at a convenient distance, an execution was then staged – in which a substitute took the priest-king's place on the cross, or in which the priest-king himself did not actually die. Towards dusk – which would have further impeded visibility – a 'body' was removed to an opportunely adjacent tomb, from which, a day or two later, it 'miraculously' disappeared.

If our scenario was accurate, where did Jesus go then? So far as our hypothesis of a bloodline was concerned, the answer to that question did not particularly matter. According to certain Islamic and Indian legends, he eventually died at a ripe old age, somewhere in the East – in Kashmir, it is claimed most frequently.

According to the letter we received, the documents found by Bérenger Saunière at Rennes-le-Château contained 'incontrovertible proof' that Jesus was alive in A.D. 45, but there is no indication as to where. One likely possibility would be Egypt, and specifically Alexandria – where, at about the same time, the sage Ormus is said to have created the Rose-Croix by amalgamating Christianity with earlier, pre-Christian mysteries. It has even been hinted that Jesus's mummified body may be concealed somewhere in the environs of Rennes-le-Château – which would explain the ciphered message in Saunière's parchments 'IL EST LÀ MORT' ('He is there dead').

We are not prepared to assert that he accompanied his family to Marseilles. In fact, circumstances would argue against it. He might not have been in any condition to travel, and his presence would have constituted a threat to his relatives' safety. He may have deemed it more important to remain in the Holy Land – like his brother, Saint James – to pursue his objectives there. In short, we can offer no real suggestion about what became of him – any more than the Gospels themselves do.

For the purposes of our hypothesis, however, what happened to Jesus was of less importance than what happened to the holy family – and especially to his brother-in-law, his wife and his children. If our scenario was correct, they, together with Joseph of Arimathea and certain others, were smuggled by ship from the Holy Land. And when they were set ashore at Marseilles, the Magdalene would indeed have brought the Sangraal – the 'blood royal', the scion of the house of David – into France.

> In researching his book, *The Hidden Tradition in Europe*, Dr Yuri Stoyanov came across an extraordinary and provocative document. This document consists of a detailed account of Cathar beliefs, particularly in the Languedoc. It was compiled by a Catholic writer – perhaps a priest – who had infiltrated high-level Cathar circles and been present at teaching sessions for initiates. In these sessions, secret and potentially explosive material was passed on to aspiring 'Parfaits'. According to the document Yuri Stoyanov discovered, the Cathars clandestinely taught that Jesus was indeed married to the Magdalene.[i]
>
> In his book, as well as in conversations with us, Yuri Stoyanov has stressed the uniqueness of the Cathar insistence on a marriage between Jesus and the Magdalene. It does not exist, he notes, among the Bogomils, the dualist 'heretics' from Eastern Europe, believed by many to be the source of Cathar beliefs. This would seem to confirm our own conclusions that the Cathars did *not* in fact derive from the Bogomils, but were indigenous to the region of the Pyrenees and the south of France. If the Magdalene, with Jesus' offspring, did find refuge with a Judaic community in that region, some knowledge of the circumstances might well have filtered down through the centuries into Cathar tradition. But it would not initially have been known to the Bogomils of Eastern Europe, who embraced a similar theological creed. The Crusades, of course, inaugurated new contacts between East and West, and new cross-fertilisations. At this point, Cathar and Bogomil teachings began to converge. Only then would the Bogomils have become privy to what Cathar tradition had inherited.
>
> i: Stoyanov, Y., *The Hidden Tradition in Europe*, London, 1994, pp.222–3.

CHAPTER THIRTEEN

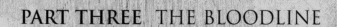

THE SECRET THE CHURCH FORBADE

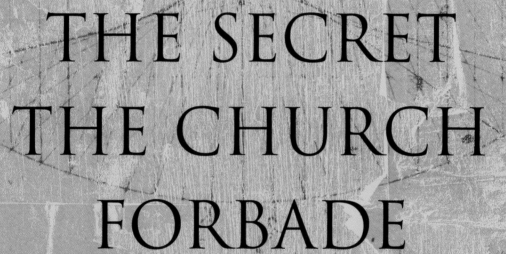

We were well aware, of course, that our scenario did not concur with established Christian teachings. But the more we researched the more apparent it became that those teachings, as they have been passed down through the centuries, represent only a highly selective compilation of fragments, subjected to stringent expurgation and revision. The New Testament, in other words, offers a portrait of Jesus and his age that conforms to the needs of certain vested interests – of certain groups and individuals who had, and to a significant degree still have, an important stake in the matter. And anything that might compromise or embarrass these interests – like the 'secret' Gospel of Mark, for example – has been duly excised. So much has been excised, as a matter of fact, that a sort of vacuum has been created. In this vacuum speculation becomes both justified and necessary.

If Jesus was a legitimate claimant to the throne, it is probable that he was supported, at least initially, by a relatively small percentage of the populace – his immediate family from Galilee, certain other members of his own aristocratic social class, and a few strategically placed representatives in Judaea and the capital city of Jerusalem. Such a following, albeit distinguished, would hardly have been sufficient to ensure the realisation of his objectives – the success of his bid for the throne. In consequence he would have been obliged to recruit a more substantial following from other classes – in the same way that Bonnie Prince Charlie, to pursue a previous analogy, did in 1745.

How does one recruit a sizeable following? Obviously by promulgating a message calculated to enlist their allegiance and support. Such a message need not necessarily have been as cynical as those associated with modern politics. On the contrary it may have been promulgated in perfectly good faith, with thoroughly noble and burning idealism. But despite its distinctly religious orientation, its primary objective would have been the same as those of modern politics – to ensure the adherence of the populace. Jesus promulgated a message which attempted to do just that – to offer hope to the downtrodden, the afflicted, the disenfranchised, the oppressed. In short it was a message with a promise. If the modern reader overcomes his prejudices and preconceptions on the matter, he will discern a mechanism extraordinarily akin to that visible everywhere in the world today – a mechanism whereby people are, and always have been, united in the name of a common cause and welded into an instrument for the overthrow of a despotic régime. The point is that Jesus's message was both ethical and political. It was directed to a particular segment of the populace in accordance with political considerations. For it would only have been among the oppressed, the downtrodden, the disenfranchised and the afflicted that he could have hoped to recruit a sizeable following. The Sadducees, who had come to terms with the Roman occupation, would have been as loath as all the Sadducees throughout history to part with what they possessed, or to risk their security and stability.

Jesus's message, as it appears in the Gospels, is neither wholly new nor wholly unique. It is probable that he himself was a Pharisee, and his teachings contain a number of elements of Pharisaic doctrine. As the Dead Sea Scrolls attest, they also contain a number of important aspects of Essene thought. But if the message, as such, was not entirely original, the means of transmitting it probably was. Jesus himself was undoubtedly an immensely charismatic individual. He may well have had an aptitude for healing and other such 'miracles'. He certainly possessed a gift for communicating his ideas by means of evocative and vivid parables – which did not require any sophisticated training in his audience, but were accessible, in some sense, to the populace at large. Moreover, unlike his Essene precursors, Jesus was not obliged to confine himself to forecasting the advent of a Messiah. He could claim to be that Messiah. And this, quite naturally, would have imparted a much greater authority and credibility to his words.

It is clear that by the time of his triumphal entry into Jerusalem Jesus had recruited a following. But this following would have been composed of two quite distinct elements – whose interests were not precisely the same. On the one hand there would have been a small nucleus of 'initiates' – immediate family, other members of the nobility, wealthy and influential supporters, whose primary objective was to see their candidate installed on the throne. On the other hand there would have been a much larger entourage of 'common people' – the 'rank and file' of the movement whose primary objective was to see the message, and the promise it contained, fulfilled. It is important to recognise the distinction between these two factions. Their political objective – to establish Jesus on the throne – would have been the same. But their motivations would have been essentially different.

When the enterprise failed, as it obviously did, the uneasy alliance between these two factions – 'adherents of the message' and adherents of the family – would seem to have collapsed. Confronted by débâcle and the threat of imminent annihilation, the family would have placed a priority on the single factor which, from time immemorial, has been of paramount importance to noble and royal families – preservation of the bloodline at all costs and, if necessary, in exile. For the 'adherents of the message' however, the family's future would have become irrelevant. For them survival of the bloodline would have been of secondary consequence. Their primary objective would have been perpetuation and dissemination of the message.

Christianity, as it evolves through its early centuries and eventually comes down to us today, is a product of the 'adherents of the message'. The course of its spread and development has been too widely charted by other scholars to necessitate much attention here. Suffice it to say that with Saint Paul, 'the message' had already begun to assume a crystallised and definitive form; and this form became the basis on which the whole theological edifice of Christianity was erected. By the time the Gospels were composed, the basic tenets of the new religion were virtually complete.

The new religion was oriented primarily towards a Roman or Romanised audience. Thus the role of Rome in Jesus's death was, of necessity, whitewashed, and guilt was transferred to the Jews. But this was not the only liberty taken with events to render them palatable to the Roman world. For the Roman world was accustomed to deifying its rulers, and Caesar had already been officially instated as a god. In order to compete, Jesus – whom nobody had previously deemed divine – had to be deified as well. In Paul's hands he was.

Before it could be successfully disseminated – from Palestine to Syria, Asia Minor, Greece, Egypt, Rome and Western Europe – the new religion had to be made acceptable to the people of those regions. And it had to be capable of holding its own against already established creeds. The new god, in short, had to be comparable in power, in majesty, in repertoire of miracles, to those he was intended to displace. If Jesus was to gain a foothold in the Romanised world of his time, he had perforce to become a fully fledged god. Not a Messiah in the old sense of that term, not a priest-king, but God incarnate – who, like his Syrian, Phoenician, Egyptian and classical counterparts, passed through the underworld and the harrowing of Hell and emerged, rejuvenated, with the spring. It was at this point that the idea of the Resurrection first assumed such crucial importance, and for a fairly obvious reason – to place Jesus on a par with Tammuz, Adonis, Attis, Osiris and all the other dying and reviving gods who populated both the world and the consciousness of their time. For precisely the same reason the doctrine of the virgin birth was promulgated. And the Easter festival – the festival of death and resurrection – was made to coincide with the spring rites of other contemporary cults and mystery schools.

Given the need to disseminate a god myth, the actual corporeal family of the 'god', and the political and dynastic elements in his story, would have become superfluous. Fettered as they were to a specific time and place, they would have detracted from his claim to universality. Thus, to further the claim of universality, all political and dynastic elements were rigorously excised from Jesus's biography. And thus all references to Zealots, for example, and Essenes, were also discreetly removed. Such references would have been, at the very least, embarrassing. It would not have appeared seemly for a god to be involved in a complex and ultimately ephemeral political and dynastic conspiracy – and especially one that failed. In the end nothing was left but what was contained in the Gospels – an account of austere, mythic simplicity, occurring only incidentally in the Roman-occupied Palestine of the first century and primarily in the eternal present of all myth.

While 'the message' developed in this fashion, the family and its supporters do not seem to have been idle. Julius Africanus, writing in the third century, reports that Jesus's surviving relatives bitterly accused the Herodian rulers of destroying the genealogies of Jewish nobles, thereby removing all evidence that might challenge their claim to the throne. And these same relatives are said to have 'migrated through the world', carrying with them certain genealogies which had escaped the destruction of documents during the revolt between A.D. 66 and 74.[1]

For the propagators of the new myth, the existence of this family would quickly have become more than an irrelevance. It would have become a potential embarrassment of daunting proportions. For the family – who could bear first-hand testimony to what really and historically happened – would have constituted a dangerous threat to the myth. Indeed, on the basis of first-hand knowledge, the family could have exploded the myth completely. Thus in the early days of Christianity all mention of a noble or royal family, of a bloodline, of political or dynastic ambitions would have had to be suppressed. And – since the cynical realities of the situation must be acknowledged – the family itself, who might betray the new religion, should, if at all possible, be exterminated. Hence the need for the utmost secrecy on the part of the family. Hence the intolerance of early Church fathers towards any deviation from the orthodoxy they endeavoured to impose. And hence also, perhaps, one of the origins of anti-Semitism. In effect the 'adherents of the message' and propagators of the myth would have accomplished a dual purpose by blaming the Jews and exonerating the Romans. They would not only have made the myth and 'the message' palatable to a Roman audience. They would also, since the family was Jewish, have impugned the family's credibility. And the anti-Jewish feeling they engendered would have furthered their objectives still more. If the family had found refuge in a Jewish community somewhere within the empire, popular persecution might, in its momentum, conveniently silence dangerous witnesses.

By pandering to a Roman audience, deifying Jesus and casting the Jews as scapegoats, the spread of what subsequently became Christian orthodoxy was assured of success. The position of this orthodoxy began to consolidate itself definitively in the second century, principally through Irenaeus, Bishop of Lyons around A.D. 180. Probably more than any other early Church father, Irenaeus contrived to impart to Christian theology a stable and coherent form. He accomplished this primarily by means of a voluminous work, *Libros Quinque Adversus Haereses* ('Five Books against Heresies'). In his exhaustive opus Irenaeus catalogued all deviations from the coalescing orthodoxy, and vehemently condemned them. Deploring diversity, he maintained there could be only one valid church, outside which there could be no salvation. Whoever challenged this assertion, Irenaeus declared to be a heretic – to be expelled and, if possible, destroyed.

A claimed descent if not from Jesus personally, then certainly from his family and from the House of David, was not unknown in Eastern Europe. It figures most prominently perhaps in the history of the Bagration dynasty. The Bagrations were said to have originated as a tribe around modern-day Lebanon and Syria during the first century A.D. They subsequently migrated northeast, across Asia Minor. By the fourth century, they had become hereditary kings of Armenia, and, later, of Georgia. They ruled as sovereigns of Georgia until 1801, when their last monarch, George XII, was imprisoned by Tsar Alexander I and his kingdom annexed by the Russian Empire. An important member of the family, Prince Petyr Ivanovich Bagration, achieved fame during the Napoleonic Wars as perhaps the greatest, and certainly the most audacious, of Russian generals. He figures prominently in Tolstoy's *War and Peace*. He participated in a number of major engagements, including Austerlitz in 1805. He saved the Russian Army from disaster at the Battle of Borodino in 1812, and died of wounds incurred there. Branches of the Bagration family survive today, in New York, in Paris, in Spain. Should a monarchy be restored in present-day Georgia, the Bagrations would possess a legitimate claim to the crown.

Medieval Byzantine sources repeatedly stress the Bagrations' Davidic descent. As part of his official title, every monarch of the Bagration dynasty was known as 'Descendant of the King and Prophet David'. Under their signatures, Bagration sovereigns would append the words: 'Of the House of Jesse, David, Solomon, Bagratide'.[i] A genealogical table of Bagration rulers shows a constant recurrence of such names as 'David' and 'Emmanuel'.

In our book, *The Messianic Legacy*, we discuss the 'post-Gospel' history of Jesus' immediate family – of his brothers, James, Jude and perhaps the figure known as Thomas ('The Twin'). We cited Julius Africanus, who refers to these relatives as 'Desposyni' or 'The Master's People', 'because of their relationship to the saviour's family.[ii] We also quoted Eusebius, to the effect that

> . . . there still survived of the Lord's family the grandsons of Jude, who was said to be His brother, humanly speaking. These were informed against as being of David's line and brought . . . before Domitian Caesar . . . Domitian asked them whether they were descended from David, and they admitted it.[iii]

Eusebius reports that the 'Desposyni' survived to become leaders of various Christian churches – according, it would seem, to a strict dynastic succession. Eusebius traces them to the time of the Emperor Trajan, A.D. 98–117. A modern Roman Catholic authority recounts a story which brings them up to the fourth century, the time of Constantine. In A.D. 318, the then Bishop of Rome, now known as Pope Sylvester, is said to have met personally with eight 'Desposyni' leaders, each of whom presided over a 'Christian' congregation. They are reported to have requested 1.) that the confirmation of Christian bishops of Jerusalem, Antioch, Ephesus and Alexandria be revoked; 2.) that these bishoprics be conferred instead on members of the 'Desposyni'; and, 3.) that Christian churches 'resume' sending money to the 'Desposyni' church in Jerusalem, which was to be regarded as the definitive Mother Church.[iv]

Not surprisingly, the Bishop of Rome rejected these requests, declaring that the Mother Church was now Rome and that Rome reserved authority to appoint her own bishops. This is said to have been the last contact between the 'Desposyni' and the coalescing orthodoxy based on Pauline thought. The 'Desposyni' then apparently disappear from the stage of history, reportedly migrating further to the northeast. They may easily have intermarried with the Bagrations. They may even have been identical with the Bagrations, who, from the end of the third century, prided themselves on being the first Christian monarchs – if not Roman Catholic monarchs – of Europe.

i: Gray, T. J-S., 'Les Bagratides. La Plus ancienne dynastie de la Chrétienté', *La Science Historique*, LXI, 1962, pp. 16–7.

ii: Eusebius, *The History of the Church*, Harmondsworth, 1965, p.55. (Eusebius, *Hist.*, I. vii).

iii: Eusebius, *op cit*, p.126. (II. xx).

iv. Martin, M., *The Decline and Fall of the Roman Church*, London, 1982, pp. 42–3.

Among the numerous diverse forms of early Christianity, it was Gnosticism that incurred Irenaeus's most vituperative wrath. Gnosticism rested on personal experience, personal union with the divine. For Irenaeus this naturally undermined the authority of priests and bishops, and so impeded the attempt to impose uniformity. As a result he devoted his energies to suppressing Gnosticism. To this end it was necessary to discourage individual speculation, and to encourage unquestioning faith in fixed dogma. A theological system was required, a structure of codified tenets which allowed of no interpretation by the individual. In opposition to personal experience and gnosis, Irenaeus insisted on a single 'catholic' (that is universal) church resting on apostolic foundation and succession. And to implement the creation of such a church, Irenaeus recognised the need for a definitive canon – a fixed list of authoritative writings. Accordingly he compiled such a canon, sifting through the available works, including some, excluding others.

Irenaeus is the first writer whose New Testament canon conforms essentially to that of the present day.

Such measures, of course, did not prevent the spread of early heresies. On the contrary, they continued to flourish. But with Irenaeus, orthodoxy – the type of Christianity promulgated by the 'adherents of the message' – assumed a coherent form that ensured its survival and eventual triumph. It is not unreasonable to claim that Irenaeus paved the way for what occurred during and immediately after the reign of Constantine – under whose auspices the Roman Empire became, in some sense, a Christian empire.

The role of Constantine in the history and development of Christianity has been falsified, misrepresented and misunderstood. The spurious eighth-century 'Donation of Constantine', discussed in Chapter 9, has served to confuse matters even further in the eyes of subsequent writers. Nevertheless, Constantine is often credited with the decisive victory of the 'adherents of the message' – and not wholly without justification. We were therefore obliged to consider him more closely, and in order to do so we had to dispel certain of the more fanciful and specious accomplishments ascribed to him.

According to later Church tradition, Constantine had inherited from his father a sympathetic predisposition towards Christianity. In fact this predisposition seems to have been primarily a matter of expediency, for Christians by then were numerous and Constantine needed all the help he could get against Maxentius, his rival for the imperial throne. In A.D. 312 Maxentius was routed at the Battle of Milvian Bridge, thus leaving Constantine's claim unchallenged. Immediately before this crucial engagement Constantine is said to have had a vision – later reinforced by a prophetic dream – of a luminous cross hanging in the sky. A sentence was supposedly inscribed across it – *In Hoc Signo Vinces* ('By this sign you will conquer'). Tradition recounts that Constantine, deferring to this celestial portent, ordered the shields of his troops hastily emblazoned with the Christian monogram – the Greek letter Chi Rho, the first two letters of the word 'Christos'. As a result Constantine's victory over Maxentius at Milvian Bridge came to represent a miraculous triumph of Christianity over paganism.

This, then, is the popular Church tradition, on the basis of which Constantine is often thought to have 'converted the Roman Empire to Christianity'. In actual fact, however, Constantine did no such thing. But in order to decide precisely what he did do, we must examine the evidence more closely.

In the first place Constantine's 'conversion' – if that is the appropriate word – does not seem to have been Christian at all but unabashedly pagan. He appears to have had some sort of vision, or numinous experience, in the precincts of a pagan temple to the Gallic Apollo, either in the Vosges or near Autun. According to a witness accompanying Constantine's army at the time, the vision was of the sun god – the deity worshipped by certain cults under the name of 'Sol Invictus', 'the Invincible Sun'. There is evidence that Constantine, just before his vision, had been initiated into a Sol Invictus cult. In any case the Roman Senate, after the Battle of Milvian Bridge, erected a triumphal arch in the Colosseum. According to the inscription on this arch, Constantine's victory was won 'through the prompting of the Deity'. But the Deity in question was not Jesus. It was Sol Invictus, the pagan sun god.[2]

Contrary to tradition, Constantine did not make Christianity the official state religion of Rome. The state religion of Rome under Constantine was, in fact, pagan sun worship; and Constantine, all his life, acted as its chief priest. Indeed his reign was called a 'sun emperorship', and Sol Invictus figured everywhere – including the imperials and banners and the coinage of the realm. The image of Constantine as a fervent convert to Christianity is clearly wrong. He himself was not even baptised until 337 – when he lay on his deathbed and was apparently too weakened or too apathetic to protest. Nor can he be credited with the Chi Rho monogram. An inscription bearing this monogram was found on a tomb at Pompeii, dating from two and a half centuries before.[3]

The cult of Sol Invictus was Syrian in origin and imposed by Roman emperors on their subjects a century before Constantine. Although it contained elements of Baal and Astarte worship, it was essentially monotheistic. In effect, it posited the sun god as the sum of all attributes of all other gods, and thus peacefully subsumed its potential rivals. Moreover, it conveniently harmonised with the cult of Mithras – which was also prevalent in Rome and the empire at the time, and which also involved solar worship.

For Constantine the cult of Sol Invictus was, quite simply, expedient. His primary, indeed obsessive, objective was unity – unity in politics, in religion and in territory. A cult, or state religion, that included all other cults within it obviously abetted this objective. And it was under the auspices of the Sol Invictus cult that Christianity consolidated its position.

Christian orthodoxy had much in common with the cult of Sol Invictus; and thus the former was able to flourish unmolested under the latter's umbrella of tolerance. The cult of Sol Invictus, being essentially monotheistic, paved the way for the monotheism of Christianity. And the cult of Sol Invictus was convenient in other respects as well – respects which both modified and facilitated the spread of Christianity. By an edict promulgated in A.D. 321, for example, Constantine ordered the law courts closed on 'the venerable day of the sun', and decreed that this day be a day of rest. Christianity had hitherto held the Jewish Sabbath – Saturday – as sacred. Now, in accordance with Constantine's edict, it transferred its sacred day to Sunday. This not only brought it into harmony with the existing régime, but also permitted it to further dissociate itself from its Judaic origins. Until the fourth century, moreover, Jesus's birthday had been celebrated on January 6th. For the cult of Sol Invictus, however, the crucial day of the year was December 25th – the festival of Natalis Invictus, the birth (or rebirth) of the sun, when the days began to grow longer. In this respect, too, Christianity brought itself into alignment with the régime and the established state religion.

The cult of Sol Invictus meshed happily with that of Mithras – so much so, indeed, that the two are often confused.[4] Both emphasised the status of the sun. Both held Sunday as sacred. Both celebrated a major birth festival on December 25th. As a result Christianity could also find points of convergence with Mithraism – the more so as Mithraism stressed the immortality of the soul, a future judgment and the resurrection of the dead.

In the interests of unity Constantine deliberately chose to blur the distinctions between Christianity, Mithraism and Sol Invictus – deliberately chose not to see any contradiction between them. Thus he tolerated the deified Jesus as the earthly manifestation of Sol Invictus. Thus he would build a Christian church and, at the same time, statues of the Mother Goddess Cybele and of Sol Invictus, the sun god – the latter being an image of himself, bearing his features. In such eclectic and ecumenical gestures, the emphasis on unity can be seen again. Faith, in short, was for Constantine a political matter; and any faith that was conducive to unity was treated with forbearance.

While Constantine was not, therefore, the 'good Christian' that later tradition depicts, he consolidated, in the name of unity and uniformity, the status of Christian orthodoxy. In A.D. 325, for example, he convened the Council of Nicea. At this council the dating of Easter was established. Rules were framed which defined the authority of bishops, thereby paving the way for a concentration of power in ecclesiastical hands. Most important of all, the Council of Nicea decided, by vote,[5] that Jesus was a god, not a mortal prophet. Again, however, it must be emphasised that Constantine's paramount consideration was not piety but unity and expediency. As a god Jesus could be associated conveniently with Sol Invictus. As a mortal prophet he would have been more difficult to accommodate. In short, Christian orthodoxy lent itself to a politically desirable fusion with the official state religion; and in so far as it did so Constantine conferred his support upon Christian orthodoxy.

Thus, a year after the Council of Nicea, he sanctioned the confiscation and destruction of all works that challenged orthodox teachings – works by pagan authors that referred to Jesus, as well as works by 'heretical' Christians. He also arranged for a fixed income to be allocated to the Church and installed the bishop of Rome in the Lateran Palace.[6] Then, in A.D. 331, he commissioned and financed new copies of the Bible. This constituted one of the single most decisive factors in the entire history of Christianity, and provided Christian orthodoxy – the 'adherents of the message' – with an unparalleled opportunity.

In A.D. 303, a quarter of a century before, the pagan Emperor Diocletian had undertaken to destroy all Christian writings that could be found. As a result Christian documents – especially in Rome – all but vanished. When Constantine, commissioned new versions of these documents, it enabled the custodians of orthodoxy to revise, edit and rewrite their material as they saw fit, in accordance with their tenets. It was at this point that most of the crucial alterations in the New Testament were probably made, and Jesus assumed the unique status he has enjoyed ever since. The importance of Constantine's commission must not be underestimated. Of the five thousand extant early manuscript versions of the New Testament, no complete edition pre-dates the fourth century.[7] The New Testament, as it exists today, is essentially a product of fourth-century editors and writers – custodians of orthodoxy, 'adherents of the message', with vested interests to protect.

THE ZEALOTS

After Constantine the course of Christian orthodoxy is familiar enough and well documented. Needless to say it culminated in the final triumph of the 'adherents of the message'. But if 'the message established itself as the guiding and governing principle of Western civilisation, it did not remain wholly unchallenged. Even from its incognito exile, the claims and the very existence of the family would seem to have exerted a powerful appeal – an appeal which, more often than was comfortable, posed a threat to the orthodoxy of Rome.

Roman orthodoxy rests essentially on the books of the New Testament. But the New Testament itself is only a selection of early Christian documents dating from the fourth century. There are a great many other works that pre-date the New Testament in its present form, some of which cast a significant, often controversial, new light on the accepted accounts.

There are, for instance, the diverse books excluded from the Bible, which comprise the compilation now known as the Apocrypha. Some of the works in the Apocrypha are admittedly late, dating from the sixth century. Other works, however, were already in circulation as early as the second century, and may well have as great a claim to veracity as the original Gospels themselves.

One such work is the Gospel of Peter, a copy of which was first located in a valley of the upper Nile in 1886, although it is mentioned by the bishop of Antioch in A.D. 180. According to this 'apocryphal' Gospel, Joseph of Arimathea was a close friend of Pontius Pilate – which, if true, would increase the likelihood of a fraudulent Crucifixion. The Gospel of Peter also reports that the tomb in which Jesus was buried lay in a place called 'the garden of Joseph'. And Jesus's last words on the cross are particularly striking: 'My power, my power, why hast thou forsaken me?'[8]

Another apocryphal work of interest is the Gospel of the Infancy of Jesus Christ, which dates from no later than the second century and possibly from before. In this book Jesus is portrayed as a brilliant but eminently human child. All too human perhaps – for he is violent and unruly, prone to shocking displays of temper and a rather irresponsible exercise of his powers. Indeed, on one occasion he strikes dead another child who offends him. A similar fate is visited upon an autocratic mentor. Such incidents are undoubtedly spurious, but they attest to the way in which, at the time, Jesus had to be depicted if he were to attain divine status among his following.

In addition to Jesus's rather scandalous behaviour as a child, there is one curious and perhaps significant fragment in the Gospel of the

Infancy. When Jesus was circumcised, his foreskin was said to have been appropriated by an unidentified old woman who preserved it in an alabaster box used for oil of spikenard. And 'This is that alabaster box which Mary the sinner procured and poured forth the ointment out of it upon the head and the feet of our Lord Jesus Christ.'[9]

Here, then, as in the accepted Gospels, there is an anointing which is obviously more than it appears to be – an anointing tantamount to some significant ritual. In this case, however, it is clear that the anointing has been foreseen and prepared long in advance. And the whole incident implies a connection – albeit an obscure and convoluted one – between the Magdalene and Jesus's family long before Jesus embarked on his mission at the age of thirty. It is reasonable to assume that Jesus's parents would not have conferred his foreskin on the first old woman to request it – even if there were nothing unusual in so apparently odd a request. The old woman must therefore be someone of consequence and/or someone on intimate terms with Jesus's parents. And the Magdalene's subsequent possession of the bizarre relic – or, at any rate, of its container – suggests a connection between her and the old woman. Again we seem to be confronted by the shadowy vestiges of something that was more important than is now generally believed.

Certain passages in the books of the Apocrypha – the flagrant excesses of Jesus's childhood, for example – were undoubtedly embarrassing to later orthodoxy. They would certainly be so to most Christians today. But it must be remembered that the Apocrypha, like the accepted books of the New Testament, was composed by 'adherents of the message', intent on deifying Jesus. The Apocrypha cannot therefore be expected to contain anything that might seriously compromise the 'message' – which any mention of Jesus's political activity, still more of his possible dynastic ambitions, manifestly would. For evidence on such controversial matters as these, we were obliged to look elsewhere.

The Holy Land in Jesus's time contained a bewildering number of diverse Judaic groups, factions, sects and sub-sects. In the Gospels, only two of these, the Pharisees and Sadducees, are cited, and both are cast in the roles of villains. However, the role of villain would only have been appropriate to the Sadducees, who did collaborate with the Roman administration. The Pharisees maintained a staunch opposition to Rome; and Jesus himself, if not actually a Pharisee, acted essentially within the Pharisee tradition.[10]

In order to appeal to a Romanised audience, the Gospels were obliged to exonerate Rome and blacken the Jews. This explains why the Pharisees had to be misrepresented and deliberately stigmatised along with their genuinely culpable countrymen, the Sadducees. But why is there no mention in the Gospels of the Zealots – the militant nationalistic 'freedom fighters' and revolutionaries who, if anything, a Roman audience would only too eagerly have seen as villains? There would seem to be no explanation for their apparent omission from the Gospels – unless Jesus was so closely associated with them that this association could not possibly be disowned, only glossed over and thereby concealed. As Professor Brandon argues: 'The Gospels' silence about Zealots . . . must surely be indicative of a relationship between Jesus and these patriots which the Evangelists preferred not to disclose.'[11]

Whatever Jesus's possible association with the Zealots, there is no question but that he was crucified as one. Indeed the two men allegedly crucified with him are explicitly described as *lestoi* – the appellation by which the Zealots were known to the Romans. It is doubtful that Jesus himself was a Zealot. Nevertheless, he displays, at odd moments in the Gospels, an aggressive militarism quite comparable to theirs. In one awkwardly famous passage, he announces that he has come 'not to bring peace, but a sword'. In Luke's Gospel, he instructs those of his followers who do not possess a sword to purchase one (Luke 22:36); and he himself then checks and approves that they are armed after the Passover meal (Luke 22:38). In the Fourth Gospel Simon Peter is actually carrying a sword when Jesus is arrested. It is difficult to reconcile such references with the conventional image of a mild pacifist saviour. Would such a saviour have sanctioned the bearing of arms, particularly by one of his favourite disciples, the one on whom he supposedly founded his church?

If Jesus was not himself a Zealot, the Gospels – seemingly despite themselves – betray and establish his connection with that militant faction. There is persuasive evidence to associate Barabbas with Jesus; and Barabbas is also described as a *lestoi*. James, John and Simon Peter all have appellations which may hint obliquely at Zealot sympathies, if not Zealot involvement. According to modern authorities, Judas Iscariot derives from 'Judas the Sicarii' – and 'Sicarii' was yet another term for Zealot, interchangeable with *lestoi*. Indeed the Sicarii seem to have been an elite within the Zealot ranks, a crack cadre of professional assassins. Finally there is the disciple known as Simon. In the Greek version of Mark, Simon is called *Kananaios* – a Greek transliteration of the Aramaic

410

word for Zealot. In the King James Bible, the Greek word is mistranslated and Simon appears as 'Simon the Canaanite'. But the Gospel of Luke leaves no room for doubt. Simon is clearly identified as a Zealot, and even the King James Bible introduces him as 'Simon Zelotes'. It would thus seem fairly indisputable that Jesus numbered at least one Zealot among his followers.

If the absence – or, rather, apparent absence – of the Zealots from the Gospels is striking, so too is that of the Essenes. In the Holy Land of Jesus's time, the Essenes constituted a sect as important as the Pharisees and Sadducees, and it is inconceivable that Jesus did not come into contact with them. Indeed, from the account given of him, John the Baptist would seem to have been an Essene. The omission of any reference to the Essenes seems to have been dictated by the same considerations that dictated omission of virtually all references to the Zealots. In short Jesus's connections with the Essenes, like his connections with the Zealots, were probably too close and too well known to be denied. They could only be glossed over and concealed.

From historians and chroniclers writing at the time, it is known that the Essenes maintained communities throughout the Holy Land and, quite possibly, elsewhere as well. They began to appear around 150 B.C., and they used the Old Testament, but interpreted it more as allegory than as literal historical truth. They repudiated conventional Judaism in favour of a form of Gnostic dualism – which seems to have incorporated elements of sun worship and Pythagorean thought. They practised healing and were esteemed for their expertise in therapeutic techniques. Finally they were rigorously ascetic, and readily distinguished by their simple white garb.

Most modern authorities on the subject believe the famous Dead Sea Scrolls found at Qumran to be essentially Essene documents. And there is no question that the sect of ascetics living at Qumran had much in common with Essene thought. Like Essene teaching, the Dead Sea Scrolls reflect a dualist theology. At the same time they lay a great stress on the coming of a Messiah – an 'anointed one' – descended from the line of David.[12] They also adhere to a special calendar, according to which the Passover service was celebrated not on Friday, but on Wednesday – which agrees with the Passover service in the Fourth Gospel. And in a number of significant respects they coincide, almost word for word, with some of Jesus's teaching. At the very least it would appear that Jesus was aware of the Qumran community and, to some extent at any rate, brought his own teachings into accord with theirs. One modern expert on the Dead Sea Scrolls believes that they 'give added ground for believing that many incidents [in the New Testament] are merely projections into Jesus' own history of what was expected of the Messiah'.[13]

Whether the Qumran sect were technically Essenes or not, it seems clear that Jesus – even if he did not undergo formal Essene training – was well versed in Essene thought. Indeed, many of his teachings echo those ascribed to the Essenes. And his aptitude for healing likewise suggests some Essene influence. But a closer scrutiny of the Gospels reveals that the Essenes may have figured even more significantly in Jesus's career.

The Essenes were readily identifiable by their white garments – which, paintings and cinema notwithstanding, were less common in the Holy Land at the time than is generally believed. In the suppressed 'secret' Gospel of Mark, a white linen robe plays an important ritual role – and it recurs later even in the accepted authorised version. If Jesus was conducting mystery school initiations at Bethany or elsewhere, the white linen robe suggests that these initiations may well have been Essene in character. What is more, the motif of the white linen robe recurs later in all four Gospels. After the Crucifixion Jesus's body 'miraculously' disappears from the tomb, which is found to be occupied by at least one white-clad figure. In Matthew it is an angel in 'raiment white as snow' (28:3). In Mark it is 'a young man in long white garment' (16:5). Luke reports that there were 'two men . . . in shining garments' (24:4), while the Fourth Gospel speaks of 'two angels in white' (20:12). In two of these accounts the figure or figures in the tomb are not even accorded any supernatural status. Presumably, these figures are thoroughly mortal – and yet, it would appear, unknown to the disciples. It is certainly reasonable to suppose that they are Essenes. And given the Essenes' aptitude for healing, such a supposition becomes even more tenable. If Jesus, on being removed from the cross, was indeed still alive, the services of a healer would clearly have been required. Even if he were dead, a healer is likely to have been present, if only as a 'forlorn hope'. And there were no more esteemed healers in the Holy Land at the time than the Essenes.

According to our scenario a mock Crucifixion on private ground was arranged, with Pilate's collusion, by certain of Jesus's supporters. More specifically it would have been arranged not primarily by 'adherents of the message', but by adherents to the bloodline – immediate family, in other words, and/or other aristocrats and/or members of an inner circle. These individuals may well have had Essene connections or have been Essenes themselves. To the 'adherents of the message', however – the 'rank and file' of Jesus's following, epitomised by Simon Peter – the stratagem would not have been divulged.

On being carried to Joseph of Arimathea's tomb, Jesus would have required medical attention, for which an Essene healer would have been present. And afterwards, when the tomb was found to be vacant, an emissary would again have been necessary – an emissary unknown to the 'rank and file' disciples. This emissary would have had to reassure the unsuspecting 'adherents of the message', to act as intermediary between Jesus and his following – and to forestall charges of grave-robbing or grave desecration against the Romans, which might have provoked dangerous civic disturbances.

Whether this scenario was accurate or not, it seemed to us fairly clear that Jesus was as closely associated with the Essenes as he was with the Zealots. At first this might seem somewhat odd, for the Zealots and the Essenes are often imagined to have been incompatible. The Zealots were aggressive, violent, militaristic, not averse to assassination and terrorism. The Essenes, in contrast, are frequently depicted as divorced from political issues, quietist, pacifist and gentle. In actual fact, however, the Zealots included numerous Essenes in their ranks – for the Zealots were not a sect but a political faction. As a political faction they drew support not only from the anti-Roman Pharisees, but from the Essenes as well – who could be as aggressively nationalistic as anyone else.

The association of the Zealots and the Essenes is especially evident in the writings of Josephus, from whom much of the available information on Palestine at the time derives. Joseph ben Matthias was born into the Judaic nobility in A.D. 37. On the outbreak of the revolt in A.D. 66 he was appointed governor of Galilee, where he assumed command of the forces aligned against the Romans. As a military commander he seems to have proved signally inept, and was promptly captured by the Roman Emperor Vespasian. Thereupon he turned Quisling. Taking the Romanised name of Flavius Josephus, he became a Roman citizen, divorced his wife and married a Roman heiress, and accepted lavish gifts from the Roman emperor – which included a private apartment in the imperial palace, as well as land confiscated from Jews in the Holy

Land. Around the time of his death in A.D. 100, his copious chronicles of the period began to appear.

In *The Jewish War* Josephus offers a detailed account of the revolt between A.D. 66 and 74. Indeed, it was from Josephus that subsequent historians learned most about that disastrous insurrection, the sack of Jerusalem and the razing of the Temple. And Josephus's work also contains the only account of the fall, in A.D. 74, of the fortress of Masada, situated at the south-western corner of the Dead Sea.

Like Montségur some twelve hundred years later Masada has come to symbolise tenacity, heroism and martyrdom in defence of a lost cause. Like Montségur it continued to resist the invader long after virtually all other organised resistance had ceased. While the rest of Palestine collapsed beneath the Roman onslaught, Masada continued to be impregnable. At last, in A.D. 74, the position of the fortress became untenable. After sustained bombardment with heavy siege machinery, the Romans installed a ramp which put them in a position to breach the defences. On the night of April 15th they prepared for a general assault. On that same night the 960 men, women, and children within the fortress committed suicide *en masse*. When the Romans burst through the gate the following morning, they found only corpses amid the flames.

Josephus himself accompanied the Roman troops who entered the husk of Masada on the morning of April 16th. He claims to have witnessed the carnage personally. And he claims to have interviewed three survivors of the débâcle – a woman and two children who supposedly hid in the conduits beneath the fortress while the rest of the garrison killed themselves. From these survivors Josephus reports that he obtained a detailed account of what had transpired the night before. According to this account the commander of the garrison was a man named Eleazar – a variant, interestingly enough, of Lazarus. And it seems to have been Eleazar who, by his persuasive and charismatic eloquence, led the defenders to their grisly decision. In his chronicle Josephus repeats Eleazar's speeches, as he claims to have heard them from the survivors. And these speeches are extremely interesting. History reports that Masada was defended by militant Zealots. Josephus himself uses the words 'Zealots' and 'Sicarii' interchangeably. And yet Eleazar's speeches are not even conventionally Judaic. On the contrary, they are unmistakably Essene, Gnostic and dualist:

Ever since primitive man began to think, the words of our

ancestors and of the gods, supported by the actions and spirit of our forefathers, have constantly impressed on us that life is the calamity for man, not death. Death gives freedom to our souls and lets them depart to their own pure home where they will know nothing of any calamity; but while they are confined within a mortal body and share its miseries, in strict truth they are dead. For association of the divine with the mortal is most improper. Certainly the soul can do a great deal even when imprisoned in the body: it makes the body its own organ of sense, moving it invisibly and impelling it in its actions further than mortal nature can reach. But when, freed from the weight that drags it down to earth and is hung about it, the soul returns to its own place, then in truth it partakes of a blessed power and an utterly unfettered strength, remaining as invisible to human eyes as God Himself. Not even while it is in the body can it be viewed; it enters undetected and departs unseen, having itself one imperishable nature, but causing a change in the body; for whatever the soul touches lives and blossoms, whatever it deserts withers and dies: such a superabundance it has of immortality.[14]

And again:

They are men of true courage who, regarding this life as a kind of service we must render to nature, undergo it with reluctance and hasten to release their souls from their bodies; and though no misfortune presses or drives them away, desire for immortal life impels them to inform their friends that they are going to depart.[15]

It is extraordinary that no scholar, to our knowledge, has ever commented on these speeches before, for they raise a multitude of provocative questions. At no point, for example, does orthodox Judaism ever speak of a 'soul' – still less of its 'immortal' or 'imperishable' nature. Indeed, the very concept of a soul and of immortality is alien to the mainstream of Judaic tradition and thought. So, too, is the supremacy of spirit over matter, the union with God in death, and the condemnation of life as evil. These attitudes derive, quite unequivocally, from a mystery tradition. They are patently Gnostic and dualist; and, in the context of Masada, are characteristically Essene.

Certain of these attitudes, of course, may also be described as in some sense 'Christian'. Not necessarily as that word subsequently came to be defined, but as it might have been applied to Jesus's original followers – those, for example, who wished to join Lazarus in death in the Fourth Gospel. It is possible that the defenders of Masada included some adherents to Jesus's bloodline. During the revolt of A.D. 66 to 74 there were numerous 'Christians' who fought against the Romans as vigorously as did the Jews. Many Zealots, in fact, were what would now be called 'early Christians'; and it is quite likely that there were some of them at Masada.

Josephus, of course, suggests nothing of this sort – although even if he once did, it would have been excised by subsequent editors. At the same time, one would expect Josephus, writing a history of Palestine during the first century, to make some mention of Jesus. Granted, many later editions of Josephus's work do contain such references; but these references conform to the Jesus of established orthodoxy, and most modern scholars dismiss them as spurious interpolations dating from no earlier than the time of Constantine. In the nineteenth century, however, an edition of Josephus was discovered in Russia which differed from all others. The text itself, translated into Old Russian, dated from approximately 1261. The man who transcribed it was not an orthodox Jew, because he retained many 'pro-Christian' allusions. And yet Jesus, in this version of Josephus, is described as human, as a political revolutionary and as a 'king who did not reign'.[16] He is also said to have had 'a line in the middle of his head in the manner of the Nazireans.'[17]

Scholars have expended much paper and energy disputing the possible authenticity of what is now called the 'Slavonic Josephus'. All things considered, we were inclined to regard it as more or less genuine – a transcription from a copy or copies of Josephus which survived the destruction of Christian documents by Diocletian and eluded the editorial zeal of the reinstated orthodoxy under Constantine. There were a number of cogent reasons for our conclusion. If the Slavonic Josephus was a forgery, for example, whose interests would it have served? Its description of Jesus as a king would hardly have been acceptable to a thirteenth-century Jewish audience. And its depiction of Jesus as human would hardly have pleased thirteenth-century Christendom. What is more, Origen, a Church father writing in the early third century, alludes to a version of Josephus which denies Jesus's Messiahship.[18] This version – which may once have been the original, authentic and 'standard' version – could well have provided the text for the Slavonic Josephus.

THE GNOSTIC WRITINGS

The revolt of A.D. 66–74 was followed by a second major insurrection some sixty years later, between 132 and 135. As a result of this new disturbance all Jews were officially expelled from Jerusalem, which became a Roman city. But even as early as the first revolt history had begun to draw a veil over events in the Holy Land, and there are virtually no records for another two centuries. Indeed the period is not dissimilar to Europe at various points during the so-called 'Dark Ages'. Nevertheless it is known that numerous Jews remained in the country, though outside Jerusalem. So, too, did a number of Christians. And there was even one sect of Jews, called the Ebionites who, while adhering generally to their faith, at the same time revered Jesus as a prophet – albeit a mortal one.

Nevertheless the real spirit of both Judaism and Christianity moved away from the Holy Land. The majority of Palestine's Jewish population dispersed in a diaspora like that which had occurred some seven hundred years before, when Jerusalem fell to the Babylonians. And Christianity, in a similar fashion, began to migrate across the globe – to Asia Minor, to Greece, to Rome, to Gaul, to Britain, to North Africa. Not surprisingly conflicting accounts of what had happened in or around A.D. 33 began to arise all over the civilised world. And despite the efforts of Clement of Alexandria, Irenaeus and their ilk, these accounts – officially labelled 'heresies' – continued to flourish. Some of them undoubtedly derived from some sort of first-hand knowledge, preserved both by devout Jews and by groups like the Ebionites, Jewish converts to one or another form of Christianity. Other accounts were patently based on legend, on rumour, on an amalgamation of current beliefs – such as Egyptian, Hellenistic and Mithraic mystery traditions. Whatever their specific sources, they caused much disquiet to the 'adherents of the message', the coalescing orthodoxy which was endeavouring to consolidate its position.

Information on the early 'heresies' is meagre. Modern knowledge about them derives largely from the attacks of their opponents, which naturally makes for a distorted picture – like the picture that might emerge of the French Resistance, for instance, from Gestapo documents.

On the whole, however, Jesus seems to have been viewed by the early 'heretics' in one of two ways. For some he was a fully fledged god, with few, if any, human attributes. For others he was a mortal prophet, not essentially different from, say, the Buddha – or, half a millennium later, Muhammad.

Among the most important of the early heresiarchs was Valentinus, a native of Alexandria who spent the latter part of his life (A.D. 136–65) in Rome. In his time Valentinus was extremely influential, numbering such men as Ptolemy among his following. Claiming to possess a body of 'secret teachings' of Jesus, he refused to submit to Roman authority, asserting that personal gnosis took precedence over any external hierarchy. Predictably enough Valentinus and his adherents were among the most belaboured targets of Irenaeus's wrath.

Another such target was Marcion, a wealthy shipping magnate and bishop who arrived in Rome around 140 and was excommunicated four years later. Marcion posited a radical distinction between 'law' and 'love', which he associated with the Old and New Testaments respectively; certain of these Marcionite ideas surfaced a full thousand years later in such works as the *Perlesvaus*. Marcion was the first writer to compile a canonical list of Biblical books – which, in his case, excluded the whole of the Old Testament. It was in direct response to Marcion that Irenaeus compiled his canonical list, which provided the basis for the Bible as we know it today.

The third major heresiarch of the period – and in many ways the most intriguing – was Basilides, an Alexandrian scholar writing between A.D. 120 and 130. Basilides was conversant with both Hebrew scriptures and Christian Gospels. He was also steeped in Egyptian and Hellenistic thought. He is supposed to have written no less than twenty-four commentaries on the Gospels. According to Irenaeus, he promulgated a most heinous heresy indeed. Basilides claimed that the Crucifixion was a fraud, that Jesus did not die on the cross, and that a substitute – Simon of Cyrene – took his place instead.[19] Such an assertion would seem to be bizarre. And yet it has proved to be extraordinarily persistent and tenacious. As late as the seventh century the Koran maintained precisely the same argument – that a substitute, traditionally Simon of Cyrene, took Jesus's place on the cross.[20] And the same argument was upheld by the priest from whom we received the mysterious letter discussed in Chapter 1 – the letter that alluded to 'incontrovertible proof' of a substitution.

If there was any one region where the early heresies most entrenched themselves, it was Egypt, and more specifically Alexandria – most learned and cosmopolitan city in the world at the time, the second largest city in the Roman Empire and a repository for a bewildering variety of faiths, teachings and traditions. In the wake of the two revolts in Judaea, Egypt proved the most accessible haven for both Jewish and Christian refugees, vast numbers of whom thronged to Alexandria. It was thus not surprising that Egypt yielded the most convincing evidence to support our hypothesis. This was contained in the so-called 'Gnostic Gospels', or, more accurately, the Nag Hammadi Scrolls.

In December 1945 an Egyptian peasant, digging for soft and fertile soil near the village of Nag Hammadi in Upper Egypt, exhumed a red earthenware jar. It proved to contain thirteen codices – papyrus books or scrolls – bound in leather. Unaware of the magnitude of the discovery, the peasant and his family used some of the codices to stoke their fire. Eventually, however, the remainder attracted the attention of experts; and one of them, smuggled out of Egypt, was offered for sale on the black market. Part of this codex, which was purchased by the C. G. Jung Foundation, proved to contain the now famous Gospel of Thomas.

In the meantime the Egyptian government nationalised the remainder of the Nag Hammadi collection in 1952. Only in 1961, however, was an international team of experts assembled to copy and translate the entire corpus of material. In 1972 the first volume of the photographic edition appeared. And in 1977 the entire collection of scrolls appeared in English translation for the first time.

The Nag Hammadi Scrolls are a collection of Biblical texts, essentially Gnostic in character, which date, it would appear, from the late fourth or early fifth century – from about A.D. 400. The scrolls are copies, and the originals from which they were transcribed date from much earlier. Certain of them – the Gospel of Thomas, for example, the Gospel of Truth and the Gospel of the Egyptians – are mentioned by the very earliest of Church fathers, such as Clement of Alexandria, Irenaeus and Origen. Modern scholars have established that some if not most of the texts in the scrolls date from no later than A.D. 150. And at least one of them may include material that is even older than the four standard Gospels of the New Testament.[21]

Taken as a whole, the Nag Hammadi collection constitutes an invaluable repository of early Christian documents – some of which can claim an authority equal to that of the Gospels. What is more, certain of these documents enjoy a claim to a unique veracity of their own. In the first place they escaped the censorship and revision of later Roman orthodoxy. In the second place they were originally composed for an Egyptian, not a Roman, audience, and are not therefore distorted or slanted to a Romanised ear. Finally they may well rest on first-hand and/or eyewitnesses sources – oral accounts by Jews fleeing the Holy Land, for instance, perhaps even personal acquaintances or associates of Jesus, who could tell their story with an historical fidelity the Gospels could not afford to retain.

Not surprisingly the Nag Hammadi Scrolls contain a good many passages that are inimical to orthodoxy and the 'adherents of the message'. In one undated codex, for example, the Second Treatise of the Great Seth, Jesus is depicted precisely as he is in the heresy of Basilides – escaping his death on the cross by dint of an ingenious substitution. In the following extract, Jesus speaks in the first person:

> I did not succumb to them as they had planned . . . And I did
> not die in reality but in appearance, lest I be put to shame by
> them . . . For my death which they think happened [happened]
> to them in their error and blindness, since they nailed their man
> unto their death . . . It was another, their father, who drank the
> gall and the vinegar; it was not I. They struck me with the reed;
> it was another, Simon, who bore the cross on his shoulder. It
> was another upon whom they placed the crown of thorns . . .
> And I was laughing at their ignorance.[22]

With convincing consistency, certain other works in the Nag Hammadi collection bear witness to a bitter and ongoing feud between Peter and the Magdalene – a feud that would seem to reflect a schism between the 'adherents of the message' and the adherents to the bloodline. Thus, in the Gospel of Mary, Peter addresses the Magdalene as follows: 'Sister, we know that the Saviour loved you more than the rest of women. Tell us the words of the Saviour which you remember – which you know but we do not.'[23] Later Peter demands indignantly of the other disciples: 'Did he really speak privately with a woman and not openly to us? Are we to turn about and all listen to her? Did he prefer her to us?'[24] And later still, one of the disciples replies to Peter: 'Surely the Saviour knows her very well. That is why he loved her more than us.'[25]

In the Gospel of Philip the reasons for this feud would appear to be obvious enough. There is, for example, a recurring emphasis on the image of the bridal chamber. According to the Gospel of Philip, 'the Lord did everything in a mystery, a baptism and a chrism and a eucharist and a redemption and a bridal chamber.'[26] Granted, the bridal chamber, at first glance, might well seem to be symbolic or allegorical. But the Gospel of Philip is more explicit: 'There were three who always walked with the Lord; Mary his mother and her sister and Magdalene, the one who was called his companion.'[27] According to one scholar, the word 'companion' is to be translated as 'spouse.'[28] There are certainly grounds for doing so, for the Gospel of Philip becomes more explicit still:

> And the companion of the Saviour is Mary Magdalene. But Christ loved her more than all the disciples and used to kiss her often on her mouth. The rest of the disciples were offended by it and expressed disapproval. They said to him, 'Why do you love her more than all of us?' The Saviour answered and said to them, 'Why do I not love you like her?'[29]

The Gospel of Philip elaborates on the matter: 'Fear not the flesh nor love it. If you fear it, it will gain mastery over you. If you love it, it will swallow and paralyse you.'[30] At another point, this elaboration is translated into concrete terms: 'Great is the mystery of marriage! For without it the world would not have existed. Now the existence of the world depends on man, and the existence of man on marriage.'[31] And towards the end of the Gospel of Philip, there is the following statement: 'There is the Son of man and there is the son of the Son of man. The Lord is the Son of man, and the son of the Son of man is he who is created through the Son of man.'[32]

CHAPTER FOURTEEN

THE GRAIL DYNASTY

On the basis of the Nag Hammadi Scrolls alone, the possibility of a bloodline descended directly from Jesus gained considerable plausibility for us. Certain of the so-called 'Gnostic Gospels' enjoyed as great a claim to veracity as the books of the New Testament. As a result the things to which they explicitly or implicitly bore witness – a substitute on the cross, a continuing dispute between Peter and the Magdalene, a marriage between the Magdalene and Jesus, the birth of a 'son of the Son of Man' – could not be dismissed out of hand, however controversial they might be. We were dealing with history, not theology. And history, in Jesus's time, was no less complex, multi-faceted and oriented towards practicalities than it is today.

The feud, in the Nag Hammadi Scrolls, between Peter and the Magdalene apparently testified to precisely the conflict we had hypothesised – the conflict between the 'adherents of the message' – and the adherents to the bloodline. But it was the former who eventually emerged triumphant to shape the course of Western civilisation. Given their increasing monopoly of learning, communication and documentation, there remained little evidence to suggest that Jesus's family ever existed. And there was still less to establish a link between that family and the Merovingian dynasty.

Not that the 'adherents of the message' had things entirely their own way. If the first two centuries of Christian history were plagued by irrepressible heresies, the centuries that followed were even more so. While orthodoxy consolidated itself – theologically under Irenaeus, politically under Constantine – the heresies continued to proliferate on a hitherto unprecedented scale.

However much they differed in theological details, most of the major heresies shared certain crucial factors. Most of them were essentially Gnostic or Gnostic-influenced, repudiating the hierarchical structure of Rome and extolling the supremacy of personal illumination over blind faith. Most of them were also, in one sense or anther, dualist, regarding good and evil less as mundane ethical problems than as issues of ultimately cosmic import. Finally most of them concurred in regarding Jesus as mortal, born by a natural process of conception – a prophet, divinely inspired perhaps but not intrinsically divine, who died definitively on the cross or who never died on the cross at all. In their emphasis on Jesus's humanity, many of the heresies referred back to the august authority of Saint Paul, who had spoken of 'Jesus Christ our Lord, which was made of the seed of David according to the flesh' (Romans 1:3).

Perhaps the most famous and profoundly radical of the heresies was Manichaeanism – essentially a fusion of Gnostic Christianity with skeins of earlier Zoroastrian and Mithraic traditions. It was founded by an individual named Mani, who was born near Baghdad in A.D. 214 to a family related to the Persian royal house. As a youth Mani was introduced by his father into an unspecified mystical sect – probably Gnostic – which emphasised asceticism and celibacy, practised baptism and wore white robes. Around A.D. 240 Mani commenced to propagate his own teachings and, like Jesus, was renowned for his spiritual healing and exorcisms. His followers proclaimed him 'the new Jesus' and even credited him with a virgin birth – a prerequisite for deities at the time. He was also known as 'Saviour', 'Apostle', 'Illuminator', 'Lord', 'Raiser of the Dead', 'Pilot' and 'Helmsman'. The last two designations are especially suggestive, for they are interchangeable with 'Nautonier', the official title assumed by the Grand Master of the Prieuré de Sion.

According to later Arab historians Mani produced many books in which he claimed to reveal secrets Jesus had mentioned only obscurely and obliquely. He regarded Zarathustra, Buddha and Jesus as his forerunners and declared that he, like them, had received essentially the same enlightenment from the same source. His teachings consisted of a Gnostic dualism wedded to an imposing and elaborate cosmological edifice. Pervading everything was the universal conflict of light and darkness; and the most important battlefield for these two opposed principles was the human soul. Like the later Cathars, Mani espoused the doctrine of reincarnation. Like the Cathars, too, he insisted on an initiate class, an 'illuminated elect'. He referred to Jesus as the 'Son of the Widow' – a phrase subsequently appropriated by Freemasonry. At the same time he declared Jesus to be mortal – or, if divine at all, divine only in a symbolic or metaphorical sense, by virtue of enlightenment. And Mani, like Basilides, maintained that Jesus did not die on the cross, but was replaced by a substitute.[1]

In A.D. 276, by order of the king, Mani was imprisoned, flayed to death, skinned and decapitated; and, perhaps to preclude a resurrection, his mutilated body was put on public display. His teachings, however, only gained impetus from his martyrdom; and among his later adherents, at least for a time, was Saint Augustine. With extraordinary rapidity, Manichaeanism spread throughout the Christian world. Despite ferocious endeavours to suppress it, it managed to survive, to influence later thinkers and to persist up to the present day. In Spain and in the south of France Manichaean schools were particularly active. By the time of the Crusades these schools had forged links with other Manichaean sects from Italy and Bulgaria. It now appears unlikely that the Cathars were an offshoot of the Bulgarian Bogomils. On the contrary, the most recent research suggests that the Cathars arose from Manichaean schools long established in France. In any case the Albigensian Crusade was essentially a crusade against Manichaeanism; and despite the most assiduous efforts of Rome, the word 'Manichaean' has survived to become an accepted part of our language and vocabulary.

In addition to Manichaeanism, of course, there were numerous other heresies. Of them all, it was the heresy of Arius which posed the most dangerous threat to orthodox Christian doctrine during the first thousand years of its history. Arius was a presbyter in Alexandria around 318, and died in 335. His dispute with orthodoxy was quite simple and rested on a single premise – that Jesus was wholly mortal, was in no sense divine, and in no sense anything other than an inspired teacher.

By positing a single omnipotent and supreme God – a God who did not incarnate in the flesh, and did not suffer humiliation and death at the hands of his creation – Arius effectively embedded Christianity in an essentially Judaic framework. And he may well, as a resident of Alexandria, have been influenced by Judaic teachings there – the teachings of the Ebionites, for example. At the same time the supreme God of Arianism enjoyed immense appeal in the West. As Christianity came to acquire increasingly secular power, such a God became increasingly attractive. Kings and potentates could identify with such a God more readily than they could with a meek, passive deity who submitted without resistance to martyrdom and eschewed contact with the world.

Although Arianism was condemned at the Council of Nicea in 325, Constantine had already been sympathetic towards it, and became more so at the end of his life. On his death, his son and successor, Constantius, became unabashedly Arian; and under his auspices councils were convened which drove orthodox Church leaders into exile. By 360 Arianism had all but displaced Roman Christianity. And though it was officially condemned again in 381, it continued to thrive and gain adherents. When the Merovingians rose to power during the fifth century, virtually every bishopric in Christendom was either Arian or vacant.

Among the most fervent devotees of Arianism were the Goths, who had been converted to it from paganism during the fourth century. The Suevi, the Lombards, the Alans, the Vandals, the Burgundians and the Ostrogoths were all Arian. So were the Visigoths, who, when they sacked Rome in 480, spared Christian churches. If the early Merovingians, prior to Clovis, were at all receptive to Christianity, it would have been the Arian Christianity of their immediate neighbours, the Visigoths and Burgundians.

Under Visigoth auspices, Arianism became the dominant form of Christianity in Spain, the Pyrenees and what is now southern France. If Jesus's family did indeed find refuge in Gaul, their overlords, by the fifth century, would have been the Arian Visigoths. Under the Arian régime, the family is not likely to have been persecuted. It would probably have been highly esteemed and might well have intermarried with Visigoth nobility before its subsequent intermarriage with the Franks to produce the Merovingians. And with Visigoth patronage and protection, it would have been secure against all threats from Rome. It is thus not particularly surprising that unmistakably Semitic names – Bera, for instance – occur among Visigoth aristocracy and royalty. Dagobert II married a Visigoth princess whose father was named Bera. The name Bera recurs repeatedly in the Visigoth-Merovingian family tree descended from Dagobert II and Sigisbert IV.

The Roman Church is said to have declared that Dagobert's son had converted to Arianism,[2] and it would not be very extraordinary if he had done so. Despite the pact between the Church and Clovis, the Merovingians had always been sympathetic to Arianism. One of Clovis's grandsons, Chilperic, made no secret of his Arian proclivities.

If Arianism was not inimical to Judaism, neither was it to Islam, which rose so meteorically in the seventh century. The Arian view of Jesus was quite in accord with that of the Koran. In the Koran Jesus is mentioned no less than thirty-five times, under a number of impressive appellations – including 'Messenger of God' and 'Messiah'. At no point, however, is he regarded as anything other than a mortal prophet, a forerunner of Muhammad and a spokesman for a single supreme God. And like Basilides and Mani, the Koran maintains that Jesus did not die on the cross, 'they did not kill him, nor did they crucify him, but they thought they did.'[3] The Koran itself does not elaborate on this ambiguous statement, but Islamic commentators do. According to most of them, there was a substitute – generally, though not always, supposed to have been Simon of Cyrene. Certain Muslim writers speak of Jesus hiding in a niche of a wall and watching the Crucifixion of a surrogate – which concurs with the fragment already quoted from the Nag Hammadi Scrolls.

JUDAISM AND THE MEROVINGIANS

It is worth noting the tenacity, even in the face of the most vigorous persecution, with which most of the heresies – and especially Arianism – insisted on Jesus's mortality and humanity. But we found no indication that any of them necessarily possessed any first-hand knowledge of the premise to which they so persistently adhered. Still less was there any evidence, apart from the Nag Hammadi Scrolls, to suggest their awareness of a possible bloodline. It was possible, of course, that certain documents did exist – documents akin to the Nag Hammadi Scrolls, perhaps even genealogies and archives. The sheer virulence of Roman persecution might well suggest a fear of such evidence and a desire to ensure that it would never see the light. But if that was the case, Rome would appear to have succeeded.

The heresies, then, provided us with no decisive confirmation of a connection between Jesus's family and the Merovingians, who appeared on the world stage some four centuries later. For such confirmation we were obliged to look elsewhere – back to the Merovingians themselves. At first glance the evidence, such as it was, seemed to be meagre. We had already considered the legendary birth of Mérovée, for example – child of two fathers, one of whom was a mysterious aquatic creature from across the sea – and guessed that this curious fable might have been intended simultaneously to reflect and conceal a dynastic alliance or intermarriage. But, while the fish symbolism was suggestive, it was hardly conclusive. Similarly the subsequent pact between Clovis and the Roman Church made considerably more sense in the light of our scenario; but the pact itself did not constitute concrete evidence. And while the Merovingian royal blood was credited with a sacred, miraculous and divine nature, it was not explicitly stated anywhere that this blood was in fact Jesus's.

In the absence of any decisive or conclusive testimony, we had to proceed cautiously. We had to evaluate fragments of circumstantial evidence, and try to assemble these fragments into a coherent picture. And we had first to determine whether there were any uniquely Judaic influences on the Merovingians.

Certainly the Merovingian kings do not seem to have been anti-Semitic. On the contrary they seem to have been not merely tolerant, but downright sympathetic to the Jews in their domains – and this despite the assiduous protests of the Roman Church. Mixed marriages were a frequent occurrence. Many Jews, especially in the south, possessed large landed estates. Many of them owned Christian slaves and servants. And many of them acted as magistrates and high-ranking administrators for their Merovingian lords. On the whole the Merovingian attitude towards Judaism seems to have been without parallel in Western history prior to the Lutheran Reformation.

The Merovingians themselves believed their miraculous power to be vested, in large part, in their hair, which they were forbidden to cut. Their position on this matter was identical to that of the Nazorites in the Old Testament, of whom Samson was a member. There is much evidence to suggest that Jesus was also a Nazorite. According to both early Church writers and modern scholars his brother, Saint James, indisputably was.

In the Merovingian royal house, and in the families connected with it, there were a surprising number of specifically Judaic names. Thus, in 577, a brother of King Clotaire II was named Samson. Subsequently one Miron 'le Lévite' was count of Bésalou and bishop of Gerona. One count of Roussillon was named Solomon, and another Solomon became king of Brittany. There was an Abbot Elisachar – a variant of 'Eleazar' and 'Lazarus'. And the very name 'Mérovée' would seem to be of Middle Eastern derivation.[4]

Judaic names became increasingly prominent through dynastic marriages between the Merovingians and the Visigoths. Such names figure in Visigoth nobility and royalty; and it is possible that many so-called 'Visigoth' families were in fact Judaic. This possibility gains further credence from the fact that chroniclers would frequently use the words 'Goth' and 'Jew' interchangeably. The south of France and the Spanish marches – the region known as Septimania in Merovingian and Carolingian times – contained an extremely large Jewish population. This region was also known as 'Gothie' or 'Gothia', and its Jewish inhabitants were thus often called 'Goths' – an error which may, on occasion, have been deliberate. By dint of this error, Jews could not be identified as such, save perhaps by specific family names. Thus Dagobert's father-in-law was named Bera, which could be a Semitic name, it means 'son' in Aramaic. And Bera's sister was married to a member of a family named Levy.[5]

Granted, names and a mystical attitude towards one's hair were not necessarily a solid basis on which to establish a connection between the Merovingians and Judaism. But there was another fragment of evidence which was somewhat more persuasive. The Merovingians were the royal dynasty of the Franks – a Teutonic tribe which adhered to Teutonic tribal law. In the late fifth century this law, codified and couched in a Roman framework, became known as Salic Law. In its origins, however, Salic Law was ultimately Teutonic tribal law and predated the advent of Roman Christianity in Western Europe. During the centuries that followed it continued to stand in opposition to the ecclesiastical law promulgated by Rome. Throughout the Middle Ages it was the official secular law of the Holy Roman Empire. As late as the Lutheran Reformation the German peasantry and knighthood included, in their grievances against the Church, the latter's disregard for traditional Salic law.

There is one entire section of the Salic Law – Title 45, 'De Migrantibus' – which has consistently puzzled scholars and commentators, and been the source of incessant legal debate. It is a complicated section of stipulations and clauses pertaining to circumstances whereby itinerants may establish residence and be accorded citizenship. What is curious about it is that it is not Teutonic in origin, and writers have been driven to postulate bizarre hypotheses to account for its inclusion in the Salic Code. Only recently, however, it has been discovered that this section of the Salic Code derives directly from Judaic Law.[6] More specifically, it can be traced back to a section in the Talmud. It can thus be said that Salic Law, at least in part, issues directly from traditional Judaic law. And this in turn suggests that the Merovingians – under whose auspices Salic Law was codified – were not only versed in Judaic law, but had access to Judaic texts.

THE PRINCIPALITY IN SEPTIMANIA

Such fragments were provocative, but they provided only tenuous support for our hypothesis – that a bloodline descended from Jesus existed in the south of France, that this bloodline intermarried with the Merovingians and that the Merovingians, in consequence, were partly Judaic. But while the Merovingian epoch failed to provide us with any conclusive evidence for our hypothesis, the epoch which immediately followed it did. By means of this 'retroactive evidence' our hypothesis suddenly became tenable.

We had already explored the possibility of the Merovingian bloodline surviving after being deposed from its thrones by the Carolingians. In the process we had encountered an autonomous principality that existed in the south of France for a century and a half – a principality whose most famous ruler was Guillem de Gellone. Guillem was one of the most revered heroes of his age. He was also the protagonist of the *Willehalm* by Wolfram von Eschenbach, and is said to have been associated with the Grail family. It was in Guillem and his background that we found some of our most surprising and exciting evidence.

At the apex of his power Guillem de Gellone included among his domains north-eastern Spain, the Pyrenees and the region of southern France known as Septimania. This area had long contained a large Jewish population. During the sixth and seventh centuries this population had enjoyed extremely cordial relations with its Visigoth overlords, who espoused Arian Christianity – so much so, in fact, that mixed marriages were common, and the words 'Goth' and 'Jew' were often used interchangeably.

By 711, however, the situation of the Jews in Septimania and north-eastern Spain had sadly deteriorated. By that time Dagobert II had been assassinated and his lineage driven into hiding in the Razès – the region including and surrounding Rennes-le-Château. And while collateral branches of the Merovingian bloodline still nominally occupied the throne to the north, the only real power resided in the hands of the so-called Mayors of the Palace – the Carolingian usurpers who, with the sanction and support of Rome, set about establishing their own dynasty. By that time, too, the Visigoths had themselves converted to Roman Christianity and begun to persecute the Jews in their domains. Thus, when Visigoth Spain was overrun by the Moors in 711, the Jews eagerly welcomed the invaders.

Under Muslim rule the Jews of Spain enjoyed a thriving existence. The Moors were gracious to them, often placing them in administrative charge of captured cities like Córdoba, Granada and Toledo. Jewish commerce and trade were encouraged and attained a new prosperity. Judaic thought coexisted, side by side, with that of Islam, and the two cross-fertilised each other. And many towns – including Córdoba, the Moorish capital of Spain – were predominantly Jewish in population.

At the beginning of the eighth century the Moors crossed the

Pyrenees into Septimania; and from 720 until 759 – while Dagobert's grandson and great-grandson continued their clandestine existence in the Razès – Septimania was in Islamic hands. Septimania became an autonomous Moorish principality, with its own capital at Narbonne and owing only nominal allegiance to the emir of Córdoba. And from Narbonne the Moors of Septimania began to strike northwards, capturing cities as deep into Frankish territory as Lyons.

The Moorish advance was checked by Charles Martel, Mayor of the Palace and grandfather of Charlemagne. By 738 Charles had driven the Moors back to Narbonne, to which he then laid siege. Narbonne, however – defended by both Moors and Jews – proved impregnable, and Charles vented his frustration by devastating the surrounding countryside.

By 752 Charles's son, Pepin, had formed alliances with local aristocrats, thereby bringing Septimania fully under his control. Narbonne, however, continued to resist, withstanding a seven-year-long siege by Pepin's forces. The city was a painful thorn in Pepin's side, at a time when it was most urgent for him to consolidate his position. He and his successors were acutely sensitive to charges of having usurped the Merovingian throne. To establish a claim to legitimacy, he forged dynastic alliances with surviving families of the Merovingian royal blood. To further validate his status he arranged for his coronation to be distinguished by the Biblical rite of anointing – whereby the Church assumed the prerogative of creating kings. But there was another aspect to the ritual of anointing as well. According to scholars, anointing was a deliberate attempt to suggest that the Frankish monarchy was a replica, if not actually a continuation, of the Judaic monarchy in the Old Testament. This, in itself, is extremely interesting. For why would Pepin the usurper want to legitimise himself by means of a Biblical prototype? Unless the dynasty he deposed – the Merovingian dynasty – had legitimised itself by precisely the same means.

In any case Pepin was confronted by two problems – the tenacious resistance of Narbonne, and the matter of establishing his own legitimate claim to the throne by referring to Biblical precedent. As Professor Arthur Zuckerman of Columbia University has demonstrated, he resolved both problems by a pact in 759 with Narbonne's Jewish population. According to this pact, Pepin would receive Jewish endorsement for his claim to a Biblical succession. He would also receive Jewish aid against the Moors. In return he would grant the Jews of Septimania a principality, and a king, of their own.[7]

In 759 the Jewish population of Narbonne turned suddenly upon the city's Muslim defenders, slaughtered them and opened the gates of the fortress to the besieging Franks. Shortly thereafter, the Jews acknowledged Pepin as their nominal overlord and validated his claim to a legitimate Biblical succession. Pepin, in the meantime, kept his part of the bargain. In 768 a principality was created in Septimania – a Jewish principality which paid nominal allegiance to Pepin but was essentially independent. A ruler was officially installed as king of the Jews. In the romances he is called Aymery. According to existing records, however, he seems, on being received into the ranks of Frankish nobility, to have taken the name Theodoric or Thierry. Theodoric, or Thierry, was the father of Guillem de Gellone. And he was recognised by both Pepin and the caliph of Baghdad, as 'the seed of the royal house of David.'[8]

As we had already discovered, modern scholars were uncertain about Theodoric's origins and background. According to most researchers he was of Merovingian descent.[9] According to Arthur Zuckerman he is said to have been a native of Baghdad – an 'exilarch', descended from Jews who had lived in Babylon since the Babylonian Captivity. It is also possible, however, that the 'exilarch' from Baghdad was not Theodoric. It is possible that the 'exilarch' came from Baghdad to consecrate Theodoric, and subsequent records confused the two. Professor Zuckerman mentions a curious assertion that the 'Western exilarchs' were of 'purer blood' than those in the East.[10]

Who were the 'Western exilarchs', if not the Merovingians? Why would an individual of Merovingian descent be acknowledged as king of the Jews, ruler of a Jewish principality and 'seed of the royal house of David', unless the Merovingians were indeed partly Judaic? Following the Church's collusion in Dagobert's assassination and its betrayal of the pact ratified with Clovis, the surviving Merovingians may well have repudiated all allegiance to Rome – and returned to what was their former faith. Their ties to that faith would, in any case, have been strengthened by Dagobert's marriage to the daughter of an ostensibly 'Visigoth' prince with the patently Semitic name of Bera.

Theodoric, or Thierry, further consolidated his position, and Pepin's as well, by an expeditious marriage to the latter's sister – Alda, the aunt of Charlemagne. In the years that followed the Jewish kingdom of Septimania enjoyed a prosperous existence. It was richly endowed with estates held in freehold from the Carolingian monarchs. It was even granted sizeable tracts of Church land – despite the vigorous protests of Pope Stephen III and his successors.

The son of Theodoric, king of the Jews of Septimania, was Guillem de Gellone, whose titles included count of Barcelona, of Toulouse, of Auvergne – and of Razès. Like his father Guillem was not only Merovingian, but also a Jew of royal blood. Royal blood acknowledged – by the Carolingians, by the caliph and, albeit grudgingly, by the pope – to be that of the House of David.

Despite subsequent attempts to conceal it, modern scholarship and research have proved Guillem's Judaism beyond dispute. Even in the romances – where he figures as Guillaume, Prince of Orange – he is fluent in both Hebrew and Arabic. The device on his shield is the same as that of the Eastern 'exilarchs' – the Lion of Judah, the tribe to which the house of David, and subsequently Jesus, belonged. He is nicknamed 'Hook-Nose'. And even amidst his campaigns, he takes pains to observe the Sabbath and the Judaic Feast of the Tabernacles. As Arthur Zuckerman remarks:

> The chronicler who wrote the original report of the siege and
> fall of Barcelona recorded events according to the Jewish calen-
> dar . . . [The] commander of the expedition, Duke William of
> Narbonne and Toulouse conducted the action with strict obser-
> vance of Jewish sabbaths and holy Days. In all of this, he
> enjoyed the full understanding and co-operation of King Louis.[11]

Guillem de Gellone became one of the so-called 'Peers of Charlemagne' – an authentic historical hero who, in the popular mind and tradition, ranked with such legendary figures as Roland and Olivier. When Charlemagne's son, Louis, was invested as emperor, it was Guillem who placed the crown on his head. Louis is reported to have said, 'Lord William . . . it is your lineage that has raised up mine.'[12] It is an extraordinary statement, given that it is addressed to a man whose lineage – so far as later historians are concerned – would seem to be utterly obscure.

At the same time Guillem was more than a warrior. Shortly before 792 he established an academy at Gellone, importing scholars and creating a renowned library; and Gellone soon became an esteemed centre of Judaic studies. It is from just such an academy that the 'heathen' Flegetanis might have issued – the Hebrew scholar descended from Solomon, who, according to Wolfman, confided the secret of the Holy

Jewish coin of the time of Antiochus VII, 138-129 B.C. The lily, stylised here, was a symbol of Judaea and perhaps the precursor of the French fleur-de-lys.

Grail to Kyot of Provence.

In 806 Guillem withdrew from active life, secluding himself in his academy. Here, around 812, he died, and the academy was later converted into a monastery, the now famous Saint-Guilhelm-le-Désert.[13] Even before Guillem's death, however, Gellone had become one of the first known seats in Europe for the cult of the Magdalene[14] – which, significantly enough, flourished there concurrently with the Judaic academy.

Jesus was of the Tribe of Judah and the royal house of David. The Magdalene is said to have carried the Grail – the Sangraal or 'royal blood' – into France. And in the eighth century there was, in the south of France, a potentate of the Tribe of Judah and the royal house of David, who was acknowledged as king of the Jews. He was not only a practising Jew, however. He was also a Merovingian. And through Wolfram von Eschenbach's poem, he and his family are associated with the Holy Grail.

THE SEED OF DAVID

The Jewish Princedom

In later centuries assiduous attempts seem to have been made to expunge from the records all trace of the Jewish Kingdom of Septimania. The frequent confusion of 'Goths' and 'Jews' seems indicative of this censorship. But the censorship could not hope to be entirely successful. As late as 1143 Peter the Venerable of Cluny, in an address to Louis VII of France, condemned the Jews of Narbonne, who claimed to have a king residing among them. In 1144 a Cambridge monk, one Theobald, speaks of 'the chief Princes and Rabbis of the Jews who dwell in Spain [and] assemble together at Narbonne where the royal seed resides.'[15] And in 1165–6 Benjamin of Tudela, a famous traveller and chronicler, reports that in Narbonne there are 'sages, magnates and princes at the head of whom is . . . a descendant of the House of David as stated in his family tree.'[16]

But any seed of David residing in Narbonne by the twelfth century was of less consequence than certain other seed living elsewhere. Family trees bifurcate,

Untitled painting of Godefroi de Bouillon wearing the crown of thorns by Claude Vignon. It was painted around 1623 for Claude de Lorraine whose coat of arms is on the right. Claude and his brother, Charles, Duke of Guise, were tutored by Robert Fludd, alleged Grand Master of the Prieuré de Sion 1595-1637.

spread, subdivide and produce veritable forests. If certain descendants of Theodoric and Guillem de Gellone remained in Narbonne, there were others who over the intervening four centuries had attained more august domains. By the twelfth century these domains included the most illustrious in Christendom – Lorraine and the Frankish kingdom of Jerusalem.

In the ninth century the bloodline of Guillem de Gellone had culminated in the first dukes of Aquitaine. It also became aligned with the ducal house of Brittany. And in the tenth century a certain Hugues de Plantard – nicknamed 'Long Nose' and a descendant of the bloodline of both Dagobert and Guillem de Gellone – became the father of Eustache, first Count of Boulogne. Eustache's grandson was Godfroi de Bouillon,

Commencement sacr parsonange enuopa lei roys fleurs delis roi en un eseu dazeur au roy clouys.

'Legend of the Fleur-de-Lys'. A fifteenth-century illumination of the legend of the divine origins of the fleur-de-lys, a symbol of the French royal line. Clovis is shown receiving the banner from his queen, Clothilde.

Left; the coat of arms for Rennes-le-Chateau Right; The Official Device of the Prieuré de Sion

Duke of Lorraine and conqueror of Jerusalem. And from Godfroi there issued a dynasty and a 'royal tradition' which, by virtue of being founded on 'the rock of Sion', was equal to those presiding over France, England and Germany. If the Merovingians were indeed descended from Jesus, then Godfroi – scion of the Merovingian blood royal – had, in his conquest of Jerusalem, regained his rightful heritage.

Godfroi and the subsequent house of Lorraine were, of course, nominally Catholic. To survive in a now Christianised world, they would have had to be. But their origins seem to have been known about in certain quarters at least. As late as the sixteenth century it is reported that Henri de Lorraine, Duke of Guise, on entering the town of Joinville in Champagne, was received by exuberant crowds. Among them, certain individuals are recorded to have chanted 'Hosannah filio David' ('Hosannah to the Son of David').

It is not perhaps insignificant that this incident is recounted in a modern history of Lorraine, printed in 1966. The work contains a special introduction by Otto von Habsburg – who today is titular Duke of Lorraine and King of Jerusalem.[17]

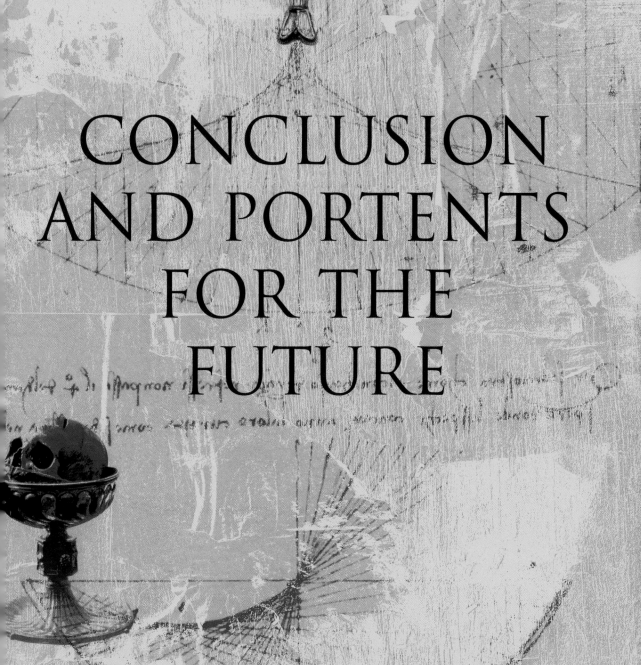

CHAPTER FIFTEEN

CONCLUSION AND PORTENTS FOR THE FUTURE

But if, for instance the statement that Christ rose from the dead is to be understood not literally but symbolically, then it is capable of various interpretations that do not conflict with knowledge and do not impair the meaning of the statement. The objection that understanding it symbolically puts an end to the Christian's hope of immortality is invalid, because long before the coming of Christianity mankind believed in a life after death and therefore had no need of the Easter event as a guarantee of immortality. The danger that a mythology understood too literally, and as taught by the Church will suddenly be repudiated lock, stock and barrel is today greater than ever. Is it not time that the Christian mythology, instead of being wiped out, was understood symbolically for once?

Carl Jung, 'The Undiscovered Self',
Collected Works, vol. 10 (1956) p. 266.

We had not, in the beginning, set out to prove or disprove anything, least of all the conclusion to which we had been ineluctably led. We had certainly not set out to challenge some of the most basic tenets of Christianity. On the contrary, we had begun by investigating a specific mystery. We were looking for answers to certain perplexing questions, explanations for certain historical enigmas. In the process we more or less stumbled upon something rather greater than we had initially bargained for. We were led to a startling, controversial and seemingly preposterous conclusion.

This conclusion compelled us to turn our attention to the life of Jesus and the origins of the religion founded upon him. When we did so, we were still not attempting to challenge Christianity. We were simply endeavouring to ascertain whether or not our conclusion was tenable. An exhaustive consideration of Biblical material convinced us that it was. Indeed we became convinced that our conclusion was not only tenable, but extremely probable.

We could not – and still cannot – prove the accuracy of our conclusion. It remains, to some extent at least, an hypothesis. But it is a plausible hypothesis, which makes coherent sense. It explains a great deal. And, so far as we are concerned, it constitutes a more historically likely account than any we have encountered of the events and personages which, two thousand years ago, imprinted themselves on Western consciousness – and, in the centuries that followed, shaped our culture and civilisation.

If we cannot prove our conclusion, however, we have received abundant evidence – from both their documents and their representatives – that the Prieuré de Sion can. On the basis of their written hints and their personal conversation with us, we are prepared to believe that Sion does possess something – something which does in some way amount to 'incontrovertible proof' of the hypothesis we have advanced. We do not know precisely what this proof might be. We can, however, make an educated guess.

If our hypothesis is correct, Jesus's wife and offspring (and he could have fathered a number of children between the ages of sixteen or seventeen and his supposed death), after fleeing the Holy Land, found a refuge in the south of France, and in a Jewish community there preserved their lineage. During the fifth century this lineage appears to have intermarried with the royal line of the Franks, thus engendering the Merovingian dynasty. In A.D. 496 the Church made a pact with this dynasty, pledging itself in perpetuity to the Merovingian bloodline – presumably in the full knowledge of that bloodline's true identity. This would explain why Clovis was offered the status of Holy Roman Emperor, of 'new Constantine', and why he was not created king, but only recognised as such.

When the Church colluded in Dagobert's assassination, and the subsequent betrayal of the Merovingian bloodline, it rendered itself guilty of a crime that could neither be rationalised nor expunged. It could only be suppressed. It would have had to be suppressed – for a disclosure of the Merovingians' real identity would hardly have strengthened Rome's position against her enemies.

Despite all efforts to eradicate it, Jesus's bloodline – or, at any rate, the Merovingian bloodline – survived. It survived in part through the Carolingians, who clearly felt more guilty about their usurpation than did Rome, and sought to legitimise themselves by dynastic alliances with Merovingian princesses. But more significantly it survived through Dagobert's son, Sigisbert, whose descendants included Guillem de Gellone, ruler of the Jewish kingdom of Septimania, and eventually Godfroi de Bouillon. With Godfroi's capture of Jerusalem in 1099, Jesus's lineage would have regained its rightful heritage – the heritage conferred upon it in Old Testament times.

It is doubtful that Godfroi's true pedigree during the time of the Crusades was as secret as Rome would have wished it to be. Given the Church's hegemony, there could not, of course, have been an overt disclosure. But it is probable that rumours, traditions and legends were rife; and these would seem to have found their most prominent expression in such tales as that of Lohengrin, for example, Godfroi's mythical ancestor – and, naturally, in the romances of the Holy Grail.

If our hypothesis is correct, the Holy Grail would have been at least two things simultaneously. On the one hand it would have been Jesus's bloodline and descendants – the 'Sang Raal', the 'Real' or 'Royal' blood of which the Templars, created by the Prieuré de Sion, were appointed guardians. At the same time the Holy Grail would have been, quite literally, the receptacle, or vessel, which received and contained Jesus's blood. In other words it would have been the womb of the Magdalene – and, by extension, the Magdalene herself. From this the cult of the Magdalene, as it was promulgated during the Middle Ages, would have arisen – and been confused with the cult of the Virgin. It can be proved, for instance, that many of the famous 'Black Virgins' or 'Black Madonnas' early in the Christian era were shrines not to the Virgin but to the Magdalene – and they depict a mother and child. It has also been argued that the Gothic cathedrals – those majestic stone replicas of the womb dedicated to 'Notre Dame' – were also, as *Le Serpent rouge* states, shrines to Jesus's consort, rather than to his mother.

The Holy Grail, then, would have symbolised both Jesus's bloodline and the Magdalene, from whose womb that bloodline issued. But it may have been something else as well. In A.D. 70, during the great revolt in Judaea, Roman legions under Titus sacked the Temple of Jerusalem. The pillaged treasure of the Temple is said to have found its way eventually to the Pyrenees; and M. Plantard, in his conversation with us, stated that this treasure was in the hands of the Prieuré de Sion today. But the Temple of Jerusalem may have contained more than the treasure plundered by Titus's centurions. In ancient Judaism religion and politics were inseparable. The Messiah was to be a priest-king, whose authority encompassed spiritual and secular domains alike. It is thus likely, indeed probable, that the Temple housed official records pertaining to Israel's royal line – the equivalents of the birth certificates, marriage licences and other relevant data concerning any modern royal or aristocratic family. If Jesus was indeed 'King of the Jews' the Temple is almost certain to have contained copious information relating to him. It may even have contained his body – or at least his tomb, once his body was removed from the temporary tomb of the Gospels.

There is no indication that Titus, when he plundered the Temple in

A.D. 70, obtained anything in any way relevant to Jesus. Such material, if it existed, might of course have been destroyed. On the other hand it might also have been hidden; and Titus's soldiers, interested only in booty, might not have bothered to look for it. For any priest in the Temple at the time, there would have been one obvious course of action. Seeing a phalanx of centurions advancing upon him, he would have left them the gold, the jewels, the material treasures they expected to find. And he would have hidden, perhaps beneath the Temple, the items that were of greater consequence – items relating to the rightful king of Israel, the acknowledged Messiah and the royal family.

By 1100 Jesus's descendants would have risen to prominence in Europe and, through Godfroi de Bouillon, in Palestine as well. They themselves would have known their pedigree and ancestry. But they might not have been able to prove their identity to the world at large; and such proof may well have been deemed necessary for their subsequent designs. If it were known that such proof existed, or even possibly existed, in the precincts of the Temple, no effort would have been spared to find it. This would explain the role of the Knights Templar – who, under a cloak of secrecy, undertook excavations beneath the Temple, in the so-called Stables of Solomon. On the basis of the evidence we examined, there would seem to be little question that the Knights Templar were in fact sent to the Holy Land – with the express purpose of finding or obtaining something. And on the basis of the evidence we examined, they would seem to have accomplished their mission. They would seem to have found what they were sent to find, and to have brought it back to Europe. What became of it then remains a mystery. But there seems little question that, under the auspices of Bertrand de Blanchefort, fourth Grand Master of the Order of the Temple, something was concealed in the vicinity of Rennes-le-Château for which a contingent of German miners was imported, under the most stringent security, to excavate and construct a hiding-place. One can only speculate about what might have been concealed there. It may have been Jesus's mummified body. It may have been the equivalent, so to speak, of Jesus's marriage licence, and/or the birth certificates of his children. It may have been something of comparably explosive import. Any or all of these items might have been referred to as the Holy Grail. Any or all of these items might, by accident or design, have passed to the Cathar heretics and comprised part of the mysterious treasure of Montségur.

Through Godfroi and Baudouin de Bouillon, a 'royal tradition' is said to have existed – which, because it was 'founded on the Rock of Sion', equalled in status the foremost dynasties of Europe. If – as the New Testament and later Freemasonry maintain – the 'Rock of Sion' is synonymous with Jesus, that assertion would suddenly make sense. Indeed it would be, if anything, an understatement.

Once installed on the throne of the kingdom of Jerusalem, the Merovingian dynasty could sanction and even encourage hints about its true ancestry. This would explain why the Grail romances appeared precisely when and where they did, and why they were so explicitly associated with the Knights Templar. In time, once its position in Palestine was consolidated, the 'royal tradition' descended from Godfroi and Baudouin would probably have divulged its origins. The king of Jerusalem would then have taken precedence over all the monarchs of Europe, and the patriarch of Jerusalem would have supplanted the pope. Displacing Rome, Jerusalem would then have become the true capital of Christendom, and perhaps of much more than Christendom. For if Jesus were acknowledged as a mortal prophet, as a priest-king and legitimate ruler of the line of David, he might well have become acceptable to both Muslims and Jews. As king of Jerusalem, his lineal descendant would then have been in a position to implement one of the primary tenets of Templar policy – the reconciliation of Christianity with Judaism and Islam.

Historical circumstances, of course, never allowed matters to reach this point. The Frankish kingdom of Jerusalem never consolidated its position. Beleaguered on every side by Muslim armies, unstable in its own government and administration, it never attained the strength and internal security it needed to survive – still less to assert its supremacy over the crowns of Europe and the Church of Rome. The grandiose design foundered; and with the loss of the Holy Land in 1291 it collapsed completely. The Merovingians were once again without a crown. And the Knights Templar were not only redundant but also expendable.

In the centuries that followed, the Merovingians – aided and/or directed and/or protected by the Prieuré de Sion – made repeated attempts to regain their heritage, but these attempts were confined to Europe. They seem to have involved at least three interrelated but essentially distinct programmes. One was the creation of a psychological atmosphere, a clandestine tradition intended to erode the spiritual hegemony of Rome – a tradition that found expression in Hermetic and esoteric thought, in the Rosicrucian manifestos and similar writings, in certain rites of Freemasonry and, of course, in the symbols of Arcadia and the underground stream. A second programme entailed political machination, intrigue and, if feasible, an overt seizure of power – the techniques employed by the Guise and Lorraine families in the sixteenth century, and by the architects of the Fronde in the seventeenth. A third programme by which the Merovingians sought to regain their heritage was dynastic intermarriage.

On first consideration it might seem that such Byzantine procedures would have been unnecessary; it might seem that the Merovingians – if they were indeed descended from Jesus – would have had no trouble establishing their supremacy. They needed only to disclose and establish their real identity, and the world would acknowledge them. In fact, however, things would not have been so simple. Jesus himself was not recognised by the Romans. When it was expedient to do so, the Church had no compunction in sanctioning the murder of Dagobert and the overthrow of his bloodline. A premature disclosure of their pedigree would not have guaranteed success for the Merovingians. On the contrary, it would have been much more likely to misfire – to engender factional strife, precipitate a crisis in faith, and provoke challenges from both the Church and other secular potentates. Unless they were well entrenched in positions of power, the Merovingians could not have withstood such repercussions – and the secret of their identity, their trump card, as it were, would have been played and lost for ever. Given the realities of both history and politics, this trump card could not have been used as a stepping stone to power. It could only be played when power had already been acquired – played, in other words, from a position of strength.

In order to re-establish themselves, therefore, the Merovingians were obliged to resort to more conventional procedures – the accepted procedures of the particular age in question. On at least four occasions these procedures came frustratingly close to success, and were thwarted only by miscalculation, by force of circumstance or by the totally unforeseen. In the sixteenth century, for example, the house of Guise very nearly managed to seize the French throne. In the seventeenth century the Fronde very nearly succeeded in keeping Louis XIV from the throne and supplanting him with a representative of the house of Lorraine. In the late nineteenth century blueprints were laid for a species of revived Holy League, which would have unified Catholic Europe – Austria, France, Italy and Spain – under the Habsburgs. These plans were thwarted by the erratic and aggressive behaviour of both Germany and Russia – who provoked a constant shift of alliances among the major powers and eventually precipitated a war which toppled all the continental dynasties.

It was in the eighteenth century, however, that the Merovingian bloodline probably came closest to the realisation of its objectives. By virtue of its intermarriage with the Habsburgs, the house of Lorraine had actually acquired the throne of Austria, the Holy Roman Empire. When Marie Antoinette, daughter of François de Lorraine, became queen of France the throne of France, too, was only a generation or so away. Had not the French Revolution intervened, the house of Habsburg–Lorraine might well, by the early 1800s, have been on its way to establishing dominion over all Europe.

It would seem clear that the French Revolution was a devastating blow to Merovingian hopes and aspirations. In a single shattering cataclysm, the carefully laid and implemented designs of a century and a half were suddenly reduced to rubble. From references in the 'Prieuré documents', moreover, it would seem that Sion, during the turmoil of the Revolution, lost many of its most precious records – and possibly other items as well. This might explain the shift in the Order's Grand Mastership – to specifically French cultural figures who, like Nodier, had access to otherwise unobtainable material. It might also explain the role of Saunière. Saunière's predecessor, Antoine Bigou, had concealed, and possibly composed, the coded parchments on the very eve of the Revolution – and then fled to Spain, where, shortly after, he died. It is thus possible that Sion, for a time at any rate, did not know precisely where the parchments were. But even if they were known to have been in the church at Rennes-le-Château, they could not easily have been retrieved without a sympathetic priest on the spot – a man who would do Sion's bidding, refrain from embarrassing questions, keep silence, and not interfere with the Order's interests and activities. If the parchments, moreover, referred to something else – something concealed in the vicinity of Rennes-le-Château, such a man would have been all the more essential.

Saunière died without divulging his secret. So did his housekeeper, Marie Denarnaud. During the ensuing years there have been many excavations in the vicinity of Rennes-le-Château, but none of them has yielded anything. If, as we assume, certain explosive items were once concealed in the environs, they would certainly have been removed when Saunière's story began to attract attention and treasure-hunters – unless these items were concealed in some depository immune to treasure-hunters, in an underground crypt, for example, under a man-made pool on private property. Such a crypt would ensure safety and be proof against any unauthorised excavations. No such excavations would be possible unless the pool were first drained; and this could hardly be done clandestinely – especially by trespassers on private land. In fact a man-made pool does exist near Rennes-le-Château – near a site called, appropriately enough, Lavaldieu (the Valley or Vale of God). This pool might well have been constructed over an underground crypt – which, in turn, might easily lead via a subterranean passageway to any of the myriad caves honeycombing the surrounding mountains.

As for the parchments found by Saunière, two of them – or, at any rate, facsimiles of two of them – have been reproduced, published and widely circulated. The other two, in contrast, have been kept scrupulously secret. In his conversation with us M. Plantard stated that they are currently in a safe deposit box in a Lloyds' bank in London. Further than that we have been unable to trace them.

And Saunière's money? We know that some of it seems to have been obtained through a financial transaction involving the Archduke Johann von Habsburg. We also know that substantial sums were made available not only to Saunière, but also to the bishop of Carcassonne, by the Abbé Henri Boudet, curé of Rennes-les-Bains. There is reason to conclude that the bulk of Saunière's revenue was paid to him by Boudet, through the intermediary Marie Denarnaud, Saunière's housekeeper. Where Boudet – a poor parish priest himself – obtained such resources remains, of course, a mystery. He would clearly seem to have been a representative of the Prieuré de Sion; but whether the money issued directly from Sion remains an unanswered question. It might equally well have issued from the treasury of the Habsburgs. Or it might have issued from the Vatican, which might have been subjected to high-level political blackmail by both Sion and the Habsburgs. In any case, the question of the money, or a treasure that engendered it, became, for us, increasingly incidental, when measured against our subsequent discoveries. Its chief function, in retrospect, had been to draw our attention to the mystery. After that, it paled to relative insignificance.

We have formulated an hypothesis of a bloodline, descended from Jesus, which has continued up to the present day. We cannot, of course, be certain that our hypothesis is correct in every detail. But even if specific details here and there are subject to modification, we are convinced that the essential outlines of our hypothesis are accurate. We may perhaps have misconstrued the meaning of, say, a particular Grand Master's activities, or an alliance in the power struggles and political machinations of eighteenth-century politics. But our researches have persuaded us that the mystery of Rennes-le-Château does involve a serious attempt, by influential people, to re-establish a Merovingian monarchy in France if not indeed in the whole of Europe – and that the claim to legitimacy of such a monarchy rests on a Merovingian descent from Jesus.

During a publicity trip to the continent for a foreign-language edition of *Holy Blood, Holy Grail*, one of us found himself in a television studio with a prominent nobleman, political 'grandee' and commentator. This distinguished individual had read our book and was eager to talk about it. As a young man, he said, prior to the Second World War, he had been in the service of his country's monarch at the time. In conversation on one occasion, our informant had asked the king which of his numerous titles he deemed most important. 'Duke of Lorraine,' the king had replied promptly (even though his claim to this title could have been disputed). When our informant asked why, the king had replied: 'Because it was the first title in Europe' – 'first', in this context, presumably meaning 'premier'. Shortly thereafter, our informant had reported this dialogue to a colleague, a fellow courtier. The latter had replied mysteriously: 'Well, of course, he is of the Secret.' Not until he read our book, our informant observed, did the meaning of those cryptic conversations become apparent to him.

Viewed from this perspective a number of the anomalies, enigmas and unanswered questions raised by our researches become explicable. So do a great many of the seemingly trivial but equally baffling fragments: the title of the book associated with Nicolas Flamel, for example – *The Sacred Book of Abraham the Jew, Prince, Priest, Levite, Astrologer and Philosopher to the Tribe of Jews who by the Wrath of God were Dispersed amongst the Gauls*; or the symbolic Grail cup of René d'Anjou, which vouchsafed, to the man who quaffed it at a single draught, a vision of both God and the Magdalene; or Andrea's *Chemical Wedding of Christian*

The Coronation of Napoleon as painted by Jacques-Louis David who emphasised the gold bees on Napoleon's robe. Above David's studio a secret society met regularly.

Rosenkreuz, which speaks of a mysterious girl-child of royal blood, washed ashore in a boat, whose rightful heritage has fallen into Islamic hands; or the secret to which Poussin was privy – as well as the 'Secret' said to 'lie at the heart' of the Compagnie du Saint-Sacrement.

During the course of our research we had encountered a number of other fragments as well. At the time they had seemed either totally meaningless or irrelevant. Now, however, they, too, make sense. Thus it would now seem clear why Louis XI regarded the Magdalene as a source of the French royal line – a belief which, even in the context of the fifteenth century, at first appeared absurd.[1] It would also be apparent why the crown of Charlemagne – a replica of which is now part of the imperial Habsburg regalia – is said to have borne the inscription 'Rex Salomon'.[2] And it would be apparent why the *Protocols of the Elders of Sion* speak of a new king 'of the holy seed of David'.[3]

During the Second World War, for reasons that have never been satisfactorily explained, the Cross of Lorraine became the symbol of the forces of Free France, under the leadership of Charles de Gaulle. In itself this is somewhat curious. Why should the Cross of Lorraine – the device of René d'Anjou – have been equated with France? Lorraine was never the heartland of France. For most of her history, in fact, Lorraine was an independent duchy, a Germanic state comprising part of the old Holy Roman Empire.

In part the Cross of Lorraine may have been adopted because of the important role the Prieuré de Sion seems to have played in the French Resistance. In part it may have been adopted because of General de Gaulle's association with members of the Prieuré de Sion – like M. Plantard. But it is interesting that, nearly thirty years before, the Cross of Lorraine figured provocatively in a poem by Charles Péguy. Not long before his death at the Battle of the Marne in 1914, Péguy – a close friend of Maurice Barrès, author of *La Colline inspirée* – composed the following lines:

Les armes de Jésus c'est la croix de Lorraine,
Et le sang dans l'artère et le sang dans la veine,
Et la source de grâce et la claire fontaine;

Les armes de Satan c'est la croix de Lorraine,
Et c'est la même artère et c'est la même veine
Et c'est la même sang et la trouble fontaine . . .

(The arms of Jesus are the Cross of Lorraine,
Both the blood in the artery and the blood in the vein,
Both the source of grace and the clear fountain;

The arms of Satan are the Cross of Lorraine,

And the same artery and the same vein,
And the same blood and the troubled fountain . . .)[4]

In the late seventeenth century the Reverend Father Vincent, an historian and antiquarian in Nancy, wrote a history of Sion in Lorraine. He
also wrote another work, entitled *The True History of Saint Sigisbert*,
which also contains an account of the life of Dagobert II.[5] On the title
page of this latter work there is an epigraph, a quotation from the
Fourth Gospel, 'He is among you and you do not know Him.'

Even before we began our research, we ourselves were agnostic, neither
pro-Christian nor anti-Christian. By virtue of our background and
study of comparative religions we were sympathetic to the core of
validity inherent in most of the world's major faiths, and indifferent to
the dogma, the theology, the accoutrements which comprise their
superstructure. And while we could accord respect to almost every
creed, we could not accord to any of them a monopoly on truth.

Thus, when our research led us to Jesus, we could approach him
with what we hoped was a sense of balance and perspective. We had no
prejudices or preconceptions one way or the other, no vested interests
of any kind, nothing to be gained by either proving or disproving anything. In so far as 'objectivity' is possible, we were able to approach
Jesus 'objectively' – as an historian would be expected to approach
Alexander, for example, or Caesar. And the conclusions that forced
themselves upon us, though certainly startling, were not shattering.
They did not necessitate a reappraisal of our personal convictions or
shake our personal hierarchies of values.

But what of other people? What of the millions of individuals across
the world for whom Jesus is the Son of God, the Saviour, the Redeemer?
To what extent does the historical Jesus, the priest-king who emerged
from our research, threaten their faith? To what extent have we violated
what constitutes for many people their most cherished understanding
of the sacred?

We are well aware, of course, that our research has led us to conclusions that, in many respects, are inimical to certain basic tenets of modern Christianity – conclusions that are heretical, perhaps even blasphemous. From the standpoint of certain established dogma we are no
doubt guilty of such transgressions. But we do not believe that we have
desecrated, or even diminished, Jesus in the eyes of those who do gen-

uinely revere him. And while we ourselves cannot subscribe to Jesus's divinity, our conclusions do not preclude others from doing so. Quite simply, there is no reason why Jesus could not have married and fathered children, while still retaining his divinity. There is no reason why his divinity should be dependent on sexual chastity. Even if he were the Son of God, there is no reason why he should not have wed and begun a family.

Underlying most Christian theology is the assumption that Jesus is God incarnate. In other words God, taking pity on His creation, incarnated Himself in that creation and assumed human form. By doing so He would be able to acquaint Himself at first-hand, so to speak, with the human condition. He would experience at first-hand the vicissitudes of human existence. He would come to understand, in the most profound sense, what it means to be a man – to confront from a human standpoint the loneliness, the anguish, the helplessness, the tragic mortality that the status of manhood entails. By dint of becoming man God would come to know man in a way that the Old Testament does not allow. Renouncing His Olympian aloofness and remoteness, He would partake, directly, of man's lot. By doing so, He would redeem man's lot – would validate and justify it by partaking of it, suffering from it and eventually being sacrificed by it.

The symbolic significance of Jesus is that he is God exposed to the spectrum of human experiences – exposed to the first-hand knowledge of what being a man entails. But could God, incarnate as Jesus, truly claim to be a man, to encompass the spectrum of human experience, without coming to know two of the most basic, most elemental facets of the human condition? Could God claim to know the totality of human existence without confronting two such essential aspects of humanity as sexuality and paternity?

We do not think so. In fact, we do not think the Incarnation truly symbolises what it is intended to symbolise unless Jesus were married and fathered children. The Jesus of the Gospels, and of established Christianity, is ultimately incomplete – a God whose incarnation as man is only partial. The Jesus who emerged from our research enjoys, in our opinion, a much more valid claim to what Christianity would have him be.

On the whole, then, we do not think we have compromised or belittled Jesus. We do not think he has suffered from the conclusions to which our research led us. From our investigations emerges a living and plausible Jesus – a Jesus whose life is both meaningful and comprehensible to modern man.

We cannot point to one man and assert that he is Jesus's lineal descendant. Family trees bifurcate, subdivide and in the course of centuries multiply into veritable forests. There are at least a dozen families in Britain and Europe today – with numerous collateral branches – who are of Merovingian lineage. These include the houses of Habsburg–Lorraine (present titular dukes of Lorraine and kings of Jerusalem), Plantard, Luxembourg, Montpézat, Montesquieu and various others. According to the 'Prieuré documents', the Sinclair family in Britain is also allied to the bloodline, as are the various branches of the Stuarts. And the Devonshire family, among others, would seem to have been privy to the secret. Most of these houses could presumably claim a pedigree from Jesus; and if one man, at some point in the future, is to be put forward as a new priest-king, we do not know who he is.

But several things, at any rate, are clear. So far as we personally are concerned, Jesus's lineal descendant would not be any more divine, any more intrinsically miraculous, than the rest of us. This attitude would undoubtedly be shared by a great many people today. We suspect it is shared by the Prieuré de Sion as well. Moreover the revelation of an individual, or group of individuals, descended from Jesus would not shake the world in the way it might have done as recently as a century or two ago. Even if there were 'incontrovertible proof' of such a lineage, many people would simply shrug and ask, 'So what?' As a result there would seem to be little point in the Prieuré de Sion's elaborate designs – unless those designs are in some crucial way linked with politics. Whatever the theological repercussions of our conclusions, there would seem, quite clearly, to be other repercussions as well – political repercussions with a potentially enormous impact, affecting the thinking, the values, the institutions of the contemporary world in which we live.

Certainly in the past, the various families of Merovingian descent were thoroughly steeped in politics, and their objectives included political power. This would also seem to have been true of the Prieuré de Sion and a number of its Grand Masters. There is no reason to assume that politics should not be equally important to both Sion and the bloodline today. Indeed all the evidence suggests that Sion thinks in terms of a unity between what used to be called Church and State – a unity of secular and spiritual, sacred and profane, politics and religion.

In many of its documents Sion asserts that the new king, in accordance with Merovingian tradition, would 'rule but not govern'. In other words he would be a priest-king, who functions primarily in a ritual and symbolic capacity; and the actual business of governing would be handled by someone else – conceivably by the Prieuré de Sion.

During the nineteenth century the Prieuré de Sion, working through Freemasonry and the Hiéron du Val d'Or, attempted to establish a revived and 'updated' Holy Roman Empire – a kind of theocratic United States of Europe, ruled simultaneously by the Habsburgs and by a radically reformed Church. This enterprise was thwarted by the First World War and the fall of Europe's reigning dynasties. But it is not unreasonable to suppose that Sion's present objectives are basically similar – at least in their general outlines – to those of the Hiéron du Val d'Or.

Needless to say, our understanding of those objectives can only be speculative. But they would seem to include a theocratic United States of Europe – a trans- or pan-European confederation assembled into a modern empire and ruled by a dynasty descended from Jesus. This dynasty would not only occupy a throne of political or secular power, but, quite conceivably, the throne of Saint Peter as well. Under that supreme authority there might then be an interlocking network of kingdoms or principalities, connected by dynastic alliance and intermarriage – a kind of twentieth-century 'feudal system', but without the abuses usually associated with that term. And the actual process of governing would presumably reside with the Prieuré de Sion – which might take the form of, say, a European Parliament endowed with executive and/or legislative powers.

A Europe of this sort would constitute a new and unified political force in international affairs – an entity whose status would ultimately be comparable to that of the Soviet Union, or the United States. Indeed it might well emerge stronger than either, because it would rest on deep-rooted spiritual and emotional foundations, rather than on abstract, theoretical or ideological ones. It would appeal not only to man's head, but to his heart as well. It would draw its strength from tapping the collective psyche of Western Europe, awakening the fundamental religious impulse.

Such a programme may well appear quixotic. But history by now should have taught us not to underestimate the potential of the collective psyche, and the power to be obtained by harnessing it. A few years ago it would have seemed inconceivable that a religious zealot – without an army of his own, without a political party behind him, without anything at his disposal save charisma and the religious hunger of a people – could single-handedly topple the modern and superbly equipped edifice of the Shah's régime in Iran. And yet that is precisely what the Ayatollah Khomeini managed to do.

We are not, of course, sounding a warning. We are not, implicitly or explicitly, comparing the Prieuré de Sion to the Ayatollah. We have no reason to think Sion sinister – as one might the demagogue of Iran. But the demagogue of Iran bears eloquent witness to the deep-rooted character, the energy, the potential power of a man's religious impulse – and the ways in which that impulse can be channelled to political ends. Such ends need not entail an abuse of authority. They may be as laudable as those of Churchill or de Gaulle were during the Second World War. The religious impulse can be channelled in any of innumerable directions. It is a source of immense potential power. And it is all too often ignored or overlooked by modern governments founded on, and often fettered to, reason alone. The religious impulse reflects a profound psychological and emotional need. And psychological and emotional needs are every bit as real as the need for bread, for shelter, for material security.

We know that the Prieuré de Sion is not a 'lunatic fringe' organisation. We know it is well financed and includes – or, at any rate, commands sympathy from – men in responsible and influential positions in politics, economics, media, the arts. We know that since 1956 it has increased its membership more than fourfold, as if it were mobilising or preparing for something; and M. Plantard told us personally that he and his Order were working to a more or less precise timetable. We also know that since 1956 Sion has been making certain information available – discreetly, tantalisingly, in piecemeal fashion, in measured quantities just sufficient to provide alluring hints. Those hints provoked this book.

If the Prieuré de Sion intends to 'show its cards', the time is ripe for it to do so. The political systems and ideologies which, in the early years of the last century, seemed to promise so much have virtually all displayed a degree of bankruptcy. Communism, socialism, fascism, capitalism, Western-style democracy have all, in one way or another, betrayed their promise, jaundiced their adherents and failed to fulfil the dreams they engendered. Because of their small-mindedness, lack of perspective and abuse of office, politicians no longer inspire confidence, only distrust. In the West today there is increasing cynicism, dissatisfaction and disillusion. There is increasing psychic stress, anxiety and despair. But there is also an intensifying quest for meaning, for emotional fulfilment, for a spiritual dimension to our lives, for something in which genuinely to believe. There is a longing for a renewed sense of the sacred that amounts, in effect, to a full-scale religious revival – exemplified by the proliferation of sects and cults, for example, and the swelling tide of fundamentalism in the United States. There is also, increasingly, a desire for a true 'leader' – not a Führer, but a species of wise and benign spiritual figure, a 'priest-king' in whom mankind can safely repose its trust. Our civilisation has sated itself with materialism and in the process become aware of a more profound hunger. It is now beginning to look elsewhere, seeking the fulfilment of emotional, psychological and spiritual needs.

Such an atmosphere would seem eminently conducive to the Prieuré de Sion's objectives. It places Sion in the position of being able to offer an alternative to existing social and political systems. Such an alternative is hardly likely to constitute Utopia or the New Jerusalem. But to the extent that it satisfies needs which existing systems do not even acknowledge it could well prove immensely attractive.

There are many devout Christians who do not hesitate to interpret the Apocalypse as nuclear holocaust. How might the advent of Jesus's lineal descendant be interpreted? To a receptive audience, it might be a kind of Second Coming.

THE END

POSTSCRIPT

Since the publication of our book, much new material has been forthcoming. Some readers, with extremely important new information, have been open and generous in passing it on to us. Others have preferred to be cryptic, enigmatic and elliptical, speaking mysteriously of unspecified knowledge they possess, or unspecified research they have done which has led to equally unspecified conclusions of a startling/amazing/shattering/definitive nature. Such hints may indeed attest to new and valid material or to an irrelevant intellectual ingenuity and a need for spurious mystification.

In any case, we have received letters from people so aggressively over-cautious and secretive that we wonder why they bothered to write to us at all. Their shroud of obscurity and opacity seems to have been generated by a fear (verging sometimes on paranoia) that they may be deprived, unscrupulously, of the fruits of their work – that we might steal the results of their research, or their decipherments, or the treasures they are convinced they have located, and leave them unacknowledged, unrecognised, unrewarded.

In *Holy Blood, Holy Grail*, we have presented our material openly. We have also supplied information about relevant sources, in order that others may be stimulated to research of their own. The time for mystification is now past. We hope that readers who have what they consider worthwhile material will be as forthcoming as we have tried to be. We urge them, if possible, to publish it themselves. Alternatively, we request them to make their findings available to us.

We hereby publicly state that no such material will be published, used or exploited by us unless some prior and mutually acceptable arrangement has been concluded with those who provide it. We also publicly state that all such material, if used by us in any way, will be duly acknowledged in a fashion that is likewise mutually acceptable. We would also like to state that we have NO interest, beyond the historical and archaeological, in any 'treasure' uncovered in connection with Rennes-le-Château. We wish only to observe and record such discoveries as and when they might be made. Any cash rewards accruing from any 'treasure' would remain with those whose information leads to the location of the relevant site.

APPENDICES

APPENDIX 1:

JEAN DE GISORS. According to the 'Prieuré documents', Jean de Gisors was Sion's first independent Grand Master, assuming his position after the 'cutting of the elm' and the separation from the Knights Templar in 1188. He was born in 1133 and died in 1220. He was at least nominal lord of the fortress of Gisors in Normandy – where meetings were traditionally convened between English and French kings and where, in 1188, a curious squabble did occur which involved the cutting of an elm. Until 1193 Jean was a vassal of the king of England – Henry II, and then Richard I. He also possessed property in England – in Sussex, and the manor of Titchfield in Hampshire. According to the 'Prieuré documents', he met with Thomas à Becket in 1169. No independent record of this meeting survives, but Becket was at Gisors in 1169 and must have had some contact with the lord of the fortress.

MARIE DE SAINT-CLAIR. Information on Marie de Saint-Clair was even more meagre than information on Jean de Gisors. Born around 1192, she was descended from Henry de Saint-Clair, Baron of Rosslyn in Scotland, who accompanied Godfroi de Bouillon on the First Crusade. Rosslyn itself was situated not far from the Templars' major preceptory in Scotland, and Rosslyn Chapel, built in the fifteenth century, became mantled with Rose-Croix and Freemasonry legends. Marie de Saint-Clair's grandmother married into the French Chaumont family – as did Jean de Gisors. The genealogies of the Chaumont, Gisors and Saint-Clair families were thus closely intertwined. There is some evidence that Marie de

Saint-Clair was, in fact, Jean de Gisors' second wife, but we could not confirm this definitely. According to the genealogies in the 'Prieuré documents', Marie's mother was one Isabel Levis. This surname, which would seem to be of Judaic origin, occurs frequently in the Languedoc, where there were Jewish settlements dating from before the Christian epoch.

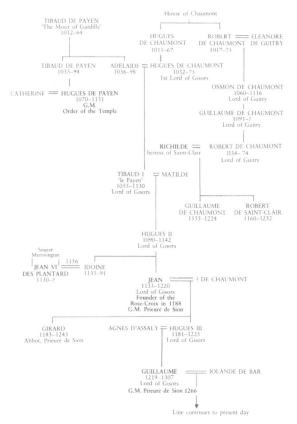

Families of Gisors, Payen amd Saint-Clair

GUILLAUME DE GISORS. Guillaume de Gisors, Jean de Gisors' grandson, was born in 1219. We had already encountered his name in connection with the mysterious head found in the Templars' Paris preceptory after the arrests in 1307. Apart from this, however, we found only one external mention of him, on a deed dated 1244, which states that he was a knight. According to the genealogies in the 'Prieuré documents', his sister married one Jean des Plantard. The 'Prieuré documents' also state that Guillaume was inducted into the Order of the Ship and the Double Crescent in 1269. This Order was created by Louis IX (Saint Louis) for nobles who accompanied him on the ill-fated Sixth Crusade. If Guillaume de Gisors was a member of it, he must therefore have been with Saint Louis during the campaign in Egypt.

EDOUARD DE BAR. Born in 1302, Edouard, Comte de Bar, was a grandson of Edward I of England and a nephew of Edward II. He was descended from a family which had been influential in the Ardennes since Merovingian times and was almost certainly connected with the Merovingian dynasty. Edouard's daughter married into the house of Lorraine, and the genealogies of Bar and Lorraine subsequently became closely intertwined.

In 1308, at the age of six (!), Edouard accompanied the duke of Lorraine into battle, was captured and not ransomed until 1314. On attaining his majority he purchased the seigneury of Stenay from one of his uncles, Jean de Bar. In 1324 he was allied in military operations with Ferry de Lorraine and Jean de Luxembourg – and the house of Luxembourg, like that of Lorraine, would seem to be of Merovingian blood. In 1336 Edouard died in a shipwreck off the coast of Cyprus.

No independent source could provide us with any link between Edouard de Bar and Guillaume de Gisors. According to the genealogies in the 'Prieuré documents', however, Edouard was grand-nephew of Guillaume's wife, Iolande de Bar. While we could not confirm this affiliation,

we found nothing to contradict it.

If, as the 'Prieuré documents' maintain, Edouard assumed Sion's Grand Mastership in 1307, he would have done so at the age of five. This is not necessarily improbable, if he was captured on the battlefield at the age of six. Until Edouard attained his majority the comté of Bar was governed by his uncle, Jean de Bar, who acted as regent. It is possible that Jean acted in the capacity of 'regent Grand Master' as well. But there would seem to be no sense in the selection of a five-year-old boy as Grand Master – unless the Grand Mastership was in some way linked to heredity or blood descent.

JEANNE DE BAR. Jeanne de Bar was born in 1295, the elder sister of Edouard. She was thus a granddaughter of Edward I of England, and a niece of Edward II. In 1310, at the age of fifteen, she was married to the earl of Warren, Surrey, Sussex and Strathern – and divorced from him some five years later, after he was excommunicated for adultery. Jeanne continued to live in England, however; and though we could find no detailed record of her activities, she seems to have enjoyed extremely cordial relations with the English throne. She seems to have had similar relations with the king of France – who in 1345 invited her back to the continent, where she became regent of the comté of Bar. In 1353 – despite the Hundred Years War and the consequent hostility between England and France – Jeanne returned to England. When the French monarch was captured at the Battle of Poitiers in 1356 and imprisoned in London, Jeanne was allowed to 'comfort' and minister to him. During his subsequent prolonged incarceration, Jeanne is said to have been his mistress, although both were elderly at the time. She died in London in 1361.

According to the 'Prieuré documents', Jeanne

de Bar presided over the Prieuré de Sion until 1351, ten years before her death. She thus appears to be the only figure on the list of Grand Masters to have resigned, abdicated, or been deposed from her position.

JEAN DE SAINT-CLAIR. Our researches yielded virtually nothing about Jean de Saint-Clair, who seems to have been a very minor figure indeed. He was born around 1329 and descended from the French houses of Chaumont, Gisors and Saint-Clair-sur-Epte. According to the genealogies in the 'Prieuré documents', his grandfather was married to Jeanne de Bar's aunt. This relationship is certainly tenuous. Nevertheless, it would seem to suggest that the Grand Mastership of Sion was still circulating exclusively within a network of interlinked families.

BLANCHE D'EVREUX. Blanche d'Evreux was in fact Blanche de Navarre, daughter of the king of Navarre. She was born in 1332. From her father she inherited the comtés of Longueville and Evreux, both immediately adjacent to Gisors; and in 1359 she became countess of Gisors as well. Ten years previously she had married Philippe VI, king of France, through whom she almost certainly knew Jeanne de Bar. She spent much of her life at the Château of Neuphle, near Gisors, and died there in 1398.

According to numerous legends, Blanche was immersed in alchemical studies and experimentation; and tradition speaks of laboratories at certain of her châteaux. She is said to have possessed a priceless alchemical work, produced in the Languedoc during the fourteenth century but based on a manuscript dating from the last days of the Merovingian dynasty seven hundred years before. She is also rumoured to have been a personal patron of Nicolas Flamel.

NICOLAS FLAMEL. Flamel's is the first name on the list of Grand Masters not to be affiliated by blood with the genealogies in the 'Prieuré documents'; and with him the Grand Mastership of Sion seems to have ceased being exclusively a family sinecure. Flamel was born around 1330 and worked for a time as a scrivener, or copyist, in Paris. By virtue of his occupation, many rare books passed through his hands, and he acquired proficiency in painting, poetry, mathematics and architecture. He also acquired an interest in alchemy, and Cabalistic and Hermetic thought.

Around 1361 Flamel, according to his own account, happened upon the alchemical text that was to transform his life. Its complete title is both puzzling and interesting – *The Sacred Book of Abraham the Jew, Prince, Priest, Levite, Astrologer and Philosopher to that Tribe of Jews who by the Wrath of God were Dispersed amongst the Gauls*. This work subsequently became one of the most famous in Western esoteric tradition. The original is said to have been deposited in the Arsenal Library in Paris. Reproductions of it have been assiduously, religiously and, it would seem, vainly studied by successive generations of would-be adepts.

According to his own account, Flamel pored over the book with no greater success for twenty-one years. At last, on a journey to Spain in 1382, he claimed to have met a converted Jew in León who elucidated the text for him. On returning to Paris he applied what he had learned, and is said to have performed his first successful alchemical transmutation at noon on January 17th – the date that recurs so persistently in connection with Saunière and Rennes-le-Château.

Whether Flamel's account is accurate or not, the fact remains that he became phenomenally wealthy. By the end of his life he owned more than thirty houses and tracts of land in Paris alone. At the same time, however, he seems to have been a modest man who did not revel in power and lavished much of his wealth on good works. By 1413 he had founded and endowed fourteen hospitals, seven churches and three chapels in Paris, and a comparable number in Boulogne – the old comté of Godfroi de Bouillon's father. This altruism, perhaps even more than his dazzling success, endeared him to posterity. As late as the eighteenth century he was revered by men like Sir Isaac Newton, who painstakingly read through his works, copiously annotated them and even copied one of them out by hand.

RENÉ D'ANJOU. We discovered no recorded contact between Flamel and René d'Anjou. At the same time, however, René himself gave us sufficient material to ponder. Although little known today, he was one of the most important figures in the years immediately preceding the Renaissance. Born in 1408, he came, in the course of his life, to hold an awesome array of titles. Among the most important were count of Bar, count of Provence, count of Piedmont, count of Guise, duke of Calabria, duke of Anjou, duke of Lorraine, king of Hungary, king of Naples and Sicily, king of Aragon, Valencia, Majorca and Sardinia. And, perhaps most resonant of all, king of Jerusalem. This latter status was, of course, purely titular. Nevertheless, it invoked a continuity extending back to Godfroi de Bouillon, and was acknowledged by other European potentates. One of René's daughters, in 1445, married Henry VI of England and became a prominent figure in the Wars of the Roses.

According to the 'Prieuré documents', René became Grand Master of Sion in 1418 at the age of ten – and his uncle, Louis, Cardinal de Bar, is said to have exercised a 'regency Grand Mastership' until 1428. Our research revealed that René was inducted into an order of some kind in 1418 –

l'Ordre du Lévrier Blanc ('White Greyhound') – but we discovered no further information of consequence about it. Certainly it might have been Sion under another name.

Sometime between 1420 and 1422 the cardinal of Lorraine created another order, l'Ordre de la Fidélité, and René was admitted as one of the original members. In 1448 René established an order of his own, the Order of the Crescent. René himself described the Order of the Crescent as a revived version of the old Order of the Ship and the Double Crescent – of which Guillaume de Gisors was a member a century and a half before. The original Knights of the Crescent included Francesco Sforza, duke of Milan and father of Leonardo da Vinci's patron; the count of Lénoncourt – whose descendant, according to the 'Prieuré documents', compiled the genealogies in the *Dossiers secrets*; and one Ferri, lord of the important fiefdom in Lorraine dating from Merovingian times and called Sion-Vaudémont. These individuals were intended by René to comprise his riposte, so to speak, to the Order of the Garter in England and the Order of the Golden Fleece in Burgundy. But for reasons that remain unclear the Order of the Crescent incurred ecclesiastical displeasure and was suppressed by the Pope.

It is from René d'Anjou that the modern Cross of Lorraine – symbol of the Free French Forces during the Second World War – ultimately derives. When he became duke of Lorraine the now familiar cross with its two horizontal bars became his personal device.

IOLANDE DE BAR. Born around 1428, Iolande de Bar was René d'Anjou's daughter. In 1445 she was married to Ferri, lord of Sion-Vaudémont and one of the original knights in René's Order of the Crescent. After Ferri's death Iolande spent most of her life at Sion-Vaudémont – which, under her auspices, was extended from a local pilgrimage centre to a sacred site for the whole of Lorraine. In the distant pagan past the place had already enjoyed such status, and a statue of Rosemerthe, an old Gallo-Teutonic Mother Goddess, was subsequently found there. Even in early Christian times the site was regarded as holy – although its name then was Mount Semita, implying something more Judaic than Christian. During the Merovingian epoch a statue of the Virgin had been erected there, and in 1070 the ruling count of Vaudémont had publicly proclaimed himself 'vassal of the Queen of Heaven'. The Virgin of Sion was officially declared 'Sovereign of the Comté of Vaudémont', festivals were held in her honour every May and she was acknowledged Protectress of all Lorraine. Our researches yielded a charter, dating from 1396, which pertains to a special chivalric confraternity based on the mountain, the Confraternity of Chevaliers de Sion – which reputedly traced[1] its origins to the old abbey on Mount Sion just outside Jerusalem. By the fifteenth century, however, Sion-Vaudémont seems to have lost some of its significance. Iolande de Bar restored to it something of its former glory.

Iolande's son, René, subsequently became duke of Lorraine. On his parents' instructions he was educated in Florence, thus becoming well versed in the esoteric tradition and orientation of the academies. His tutor was Georges Antoine Vespucci, one of Botticelli's chief patrons and sponsors.

SANDRO FILIPEPI. Better known as Botticelli, Sandro Filipepi was born in 1444. With the exception of Nicolas Flamel, his is the first name on the list of Sion's alleged Grand Masters not to be directly affiliated with the families whose genealogies figure in the 'Prieuré documents'. At the same time, however, he seems to have enjoyed an extremely close rapport with some of those families. Among his patrons were the Medicis, the Estes, the Gonzagas and the Vespuccis – Georges Antoine Vespucci, patron of Botticelli, was teacher of Iolande de Bar's son, the future duke of Lorraine, who studied in Florence. Botticelli himself studied under Filippo Lippi and Mantegna, both of whom had been patronised by René d'Anjou. He also studied under Verrocchio, an alchemist and exponent of Hermetic thought, whose other pupils included Leonardo da Vinci.

Like most people we did not at first think of Botticelli in 'occult' or esoteric terms. But recent scholars of the Renaissance – Edgar Wind, for instance, and Frances Yates – have effectively argued an esoteric predisposition in him, and we deferred to the persuasiveness of their conclusions. Botticelli does seem to have been an 'esotericist', and the greater part of his work reflects an embodiment of esoteric principles. One of the earliest known decks of Tarot cards is ascribed to Botticelli or his tutor, Mantegna. And the famous painting 'Primavera' is, among many other things, an elaboration on the theme of Arcadia and the esoteric 'underground stream'.

LEONARDO DA VINCI. Born in 1452, Leonardo was well acquainted with Botticelli – in large part through their joint apprenticeship to Verrocchio. Like Botticelli, he was patronised by the Medicis, the Estes and the Gonzagas. He was also patronised by Ludovico Sforza, son of Francesco Sforza, one of René d'Anjou's closest friends and an original member of the Order of the Crescent.

Leonardo's esoteric interests and orientation, like Botticelli's, have by now been well established. Frances Yates, in conversation with one of our researchers, described him as an early

'Rosicrucian'. But in Leonardo's case esoterica would appear to extend even further than in Botticelli's. Even Vasari, his biographer and contemporary, describes him as being of 'an heretical cast of mind'. What precisely might have constituted his heresy remains unclear. During the last few years, however, certain authorities have ascribed to him an ancient heretical belief that Jesus had a twin. Certainly there is evidence for this contention, in a cartoon sketch called 'The Virgin with Saint John the Baptist and Saint Anne', and in the famous 'Last Supper' – where there are, in fact, two virtually identical Christs. But there is no indication of whether the doctrine of Jesus's twin is to be taken literally or symbolically.

Between 1515 and 1517 Leonardo, as a military engineer, was attached to the army of Charles de Montpensier and de Bourbon, Constable of France, Viceroy of Languedoc and Milan and alleged to be the next Grand Master. In 1518 he established himself at the Château of Cloux, and again seems to have been in proximity to the Constable, who was living nearby at Amboise.

> Many of our readers sent in fragments of intriguing information. One such pertained to Leonardo. In the first edition of *Lives of the Artists*, published in 1550, Vasari wrote that Leonardo formed '. . . a doctrine so heretical that he depended no more on . . . any religion'. This sentence was excised from the second edition of the book, which appeared in 1568, and from all subsequent editions thereafter. But all subsequent editions, including that used for the modern paperback translation, report that Leonardo, when old and infirm, confessed and repented[i] and, immediately before his death, received the Holy Sacraments. This is a give-away. Without the sentence excised from the first edition, one would not know what it was he confessed and repented. One would not even have any reason to think he confessed and repented anything in particular.
>
> i: Vasari, G., *Lives of the Artists*, trans. G. Bull, London, 1987, p.270.

CONNÉTABLE DE BOURBON. Charles de Montpensier and de Bourbon, Duke of Châtellerault, Constable of France, was probably the single most powerful lord in France in the early sixteenth century. Born in 1490, he was the son of Claire de Gonzaga; and his sister married the duke of Lorraine, grandson of Iolande de Bar and great-grandson of René d'Anjou. Among Charles's personal entourage was one Jean de Joyeuse, who, through marriage, had become lord of Couiza, Rennes-le-Château and Arques, near where the tomb identical to the one in Poussin's painting stands.

As Viceroy of Milan, Charles was in contact with Leonardo da Vinci; and this contact seems to have continued later, near Amboise. In 1521, however, Charles incurred the displeasure of François I of France, and was forced to abandon his estates and flee the country incognito. He found a refuge with Charles V, Holy Roman Emperor, and became a commander of the imperial army. In this capacity he defeated and captured the French king at the Battle of Pavia in 1525. Two years later he died while besieging Rome.

FERDINAND DE GONZAGUE. Ferrante de Gonzaga, as he is more commonly known, was born in 1507, the son of the duke of Mantua and of Isabelle d'Este – one of Leonardo's most zealous patrons. His primary title was count of Guastalla. In 1527 he assisted his cousin, Charles de

Montpensier and de Bourbon, in the latter's military operations. Some years later he seems to have been covertly in league with François de Lorraine, Duke of Guise, who came within a hair's-breadth of seizing the French throne. Like virtually all the Gonzagas of Mantua, Ferrante was an assiduous devotee of esoteric thought.

At the same time, he also confronted us with the only fragment of ostensibly wrong information we encountered in the whole of the 'Prieuré documents'. According to the list of Sion's Grand Masters in the *Dossiers secrets*, Ferrante presided over the Order until his death in 1575. According to independent sources, however, he is believed to have died near Brussels in 1557. The circumstances surrounding his death are extremely vague, and it is possible, of course, that he did not die in 1557 at all, but merely went to ground. On the other hand, the date in the *Dossiers secrets* may be a genuine error. What is more, Ferrante had a son, César, who did die in 1575, and who may somehow have become confused with his father – deliberately or otherwise. The point is that we found no other such apparently glaring inaccuracies in the 'Prieuré documents', even when the subject was far more obscure and less susceptible to contradiction from independent sources. It seemed almost inconceivable to us that an error in this particular instance could occur through mere carelessness or oversight. On the contrary it was almost as if the error, by so flagrantly confuting accepted accounts, was intended to convey something.

LOUIS DE NEVERS. Louis, Duke of Nevers, was, in fact, Louis de Gonzaga. Born in 1539, he was the nephew of Ferrante de Gonzaga, his predecessor on the list of Sion's Grand Masters. His brother married into the Habsburg family and his daughter married the duke of Longueville, a title formerly held by Blanche d'Evreux; his great-niece married the duke of Lorraine and devoted considerable interest to the old sacred site of Sion-Vaudémont. In 1622 she had a special cross installed there, and in 1627 a religious house and school were founded.

During the Wars of Religion Louis de Nevers was closely allied to the house of Lorraine and its cadet branch, the house of Guise – who effectively exterminated the old Valois dynasty of France and nearly obtained the throne for themselves. In 1584, for example, Louis signed a treaty with the duke of Guise and the cardinal of Lorraine, pledging mutual opposition to Henri III of France. Like his colleagues, however, he became reconciled to Henri IV, and served as Superintendent of Finances to the new monarch. While acting in this capacity, he would have functioned in close contact with Robert Fludd's father. Sir Thomas Fludd was Treasurer of the military contingent sent by Elizabeth I of England to support the French king.

Louis de Nevers, like all the Gonzagas, was deeply versed in esoteric tradition and is believed to have associated with Giordano Bruno – who, according to Frances Yates, was involved in certain secret Hermetic societies which anticipated the 'Rosicrucians'. In 1582, for example, Louis was in England, consorting with Sir Philip Sidney (author of *Arcadia*) and John Dee, the foremost English esotericist of his age. A year later Bruno visited Oxford and consorted with the same people, and, Frances Yates maintains, furthered the activities of their clandestine organisation.

ROBERT FLUDD. Born in 1574, Robert Fludd inherited John Dee's mantle as England's leading exponent of esoteric thought. He wrote and published prolifically on a broad spectrum of esoteric subjects, and developed one of the most comprehensive formulations of Hermetic philosophy ever written. Frances Yates suggests that some of his work may be 'the Seal or secret code of a Hermetic sect or society'. Although Fludd himself never claimed to be a member of the 'Rosicrucians', then causing a sensation on the continent, he warmly endorsed them, declaring that the 'highest good' was the 'Magia, Cabala and Alchymia of the Brothers of the Rosy Cross'.

At the same time Fludd rose to an esteemed position in the London College of Physicians and his friends included William Harvey, who discovered the circulation of the blood. Fludd also enjoyed the favour of James I and Charles I, both of whom granted him rent from lands in Suffolk.

Fludd's father had been associated with Louis de Nevers. Fludd himself was educated at Oxford, where John Dee and Sir Philip Sidney seem to have established an enclave of esoteric interests a few years before. Between 1596 and 1602 Fludd travelled extensively in Europe, consorting with many people subsequently involved in the 'Rosicrucian' movement. Among these was one Janus Gruter, a close personal friend of Johann Valentin Andrea.

In 1602 Fludd received an interesting and, for our purposes, significant commission. He was specifically called to Marseilles, to act as personal tutor to the sons of the duke of Guise, particularly Charles, the young duke of Guise. His association with Charles appears to have continued as late as 1620.

In 1610 Charles, Duke of Guise, married Henriette-Catherine de Joyeuse. The latter's possessions included Couiza, at the foot of the mountain on which Rennes-le-Château is situated. And they included Arques, site of the tomb identical to the tomb in Poussin's painting. Some twenty years later, in 1631, the duke of Guise,

after conspiring against the French throne, went into voluntary exile in Italy, where he was soon joined by his wife. In 1640 he died. But his wife was not allowed to return to France until she consented to sell Couiza and Arques to the crown.[2]

JOHANN VALENTIN ANDREA. Andrea, the son of a Lutheran pastor and theologian, was born in 1586 in Württemburg, which bordered on Lorraine and the Palatinate of the Rhine. As early as 1610 he was travelling about Europe and was rumoured to be a member of a secret society of Hermetic or esoteric initiates. In 1614 he was ordained deacon of a small town near Stuttgart, and seems to have remained there, unscathed, through the turmoil of the Thirty Years War (1618–48) that followed.

ROBERT BOYLE. Robert Boyle was born in 1627, the youngest son of the earl of Cork. Later he would be offered a peerage of his own, and declined it. He was educated at Eton, where his provost, Sir Henry Wotton, was closely connected with the 'Rosicrucian' entourage of Frederick of the Palatinate.

In 1639 Boyle embarked on a prolonged European tour. He spent some time in Florence – where the Medicis, resisting papal pressures, continued to extend support for esotericists and scientists, including Galileo. And he passed twenty-one months in Geneva – where he acquired a number of esoteric interests, including demonology. During his sojourn in Geneva he obtained a work, 'The Devil of Mascon', which he had translated by one Pierre du Moulin, who was to become a lifelong friend. Du Moulin's father was personal chaplain to Catherine de Bar, wife of Henry de Lorraine, Duke of Bar. Subsequently, the elder du Moulin obtained the assiduous patronage of Henri de la Tour d'Auvergne,

Viscount of Turenne and Duke of Bouillon.

On his return to England in 1645, Boyle immediately established contact with the circle of Samuel Hartlib, Andrea's close friend and correspondent. In letters dated 1646 and 1647, he speaks repeatedly of the 'Invisible College'. He declares, for example, that 'the cornerstones of the *Invisible* or (as they term themselves) the Philosophical College, do now and then honour me with their company.'

By 1654 Boyle was at Oxford, where he consorted with John Wilkin, former chaplain to Frederick of the Palatinate. In 1660 Boyle was among the first public figures to offer allegiance to the newly restored Stuarts, and Charles II became patron of the Royal Society. In 1668 he established himself in London, living with his sister – who was related by marriage to John Dury, another friend and correspondent of Andrea. At his London premises Boyle received numerous distinguished visitors – including Cosimo III de' Medici, subsequently ruler of Florence and grand duke of Tuscany.

During these years Boyle's two closest friends were Isaac Newton and John Locke. He is said to have taught Newton the secrets of alchemy. In any case the two of them met regularly to discuss the subject and study alchemical works. Locke, in the meantime, shortly after making Boyle's acquaintance, embarked for a lengthy stay in the south of France. He is known to have made special visits to the graves of Nostradamus and René d'Anjou. He is known to have wandered in the vicinity of Toulouse, Carcassonne, Narbonne – and, quite conceivably, Rennes-le-Château. He is known to have associated with the duchess of Guise. He is known to have studied Inquisition reports on the Cathars, as well as the history of the legends according to which the Magdalene brought the Holy Grail to Marseilles. In 1676 he visited the Magdalene's alleged residence at Saint Baume.

While Locke explored the Languedoc, Boyle maintained a voluminous correspondence with the continent. Among his papers there are letters comprising half of a sustained exchange with an elusive and otherwise unknown individual in France – one Georges Pierre, quite possibly a pseudonym. These letters deal extensively with alchemy and alchemical experimentation. More important, however, they speak of Boyle's membership of a secret Hermetic society – which also included the duke of Savoy and du Moulin.

Between 1675 and 1677 Boyle published two ambitious alchemical treatises – *Incalescence of Quicksilver with Gold* and *A Historical Account of a Degradation of Gold*. In 1689 he published an official statement declaring he could not receive visitors on certain days which he had set aside for alchemical experimentation. This experimentation, he wrote, was to

> comply with my former intention to leave a kind of Hermetic legacy to the studious disciples of that art and to deliver candidly in the annexed paper some processes, chemical and medical, that are less simple and plain than those barely luciferous ones I have been wont to affect and of a more difficult and elaborate kind than those I have hitherto published and more of a kind to the noblest Hermetic secrets or as Helmont styles them 'arcana majora'.[3]

He adds that he intends to speak as plainly as he can, 'though the full and complete uses are not mentioned, partly because, in spite of my philanthropy. I was engaged to secrecy.'[4]

The 'annexed paper' to which Boyle alludes

was never found. It may well have passed into the hands of Locke or, more likely, Newton. On his death in 1691 Boyle entrusted all his other papers to these two confidants, as well as samples of a mysterious 'red powder' which figured prominently in much of Boyle's correspondence and in his alchemical experiments.

ISAAC NEWTON. Isaac Newton was born in Lincolnshire in 1642 – descended from 'ancient Scottish nobility', he himself insisted, although no one seems to have taken this claim very seriously. He was educated at Cambridge, elected to the Royal Society in 1672 and made Boyle's acquaintance for the first time in the following year. In 1689–90 he became associated with John Locke and an elusive, enigmatic individual named Nicholas Fatio de Duillier. Descended from Genevan aristocracy, Fatio de Duillier seems to have wafted with cavalier insouciance through the Europe of his time. On occasion, he appears to have worked as a spy, usually against Louis XIV of France. He also appears to have been on intimate terms with every important scientist of the age. And from the time of his appearance in England, he was Newton's single closest friend. For at least the next decade their two names were inextricably linked.

In 1696 Newton became Warden of the Royal Mint and was subsequently instrumental in fixing the gold standard. In 1703 he was elected President of the Royal Society. Around this time he also became friendly with a young French Protestant refugee named Jean Desaguliers, who was one of the Royal Society's two Curators of Experiments. In the years that followed, Desaguliers became one of the leading figures in the astonishing proliferation of Freemasonry throughout Europe. He was associated with leading Masonic figures like James Anderson, the Chevalier Ramsay and Charles Radclyffe. And in 1731, as Master of the Masonic Lodge at The Hague, he presided over the initiation of the first European prince to become a member of 'the craft'. This prince was François, Duke of Lorraine – who, after his marriage to Maria Theresa of Austria, became Holy Roman Emperor.

There is no record of Newton himself having been a Freemason. At the same time, however, he was a member of a semi-Masonic institution, the 'Gentleman's Club of Spalding' – which included such notables as Alexander Pope. Moreover certain of his attitudes and works reflect interests shared by Masonic figures of the period. Like many Masonic authors, for example, he esteemed Noah, more than Moses, as the ultimate source of esoteric wisdom. As early as 1689 he had embarked on what he considered one of his most important works, a study of ancient monarchies. This work, *The Chronology of Ancient Kingdoms Amended*, attempted to establish the origins of the institution of kingship, as well as the primacy of Israel over other cultures of antiquity. According to Newton, ancient Judaism had been a repository of divine knowledge, which had subsequently been diluted, corrupted and largely lost. Nevertheless, he believed that some of it had filtered down to Pythagoras, whose 'music of the spheres' he regarded as a metaphor for the Law of Gravity. In his attempt to formulate a precise scientific methodology for dating events in both Scripture and classical myth, he employed Jason's quest for the Golden Fleece as a pivotal event; and like other Masonic and esoteric writers, he interpreted that quest as an alchemical metaphor. He also endeavoured to discern Hermetic 'correspondences' or correlations between music and architecture. And, like many Masons he ascribed great significance to the configuration and dimensions of Solomon's Temple. The dimensions and configuration of the Temple he believed to conceal alchemical formulae; and he believed the ancient ceremonies in the Temple to have involved alchemical processes.

Such preoccupations on Newton's part were something of a revelation to us. Certainly they do not concur with his image as it is promulgated in our own century – the image of the scientist who, once and for all, established the separation of natural philosophy from theology. In fact, however, Newton, more than any other scientist of his age, was steeped in Hermetic texts and, in his own attitudes, reflected Hermetic tradition. A deeply religious person, he was obsessed by the search for a divine unity and network of correspondences inherent in nature. This search led him into an exploration of sacred geometry and numerology – a study of the intrinsic properties of shape and number. By virtue of his association with Boyle, he was also a practising alchemist – who, in fact, attributed a paramount importance to his alchemical work.[5] In addition to personally annotated copies of the 'Rosicrucian' manifestos, his library included more than a hundred alchemical works. One of these, a volume by Nicolas Flamel, he had laboriously copied in his own hand. Newton's preoccupation with alchemy continued all his life. He maintained a voluminous and cryptic correspondence on the subject with Boyle, Locke, Fatio de Duillier and others. One letter even has certain key words excised.

If Newton's scientific interests were less orthodox than we had at first imagined, so were his religious views. He was militantly, albeit quietly, hostile to the idea of the Trinity. He also repudiated the fashionable Deism of his time, which reduced the cosmos to a vast mechanical machine constructed by a Celestial Engineer. He questioned the divinity of Jesus and avidly collected all manuscripts pertaining to the issue. He doubted the complete authenticity of the New Testament, believing certain passages to be corruptions interpolated in the fifth century. He was deeply intrigued by some of the early Gnostic heresies and wrote a study of one of them.[6]

Prompted by Fatio de Duillier, Newton also displayed a striking and surprising sympathy for the Camisards, or Prophets of Cévannes, who, shortly after 1705, began appearing in London. So called because of their white tunics, the Camisards, like the Cathars before them, had arisen in the south of France. Like the Cathars they were vehemently opposed to Rome and stressed the supremacy of 'gnosis', or direct knowledge, over faith. Like the Cathars they queried Jesus's divinity. And like the Cathars they had been brutally suppressed by military force – in effect, an eighteenth-century Albigensian Crusade. Driven out of the Languedoc, the heretics found refuge in Geneva and London.

A few weeks before his death Newton, aided by a few intimate friends, systematically burned numerous boxes of manuscripts and personal papers. With considerable surprise, his contemporaries noted that he did not, on his death-bed, request last rites.

CHARLES RADCLYFFE. From the sixteenth century the Radclyffes had been an influential Northumbrian family. In 1688, shortly before he was deposed, James II had created them earls of Derwentwater. Charles Radclyffe himself was born in 1693. His mother was an illegitimate daughter of Charles II by the king's mistress, Moll Davis. Radclyffe was thus, on his mother's side, of royal blood – a grandson of Charles II. He was cousin to Bonnie Prince Charlie and to George Lee, Earl of Lichfield – another illegitimate grandson of the Stuart king.

Not surprisingly, therefore, Radclyffe devoted much of his life to the Stuart cause.

CHARLES DE LORRAINE. Born in 1712, Charles de Lorraine was François's brother and junior by four years. It is probable that both brothers had been exposed, in boyhood, to a Jacobite influence, for their father had offered protection and refuge at Bar-le-Duc to the exiled Stuarts. In 1736, when François married Maria Theresa, Charles became brother-in-law to the future Austrian empress. Eight years later, in 1744, he consolidated this relationship by marrying Maria Theresa's sister, Marie Anne. In the same year, he was appointed governor-general of the Austrian Netherlands (now Belgium) and commander-in-chief of the Austrian Army.

François, on his marriage, had formally renounced all claim to Lorraine, which was entrusted to a French puppet. In exchange he received the archduchy of Tuscany. Charles, however, adamantly refused to acknowledge this transaction, refused to renounce his claim to Lorraine. Given François's abdication, he was thus, in effect, titular duke of Lorraine. And in 1742 he advanced with an army of 70,000 troops to recapture his native soil. He would most likely have done so, had he not been obliged to divert his army to Bohemia in order to thwart a French invasion.

In the military operations that followed Charles proved himself a skilled commander. Today he would no doubt be regarded as one of the better generals of his age, were it not his misfortune to be pitted repeatedly against Frederick the Great. It was against Charles that Frederick won one of his most dazzling and decisive victories, the Battle of Leuthen in 1757. And yet Frederick regarded Charles as a worthy and 'redoubtable' adversary, and spoke of him only in glowing terms.

Following his defeat at Leuthen, Charles was relieved of command by Maria Theresa and retired to his capital of Brussels. Here he established himself as a patron of the arts and assembled a glittering court around him – an elegant, gracious and highly cultivated court which became a centre for literature, painting, music and the theatre. In many respects this court resembled that of Charles's ancestor, René d'Anjou; and the resemblance may well have been deliberate.

In 1761 Charles became Grand Master of the Teutonic Order – a latter-day chivalric vestige of the old Teutonic Knights, the Templars' Germanic protégés who had been a major military power until the sixteenth century. Later, in 1770, a new Coadjutor of the Teutonic Order was appointed – Charles's favourite nephew, Maximilian. During the years that followed, the bond between uncle and nephew was extremely close; and in 1775, when an equestrian statue of Charles was raised in Brussels, Maximilian was again in attendance. The official unveiling of this statue, which had been very precisely scheduled, was on January 17th[7] – the date of Nicolas Flamel's first alchemical transmutation, of Marie de Blanchefort's tombstone, of Saunière's fatal stroke.

MAXIMILIAN DE LORRAINE. Born in 1756, Maximilian de Lorraine – or Maximilian von Habsburg – was Charles de Lorraine's favourite nephew and Maria Theresa's youngest son. As a youth he had seemed destined for a military career, until a fall from a horse left him crippled in one leg. As a result he turned his energies to the Church, becoming, in 1784, bishop of Münster, as well as archbishop and imperial elector of Cologne. On the death of his uncle, Charles, in 1780 he also became Grand Master of the Teutonic Order.

In other respects, too, Maximilian followed in his uncle's footsteps. Like Charles he became an assiduous patron of the arts. Among his protégés were Haydn, Mozart and the young Beethoven. The latter even intended to dedicate the First Symphony to him. By the time the work was finished and published, however, Maximilian had died.

Maximilian was an intelligent, tolerant and easy-going ruler, beloved by his subjects and esteemed by his peers. He seems to have epitomised the ideal of the enlightened eighteenth-century potentate and was probably one of the most cultured men of his age. In political matters he appears to have been particularly lucid, and urgently sought to warn his sister, Marie Antoinette, of the storm then just beginning to gather in France. When the storm broke, Maximilian did not panic. In fact, he seems to have been generally sympathetic to the original objectives of the Revolution, while at the same time providing a haven for aristocratic refugees.

Although Maximilian declared that he was not a Freemason, this statement has often been questioned. Certainly he is widely suspected of having belonged to one or another secret society – despite his position in the Church and Rome's vigorous prohibition of such activities. In any case he is known to have openly consorted with members of the 'craft' – including, of course, Mozart.

Like Robert Boyle, Charles Radclyffe and Charles de Lorraine, Maximilian appears to reflect a certain pattern in the list of Sion's alleged Grand Masters – a pattern which in fact extends back to the Middle Ages. Like Boyle, Radclyffe and his own uncle, Maximilian was a youngest son. The list of alleged Grand Masters includes a number of younger or youngest sons – many of whom appear in lieu of more famous elder brothers.

Like Radclyffe and Charles de Lorraine, Maximilian kept a relatively low profile, working quietly behind the scenes and acting – assuming Sion's Grand Master acts at all – through intermediaries and mouthpieces. Radclyffe, for example, appears to have acted through the Chevalier Ramsay, then through Hund. Charles de Lorraine would seem to have acted through his brother, François. And Maximilian seems to have acted through cultural figures, as well as through certain of his own numerous siblings – Marie-Caroline, for instance, who, as queen of Naples and Sicily, was largely responsible for the spread of Freemasonry in those domains.

CHARLES NODIER. Born in 1780, Charles Nodier seems to inaugurate a pattern that obtains for all Sion's alleged Grand Masters after the French Revolution. Unlike his predecessors he not only lacks noble blood, but seems to have had no direct contact whatever with any of the families whose genealogies figure in the 'Prieuré documents'. After the French Revolution the Prieuré de Sion – or at least its purported Grand Masters – would appear to have been divorced both from the old aristocracy and from the corridors of political power; or so, at any rate, our research led us to conclude at the time.

Nodier's mother was one Suzanne Paris, who is said not to have known her parents. His father was a solicitor in Besançon and, before the Revolution, a member of the local Jacobite Club. After the outbreak of the Revolution, Nodier senior became Mayor of Besançon and President of the town's Revolutionary Tribunal. He was also a highly esteemed Master Mason, in the forefront of Masonic activity and politics at the time.

Charles Nodier displayed an extraordinary precocity, allegedly becoming involved in – among other things – cultural and political affairs at the age of ten! By the age of eighteen, he had established a literary reputation and continued to publish prolifically for the rest of his life, averaging a book a year. His work covers an impressive diverse spectrum – travel journals, essays on literature and painting, studies of prosody and versification, a study of antennae in insects, an inquiry into the nature of suicide, autobiographical reminiscences, excursions into archaeology, linguistics, legal questions and esoterica, not to mention a voluminous corpus of fiction. Today Nodier is generally dismissed as a literary curiosity.

Although initially sympathetic to the Revolution, Nodier quickly turned against it. He performed a similar volte-face in his attitude towards Napoleon, and by 1804 was vociferous in his opposition to the emperor. In that year he published, in London, a satirical poem, *The Napoléone*. Having produced this seditious tract, he then, oddly enough, set about calling attention to the fact that he had done so. The authorities at first paid no attention to him, and Nodier seems to have gone inordinately out of his way simply to get arrested. At last, after writing a personal letter to Napoleon in which he professed his guilt, he was imprisoned for a month, then sent back to Besançon and kept under half-hearted surveillance. Nevertheless, Nodier claimed later that he had continued to oppose the régime, becoming involved in two separate plots against Napoleon, in 1804 and again in 1812. Although he was given to boasting and bravado, this claim may not have been without substance. Certainly he was friendly with the instigators of the two plots, whom he had met in Besançon during his youth.

VICTOR HUGO. Hugo's family was originally from Lorraine – of distinguished aristocratic descent, he later insisted – but he himself was born in Besançon, that hotbed of subterranean subversive activity, in 1802. His father was a general under Napoleon, but maintained very cordial relations with the conspirators involved in the plot against the emperor. One of these conspirators, in fact, was Madame Hugo's lover, cohabiting with her in the same house and playing an important role in her son's development, being the young Victor's godfather and mentor. Thus Hugo had been exposed to the world of intrigue, conspiracy and secret societies from the age of seven.

By the age of seventeen he was already a fervent disciple of Charles Nodier; and it was from Nodier that he acquired his erudite knowledge of Gothic architecture, which figures so saliently in *The Hunchback of Notre Dame*. In 1819 Hugo and his brother established a publishing house in conjunction with Nodier, and this house produced a magazine under Nodier's editorial direction. In 1822 Hugo married in a special ceremony at Saint Sulpice. Three years later he and Nodier, with their wives, embarked on a prolonged journey to Switzerland. In the same year, 1825, the two friends travelled together to attend the coronation of Charles X. In the years that followed Hugo formed his own salon, modelled on Nodier's and patronised by most of the same celebrities. And when Nodier died in 1844 Hugo was one of the pallbearers at the funeral.

Like Newton, Hugo was a deeply religious man, but his religious views were highly unorthodox. Like Newton, he was militantly antitrinitarian and repudiated Jesus's divinity. As a result of Nodier's influence, he was immersed all his life in esoterica, in Gnostic, Cabalistic and Hermetic thought – a preoccupation that figures prominently in his poetry and prose. And he is known to have been connected with a so-called 'Rose-Croix' order, which also included Éliphas Lévi and the young Maurice Barrès.

Hugo's political attitudes have always been a source of perplexity to critics and historians, and are too complex, too inconsistent, too contingent on other factors, to be discussed here. We found it significant, however, that, despite his personal admiration for Napoleon, Hugo was a staunch royalist, who welcomed the restoration of the old Bourbon dynasty. Yet at the same time he seems to have regarded the Bourbons as desirable only in a provisional way – a kind of stop-gap measure. On the whole, he appears to have despised them, and was particularly fierce in his condemnation of Louis XIV. The ruler whom Hugo most enthusiastically endorsed – indeed, the two were close personal friends – was Louis-Philippe, the 'Citizen King' elected to preside over a popular monarchy. And Louis-Philippe was allied by marriage to the house of Habsburg-Lorraine. His wife, in fact, was Maximilian de Lorraine's niece.

M. Plantard offered some interesting information. Victor Hugo, he said, had been inducted into the Prieuré de Sion at a conventicle at Blois on 2 May 1825, sponsored by Charles Nodier. In June 1829, Hugo supposedly presided over the admission into the order of Théophile Gautier, who had been proposed by two other prominent literary figures, Gérard de Nerval and Pétrus Borel. On 22 July 1844, at a conventicle at Sainte Madeleine, Hugo was himself elected Grand Master and successor to Nodier. According to M. Plantard, an attempt was made a year later to implicate him in scandal and depose him. When thwarted, Gautier, the alleged instigator of this design, fled Paris and embarked on a journey to Algeria.

None of this, of course, can be verified without considerable research, and perhaps not even then. Neither is it, in itself, of much apparent importance. But it is striking simply by virtue of its meticulous precision of detail. It was just this kind of precision that we encountered throughout our research of the Prieuré de Sion; and it was just this kind of precision that convinced us to take the Prieuré seriously. Granted, a novelist might fabricate a comparable precision. But M. Plantard had no aesthetic justification for doing so. Neither did he stand to gain financially or in any other way. In the absence of any plausible reason for fabrication, we had no reason to doubt his word. While we were not prepared to accept it unreservedly, we were not prepared summarily to discount it either.

CLAUDE DEBUSSY. Debussy was born in 1862; and though his family was poor, he quickly established wealthy and influential contacts. While still in his teens, he was performing as pianist in the château of the French president's mistress, and seems to have become acquainted with the head of state as well. In 1880 he was adopted by the Russian noblewoman who had patronised Tchaikovsky, and travelled with her to Switzerland, Italy and Russia. In 1884, after winning a coveted musical prize, he studied for a time in Rome. Between 1887 and 1906, he lived mostly in Paris, but the years preceding and following this period were devoted to extensive travelling. These travels are known to have brought him into contact with a number of eminent people. We endeavoured to determine whether any of them were connected with the families whose genealogies figure in the 'Prieuré documents', but our efforts, for the most part, proved futile. Debussy, it transpired, was curiously secretive about his aristocratic and political associates. Many of his letters have been suppressed; and in those that have been published important names and often whole sentences have been scrupulously excised.

Debussy seems to have made Hugo's acquaintance through the symbolist poet, Paul Verlaine. He later set a number of Hugo's works to music. During his time in Paris he became an integral member of the symbolist circles, who dominated the cultural life of the French capital. These circles were sometimes illustrious, sometimes odd, sometimes both. They included the young cleric, Émile Hoffet – through whom Debussy came to meet Bérenger Saunière; Emma Calvé, the esoterically oriented diva; the enigmatic magus of French symbolist poetry, Stéphane Mallarmé – one of whose masterpieces, *L'Après-Midi d'un Faune*, Debussy set to music; the symbolist playwright, Maurice Maeterlinck, whose drama, *Pelléas et Mélisande*, Debussy turned into a world-famous opera; and the flamboyant Comte Philippe Auguste Villiers de l'Isle-Adam, who wrote the 'Rosicrucian' play, *Axel*. Although his death in 1918 prevented its completion, Debussy began to compose a libretto for Villiers's occult drama, intending to turn it, too, into an opera. Among his other associates were the luminaries who attended Mallarmé's famous Tuesday night *soirées* – Oscar Wilde, W. B. Yeats, Paul Valéry, André Gide, Marcel Proust.

In themselves, Debussy's and Mallarmé's circles were steeped in esoterica. At the same time, they overlapped other circles that were more esoteric still. Thus Debussy consorted with virtually all the most prominent names in the so-called 'French occult revival'.

It is worth noting, perhaps, a review he wrote in 1903, which refers to Wagner's *Die Walküre*. In a parenthetical comment on one scene in the opera, Debussy says: 'Perhaps it's

to destroy that scandalous legend that Jesus Christ died on the Cross . . .'[i]

i: *Debussy on Music*, collected by F. Lesure, trans. R.L. Smith, London, 1977, p.171.

JEAN COCTEAU. Born in 1889, Cocteau seemed to us a most unlikely candidate for the Grand Mastership of an influential secret society. But so, too, did some of the other names when we first encountered them. For nearly all those other names certain relevant connections gradually became apparent. In Cocteau's case few such connections did.

It is worth noting, however, that Cocteau was raised in a milieu close to the corridors of power – his family was politically prominent and his uncle was an important diplomat. Despite his subsequent bohemian existence, he never completely divorced himself from these influential spheres. Outrageous though his behaviour sometimes was, he retained close contact with individuals highly placed in aristocratic and political circles. Like many of Sion's alleged Grand Masters – Boyle, Newton, Debussy, for instance – he appeared to remain sublimely aloof from politics. During the German Occupation he took no active part in the Resistance, but made apparent his antipathy to the Pétain régime. And after the war he seems to have enjoyed considerable currency with de Gaulle, whose brother commissioned him to deliver an important lecture on the state of France. For us, the most convincing testimony of Cocteau's affiliation with the Prieuré de Sion resides in his work – in the film *Orphée*, for instance, in such plays as *The Eagle has Two Heads* (based on the Habsburg Empress Elisabeth of Austria) and in the decoration of such churches as Notre Dame de France in London. Most convincing of all, however, is his signature appended to the statutes of the Prieuré de Sion.

APPENDIX 2

THE COMTE DE CHAMBORD AND THE FRENCH THRONE

One individual whom we neglected to discuss properly in the text of *Holy Blood, Holy Grail* was the Comte de Chambord. As the reader may remember, Chambord's name was linked to the story of Béranger Saunière, and thus with the point of departure for any investigation of the mystery of Rennes-le-Château. It was known, for example, that one of Saunière's sponsors and patronesses was the widow of the Comte de Chambord. And when Saunière was visited at Rennes-le-Château by Archduke Johann Stefan von Habsburg (Baron von Brandhof and Comte de Méran), the archduke identified himself as 'Monsieur de Chambord'. It was as 'M. de Chambord' that the archduke, acting for the real Chambord's widow, continued to visit Saunière regularly every year – to monitor the progress of the priest's research, and to make annual payments of some 20,000 francs. Altogether, 'M. de Chambord' paid more than a dozen visits to Rennes-le-Château. He himself survived until 1947. According to 'the Prieuré documents', he was searching – on behalf of both Chambord's family and his own – for formal proofs of Merovingian descent, which could then be used 'to upset the political givens of France'.[1] But who exactly was the Comte de Chambord, in whose name all this activity occurred?

In 1793, Louis XVI and his wife, Marie Antoinette, met their deaths under the guillotine. Their son, who might have been Louis XVII, disappeared. According to some accounts, he was murdered – in the Temple of Paris, the one-time preceptory of the Knights Templar. According to other accounts, the prince was spirited away to safety. But whatever became of him, he was never heard of again, and his fate remains one of the enigmas of European history. In the meantime, the dead king's two brothers – the elder also named Louis, the younger named Charles – escaped into exile abroad.

When Napoleon abdicated in 1814, the Bourbon monarchy was restored, and the guillotined king's brother ascended the throne as Louis XVIII. On Louis' death in 1824, the youngest of the brothers, Charles, succeeded him as Charles X. Charles' son had been assassinated in 1820. Just before his death, however, he had sired a son of his own, Henri-Dieudonné d'Artois, Duc de Bordeaux. A year later, in 1821, this child received the title of Comte de Chambord. The Comte de Chambord was thus the grandson of King Charles X of France. He was also to be the last direct claimant to the throne in the Bourbon line of succession which had begun with Henri IV in 1589.

The young count's grandfather, Charles X, ruled with signal ineptitude, even by the standards of earlier Bourbon sovereigns. In a France that had experienced revolution, empire, secularisation, a separation of Church and State, an increasingly influential popular voice and a fledgling constitutional democracy, Charles attempted to invoke divine right and absolute monarchy. The resulting revolution, which erupted on 28 July 1830, was inevitable. Charles was forced to abdicate, expecting that his grandson, the Comte de Chambord, would succeed him as Henri V. But the French Chamber of Deputies refused to accept this succession. Instead, it *voted* to confer the crown on the Duc d'Orléans, who became Louis-Philippe, the so-called 'citizen king'. The French monarchy, formerly hereditary, had now become elective; and the Comte de

Chambord was disenfranchised, barred from what he believed to be his inheritance.

The count was ten years old at the time. He and his deposed grandfather found refuge for a time in Britain, in Edinburgh, where the Crown made Holyrood Palace available to them. From there, they moved to Prague, residing in the Hradcany Palace, where Charles, in 1836, died. On his grandfather's death, the sixteen-year-old Comte de Chambord received a new tutor – none other than General Armand, Marquis d'Hautpoul, nephew of Marie de Negri d'Ables or Marie de Blanchefort. Hautpoul, it will be remembered, had resigned from his post as commandant of the Staff College in protest at the election of Louis-Philippe.

In the years that followed, the Comte de Chambord, still rancorous at the loss of his inheritance, migrated from one place of exile to another – in Austria, for example, in Rome, in Bohemia. In 1841, he found his way to London, living in Belgrave Square. Two years later, however, he antagonised the young Queen Victoria, a supporter of Louis-Philippe, by organising a demonstration on his own behalf in Belgravia. Shortly thereafter, he returned to the continent.

In 1846, Chambord, now aged twenty-six, married the Archduchess Maria-Therese von Habsburg-Este, sister of the Duke of Modena, ruler of Habsburg possessions in northern Italy. The count and his new wife established their residence at Wiesbaden. Among their entourage was the then Marquis de Cherisey.[2] Among their other visitors and courtiers were members of several families that have figured recurrently throughout our story – of the Noailles and Joyeuse families, for example. In the seventeenth century, the Duc de Joyeuse had married the Duchesse d'Arques, chateleine of the land on which the tomb at Arques – the tomb in Poussin's painting, with

Rennes-le-Château in the background – was situated. After migrating to Rome, the Duc de Joyeuse and the Duchesse d'Arques had become Poussin's patrons.

In 1848, France was again swept by revolution; but any dreams the Comte de Chambord harboured of obtaining the throne were thwarted when Louis Napoleon was elected President of the Second Republic. Four years later, the republic was transformed by referendum into the Second Empire, and Louis Napoleon became the Emperor Napoleon III. For the next two decades, Chambord was forced to watch from exile as France became the cultural capital of Europe and, so it seemed, the supreme power on the continent. The Crimean War (1854–6) ended inconclusively, but it yielded a dividend in propaganda of some impressive military victories – at the Alma, for example, at Balaclava and at Inkerman. These, granted, were primarily achievements of British troops; but the French Army, to the extent that it was involved, acquitted itself well, and France could therefore bask in the glory. Further glory, rather more deserved, was won in 1859, when French soldiers defeated the Austrians at the battles of Magenta and Solferino, and liberated northern Italy from Habsburg control.

In 1870, the aura of French invincibility was deflated by Bismarck's military machine in the Franco-Prussian War. After a series of humiliating defeats, Napoleon III was forced to abdicate, the Second Empire collapsed and a revolutionary provisional government in Paris declared a republic. In the aftermath of this débâcle, the Comte de Chambord's opportunity seemed at last to have come. In October 1873, he was offered the throne of France – on condition that he accepted the Tricolour flag and the principles of the French Revolution. Remaining fettered to his absolutist values, the count refused these conditions. The offer of the throne was withdrawn and in February 1875, the Third French Republic was officially proclaimed. Chambord survived, more embittered than ever, until 1883. During his final illness, his supporters flocked to pray for him at Lourdes and at Paray-le-Monial, centre of the Hieron du Val d'Or, which figures in the text of *The Holy Blood and the Holy Grail*. Within two years of her husband's death, Chambord's widow, née Maria-Theresa von Habsburg, despatched her relative, Johann Stefan von Habsburg, to Rennes-le-Château.

What was he seeking on her behalf? According to the 'Prieuré documents', formal proofs of Merovingian descent in the parchments discovered by Béranger Saunière. But such proofs would hardly have authenticated the claims of a Bourbon pretender such as Chambord. They might, however, have authenticated the Merovingian descent, and thus the claims, of the Habsburgs. It is difficult to assess the impact such authentication might have had on 'the political givens of France'. But in 1914, the issue became academic when France found herself at war with the Habsburg imperium. This, of course, would have put Saunière in a compromising position. It would also explain the rumours of German and Austrian spies in the vicinity of Rennes-le-Château. It would explain the interest not only of the Habsburgs, but also of the Hohenzollerns, in the mystery. It would explain why, according to one well-informed source, the French Ministry of War maintained a dossier on Saunière and his alleged contacts with enemy agents. And it might shed some light on the mysterious circumstances attending Saunière's death in 1917.

APPENDIX 3
Eastern European Literary Figures

Alexander Lernet-Holenia is virtually unknown in the English-speaking world. Even among those conversant with Austrian literature, his status is regarded as equivocal – the status of a gifted dilettante, rather than that of a major artist. He was born in 1897, roughly contemporary with Joseph Roth and Heimito von Doderer, and died in 1976. Like Roth and Doderer, he spent his childhood and boyhood under the old Habsburg imperium, then witnessed the collapse of the once mighty and seemingly immutable empire. Like Roth and Doderer, he could be scathingly critical of the defunct régime, while, at the same time, pining nostalgically for the golden days of its twilight.

Lernet-Holenia began publishing poetry when both he and the century were still in their twenties. His early verse earned praise from such luminaries as Rilke and Hofmannsthal. In the 1930s, while not abandoning poetry, he began to turn first to drama, then to prose fiction; and though he regarded his poetry as his major achievement, it is primarily for his novels that he is remembered today. Whilst not being devoid of literary significances, these are hardly works of monumental stature. But we mention them here because certain of them address – sometimes in a tantalisingly oblique fashion – themes relevant to the mystery of Rennes-le-Château. In 1936, for example, 20 years before Pierre Plantard de Saint-Clair and his entourage began extolling the importance of the Merovingian bloodline, Lernet-Holenia published a novel entitled (in English) *The Resurrection of Maltravers*. The text includes such passages as the following:

Legend had it that the Maltraverses are ultimately descended from no lesser a being than Merowech, the son of an ocean demon, who had overpowered the Queen of the Franks as she bathed in the sea. When the Carolingians seized power in France (the Merowingians were said to be so incapable of maintaining the regency that, purely for prestige purposes, they had simply driven around the country in two-wheeled oxcarts, the kind used during the migration of the peoples) – when the Carolingians seized the throne, some of the lst Merowingians fled to Norman territory, from where they upheld their hereditary claims. They continued to bear the most ancient French coat-of-arms, the golden toads, which eventually evolved into lilies. The dukes of Normandy enfeoffed them with the Comté de Maltravers. The 'heirs of the toads' recovered from the decay of their house and soon became such a powerful shield for the dukes of Normandy that they were surnamed 'Fortescue', for 'Fortescue' means 'powerful shield'. And their motto was: Arise and Take Your Inheritance.

They never did. But when the Normans conquered England, the Fortescue-Maltraverses went along, and they received County Surrey before it was given to the Howards. Eventually they lost Comté de Maltravers in northern France, and it passed into the hands of the Sommerstorffs, a family from Cleve. Around the time of the Turkish Wars, a certain Hugh Fortescue-Maltravers, a younger son of the dynasty, arrived in Hungary, joined the fight against the Turks, became a general, and was made a count of *ancienne noblesse* by the Emperor, but without the predicate of 'illustrious' for the other families protested, even though they themselves bore that title more or less illegitimately. However, the Emperor presented him with several estates in northern Hungary, including Skalitz and Sobotitz.

As the reader will no doubt realise, none of the proper names cited in this passage occurs in the text of *The Holy Blood and the Holy Grail*. They may be anagrams. They may be puns in any of several languages known to Lernet-Holenia. They may involve word games of some other kind – or codes such as those that have figured in our story from Henri Boudet to the Marquis de Cherisey. But the theme of a blood descent from the Merovingians – described elsewhere in the text as the original aristocracy and first family of Europe – is clear enough. So, too, is another reference in the text which equates the Merovingians explicitly with the 'Grail family'. Yet despite the emphasis accorded them, the Merovingians are ultimately incidental to Lernet-Holenia's novel, which moves off in other directions, to confront other subject matter. The Merovingian allusions are tossed in as provocative non-sequiturs – as if Lernet-Holenia were confiding a sly wink to someone, indicating that he knew something. One might, of course, see a number of incidents in the narrative – perhaps the narrative in its entirety – as an allegory. But it is not feasible, in this postscript, to embark on detailed literary analysis and interpretation. All we can do here is recommend *The Resurrection of Maltravers*, as well as other works in Lernet-Holenia's corpus, to our readers.

If Lernet-Holenia is a relatively minor literary figure, other writers in his Viennese circle were of considerably greater consequence. One of these is Heimito von Doderer (1896–1966). Doderer's status may not be comparable to that of the slightly older novelists Robert Musil and Hermann Broch, who dominated Viennese literary society during the thirties. But he is still a major figure, with an assured place in any syllabus of twentieth-century German-language prose fiction. Although he, too, is little known in the English-speaking world, one of his two most important works, *The Demons*, has appeared in English translation, as have two more ephemeral texts. Still untranslated is the earlier of his two most ambitious novels, *Die Strudlhofstiege*, published in German in 1951. Also untranslated is his most bizarre and opaque narrative, *The Merovingians, or The Total Family*, published in German in 1962. Again, it is not feasible here to embark on any detailed literary analysis. Suffice to say that the work, despite its title, is not set in Merovingian times. On the contrary, it is a complex symbolic and perhaps allegorical story, incorporating much discursive digression and recounting various events of Merovingian history in nineteenth-century bourgeois dress. It will prove fertile territory for readers sufficiently fluent in German to cope with Doderer's ornate, baroque and sometimes labyrinthine prose.

Such readers may well ask themselves why two pro-Habsburg Austrian novelists, working in Vienna between the 1930s and the 1960s, should be so conversant and preoccupied with Merovingian themes. And such readers may also be prompted to look at some of the other writers in Doderer's and Lernet-Holenia's literary circle – at Musil's closest friend and disciple, for example, Albert Paris Gütersloh, whose major novel, *Sun and Moon*, still awaits translation.

Lernet-Holenia, Doderer and their circle made us wonder whether the story we had traced in France might not have been echoed elsewhere – specifically in Habsburg and former Habsburg domains. Until the early nineteenth century, these domains had included modern day Belgium, formerly the Austrian Netherlands. Here, after all, was the original heartland of the Merovingians. From here had issued numerous families claiming Merovingian descent – including that of the Marquis de Cherisey. In the eighteenth century, Charles de Lorraine, cited as Grand Master of the Prieuré de Sion, had been Governor-General of the Austrian Netherlands. And Belgium was also the birthplace of several symbolist figures of the *fin-de-siècle* who moved in the circles of Debussy and Emma Calvé – Emile Verhaeren, for example, and, of course, Maurice Maeterlinck, on whose 'Merovingian' drama, *Pelléas and Melisande*, Debussy based his opera. Much of this territory has yet to be explored. But it was from a very different quarter of the former Habsburg empire that the most startling and significant discovery was to issue. We owe this discovery to Sonia Kanikova, co-editor of *The Everyman Companion to East European Literature* (Dent, 1993).

Ms. Kanikova called our attention to a Czech novelist, one Prokop Chocholaušek, who was born in 1819 and died in 1864. Chocholaušek is an extremely obscure figure and an extremely minor one, of questionable literary consequence. From Ms. Kanikova's description of him, he would seem to have been a kind of downmarket and cack-handed Bohemian imitator of Sir Walter Scott, who churned out a series of meticulously researched but artistically inept historical narratives, often on chivalric themes. In 1842 – when the Parisian circle of Charles Nodier, Gérard de Nerval, Petrus Borel, Théophile Gautier and

Victor Hugo was flourishing – Chocholaušek published a novel entitled (in translation) *The Templars in Bohemia*.[1]

According to Pierre Plantard de Saint-Clair, the Marquis de Cherisey and their associates, the Knights Templar had been created as a kind of executive arm, and public persona, for the Ordre de Sion. The Ordre de Sion was said to be the real power behind the Templars until 1188, at which time they were, so to speak, cut free. In 1188, the Ordre de Sion was said to have become the Prieuré de Sion and continued as such to the present. In our own research, we found much circumstantial evidence to support these assertions, but no definitive confirmation, no testimony independent of the Prieuré's own statements. We found, for example, original charters pertaining to the Ordre de Sion dating from the twelfth and thirteenth centuries, but there was no explicit mention of a link with the Templars. We found other references to Sion as late as the seventeenth century, when one of their premises at Orléans was turned over to the Jesuits. After the seventeenth century, however, we found no allusions to any Ordre or Prieuré de Sion until the modern day organisation surfaced, under M. Plantard de Saint-Clair's auspices, in 1956.

In *The Templars in Bohemia*, published in 1842, Prokop Chocholaušek is quite explicit. At the beginning of the Crusades, he states, nine knights under the leadership of Hughes de Payn established themselves as the Knights of Sion, or the Ordre de Sion. They were to become the clandestine nucleus behind the Knights Templar, who were created as their public façade. Sion figures by name throughout Chocholoušek's novel. When Templar functionaries greet each other, for example, they do so with the words 'Hail, Sion!' or 'Glory to Sion!'.

For readers with a knowledge of Czech, Prokop Chocholaušek is likely to prove a happy hunting-ground indeed. We, unfortunately, possess no such knowledge. We are left baffled by the question of how and where an obscure Bohemian novelist of the early to mid-nineteenth century came by his information.

APPENDIX 4

THE ORDER OF THE FLEUR DE LYS

In our book *The Temple and the Lodge*, the Montgomery family emerged as having played a salient role in the origins and coalescence of what later became Freemasonry: and although the point was not made explicitly in that book, the reader will undoubtedly have noted numerous links between the Montgomery family and various other families associated with the Prieuré de Sion. When we wrote *Holy Blood, Holy Grail*, however, we were not yet aware of the Montgomery family's significance. In consequence, only one Montgomery figured in our text. This was Gabriel, who, in 1559, at a jousting tournament, killed the French Valois King Henri II with a lance thrust through the eyes – a lance thrust eerily reminiscent of the one which supposedly killed the Merovingian King Dagobert II in A.D. 679. It was his ostensibly accurate prediction of the French monarch's death that, at a single stroke, established Nostradamus' reputation as a prophet and seer. As we pointed out in the text, however, there have been persuasive suggestions that Nostradamus was in fact working as an agent for the House of Lorraine, and that his supposed prophecy was not a prophecy at all, but a blueprint for action. There have been similar suggestions that Gabriel de Montgomery, who brought the prophecy to fulfilment, was also working for the House of Lorraine.

After *Holy Blood, Holy Grail* was published, we were contacted by a member of the Montgomery family. He made available a corpus of intriguing material, some of which found its way into *The Temple and the Lodge* and reinforced the conclusions of that book. He also recounted a narrative which had surfaced among Montgomery family papers – a nineteenth-century translation or transcription of a much earlier text. According to this narrative, a man named Yeshua ben Joseph, at some point during the Roman occupation of Palestine, was married to a woman known as Miriam of Bethany. Miriam was described as a priestess of a 'female cult'. In the aftermath of a revolt against the Romans – the narrative did not specify which revolt – Miriam was captured. Because she was pregnant, however, she was spared execution, was smuggled out of Palestine and eventually found refuge in Gaul, where she bore a daughter. No subsequent mention was made of Yeshua ben Joseph – who presumably died in the revolt or was executed for his part in it. This narrative effectively speaks for itself. It is impressively close to the conclusions we proffered in *Holy Blood, Holy Grail*.

Our informant also provided us with detailed material on a neo-chivalric order known as the Order of the Fleur de Lys. It was reportedly founded in 1439 by René d'Anjou, Cosimo de Medici and an unidentified member of the Montgomery family – one of the numerous Scots fighting on the continent at the time. The order was said to have been suppressed by Pope Sixtus IV in 1478 and been dormant for the better part of a century. When it surfaced again in 1556, its members are said to have included James Hamilton, Robert Seton, William de Gonzaga, Louis de Gonzaga and one F. von Habsburg. Along with the Montgomery family, the Hamiltons and the Setons were among the inter-

locking network of Scottish aristocrats associated with the origins of Freemasonry. Louis de Gonzaga, Duc de Nevers, is listed as one of the Prieuré de Sion's Grand Masters. His brother, William, was married to Eleanore von Habsburg, daughter of the Emperor Ferdinand I. William's granddaughter was to marry another Habsburg, the future Emperor Ferdinand II.

The primary objective of the Order of the Fleur de Lys was, apparently, to campaign against the Turks in what is now Serbia – which would seem to explain the fleur de lys on the present Bosnian flag. But the order also appears to have become embroiled in French politics of the sixteenth and seventeenth centuries. Its members around 1560 are said to have included Gabriel de Montgomery, whose lance thrust killed Henri II, and at least 30 other personnel from the Scots Guard – ostensibly the personal bodyguard of Valois monarchs, but secretly aligned with the Valois' rivals, the House of Guise-Lorraine. Some 90 years later, during the Fronde, the Order of the Fleur de Lys was still reportedly aligned with the House of Lorraine.

According to our informant, his knowledge derived from his uncle, the late Brigadier John Montgomery, who was private secretary to Leopold, King of the Belgians between the two world wars of this century and last Grand Master of the Order of the Fleur de Lys. For the last 30-odd years, the order has apparently been dormant, but is now being revived. Since its inception, its Grand Masters have been the following:

1439–1480 René d'Anjou

1480–1485 Ludovico Sforza, Duke of Milan

1485–1508 René II de Lorraine

1508–1527 Charles de Montpensier, Connétable de Bourbon

1527–1556 Ferrante de Gonzaga

1556–1572 Hugh Montgomery, 2nd Earl of Eglington

1572–1585 David de Seton

1585–1595 Robert de Saint-Clair

1595–1640 Charles de Guise, Duke of Lorraine

1640–1675 Henri de la Tour Bouillon

1675–1689 John Graham of Claverhouse, Viscount Dundee

1689–1715 Hugh Montgomery of Mount-Alexander

1716–1730 John Erskine of Mar

1730–1746 Charles Radclyffe, Earl of Derwentwater

1746–1757 John Erskine of Mar

1757–1768 Alexander Montgomery, Earl of Eglington

1768–1800 Maximillian von Habsburg

1800–1815 Hugh Montgomery of Grey Abbey

1815–1825 George Beaumont

1825–1838 Robert Montgomery of Comber

1838–1862 Archibald Montgomerie of Eglington and Winton

1862–1875 Louis Napoleon

1875–1900 Robert Dundee of Braxfield

1900–1914 Robert Hamilton of Hamilton

1914– Leopold, King of the Belgians

Some of these names, especially those towards the latter part of the list, are unknown to us. But the list also includes five figures – René d'Anjou, Connétable de Bourbon, Ferrante de Gonzaga, Charles Radclyffe and Maximillian von Habsburg – who are cited as Grand Masters of the Prieuré de Sion. And a number of other names are closely connected with the story recounted in our book. Ludovico Sforza, for example, was the patron of Leonardo de Vinci, and Leonardo is named as one of the Prieuré's Grand Masters. René II of Lorraine (and Anjou) was the son of Ioland de Bar, also on the Prieuré's Grand Master list, and, through his marriage to Jeanne d'Harcourt de Montgomery, father of Claude de Guise. Charles de Guise, Duke of Lorraine, was married to the Duchess d'Arques, whose lands included the site of the tomb in Poussin's painting and who became Poussin's patroness in Rome. John Graham of Claverhouse, Viscount Dundee, was found dead on the battlefield of Killiecrankie reportedly with an original pre-1314 Templar cross.

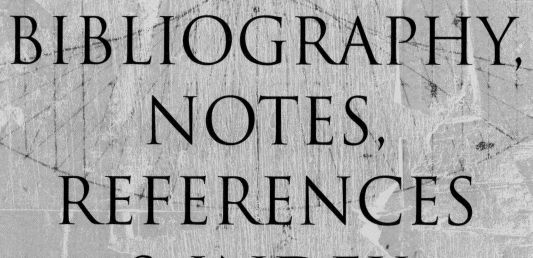

BIBLIOGRAPHY,
NOTES,
REFERENCES
& INDEX

1 'THE PRIEURÉ DOCUMENTS'

Antoine l'Ermite, *Un Trésor mérovingien à Rennes-le-Château* (Anvers, 1961).

Beaucean, Nicolas, *Au Pays de la Reine Blanche* (Paris, 1967).

Blancasall, Madeleine, *Les Descendants mérovingiens ou l'énigme du Razès Wisigoth* (Geneva, 1965).

Boudet, Henri, *La Vraie Langue celtique* (Carcassonne, 1886).

Boudet, Henri, *La Vraie Langue celtique*, facsimile edition with preface by Pierre Plantard de Saint-Clair (Paris, 1978).

Chérisey, Philippe de, *Circuit* (Liège, 1968).

Chérisey, Philippe de, *L'Enigme de Rennes* (Paris, 1978).

Chérisey, Philippe de, *L'Or de Rennes pour un Napoléon* (Liège, 1975).

Delaude, Jean, *Le Cercle d'Ulysse* (Toulouse, 1977).

Feugère, Pierre, Saint-Maxent Louis and Koker, Gaston de, *Le Serpent rouge* (Pontoise, 1967).

Hisler, Anne Lea, *Trésor au pays de la Reine Blanche* (1969).

Hisler, Anne Lea, *Rois et gouvernants de la France* (Paris, 1964).

Lobineau, Henri, *Généalogie des rois mérovingiens et origine des diverses familles françaises et étrangères de souche mérovingienne* (Geneva, 1956).

Lobineau, Henri, *Dossiers secrets d'Henri Lobineau* (Paris, 1967).

Myriam, D., 'Les Bergers d'Arcadie', *Le Charivari*, no. 18 (Paris, 1973).

Roux, S., *L'Affaire de Rennes-le-Château* (Levallois-Perret, 1966).

Stublein, Eugène, *Pierres gravées du Languedoc* (Limoux, 1884). Reproduction of plates XVI to XXIII by Abbé Joseph Courtauly (Villarzel-du-Razès, 1962).

2 GENERAL REFERENCES

Addison, C. G., *The History of the Knights Templars* (London, 1842).

Alart, M., 'Suppression de l'Ordre du Temple en Roussillon,' *Bulletin de la socété agricole, scientifique et littéraire des Pyrénées Orientales*, vol. 15 (Perpignan, 1867).

Albon, M. de, *Cartulaire général de l'Order du Temple* (Paris, 1913).

Allegro, J. M., *The Dead Sea Scrolls*, 2nd edn (Harmondsworth, 1975).

Allegro, J. M., *The Treasure of the Copper Scroll* (London, 1960).

Allier, R., *La Cabale des dévots, 1627–1666* (Paris, 1902).

Allier, R., *Une Société secrete au XVIIe siècle. La Compagnie du Très-Saint Sacrement* (Paris, 1909).

Anderson, J., *The Constitutions of the Free Masons* (Paris, 1723).

Andressohn, J. C., *The Ancestry and Life of Godfrey of Bouillon* (Bloomington, 1947).

Annuaire ecclésiastique (Paris, 1896).

Anselm, Le P., *Historie généalogique et chronologique de la maison royale de France*, 9 vols. (Paris, 1726–33).

Arbois de Jubainville, M. H. d', *Histoire des ducs et des comtes de Champagne*, 7 vols. (Paris, 1859–69).

Arcons, C. d', *Du Flux et reflux de la mer et des longitudes avec des observations sur les mines métalliques de France* (Paris, 1667).

Aubert de la Chenaye des Bois, F. A., *Dictionnaire de la noblesse*, 19 vols., 3rd edn (Paris, 1863–76).

Auguste, A., *La Compagnie du Saint-Sacrement à Toulouse* (Paris, 1913).

Bander, P., *The Prophecies of St Malachy and St Columbkille*, 4th edn (Gerards Cross, 1979).

Barber, M., *The Trial of the Templars* (Cambridge, 1978).

Barber, R., *King Arthur in Legend and History* (Ipswich, 1973).

Barber, R., *The Knight and Chivalry*, 2nd edn (Ipswich, 1974).

Baring-Gould, S., *Curious Myths of the Middle Ages* (London, 1881).

Barral, A. de, *Légendes capétiennes* (Tours, 1884).

Barthélemy, E. de, *Obituaire de la Commanderie du Temple de Reims* (Paris, 1882).

Begouen, Comte de, *Une Société émule de la Compagnie du Saint-Sacrament: L'AA de Toulouse* (Paris, 1913).

Bernadac, C., *Le Mystère Otto Rahn* (Paris, 1978).

Bernstein, H., *The Truth about 'The Protocols'* (New York, 1935).

Birch, T,. *The Life of Robert Boyle* (London, 1744).

Blunt, A., *Nicolas Poussin*, 2 vols. (London, 1967).

Bouquet, M. (ed.), *Recueil des historiens des Gaules et de la France*, vol. 15 (Paris, 1738).

Brandon, S. G. F., *Jesus and the Zealots* (Manchester, 1967).

Brandon, S. G. F., *The Trial of Jesus of Nazareth* (London, 1968).

Brownlee, W. H., 'Whence the Gospel According to John', in James H. Charlesworth (ed.), *John and Qumran* (London, 1972).

Bruel, A., 'Chartes d'Adam, Abbé de N-D du Mont-Sion et le Prieuré de Saint-Samson d'Orléans', *Revue de L'Orient Latin*, vol. 10 (Paris, 1905).

Bull, N. J., *The Rise of the Church* (London, 1967).

Calmet, Dom, 'Des Divinités payennes', in *Oeuvres inédites de Dom A. Calmet*, 1st ser. (Saint-Dié, 1876).

Carpenter, R., *Folk-tale, Fiction and Saga in the Homeric Epics* (Los Angeles, 1946).

Carrière, V., *Histoire et cartulaire des Templiers de Provins* (Paris, 1919).

Catel, G. de, *Mémoires de l'histoire du Languedoc* (Toulouse, 1633).

Chadwick, H., *The Early Church* (Harmondsworth, 1978).

Chadwick, H., *Priscillian of Avila* (Oxford, 1976).

Le Charivari, no. 18 (Paris, Oct.–Dec. 1973).

Chassant, A., and Tausin, H., *Dictionnaire des devises historiques et héraldiques* (Paris, 1878).

Chatelain, U. V., *Le Surintendant Nicolas Foucquet* (Paris, 1905).

Chaumeil, J.-L., *Le Trésor du triangle d'or* (Paris, 1979).

Chrétien de Troyes, *Le Conte del Graal*, published as *The Story of the Grail*, trans. Robert W. Linker, 2nd edn (Chapel Hill, 1952).

Cochet, Abbé, *Le Tombeau de Childeric Ier* (Paris, 1859).

Cohn, H., *The Trial and Death of Jesus* (New York, 1971).

Cohn, N., *The Pursuit of the Millennium* (St Albans, 1978).

Cohn, N., *Warrant for Genocide* (Harmondsworth, 1970).

Collin, H., 'Après Azincourt. Bar, capital ducale, et la compagnie du Lévrier Blanc,' *Bulletin des sociétés d'histoire et d'archéologie de la Meuse*, no. 12 (Bar-le-Duc, 1975).

Courrent, P., *Notice historique sur les bains de Rennes* (Carcassonne, 1934).

Curzon, H. de, *La Règle du Temple* (Paris, 1886).

Cutts, E. L., *The Sepulchral Slabs and Crosses of the Middle Ages* (London, 1849).

Daraul, A., *A History of Secret Societies* (New York, 1969).

Delaborde, H. F., *Jean de Joinville et les seigneurs de Joinville* (Paris, 1894).

Demay, G., *Inventaire des sceaux de la Normandie* (Paris, 1881).

Denyau, R., *Histoire polytique de Gisors et du pays de Vulcsain* (Gisors, 1629). Manuscript in Bib. De Rouen, Coll. Montbret 2219, V 14a.

Descadeillas, R., 'Mythologie du trésor de Rennes', *Mémoires de la société des arts et des sciences de Carcassonne*, 4th ser., vol. 7, part 2 (Carcassonne, 1974).

Descadeillas, R., *Rennes et ses derniers seigneurs* (Toulouse, 1964).

Didrit, Abbé Th., 'La Montagne de Sion-Vaudémont et son sanctuaire', *Mémoires de la société d'archéologie Lorraine*, 3rd ser., vol. 27 (Nancy, 1899).

Digot, A., *Histoire de Lorraine*, 3 vols (Nancy, 1856).

Digot, A., *Histoire du royaume d'Austrasie*, 4 vols (Nancy, 1863).

Digot, A., 'Mémoire sur les établissements de l'Order du Temple en Lorraine', *Mémoires de la société d'archéologie Lorraine*, 2nd ser., vol. 10 (Nancy, 1868).

Digot, P., *Notice historique sur Notre-Dame-de-Sion* (Nancy, 1856).

Dill, S., *Roman Society in Gaul in the Merovingian Age* (London, 1926).

Dobbs, B. J. T., *The Foundations of Newton's Alchemy* (Cambridge, 1975).

Dodd, C.H., *Historical Tradition in the Fourth Gospel* (Cambridge, 1963).

Dodu, G., *Histoire des institutions dans le royaume latin de Jérusalem* (Paris, 1894).

Doinel, J.-S., *Note sur le Roi Hildérik III* (Carcassonne, 1899).

Drummond, J. S., *The Twentieth Century Hoax* (London, 1961).

Dumas, F., *Le Tombeau de Childeric* (Paris, n.d.).

Einhard, *The Life of Charlemagne*, in *Two Lives of Charlemagne*, trans. Lewis Thorpe (Harmondsworth, 1979).

Eisenstein, E. L., *The First Professional Revolutionist: Filippo Michele Buonarroti* (Harvard, 1959).

Eisler, R., *The Messiah Jesus and John the Baptist*, trans. A. H. Krappe (London, 1931).

Erdeswick, S., *A Survey of Staffordshire*, new edn (London, 1844).

Esquieu, L., 'Les Templiers de Cahors', in *Bulletin de la société des études littéraires, scientifiques et artistiques du Lot*, vol. 22 (Cahors, 1897).

Evison, V. I., *The Fifth-century Invasions South of the Thames* (London, 1965).

Fédié, L., *Le Comté de Razès et le Diocèse d'Alet* (Carcassonne, 1880; reprinted Brussels, 1979).

Finke, H., *Papsttum und Untergang des Templerordens*, 2 vols. (Münster, 1907).

Folz, R., 'Tradition hagiographique et culte de Saint Dagobert, roi des Francs', *Le Moyen Age*, 4th ser., vol. 18 (Brussels, 1963).

Fortune, D., *The Mystical Qabalah*, 9th edn (London, 1970).

Frappier, J., *Chrétien de Troyes* (Paris, 1968).

French, P. J., *John Dee: The World of an Elizabethan Magus* (London, 1972).

Fry, L., *Waters Flowing Eastward, the War against the Kingship of Christ* (London, 1965).

Genealogy of Genevill of Trime, manuscript in Brit. Lib., Harley 1425, f. 127.

Gérard, P., and Magnou, É., *Cartulaires des Templiers de Douzens* (Paris, 1965).

Gilles, M., *Histoire de Sablé* (Paris, 1683).

Goodenough, E. R., *Jewish Symbols in the Greco-Roman Period*, 12 vols. (New York, 1953).

Gospel of the Infancy of Jesus Christ, in *The Lost Books of the Bible*, ed. Rutherford H. Platt (New York, 1974).

Gospel of Peter, in *The Lost Books of the Bible*, ed. Rutherford H. Platt (New York, 1974).

Gould, R. F., *The History of Freemasonry*, 6 vols. (London, n.d.).

Gout, P., *Le Mont-Saint-Michel*, 2 vols. (Paris, 1910).

Graves, R., *The Greek Myths*, 2 vols., rev. edn (Harmondsworth, 1978).

Graves, R., *King Jesus*, 4th edn (London, 1960).

Graves, R., *The White Goddess*, enlarged edn (London, 1977).

Gregory of Tours, *The History of the Franks*, trans. Lewis Thorpe (Harmondsworth, 1977).

Greub, W, 'The Pre-Christian Grail Tradition of the Three Kings', *Mercury Star Journal*, vol. 5, no. 2 (Summer 1979). (Extract from *Wolfram von Eschenbach und die Wirklichkeit des Grals*.)

Grousset, R., *Histoire des croisades et du royaume franc de Jérusalem*, 3 vols. (Paris, 1934–6).

Hagenmeyer, H., *Le Vrai et le faux sur Pierre l'Hermite*, trans. Furcy Raynaud (Paris, 1883).

Halevi, Z., *Adam and the Kabbalistic Tree* (London, 1974).

Halsberghe, G. H., *The Cult of Sol Invictus* (Leiden, 1972).

Hay, R. A., *Genealogie of the Saintclaires of Rosslyn* (Edinburgh, 1835).

Henderson, G. D., *Chevalier Ramsay* (London, 1952).

The Interlinear Greek–English New Testament, trans. Alfred Marshall, 2nd edn (London, 1967).

Iremonger, F.A., *William Temple Archbishop of Canterbury, His Life and Letters* (London, 1948).

Irenaeus of Lyons, *Five Books of S. Irenaeus, Bishop of Lyons, against Heresies*, trans. John Keble (London, 1872).

Jacobus de Voragine, *The Golden Legend*, ed. F. S. Ellis (London, 1900).

Jaffus, F., *La Cité de Carcassonne et les trésors des Wisigoths* (Carcassonne, 1867).

Jean de Joinville, *Life of Saint Louis*, in *Chronicles of the Crusades*, trans. Margaret R. B. Shaw (Harmondsworth, 1976).

Jeantin, J.-F.-L., *Les Chroniques de l'Ardenne et des Woëpvres*, 2 vols. (Paris, 1851).

Johann von Würzburg, *Description of the Holy Land, by John of Würzburg, AD 1160–1170*, trans. Aubrey Stewart, *Palestine Pilgrims Text Society*, vol. 5 (London, 1897).

Josephus, *The Jewish War*, trans. G. A. Williamson (Harmondsworth, 1978).

Jourdanne, G., *Folk-Lore de l'Aude*, 2nd edn (Paris, 1973).

Joyce, D., *The Jesus Scroll* (London, 1975).

King, F., *The Secret Rituals of the O.T.O.* (London, 1973).

Klausner, J. G., *Jesus of Nazareth* (London, 1925).

The Koran, trans. N. J. Dawood (Harmondsworth, 1977).

Labouisse-Rochefort, A. de, *Les Amours, à Éléonore*, 2nd edn (Paris, 1818).

Labouisse-Rochefort, A. de, *Voyage à Rennes-les-Bains* (Paris, 1832).

Lacordaire, J. B. H., *St Mary Magdalen* (London, 1880).

Lalanne, L., *Dictionnaire historique de la France* (Paris, 1877).

Lanigan, J., *An Ecclesiastical History of Ireland*, 4 vols., 2nd edn (Dublin, 1829).

Làuth, F., 'Tableau de l'au delà', *Mémoires de la société des arts et des sciences de Carcassonne*, 3rd ser., vol. 5 (Carcassonne, 1937–40).

Lecoy de la Marche, R. A., *Le Roi René*, 2 vols. (Paris, 1875).

Lees, B. A., *Records of the Templars in England in the Twelfth Century* (London, 1935).

Le Forestier, R., *La Franc-Maçonnerie occultiste* (Paris, 1928).

Le Forestier, R., *La Franc-Maçonnerie templière et occultiste aux XVIIIe et XIXe siècles* (Paris, 1970).

Le Maire, F., *Histoire et antiquitez de la ville et duché d'Orléans*, 2 vols., 2nd edn (Orleans, 1648).

Léonard, E.-G., *Introduction au cartulaire manuscrit du Temple* (Paris, 1930).

Lépinois, E. de, 'Lettres de Louis Fouquet à son frère Nicolas Fouquet,' in *Archives de l'art français*, 2nd ser., vol. 2 (Paris, 1861–6).

Levillain, L., 'Les Nibelungen historiques', *Annales du Midi*, year 49 (Toulouse, 1937) and year 50 (Toulouse, 1938).

Lilley, A. L., *Modernism: A Record and Review* (London, 1908).

Lizerand, G., *Dossier de l'affaire des Templiers* (Paris, 1923).

Lobineau, G. A., *Histoire de Bretagne*, 2 vols. (Paris, 1707).

Loomis, R. S., *Arthurian Tradition and Chrétien de Troyes* (New York, 1949).

Loomis, R. S., *The Grail* (Cardiff, 1963).

Loyd, L. C., *The Origins of some Anglo-Norman Families*, ed. C. T. Clay and D. C. Douglas (Leeds, 1951).

Lucie-Smith, E., *Symbolist Art* (London, 1977).

The Mabinogion, trans. Jeffrey Gantz (Harmondsworth, 1977).

Maccoby, H., *Revolution in Judaea* (London, 1973).

Maddison, R. E. W., *The Life of the Honourable Robert Boyle, F.R.S.* (London, 1969).

Manuel, F. E., *A Portrait of Isaac Newton* (Cambridge, Mass., 1968).

Marie, F., *Rennes-le-Château, étude critique* (Bagneux, 1978).

Marot, P., *Le Symbolisme de la croix de Lorraine* (Paris, 1948).

Mazières, Abbé M.-R., 'Une curieuse affair du XIIe siècle, celle du "Puig des Lépreux" à Perpignan,' *Mémoires de la société des arts et des sciences de Carcassonne*, 4th ser., vol. 4 (Carcassonne, 1960–62).

Mazières, Abbé M.R., 'Un Épisode curieux, en terre d'Aude, du process de templiers', *Memories de la société des arts et des sciences de Carcassonne*, 4th ser., vol. 4 (Carcassonne, 1960–62).

Mazières, Abbé M.-R., 'Recherches historiques à Campagne-sur-Aude', *Mémoires de la société des arts et des sciences de Carcassonne*, 4th ser., vol. 4 (Carcassonne, 1960–62).

Mazières, Abbé M.-R., 'La Venue et le séjour des Templiers du Roussillon à la fin du XIIIme siècle et au début du XIVme dans la vallée du Bézu (Aude)', *Mémoires de la société des arts et des sciences de Carcassonne*, 4th ser., vol. 3 (Carcassonne, 1957–9).

Melville, M., *La Vie des Templiers*, 2nd edn (Paris, 1974).

Michelet, M., *Procès des Templiers*, 2 vols (Paris, 1851).

Michell, H., *Sparta* (Cambridge, 1964).

The Nag Hammadi Library in English, trans. by members of the Coptic Gnostic Library Project of the Institute for Antiquity and Christianity, dir. James M. Robinson (Leiden, 1977).

Nantes, G., de, *Liber Accusationis in Paulum Sextum* (St Parres les Vaudes, 1973).

Nelli, R., *Les Cathares* (Toulouse, 1965).

Nelli, R., *Dictionnaire des hérésies méridionales* (Toulouse, 1968).

Nelli, R., *La Philosophie du catharisme* (Paris, 1978).

Niel, F., *Les Cathars de Montségur* (Paris, 1973).

Nilus, S., *Protocols of the Learned Elders of Zion*, trans. Victor E. Marsden (London, 1923).

Nodier, C., *Contes*, ed. Pierre-Georges Castex (Paris, 1961).

Nodier, C., *History of the Secret Societies of the Army* (London, 1815). Published anonymously.

Nodier, C., *Voyages pittoresques at romantiques dans l'ancienne France, Normandy*, 3 vols (Paris, 1820–78).

Noonan, J. T., *Contraception* (New York, 1967).

Oldenbourg, Z., *Massacre at Montségur* (London, 1961).

Olry, M. E., 'Topographie de la montagne de Sion-Vaudémont', *Mémoires de la société d'archéologie Lorraine*, 2nd ser., vol. 10 (Nancy, 1868).

Orr, J., *Les Oeuvres de Guiot de Provins* (Manchester, 1915).

Ort, L. J. R., *Mani: A Religio-historical Description of his Personality* (Leiden, 1967).

Oursel, R., *Le Procès des Templiers* (Paris, 1959).

Pagels, E., *The Gnostic Gospels* (London, 1980).

Pange, J. de, *L'Auguste Maison de Lorraine* (Lyons, 1966).

Paoli, M., *Les Dessous d'une ambition politique* (Nyon, 1973).

Parrinder, G., *Jesus in the Qur'an* (London, 1965).

Perey, L., *Charles de Lorraine et la cour de Bruxelles* (Paris, 1903).

The Perlesvaus, trans. Sebastian Evans as *The High History of the Holy Grail*, new edn (London, 1969).

Peyrefitte, R., 'La Lettre secrète', *Le Symbolisme*, no. 356 (Paris, April–June 1962).

Phipps, W. E., *The Sexuality of Jesus* (New York, 1973).

Phipps, W. E., *Was Jesus Married?* (New York, 1970).

Pincus-Witten, R., *Occult Symbolism in France: Joséphin Péladan and the Salons de la Rose-Croix* (London, 1976).

Pingaud, L., *La Jeunesse de Charles Nodier* (Besançon, 1914).

Piquet, J., *Des Banquiers au moyen âge: les Templiers* (Paris, 1939).

Plot, R., *The Natural History of Staffordshire* (Oxford, 1686).

Ponsich, P., 'Le Conflent et ses comtes du IXe au XIIe Siècle', *Etudes Roussillonnaises*, first year, no. 3–4 (Perpignan, July–Dec. 1951).

Poull, G., *La Maison ducale de Bar*, vol. 1 (Rupt-sur-Moselle, 1977).

Powicke, F. M., *The Loss of Normandy*, 2nd edn (Manchester, 1961).

Procopius of Caesarea, *History of the Wars*, trans. H. B. Dewing (London, 1919).

Prutz, H. G., *Entwicklung und Untergang des Tempelherrenordens* (Berlin, 1888).

Quatrebarbes, T., de, *Oeuvres completes du roi René*, 4 vols. (Angers, 1845).

Queste del Saint Graal, trans. P. M. Matarasso as *The Quest of the Holy Grail* (Harmondsworth, 1976).

Rabinowitz, J. J., 'The Title *De Migrantibus* of the *Lex Salica* and the Jewish *Herem Hayishub*', *Speculum*, vol. 22 (Cambridge, Mass., Jan. 1947).

Rahn, O., *Croisade contre le Graal*, trans. Robert Pitrou (Paris, 1974).

Rahn, O., *La Cour de Lucifer*, trans. René Nelli (Paris, 1974).

René d'Anjou, *Le Livre du cuer d'amours espris*, manuscript in Nat. Bib. Vienna, Cod. Vind. 2597.

Rey, E.-G., 'Chartes de l'Abbaye du Mont-Sion,' *Mémoires de la Société nationale des antiquaires de France*, 5th ser., vol. 8 (Paris, 1887).

Rey, E.-G., *Les Familles d'Outre-mer* (Paris, 1869).

Richey, M. F., *Studies of Wolfram von Eschenbach* (London, 1957).

Robert de Boron, *Roman de l'Estoire dou Saint Graal*, trans. Frederick J. Furnival as *The History of the Holy Graal* (London, 1861).

Roberts, J. M., *The Mythology of the Secret Societies* (St Albans, 1974).

Roche, D., 'La Capitulation et le bûcher de Montségur', in *Mémoires de la société des arts et des sciences de Carcassonne*, 3rd ser, vol. 7 (Carcassonne, 1944–6).

Roethlisberger, B., *Die Architektur des Graltempels im Jungen Titurel* (Nendeln, 1970).

Roger de Hoveden, *The Annals of Roger de Hoveden*, trans. H. T. Riley, 2 vols. (London, 1853).

Röhricht, R., *Regesta Regni Hierosolymitani* (Innsbrück, 1893).

Rosnay, F. de, *Le Hiéron du Val d'Or* (Paray-le-Monial, 1900).

Rougement, D. de, *Love in the Western World* (New York, 1940).

Runciman, S., *A History of the Crusades*, 3 vols. (Harmondsworth, 1978).

Runciman, S., *The Medieval Manichee* (Cambridge, 1969).

Sabarthès, A. (ed.), *Dictionnaire topographique du département de l'Aude* (Paris, 1912).

Saint-Clair, L. A. de, *Histoire Généalogique de famille de Saint-Clair* (Paris, 1905).

Sainte-Marie, L. de, *Recherches historiques sur Nevers* (Nevers, 1810).

Saxer, V., *Le Culte de Marie Madeleine en Occident*, 2 vols, (Paris, 1959).

Schonfield, H. J., *The Passover Plot* (London, 1977).

Schottmüller, K., *Der Untergang des Templer-Ordens*, 2 vols. (Berlin, 1887).

Sède, G. de, *L'Or de Rennes* (Paris, 1967). (Also published in paperback as *Le Trésor maudit*.)

Sède, G. de, *La Race fabuleuse* (Paris, 1973).

Sède, G. de, *Signé: Rose + Croix* (Paris, 1977).

Sède, G. de, *Les Templiers sont parmi nous* (Paris, 1976).

Sède, G. de, *Le Vrai Dossier de l'énigme de Rennes* (Vestric, 1975).

Seward, D., *The Monks of War* (St Albans, 1974).

Shah, I., *The Sufis* (London, 1969).

Simon, E., *The Piebald Standard* (London, 1959).

Smith, M., *The Secret Gospel* (London, 1974).

Smith, M., *Jesus the Magician* (London, 1978).

Soultrait, G. de (ed.), *Dictionnaire topographique du département de la Nièvre* (Paris, 1865).

Staley, E., *King René d'Anjou and his Seven Queens* (London, 1912).

Steegmuller, F., *Cocteau: A Biography* (London, 1970).

Sumption, J., *The Albigensian Crusade* (London, 1978).

Taylor, A. J. P., *The War Plans of the Great Powers, 1880–1914* (London, 1979).

Thomas, K., *Religion and the Decline of Magic* (Harmondsworth, 1980).

Thory, C. A., *Acta Latomorum ou chronologie de l'histoire de la franche-maçonnerie Française et étrangère*, 2 vols. (Paris, 1815).

Tillière, N., *Histoire de l'Abbaye d'Orval* (Orval, 1967).

Topencharon, V., *Boulgres et Cathares* (Paris, 1971).

Ullmann, W., *A History of Political Thought: The Middle Ages*, rev. edn (Harmondsworth, 1970).

Vachez, A., *Les Familles chevaleresques du Lyonnais* (Lyon, 1875).

Vaissete, J. J., 'Dissertation sur l'origine des Francs', *Collection des Meilleurs Dissertations*, vol. 1 (Paris, 1826).

Vaissete, J. J., and Vic, C. de, *Histoire générale de Languedoc avec des notes et les pièces justificatives*, under direction of Edouard Dulaurier (Toulouse, 1872–1905).

Vazart, L., *Abrégé de l'histoire des Francs, les gouvernants et rois de France* (Paris, 1978).

Vermes, G., *The Dead Sea Scrolls in English*, 2nd edn (Harmondsworth, 1977).

Vermes, G., *Jesus the Jew* (London, 1977).

Vincent, Le R. P., *Histoire de l'anciene image miraculeuse de Notre Dame de Sion* (Nancy, 1698).

Vincent, Le R. P., *Histoire fidelle de St Sigisbert XII roy, d'Austrasie, et III du nom. Avec un abrégé de la vie du Roy Dagobert son fils* (Nancy, 1702).

Vogüé, M. de, *Les Églises de la terre sainte* (Paris, 1860).

Waite, A. E., *The Hidden Church of the Holy Grail* (London, 1909).

Waite, A. E., *A New Encyclopaedia of Freemasonry*, 2 vols. (London, 1921).

Waite, A. E., *The Real History of the Rosicrucians* (London, 1887).

Walker, D. P., *The Ancient Theology* (London, 1972).

Walker, D. P., *Spiritual and Demonic Magic from Ficino to Campanella* (London, 1975).

Wallace-Hadrill, J. M., *The Long-haired Kings* (London, 1962).

Ward, J. S. M., *Freemasonry and the Ancient Gods*, 2nd edn (London, 1926).

Weston, J. L., *From Ritual to Romance* (Cambridge, 1920).

William, Count of Orange, ed. Glanville Price (London, 1975).

William of Tyre, *A History of Deeds Done Beyond the Sea*, trans. Emily Atwater Babcock and A. C. Krey, 2 vols. (New York, 1943).

Wind, E., *Pagan Mysteries in the Renaissance*, rev. edn (Oxford, 1980).

Winter, P., *On the Trial of Jesus* (Berlin, 1961).

Wolfram von Eschenbach, *Parzival*, trans. Helen M. Mustard and Charles E. Passage (New York, 1961).

Wolfram von Eschenbach, *Willehalm*, trans. R. Fink and F. Knorr (Jena, 1944).

Yates, F. A., *The Art of Memory* (Harmondsworth, 1978).

Yates, F. A., *Giordano Bruno and the Hermetic Tradition* (London, 1978).

Yates, F. A., *The Rosicrucian Enlightenment* (St Albans, 1975).

Yates, F. A., *The Occult Philosophy in the Elizabethan Age* (London, 1979).

Zuckerman, A. J., *A Jewish Princedom in Feudal France* (New York, 1972).

NOTES AND REFERENCES

NOTE
The full bibliographical details, when not cited here, are to be found in the Bibliography.

1 VILLAGE OF MYSTERY

1 Gérard de Sède, *L'Or de Rennes*. Robert Charroux, *Trésors du monde* (Paris, 1962), pp. 247 ff.

2 *Annuaire Ecclesiastique*, p. 282.

3 De Sède, *L'Or de Rennes*, p. 28. The painting was supposedly of 'Saint Antoine l'Hermite'. De Sède himself said in conversation that the painting was the 'Temptation of Saint Anthony', but no one knew which one. Later our researches indicated that it was in fact 'Saint Anthony and Saint Jerome in the Desert'.

4 Fédié, *Le Comté de Razès*, pp. 3 ff. The figure of 30,000 inhabitants is given by de Sède in *L'Or de Rennes*, p. 17. He gives no source.

5 Procopius, *History of the Wars*, book v, xii.

6 We have twice had the relevant archives in the Vatican checked and on both occasions our researchers reported that no reference to Saunière could be found. There is not even any record of his existence, a curious lacuna in the normally detailed Vatican records. It suggests that all information regarding this priest has been extracted deliberately.

7 Lépinois, 'Lettres de Louis Fouquet', pp. 269 ff. The letter was kept in the archives of the Cossé-Brissac family, who have been prominent in Freemasonry since the eighteenth century.

8 Delaude, *Cercle d'Ulysse*, p. 3. The author says that the tomb is cited in a *mémoire* by the Abbé Delmas dating from the seventeenth century. This work is undoubtedly the *mémoire* of Delmas dated 1709. This manuscript was originally deposited with the *Académie celtique*, then vanished for some time. Earlier this century it reappeared and part was published in Courrent, *Notice historique*, pp. 9–17. However, this extract does not mention the tomb. It can only be supposed that the missing pieces contain the information, but the Delmas manuscript is now in private possession in Limoux, and has not been made available to us for reference.

2 THE CATHARS AND THE GREAT HERESY

1 In 1888, while working at the Municipal Library of Orleans, Doinel found a manuscript dating from 1022, written by a Gnostic who was later in the same year burned at the stake. Reading this manuscript converted Doinel into an avid Gnostic. See Lauth, 'Tableau de l'au dela', pp. 212 ff.

2 Manichaeans had long been involved in the use of various forms of birth control, and were also accused of justifying abortion. These practices were almost certainly part of the latter Cathar teaching. Noonan makes the point that the Church's condemnation of contraception had been reaffirmed during its condemnation of the Cathars. See Noonan, *Contraception*, p. 281, Chadwick, *Priscillian*, p. 37.

3 De Rougement, *Love in the Western World*, p. 78.

4 In A.D. 800 Manichaeans were still being condemned in the West. In 991 Gerbert d'Aurillac, later Pope Sylvester II, expressed Manichaean beliefs. See Runciman, *The Medieval Manichee*, p. 117, Niel, *Les Cathars de Montségur*, pp. 26 ff.

5 Jean de Joinville, *Life of Saint Louis*, p. 174.

6 Niel, *Les Cathars de Montségur*, pp. 291 ff.

7 The Manichaeans had a sacred festival called the *Berma*, which was celebrated during March. Niel suggests that this was the festival held at Montségur on March 14th, adding that in 1244 the spring equinox fell on this date: Niel, *Les Cathars de Montségur*, pp. 276 ff. The Manichaeans apparently used a special book of drawings which expressed Mani's teachings, perhaps symbolically. It contained pictures showing the dualism between the Sons of Light and the Sons of Darkness. This book was used during the *Berma* festival. Perhaps a similar book of symbols constituted part of the Cathar treasure. See Ort, *Mani*, pp. 168 ff., 180 and 253 ff.

8 See Waite, *Holy Grail*, pp. 524 ff. For criticism, see his 1933 edition, pp. 396 ff.

9 Nelli, *Dictionnaire des hérésies*, pp. 216 ff. The writer most involved with these types of connections was Otto Rahn, author of *Croisade contre le Graal*, and *La Cour de Lucifer*. Otto Rahn claimed that the Grail castle in Wolfram von Eschenbach's *Munsalvaesche* is Montségur. Rahn's books were first published in German in the 1930s. Rahn himself joined the SS, rising to the rank of Colonel. His researches into the Cathars and the Grail had the support of Alfred Rosenberg, major racial philosopher, spokesman for the Nazi party and friend of Hitler. Rahn disappeared in 1939, allegedly committing suicide on the peak of Mount Kufstein. However, a French researcher has turned up several documents relating to Rahn, the latest dated 1945. See Bernadac, *Le Mystère Otto Rahn*. If these documents indeed refer to the author Otto Rahn, it is interesting to speculate whether he was behind the mysterious German excavations carried out at Montségur and other Cathar sites during the Second World War.

3 THE WARRIOR MONKS

1 Runciman, *History of the Crusades*, vol. 2, p. 477.

2 Esquieu, 'Les Templiers de Cahors', p. 147, n. 1, explains that Hugues de Payen was not born in Champagne but in the château of Mahun, near Annonay in the lower Rhône valley (Ardèche). His birth record has been found and the date of birth given is February 9th, 1070. Presumably he later moved to Champagne.

3 William of Tyre, *History of Deeds Done Beyond the Sea*, vol.

1, pp. 525 ff.

4 Addison, *History of the Knights Templars*, p. 19. For a copy of the original rule see Curzon, *La Règle du Temple*.

5 Addison, *History of the Knights Templars*, p. 19.

6 This date has been challenged, it has been argued that it must date from no earlier than 1152.

7 King Richard I was a close friend of the Order, and lived with them during his stay in Acre. When he left the Holy Land in 1192, he left disguised as a Templar, setting sail in a Templar ship, and accompanied by four members of the Order. See Addison, *History of the Knights Templars*, p. 148.

8 Daraul, *History of Secret Societies*, pp. 46 ff. Daraul neglects to supply a source.

9 See Piquet, *Des Banquiers au moyen âge*. The initial function was to facilitate the pilgrimage to the Holy Land. See also Melville, *Vie des Templiers*, pp. 87 ff. The first loan was recorded in 1135. Seward, *The Monks of War*, p. 213, says, 'The Poor Knights' most lasting achievement, their contribution towards the overthrow of the church's attitude to usury, was economic. No medieval institution did more for the rise of capitalism.' Usary was prohibited, so the interest on loans was calculated beforehand and included in the total amount borrowed. If land was used as collateral, the Templars received all the income from this land until the full loan was repaid.

10 Melville, *Vie des Templiers*, p. 220.

11 See Mazières, 'La Venue et le séjour des Templiers', p. 235.

12 Blanchefort was destroyed during the Albigensian Crusade, falling some time before 1215, at which date its lands were given by Simon de Montfort to Pierre de Voisins. The lord of Blanchefort had fought at the side of Raymond-Roger Trencavel, the Cathar leader. See Fédié, *Le Comte de Razès*, p. 151. Bertrand de Blanchefort himself, often in conjunction with the earlier Trencavel, was involved in donations of money and property to the Templars. These transactions are recorded before he joined the Order, while he was still married to his wife Fabrissa. See Albon, *Cartulaire général*, p. 41 (Charter LVI 1133–4). Mention of Bertrand's wife and his two brothers, Arnaud and Raymond, can be found in the same work, Charter CLX 1138, p. 112.

13 Mazières, 'La Venue et le séjour des Templiers', pp. 243 ff. See also Mazières, 'Recherches historiques', p. 276. A document found in the archives of the Bruyères and Mauléon family records how the Templars of Campagne and Albedune (Le Bézu) established a house of refuge for Cathar 'bonhommes'. This document and others disappeared during the war, sometime in November 1942.

14 See for example Léonard, *Introduction au cartulaire*, p. 76. The preceptor of the Temple at Toulouse at the beginning of the Albigensian Crusade was of the Cathar Trencavel family.

15 One way that the Order could well have received advance warning of the catastrophe was via Jean de Joinville. He was seneschal of Champagne and so would have received Philippe le Bel's secret orders to carry out the arrests. He was known to be sympathetic to the Templars, and his uncle, André, had been a member of the Order and preceptor of Payns in the 1260s (Léonard, *Introduction au cartulaire*, p. 145). Jean wrote of a mysterious oath mentioning spitting on the cross, at the time that the Templars were being accused of it. Furthermore he hinted very strongly that Saint Louis knew of this fifty years before, and refused to condemn it. (See Jean de Joinville, *Life of Saint Louis*, p. 254.) Jean organised a league of nobles to oppose the excesses of the French king against the Temple. The league was rendered superfluous by the king's death.

16 When the arresting officers, accompanied by the king himself, took the Paris Temple in 1307, they found neither the money of the Order nor the documents. The treasurer of the Order was Hugues de Peraud, and under him served Gérard de Villers, the preceptor of France. In 1308 seventy-two Templars were taken to Poitiers to give evidence before the pope himself (the number of Templars is given in the Papal Bull, *Faciens misericordam*). Not all the depositions taken at the time have survived. It is quite possible that many vanished when all the Vatican secret archives, including all documents relating to the Templars, were taken to Paris by order of Napoleon. Such was the chaos that shopkeepers were found wrapping their goods in the precious documents. Thirty-three depositions by Poitiers were published by the German historian, Conrad Schottmüller, in 1887, and a further seven by Heinrich Finke in 1907. In this last group there is a curious statement by a Jean de Châlons. He claimed that Gérard de Villers had foreknowledge of the arrests, had fled the Temple accompanied by fifty knights and gone to sea in eighteen galleys of the Order. He adds that Hugues de Châlons had left with all the treasure of Hugues de Peraud – *cum toto thesauro fratris Hugonis de Peraudo*. This, he said when questioned, had remained secret because those Templars who knew of it feared they would be killed if they spoke. See Finke, *Papsttum und Untergang des Templerordens*, vol. II, p. 339.
There is some evidence to support such an assertion. When the Templars were arrested that dawn, certain had not been present and were captured a few days later. Gérard de Villers and Hugues de Châlons were not recorded as being captured. See Barber, M., *Trial of the Templars*, p. 46.

17 This story is reported by Waite, *New Encyclopaedia of Freemasonry*, vol. 2, p. 223.

18 Wolfram von Eschenbach, *Parzival*, p. 251.

19 Shah, *The Sufis*, p. 225. See also the introduction to Shah's book by Robert Graves, who, on p. xix, explains the play on words linking black with wise in Arabic. Graves claims that the three black heads on the family shield of Hugues de Payen are such a device with a dual

20 Oursel, *Le Procès des Templiers*, p. 208.

21 Lobineau, H., *Dossiers secrets*, planche no. 4, *Ordre de Sion*, gives a quote from p. 292 of the *Livre des constitutions* (of the Ordre de Sion) where the head is called CAPUT LVIII ♍ – Head 58 Virgo.

22 This version is from Ward, *Freemasonry and the Ancient Gods*, p. 305.

23 Roger de Hoveden, *Annals*, vol. II pp. 248 ff. For a detailed discussion of the *Yse* stories see Barber, M., *Trial of the Templars*, pp. 185 ff. He does not consider that the story has any relevance to the history of the Templars, suggesting it was a fragment of common folklore used as a weapon against the Order.

24 Barber, M., *Trial of the Templars*, p. 249. The list is abridged.

25 Michelet, *Procès des Templiers*, vol. II, p. 384, deposition of Jean de Chaumes.

26 Schottmüller, *Der Untergang des Templer-Ordens*, vol. III, p. 67, deposition of Deodatus Jefet.

27 Michelet, *Procès des Templiers*, pp. 383 ff, deposition of Fulk de Troyes.

28 Jean de Joinville, *Life of Saint Louis*, p. 254. See also ch. 3, n. 15.

29 Albon, *Cartulaire general*, p. 2 (Charter III, 1125) mentions a Templar named *Roberti* – who could possibly have been the Robert who became Grand Master after the death of Hugues de Payen. On p. 3 (Charter IV 1125) there is mention of Templars *Henrico et Roberto*. This then adds two names to Fulk d'Anjou and Hugues de Champagne, making at least four recruits.

30 Bouquet, *Recueil des Historiens*, vol. 15 (*Epistolae Ivonis Carnotensis Episcopi*), p. 162, no. 245.

31 'The *milice du Christ*, the evangelical soldiery in this letter is none other than the Order of the Temple. But in 1114 the Order of the Temple was not yet established . . .' Arbois de Jubainville, *Histoire . . . de Champagne*, vol. II, pp. 113–14, no. 1.

32 The school was founded by the famous medieval Rabbi, Rashi (1040–1105).

33 Allegro, *Treasure of the Copper Scroll*, pp. 107 ff.

34 Arbois de Jubainville, *Histoire . . . de Champagne*, vol. II, pp. 87 ff.

35 Ibid., pp. 98 ff., n. 1.

36 Personal communication to Henry Lincoln by Abbé Mazières.

37 Arcons, *Du Flux et reflux*, pp. 355 ff. See also Catel, *Mémoirs . . . du Languedoc*, book I, p. 51.

38 Mazières, 'La Venue et le séjour des Templiers', pp. 234 ff.

39 Personal communication to Henry Lincoln by Abbé Mazières.

4 SECRET DOCUMENTS

1 Descadeillas, *Rennes et ses derniers seigneurs*.

2 See Descadeillas, 'Mythologie', and de Sède, *Le Vrai Dossier*.

3 Paoli, *Les dessous*, p. 86.

4 *Le Monde* (Feb. 21st, 1967), p. 11. *Le Monde* (Feb. 22nd, 1967), p. 11. *Paris-Jour* (Feb. 21st, 1967), no. 2315, p. 4.

5 Feugère, Saint-Maxent and Koker, *Le Serpent rouge*, p. 4.

5 THE ORDER BEHIND THE SCENES

1 Grousset, *Histoire des croisades*, vol. III, p. xiv.

2 Vogüé, *Les Eglises*, p. 326.

3 Vincent, *Histoire de l'anciene image*, pp. 92 ff.

4 Röhricht, *Regesta*, p. 19, no. 83.

5 Ibid., p. 25, no. 105.

6 Tillière, *Histoire . . . d'Orval*, pp. 3 ff.

7 Jeantin, *Les Chroniques*, vol. 1, p. 398. In Hagenmeyer's *Le Vrai et le faux sur Pierre l'Hermite*, it is claimed that before becoming a monk Peter was a minor noble, owning the fief of Achères near Amiens and was a *vassal of Eustache de Boulogne*, Godfroi's father. See pp. 58 ff. Hagenmeyer, however, does not accept that Peter was the tutor of Godfroi.

Peter obviously had considerable prestige, for after the taking of Jerusalem the crusading army embarked on another campaign leaving Peter in charge of the city.

8 William of Tyre, *History of Deeds Done Beyond the Sea*, vol. 1, p. 380. See also Runciman, *History of the Crusades*, vol. 1, p. 292. This same bishop from Calabria was a friend of one Arnulf, a very minor ecclesiastic, who, with the help of the bishop, was later elected the first Latin Patriarch of Jerusalem!

A strange group survived from the earlier 'people's crusade' called *Tafurs*, who earned a certain notoriety when some of their members were accused of cannibalism by the emir of Antioch. Of this group there was an inner 'college' presided over by a *King Tafur*. The contemporary chronicles present *King Tafur* as a man that even the crusade princes approached with humility, even reverence. It was this *King Tafur* who is said to have performed the coronation of Godfroi de Bouillon. Moreover, *King Tafur* was said to be associated with Peter the Hermit. Could it be possible that this inner group, and the king, were the representatives from Calabria? The name *Tafur*, could, with one letter change, be an anagram for *Artus*, a ritual name. For a summary of the influence of the *Tafurs* see Cohn, N., *Pursuit of the Millennium*, pp. 66 ff.

9 Lobineau, H., *Dossiers secrets*, planche no. 4.

10 Ibid.

11 Archives du Loiret, série D. 357. See also Rey, E.-G., 'Chartes . . . du Mont-Sion', pp. 31 ff., and Le Maire, *Histoire et Antiquitez*, part 2, ch. XXVI, pp. 96 ff.

12 Yates, *Rosicrucian Enlightenment*.

13 See for example Yates, *Giordano Bruno*, pp. 312 ff., and Yates, *Occult Philosophy*, p. 38. In both these works

Frances Yates explores the transmission of Hermetic thought and the secret societies which grew up around the central figures involved.

14 We have this information from 'Prieuré' sources. We have seen the manuscript in question at the Bibliothèque de Rouen, *Histoire polytique de Gisors et du pays de Vulcsain* by Robert Denyau, 1629 (Collection Montbret 2219, V 14a).

15 Röhricht, *Regesta*, p. 375, no. 1440.

16 Bruel, *Chartes d'Adam*, pp. 1 ff.

17 Lobineau, H., *Dossiers secrets*, planche no. 4.

18 Oursel, *Le Procès des Templiers*, p. 208.

19 Rey, E.-G., *Chartes . . . du Mont-Sion*, pp. 34 ff.

20 It is perhaps worth comparing the given lists of Grand Masters of the Knights Templar.

A The list as given in Henri Lobineau, *Dossiers secrets*:

> Hugues de Payen, 1118–31
> Robert de Bourgogne, 1131–50
> Bernard de Tremblay, 1150–53
> Bertrand de Blancafort, 1153–70
> Janfeders Fulcherine, 1170–71
> (= Gaufridus Fulcherius/Geoffroy Foucher)
> François Othon de St Amand, 1171–9
> Théodore de Glaise, 1179–84
> (= Theodoricus/Terricus)
> François Gérard de Riderfort, 1184–90

B The list as given in a modern source – Seward, *Monks of War*, p. 306.

> Hugues de Payen, 1118–36
> Robert de Craon, 1136–46
> Everard des Barres, 1146–52
> Bernard de Tremelai, 1152–3
> André de Montbard, 1153–6
> Bertrand de Blanquefort, 1156–69
> Philippe de Milly, 1169–70
> Eudes de St Amand, 1170–9
> Arnold de Torroge, 1179–85
> Gérard de Ridefort, 1185–91

It is worth reviewing a specimen of the evidence which supports the Prieuré list, using the first Grand Master as an example. The date of death for Hugues de Payen differs. The Prieuré list puts it at 1131, while the modern list claims 1136. This latter date cannot be proved and, in fact, would appear to be wrong. 1136 is given in *L'Art de vérifier les dates*, vol. 5 (Paris, 1818), p. 338 and the normally stated day of death, May 24th, is given in the thirteenth-century *Obituaire de la commanderie . . . de Reims* (see Barthélemy), p. 321. However, this early document does not give any year of death. So scholars have been dependent upon the surviving charters signed by Hugues de Payen. These charters indicate that in fact

Hugues did die around 1131, or shortly thereafter. In Albon, *Cartulaire général*, several charters are given which have been signed by Hugues. He uses his full name, generally given as *Hugo de Pagano*. The last charter signed in this way is dated 1130 (Albon, *Cartulaire général*, pp. 23 ff.). It would appear likely that he died some time following this date and before 1133, the year in which a charter appeared mentioning, but not signed by, *Hugoni, magistro militum . . . Templi* (Albon, *Cartulaire général*, p. 42). This charter has generally been attributed to Hugues de Payen, but it seems more likely that it is in fact referring to Hugues Rigaud, who appears in many other charters reproduced by M. d'Albon, and indeed, is now considered to have been the common master of Saint-Sépulchre and the Temple, or the Temple in Jerusalem, from 1130 to 1133. See Gérard and Magnou, *Cartulaire*, p. xxxviii. So the Prieuré list appears to have the evidence in its favour. It should also be noted that at no point does William of Tyre ever list Everard des Barres or André de Montbard as Grand Masters of the Knights Templar – which subsequent historians, on a highly questionable basis, do.

6 THE GRAND MASTERS AND THE UNDERGROUND STREAM

1 Lobineau, H., *Dossiers secrets*, planche no. 4, Ordre de Sion.

2 Loyd, *Origins of Anglo-Norman Families*, pp. 45 ff. And Powicke, *Loss of Normandy*, p. 340.

3 Roger de Hoveden, *Annals*, vol. I, p. 322. It reads, 'Thomas, the archbishop of Canterbury, and some of his fellow-exiles, came to an interview with the legates, on the octave of Saint Martin, between Gisors and Trie . . .' This meeting-place between the two adjacent castles is the site of the famous elm tree which was later cut down. In his *Voyages Pittoresques* (*Normandy*, vol. 2, p. 138) Charles Nodier says that 'St Thomas de Canterbury had there (under the Gisors elm) prepared for his martyrdom.' It is unclear exactly what he is implying here but it is provocative.

4 Lecoy de la Marche, *Le Roi René*, vol. I, p. 69. The duke of Lorraine had no son, and by the conventions of the times it was to René that Jeanne was referring.

5 See Staley, *King René d'Anjou*, pp. 153 ff.

6 Staley, *King René d'Anjou*, p. 29. René himself carved the inscription.

7 Sir Philip Sidney was an associate of John Dee and also steeped in Hermetic thought. Frances Yates considers John Dee to be the source of the Rosicrucian manifestos – Yates, *Occult Philosophy*, pp. 170 ff. For further information on Sidney and Dee see French, *John Dee*. Sidney then was well aware of the 'underground stream' flowing through European culture.

8 All the manifestos are printed in Waite, *Real History of the Rosicrucians*.

9 Yates, *Rosicrucian Enlightenment*, p. 125.

10 Ibid., p. 192.

11 Some letters exist, which are held by the Royal Society, written to Robert Boyle regarding a group called the *Sacred Cabalistic Society of Philosophers* who admitted him as a member. It appears to be based in France. See Maddison, *Life of . . . Robert Boyle*, pp. 166 ff.

12 Yates, *Rosicrucian Enlightenment*, pp. 223 ff. Frances Yates explains the connecting links between the Rosicrucian movement and the Royal Society.

13 For further information on Ramsay see Walker, *The Ancient Theology*, pp. 231 ff., and Henderson, *Chevalier Ramsay*.

14 The text of the Oration is published in Gould, *History of Freemasonry*, vol. 5, pp. 84 ff.

15 Waite, *New Encyclopaedia of Freemasonry*, vol. 2, pp. 353 ff., and Le Forestier, *La Franc-Maçonnerie*, pp. 126 ff.

16 This list is reproduced in Thory, *Acta Latomorum*, vol. 2, p. 282. The list follows Sion's list only until the split in 1188. The Grand Master at that time was Gérard de Ridefort.

17 Nodier, *Voyages Pittoresques, Normandy*, vol. 2, pp. 137 ff.

18 Pingaud, *La Jeunesse de Charles Nodier*, p. 39.

19 Ibid., pp. 231 ff., contains the rules of the society. Some are curious. Rule 18 states, 'The brothers of the Society of the Philadelphes have a particular liking for the colour sky-blue, the figure of the pentagram and the number 5.'

20 Ibid., p. 47.

21 Nodier, *Contes*, pp. 4 ff.

22 Nodier, *History of Secret Societies*, p. 105.

23 Ibid., p. 116.

24 The most significant figure in secret societies of the period was Filippo Michele Buonarroti (a descendant of Michelangelo's brother) who began his career as a page to the archduke of Tuscany (son of François de Lorraine) and became involved in Freemasonry. At the outbreak of the French Revolution he went to Corsica, where he stayed until 1794 and became acquainted with Napoleon. From the early 1800s he set up a succession of secret societies. He founded so many that historians have no idea of the actual number founded. One comments that 'Buonarroti was a true divinity, if not omnipotent – at least omnipresent', Eisenstein, *The First Professional Revolutionist . . . Buonarroti*, p. 48, quoting Lehning. He shared many mutual friends with Nodier and Hugo – Petrus-Borel, Louis Blanc, Célestin Nanteuil, Jehan Duseigneur, Jean Gigoux, so it is most likely that they knew each other. In fact the absence of any record of them meeting is highly suspicious, given the status which Buonarroti commanded later in his life in Paris.

See also Roberts, *Mythology of the Secret Societies*, pp. 233 ff., 'for thirty years without ever stopping, like a spider in his hole, spinning the threads of a conspiracy that all the governments have broken, each in turn, and that he never tires of renewing.' Eisenstein, *The First Professional Revolutionist . . . Buonarroti*, p. 51.

It is most likely that Buonarroti and Nodier were both in the Prieuré de Sion – especially as one of Buonarroti's organisations was the Philadelphes, the same name Nodier used for his order.

25 See Chapter 7, n. 33.

26 Lucie-Smith, *Symbolist Art*, p. 110. For Péladan's life and associates see Pincus-Witten, *Occult Symbolism in France*.

27 Lucie-Smith, *Symbolist Art*, p. 111.

28 This was his comment when asked to do the painting which now forms part of a chapel in the church of Notre Dame de France, London.

29 See Bander, *Prophecies of St Malachy*, p. 93. The Latin phrase is *Pastor et Nauta* – the word *nauta* can mean either 'seaman' or 'navigator', which in old French is 'nautonnier'.

30 'Inde a primis' published in *L'Osservatore Romano* (July 2nd, 1960), p. 1. An English translation can be found in *Review for Religious*, vol. 20 (1961), pp. 3 ff.

7 CONSPIRACY THROUGH THE CENTURIES

1 Lobineau, H., *Dossiers secrets*, planche no. 4, Ordre de Sion.

2 De Sède, *Les Templiers*, pp. 220 ff. For the story of Lhomoy see de Sède, pp. 20 ff. and 231 ff. See also Chaumeil, *Triangle d'or*, pp. 19 ff.

3 Le Maire, *Histoire et Antiquitez*, part 2, ch. XXVI, pp. 96 ff.

4 The cardinal of Lorraine was behind the amnesty in favour of Huguenots given at Amboise on March 7th, 1560. The cardinal also secretly gave money to certain Protestant groups.

5 It was through René d'Anjou that the double-barred cross became associated with Lorraine. René had adopted this cross as his emblem, using it on his seals and coinage. The popularity of the cross dates from its use by René II, duke of Lorraine, at the battle of Nancy in 1477. See Marot, *Le Symbolisme*, pp. 1 ff.

6 Nostradamus moved in circles connected with the house of Lorraine. He lived for some years at Agen, and Jean de Lorraine was bishop of Agen at the time, as well as head of the Inquisition in France. Research indicates that Nostradamus received warning of the Inquisition's interest in him, and all factors point to Jean, cardinal of Lorraine having been the source of that warning. Moreover Nostradamus's friend Scaliger in Agen was a friend of the cardinal and also acquainted with the Hermeticist and creator of the 'Memory Theatre', Giulio Camillo (see Yates, *Art of Memory*, ch. 6). The cardinal of Lorraine was well acquainted with Camillo. Also two court poets, Pierre de Ronsard and Jean Dorat, were friends of Nostradamus. Ronsard wrote several poems in praise of Nostradamus and the cardinal. The cardinal supported both these poets. It was Jean Dorat who sent Jean-Aimé de Chavigny to Nostradamus as his secretary. Much research into these connections is presented in the

novel *The Dreamer of the Vine*, by Liz Greene (London, 1979).

7 Quatrain v: 74, for example, relates probably to Charles Martel driving back the Saracens, and beating them at the battle of Poitiers in 732. Quatrain III: 83 may well refer to the long-haired Merovingian kings taking the kingdom of Aquitaine, which they did after 507. Many of the quatrains and presages mention the *Rases* which seems to be a pun both on the area of the Razès and the exiled Counts, the 'shaven ones', the Merovingian descendants.

8 De Sède, *La Race fabuleuse*, pp. 106 ff. De Sède's credibility in this book tends to be somewhat undercut by his rather unlikely claim that the Merovingians were extra-terrestrials! In conversation he was asked the source for his assertion that Nostradamus spent time at Orval. He replied that a man named Eric Muraise had a manuscript proving this, which de Sède had personally viewed. We questioned some of the monks at the Abbey of Orval about the possibility of Nostradamus having been there. They shrugged, and said it was a tradition, but they had no evidence either to prove or disprove it. It was possible, one said wearily.

9 Allier, *La Cabale*, pp. 99 ff. The author states that it was the Compagnie which suggested to Olier that he found Saint Sulpice.

10 Allier, *La Cabale*, p. 33.

11 Auguste, *La Compagnie . . . à Toulouse*, pp. 20 ff.

12 Allier, *La Cabale*, p. 3.

13 Lobineau, H., *Dossiers secrets*, planche no. 1, 1100–1600, no., planche no. 19, 1800–1900.

14 Sainte-Marie, *Recherches historiques*, p. 243.

15 Soultrait (ed.), *Dictionnaire topographique . . . de la Nièvre*, pp. 8, 146. The hamlet of Les Plantards was near to Sémelay, later the birthplace of Jean XXII des Plantard.

16 See the *Bulletin de la société nivernais des lettres, sciences et arts*, 2eme série, tome VII (1876), pp. 110, 139, 140–41, 307. See also Chaumeil, *Triangle d'or*, pp. 80 ff. and illustrations of coins discovered on the site.

17 These are examples of the factors which have led subsequent authors to regard Fouquet as being the likely candidate for the Man in the Iron Mask. Much persuasive evidence exists to support the assertion.

18 Blunt, *Poussin*, vol. I, p. 170.

19 This painting is illustrated in Ward, *Freemasonry and the Ancient Gods*, facing p. 134. It is in the possession of the Supreme Grand Royal Arch Chapter of Scotland, Edinburgh.

20 Delaude, *Cercle d'Ulysse*, p. 3.

21 Gout, *Mont-Saint-Michel*, pp. 141 ff. Robert de Torigny, Abbé 1154–86, wrote some 140 volumes during his life, a large number of which were dedicated to the history of the region. During his rule the number of monks at the abbey doubled and it became a 'sanctuary of science'. He was a close friend of both Henry II and Becket and, given their close association with the Prieuré de Sion, the Templars and Gisors, it would be surprising if Robert were not also *au fait* with them. If the Plantard family did indeed use the motto as suggested, one would expect Robert to have recorded it, since the Plantard family not only seem to have been resident in Brittany at the time, but Jean VI des Plantard in 1156 (according to Henri Lobineau) married Idoine de Gisors, the sister of Jean de Gisors, Ninth Grand Master of the Ordre de Sion, founder of the Ordre de la Rose-Croix. History records Idoine, but not her husband – which does not allow us to find which title the Plantard family were using in the twelfth century.

We were not able to find any mention of the Plantard family, nor any trace of Robert's genealogical surveys. His manuscripts have been scattered but lists of them exist, though none of them includes obviously genealogical material. We were later told that the relevant manuscript was in the 'private' archives of Saint Sulpice, Paris. Hardly a satisfactory ending to this line of investigation.

22 Myriam, 'Les Bergers d'Arcadie', in *Le Charivari*, no. 18, pp. 49 ff.

23 Thory, *Acta Latomorum*, vol. 2, pp. 15 ff. Gould, *History of Freemasonry*, vol. 2, p. 383.

24 Erdeswick, *A Survey of Staffordshire*, p. 189.

25 Peyrefitte, 'La Lettre Secrète', pp. 197 ff. The letter in question was attached to a Bull of Excommunication issued by the pope on April 28th, 1738.

26 The Oriental Rite of Memphis first appeared in 1838, when Jacques Etienne Marconis de Nègre established the Grand Lodge Osiris in Brussels. The underlying legend of the Rite was that it descended from the Dionysian and Egyptian mysteries. The sage Ormus is said to have combined the mysteries with Christianity to produce the original Rose-Croix. The Oriental Rite of Memphis was a system of ninety-seven degrees, producing such august titles as Commander of the Luminous Triangle, Sublime Prince of the Royal Mystery, Sublime Pastor of the Hutz, Doctor of the Planispheres, and so on. See Waite, *New Encyclopaedia of Freemasonry*, vol. 2, pp. 241 ff. The Rite was eventually reduced to thirty-three degrees, calling itself the *Ancient and Primitive Rite*. It was taken to the United States circa 1854–6 by H. J. Seymour, and to England in 1872 by John Yarker. It was later associated with the Ordo Templi Orientis. The magazine of the Rite of Memphis, the *Oriflamme*, advertised the O. T. O. in its issues. In 1875 the Rite was amalgamated with the *Rite of Misraim*. In *History of the Ancient and Primitive Rite of Masonry* (London, 1875) the Rite of Memphis is said to derive from that of the *Philadelphians* of Narbonne, established in 1779.

27 See also Genesis 28:18, where Jacob anoints a stone pillar.

28 Pitois, as librarian to the Ministry of Public Education, was given the task of sorting through all the books from the monasteries and provincial libraries brought to Paris. He and Charles Nodier pored over them, and claimed to have made interesting discoveries daily.

29 Jean-Baptiste Hogan.
30 It is quite possible that the doctrine of papal infallibility, formally stated for the first time on July 18th, 1870, was part of the Roman Catholic church's reaction to Modernist tendencies, as well as to Darwinian thought and the increasing continental power of Lutheran Prussia.
31 Iremonger, *William Temple*, p. 490.
32 A short biography of Hoffet is given in Descadeillas, *Mythologie*, pp. 85 ff. Hoffet was born in Schiltigheim, Alsace on May 11th, 1873. In 1884 he began his studies at Paris at the Maîtrise de Montmartre, later continuing them at the Petit Séminaire de Notre-Dame de Sion, where he prepared to enter the Church. He began his novitiate at Saint-Gerlach in Holland and entered the religious Order of *Oblats de Marie* in 1892. At Liège he was ordained as a priest in 1898. He worked then as a missionary, firstly in Corsica then back in France. In 1903–4 he was in Rome. He returned to Paris to live in 1914, and died there in March 1946. He wrote prolifically, particularly for specialist magazines on religious history. He was a linguist, fluent in Greek, Hebrew and Sanskrit. De Sède, *Le Vrai Dossier*, pp. 33 ff., reports that Descadeillas, while publicly disparaging any idea of a 'mystery' at Rennes, nevertheless in 1966 wrote to the authorities of the *Oblats de Marie* to ask whether there was any proof that Hoffet ever preached in Rennes-le-Château. De Sède reports that the archivist of Hoffet's Order wrote, 'Hoffet is the author of some very interesting studies on Freemasonry, of which he had made a particular study, and I have unearthed a number of his manuscripts . . . I have ordered that the particularly interesting documents be placed in security.' See also Chaumeil, *Triangle d'or*, pp. 106 ff.
33 Papus was born in Spain on July 13th, 1865. In 1887 he joined the Theosophical Association but in 1888 left to found his own group – on Martinist principles. In the same year he was one of the founding members of the *Ordre Kabbalistic de la Rose-Croix*, along with Péladan and Stanislas de Guaïta. In 1889, together with these two and Villiers de l'Isle-Adam he founded the review *L'Initiation*. In 1891 a 'supreme council' of the Martinist Order was formed in Paris with Papus as Grand Master. At about this time Papus helped Doinel found the Gnostic Catholic Church. In 1895 Doinel withdrew, leaving the church in the care of Papus and two others, under the jurisdiction of a patriarch. Doinel then went to Carcassonne. This same year Papus became a member of the *Order of the Golden Dawn*, in the Paris lodge *Ahathoor*. During the 1890s Papus was a friend of Emma Calvé. In 1899 one of his close friends, Philippe de Lyon, went to Russia and established a Martinist lodge at the imperial court. In 1900 Papus himself went to St Petersburg, where he became a confidant of the czar and czarina. He visited Russia on at least three occasions, the last being in 1906. During this time he made the acquaintance of Rasputin.
    Papus later became Grand Master in France of the Ordo Templi Orientis and the lodge of Memphis and Misraim. He died on October 25th, 1916.
34 Nilus, *Procotols*. This work had, by the 1960s, been through some eighty-three editions which would tend to suggest that anti-Semitism is rife in Great Britain. The publishing company, Britons Publishing (now part of Augustine Publishing, a Catholic traditionalist press) also had such titles as *Jews' Ritual Slaughter* (price 3d), *Jews and the White Slave Traffic* (price 2d).
35 For the history of the Protocols see Cohn, *Warant for Genocide*, and Bernstein, *Truth about 'The Protocols'*, which reproduces in full translations of the various suggested sources for the Protocols. The standard anti-Semitic history is detailed in Fry, *Waters Flowing Eastward*. This is a controversial document by any standards. It gives, amongst other things, a photograph 'proving' that Czar Nicolas II was killed in ritual murder by a Jewish Cabalist! To see this type of illiterature still being published in 1965 is somewhat disconcerting.
36 Nilus, *Protocols*, no. 13.
37 Lodge of Memphis and Misraim. See n. 33.
38 Nilus, *Protocols*, no. 24. This statement does not appear in some earlier editions of the *Protocols*.
39 Nilus, *Protocols*, no. 24.
40 Blancasall, *Les Descendants*, p. 6.
41 See the preface by Pierre Plantard de Saint-Clair in the 1978 Belfond reprint of Boudet, *La Vraie Langue celtique*.
42 Chaumeil, *Triangle d'or*, p. 136.
43 See Rosnay, *Le Hiéron du Val d'Or*.
44 Chaumeil, *Triangle d'or*, pp. 139 ff.

8 THE SECRET SOCIETY TODAY

1 Philippe de Chérisey, an associate of Pierre Plantard de Saint-Clair, has written an allegorical 'novel' called *Circuit*. The subject matter ranges from Atlantis to Napoleon. It has twenty-two chapters, each taking its title from one of the Tarot major trumps. It exists in a single example at the Versailles annexe of the Bibliothèque Nationale, Paris. Part involves the story of two symbolic personages, Charlot and Madeleine, who find a treasure at Rennes-le-Château. See Chaumeil, *Triangle d'or*, pp. 141 ff. for this extract.
2 *Prieuré de Sion: Statutes*, Articles XI and XII. Received by the Sous-Prefecture, Saint-Julien-en-Genevois, May 7th, 1956. File number KM 94550.
3 *Midi Libre* (Feb. 13th, 1973), p. 5.
4 Myriam, 'Les Bergers d'Arcadia', *Le Charivari*, no. 18, pp. 49 ff.
5 Contained in Henri Lobineau, *Dossiers secrets*, p. 1.
6 Ibid.
7 Ibid.
8 Roux, S., *L'Affaire de Rennes-le-Château*. In another part of

the *Dossiers secrets*, a page written by one Edmond Albe, S. Roux is identified as the Abbé Georges de Nantes. In his book Mathieu Paoli claims (*Les Dessous*, p. 82) the same identification. Georges de Nantes is the head of the 'Catholic Counter-Reformation in the XXth Century', and also author of the sustained attack on Pope Paul VI, *Liber Accusationis in Paulum Sextum*. In this he accuses Pope Paul of being an heretic. He would seem in fact to be in much the same camp as M. Lefebvre. Intrigued that this identification appeared to be uncontested, we wrote to Abbé Georges Nantes, giving him the quote from Paoli's book, requesting comments, and asking whether he would confirm or deny M. Paoli's assertion. The Abbé de Nantes wrote back, saying that he gets asked from time to time for explanations concerning this text and he could only repeat that he has nothing to do with S. Roux. Moreover, he added, 'Such a text is a true tissue of absurdities. How could you take it seriously?'

9 Roux, *L'Affaire de Rennes-le-Château*, p. 1.

10 Ibid., p. 2.

11 Ibid.

12 Delaude, *Cercle d'Ulysse*, p. 6 (v).

13 *Guardian* (London, Sept. 11th, 1976), p. 13.

14 Mgr Brunon, who replaced Lefebvre as bishop of Tulle, said that in his opinion Lefebvre was being manipulated by others. See the *Guardian* (London, Sept. 1st, 1976), p. 4. Gianfranco Svidercoschi, described by *The Times* as being 'an experienced and usually well informed Vatican correspondent', declared the Pope to be aware that 'Mgr Lefebvre was being conditioned surreptitiously by other people'. See *The Times* (London, Aug. 31st, 1976), p. 12.

15 *Guardian* (Aug. 30th, 1976), p. 16. Intrigued by this, we wrote to Father Peter Morgan, asking him if he would clarify this matter. Father Morgan did not reply.

16 This information was published in the daily papers of 19 and 20 January 1981. The article cited came from the review *Haut-Anjou*.

17 Our latest information is that they were transferred to Paris 13 October 1979 and are held in a safe deposit box in the 'Caisse d'Epargne', at 4 Place de Mexico, Paris.

18 *Le Charivari*, no. 18, pp. 56 ff.

19 The old statutes were registered with the Sub-Prefecture on May 7th, 1956. According to the second issue of *Circuit* dated June 3rd, 1956, a meeting was held that week to discuss statutes. The statutes bearing Cocteau's signature are dated June 5th, 1956.

20 *Bonne Soirée*, no. 3053 (Aug. 14th, 1980), p. 14.

21 We have, during the writing of this book, consulted a large number of works dealing with the genealogies of noble families, both ancient and contemporary. We have never found a single reference to the title Plantard de Saint-Clair. However, this failure to find his name doesn't invalidate the claim, especially since he admits it to have been clandestine for centuries.

22 *Le Charivari*, no. 18, p. 60, *Gisors et son secret*.

23 M. de Sède's major work, *Les Templiers sont parmi nous*, contains a section at the back entitled, 'Point de vue d'un Hermétiste'. This section consists of a lengthy interview with Pierre Plantard de Saint-Clair in which de Sède not only poses a multitude of questions but also acknowledges Plantard as a seemingly definitive authority. M. Plantard also seems to have been involved in de Sède's book on Rennes-le-Château. During the making of the film *The Lost Treasure of Jerusalem?* for the BBC, we received from de Sède's publishers a mass of visual material which had been used in the book. All the photographs were stamped 'Plantard' on the reverse. This would suggest that this material had presumably been in Plantard's possession and he had entrusted it to de Sède.

24 *Le Charivari*, no. 18, p. 55.

25 Ibid.

26 Ibid., p. 53.

27 We received from M. Plantard a photocopy of a legally certified deposition by a named member of the Légion d'Honneur and officer in the French Resistance during the Second World War. It states that Pierre Plantard clandestinely produced the resistance journal *Vaincre* from 1941. It furthermore states that M. Plantard was imprisoned by the Gestapo at Fresnes from October 1943 until February 1944. This deposition is stamped and dated May 11th, 1953.

Checking this did not prove to be a straightforward task. Firstly there were many journals named *Vaincre* published by various resistance groups during the war. However, the magazine involved would seem to be the *Vaincre* issued by the Comité Local du Front National de Lutte pour l'Indépendance de la France, a copy of which is in the Bibliothèque Nationale, Paris, dated April 1943. It was produced in Saint-Cloud, Paris.

We wrote to the historical service of the French Army asking for details on the resistance activities of M. Plantard. We received a letter from the French Ministry of Defence informing us that this information was personal and confidential.

28 See Vazart, *Abrégé de l'histoire des Francs*, pp. 271, 272, nn. 1 and 2. The latter note contains the text of the letter from General de Gaulle.

29 This information came with Jean-Luc Chaumeil, in conversation with him. We sought to check on M. Paoli, beginning with Swiss television, as we knew he had worked for them at the time he wrote his book. The administrative chief of Radio-Télévision Suisse Romande told us that M. Paoli had left in 1971. He was said to have gone to Israel and worked for Israeli television at Tel Aviv. The trail unfortunately ended here.

30 Paoli, *Les Dessous*, p. 86.

31 The copies of *Circuit*, some of which are available at the Versailles Annexe, are a prime example of the obscure manner in which the story has been made available.

The first series of *Circuit* begins on May 27th, 1956, and runs weekly until a special edition which follows issue number 11 and is dated September 2nd, 1956. The magazines are mimeographed and generally consist of two to four pages. They issue from Sous-Cassan, Annemasse, and each has an introduction by Pierre Plantard. Many contain the minutes of the meetings held to discuss the drawing up and registration of the statutes of the Prieuré de Sion with the Sub-Prefecture at Annemasse, though the name of the Prieuré is not mentioned once. In fact, the ostensible concern of all the issues of the magazine is low-cost housing. The organisation behind the magazine is not called the Prieuré de Sion, but the Organisation for the Defence of the Rights and the Liberty of Low-Cost Homes! (A certain sense of humour pervades many of the Prieuré documents.) At the same time, however, names which appear in Sion's statutes appear in these issues of *Circuit*. There was one issue, however (no. 8, July 22nd, 1956), which contained an article by a certain M. Defago (who appears on Sion's Statutes as Treasurer) about astrology, explaining a system using thirteen astrological signs rather than twelve. The thirteenth sign is one called Ophiuchus, and is placed between Scorpio and Sagittarius.

The second issues of *Circuit* appeared in 1959 and are called the *Cultural Periodical of the Federation of French Forces*. Many of them have disappeared. We found Numbers 2 (August 1959), 3 (September 1959), 5 (November 1959) and 6 (December 1959). Mathieu Paoli records the existence of a Number 1 (July 1959) and a Number 4. In addition there is mention of a Number 8 in *Le Charivari*. It thus appears that someone has removed certain issues.

The magazines contain articles on subjects ranging from Atlantis to astrology. Some contain political predictions for the years ahead computed astrologically by Pierre Plantard. On the reverse, all the magazines are stamped with the symbol of the organisation and the stamp of 'Plantard'.

32 Vazart, *Abrégé de l'histoire des Francs*, p. 271.
33 Paoli, *Les Dessous*, p. 94.
34 Ibid.
35 Ibid., pp. 94 ff.
36 Ibid., p. 102.
37 Ibid., p. 103.
38 Ibid., p. 112.

9 THE LONG-HAIRED MONARCHS

1 Cochet, *Le Tombeau de Childeric Ier*, Dumas, *Le Tombeau de Childeric*.
2 According to Cochet, *Le Tombeau de Childeric Ier*, p. 25, Leopold Wilhelm (who was also Grand Master of the Teutonic Knights) kept twenty-seven of the bees for himself, while giving up the rest. We may be speculating too far but it is interesting to note that the Prieuré de Sion at the time had twenty-seven commanderies.
3 Our first inkling that Napoleon was connected with this story came with the numerous references in the *Dossiers'* genealogies which noted among their sources the work

of an Abbé Pichon. Between 1805 and 1814, Pichon completed a study of the Merovingian descent from Dagobert II until November 20th, 1809, when Jean XXII des Plantard was born in Sémelay (Nièvre). His sources were stated to be documents discovered following the French Revolution. Additional information was contained in the *Alpina* publication of Madeleine Blancasall, which stated (p. 1) that Abbé Pichon was commissioned by Sieyès (Official of the Directory, 1795–9) and Napoleon. A comprehensive body of material is contained in *L'Or de Rennes pour un Napoléon* by Philippe de Chérisey, which is now on microfiche at the Bibliothèque Nationale, Paris. Briefly Chérisey says that the Abbé Sieyès, via Pichon's researches on the captured royal archives, knew of the survival of the Merovingians. He told the story to Napoleon, whom he then urged to marry Joséphine, the ex-wife of a Merovingian descendant, Alexandre de Beauharnais. Napoleon later adopted her two children, who carried the 'blood royal'.

Later Napoleon commissioned Abbé Pichon (whose real name is said to be François Dron) to complete a definitive genealogy. Napoleon was interested, among other things, in the indications that the Bourbon dynasty was in fact illegitimate. And his coronation as Emperor of the French (not of France), in a ceremony with significant Merovingian resonances, is said to be a result of Sieyès's and Pichon's studies. If this is so, Napoleon was setting up a foundation for a renewed Merovingian empire. Being childless by Joséphine, he then married Marie Louise, the daughter of the Habsburg Austrian Emperor, of Merovingian descent. She bore his son, Napoleon II, who carried the 'blood royal' of the Merovingians. The latter however died childless. But the future Napoleon III, son of Louis Bonaparte and Hortense de Beauharnais (daughter of Joséphine by her first marriage) also carried the 'blood royal'.

Chérisey also implies coyly that Archduke Karl (brother of Napoleon's wife) was bribed to lose the battle of Wagram in 1809 in exchange for part of the Merovingian treasure which Napoleon had found in the Razès. This treasure was later discovered at Petroassa in 1837, then a Habsburg domain. Given the Merovingian descent of the Habsburgs, it is clear to see why they would value it.

4 Carpenter, *Folktale, Fiction and Saga*, pp. 112 ff.
5 The Roman name for Artemis was Diana, and another name for the Arduina cult was 'Diana of the Ardennes'. A huge statue to her existed until it was destroyed by Saint Vulfilau in the sixth century. Her cult was a moon cult, with images of her carrying the crescent moon. She was also considered to be the deity of fountains and springs. The foundation of the Abbey of Orval, which legend intertwines with a mystic spring, may well suggest some vestige of a Diana/Arduina cult. See Calmet, 'Des Divinités', pp. 25 ff.
6 For example see Gregory of Tours, *History of the Franks*,

book V, ch. 44.

7   Wallace-Hadrill, *The Long-haired Kings*, pp. 203 ff.

8   Ibid., p. 158.

9   Dill, *Roman Society in Gaul*, p. 88.

10 Wallace-Hadrill, *The Long-haired Kings*, p. 171.

11 The major sources for the life of Dagobert II are Digot, *Histoire de royaume d'Austrasie*, vol. 3, pp. 220 ff., and pp. 249 ff., (ch. XV) and pp. 364 ff., Folz, 'Tradition hagiographique', and Vincent, *Histoire fidelle de St Sigisbert*.

12 Lanigan, *An Ecclesiastical History*, vol. 3, p. 101.

13 Henri Lobineau, *Dossiers secrets*, planche no. 1, 600–900; Blancasall, *Les Descendants*, p. 8 and tableau no. 1.

14 De Sède's statement receives some support from the known facts about Saint Amatus's life. He incurred the enmity of the same Ebroin, Mayor of the Palace to King Thierry III, who was behind the assassination of Dagobert II. He was displaced from his bishopric at about the same time that Dagobert returned to his rightful heritage. The coincidence of dates could well reflect his involvement in Dagobert's return. Dagobert would have been most likely to travel back to his kingdom via Saint Amatus's bishopric. To travel directly up from the Razès would involve travelling through the territory of Thierry III, something he would have avoided.

15 Henri Lobineau, *Dossiers secrets*, planche no. 2, 1500–1650. Blancasall, *Les Descendants*, p. 8. This treasure joins the list of the other treasures either once or still in the Rennes-le-Château area.

16 Wallace-Hadrill, *The Long-haired Kings*, p. 238.

17 Called *Satanicum* in the Latin charters, a name derived from a Temple to Saturn once situated there.

18 See n. 16.

19 For an exploration of the cult see Folz, 'Tradition hagiographique'.

20 Digot, A., *Histoire du royaume d'Austrasie*, vol. 3, pp. 370 ff.

21 Interestingly Jules Doinel, creator of the Gnostic Catholic Church and librarian at Carcassonne, published in 1899 a short work deploring the displacement of the Merovingians by the Carolingians. See Doinel, *Note sur le Roi Hildérik III*.

22 Wallace-Hadrill, *The Long-haired Kings*, p. 246.

23 Ibid., p. 248.

24 Einhard, *Life of Charlemagne*, p. 81.

25 Paoli, *Les Dessous*, p. 111.

26 Dagobert II was 'rediscovered' in 1646 by Adrien de Valois. He was fully restored to the genealogies of the Merovingians by the Jesuit Bollandiste Henschenius, in *Diatriba de tribus Dagobertus*, in 1655. See Folz, 'Tradition hagiographique', p. 33. It is interesting, given this lack of knowledge of Dagobert II at the time, that Robert Denyau mentions him in the *Calendarium Martyrology* appended to his *Histoire . . . de Gisors*, dated 1629.

27 Delaude, *Cercle d'Ulysse*, p. 4. This charter supposedly originates from *Villas Capitanarias* later called Trapas, and relates to the foundation of the monastery Saint Martin d'Albières. We tried to locate the charter without success. The archives of Capitanarias are held in the Archives de l'Aude, Series H. But the charter does not appear. Thus it was with interest that we noted a letter to M. Jean Delaude, asking for his source of information on the document. The writer of this letter was a member of the University of Lille. Jean Delaude replied that the charter existed in the French National Archives, that it was uncatalogued, and that even with the help of an archivist, it had taken him two months to trace it. Although all such archival collections contain vast amounts of uncatalogued material, he gave no information on how this charter could be traced by anyone else. See Chérisey, *L'Enigme de Rennes*, letters number 4 and 5 (1977).

28 Ponsich, *Le Conflent*, p. 244.

29 Ibid., fig. 1. See also Vaissete, *Histoire générale de Languedoc*, vol. 2 (notes), p. 276.

30 Vaissete, *Histoire générale de Languedoc*, vol. 3, pp. 4 ff.

31 The earliest report of this legend appears in the "Regius Manuscript" dating from around 1390. See Pick, F.L. and Knight G.N., *"The Pocket History of Freemasonry"*, pp. 30 ff.

32 The title of Godfroi de Bouillon's duchy, Basse-Lorraine, was dropped in 1190, the suzeraines called themselves dukes of Brabant. So the duchess of Brabant is no doubt a variant of the duchess of Bouillon.

33 The standard French genealogical work is Anselm, *Histoire généalogique et chronologique*, which details the history of the house of Boulogne in vol. VI, pp. 247 ff. It is with Godfroi's grandfather, Comte Eustache Ier de Boulogne, that the confusion begins. His father is not recorded, only the name of his mother, Adeline, and her second husband, Ernicule, Count of Boulogne. Ernicule adopted the young Eustache, making him heir. His true father is lost to history.

The *Dossiers secrets* (planche no. 2, 900–1200) record his true father as Hugues des Plantard ('Long Nose') who was assassinated (according to Abbé Pichon) in 1015.

10 THE EXILED TRIBE

1   Graves, *White Goddess*, p. 271.

2   The full text is as follows: UN JOUR LES DESCENDANTS DE BENJAMIN QUITTÈRENT LEUR PAYS, CERTAINS RESTÈRENT, DEUX MILLE ANS APRÈS GODEFROY VI, DEVIENT ROI DE JÉRUSALEM ET FONDÉ L'ORDRE DE SION – De cette legende merveilleuse qui orne l'histoire, ainsi que l'architecture d'un temple dont le sommet se perd dans l'immensité de l'espace et des temps, dont POUSSIN à voulu exprimer le mystère dans ses deux tableaux, les 'Bergers d'Arcadie', se trouve sans doute le secret du trésor devant lequel, les descendants paysans et bergers du fier sicambre, méditent sur 'et in arcadia ego', ✡ et le Roi *'Midas'*. Avant 1200 a notre ère – Un fait important est, l'arrivée des Hébreux dans la terre promise et leur lente installation en Caanan. Dans

la Bible, au Deuteronome 33; il est dit sur BENJAMIN: C'est le bien aimé de l'Eternal, il habitera en sécurité auprès de lui, l'Eternal le couvrira toujours, et résidera entre ses épaules. ✝. Il est encore did à Josué 18 que le sort donna pour héritage aux fils de BENJAMIN parmi les quatorze villes et leur villages: JEBUS de nos jours JERUSALEM avec ses trios points d'un triangle: GOLGOTHA SION et BETHANIE.

〰 Et enfin il est écrit, aux Juges 20 et 21: 'Aucun de nous ne donnera sa fille pour femme à un Benjamite . . . O Eternel, Dieu d'Israël, pourquoi est-il arrivé en Israël qu'il manque aujourd'hui une tribu d'Israël' 〰

A la grande énigme de l'Arcadie VIRGILE qui était dans le secret des dieux, lève le voile aux Bucoliques X-46/50: 'Tu procul a patria (nec sit mihi credere tantum). Alpinas, a, dura, nives et frigora Rheni me sine sola vides. A, te ne frigora laedant! A tibi ne teneras glacies secet aspera plantas!'

✡

SIX PORTES ou le sceau de l'Etoile, voici les secrets des parchemins de l'Abbé SAUNIÈRE, Curé de Rennes-le-Château et qu'avant lui le grand initié POUSSIN connaissait lorsqu'il réalisa son oeuvre à la demande du PAPE, l'inscription sur la tombe est la même.' – Lobineau, *Dossiers secrets*, planche no. 1, 400–600.

3 Graves, *Greek Myths*, vol. 1, p. 203, no. 1.
4 Michell, *Sparta*, p. 173. The Spartans worshipped both Artemis and Aphrodite as a warrior goddess. The latter is the form often assumed by Ishtar and Astarte, indicating the probability of Semitic influence.
5 2 Maccabees 5:9.
6 1 Maccabees 12:21.
7 'Semitic' was first coined in 1781 by Schlözer, a German scholar, to indicate a group of closely related languages. Those who spoke these tongues became called 'Semites'. The word derives ultimately from *Shem*, son of Noah. If the mountain in question held a Jewish colony, it would have been called the 'Mountain of Shem'. But there is also a more mundane possibility. The Latin word 'Semita' means path or way, and this alternative must be considered.

11 THE HOLY GRAIL

1 These very likely had some connection with Otto Rahn, see Chapter 2, n. 9.
2 Philippe d'Alsace, Count of Flanders often visited Champagne, and in 1182 tried unsuccessfully to marry Marie de Champagne (daughter of Eleanor d'Aquitaine) who had been widowed the year before. *Le Conte del Graal* probably dates from about his time.There is a connection between the house of Alsace and that of Lorraine. Gérard d'Alsace, on the death of his brother in 1048, became the first hereditary duke of Haut-Lorraine, today simply Lorraine. All subsequent dukes of Lorraine traced their ancestry back to him.
3 see Loomis, *The Grail*, pp 233

4 An argument for this is put forward by Barber, R., *Knight and Chivalry*, p. 126.
5 *Perlesvaus*, p. 359.
6 Ibid., p. 2.
7 Ibid., p. 214.
8 Ibid., p. 360.
9 Ibid., pp. 199 ff.
10 Ibid., p. 82.
11 Ibid., p. 89.
12 Ibid., p. 268.
13 Ibid., p. 12.
14 Wolfram von Eschenbach, *Parzival*, pp. 243 ff.
15 Ibid., p. 251.
16 Ibid., p. 253.
17 Ibid., p. 129.
18 Ibid., p. 130.
19 Ibid., pp. 251 ff.
20 Ibid., p. 251, n. 11.
21 Ibid., p. 252.
22 Ibid., p. 252.
23 Rahn, *Croisade contre le Graal*, pp. 77 ff., and *La Cour de Lucifer*, p. 69.
24 Wolfram von Eschenbach, *Parzival*, pp. 263 ff.
25 Ibid., p. 264.
26 Ibid., p. 426.
27 Barral, *Légendes Capétiennes*, p. 64.
28 It is interesting that the French city of Avallon dates back to Merovingian times. It was the capital of a region, then a comté, which was part of the kingdom of Aquitaine. It gave its name to the whole region – the Avallonnais.
29 Greub, 'The Pre-Christian Grail Tradition', p. 68.
30 Halevi, *Adam and the Kabbalistic Tree*, pp. 194, 201. Fortune, *Mystical Qabalah*, p. 188.
31 It is sometimes said that the Christian and Cabalistic traditions did not come together until the fifteenth century in the hands of such writers as Pico della Mirandola. However, the *Perlesvaus* would seem to prove that they had fused by the beginning of the thirteenth century. This is an area which needs more study. The particular images in the *Perlesvaus* are those normally associated with the Cabalah as it is used magically.
32 *Queste del Saint Graal*, p. 34.
33 It may perhaps be echoing the fact that King Dagobert spent much of his youth in Britain.
34 *Queste del Saint Graal*, introduction, pp. 16 ff.

12 THE PRIEST-KING WHO NEVER RULED

1 Smith, *Secret Gospel*, pp. 14 ff.
2 Ibid., pp. 15 ff.
3 Ibid., p. 16.
4 Ibid., pp. 16 ff. The youth naked save for a linen cloth appears later in Mark 14:51–2. When Jesus is betrayed in Gethsemane, he is accompanied by 'a certain young man, having linen cloth cast about his naked body'.
5 The oldest manuscripts of the Scriptures, including the

Codex Vaticanus and the *Codex Sinaiticus*, do not have the present ending to Mark. In both of them Mark's gospel finishes at 16:8. Both date from the fourth century, the time when the whole Bible was collected into one volume for the first time.

6 Philo Judaeus, *Embassy to Gaius*, xxxviii, 301–3.
7 Maccoby, *Revolution in Judaea*, p. 99.
8 Dodd, *Historical Tradition in the Fourth Gospel*, p. 423.
9 Brandon, *Jesus and the Zealots*, p. 16.
10 Vermes, *Jesus the Jew*, p. 99.
11 Charles Davis, reported in the *Observer* (London, March 28th, 1971), p. 25.
12 Phipps, *Sexuality of Jesus*, p. 44.
13 Smith, *Jesus the Magician*, pp. 81 ff.
14 Brownlee, 'Whence the Gospel According to John', p. 192.
15 Schonfield, *Passover Plot*, pp. 119, 134 ff.
16 Ibid., p. 256.
17 The standard tradition is given in Jacobus de Voragine, *The Golden Legend*, in the *Life of S. Mary Magdalen*, pp. 73 ff. This dates from 1270. The earliest written form of this tradition would appear to be the 'Life of Mary Magdalen' by Rabanus (776–856), Archbishop of Mainz. It is in *The Antiquities of Glastonbury*, by William of Malmesbury, that the extension of the legend – Joseph of Arimathea coming to Britain – first occurs. It is often considered a later addition to William's account.
18 Vermes, *Jesus the Jew*, p. 21, mentions that in Talmudic sayings the Aramaic noun denoting *carpenter* or *craftsman* (naggar) stands for *learned man* or *scholar*.
19 Maccoby, *Revolution in Judaea*, pp. 57 ff., quotes Philo of Alexandria describing Pilate as 'cruel by nature'.
20 Cohn, H., *Trial and Death of Jesus*, pp. 97 ff.
21 All scholars concur that no such privilege existed. The purpose of the fiction is to increase the guilt of the Jews. See Brandon, *Jesus and the Zealots*, p. 259, Cohn, H., *Trial and Death of Jesus*, pp. 166 ff. (Haim Cohn is an ex-attorney-general of Israel, member of the Supreme Court, and lecturer on historical law), and Winter, P., *On the Trial of Jesus*, p. 94.
22 As Professor Brandon says (*Jesus and the Zealots*, p. 328) all inquiry concerning the historical Jesus must start from the fact of his execution by the Romans for sedition. Brandon adds that the tradition of his being 'King of the Jews' must be accepted as authentic. In view of its embarrassing character, the early Christians would not have invented such a title.
23 Maccoby, *Revolution in Judaea*, p. 216.
24 Brandon, *Trial of Jesus*, p. 34.
25 Joyce, *Jesus Scroll*, p. 106.
26 For crucifixion details see Winter, *On the Trial of Jesus*, pp. 62 ff., and Cohn, H., *Trial and Death of Jesus*, pp. 230 ff.
27 See Schonfield, *Passover Plot*, pp. 154 ff., for details.
28 An argument for this identification is given by Allegro, *The Copper Scroll*, pp. 100 ff.
29 Cohn, H., *Trial and Death of Jesus*, p. 238.
30 See *The Interlinear Greek–English New Testament*, p. 214

(Mark 15:43, 45).

13 THE SECRET THE CHURCH FORBADE

1 Eisler, *Messiah Jesus*, pp. 606 ff.
2 Chadwick, *The Early Church*, p. 125.
3 Goodenough, *Jewish Symbols*, vol. 7, pp. 178 ff.
4 See Halsberghe, *The Cult of Sol Invictus*. The author explains that this cult was brought to Rome in the third century A.D. by the Emperor Elagabalus. When Aurelian introduced his religious reform it was in fact a re-establishment of the cult of Sol Invictus as originally introduced.
5 218 for, 2 against. The Son was then pronounced identical with the Father.
6 It was not until 384 that the Bishop of Rome called himself 'Pope' for the first time.
7 There is a possibility that some may be discovered. In 1976 a large repository of old manuscripts was discovered at the monastery of Saint Catherine on Mount Sinai. The find was kept quiet for some two years before news was leaked to a German newspaper in 1978. There are thousands of fragments, some dating from before A.D. 300, including eight missing pages from the *Codex Sinaiticus* now in the British Museum. The monks who hold the bulk of the material have granted access only to one or two Greek scholars. See *International Herald Tribune* (April 27th, 1978).
8 Gospel of Peter, 5:5.
9 Gospel of the Infancy of Jesus Christ, 2:4.
10 Maccoby, *Revolution in Judaea*, p. 129. The author adds that the portrayal of Jesus as anti-Pharisee was probably part of the attempt to show him as a rebel against the Jewish religion rather than as a rebel against Rome.
11 Brandon, *Jesus and the Zealots*, p. 327. See also Vermes, *Jesus the Jew*, p. 50, 'Zealot or not, Jesus was certainly charged, prosecuted and sentenced as one.'
12 Allegro, *Dead Sea Scrolls*, p. 167.
13 Ibid., p. 175.
14 Josephus, *Jewish War*, p. 387.
15 Ibid., p. 387.
16 Ibid., appendix, p. 400.
17 Eisler, *Messiah Jesus*, p. 427.
18 Ibid., p. 167.
19 Irenaeus, *Five Books . . . against Heresies*, p. 73.
20 *Koran*, 4:157. See also Parrinder, *Jesus in the Qur'an*, pp. 108 ff.
21 Pagels, *Gnostic Gospels*, pp. xvi ff.
22 The Second Treatise of the Great Seth, in Robinson, J., *Nag Hammadi Library in English*, p. 332.
23 The Gospel of Mary, in Robinson, J., *Nag Hammadi Library in English*, p. 472.
24 Ibid., p. 473.
25 Ibid.
26 The Gospel of Philip, in Robinson, J., *Nag Hammadi Library in English*, p. 140.
27 Ibid., pp. 135 ff.

28 Phipps, *Was Jesus Married?*, pp. 136 ff.
29 The Gospel of Philip, in Robinson, J., *Nag Hammadi Library in English*, p. 138.
30 Ibid., p. 139.
31 Ibid.
32 Ibid., p. 148.

14 THE GRAIL DYNASTY

1 Parrinder, *Jesus in the Qur'an*, pp. 110 ff.
2 Blancasall, *Les Descendants*, p. 9.
3 *Koran*, 4:157.
4 There was the sacred Bull of Meroe, at Heliopolis. That bulls were regarded highly by the Sicambrians is shown by the fact that a gold bull's head was found buried with Childeric, the father of Clovis.
5 Henri Lobineau, *Dossiers secrets*, planche no. 1, 950–1400, n. 1.
6 Rabinowitz, 'De Migrantibus'.
7 Zuckerman, *Jewish Princedom*, pp. 36 ff.
8 Zuckerman, *Jewish Princedom*, p. 59.
9 Ponsich, 'Le Conflent', p. 244, n. 10. See also Levillain, 'Nibelungen', year 50 (1938) genealogy facing p. 46.
10 Zuckerman, *Jewish Princedom*, p. 81.
11 Ibid., p. 197.
12 *William, Count of Orange, The Crowning of Louis*, p. 4 (9).
13 Part of it now forms 'The Cloisters' in New York.
14 Saxer, *Marie Madeleine*, vol. 2, p. 412. The cult, observing the day of January 19th, dates from at least A.D. 792–5.
15 Zuckerman, *Jewish Princedom*, p. 64.
16 Ibid., p. 58.
17 Pange, *Maison de Lorraine*, p. 60.

15 CONCLUSION AND PORTENTS FOR THE FUTURE

1 Lacordaire, *St Mary Magdalen*, p. 185.
2 *Enclyclopaedia Britannica*, 14th edn (1972), *Crown and Regalia*, fig. 2.
3 Nilus, *Protocols*, no. 24.
4 Péguy, Charles, 'La Tapisserie de Sainte Genevière', in *Oeuvres poétiques complètes* (Paris, 1957), p. 849.
5 Saint Sigisbert was the father of Dagobert II.

APPENDIX 1:

1 See Digot, P., *Notre-Dame-de-Sion*, p. 8. We obtained a copy of the original charter of this Order, the records being held in the Bibliothèque Municipale, Nancy.
2 Fédié, *Le Comté de Razès*, p. 119.
3 Birch, *Life of Robert Boyle*, p. 274.
4 Ibid.
5 See Manuel, *Portrait of Isaac Newton*, and Dobbs, *Foundations of Newton's Alchemy*.
6 Newton was also a supporter of the Socinians, a religious group who believed that Jesus was divine by office rather than by nature. They were Arian in orientation. Newton himself was described as an Arian.
7 Perey, *Charles de Lorraine*, p. 287.

APPENDIX 2:

1: Deloux, J-P., and Brétigny, J., *Rennes-le-Château: capitale secrète de l'histoire de France*, Paris, 1982, p.5 and 11.
2: Anne, T., *M.Le Comte de Chambord à Wiesbaden*, Paris, 1851, p.204.

APPENDIX 3

1: Chocholaušek, P., *Templáriv Chechách*, Prague, 1842, pp.5–12.

INDEX